A Life in
Letters

Sophie Ratcliffe is Fellow and Tutor in English at Lady Margaret Hall, University of Oxford, specialising in nineteenth- and twentieth-century literature. She also reviews fiction and criticism for the national press. She lives in Oxford with her husband and two young children.

Praise for *P. G. Wodehouse: A Life in Letters*

'In this new collection . . . Sophie Ratcliffe has rolled up her sleeves and waded into the fr.. . . . she has succeeded marvellously. When it comes to the world of Wodehouse, ...cliffe knows her stuff. She has embroidered this plump selection of letters with an ... ninating but unobtrusive critical apparatus.'   *Literary Review*

'...body requiring evidence of how much work P.G. Wodehouse put into his comic .. should read his letters. In her introduction to this definitive compendium of ...house's correspondence, Sophie Ratcliffe warns that [the letters] display only ... casions the extraordinary stylistic elan that one finds in fiction. Indeed they ... hough when the extraordinary elan bubbles briefly to the surface, it is worth ... g for.'   *Scotland on Sunday*

'... authoritative edition of generous selections – from "Plum's" prolific pen, from ...cr.oldays at Dulwich College in 1899 throughout his long Anglo-American career as a novelist and musical comedy lyricist to his last letters from Long Island in 1975 – is acutely attuned to his contradictions of character and his desire to please at the expense of absolute veracity.'   *The Times*

'An intriguing picture of a great 20th-century writer . . . In its peculiar English way, it has a strange intimacy, the perverse fruit of Wodehouse's instinctive, Jeevesian, discretion.'   *Guardian*

BOOKS BY P. G. WODEHOUSE

FICTION

Aunts Aren't Gentlemen
The Adventures of Sally
Bachelors Anonymous
Barmy in Wonderland
Big Money
Bill the Conqueror
Blandings Castle and Elsewhere
Carry On, Jeeves
The Clicking of Cuthbert
Cocktail Time
The Code of the Woosters
The Coming of Bill
Company for Henry
A Damsel in Distress
Do Butlers Burgle Banks
Doctor Sally
Eggs, Beans and Crumpets
A Few Quick Ones
French Leave
Frozen Assets
Full Moon
Galahad at Blandings
A Gentleman of Leisure
The Girl in Blue
The Girl on the Boat
The Gold Bat
The Head of Kay's
The Heart of a Goof
Heavy Weather
Ice in the Bedroom
If I Were You

Indiscretions of Archie
The Inimitable Jeeves
Jeeves and the Feudal Spirit
Jeeves in the Offing
Jill the Reckless
Joy in the Morning
Laughing Gas
Leave it to Psmith
The Little Nugget
Lord Emsworth and Others
Louder and Funnier
Love Among the Chickens
The Luck of the Bodkins
The Man Upstairs
The Man With Two Left Feet
The Mating Season
Meet Mr Mulliner
Mike and Psmith
Mike at Wrykyn
Money for Nothing
Money in the Bank
Mr Mulliner Speaking
Much Obliged, Jeeves
Mulliner Nights
Not George Washington
Nothing Serious
The Old Reliable
Pearls, Girls and Monty Bodkin
A Pelican at Blandings
Piccadilly Jim
Pigs Have Wings

Plum Pie
The Pothunters
A Prefect's Uncle
The Prince and Betty
Psmith, Journalist
Psmith in the City
Quick Service
Right Ho, Jeeves
Ring for Jeeves
Sam the Sudden
Service with a Smile
The Small Bachelor
Something Fishy
Something Fresh
Spring Fever
Stiff Upper Lip, Jeeves
Summer Lightning
Summer Moonshine
Sunset at Blandings
The Swoop
Tales of St Austin's
Thank You, Jeeves
Ukridge
Uncle Dynamite
Uncle Fred in the Springtime
Uneasy Money
Very Good, Jeeves
The White Feather
William Tell Told Again
Young Men in Spats

OMNIBUS

The World of Blandings
The World of Jeeves
The World of Mr Mulliner
The World of Psmith
The World of Ukridge
The World of Uncle Fred
Wodehouse Nuggets
(edited by Richard Usborne)
The World of Wodehouse Clergy
Weekend Wodehouse

PAPERBACK OMNIBUSES

The Golf Omnibus
The Aunts Omnibus
The Drones Omnibus
The Clergy Omnibus
The Hollywood Omnibus
The Jeeves Omnibus 1
The Jeeves Omnibus 2
The Jeeves Omnibus 3
The Jeeves Omnibus 4
The Jeeves Omnibus 5

POEMS

The Parrot and Other Poems

LETTERS

Yours, Plum

AUTOBIOGRAPHICAL

Wodehouse on Wodehouse (comprising Bring on the Girls, Over Seventy, Performing Flea)

BY SOPHIE RATCLIFFE

On Sympathy (Oxford University Press, 2008)

P. G. Wodehouse
A Life in Letters

Edited by Sophie Ratcliffe

arrow books

Published in the United Kingdom by Arrow Books in 2013

13 5 7 9 10 8 6 4 2

Copyright © Trustees of the Wodehouse Estate 2011

Introduction, selection and other editorial matter © Sophie Ratcliffe 2011

Sophie Ratcliffe has asserted her right under the Copyright, Designs
and Patents Act, 1988 to be identified as the author of this work.

First published in the United Kingdom in 2011 by Hutchinson

Arrow Books
Random House, 20 Vauxhall Bridge Road,
London SW1V 2SA

www.randomhouse.co.uk

Addresses for companies within The Random House Group Limited
can be found at: www.randomhouse.co.uk/offices.htm

The Random House Group Limited Reg. No. 954009

A CIP catalogue record for this book
is available from the British Library

ISBN 9780099514794

The Random House Group Limited supports the Forest Stewardship Council®
(FSC®), the leading international forest-certification organisation.
Our books carrying the FSC label are printed on FSC®-certified paper.
FSC is the only forest-certification scheme supported by the leading
environmental organisations, including Greenpeace.
Our paper procurement policy can be found at:
www.randomhouse.co.uk/environment

Printed and bound by CPI Group (UK) Ltd, Croydon, CR0 4YY

For all Wodehouse's heroines,
imaginary and real, especially Leonora

Contents

Illustrations

ILLUSTRATIONS IN THE TEXT   PAGE

The editor and publisher are grateful to the following for permission to reproduce photographs: plates 2, 3, 17, 24, 28, 29, 32, 39, and p. 70, p.299, p. 300, Wodehouse Estate; plate 6, courtesy of HSBC holdings plc; plates 7, 11, 12, 18, 20, 25, 27, 30, 37 and pages 33, 55, 69, 95, 130, 300, courtesy of Tony Ring; plate 8, image courtesy of Mellors and Kirk Fine Art Auctioneers; plate 9, courtesy of N. T. P. Murphy; plate 10, courtesy of Richard Perceval-Maxwell; plate 13, by kind permission of Emsworth Maritime and Historical Trust (Emsworth Museum); plate 14, courtesy of Timothy Bradshaw; plate 15, courtesy of Ann Garland and Linda Eaton; plate 16, Source: Library and Archives Canada/Department of Employment and Immigration fonds/RG 76, Microfilm T-4790; plate 21, © National Portrait Gallery, London; plate 22, courtesy of *Tatler*; plate 23, © Sasha/Hulton Archives/Getty Images; plate 25, © Warner Bros. Entertainment; plate 26, © Popperfoto/Getty Images; plate 30, © Warner Bros. Entertainment; plate 33, National Archives; plate 34, courtesy of Reinhild von Bodenhausen; plate 35, © The Advertising Archive; page 42, The Morgan Library and Museum, New York; pages 45, 48 and 186, with kind permission of the Governors of Dulwich College; page 67, The Bodleian Library, Oxford; page 70, Henry W. and Albert A. Berg Collection of English and American Literature, The New York Public Library, Astor, Lenox and Tilden Foundations; pages 293 and 299, Columbia University Library. Every effort has been made to contact all copyright holders. If notified, the publisher will be pleased to rectify any errors or omissions at the earliest opportunity.

Acknowledgements

To begin, I owe a great debt to P. G. Wodehouse's step-grandson, Sir Edward Cazalet, and to the Trustees of the Wodehouse Estate. I have been fortunate enough to have had the Estate's wholehearted support combined with complete editorial freedom. My grateful thanks also to the entire Cazalet family – Camilla, David, Hal and Lara – for their warmth, patience and encouragement as the project progressed.

In 2004, Robert McCrum's biography, *Wodehouse: A Life*, appeared. It contains a wealth of new material about Wodehouse. My book often draws on his knowledge and prior research; I am grateful for his enthusiasm and generosity throughout the time I have been working on this book.

I have benefited hugely from the kindness of two experts in the field of Wodehouse studies. Lt. Colonel Norman Murphy, author of, among others, the superb *Wodehouse Handbook*, has patiently and with great humour commented on drafts, saved me from numerous errors and omissions, and provided vital and fascinating advice on the context surrounding Wodehouse's writing life. Tony Ring, author of *The Wit and Wisdom of P. G. Wodehouse* and co-editor of *The Wodehouse Concordance*, has also been extraordinarily generous with his time, knowledge, and the contents of his archive. He again has corrected and augmented numerous drafts of this book with a razor-sharp eye for detail, and has been particularly helpful in discussing both Wodehouse's financial affairs and his theatrical ventures. Without the knowledge and kindness of both these men this would have been a far lesser book, and the writing of it far less enjoyable. Grateful thanks, also, both to Elin Murphy for her generous support, and her timely help with the introduction, and to Elaine Ring, for her own wisdom, wit and kindness. All errors, of course, remain mine.

My editor, Anthony Whittome, rightly saw the way in which this book should be constructed. He has been astute, critical, patient and unfailingly encouraging. I have been enormously fortunate to work with him. My thanks, also, to Caroline Gascoigne, Joanna Taylor, Neil Bradford, Phil Brown, and Paulette Hearn at Hutchinson.

To my agent, Peter Straus, at Rogers, Coleridge & White, grateful thanks for his incisive intelligence, advice and forbearance, from the genesis of this book to its completion.

I have benefited from the generosity of three institutions during the course of editing this book. The British Academy permitted me to combine my Postdoctoral research with my research on this Wodehouse edition. Keble College provided financial and intellectual support in the early stages of the book. Christ Church – my current academic home – generously provided a grant to enable its completion.

I must also thank the following libraries for allowing me access to material in their collections: the Henry W. and A. Albert Berg Collection of English and American Literature at The New York Public Library (Berg); the Louis Wilson Library, University of North Carolina at Chapel Hill (Chapel Hill); the Special Collections Research Center, University of Chicago Library (Chicago); The Rare Book and Manuscript Library, Columbia University (Columbia); the Division of Rare and Manuscript Collections, Cornell University Library (Cornell); Dulwich College Archives (Dulwich); Emsworth Museum, Emsworth Maritime and Historical Trust, Emsworth, Hampshire (Emsworth); the Pierpont Morgan Library, New York (Morgan); Oriel College Archive, Oxford (Oriel); Oxford University Archives, Bodleian Library, Oxford (OUA); Harry Ransom Humanities Research Center, University of Texas at Austin, Texas (Ransom); Special Collections, Morris Library, Southern Illinois University, Carbondale (Southern Illinois); UCL Library Services, London (UCL); Wheaton College Special Collections, Wheaton, Illinois (Wheaton).

Finding certain Wodehouse letters has proved a challenge. I have been helped greatly by the following people: Tony Aldridge of Hawthorn Books, Curtis Armstrong, James Bantin, Hilary Bruce, Gus Caywood, Jeff Coates, Mark Everett, Kris Fowler, Mike Griffith, S. Richard Heymann, Mark Hinton, Christopher Langley, Calista Lucy, Mellors and Kirk Auctioneers, Rupert Neelands at Christie's, Michael Pointon, Matthew Prichard, Peter Selley and Meg Ford at Sotheby's, Tim Straker, Lucia Stuart, Dr Richard Sveum, Kristin Thompson, Barbara Way and Mandy Wise. I am grateful to Pauline Grant for all her help with negotiating the Wodehouse archive and for the copying of many letters.

Particular thanks to Nigel Wodehouse, Dr Ronald Levine, Richard Perceval-Maxwell and Tom Sharpe. I am also enormously grateful to the descendants of Alice Dovey – Linda Eaton and Ann Garland – and the grandchildren of Leslie Havergal Bradshaw – Dove and Timothy Bradshaw – who have provided vital new material and letters. Reinhild von Bodenhausen's record of her time with Wodehouse, *P. G. Wodehouse: The Unknown Years*, has also proved immensely useful. I am grateful for her permission to quote from this work and from her mother's diaries.

Many individuals have helped with queries, a number of them responding with dizzying speed and accuracy. These include Mary Alexander, Dorothy Bone, Susan Collicott, John Dawson, Peter Day, Daniel Garrison, Murray Hedgcock, David Jasen, Sara Kinsey, Ian Michaud, Christopher Pelling, Rob Petre, Jeremy Schuman, Colin Shindler and Jean Tillson.

The collation and transcription of these letters was a large task. I have been ably assisted by Alice Ferns, James Fotherby, Soraya Gillani, Kirsty Martin, Thomas Morris, Andrew Murray and Kate Womersley. I take it as a testament to the continuing interest in Wodehouse as a writer that numerous Oxford undergraduates volunteered to give up their time to help with the sorting of thousands of letters. My particular thanks to Charlie Annis, Roxanne Brennan, Alexander Bubb, Kate Derycker, Simone Docherty, Kayleigh Fitzgerald, Rebecca Gibson, Holly Guest, Alexandra Hawley, Isla Jeffrey, Lauren Johnson, Hannah Martin and Martin Parlett.

I have, throughout this process, had the good fortune to have the most intellectually imaginative and committed research assistant in the shape of Miranda Ward. I cannot begin to thank her for everything that she has done, above and beyond the call of duty. A number of the discoveries in this book are hers.

On a personal level I owe thanks to many colleagues and friends, including Sally Bayley, Jonathan Bickford, Mishtooni Bose, Marc Brodie, Paddy and Rebecca Bullard, Christopher and Gillian Butler, Rachel Buxton and Jenny Wheeldon, Xander Cansell, Robert Douglas-Fairhurst, Claudia Fitzgerald, Susan and Nigel Fotherby, Ralph Hanna, Clive James, John Lyon, Peter McDonald, Edward Mendelson, John Mitchinson, Diane Purkiss, Olwen Renowden, Deborah Rogan, Richard Rutherford, Helen Small and Brian Young. Research in American archives and libraries was made possible through the generous hospitality and friendship of Philip Rosenbaum and Erin Blondel.

Six people who helped to make this book in different ways are not here to see the end result: my father Andrew Ratcliffe, whose copy of *The Inimitable Jeeves* was the first Wodehouse I ever read; Nigel Williams provided access to hard-to-discover Wodehouse letters; Patrick Wodehouse kindly provided me with crucial family material; Angus Thuermer looked for photographs and letters; Alan Schuman saw the point of this book and was its unwavering champion; Frederick Vincent, a true gentleman, swapped his favourite Wodehouse novels with me some years before this book began.

My mother and step-father, Rel and Harry Cowen, have been unstinting with their time and love to help me to get this book finished. Yvonne Leeds has been a steadfast support, full of good sense and humour. I couldn't have managed without her. Two-year-old Ivo Schuman has provided many diversions, and has been a constant reminder of the importance of the life that surrounds all letters. His sister, Ottilie, showed consideration and chutzpah in equal measure, timing her arrival to coincide with that of the second proofs.

Finally, and most of all, my thanks to my husband, Dr Andrew Schuman. The editing of this book has spanned all the years he has known me, and he has given up night after night to researching, deciphering handwriting, proofing and correcting. He tenaciously followed missing leads long after I had given them up, and made a number of crucial discoveries as a result. He has brought much intelligence, imagination and belief to this project. Thanks are far too small for what I owe him, but I send them anyway, with – as ever and always – all of my love.

P. G. WODEHOUSE · *A Life in Letters*

Introduction

When it comes to letter-writing, P. G. Wodehouse's Bertie Wooster belongs to the minimalist school:

Dear Freddie, —
Well, here I am in New York. It's not a bad place. I'm not having a bad time. Everything's not bad. The cabarets aren't bad. Don't know when I shall be back. How's everybody? Cheerio! —

Yours,

Bertie.

PS. — Seen old Ted lately?

'Not that I cared about old Ted', he adds, 'but if I hadn't dragged him in I couldn't have got the confounded thing on to the second page.'[1]

Receiving post is, for Bertie, equally confounding. This is partly a matter of timing; morning, after all, is never the best time for reading, especially if you have a 'bit of a head on'.[2] But it is also because the letter, in the world of Wodehouse, is an intrusive presence – a symbol of reality permeating the all-too-secure haven of one's bachelor flat, gentlemen's club or country seat. Whether it hails from an aunt, fiancée or amorous peer of the realm, the envelope by the toast rack is a threatening sight – a crumb in the butter of the Wodehousean Eden.

Wodehouse's own attitude to letters was more positive. Many different exchanges – ranging from notes to his family to business letters and discussions of plot design – offer a fascinating and unique insight into a twentieth-century writing life, and the history of his time. Wodehouse exchanged letters with numerous well-known figures – including artists and writers such as Ira Gershwin, Evelyn Waugh, George Orwell and Agatha Christie. He also kept up a regular correspondence with his friends and family, especially his beloved step-daughter, Leonora, or 'Snorky'.

While some might assume that Wodehouse's novels are conventional, beneath the mostly male upper-crust there is some radical table-turning. Butlers bail their masters out, passion wins over reason, and girls, invariably, know more than boys. The letters reveal the roots of this reversal. Wodehouse was a self-made man who married a chorus-girl, spent time with Hollywood movie stars, and endured Nazi imprisonment and journalistic accusations of treason. This was a life that was much more eventful than many – especially many of his younger generations of readers – might assume. As for the man himself, this 'laureate of repression' could be affectionate, naughty and tender in correspondence.[3]

A number of these letters touch on Wodehouse's feelings about love. Bertie Wooster declares that there are two sorts of men. Those who would like to find a woman in their bedroom, and those who would rather not. From accounts of his own marriage, Wodehouse was, in many ways, of the second sort. Nevertheless, his early letters to his friend Leslie Bradshaw contain some revealing details about his romantic encounters, while in his later letters he speculates, from time to time, on other people's sex lives, marriages and divorces.

Solvency is also a key theme of his correspondence – the getting, losing and spending of money dominates his letters as much as it does his plots. Ever since missing out on his place at Oxford, Wodehouse was driven by the idea of bringing in the 'boodle' – and he was hugely successful as an earner.[4] The correspondence follows his financial fortunes, his crises with the taxman, his affectionate reflections on his wife's spending, and his gifts to friends and family.

Elsewhere, letters demonstrate the difficulties of plotting, the complexities of character creation and also the moments of inspiration. When Jeeves, 'the perfect omniscient nanny', first entered the Wodehouse oeuvre, he came in with the utmost discretion.[5] As Wodehouse told Lawrence Durrell, '[i]t never occurred to me that Jeeves would do anything except open doors and announce people.'[6]

Whether delivering an account of the difficulties of getting a small glass of whiskey during Prohibition, or giving the 'low down on the Riviera',[7] Wodehouse offers characteristically comic accounts of living, writing and socialising in England, America and France through the 1920s and 1930s – as well as an extraordinary account of his life in a German internment camp, in Nazi Berlin, and in occupied and post-liberation Paris.

Given Wodehouse's acknowledged skill as a novelist, it is perhaps surprising that it has taken so long for so many of these letters to be collected in one volume.[8] The delay comes in part from Wodehouse's unusual place in the English canon. An acknowledged master of the English comic novel, praised by philosophers such as Ludwig Wittgenstein and Anthony Quinton, and writers such as T. S. Eliot and W. H. Auden, he has also always been an unashamedly popular writer – one whom readers have, on the whole, simply enjoyed, rather than studied. From one perspective, Wodehouse merits a scholarly volume, directed at an academic audience – from another, he deserves a letters book aimed at the general reader. This edition seeks to serve both readerships.

Wodehouse is also a writer whose works resist a certain sort of biographical approach. He disliked investigations into his personal life and circumstances, partly because he found them intrusive. (He wrote to his friend William Townend that their unedited correspondence should eventually 'be destroyed. Gosh', he added, 'it would be awful if some of the things I've written you were made public').[9] And he also intimated that biographical context was, to a degree, irrelevant to understanding a work of art. Writing about Shakespeare, he noted that 'a thing I can never understand is why all the critics seem to assume that his plays are a reflection of his personal moods and dictated by the circumstances of his private life. You know the sort of thing I mean. They say "*Timon of Athens* is a gloomy bit of work. That means that Shakespeare was having a lousy time when he wrote it." I can't see it. Do you find that your private life affects your work? I don't.'[10]

Indeed, while the Edwardian England of Wodehouse's early adulthood permeates his works, his personal circumstances and the tenor of his fictional worlds are not always an easy match. One of the surprises of this correspondence is the occasional, startling disparity between life and art. Take his masterly *Joy in the Morning*, written during one of the most difficult periods of his life. Just weeks after leaving Nazi internment, Wodehouse was still able to conjure up the 'embowered' hamlet of Steeple Bumpleigh, 'in the midst of smiling fields and leafy woods'. While he struggled with the weight of national disapproval, his halcyon fictional world had only one cloud on the horizon – the 'somewhat sticky affair' of Bertie, Florence Craye and 'Stilton' Cheesewright – effortlessly resolved by the shimmering Jeeves.[11]

Parallels between Wodehouse's correspondence and his fiction run at a deeper level. Wodehouse may have famously parodied the modernist poets, but he has more in common with T. S. Eliot than he might have admitted. For Wodehouse, as for Eliot, the aim of the written text was not to express, but to 'escape' from emotion.[12] It is, as he told a friend, 'hopeless to try and put down on paper what one is feeling'.[13] From Wodehouse's earliest works, we find that the idea of internal psychology, in what he referred to as 'the Henry James style', is parodied and resisted.[14]

His letters have a similar emotional reticence. It was Dr Johnson, one of Wodehouse's earliest literary loves, who wrote that a man's soul, 'lies naked' in his letters.[15] Wodehouse's attitude to nudity was a wary one: 'You know my views on nudes', he once wrote to a friend, 'I want no piece of them.'[16] Wodehouse's letters are usually clad in the epistolary equivalent of Bertie's heliotrope pyjamas, carefully buttoned up to disguise true feeling.

The 'cladding', for Wodehouse, has always been his extraordinary written style. Drawing on the techniques of such writers as Dickens and Thackeray, Conan Doyle and O. Henry, as well as lesser-known but popular late nineteenth- and early twentieth-century authors such as W. W. Jacobs and Barry Pain, Wodehouse's fiction offers something unique in the history of English prose. He is, as Stephen Medcalf argues, 'the greatest and most original' of a group of writers (the list includes G. K. Chesterton, Evelyn Waugh and John Betjeman) who may have eschewed the techniques of modernism, but who still provide stylistic paths through the same insecurity that the modernists exposed.[17]

While such a style is difficult to analyse (one critic has compared the act to 'taking a spade to a *soufflé*'), there are a variety of figures of speech that recur throughout Wodehouse's fiction, and his letters.[18] One is the way in which he deflects emotion away from the self. When disaster occurs in the shape of income-tax demands or illness, it is the 'home' that metonymically laments. When he expresses admiration for his wife, her outfits – rather than her body – garner the praise. Such manoeuvres are perfected in his fiction, with his use of the transferred epithet – a technique that casts the state of mind of the protagonist onto a nearby, unlikely inanimate object. We have, for example, 'I balanced a thoughtful lump of sugar on my teaspoon';[19]

'he uncovered the fragrant eggs and b. and I pronged a moody forkful'[20] – or the memorable ablutions in *Jeeves and the Feudal Spirit*:

> As I sat in the bath-tub, soaping a meditative foot and singing, if I remember correctly, 'Pale Hands I Loved Beside the Shalimar', it would be deceiving my public to say that I was feeling boomps-a-daisy.[21]

The shifting of affect, from mind to limb, is not only absurdly incongruous; it has the effect of holding the emotion in question at arm's (or leg's) length. The pace of this sentence is also ingenious. It suspends its meaning, clause after clause, building up our expectations, till it sinks, like a punctured rubber duck, on 'boomps-a-daisy'. It is a phrase as unexpected – after the precision of 'if I remember', the mystique of 'Shalimar' and the rhetorical nod to 'my public' – as it is daft. But Bertie isn't even feeling 'boomps-a-daisy'; it is part of his charm that his low mood is described not only tangentially, captured in the shape of his 'meditative' foot, but through negative inference and euphemism.

Discretion also governs another feature of the typically Wodehousean syntax – his use of abbreviation. Terms such as 'posish', 'eggs and b.', 'f.i.h.s' ('fiend in human shape') and 'festive s.' ('festive season') appear both in Wodehouse's fiction and in his letters, and there is a perfectly balanced comic tension about these coded syntactical tics. The unsaid-but-understood creates a clubby feeling of intimacy between writer and reader. But there is also something subtly self-deprecating about the Wodehousean abbreviations – as if he is creating a voice that is necessarily compacted, determined not to draw too much attention to itself. As Basil Boothroyd points out, both Wodehouse's heroes and Wodehouse himself 'are vulnerable at heart'.[22]

Wodehouse is a writer who could easily have chosen to write quite a different sort of fiction – one ballasted by an armoury of academic knowledge. A brilliant scholar, disappointed in his hopes for university, he had an immense grasp of literature, philosophy and Classics. Well into his later years, his letters reveal that he spent time reading Balzac, Austen, Fielding, Smollett and Faulkner, and throughout his career his writing demonstrates this literary breadth. But this is not the dense allusive erudition that one finds in writers such as Ezra Pound or

Gertrude Stein. Balancing Byron and Shelley, Plato and Maeterlinck against contemporary slang, Wodehouse moves seamlessly between registers, both celebrating and diminishing the world of high art.

Wodehouse's pre-eminent stylistic flourish is his use of metaphor and simile. Page after page of his novels contain sparklingly unusual stretches of the imagination – 'Ice formed on the butler's upper slopes'; a man 'wilts' like 'a salted snail' – and one finds the same in his letters.[23] 'Things', he tells a friend, 'are beginning to stir faintly, like the blood beginning to circulate in a frozen Alpine traveller who has met a St Bernard dog and been given a shot from the brandy flask';[24] returning to New York, he reflects, 'was like meeting an old sweetheart and finding she has put on a lot of weight'.[25] It is a technique that does more than simply amuse. Some of Wodehouse's similes and metaphors are so extraordinary that they approach the absurd. Style, for Wodehouse, is a carefully crafted form of ludic release, and it is in the very texture of his sentences that one can see the originality of his mind at work.

Nevertheless, the letters in this volume have a very distinct stylistic difference from Wodehouse's fiction. Often written at speed, the letters show Wodehouse without his crafted style in place. Moments of great emotion break through: his excited optimism at the prospect of winning a scholarship to Oxford; his terrible disappointment when he learned that a 'varsity life was not to be his lot after all; his stoicism in the face of romantic disappointment; his devastation at the death of his step-daughter; his bewildered outrage and sorrow at the public response to his wartime errors.

Apart from a hiatus during the years 1915–1917, for which unaccountably no letters survive, the correspondence provides an extraordinarily detailed account, not only of Wodehouse's activities, but of his evolution as a writer: his early success in schoolboy magazines (*Mike Jackson* and *Psmith*), his rapid development as a writer in Edwardian journalism, his battles to make his mark with New York periodicals, his writing for *Playboy* magazine, and his love of 1970s TV soaps. New sources for Wodehouse's characters, from to Billie Dore to T. Patterson Frisby, are revealed – and new caches of correspondence provide important insights into his years in New York and Berlin.

It is all too often forgotten that Wodehouse was a famous lyricist and playwright as well as a novelist. As the critic Mark Steyn notes, '[h]ad

Wodehouse died in 1918 he would have been remembered not as a British novelist but as the first great lyricist of the American musical.'[26] Wodehouse read his way through Shakespeare each year – and he adored the works of W. S. Gilbert. This book of letters has a dramatic quality of its own, with its fair share of characters standing in the wings. Wodehouse's friend and one-time collaborator, Herbert Westbrook, one of the inspirations for his comic hero Ukridge, was an influential backstage presence in Wodehouse's life. The imperious theatrical producer, Florenz Ziegfeld, was partially responsible for the numerous changes of address that we find in Wodehouse's correspondence, frequently sending verbose telegrams summoning Wodehouse from across the Atlantic to rescue his latest production. Elsewhere in these letters, we catch glimpses of Wodehouse's dealings with wayward literary agents, stroppy actresses and loyal wartime comrades. And there is his huge range of enduring non-human attachments – Wonder and Squeaky, Bimmy and Bill, his adored dogs and cats. The most important of all behind-the-scenes presences was his wife, Ethel. In the letters, we see her negotiating prices for Wodehouse's serials, rethinking his plot ideas and liaising with agents, before heading to the local casino. Wodehouse, meanwhile, was often to be found cutting a letter short because of Ethel's pressing demands. I must stop now, he told his friend, the novelist Denis Mackail, as Ethel is 'yowling in the passage that my cocktail is ready.'[27]

There is a further staginess to these letters, for Wodehouse is often to be found ventriloquising a specific persona according to the perceived preference of his correspondent. With his friend Eric George, he adopts the role of a passionate but jilted inamorata out of a Thackeray sketch, then switches to the character of an ersatz Sam Weller, before brandishing his literary knowledge like an undergraduate manqué; to Leonora, he is both an adoring father and good 'pal', full of slang and silliness; when writing to Denis Mackail, Wodehouse can be unusually sarcastic and catty. Meanwhile letters to the dashing Guy Bolton have an uncharacteristic machismo about them, containing innuendos, dirty jokes and – somewhat implausibly – a mention of the 'brave old days' when Wodehouse 'used to have the clap'.[28] Indeed, reading these letters, one feels that Wodehouse comes close to Keats (a poet often quoted in his novels): he is a writer with 'no self at all', constantly shape-shifting to suit his audience.[29]

Of course, the central drama of Wodehouse's life was one in which he was an unwitting player. The story of his internment by the Nazis, and the subsequent controversy that ensued after he had made a series of humorous broadcasts on German radio, is well known. These letters, many of which have never been seen before, offer an unprecedented insight into the ways in which Wodehouse negotiated, or failed to negotiate, the complexities of wartime Berlin and occupied Paris – and his deep fear of losing his public as a result of his error of judgement.

Given Wodehouse's lack of any real involvement in the major political events of the twentieth century, it is often asked whether there is any political aspect to his writing – indeed critics may ask how to negotiate an oeuvre that seems to resist politics so determinedly. Wodehouse's method of writing a novel was, he claims in a letter, 'making the thing frankly a fairy story and ignoring real life altogether'.[30] As Evelyn Waugh writes, when reading about Wodehouse's characters

> We do not concern ourselves with the economic implications of their position; we are not sceptical about their quite aston-ishing celibacy. We do not expect them to grow any older, like the Three Musketeers or the Forsytes. We are not interested in how they would 'react to changing social conditions' as publishers' blurbs invite us to be interested in other sagas. They are untroubled by wars. [...] They all live, year after year, in their robust middle twenties; their only sickness is an occasional hangover. It is a world that cannot become dated because it has never existed.[31]

Wodehouse's work, however, can be seen as more than simply escapist, providing us, as it does, with the notion of an alternative universe. He is, as Auden notes, one of the 'great English experts on Eden' – he 'proclaims the dream of a world where things could be otherwise'.[32]

As for the politics of the man himself, these letters demonstrate something of Wodehouse's particular brand of good nature, mixed with naïveté and blindness – and 'a complete unawareness that anyone could be as ungentlemanly as the Nazis actually were'.[33] Wodehouse's comments on international events range in character from patriotic interest to somewhat disengaged bemusement. One thing the letters make clear, however, is his lack of snobbery and prejudice. Wodehouse writes as readily to ex-housekeepers as to aristocrats, and his letters are always warm, interested, and invariably concerned with the welfare of his correspondent. Indeed, one of the reasons why Wodehouse's personal sense of politics was so hazy was that he never seemed able to conceive of, or interest himself in, the notion of others in the context of any sort of group at all; his concern was wholly with the individual.

Looking through these letters, a reader might be struck by the work-aday nature of Wodehouse's correspondence. He is, at times, downright ordinary. While the letters are consistently interesting for the detail they contain and the light they shed upon his times, they display only on occasions the extraordinary stylistic élan that one finds in his fiction. The particular qualities that make up Wodehouse's character as both a man and a writer explain this resistance to extensive rhetorical flair. The ethics of Wodehouse's entire oeuvre are, as critics have noted, an ethics of humility. It is, after all, Bertie's humility 'with all its complicated to and fro of self-realisation and avoidance of self-realisation' that makes him, for us, an interesting character.[34] And there is a humility in Wodehouse's writing from the largest scale – he happily adopts the role of a popular genre writer – to the level of an individual sentence. Wodehouse may play with the everyday cliché, but he never derides it. The rhythms of everyday speech, are, for him, a form of communion. He was a humble man, and the modesty of his letters reflects this.

Born in 1881, the year in which the first telephone company was formed, Wodehouse grew up at a time of phenomenal change in methods of communication, and he was acutely aware of the expressive capacities – or failures – of varying media. 'You can't', as he wrote in a 1923 lyric 'make love by wireless':

It's like eggs without the ham
There is nothing girls desire less
Than a cold Marconigram;

For it's something you can't speak to
From a someone you can't see;
It's like a village church that's spireless,
Or a Selfridge's that's buyerless

Or a Pekinese that's sireless
And it isn't any good to me![35]

But Wodehouse was no technophobe. Like his contemporary, James Joyce, Wodehouse relishes the comic possibilities that such new media allow a writer. One thinks, for example, of Monty Bodkin's garbled telephone call to Lord Emsworth in *Heavy Weather*, alerting him to an imminent pig-napping, or Smallwood Bessemer's whistle-stop proposal in 'Tangled Hearts':

'Miss Flack?'
'Hello?'
'Sorry to disturb you at this hour, but will you marry me?'
'Certainly. Who is that?'[36]

Telegrams also provide a rich vein of humour. Aunt Dahlia's epic telegram exchanges with her 'fat-headed nephew' in *Right Ho, Jeeves* are a case in point. Or Madeline Bassett's lyrical telegraphese – 'Please come here if you wish but, Oh Bertie, is this wise? [...] Surely merely twisting knife wound' (in which, as Stephen Medcalf writes, the humour 'lies in the idiocy of omitting "in the", after putting in "Oh Bertie"').[37] Elsewhere, we see Wodehouse's comic riffs on the public letter form in *Over Seventy*, and his mocking of cliché in *Pearls, Girls and Monty Bodkin*, in which Chimp Twist is left to brood on a picture postcard presenting 'a charming picture of the Croisette at Cannes' bearing the unusual inscription: 'Having a wonderful time. Glad you're not here'.[38]

Wodehouse's writing career took off at a point when there was a boom in the appearance of the 'open' or 'public' letter. The daily paper, as Matthew Rubery notes, was an interactive entity, full of personal announcements, advertisements and 'brief stories written in the blood of broken hearts'.[39] Wodehouse himself was briefly an 'agony uncle' for the journal *Tit-Bits*, and he took a particular delight in the psychology of the public letter writer, as his 1904 *Punch* article 'Balm for the Broken-Hearted' reveals. The article is allegedly constructed from the contents of an editorial waste-paper basket, containing readers' responses to a 'broken-hearted' correspondent who had written to the paper during the previous week:

SIR,—The accident of which your correspondent complains is one that might happen to anybody. All that he needs, in my opinion, is a little perseverance and determination. Perhaps travel would prove as efficacious in curing him as it was in curing me under similar circumstances. The object of my devotion was a lady whose refined singing and dancing had created something of a furore at the music-halls. My life was temporarily blighted by the discovery that she was already married, and that her youngest son was then playing *Hamlet* in the provinces. But I soon recovered on joining my ship and going for my first voyage, and since then her memory has cost me scarcely a pang. Like the good sailor I am, I have now a wife at Marseilles, a second at Amsterdam, a third in London, and others at Nagasaki, New York, Athens, Archangel, and, I believe, Constantinople.

I am, yours, &c., VIKING.

Sir,—Your correspondent might derive consolation from the history of the Israelite kings. King SOLOMON was in all probability jilted—perhaps frequently—in his salad days. Yet in the end, by persevering and not giving way, he amassed the substantial total of one thousand (1,000) wives. Without counselling him actually to go and do likewise, I should like to point out to your correspondent that *this is the right spirit*.

Yours, &c., THEOLOGIAN.

MY VERY DEAR SIR,—Take my advice, and look on the bright side. What seems a misfortune at first sight, often proves in the end to be a blessing. Many years ago I was engaged for six months to a lady who afterwards refused to marry me. What was the result? Misery? Gloom? Not a bit of it. I wrote and placed to great advantage articles on 'How to Propose', 'Buying the Ring', 'Do Girls like Presents?', 'The £ s. d. of Courtship', 'Should Kisses be Taxed?' and 'How to Write a Love-letter'; also two hundred and four sets of verse, and a powerful story called *The Jilting of Joshua Jenkins*. I attribute to my engagement and the experience I derived from it my present position of sub-editor on *Blogg's Weekly Nuggets. Verb. Sap.*

Yours in haste, ENERGETIC JOURNALIST.[40]

All these written forms – the public letters, the telegrams, the postcards – feature in this book, and it is one of the pleasures and challenges of this edition to attempt to convey Wodehouse's pride in impressively headed notepaper, his marginal doodles, and his frustration with his beloved Royal typewriter. One imagines that the felicitously mistaken euphony of a 1932 telegram, instructing his agent to 'PUBLISH OMNIBUSH' signed 'SODEHOUSE', would have made Wodehouse smile.[41] A full sight of Wodehouse's extant correspondence gives a sense of the rate at which he was working and writing. He was often typing several letters a day – almost every day of his life. And, despite a (fictional) anecdote in which he claimed that he tossed all his letters out of the window, relying on the public's goodwill to post them, he was an assiduous and careful correspondent.[42]

There are many such confected anecdotes in Wodehouse's autobiographical works. They appear not through any innate mendacity, but from his almost compulsive desire to please his readers. 'We shall have to let truth go to the wall if it interferes with entertainment', he told Guy Bolton, as they planned their autobiographical memoir, *Bring on the Girls*.[43] Indeed, any editor setting out to work on Wodehouse's correspondence from a biographical perspective is conscious that Wodehouse likes to 'improve' his primary material. The 'letters' from Wodehouse, collected by his friend William Townend and published under the title *Performing Flea*, are a prime example – radically rewritten, as Wodehouse told his editor, to be 'full of anecdotes about celebrities – which the public loves – and a lot of funny stories'.[44] The letters are also heavily cut, to remove what Wodehouse saw as the 'frightfully dull' focus on 'Pekes and footer'.[45]

The original copies of Wodehouse's letters are kept in a variety of locations. A large number are held in the Wodehouse Archive. Many are in private hands, and a quantity in library collections across the world. Their forms are various and fascinating, ranging from handwritten and typed letters, to telegrams, novelty Christmas cards, postcards, and scribbled notes, letters embedded in government papers – and not a few transcribed by admiring friends.

Given the adverse comments that have been levelled at Wodehouse over the years, transparency has been of paramount importance in the preparation of this edition. I have been fortunate to have the full support and cooperation of the Wodehouse Estate, which granted me the freedom to publish any and every part of any Wodehouse letter. But the vast size of Wodehouse's correspondence has necessarily made this a selected edition. Letters have been chosen for inclusion on the basis of their individual merit – either in terms of the information that they offer about Wodehouse's life, the evolution of his style, or times in which he lived. Cuts within individual letters have also been essential, but passages have only been removed if they are irrelevant to the main thrust of the letter, or to Wodehouse's biographical or artistic narrative. I have made a particular point of leaving the letters that Wodehouse sent during the war years as complete as space will allow.

One of the problems in editing Wodehouse's letters is the effect it has on their particular rhythm and tone. Given that Wodehouse is the subject of this book of letters, cuts have obviously been made to make him the primary focus. This has the effect of diminishing one of the key aspects of his correspondence – his concern for other people. There is almost no letter that does not begin and end with Wodehouse's often extensive concerns for, and enquiries about, the person to whom he is writing. Bill Townend's eczema, Rene's arthritis, Lily's finances and the state of Denis's dog's bowels are all part of the substance of his letters.

A final editorial decision relates to the question of when a letter actually qualifies as being a letter; whether, for instance, one should include letters that were written but never posted, letters that were posted but never received, or letters that exist only in the form of copies – transcribed within the letters of others. I have included all of the above in this edition, with the view that the journey a letter has taken, or not taken, may be illuminating in its own way. A particularly intriguing history surrounds one of the critical letters in this book – a note that was written by Wodehouse when under prison guard in Paris. The letter was an affectionate and cheerful one, intended to reassure Ethel of his safety and to raise her spirits in the frightening atmosphere of newly liberated Paris. Wodehouse gave the letter to a messenger – but it was in fact never delivered as intended. Instead, some forty-seven years later, an envelope arrived in Remsenburg, Long Island, addressed to Lady Wodehouse. The Frenchman who had been charged with its delivery had, for some reason, been unable to carry out his mission, and the document only came to light after his death.

Wodehouse himself had died just two years earlier – but the delivery of this love letter from beyond the grave seems a small material tribute to his fictional world where all, in the end, comes right. As Wodehouse's Ginger Kemp puts it, 'such is the magic of a letter from the right person'.[46]

1 'The Aunt and the Sluggard' (*Strand* and *SEP* 1916), repr. in *Carry On, Jeeves* (1925).

2 See 'Doing Clarence a Bit of Good' (*Strand* 1913; *Pictorial Review* 1914), repr. in *My Man Jeeves* (1919).

3 The phrase is Robert McCrum's. See *Wodehouse: A Life* (London: Viking, 2004), p. 139.

4 See PGW's early letter to Eric George, October 1899 (Morgan).

5 The description is W. H. Auden's. See 'Balaam and His Ass' (1954), repr. in *The Dyer's Hand* (New York: Vintage, 1948), p. 144.

6 PGW to Lawrence Durrell, 19 May 1948 (Southern Illinois).

7 PGW to Leonora Cazalet, 2 April 1921 and 30 March 1925 (Wodehouse Archive).

8 There have been two earlier collections of Wodehouse's letters. Frances Donaldson's *Yours, Plum: The Letters of P. G. Wodehouse* (1990) is limited to the letters located in the Wodehouse Archive, and its thematic arrangement makes it necessarily highly selective; *Performing Flea* (1953) contains solely Wodehouse's letters written to William Townend.

9 PGW to William Townend, 23 March 1955 (Dulwich).

10 PGW to William Townend, 24 February 1945 (Dulwich).

11 *Joy in the Morning* (1946), Chapter 1.

12 'Poetry is not a turning loose of emotion, but an escape from emotion', T. S. Eliot, 'Tradition and the Individual Talent' (1919) in *Selected Essays* (London: Faber, 1969), p. 21.

13 PGW to Denis Mackail, 18 November 1949 (Wodehouse Archive).

14 See P. G. Wodehouse, 'Stone and the Weed', *The Captain* (May 1905), repr. in *Tales of Wrykyn and Elsewhere* (London: Porpoise, 1997), p. 315.

15 Dr Johnson to Hester Thrale, 27 October 1777. See *Letters To and From the Late Samuel Johnson L.L.D.*, published by Hester Lynch Piozzi (London: A. Strachan, 1788), p. 11.

16 PGW to Denis Mackail, 7 November 1945 (Wodehouse Archive).

17 Stephen Medcalf, 'The Innocence of P. G. Wodehouse' in *The Modern English Novel: the Reader, the Writer and the Work*, ed. Gabriel Josipovici (London: Open Books, 1976), p. 188.

18 See *Punch, or the London Charivari*, 1 February 1933, vol. 184, p. 140.

19 *Joy in the Morning*, Chapter 5.

20 'Jeeves and the Impending Doom', in *Very Good, Jeeves* (1930).

21 *Jeeves and the Feudal Spirit*. See Chapter 1.

22 Basil Boothroyd, 'The Laughs' in *A Homage to P. G. Wodehouse* (London: Barrie and Jenkins, 1973), p. 62.

23 *Pigs Have Wings* (1952), Chapter 5; *Bertie Wooster Sees It Through* (1954), Chapter 19.

24 PGW to Guy Bolton, 1 September 1945 (Wodehouse Archive).

25 PGW to William Townend, 11 May 1947 (Dulwich).

26 Mark Steyn, *Broadway Babies Say Goodnight* (London: Faber, 1997), p. 53.

27 PGW to Denis Mackail, 26 January 1946 (Wodehouse Archive).

28 PGW to Guy Bolton, 16 October 1959 (Wodehouse Archive).

29 'the poet has [...] no identity [...] he has no self [...] When I am in a room with People [...] the identity of every one in the room begins so to press upon me that I am in a very little time annihilated', John Keats to Richard Woodhouse, 27 October 1818, repr. in *Selected Letters of John Keats*, ed. Grant F. Scott (Cambridge, Mass.: Harvard University Press, 2005), p. 195.

30 PGW to William Townend, 23 January 1935 (Dulwich).

31 Evelyn Waugh, 'An Angelic Doctor: The Work of P. G. Wodehouse' (1939), repr. in *The Essays, Articles and Reviews of Evelyn Waugh*, ed. Donat Gallagher (London: Methuen, 1983), p. 255.

32 W. H. Auden, 'Dingley Dell & The Fleet', repr. in *The Dyer's Hand*, p. 411. My second quotation is taken from Theodor Adorno's 'Lyric Poetry and Society' (1951) in *Telos* 20 (1974), p. 5.

33 Medcalf, p. 189.

34 Medcalf, p. 197.

35 'You Can't Make Love By Wireless' from *The Beauty Prize* (1923). See *The Complete Lyrics of P. G. Wodehouse*, edited by Barry Day (Oxford: Scarecrow, 2004), pp. 325–6.

36 'Tangled Hearts' in *Nothing Serious* (1950).

37 P. G. Wodehouse, *The Code of the Woosters*, Chapter 2; Medcalf, p. 197.

38 *Pearls, Girls and Monty Bodkin* (1972), Chapter 3.

39 'Our Wants', *Punch* 3 (1842), p. 140.

40 P. G. Wodehouse, 'Balm for the Broken-Hearted', *Punch, or the London Charivari*, vol. 126, 24 February 1904, p. 135.

41 PGW to Paul Reynolds, 27 April 1932 (Columbia).

42 See *Bring on the Girls* in *Wodehouse on Wodehouse* (London: Penguin, 1981), p. 139.

43 PGW to Guy Bolton, 4 November 1952 (Wodehouse Archive).

44 PGW to J. D. Grimsdick, 23 March 1953 (Dulwich).

45 PGW to William Townend, 23 March 1955 (Dulwich).

46 *The Adventures of Sally* (1922), Chapter 11.

Editorial Policy

All cuts are marked with an ellipsis, with the exception of postscripts that are, on occasion, silently omitted. Silent corrections are made for most typographical errors, save in the case of misspelled names, where it is thought that the mistake might reveal something about the relationship. The layout of Wodehouse letters varies and on occasion no date or address is given. Where it seems appropriate or necessary, an approximate date may be supplied in square brackets. If present in the original, dates have been justified to the left, and all addresses to the right. Addresses have not been standardised, but are given as they appear on the original letter. If a salutation or signature is omitted, this signals that a significant cut has been made at either the beginning or end of a letter, or both. Wodehouse's occasional intentional comic grammatical lapses ('look what he done') and idiosyncratic spelling, ('dam' for 'damn', 'lyrist' for 'lyricist') have been preserved and left unmarked, so as not to clutter the reading texture. All sources for the letters are given at the end of the book, together with references for any quotations within the commentary.

Selected Recipients

LILLIAN SARAH BARNETT
(1880–1974)

Known to Wodehouse as 'Lily', Lillian Barnett was Wodehouse's housekeeper at his house in Emsworth – 'Threepwood'. Wodehouse continued to maintain his house in England for a time while he was in America, and often wrote to Lily to send over necessary possessions and organise minor administrative matters – and to get news of England, as he found himself 'frightfully homesick at times'. Indeed, Wodehouse's letters are less those of an employer than of a friend. Personal, affectionate and helpful, he informs her of his latest theatrical or writing ventures, asks after her husband, Bert (the local postman), and attempts to help find work for her children. The correspondence continued throughout Wodehouse's life, long after his house at Emsworth was given up.

ANGA VON BODENHAUSEN
(1900–1976)

Of Scottish descent, and a member of a respected German aristocratic family, Anga von Bodenhausen was a widow when she met Wodehouse. She lived in Degenershausen, an estate in the Harz mountains in Germany, with her young daughter, Reinhild. Anga took Wodehouse in as a house-guest in 1941, following the outcry surrounding his Berlin broadcasts. He returned to her house during the summer of 1942.

Fervently anti-Nazi, Anga later became engaged to her cousin, Raven von Barnikow, who was peripherally involved in the assassination attempt upon Hitler. Wodehouse corresponded with Anga on his return to Berlin, and also later, when he and Ethel moved from Berlin to Paris. After Germany's defeat, Degenershausen fell into the hands of the Russians, and Anga von Bodenhausen was advised to surrender the property and make her escape. Moving through Bavaria, and then on to Berlin, Anga and her daughter suffered much hardship and near-starvation. They lost touch with the Wodehouses, and eventually found safety and a home in Holstein.

GUY BOLTON
(1882–1979)

Born in Kent, Bolton's childhood was blighted by the early death of his mother, who was an alcoholic. His father moved the family from England to Manhattan in 1893. Bolton dreamed of being a writer, but initially found himself working in his father's engineering business, before qualifying as an architect. He had his first magazine story accepted in 1904. Married by 1908, and soon with two children to support, he continued to work in his father's architectural firm, while collaborating on plays. Encouraged by a 1911 success, he gave up his day job to write for the theatre full-time. In 1914, he first met and began to write lyrics for the composer Jerome Kern. In 1915, Kern and Bolton joined forces with Wodehouse, and an immensely successful three-way collaboration began on a series of musical comedies which played at the Princess Theatre in New York. These included such hits as *Sally*, *Oh, Boy!*, and *Oh, Lady! Lady!!* Wodehouse and Bolton remained close friends for the rest of their lives, working and travelling together during an intensive period between 1915 and the early 1920s. Bolton recalls that working with Wodehouse was 'delightfully easy ... Ideas came and were dropped or seized on ... we were always laughing'.

Bolton continued to write straight plays, musical comedies and novels throughout his life. He sustained a long correspondence with Wodehouse, which touches frequently on the subject of work, as well as their other shared passion – dogs.

Bolton's romantic life was often complicated. Extremely handsome, he was drawn to many women and divorced three times, but his fourth marriage in 1937 to Virginia DeLanty, a former chorus-girl, was to last until his death.

(1892–1950)

Bradshaw and Wodehouse first met in New York in 1909 and their friendship began when Bradshaw, a fellow Englishman, interviewed Wodehouse for a feature for the boys' magazine, *The Captain*, in 1910. Bradshaw's father had worked his way up from cabin boy to a captain of the Red Star Shipping Line, and his mother was a nurse from Liverpool. The family moved to New York in 1907. Bradshaw's mother was a Christian Scientist, and both parents had strong views about their son's aims in life.

Bradshaw worked as a journalist and editor for various New York publications, and also as private secretary and amanuensis for the financier and writer, Thomas Lawson, in Boston. When in New York, Bradshaw often stayed with Wodehouse, and acted as his literary agent on an informal basis. Wodehouse dedicated his novel, *Psmith in the City*, to Bradshaw in 1910. Bradshaw reciprocated with a dedication to Wodehouse in his school novel, *The Right Sort*, in 1912. After a difficult romance, Bradshaw married the American, Olive Marie Barrows, in 1915.

SIR EDWARD CAZALET
(1936–)

The second child of Leonora Cazalet. Folklore in the village of Shipbourne, Kent, tells of Wodehouse patiently following Edward's nanny and pram round Shipbourne Green before setting off on his own normal daily six-miler. Edward in his early days became very involved with his father, Peter's, racing stable, riding as an amateur steeplechase jockey. Later he became a barrister and subsequently a High Court judge. Wodehouse loved hearing about Edward's cases and, at times, he would ask for guidance when dealing with legal matters in his plots. (On one occasion Edward recalls telling Wodehouse that he had been unable to trace any record of a policeman's helmet ever having been stolen.)

Edward would visit Wodehouse in Long Island, armed with the latest thrillers or bestsellers: Agatha Christie, Dick Francis and Anthony

Powell were much favoured. After lunch he would go out with Plum on his afternoon walks, accompanied by at least two dogs and meeting other canine friends of theirs in the neighbourhood. In the evening two pre-dinner martinis each was the norm.

In 1965, Edward married Camilla Gage, and Wodehouse greatly enjoyed discussing Shakespeare with her. She recalls that he 'preferred the comedies to the tragedies' and that, overall, he thought *Love's Labour's Lost* was one of the most underrated of Shakespeare's plays.

Edward now helps to run the Wodehouse Estate, which continues to have a remarkable turnover of Wodehouse's books, translated into at least thirty languages.

LEONORA CAZALET (FORMERLY WODEHOUSE NÉE ROWLEY) (1904–1944)

Daughter of Leonard Rowley and Ethel Newton, Leonora was educated in England, France and America. Her father died in 1910, when Leonora was only six, but she was formally adopted by Wodehouse five years later. She soon became his adored daughter. Jokingly referred to as his 'confidential secretary and advisor', Leonora frequently advised him on his manuscripts, and accompanied him on business trips. She was a talented writer in her own right, albeit with a very small output, and published under the pseudonym, 'Leol Yeo'. She also worked briefly for MGM studios in Hollywood. Leonora was remembered as an extraordinarily intelligent, charming and attractive person – an individual full of 'humanity', with 'no understanding or feeling for class barriers', who was 'interested in everyone she met'.

Leonora married Peter Cazalet in 1932, and had two children – Sheran and Edward. She died unexpectedly, and suddenly, in 1944, before her fortieth birthday. On hearing of her death, Wodehouse was reported to have said, 'I thought she was immortal'. Wodehouse never recovered from her loss. When her son, Edward, once asked him if he could write a short memoir about her he said, a few days later, in a voice close to tears, that he just could not manage this because he found it too painful.

(1899–1989)

The sister of Wodehouse's son-in-law, Peter Cazalet, Thelma Cazalet joined her brother, Victor, in the House of Commons in 1931 and was an active and regular speaker on a number of issues – in particular, education, women's rights and the arts. She was married in 1939 to the journalist and broadcaster, David Keir. In May 1945, she was appointed Parliamentary Secretary to the Minister of Education in the short-lived post-war caretaker government. The 1945 general election was to sweep the coalition government from power – ending her parliamentary career. Thereafter she became a member of the Arts Council, a Governor of the BBC, and President of the Equal Pay Campaign Committee. She was appointed a CBE in 1962.

For Wodehouse's ninetieth birthday, she edited the collection, *Homage to P. G. Wodehouse* – a series of congratulatory essays from twelve well-known writers, including John Betjeman, Auberon Waugh and Malcolm Muggeridge.

SIR ARTHUR CONAN DOYLE
(1859–1930)

Doyle began writing while pursuing a career as a medical surgeon. Service as a ship's doctor gave him a range of experiences, many of which fed into his later writing. In 1885 he settled in Portsmouth and built up a successful practice, and also a reputation as a writer of short stories. His first Sherlock Holmes story, *A Study in Scarlet*, was published when Wodehouse was only six years old. By 1891, Doyle had moved to London, and his work was a hit with the readers of *The Strand Magazine*. Doyle was always one of Wodehouse's great writing heroes, and a major influence on his early work. Quotations from Doyle's work appear thoughout Wodehouse's writing, from his first novel, *The Pothunters*, to his last complete book, *Aunts Aren't Gentlemen*. The pair played cricket together at Lord's, and also at Doyle's country house, and met for lunch occasionally during the 1920s, where the conversation sometimes turned to their shared interest in spiritualism.

ERIC BEARDSWORTH GEORGE
(1881–1961)

Also known as 'Jimmy', Eric George was in the year above Wodehouse at Dulwich College. He left in 1899 to take up a place at Oriel College, Oxford. Wodehouse's own nickname for George – 'Jeames' – is taken from Thackeray's parodic *Punch* sketches, 'The Diary of C. Jeames de la Pluche Esq.' (1845). The sketches tell the story of a footman turned millionaire. In their correspondence, Wodehouse adopts the phrases and voice of one of Jeames' spurned female admirers. George went on to exhibit at the Royal Academy, specialising in the male nude figure, and religious subjects. His epic poem, *Cephalus and Procris: An Episode between Two Wars*, was published in 1954.

IRA GERSHWIN
(1896–1983)

Born in New York, Ira began his working life in a hotel owned by his father, and started writing lyrics at the request of his younger brother, the composer, George. To begin with, he was much in George's shadow, but by 1924, Broadway billboards gave joint credit to both the Gershwins on the smash hit *Lady, Be Good*, soon to be followed by numerous Broadway successes. Ira went on to write such well-known lyrics as 'The Man I Love', ''S Wonderful' and 'I Got Rhythm'. Wodehouse first collaborated with the Gershwin brothers on the 1926 musical, *Oh, Kay!*, and Ira Gershwin was one of the many lyricists who would later pay tribute to Wodehouse as a mentor and inspiration. The pair met again in Hollywood in the 1930s and continued to correspond for the rest of their lives.

LADY HORNBY (NÉE CAZALET)
(1934–)

Sheran and her younger brother Edward were regularly visited by their grandparents Ethel and P. G. Wodehouse in the years before the war, and Wodehouse particularly enjoyed going for long walks with his young granddaughter when staying with the family. From the mid-1950s, Sheran was making frequent visits to America to see the Wodehouses. In the late 1950s, she began work for the BBC, ultimately becoming part of a team running one of its main contract departments. She remembers that Wodehouse often questioned her closely about her work in the television and theatre worlds, and the pair would go to New York together, to see the latest shows. In 1967, Sheran married Simon Hornby, later to be Chairman and Chief Executive of W.H. Smith. Hornby was a major Wodehouse enthusiast and later a Patron of the P. G. Wodehouse Society. He regularly joined her on her visits to Long Island.

DENIS GEORGE MACKAIL
(1892–1971)

Grandson of the artist Edward Burne-Jones, Mackail was born into an academic and literary family. After an Oxford education, financial constraints forced him to put his literary ambitions aside, and he found himself working as a civil servant and later in the print room of the British Museum. Nevertheless, his first novel, *What Next?*, found immediate success, and enabled him to give up work and write full-time. Wodehouse and Mackail frequently exchanged letters, discussing not only work, but also their shared love of Pekingese dogs. Denis had a long and happy marriage to Diana Granet, and Ethel was also close to the couple. Despite the overall warmth of their correspondence, in later years, Wodehouse seemed to find the sarcastic strains of Mackail's letters grating.

SIR EDWARD MONTAGUE COMPTON MACKENZIE
(1883–1972)

After attempts at poetry and theatrical writing, Mackenzie began to find success as a novelist in the period just before the First World War. Service in the Royal Marines interrupted his writing, but provided him with much material for later novels. After the war he settled in

Scotland, became a founder member of the National Party of Scotland in 1928, and went to live on the Hebridean island of Barra (which was later to inspire his most enduring novel, *Whisky Galore*).

Mackenzie first came across Wodehouse in 1899, when both writers were still schoolboys. Mackenzie recalls reading of Wodehouse's exploits on the rugby pitch as 'an outstanding forward' for a rival school team. Mackenzie went on to admire Wodehouse's fiction greatly – and when Wodehouse praised Mackenzie's 1919 comic novel *Poor Relations* as the 'best comic novel for a long time', Mackenzie recalled that it was 'the greatest pleasure he had ever received from a review during my life'.

The pair became friends, and Mackenzie was invited to lunch parties at Norfolk Street, finding himself captivated by Leonora – 'the most brilliant young woman I had ever known'. Mackenzie was a staunch supporter of Wodehouse during the difficult war years, and wrote to the *Daily Telegraph* to counter A. A. Milne's attack on Wodehouse's broadcasts from Berlin.

Mackenzie was, like Wodehouse, a prolific writer, and the pair exchanged occasional congratulatory letters throughout their careers.

MALCOLM MUGGERIDGE
(1903–1990)

British journalist, broadcaster and author, best known in his later life as an outspoken television presenter. After travelling widely to report on worldwide news stories, Muggeridge joined the Intelligence Corps, and served in Mozambique, North Africa, Italy and Paris during World War Two. When Wodehouse was interrogated by MI5 about his wartime broadcasts, Muggeridge was assigned to the Wodehouses as a liaison officer. He soon became good friends with the couple, helping them negotiate the difficulties of post-liberation Paris – as well as introducing Wodehouse to George Orwell.

Wodehouse was always intensely grateful for Muggeridge's help and support during these war years. Muggeridge became editor of *Punch* magazine in 1953, and commissioned a number of articles from Wodehouse, which later became part of Wodehouse's autobiography, *Over Seventy*.

JAMES BRAND PINKER
(1863–1922)

Pinker began his career as a clerk in Tilbury Docks, then worked as a journalist in Constantinople before becoming the editor of *Pearson's Magazine*. After only a year as editor, he left to found his literary agency in London in 1896. Pinker was one of the very first professional literary agents, and his clients included Henry and William James, Arnold Bennett, Joseph Conrad, George Gissing, H.G. Wells, D.H. Lawrence, Edith Wharton and James Joyce. His entry in the 1901 *Literary Year Book* noted that he had a particular reputation for 'helping young authors in the early stages of their career, when they most need the aid of an advisor with a thorough knowledge of the literary world and the publishing trade'.

PAUL REVERE REYNOLDS
(1864–1944)

A Harvard-educated philosophy graduate who studied under William James, this 'tall, spare, awkward, shy' man was the unlikely founder of America's first and (for its time) most successful literary agency. Wodehouse became Reynolds' client in 1915, and joined a list that included Stephen Crane, George Bernard Shaw, Willa Cather, Booth Tarkington, H. G. Wells, and F. Scott Fitzgerald. Reynolds' offices were as modest as his persona. His son recalls that he leased 'four small, dirty, badly furnished rooms', always worked in his starched collar and suit, and rarely stopped for lunch. The office telephone was almost redundant; Reynolds preferred letters, replying remarkably promptly and carefully to even the smallest written enquiry. He was unceasingly attentive to Wodehouse, and dealt efficiently and tactfully both with major deals with magazine editors, and with minor requests – sending flowers to Ethel on Wodehouse's behalf, or dealing with unpaid bills.

(1928–)

A British writer, famous for his satirical novels, such as *Riotous Assembly* (1971), *Indecent Exposure* (1973) and *Porterhouse Blue* (1974). Wodehouse admired Sharpe's work and a correspondence began in the 1970s, in which Wodehouse confided his insecurities about the plots of his novels, his reflection that if he 'had gone to Oxford', he wouldn't have become a writer – and his honest opinion that William Townend's writing was 'frightfully dull'.

WILLIAM TOWNEND
(1881–1961)

Known in early correspondence as V.T., 'Villiam', and later as Bill. Wodehouse shared an attic study with Townend at Dulwich College, and slept in the same dormitory in Elm House. Townend left Dulwich in 1899 to train to become a commercial artist, and provided illustrations for Wodehouse's early serial, *The White Feather*. He married Irene Ellam, known as 'Rene', in 1915. Townend spent his twenties in America and Canada, before returning home. He published many short stories and novels but never found success on a wide scale. A book of Wodehouse's letters to Townend, *Performing Flea*, edited by Townend himself, was published in 1953.

It was Wodehouse who persuaded Townend to give up painting for writing. Wodehouse always felt some responsibility towards his friend as a result. Their extensive correspondence over fifty years shows that Wodehouse gave him much advice and encouragement, as well as writing to publishers on his behalf – and quietly subsidising him. The pair often discussed each other's emerging plots, and Townend offered Wodehouse numerous ideas for his stories.

Born in London, the son of publisher and editor, Arthur Waugh, Evelyn went up to Oxford in 1922. Although he initially resisted the idea of becoming a writer, his 1928 success *Decline and Fall* was followed by novels that included *Vile Bodies* (1930), *Black Mischief* (1932) and *Brideshead Revisited* (1945). Waugh had admired Wodehouse for many years, writing in his diary in 1940 that he 'read P. G. Wodehouse (who has been lost along with the Channel ports) [...] and forgot the war'. The pair first met when Waugh visited New York after the war, and they became friends.

Waugh's championing of Wodehouse culminated in a 1961 radio tribute, in which he condemned the Establishment's treatment of Wodehouse during the war, and celebrated his 'idyllic' fictional world. In Wodehouse's later years, the pair bonded over their mutual dislike of journalists. Wodehouse was to commemorate Waugh's infamous public row with two journalists from the *Daily Express* in verse. Waugh referred to Wodehouse, both affectionately and respectfully, as 'Dr Wodehouse' – in reference to his honorary Oxford D.Litt. Wodehouse's library contained all of Waugh's novels, one of which is inscribed to 'the Master of Our Profession'. One 'has to regard a man as a Master', Waugh wrote, 'who can produce on average three uniquely brilliant and entirely original similes to every page'.

CHAPTER ONE

Childhood

Throughout their marriage, P. G. Wodehouse and his wife Ethel left small notes around the house for each other. Some were affectionate, others more workaday. One from Ethel, written long after her husband had gone to bed, reads as follows:

3.30am
My Darling
Pears for your breakfast and please <u>first</u>
drink the small glass of <u>fresh</u> orange juice.
Took hours to squeeze.
All the love I have.
Bunny[1]

The tone here says much about this relationship. Ethel's emotional candour made her a good match for a man who, even in his most personal letters, gave little away. It was a marriage that brought Wodehouse long-lasting happiness, providing him with inspiration, domestic security and a type of loving affection that bordered on the maternal.

Pelham Grenville was born into a very different atmosphere. His was a typical Victorian childhood, where feelings remained unspoken and distances were kept. The third of four sons, he arrived prematurely on 15 October 1881, when his mother was visiting relatives in Guildford [see plate 1]. His first lodgings were unassuming, but behind the façade of the tall Victorian end-of-terrace house at 59 Epsom Road, one of the most remarkable writers of the twentieth century made his entrance.

Though not wealthy, the Wodehouses were established members of that very specific, but long vanished, sector of society – the Victorian 'gentry' – defined by its particular ideas of morality, education, status and propriety. The Wodehouse family line itself could be traced back to Agincourt, while his mother's family, the Deanes, were related to

Cardinal Newman. Eleanor displayed a surprisingly romantic streak in her choice of names for her sons. Philip Peveril, her eldest, took his name from Walter Scott's 1823 novel *Peveril of the Peak* – an allusion to the fact that he was born overseas, the first white child born on the Peak in Hong Kong. The choices for the two middle sons were less literary but equally striking. Armine was an old family name from the Wodehouse line, while Pelham (always known to his friends as 'Plum') was named after his godfather, Colonel Pelham von Donop. But with Wodehouse's middle name – Grenville – Eleanor once again showed her poetic side, conjuring one of Tennyson's heroes; and with Richard Lancelot, her youngest child, Eleanor returns to Tennyson and Arthurian legend.

The names might have been unusual, but Wodehouse's father, Henry Ernest – known as Ernest – was 'as normal as rice pudding' and determined to give his sons a childhood to match.[2] This was a world of tapioca and high tea, of moral edification and steely discipline. The only thing conspicuously – but critically – missing from Wodehouse's upbringing was the presence of his parents.

Ernest was one of many ambitious young Victorian men who had chosen to forge a career in the Colonies. After joining the Civil Service in 1867, he had been sent to Hong Kong. A post in such a location was 'rather like being awarded your Second Eleven colours; for the First Eleven always went to India'.[3] Nevertheless, there was much for a civil servant to do in 1860s Hong Kong. Crime flourished, piracy was rife, and the numerous opium dens and brothels needed to be kept under licence. Both the Anglo-Chinese police force and higher-ranking members of the British Administration had been perceived as corrupt, and Whitehall was attempting reforms. Initially appointed as an interpreter, Ernest was given the important job of commanding the Chinese section of the police force.[4] He met and married Eleanor Deane in 1877, and soon became a respected magistrate [see plate 3].

After Pelham's birth, Eleanor took her third son back to 'The Homestead', their bungalow in Hong Kong, and for the first two years of his life he was placed in the care of an 'ayah', or Chinese nursemaid. Meanwhile, Armine and Peveril were set up in a house in England under the care of a nurse named Emma Roper. Eleanor kept a close eye on the situation, as her parents were living in the house next door.

Once Pelham was three years old, he was brought back from Hong Kong to join his brothers. 'Nanny Roper' was remembered by Wodehouse as being 'very severe in her manner, making the boys dress formally every day and keeping them spotlessly clean'.[5] Some firmness was probably necessary; a childhood friend recalled that the 'little Wodehouses', especially Pelham, were 'very naughty' [see plate 2].[6] A few years later, the children were moved on to what was known as a 'Dame School' – a privately run establishment in a family home, in which small numbers of children received education and accommodation. Overseen by the Prince sisters, and based in Croydon, a suburb of South London, 'Elmhurst' (as it was later known) catered specifically for the families of colonial civil servants. Later, Wodehouse remembered his Croydon school as the place in which he first encountered the feisty nature of the Cockney housemaid, immortalised in figures such as *Uncle Dynamite*'s Elsie Bean.[7]

Many Victorian children whose parents were British nationals overseas received this sort of education *in loco parentis*. Indeed, separation from one's parents under such circumstances was the norm. The climate of the tropics was hazardous for infants, and Hong Kong had particularly acute problems in terms of drainage and sanitary provision. Parental leave was at four- or five-year intervals, and travel from Hong Kong to England by ship took over two months. A number of children endured far worse than Wodehouse. The young Kipling, a decade earlier, was sent back from Bombay at the age of three, and was cruelly treated. Looking back on the sudden separation from his parents, Kipling recalls the experience as akin to having 'lost all [his] world'.[8] Wodehouse, by contrast, reflected cheerfully on his early years. He had, he admits, no shortage of familial contact. Holidays from school were spent visiting his numerous relatives. The Wodehouse boys had no fewer than fifteen uncles and twenty aunts. But this was contact of a desultory sort:

Looking back, I can see that I was just passed from hand to hand. It was an odd life with no home to go to, but I have always accepted everything that happens to me in a philosophical spirit; and I can't remember ever having been unhappy in those days. My feeling now is that it was very decent of those aunts to put up three small boys for all those years. We can't have added much entertainment to their lives. The only thing you could say for us is that we never gave any trouble.[9]

Wodehouse's breeziness is accented by his characteristically 'decent' understatement. Things in his world are always 'odd' rather than 'terrible'. But sadness seeps through. The Wodehouse children sound like so much unwanted luggage. There is a touch of strained parody about the final phrase – 'we never gave any trouble' – as if the voices of many disapproving aunts are still ringing in his ears. Perhaps most significant is the thin comfort blanket of amnesia: 'I can't remember ever having been unhappy'. There were, one suspects, muffled tears at bedtime for his own 'lost world', preface to emotional withdrawal.

For even by Victorian standards, Ernest and Eleanor's absence was a long one. The separation was to create a coolness between Wodehouse and Eleanor. 'We looked upon mother', he recalls, 'more like an aunt. She came home very infrequently'.[10] The fact that there are no extant letters between Wodehouse and his parents, either from his childhood or from his later life, may indicate something about these particular relationships. While it is not clear what sort of correspondent Eleanor Wodehouse might have been, she was, by all accounts, a distant and unsentimental mother.

This question of emotional containment echoes through Wodehouse's writing. Brought up in the midst of the Victorian cult of childhood, Wodehouse would have been surrounded by commodified images such as the Pears' Soap 'Bubbles' boy, and the lisping 'sweet innocence' of the children's classic *Helen's Babies*.[11] Those of tender years, in Wodehouse's fiction, are portrayed with less sentiment. 'I can't handle anything except rather tough children, if I am to get comedy', Wodehouse admitted.[12] For Wodehouse, being a child – and being tough – went hand in hand.

While he kept his sons at arm's length, Ernest Wodehouse planned their education with some care, particularly as his second son, Armine, was seen to be academically brilliant. Pelham was left more to his own devices, and read children's popular works voraciously. I was 'soaked in Anstey's stuff', he recalls.[13] Familiar with Victorian classics such as *Tom Brown's School Days*, he also read and loved the moral bestseller

Eric, or Little by Little, and was gripped by the school stories which appeared in the weekly penny magazine *The Boy's Own Paper.*[14]

But even in his earliest years Wodehouse went a step beyond the average schoolboy, independently tackling Pope's translation of the *Iliad* at the age of six, and writing his own brand of epic 'poertory', of which a remnant survives:

> Oh ah that Sorryful
> day
> When on the battel
> field the pets did
> lay in sorryful
> disgrace.
> With red blud
> Streaming past
> There life ros
> pasing fast
> And in the
> camp there lay
> Thousands of dead
> Men.
>
> P.G. Wodehouse
>
> this is a bit of
> poertory I Made
> up

In 1889, a change was called for. Peveril, Wodehouse's eldest brother, was suffering from a 'weak chest', and the Wodehouse children were moved to a school in Guernsey as part of a 'package deal', where they might 'benefit' from the sea air. Wodehouse remembers it as 'a delightful place. [...] My recollections are all of wandering about the island.' The only disappointment, he recalls, was 'the awful steamer trips back to England for the holiday'.

Vacations, Wodehouse recalls, would be spent with 'various aunts, some of whom I liked but one or two were very formidable Victorian women'.[15] Wodehouse was aware that he should 'Never complain!' He chose, instead to 'note every detail and write it down'.[16] The young Wodehouse may not have always had a pencil to hand, but it is clear from his fiction that he was continually observing his surroundings, and making mental notes, particularly on the matter of Aunts. It is, of course, Bertie Wooster who is most particularly plagued by the Auntly phenomenon – and his confrontation with an intimidating vista at Deverill Hall has something of a child's perspective about it:

> As far as the eye could reach, I found myself gazing on a surging sea of aunts. There were tall aunts, short aunts, stout aunts, thin aunts, and an aunt who was carrying on a conversation in a low voice to which nobody seemed to be paying the slightest attention.[7]

Bertie's Aunt Agatha, 'the nephew-crusher' who 'chews broken bottles and kills rats with her teeth', was, Wodehouse later confirmed, his Aunt Mary Deane, 'the scourge of my childhood'.[8] Another Deane sister, Louisa, was one of the models for the kindlier Aunt Dahlia.

'In this life', as Bertie phlegmatically muses, 'it is not aunts that matter but the courage which one brings to them'.[19] Indeed, Wodehouse's familiarity with the figure of the aunt was a felicitous coincidence for a comic writer. For the relationship's distance allowed him to exploit the plot potential of the family structure with a light touch. As Richard Usborne notes, '[i]t is funny when Bertie slides down drainpipes, or to America, to escape his Aunt Agatha's wrath. It would be sad if he were thus frightened by his mother'.[20]

Being a nephew, for Wodehouse, brought other literary benefits. Wodehouse's aunts did a great deal of visiting, particularly as four of them were vicars' wives. Wodehouse was often taken along on these social rounds, which included making calls to the local Great Houses. 'Even at the age of ten', Wodehouse remembers, ' I was a social bust, contributing little or nothing to the feast of reason and flow of soul. [...] There always came a moment when my hostess, smiling one of those painful smiles, suggested that it would be nice for your little nephew to go and have tea in the servants' hall. And she was right. I loved it. My mind today is fragrant with memories of kindly footmen and vivacious parlour-maids. In their society, I forgot to be shy and kidded back and forth with the best of them. [...] Sooner or later in would come the butler [...] "The young gentleman is wanted", he would say morosely, and the young gentleman would shamble out'.[21] It was in this way that Wodehouse gained so much knowledge of the life of servants behind the baize door. Characters such as the portly Beach, the Blandings butler, Angus McAllister, the gardener and 'human mule', and the chef Anatole, 'God's gift to the gastric juices', all owe their provenance to these childhood visits.

At twelve, Wodehouse was moved from Guernsey to a small private school at Kearsney, near Dover. 'I was supposed to be going into the Navy', he recalls.[22] The school was not a success at the time, but Wodehouse was later to use Malvern House as the alma mater of Bertie Wooster and several of his friends. Armine, meanwhile, was sent to a more academic boarding school in South London, Dulwich College. It was on another of Wodehouse's unhappy holidays, paying a visit to his elder brother, that Wodehouse first saw and fell in love with Dulwich. He pleaded with his father to allow him to attend. It was to be the beginning of 'six years of unbroken bliss'.[23]

1 Ethel Wodehouse to PGW, u.d. (Wodehouse Archive).

2 *Over Seventy* (1957), repr. in *Wodehouse on Wodehouse* (Harmondsworth: Penguin, 1981), p. 474.

3 Benny Green, *P. G. Wodehouse: A Literary Biography* (New York: Rutledge, 1981), p. 8.

4 See Colin Crisswell and Mike Watson, *The Royal Hong Kong Police Force* (London: Macmillan, 1982), p. 57.

5 David Jasen, *Portrait of a Master* (New York: Mason & Lipscomb, 1974), p. 5.

6 P. G. Wodehouse, *Notes and Phrases* (Wodehouse Archive).

7 See N. T. P. Murphy, *The Wodehouse Handbook*, Vol. I (London: Popgood & Groolley, 2006), p. 16.

8 Rudyard Kipling, 'Baa Baa Black Sheep', *The Week's News* (Allahabad), 21 December 1888.

9 Jasen, p. 8.

10 Jasen, p. 5.

11 The comment about *Helen's Babies* is George Orwell's. See 'Riding Down from Bangor', *Tribune*, 22 November 1946.

12 PGW to Paul Reynolds, 3 December 1937 (Columbia).

13 PGW to Richard Usborne, 9 May 1958 (Wodehouse Archive).

14 PGW to Richard Usborne, 3 June 1955 (Wodehouse Archive).

15 Jasen, p. 8.

16 This was P. G. Wodehouse's adult advice to a ten-year-old German girl, Reinhild von Bodenhausen, in 1941. See *P. G. Wodehouse: The Unknown Years* (Stamford Lake: Sri Lanka, 2009), p. 14.

17 P. G. Wodehouse, *The Mating Season* (1949), Chapter 1.

18 PGW to Richard Usborne, 14 January 1955 (Wodehouse Archive).

19 *The Mating Season*, Chapter 1.

20 Richard Usborne, *Wodehouse at Work* (London: Herbert Jenkins, 1961), p. 31.

21 *Over Seventy*, p. 512.

22 PGW to Richard Usborne, 1 September 1956 (Wodehouse Archive).

23 *Over Seventy*, p. 477.

CHAPTER TWO

Dulwich

Wodehouse arrived at Dulwich College when he was twelve and a half, and the six years spent there, he recalls, 'went like a breeze'.[1] He described it as 'a resolutely middle-class school'. Its pupils were sons of 'respectably solvent' parents, who had sent their sons to be educated in the knowledge that 'we all had to earn our living later on'.[2] With this ethos came a spirit of determined hard work, strong discouragement of 'putting on side', and good sportsmanship. Situated in the suburbs of South-East London, the imposing red-brick Victorian building is surrounded by sixty-five acres of rolling green fields, chestnut-lined avenues and cricket pitches. At the time Wodehouse arrived, the school was thriving, with more than six hundred boys.

Much of its success could be attributed to its extraordinary headmaster, Arthur Herman Gilkes. Wodehouse recalls Gilkes as 'a man with a long white beard who stood six-foot-six in his socks and he had one of those deep musical voices. I can still remember how he thrilled me when he read us that bit from Carlyle's *Sartor Resartus* which ends "But I, mine Werther, am above it all". It was terrific. But he also scared the pants off me!'[3] Gilkes had a magnetic presence, instilling the importance of fair play, as well as a love of sport and a thirst for knowledge. Harsh on slang and smoking, he was also generous and charismatic. He was often to be found umpiring on the cricket pitch, or giving the boys individual 'tutorials' for which they had to read an essay aloud – an experience which was, Wodehouse remembered, 'akin to suicide'.[4]

At Dulwich, things went well from the start. Wodehouse excelled in the open examination, winning a £20 scholarship, and was placed in a form of boys older than himself. While Wodehouse's brother, Armine, flourished in the sixth form, Gilkes took Wodehouse minor under his wing, banning him from cycling (due to his poor eyesight) and suggesting boxing as an alternative. But it was during his years in the sixth form that Wodehouse made his mark. He represented the school in the First XV for rugby football and the First XI at cricket, and also busied himself writing poetry. In 1899, he was chosen to be one of the editors of the school magazine, under the eye of William Beach Thomas, a Dulwich master later to become a famous war correspondent.

Wodehouse relished the social and gastronomic aspect of school as well. For most of his time he was a boarder, initially sharing a dormitory, and then a study bedroom, with one or two other boys. There were 'open fires in winter, a kettle for tea or cocoa, a toasting fork, a twice-daily delivery of bread, milk, and what the boys called "spreads" such as dripping, meat extracts, or honey. There was a Buttery in the Centre Block for milk and jam or chocolate "splits" during morning break, and "warm" cake for afternoon tea; and there was a meat meal and often sponge or suet puddings [...] at long trestle tables in the Great Hall at 6pm.'[5]

Though Pelham Grenville was seen as the more sportingly inclined of the brothers, he had his heart set on a place at Oxford, and was equally committed to his studies. 'We might commit mayhem on the football field, but after the game was over we trotted off to our houses and wrote Latin verse.'[6] He also showed an early thirst for literary journalism and remembered 'stroll[ing] down to the station' after school, to 'read the weeklies and the magazines on the bookstall' [see plate 4].[7] The shelves would have been full. The Education Acts of the 1870s led to an explosion in the numbers of newspapers and journals catering for every sector of society. Writing in 1955, Wodehouse recalls the number of boys' magazines. *Chums* was a particular favourite, a weekly periodical modelled on *The Boy's Own Paper*, which included advice on 'How to Train for the Football Season' and 'The Right Way to Carry a Boa-Constrictor', as well as serials which made 'an enormous impression' on him as a young reader, such as Max Pemberton's *Iron Pirate* and Robert Louis Stevenson's *Treasure Island*.

> Then – in 1900 – the *Captain* appeared, and in the first number was a serial by Fred Swainson called *Acton's Feud*. It began, I remember, 'Shannon, the old international, had brought a hot side down to play the school ...' and if there has ever been a better opening line than that, I have never come across it. It was

something entirely new in school stories – the real thing – and it inflamed me to do something in that line myself. If it hadn't been for *Acton's Feud*, I doubt if I would ever have written a school story.[8]

Wodehouse's first piece of published writing – an essay entitled 'Some Aspects of Game-Captaincy' – appeared as a prize-winning contribution to *The Public School Magazine* when he was still at Dulwich. His fee – 10/6 – was recorded in a notebook entitled *Record of Money Received for Literary Work*, in which he was to log his income for the next seven years. The essay is a masterpiece of classification, characterising the various types of football-playing schoolboys according to their genus: 'the keen and regular player', 'the partial slacker, and lastly, the entire, abject and absolute slacker'.[9] Almost all of Wodehouse's early published writings – *The Pothunters*, *Tales of St Austin's*, *The Gold Bat* and *The Head of Kay's* – were school stories and, like his very first piece, were based on his life at Dulwich and the fiction that he read during his time there.

Apart from a certain frostiness on the part of 'Scotty Gibbon', the football captain, or the 'scratching' of the annual match against Bedford owing to poor weather, there was little to mar the Dulwich years.[10] The biggest potential shadow came early on in his time at the school, with the news of his parents' return. In 1895, Ernest retired early from the Civil Service due to ill-health, and the Wodehouses took a house near the school at 62 Croxted Road, where Wodehouse was later to set several of his novels. Pelham had to adapt quickly, not only to life as a day boy, but also to living with his parents and a new younger brother, Dick, who had been born in 1892. Relations with Ernest, Wodehouse remembers, were always amicable, despite his father's habit of occupying the toilet for two hours every morning. He found his mother to be a more difficult character. 'I met her as virtually a stranger', he recalls, 'and it was not easy to establish cordial relations'.[11] But London life did not suit Ernest and Eleanor, and within a year they moved to the countryside, settling in the Old House in the Shropshire village of Stableford. Wodehouse returned to being a boarder.

An English family home meant that finally the Wodehouse boys could be reunited in the school holidays. Wodehouse loved the countryside, and often used it as the backdrop for his school stories, drawing on the architecture and spirit of Dulwich and relocating them to Shropshire.[12] Even while home for the vacation, he was keen to stay in touch with his school friends. Wodehouse was popular with all of his year, but he formed a particular bond with two boys, Eric Beardsworth George and William Townend, both of whom were later to become artists and writers. Together, they styled themselves the 'three genii'. Wodehouse and Townend's friendship (rather like that of Bertie Wooster and Bingo Little) would last a lifetime [see plate 5].

Wodehouse often returned to his old school to attend rugby and cricket matches, and followed the progress of his old school teams with keen interest. In many ways, Wodehouse never left Dulwich at all. 'I sometimes feel', Wodehouse confided, 'as if I were a case of infantilism. I haven't developed mentally at all since my last year at school. All my ideas and ideals are the same. I still think the Bedford match the most important thing in the world.'[13]

1 PGW to William Townend, 7 March 1946 (Dulwich).
2 Jasen, p. 11.
3 Jasen, pp. 18–19.
4 Margaret Slythe, 'P. G. Wodehouse: The Dulwich Factor', *Plum Lines,* Vol. 29, No. 4 (Winter 2008), p. 8.
5 Ibid., p. 9.
6 Jasen, p. 15.
7 PGW to Saville, 31 August 1969 (private archive).
8 PGW to Richard Usborne, 3 June 1955 (Wodehouse Archive).
9 P. G. Wodehouse, 'Some Aspects of Game-Captaincy', *The Public School Magazine,* February 1900, p. 12.
10 PGW to Richard Usborne, 11 January 1952 (Wodehouse Archive).
11 Jasen, p. 9.
12 'Preface' (1969) to *Something Fresh* (1915).
13 PGW to William Townend, 9 February 1933 (Dulwich).

1899–1900:
'set thy beetle-crusher on the ladder of fame'

'All through my last term at Dulwich I sprang from my bed at five sharp each morning, ate a couple of petit beurre biscuits and worked like a beaver at my Homer and Thucydides.' Aged seventeen, Wodehouse was preparing for university scholarship examinations, aiming to win a place at an Oxford college. Eric George had been in the year above Wodehouse, and had left Dulwich in 1899 to take up a place at Oriel, which was now Wodehouse's college of choice. Armine was also up at Oxford, having won a scholarship to Corpus Christi College that year.

The slangy intimacy of this early correspondence takes its tone from the prevailing culture of schoolboy expression, which would be familiar to any reader of The Boy's Own Paper. *Wodehouse combines this with his borrowings from, and homage to, established writers of the Victorian age. Wodehouse's nickname for George – 'Jeames' – is taken from Thackeray's parodic* Punch *sketch, 'The Diary of C. Jeames de la Pluche Esq.' (1845), the story of a footman turned millionaire. In a playful extended allusion to his separation from Eric George, Wodehouse impersonates Jeames' jilted admirer, the 'hilliterit cookmaid', Maryanne Hoggins, who laments Jeames' absence in doggerel – 'But O! imagine vot I felt / Last Vensday veek as ever were; I gits a letter, which I spelt / "Miss M. A. Hoggins, Buckley Square."'*

TO ERIC GEORGE

Old House,
Stableford,
Salop.

[Summer 1899]

My only Jeames.
I am badly in need of some funny drorks to write pottery about.[1] Send some at your earliest convenience, or sooner if you can.

I am vorking till Vensday at St Margaret's Bay.[2] I am going to try for a Schol at Oriel. At least that is my ambition. I don't think I shall get one. When does the exam come off, do you know? It would be ripping if we could both (or as the Scotch say 'baith') be at the same college. 'It would be monstrous nice now'. I wrote a pome to you some time ago about the inadvisability of painting 'them saints & suchlike'. It is since dead!

Do you know, Jeames, I think your pome anent Mr Roop is a gem of the first water.[3] I consider the splendid burst of triumphant joy in the last line, where our author says 'There ain't no wulgar among the blest' is without a par (or ma) in the English langwidge! Have just finished *Pendennis* & *Esmond*. Rattling good books both of them. Now how kind it is of me to encourage an obscure author by such a favourable criticism, isn't it. I presume you know both by heart. I think that place where Blanche says to Foker: 'How lovely it must be to have a Father, Mr Foker!' & he says: '<u>Oh! uncommon</u>!!' is grand.[4] I heard from our unique V.T. some time ago & answered his letter with promptitude, so to speak. He is rather sick at leaving. I think it shows what an awfully fine chap he is that he gives up going to Varsity. I know he would have liked to go awfully, poor chap. I don't know what I shall do without him at the House.[5] We used to have rows every other day, but they never lasted long, generally departing with his toothache!

I read some Browning today. I still like Tennyson better, though. I think some of the descriptions of nature in T. are absolutely whacking. Eg in the 'Voyage of Maeldune',

'The whole isle-side flashing down from the peak without ever a tree'.

Heck mon, its just beutiful! [*sic*]

Goodbye now.

Write soon and often.

Yrs till chaos

P. G. Wodehouse.

1 George was a talented artist. His letters to his friends were abundantly illustrated with 'drorks'.
2 PGW was presumably staying with his Aunt Edith Deane and her husband, Commander Augustus Bradshaw, who took a house at St Margaret's Bay in Kent.
3 George's poem about 'Mr Roop', a joke between the pair, alludes to the Indian 'rupee'. Until his retirement and return to England in 1895, PGW's father, Ernest Wodehouse, had been a judge in Hong Kong, and his Civil Service pension was paid in rupees. PGW recalls

that this currency 'was always jumping down and throwing fits [...] "Watch that rupee!"
was the cry in the Wodehouse family' (*Over Seventy*, p. 477).

4 W. M. Thackeray, *The History of Henry Esmond* (1852). PGW quotes Miss Amory's
declaration: 'Oh how delightful it must be to have a father – a father, Mr Foker!' from
The History of Pendennis (1848).

5 William Townend (V.T.), PGW's best friend at Dulwich College, had turned down
a place at Cambridge University ('Varsity') in order to study to be a commercial artist.

P. G. Wodehouse to Eric Beardsworth George, summer 1899.

Old House.
Stableford.
Salop.

Sept. 1899.

Jeames, friend of me boyhood, & companion of me youthful years, list, I prithee. Your letter was very welcome & prompt. I have not answered it before because I have been <u>wurking</u>! That scholarship at Horiul, Jeames me lad, is a certainty. I <u>am</u> a genius. I always knew it.

I haven't read *Faust* but I have read *Palamon and Arcite* right through, 3000 lines if it's an inch! It is rather a good poem full of blud and luv!

I will apprise you of the visiting Sunday when I get back, as I don't know yet when it is. It has always been the ambition of my life to share your 'storied urn & animated bust'.[1] I shall sponge on you frightfully when I come up for my Schol! I am going to spend nearly all next term up at Oxford trying for various Schols! Ho yus, Jeames, I mean to do it in style.

Have you done your Saints yet? If not have you done anythink in the papers?

I come back to school on Tuesday. I arrive about 5, so if I come to drag you out for a walk, be not afraid with any amazement, as they say in the marriage service.[2] Which I know you've been married <u>heaps</u> of times, Jeames, so you ought to know it.

I heard yesterday that Shakespeare was not alive. It steeped me in profound gloom. But I thought eftsoons that I was alive so it was all right for the Literature of the World. I am writing a 9-act tragedy called *Julius Othello or Lycidas regained*. Talking of Browning, Jeames, (not that we were talking of him), he is not nearly so obscure as a bloke called Henley.[3] Have you read any of his rot. Here is a sample: –

'A sigh sent wrong,
A kiss that went astray,
A pain life-long
So they say!'

Iggsplane this, men & angels, as Thackeray says. Isn't it rot?[4] Have you read *Esmond*. I liked it awfully. Have you ever noticed that Thackeray can't draw a good woman without making her a lunatic like Mrs Pendennis, who never says anything without raising her eyes in soulful ecstasy or silent pain to the ceiling. It is wery vearin', as you remark.

You will just have time for a letter before I come back. Mind you write. Goodbye now

Yrs through the ever-rolling streeemes of tyme,[5]

    P. G. Wodehouse (+ his mark)

P. S. When you say *Faust*, do you mean Marlowe's play? Reply paid.

PGW

1 Dryden's long poem *Palamon and Arcite* (1700). Thomas Gray's 'Elegy Written in a Country Churchyard' (1751) – 'Can storied urn or animated bust / Back to its mansion call the fleeting breath' – evokes the idea of hidden genius, 'some mute inglorious Milton' that never saw the light.
2 'Wives, submit yourselves unto your husbands, as it is fit in the Lord [...] even as Sarah obeyed Abraham, calling him lord; whose daughters ye are as long as ye do well, and are not afraid with any amazement', 'The Form of Solemnisation of Matrimony', *The Book of Common Prayer*.
3 William Ernest Henley's *Poems* had been published in 1897.
4 For 'Iggsplane this, men and angels', see Thackeray's *Epistles to the Literati* (1840).
5 The joke on 'Time, like an ever-rolling stream', from Watt's hymn 'O God, Our help in Ages Past', would have been recognised by all Dulwich College boys. Daily attendance at Chapel was central to public school life.

In 1899, Wodehouse became one of the five editors of the Dulwich College school magazine, The Alleynian – *an achievement that he compares, by way of an allusion to Samuel Johnson's 'The Vanity of Human Wishes', to that of Charles XII of Sweden ('He left the Name, at which the World grew pale / To point a Moral, or adorn a Tale'). Wodehouse's comic poetry, modelled on his literary hero, W. S. Gilbert, was published in the magazine.*

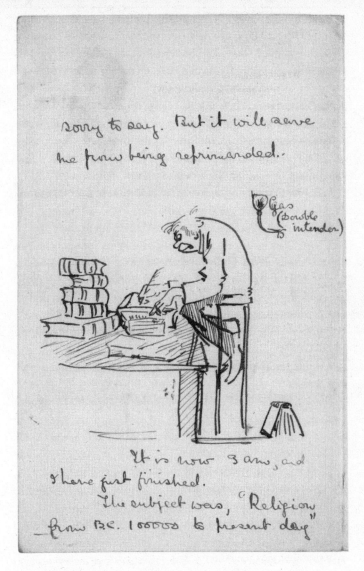

A sketch from a letter from Eric Beardsworth George, depicting life at Oriel.

Today

Jeames of me boyhood's hours, best congraggers on the commission to illustrate a real live book. Thou art the first of the 3 genii to set thy beetle-crusher on the ladder of Fame! By the time I begin to write you will be such a terror to the publishers etc that you will get me countless commissions, or I'll know the reason why, so to speak.

I am a heditor myself, Jeames, now. I write those Editorials in the *Alleynian* at which the world grows pale.

Oh! you young Warsity blud, you! I will leap up to Oxon for the Half term like a young sparrow. I shall have to get leave, unless you can prove you are an uncle or parent of mine. If you see Mr J KB Dawsoon break it to him gently that I can't find a photo at present, but have ordered a cart-load for him from Bayfield's. I am getting werry emaciated now, has I am training for the Bedford match.[1]

I am werry proud, having seen myself in the *Tonbridgian* called 'the school Lorryit'. 'Sblood![2]

What do you think of Ernest Prater's drorks? They are monstrous nice, I think.[3]

The gay Billiam T. has got to draw 6 hours a day for his two years![4] Losh, mon, it's uncanny.

> I sing by night, I sing by day!
>   My voice gets werry hoarse!
> I love to watch the salmon play,
> Then gaily wend my homeward way,
>   Refreshed with onion-sauce.

> My mother bids me bind my hair.
>   Shall Britons ever slave?
> Never! and so I always spare
> The life of every ex-Lord-Mayor
>   Beneath the ocean wave.

(Poetry)

I find life werry hollow, Jeames, now you have gone to Warsity. I sit & smoke & spit. At other times I stand & smoke & spit, and sigh!

Simple Fare (a pome).

I loathe all needless luxuries,
I loathe your regal bread & cheese,
I also loathe with loathing utter
Your enervating bread & butter.

Be mine a simple hardy fare,
A devilled kidney here & there,
Château Lafitte [*sic*] & ancient port.
Such is the fare I've always sought.

My friends declare I'm growing stout,
My doctor darkly hints at gout,
But till I seek the realms above,
Such simple fare I'll always love.

Yrs till the mausoleum
P. G. Wodehouse-Shakespeare

P.S. Write soon & send some pictures for pomes. PGW.

---

1 Another Dulwich College boy, J. K. B. Dawson had gone up to Exeter College in July 1899.
2 In one of the earliest reviews of PGW's work, the magazine of a rival public school reports that *The Alleynian* contains a poem by 'the school laureate "P.G.W." [...] on purely Hypothetical subjects, which is in our opinion a trifle obscure, to say nothing of a rather ambiguous rhyme', *The Tonbridgian*, 1899 (July), p. 1647.
3 Ernest Prater (1864–1950), an illustrator for, among others, *The Strand*, *Pall Mall Gazette* and *The Boy's Own Paper*.
4 William Townend.

Eric George's illustration of candidates heading for Oxford examinations,
bearing their cribs and 'Key to Euripides'.

The scholarship examinations were fiercely difficult, and Wodehouse had been preparing for months. The papers of 1899 required candidates to translate extracts from Plato, Thucydides, Theognis, Cicero, Propertius and the younger Pliny, as well as to write essays on 'The Literary Man as Statesman', the comparative 'aims and achievements of Frederick the Great and Napoleon' and the extent to which 'the modern novel [is] a substitute for the Elizabethan drama'. But Wodehouse was never to go to Oxford, or even to take the scholarship exams. '[J]ust as scholarship time was approaching, with me full to the brim with classic lore [...] it seemed to my father that two sons at the University would be a son more than the privy purse could handle.'

Wodehouse never elaborated on his father's reasons for preventing him from going to Oxford; it was an unspeakable blow. For years, he had been reading stories in the pages of The Captain *about the joys of being a ''Varsity "man"'. For his fictional heroes in* The Captain, *life at the 'quaint old coll' was like Dulwich, only better – 'almost like going to Elysium'. Wodehouse's brother, Armine, was already excelling at Oxford – he went on to achieve a double First (first class degree) in Classics as well as to win the Newdigate Prize for English verse.*

Ernest's plans for his third son were quite different. Wodehouse was to leave Dulwich and become a clerk in the Hongkong and Shanghai Banking Corporation. For Ernest, the path before his son now seemed set. Pelham Grenville would begin in the bank's London office. And before too long, it was expected that he would follow in his father's footsteps, heading out to the Far East.

TO ERIC GEORGE

> Elm Lawn[1]
> Dulwich Common
> <u>SE</u>

Friend of me boyhood, here's some dread news for you. My people have not got enough of what are vulgarly but forcibly called 'stamps' to send me to Varsity. Damn the last owed is wot I know you will say. Oh! money, money, thy name is money! (a most lucid remark). I am going into the Hong Kong & Shanghai Bank. For two yrs I will be in

England from the time I am 19. So I will have 2 yrs to establish myself on a pinnacle of fame as a writer.

I vote you get your publisher pal to start a paper. (NB this is wrote serious.) You & WT could do the drorks, & you & I could do the writing. 'Tis a gorgeous scheme. I have a brain that could fill 3 papers with eloquence wit & satire if need be. You have a pencil & brush like those of Rossetti & E T Reed combined.[2] Damn it, man, (so to speak!) it's a grand scheme. For about £15 you can get 1000 copies published. We will get 1000 people to pay a yearly subscription at 6d per week & there you are. You clear £10 per week. It is an amazingly fine scheme. Write and criticize it.

V.T. was down here on Wednesday, drunk as usual. I hit him on the chest, knocked his bowler in & went on my way with a lightened heart, feeling I had not vasted my morning.

Write an illustrated letter to me soon. Also send me some drawings (small) to write pomes on.

I am going to send some pomes to a few editors soon. Let us hope the boodle will flow in. I think *Pearson's Weekly* is about my form, or perhaps *Pick-Me-Up*.[3] NB our paper will consist of interviews, pomes, drorks (comic & serious), an editorial, & reviews of books. That is about all.

Goodby enow

Write soon

Yrs till Chaos

P. G. <u>Wodehouse</u>

---

1 Elm Lawn was PGW's boarding house.
2 Edward Tennyson Reed (1860–1933), *Punch* cartoonist and parliamentary caricaturist.
3 PGW refers to some of the newer Victorian periodicals – Cyril Pearson (previously at Newnes) launched his journal in 1890; *Pick-Me-Up*, another British weekly, began in 1888 and by 1897 was retailing at a penny per issue.

CHAPTER THREE

Early Career

By January 1901, the nation was in mourning for Victoria. As the evening lamps were lit, shopkeepers carefully dusted the black and purple banners that hung from their windows, and a young black-suited Wodehouse would have made his way home from work. It was a distance of about five miles through the London streets, tracing the Thames's curve from the dust of the City centre to the unfashionable end of the King's Road. The walk must have seemed long to Wodehouse. The beginning of the Edwardian era brought little that was new for him, and life at the Hongkong and Shanghai Bank was as dull as he had feared. He was, he recalls, 'the most inefficient clerk whose trouser seat ever polished the surface of a high stool'. Assigned, initially, to the postage department, Wodehouse was moved on to 'Fixed Deposits', 'drifted to Inward Bills [...] and then to Outward Bills and to Cash, always with a weak, apologetic smile on my face', and a 'total inability to grasp what was going on'.[1]

Though he detested the work, he enjoyed playing in the bank's rugby and cricket teams [see plate 6] and life at the bank was, for Wodehouse, not entirely wasted. Within a few years, it was to provide crucial material for his fiction. In 1908, the Hongkong and Shanghai Bank reappears in print, thinly disguised as the 'New Asiatic Bank' in his 1908 serial, *The New Fold*. There, at the Asiatic, Wodehouse's hero Mike sits disconsolately, punching postage stamps and 'reading a surreptitious novel behind a pile of ledgers' [see plate 7].[2]

Mike's plight would have struck a chord with many readers. He was the sort of young man that *The Captain* magazine had described: forced to leave school with 'no capital, no influence [...] in a world where he is not much wanted'.[3] Wodehouse, like Mike, was just one of thousands of nobodies lost in the maze of early Edwardian bureaucracy. From Grossmith's Mr Pooter in the late 1880s to Eliot's 'young man carbuncular' in 1922, the writing of this period is full of such figures – anonymous clerks in their ill-fitting frock coats, clutching their bowler hats and dreams. But Wodehouse wanted something more. He wanted to make fiction, not be the stuff of it. As he opened the door to his 'horrible lodgings' in Markham Square, he would scan the hall table for replies to the stories and articles that he had written, longhand, and sent out the week before.

The field of opportunity, for Wodehouse, was huge, as the early 1900s saw a further boom in print journalism. Print made its way into everyone's lives – from the advertisements for Eno's Fruit Salts on the sides of the horse-drawn omnibuses to the dense small-print weekly newspapers, full of reader's queries, pictures, prizes and gossip – and everyone wanted to be in print.

There was, for Wodehouse, little to celebrate at the end of the working day. His mail consisted, almost entirely, of rejection slips, which he used, with characteristic creativity, to paste to the walls of his bed-sitting room. 'I could', he recalls, 'have papered the walls of a good-sized banqueting hall.' Struck down with mumps, and recuperating at his parents' house in Shropshire in the summer of 1901, he produced no fewer than nineteen short stories – all of which the 'editors were compelled to decline owing to lack of space'.[4] But, gradually, there were successes. Wodehouse drew on what he knew at this period – his schooldays at Dulwich – and his stories of honour, good sportsmanship and derring-do were accepted by a number of national magazines aimed at the schoolboy market. He was also getting 'an occasional guinea' for small pieces aimed at the adults, with articles placed in the hugely successful weekly compilation *Tit-Bits*, and its rival *Answers*. By 1902, one of his school serials, *The Pothunters*, was published in book form.

Two crucial things made all the difference to Wodehouse in these early years. The first was the kindness of an established journalist, William Beach Thomas. After a brief spell as a Dulwich schoolmaster, Beach Thomas was now working for the *Globe* newspaper, an intensive job for a man who hated city life. Whenever he wanted to get away from town for a few days, he asked his former pupil to fill in for him. It was easy enough for Wodehouse to call in sick at the bank, and head over to the *Globe* offices on the Strand for a spot of moonlighting. Then came Beach Thomas's annual holiday – he needed cover at the *Globe* for three weeks. However atrocious a clerk Wodehouse was, someone would notice a three-week absence. There was, for Wode-house, no contest. With no steady job to go to, he placed his faith in his freelance writing, and decided to 'chuck the bank'.[5] His excitement is reflected in the inscription that he wrote in a copy of *The Pothunters* given to his friend Bill Townend: 'these first fruits of a GENIUS at which the WORLD will (shortly) be AMAZED (You see if it won't)'. It was the right move. By 1903, he was a fully fledged journalist, working on the permanent staff of the *Globe* on a column named 'By the Way' – a humorous round-up of the day's news, which appeared on its front page.

The second turning-point came a year later, in the shape of another aspiring fellow writer and schoolmaster – Herbert Wotton Westbrook [see plate 9]. Handsome, charismatic, and permanently broke, West-brook turned up unannounced at Wodehouse's digs clutching a letter of introduction from a friend. He found the young author hard at it, 'sitting at a table, a woollen sweater wrapped around his feet, working on a poem for *Punch* by the light of a green-shaded oil lamp'.[6] Westbrook was ambitious but lazy, known to his friends as the 'King of Slackers'. Westbrook drew on Wodehouse's advice and encouragement, but also, as time went on, borrowed and pawned Wodehouse's belongings – and was even prone to pilfering his plots.

But Westbrook was not without his uses. An invitation to visit the small prep school where Westbrook taught was exactly what Wodehouse needed as an escape from London life. Emsworth House School soon became Wodehouse's rural retreat; he lodged above the school stables, played cricket with the Emsworth boys, and later adopted the name Emsworth for Clarence, the pig-loving 9th Earl and Seigneur of Blandings Castle. Soon Wodehouse was spending most of his time in Hampshire, sharing rooms with Westbrook, and sending his copy up to London by train.

Westbrook provided more than just company. The pair began to work together – both at the offices of the *Globe*, where Westbrook was appointed as Wodehouse's deputy – and on various freelance projects and novels. With his entrepreneurial schemes and scams, and state of déshabillé, Westbrook was also ideal raw material for Wodehouse's fiction, becoming one of the models for his first great fictional character – Ukridge. Indeed, his influence was a lasting one. The spectre of 'Brook', or 'Old Brook' – a man with talent but without the stamina to see it through – hangs over Wodehouse's letters, the spirit of unful-filled potential, goading him to work harder. Wodehouse was also to become good friends with the owner of the school, Baldwin King-Hall, affectionately known as 'Baldie', and his sister Ella [see plate 10].

Wodehouse was working feverishly – and beginning to see results. By 1904, his second school novel, *A Prefect's Uncle*, had been published, together with a further school story (*The Gold Bat*) and a book for children. He was turning, by his own joking admission, into 'something of a capitalist'.[7]

In 1904 he also realised a long-held ambition – to see New York. He made his first trip to America in April on a budget, travelling 'second class with three other men in the cabin' and took the oppor-tunity to get an insider's view of the American boxing circuit.[8] New York was 'like being in heaven without having to go to all the bother and expense of dying'.[9] On his return, Wodehouse found himself appointed as editor of the 'By the Way' section of the *Globe* newspaper, and contributed a lyric to a new West End show. Writing in his note-book on 13 December 1904, Wodehouse 'set it down': 'I have arrived. Letter from Cosmo Hamilton congratulating me on my work and promising commission to write lyrics for his next piece. I have a lyric in *Sergeant Brue*, a serial in *The Captain*, 5 books published, I am editing "By the Way", *Pearson's* have two stories and two poems of mine, I have finished the "Kid Brady" stories, and I have a commission to do a weekly poem for *Vanity Fair*.'[10]

Back in England, Wodehouse managed to combine fiction and writing lyrics for musicals with a new post as the resident lyricist at the Aldwych Theatre in London. The year 1906 saw success as a novelist on a wider scale, as Ukridge made his first appearance in Wodehouse's outstanding tale of romance and poultry, *Love Among the Chickens*. *Not George Washington*, Wodehouse's and Westbrook's autobiographical account of London literary life, was published in 1907. The following year, Wodehouse turned to his friend Townend for help with plotting a potboiler, *The Luck Stone*, a schoolboy romp with a touch of murder-mystery about it, inspired by Anstey's colonial tale, *Baboo Jabberjee* [see plate 11].

With such success, Wodehouse could easily have become quite a man about town, and he was certainly beginning to acquire the trappings.

The sheet music for Wodehouse's lyric in the musical *Sergeant Brue* (1904), with Wodehouse incorrectly billed.

In 1906, he bought (and promptly crashed) a Darracq motor car from his friend the theatrical manager Seymour Hicks. His theatrical connections would place him in the vicinity of a number of attractive young women. But there is, in these early letters, little sign of romance. It is perhaps no coincidence that the entire plot of *Not George Washington* revolves around ways not to find, but to avoid, a girl. One might imagine that Wodehouse's sentiments echoed those of his narrator, James Orlebar Cloyster, who finds himself faced with the idea of love and wondering: 'Did I really want to give up all this? The untidiness,

the scratch meals, the nights with [friends].'[11] For Wodehouse, as for
Cloyster, the answer was no. Indeed, the twenty-something Wodehouse
sought out the company of those who allowed him to play out aspects
of his younger self. His old Dulwich friend Bill Townend provided
cocoa and chats over the footer results. And he often spent time with
the daughters of his family friends, the Bowes-Lyons. The Bowes-Lyon
sisters remembered Wodehouse as a much-loved guest, who turned
up for tea with copies of the latest children's books and joking proposals
of marriage. 'I think', Effie wrote, noting the childlike side of the man,
'he could be friends with us because we were little girls.'[12] The girls
were also a source of inspiration for Wodehouse. Some of his vignettes
– 'Effie and Teenie are always quoting from the last book they have
read. Eg. Effie, after reading *Macbeth*, calls T. "Young fry of treachery"'
– have an almost Woosterian feel about them [see plate 8].[13]

If there is a unifying spirit to these early letters, it is that of a man
trying to grow into himself. 'I am always quite at my ease', he wrote
in his private notebooks '(a) with people whose liking I don't want to
win (b) with people who are clever in a way that doesn't impress.' 'We
all act through life', Wodehouse added in another note, 'and each of
us selects the special audience he wishes to impress.'[14] And Wodehouse
in his twenties wanted to impress just about everyone. Dignified letters
to publishers are followed by slangy notes to friends. One sees, in this
correspondence, Wodehouse as both adult and adolescent – fiercely
independent and ambitious, but still clinging nervously to his Dulwich
College roots. Throughout this period, Wodehouse's professional
persona still carries with it a schoolboyish anxiety about doing the
right thing. It is this insecurity that makes Wodehouse's final letter
to his illustrious literary agent, J. B. Pinker, all the more remarkable.

In 1909, Wodehouse arrived on his second visit to New York. *Love
Among the Chickens* had been sold to an American publisher, and he
set out to find new writing opportunities. Such was Wodehouse's
confidence that he had resigned from his post at the *Globe*. His previous
letters to J. B. Pinker had been respectful, earnest, and self-consciously
over-written. But in his final note Wodehouse has an uncharacteristic
swagger about him. His tone is almost off-hand – 'I hadn't', he says,
'had time in the hurry of my departure to call.' Though staying at a
friend's apartment on East 58th Street, the note is dashed off, longhand,

on writing paper swiped from the luxurious Waldorf Astoria hotel. He was entering a world 'where dollar bills grew on trees and nobody asked or cared who anybody else's father might be'.[15] Wodehouse might not yet have arrived, but he certainly thought he was on his way.

1 *Over Seventy*, p. 478.
2 *The New Fold* was published in 1908–9, becoming the 1910 novel *Psmith in the City*. See Chapter 13.
3 'When You Leave School: Something in the City', *The Captain*, July 1899, pp. 394–7, at p. 394.
4 *Over Seventy*, p. 479.
5 PGW to Richard Usborne, 11 January 1952 (Wodehouse Archive).
6 Jasen, p. 29.
7 *Over Seventy*, p. 481.
8 PGW to William Townend, 11 September 1946 (Dulwich).
9 *America, I Like You* (New York: Simon and Schuster, 1956), p. 36.
10 *Money Received for Literary Work* (Wodehouse Archive). Cosmo Hamilton, a friend, playwright and novelist who worked on many of the musical successes of the day; *Sergeant Brue* was playing at the Strand Theatre; PGW's 1904 *The Captain* serial was *The Gold Bat*; the 'Kid Brady' stories, published in *Pearson's* from 1905 to 1907, revolve around a former cowboy turned lightweight boxer.
11 P. G. Wodehouse and Herbert Westbrook, *Not George Washington* (1907), Chapter 8.
12 N. T. P. Murphy, *In Search of Blandings* (London: Secker & Warburg, 1986), p. 132.
13 *Phrases and Notebooks* (Wodehouse Archive).
14 Ibid.
15 See *Piccadilly Jim* (1917), Chapter 6. The novel first appeared as a serial in the *Saturday Evening Post* in 1916.

1901–1909:
'Got a plot, thanks'

Buoyed by the publication of The Pothunters, *Wodehouse was discussing a new contract with his publishers.*

TO MESSRS. A. & C. BLACK

23 Walpole St.
S.W.

December 8. 1902

Dear Sir.

In reply to your letter of today, I beg to acknowledge receipt of your cheque for £6.18.7. I must thank you for your very liberal proposal with regard to my next book, and I shall be only too glad to avail myself of it. I have finished a public school story of almost exactly the same length as *The Pothunters*, and can forward it immediately if you wish it. The title of the book is *The Bishop's Uncle* and like *The Pothunters* it deals chiefly with the outdoor life of the public school.¹ There is a great deal of cricket in the book, in fact, strictly speaking, it is nearly all cricket, for very little else except that game goes on in the Summer Term at school. This being the case, it occurs to me that the book might do better if brought out in the Summer, though of course my knowledge of the science of publishing is very slight. At any rate I will wait until I hear from you before forwarding it. I should very much like Mr R. N. Pocock to illustrate it, if you have no objection. We worked together for so long on the *Public School Magazine* that we both see things from the same point of view as regards public school matters. I hope, if you do not like *The Bishop's Uncle* at first sight, that you will let me revise it. I can generally improve on my work at a second attempt. I am doing a good deal of work for *Punch* now, and the editor sends back two out of every three of my MSS to be altered, and he always takes them when I return them in their corrected form.

I should be very glad to receive 10% on the Cheap American edition of *The Pothunters*.

Yrs. faithfully

P. G. Wodehouse.

1 This was to be retitled *The Prefect's Uncle* (1903).

Throughout his early career, Wodehouse's friendship with Townend and Herbert Wotton Westbrook was vital. There was, however, always a competitive edge between Westbrook and Wodehouse, especially over ideas for stories. One night, in Westbrook's Rupert Street digs, Townend told the story of one of his old acquaintances, Carrington Craxton, a man who 'drank too much' and 'sponged, more or less on people', and tried to start a chicken farm. Both Wodehouse and Westbrook saw potential in the sketch, and each wished to develop it into a novel.

TO WILLIAM TOWNEND

22 Walpole Street,

S.W.[1]

March 3. 1905

Dear Willyum,

This is great about our Westy. Damn his eyes. What gory right has he got to the story any more than me? Tell him so with my love. As for me, a regiment of Westbrooks, each slacker than the last, won't stop me. I have the thing mapped out into chapters, & shall go at it steadily. At present it isn't coming out quite so funny as I want. Chapter One is good, but as far as I have done of Chapter Two, introducing Ukridge, doesn't satisfy me. It is flat. I hope, however, to amend this.

[...]

Do send along more Craxton stories (<u>not</u> improper ones).[2] I am going to pad book out with them, making Ukridge an anecdotal sort of man. If they are <u>mildly</u> improper, it's all right. Do come up on 10th. You needn't bring Westy though. I am very much fed up with him just now, as he has been promising all sorts of things in my name without my knowledge to some damned cousins of his, the Goulds, which might have made a lot of worry for me. I say, I boxed 2 rounds with Brougham in the Junior Study tonight, & he put it all over me. In the second round he was giving me particular Hell. I believe that he might do something if he got down to 10 st. & went up.[3]

R.S.V.P. I have locked up your MS in case of a raid by Westy. Don't give him all the information you've given me. Not that he would ever get beyond chapter 2, though. His intention of rushing through his book doesn't worry me much!

Yours

PGW

1 PGW's London digs from 1902 to 1904. He uses this address (changed by one number) in *Not George Washington*: 'A fairly large bed-sitting room was vacant at No. 23. I took it, and settled down seriously to make my writing pay' (Chapter 3).

2 Many years later, Townend described the Craxton of 1902: 'he was the worst football player that ever lived [...] he played in a sweater, old-fashioned knickerbockers [...] brown stockings. [...] And his pince-nez really were secured by ginger-beer wire. [...] He could not keep his feet, he could not run [...] and the boys on the touch line were convulsed', William Townend to PGW, 22 March 1957 (Dulwich).

3 Wodehouse kept up his boxing with the boys at Emsworth House School.

The novel was to become Love Among the Chickens. *While Craxton provided the inspiration for Ukridge (the hero of the novel, famous for his chaotic money-making schemes and equally careless wardrobe), his character was fleshed out by Wodehouse's perceptions of Westbrook himself. Once the novel was completed, Wodehouse realised that he needed an agent, and a sharper focus on placing and marketing his work.*

'By the Way' Room
Offices of 'The Globe'
367 Strand
<u>W.C.</u>

January 16. 1906

Dear Sir.

I rang you up on the telephone today to ask if you would handle my work. I have made a sort of corner in public-school stories, and I can always get them taken either by the *Windsor* or one of the Pearson magazines or the *Captain*.[1] I get about £2.10 a thousand words for them, but I fancy that judicious management could extract more.[2] I should be very glad if you could find time to place them for me.

I have also written a novel of about 70,000 words.[3] I have had this typed once, and a friend of mine on the *New York World* is handling the typed copy in America. Would it be necessary to have this M.S. re-typed for England? The copy I have by me is perfectly clearly written.

Yours faithfully

P. G. Wodehouse

1 *The Windsor Magazine*, 'an Illustrated Monthly for Men and Women' (1895–1939), featuring writers such as Arnold Bennett, Jerome K. Jerome, Rudyard Kipling and Jack London. *The Captain, a Magazine for Boys and 'Old Boys'* (1899–1924) aimed at the public school market, and those who sought to identify with them, with the emphasis on Muscular Christianity, Imperialism and good sportsmanship.
2 £2.10 – about £175 by today's standards.
3 *Love Among the Chickens* (1909); published in the USA as a serial in 1908–9.

Offices of 'The Globe'
367 Strand
W.C.

May 4. 1906

Dear Mr Pinker.

I think the best thing would be to take the £2.2 & then sell the story elsewhere later on, as he suggests. After all, there's not much difference between £2.2 & £3.3, and when I am a great man we will sell 'Signs and Portents' for much gold.[1]

You might try & make him raise it to £2.10; but failing that take the £2.2. Have *Pearson's* taken 'The Renegade'? I heard from Everett that they were reading it.[2] By the way, I have a school story, *The White Feather*, strong plot, scintillating humour, length 50,000 words, just finished as serial in *The Captain*. Couldn't you sound a few publishers about it before sending it round? Sort of accept tenders for it. Or can this only be done with men like Doyle & Kipling?[3]

Yours sincerely

P. G. Wodehouse

1 PGW's 'Signs and Portents: A Cricket Story', published in *Stage and Sport* on 19 May 1906.
2 Wodehouse's story 'The Renegade' was not taken by *Pearson's* and has not survived.
3 *The White Feather*, the tale of a schoolboy's redemption from cowardice through boxing prowess, was published in the UK by A. & C. Black in 1907.

In 1906–7, Wodehouse and Westbrook collaborated on the novel Not George Washington. *Despite this, their difficult friendship continued. 'Brook' is 'a complete shit', Wodehouse confided to Townend. As the following letter shows, Wodehouse was scrupulous in observing the boundaries of intellectual property. Westbrook took a more relaxed approach to questions of ownership, helping himself to various items belonging to Wodehouse and inviting unwelcome house guests to the 'various houses' that they shared in Emsworth.*

It was during this period that Wodehouse developed one of his most memorable characters – the immaculately dressed, monocle-wearing Rupert

Eustace Psmith. Psmith was 'a kind of supercharged, upper-class version of the "masher" or "knut" of the Edwardian comic paper'. Wodehouse elaborated this classic figure by adding characteristics of the flamboyant Edwardian theatre impresario Rupert D'Oyly Carte. Wodehouse introduced Psmith in his 1908 serial The Lost Lambs, *which was eventually to become the second part of his novel* Mike.

TO CASSELL & CO., LONDON

The Globe,
367, Strand. W.

August 3. 1907

Dear Sir,

The fact that the preliminary notices of *Not George Washington* have gone out with the names wrong is a pity: but all the same I must make a point of having them altered. To say that the book is by P. G. Wodehouse and H. Westbrook is absolutely out of question [*sic*] unless you care to insert the enclosed preface.[1] If you do, then let the order of the names stand. If not, they must be altered. I absolutely refuse to give people the impression that I wrote the book with some slight help from Mr. Westbrook when my share in it is really so small.

Will you also please insert the enclosed dedication.

Yours faithfully,

P. G. Wodehouse

1 PGW's suggested correction read 'The order in which the authors names are placed on the title page of this book is wrong, and is due to a mistake. The central idea, the working out of the plot and everything that is any good at all in the book are by "H. Westbrook". The rest is by "P. G. Wodehouse".' In the end, this prefatory note was not necessary as Westbrook's name was placed first.

Not George Washington *was dedicated to Ella King-Hall, the sister of the owner of Emsworth House School. Although Ella was sixteen years older than Wodehouse, he was, according to the King-Hall family, 'half in love' with her. Ella was a talented writer and musician, and the pair collaborated on a musical sketch,* The Bandit's Daughter, *which survived only a few nights of its London run in Camden Town.*

Constitutional Club,
Northumberland Avenue,
W.C.[1]

[1908]

Dear Bill.

It's all right. Got a plot, thanks. Not much good, but will do. May have to call on you for one or two isolated episodes, possibly, if you can manage, but think I'm all right.

[...]

Go over to Emsworth & see the extraordinary deadbeat old Brook has brought to Tresco.[2] Old College tutor of his, absolutely on rocks, has been sleeping on Blackfriars Bridge. Drink, etc. Sort of Craxton, only <u>awful</u> bore. Well worth a visit of inspection, though. It will make you laugh to see Brook & him slouching off to the pub together, each looking seedier than the other. Mind you go.

Send stuff <u>here</u> this week, as shall be in London probably till the deadbeat gets out of Tresco.

Yrs,

PGW

1 The Constitutional Club, PGW's London address, became the model for the Senior Conservative Club in his Blandings novels, 'celebrated for the steadfastness of its political views, the excellence of its cuisine, and the Gorgonzolaesque marble of its main staircase' (*Psmith in the City*).
2 Tresco, the name of PGW's country 'residence' in Emsworth, which he shared with Westbrook. He subsequently rented and then bought Threepwood, a villa next to Emsworth School. Threepwood was to be immortalised in PGW's choice of names for his characters in his Blandings Castle stories – the Threepwood dynasty includes Galahad, as well as Clarence, Lord Emsworth.

One of Wodehouse's many collaborative sidelines included freelancing for Tit-Bits – a mass-circulation weekly, which included stories and human-interest features. The most popular page was the 'Answers to Correspondents' – an early Edwardian agony column – which Wodehouse handled with his friend Bill Townend. Such pages had been common in the Victorian penny journals. The novelist Wilkie Collins considered these pages both fascinating and highly comic. 'There is no earthly subject that it is possible to discuss, no private affair that it is possible to conceive, which the amazing Unknown Public will not confide to the Editor in the form of a question, and which the editor will not set himself seriously and resolutely to answer. Hidden under cover of initials, or Christian names, or conventional signatures, such as Subscriber, Constant Reader, and so forth, the editor's correspondents seem, many of them, to judge by the published answers to their questions, utterly impervious to the senses of ridicule or shame. Young girls beset by perplexities which are usually supposed to be reserved for a mother's or an elder sister's ear only, consult the editor. Married women who have committed little frailties, consult the editor. Male jilts in deadly fear of actions for breach of promise of marriage, consult the editor. Ladies whose complexions are on the wane, and who wish to know the best artificial means of restoring them, consult the editor'. The actual editor, George Newnes, had a different view. He saw the page as the most important in the paper. It was his way of keeping in touch with his public – and it was crucial to him that the queries from his readers were sympathetically handled. Wodehouse, like Collins, took the page less seriously, including fictional correspondents along with the actual, and publicising his own works. It was not long before Wodehouse was dismissed from this particular job. Newnes decided to keep such work 'in house'.

George Newnes Limited
Editorial Department
Tit-Bits
8, 9, 10 & 11 Southampton Street
Strand
London

August 29. 1908

A Lover's Trials. – CITIZEN'S grievance is against aunts. Not his own aunts, but those of his *fiancée*. They insist on accompanying him and the young lady, apparently thinking they are doing the latter a kindness. —— CITIZEN has our sympathy. A little personal reminiscence may interest him. A short time ago we dragged our tired limbs to the Franco-British Exhibition, and there treated ourselves to a trip on the Spiral Railway. As the car reached the top, a young lady, hitherto silent, gave out the following remark to her companion: 'Well, Henry', she said, 'thank goodness, we've managed to lose the auntie at last.' Does CITIZEN see the point?

Wilkie Bard (Druriolanus). – Yes, your friend was right. Wilkie Bard will be the principal comedian in the next Drury Lane pantomime.[1]

Queer Quarrels (Albert). – Of all disputes this is the silliest. ALBERT loves a red tie. He says it suits his complexion. His wife hates the colour, and wants him to wear purple. She says it is so much more gentlemanly. —— Why not compromise? Would not a tie of alternate purple and red stripes solve the problem? It would be *chic* and *je ne sais quoi* (not to mention *verb. sap.*) without being ostentatious.[2] Besides, anything for a quiet life.

American Policemen (U.S.A.). – American policemen have different methods from London policemen, but it must be remembered that they have a different public to handle. The London constable takes it for granted that a word from him will be sufficient, and he is generally right. The American policeman finds it safer to rely on a stout arm and a stouter truncheon.[3]

Top-Hats (Well-Dressed, Kensington). – Our chief objection to the top-hat is its discomfort. Not that we think it is altogether a thing of beauty.[4] But, of course, it does lend a certain air of respectability.

1 Wilkie Bard (1874–1944), pantomime dame and British music hall artist, specialising in 'coster songs' and tongue-twisters. Bard did indeed make his reputation in the 1908 Drury Lane pantomime, with his popular tongue-twister, 'She sells sea shells on the sea shore'.
2 Albert's tie dilemma recalls the description of Rosie's outfit in 'The Spring Frock' which 'had no poetry, no meaning, no chic, no je-ne-sais-quoi' (*The Strand Magazine*, December 1919).
3 The play on the literal and figurative meanings of 'stout' and 'stouter' reappears in 'Honeysuckle Cottage' (1925), repr. in *Meet Mr Mulliner* (1927).
4 'A thing of beauty is a joy forever', John Keats, 'Endymion' (1818).

would occur when this office was invaded by scores of indignant picture-postcard collectors – all wishing to know the reason why we had selected Miss Dash instead of Miss Blank, Miss Asterisk, or a hundred others? You are a thoughtless person, J. B. T. Our answer to your question is, "Every actress is our most beautiful actress."

Short-Sight (Depressed). – Nonsense. What is there to be depressed about because an oculist has told you you must play cricket in spectacles? Scores of fine players do. Look at R. A. Young and Killick, also J. N. Crawford, whom many people consider one of the three best all-round cricketers in the world.

Little Accomplishments (D. D. L.). – D. D. L. has a cousin who can write the Lord's Prayer on a piece of paper the size of a threepenny-bit. Not a bad performance, but not of much use to anybody, we should think.

Fire Insurance (W. G.). – If a tenant is bound by agreement to insure in the landlord's name and the tenant sets fire to the buildings, can the landlord claim from the insurance company? ——Consult the policy. If the policy contains an exception to the effect that the company will not be liable "for incendiarism," the landlord's only satisfaction will be to prosecute for arson.

Independence Day (Not George Washington). – Yes, you are quite right. The list of casualties every Fourth of July in the United States is enormous. In fact, what with Independence Day rejoicings and Chicago beef, it is a wonder that there are enough Americans left to make a decent railway accident. This year's figures are seventy-one killed and 2,264 injured – a record since 1889.

Christian Science (J. Grant). – Yes: the mind can, of course, exercise a wonderful effect in subduing illness, but when it comes to saying there is no such thing as pain—— Have you ever heard the story of the Christian Science lady and the small boy, whom she found writhing about after a heavy meal of green apples? "My lad," she said, "there is no such thing as pain." "Ain't there just!" he replied, twisting himself into a lover's knot; "I've got positive inside information to the contrary."

Rural Beliefs (Farmer). – When will people learn that hedgehogs and moles are not injurious to agriculture? Hedgehogs eat mice, snails, and wire-worms. We should not care to do it ourselves, but the hedgehogs are all for it, and consequently ought to be numbered among the few friends the farmer has.

Passing the Doctor. – PATRIOT asks us if we do not think the medical examination that all would-be recruits have to undergo too severe. ——Not at all. Of course, it is all very well to say that anyone who has learned to shoot can kill a man at 600yds. or 700yds., whatever the state of his heart or lungs. But a soldier has not only to shoot. He has to march fifteen or twenty miles at a stretch over difficult country before he starts shooting. A man must be fit and well to do this. Hence, doctors have to be strict.

Arbitration (U.S.A.). – Yes. On two occasions we have had quarrels with the United States that might have led to war. One was after the Civil War in the 'sixties, when the States claimed damages from us for the destruction inflicted on their shipping by the privateer *Alabama*. The other was in 1896, when there was a dispute over the Venezuelan frontier.

A page from *Tit-Bits*, 'Answers to correspondents', 15 August 1908. Note the appearance of 'Not George Washington' as the pseudonym of the 'Independence Day' correspondent.

May 6. 1908

Dear Bill.

Here's a go. I've been commissioned by *Chums* to do a serial (70,000 words) by July. They want it not so public-schooly as my usual, & with rather a lurid plot. For Heaven's sake rally to the old flag & lend a hand with the plot.[1] I've written off today earnestly recommending you for the pics on the strength of *The White Feather*, & this time I think it really may come off (Beroofen),[2] as I am to them practically old man Kip doing the story as a bally favour.[3]

In any case, give me an idea or two for the plot. I enclose root idea.

I have asked them to write to you. If they give you the pics to do, wire to me at once, as it will buck me up.

Yours

PGW

P.S. Your reward will be my blessing & at least a fiver, as in case of *Lost Lambs*, which, by the way, I have only just finished with <u>incredible</u> sweat.[4]

RSVP

1 PGW's commission was to become *The Luck Stone*, published under the pseudonym Basil Windham. *Chums* published the serial in nineteen weekly instalments from September 1908 to January 1909.
2 *Unberufen* – 'touch wood' (German). The joke can be traced back to an 1891 *Punch* sketch. PGW uses 'beroofen' again in *The Gem Collector* (1909; US title, *The Intrusion of Jimmy*), and still remembers it in 1934 for Aunt Dahlia in *Right-Ho, Jeeves*.
3 Old Man Kip – Rudyard Kipling. See 'The Sing-Song of Old Man Kangaroo', in *Just-So Stories* (1902). Though he was only forty-three years old in 1908, Kipling's success made him, in PGW's eyes, one of the grand old men of the literary establishment.
4 *The Lost Lambs* (which was later to become the second part of *Mike*) was published in *The Captain* from April to September 1908.

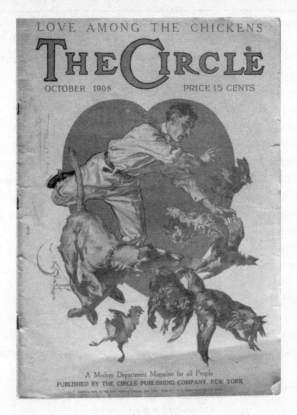

LOVE AMONG THE CHICKENS

THE CIRCLE

OCTOBER 1908   PRICE 15 CENTS

A Modern Department Magazine for all People
PUBLISHED BY THE CIRCLE PUBLISHING COMPANY, NEW YORK

Wodehouse's *Love Among the Chickens*, in American serialised form.

The Luck Stone *was not as great a success as Wodehouse's other works.* 'Although the plot is excellent', *his publisher noted,* 'the general atmosphere is hardly up to the standard of Mike.' *The manuscript was sent back to Wodehouse, with a request that he rewrite it with a view to turning it into a novel. As the decade drew to a close, Wodehouse headed for New York and attempted to track down his American literary agent, A. E. Baerman, who had promised (but not delivered) a $1,000 advance on an American edition of* Love Among the Chickens. *The novel was described by a reviewer as* 'a merry tale, cleverly told' *full of* 'ludicrous situations [...] kept in fine restraint'. *In the battle of Westbrook v. Wodehouse, Wodehouse had won hands down. Now he needed to find his way in New York, alone.*

36 East 58th Street
New York

May 11. 1909

Dear Mr Pinker.
I hadn't time in the hurry of my departure to call.

I am having a very good time here, & am thinking of stopping some time. I'll be sending you over some MSS shortly. This is the place for money. I have just sold that 'Out of School' story to *Ainslee's* for $100 (£20). *Love Among the Chickens* comes out here as a book today, & is to be boomed largely.

Yours sincerely

P. G. Wodehouse.

P. G. Wodehouse to J. B. Pinker, 11 May 1909.

CHAPTER FOUR

New York

Despite the excitement of the New York hustle, Wodehouse must have sorely missed his friends – the regular Sunday cocoa nights in Bill Townend's Clapham digs where they talked about plots over hot buttered toast; cricket and dirty jokes with the dilettante Westbrook; comforting chats with Lily, the Emsworth housekeeper [see plate 13]. There was no shortage of companions in New York. Wodehouse soon tired of his slippery agent, Abe Baerman, but Norman Thwaites, from the *New York World*, lent him an apartment and gave him introductions into journalism, while Baerman's replacement, the hard-drinking, hard-boiled Seth Moyle, offered a glimpse of the edgier side of Manhattan life. It was, however, a few months before he found his true confidant – the seventeen-year-old British-born New Yorker, Leslie Havergal Bradshaw [see plate 14].

An aspiring fellow writer, Bradshaw was a hardworking dreamer. With a demanding employer, an impossible family and – in due course – a fearsome fiancée, he came to be, for Wodehouse, a Bingo Little and a Jimmy Pitt rolled into one. Bradshaw had moved to New York three years earlier. Like Wodehouse, he wrote for *The Captain* – and the pair met when Bradshaw was sent to write a feature article for the boys' magazine. The result is part feature article, part eulogy:

> He is just what I imagined: tall, big and strong; a young man, with dark hair, rather light blue eyes, a healthy colour, and the most friendly, genial, likeable manner in the world [...] He has a big hand and shakes with you vigorously. [...] I had an awfully hard job to tear myself away. I finally did go. But first he gave me a cheery promise to look me up at my home a few days later. Since then, I have seen him frequently and have been the recipient of much kindness from him.[1]

This was a writing partnership as well as a friendship. Wodehouse helped Bradshaw with his plots; Bradshaw used his literary contacts to act as Wodehouse's unofficial agent.

Wodehouse soon moved out of Thwaites' apartment and into the bohemian Hotel Earle in Greenwich Village, where he worked feverishly at his novel, which was to be published in America as *A Gentleman of Leisure*.[2] During this period, the restlessness that was to mark Wodehouse's life for the next twenty years began to emerge. Soon after selling a number of stories, he returned to England and showed signs of settling down, buying a cottage next to Emsworth House School. He even started working back at the *Globe* with Westbrook, and enjoyed the summer cricket season, playing alongside writers such as Conan Doyle and J. M. Barrie. But just as life was beginning to seem established, Wodehouse received a request concerning the dramatisation of *A Gentleman of Leisure* for the American stage, and booked another passage back to New York.

These years, in which Wodehouse 'sort of shuttled to and fro across the Atlantic', were made possible by the efficiency of the transatlantic ocean-liner.[3] This was the age of ocean travel, and the sea was – for Wodehouse – a source of inspiration. Many of his early novels draw on the maritime atmosphere, from the frenzied bustle of the Paddington boat-train, to the heft and sway of the sea; the tremor of the engines in the dining saloon, and 'that faint, but well-defined, smell of cooked meats' that pervades the floating vessel.[4]

Wodehouse made the most of his peripatetic existence. The 'first truly Anglo-American author', many of his articles during this period were placed in both American publications (such as *Cosmopolitan* and *McClure's*) and British periodicals (such as *The Strand*).[5] One of Wodehouse's gifts was his ability to capture a nation's characteristics – and to exaggerate them. He offered his American audiences classic scenes of English tearooms and top hats, while his English readers enjoyed the excitement of Times Square, Brooklyn housebreakers and 'magnificently aloof' taxi-chauffeurs.[6]

Around this time, Wodehouse began work on a new set of stories with a distinctive protagonist – Reggie Pepper. The prototype for Bertie Wooster, Pepper was modelled on the English 'dude' parts that Wodehouse had seen on the New York stage – and the stock Edwardian aristocrat roles that he had seen played by the comedian George Grossmith Jr [see plate 12]. [7]

In the end, Wodehouse was to make – at least for a while – a home in America. But this was an accidental act of homemaking. By October 1914, the 'slight friction threatening in the Balkans' had turned into full-blown conflict. [8] At the point war was declared, Wodehouse found himself on, of all places, a German ocean liner. He was travelling back to America on the same boat as the actor John Barrymore and was attempting to score a feature interview.

Wodehouse was never to see active service. As he told his biographer, 'I was rejected for service because of my eyes.' After the call for conscription was introduced in America he 'tried to enlist again [...] but was rejected once more'. [9] In many ways, his geographical location provided shelter from the realities of war. Indeed, his only on-the-record comment was in an interview in *The New York Times* in which he declares that – paradoxically – the 'tragedy of war' is 'going to have a great effect on the attitude towards humour of the British public. People will become so depressed that they will become less critical of the methods used to cheer them up.' [10]

Wodehouse's personal 'war' was dominated by his attempts to break into the American market. By 1915, he had had numerous pieces printed in the American 'pulps' – such as *Argosy*, *Munsey's* and *People's*. These magazines were cheap and widely circulated, but they also bought their stories from authors at cheaper rates. Wodehouse was still chasing that elusive prize – to land a serialised novel in one of what were known as the 'slick papers'.

Wodehouse's life in Manhattan was a highly social one. Parties began in the small hours, when Thwaites returned from the *New York World* offices; nights were spent playing records on Bradshaw's gramophone, and entertaining glamorous New York actresses. But by 1913 most of Wodehouse's friends had started to pair off. Thwaites had a girlfriend. Westbrook had unexpectedly married Wodehouse's Emsworth friend, Ella King-Hall. Bradshaw was particularly preoccupied, engaging in an almost daily tempestuous correspondence with his fiancée, Olive. Wodehouse's own romantic forays were more short-lived. He would remember his first real attachment, to the actress and singer Alice Dovey, all his life [see plate 15]. 'I shall never forget how wonderful she was, with her charm, and her sense of comedy, and her beautiful voice'. 'All the heroines in my books are more or less drawn from her', he later wrote, and his nickname for Alice, 'Billie', was given to the irrepressible Billie Dore in *A Damsel in Distress*.[11] Wodehouse immortalises his feelings for Alice in his unusually sentimental short story 'In Alcala'. Set in a bleak boarding house, and featuring an awkward British writer and an attractive American actress, the story has many biographical resonances. But given that Wodehouse's proposal of marriage to Alice Dovey was turned down, one suspects the moment in which the hero 'shower[s]' his lover's 'upturned face with kisses' was wishful thinking.[12]

There are mentions of other women. A relationship with a London widow is intriguingly filtered through a correspondence with her eleven-year-old daughter; a dinner engagement with another widow – this time a well-known actress – and a meeting with a London lady journalist apparently came to nothing.[13] Loneliness began to set in. 'Solitude had not hurt him till now', Wodehouse wrote.[14] A letter to Bradshaw complains of life's infernal monotony.[15] By the end of the year, the realities of bachelor life were beginning to pall.

1 'Impressions of P. G. Wodehouse', *The Captain*, March 1910, vol. XXII, no. 132, pp. 500–1.
2 The book had numerous variant titles in stage, serial and book versions, in the US and UK, including *The Gem Collector*, *A Gentleman of Leisure* and *A Thief for a Night*.
3 Jasen, p. 47.
4 *The Girl on the Boat* (1922), Chapter 6.
5 Barry Phelps, *P. G. Wodehouse: Man and Myth* (Constable: London, 1992), p. 99.
6 *The Intrusion of Jimmy* (1910), Chapter 6.
7 See Murphy, pp. 125–6.
8 *The Inimitable Jeeves* (1923), Chapter 1.
9 These are PGW's own words. See Jasen, p. 53. Other biographers give conflicting and sometimes conjectural accounts of PGW's attempts to enlist. See Frances Donaldson, *P. G. Wodehouse: A Biography* (New York: Knopf, 1982), p. 107, and Phelps, p. 101. The only concrete record is that of his registration in America in September 1918. See Robert McCrum, *Wodehouse: A Life* (London: Viking, 2004), pp. 108 and 439.
10 Joyce Kilmer, 'War Will Restore England's Sense of Humour', *The New York Times*, 7 November 1915.
11 PGW to Ann Garland, 12 February 1969 (private archive).
12 'In Alcala' (1911), repr. in *The Man Upstairs and Other Stories* (1914).
13 In a letter to Bradshaw, PGW notes that he is 'going to ask Daisy Wood to dinner'. Wood was a recently widowed British music hall artiste, and sister of the music hall comedienne Marie Lloyd, PGW to L. H. Bradshaw, 22 November 1912 (private archive).
14 'In Alcala'.
15 PGW to L. H. Bradshaw, 1 September 1914 (private archive).

1909–1914:
'American hustle'

The Earle
103 Waverly Place
One door from Washington Sq. North
New York

Sept 7. 1909

Dear Bradshaw.
Here I am. As Wilkie Bard was singing when I left England, 'I'm here if I'm wanted'.[1]

I am in most of the day. Why not drop in on your way home?

Yrs

P. G. Wodehouse

1 Wilkie Bard's 'The Policeman' ('I'm there if I'm wanted') was a popular hit song in 1908.

The Earle
103 Waverly Place
One door from Washington Sq. North
NEW YORK

November 9. 1909

<u>Tuesday.</u>
Dear Bradshaw.
Thanks awfully for your letter. It's ripping of you wanting to give me a leg-up, but I'm afraid it wouldn't do. So far from wanting to get my boys' books published this side, I look on them as a guilty past which I must hush up. I want to start here with a clean sheet as a writer of

grown-up stories. The *Captain* books are all right in their way, but their point of view is too immature. They would kill my chances of doing anything big. I don't want people here to know me as a writer of school-stories. I want to butt into the big league. It wouldn't do me much good people saying I was better than Andrew Home when I want them to say I'm better than O. Henry.[1] The school stories have served their time, and it could hurt my chances to have them bobbing up when I'm trying to do bigger work. I have given up boys stories absolutely.

I think I saw the Pilgrims in Broadway today. At least there was a group of apparent Britons, with one man on crutches.[2]

I hope the serial is going strong. I return the synopsis.

Yours ever

P. G. Wodehouse

1 Andrew Home, writer of school stories, with titles including *From Fag to Monitor* (1896), *By a School Boy's Hand* (1904) and *Bravo Bob* (1909). See Bradshaw's 1910 *Captain* interview, which claims that '[t]he best magazines such as the *Cosmopolitan*, *Collier's Weekly*, &c., are printing [Wodehouse's] stories. The former, in fact, calls him "A second O. Henry" (O. Henry is considered to be the greatest short-story writer in America today).'
2 'The Pilgrims of England', an English football team, were touring the USA in late 1909. A match report in the 3 November 1909 edition of the *Inquirer* noted that, by this point in the tour, a number of the British players 'were in a more or less crippled condition'. They were, nevertheless, victorious in most of their matches, gaining much press attention.

TO LESLIE HAVERGAL BRADSHAW

Dear Bradshaw,

Thanks awfully for mags. Use any public school stuff you like in accompanying notebooks but don't swipe me other notes![1]

Yours ever

PGW

P.S. I'm getting in a piano. You must come & play it.

1 PGW's notebooks, which he had been keeping since he had left Dulwich College. Entitled *Phrases and Notes*, they include conversations with a London bus driver and a policeman, as well as accounts of football, cricket matches and incidents at his old school. Many of the notes formed the basis of his later short stories.

Hotel Earle
103 Waverly Place
One door from Washington Sq. North
NEW YORK

April 29. 1910

Dear Bradshaw.

The announcement in the *Argosy* looks great.[1] You certainly are going strong. I'm not certain about next week. I'll write if it can be managed, but I shall probably be pretty busy with *Psmith*, which is giving me trouble.[2]

The fight was awfully good. Ketchel finished up in great style, & had a clear lead on points at the end.[3]

Yours ever

P.G.W.

1 The 'announcement' in *The Argosy* refers to Bradshaw's forthcoming story 'Mrs Allison's Day of Excitement', which ran in the July issue.
2 PGW's reference to *Psmith* may refer to what eventually became the US version of *The Prince and Betty*, which incorporated part of the plot of *Psmith, Journalist*.
3 PGW wrote about boxing for the *Daily Express* in England. Polish-American boxer Stanislaw Kiecal (1886–1910), better known as Stanley Ketchel, fought six times in 1910 before his murder in October of that year.

Bradshaw was temporarily on the staff of Success *magazine, a mass-market monthly, which espoused the virtue of self-reliance. Wodehouse often used him, and other friends, as informal literary agents, attempting to get them to negotiate publication of his stories. Wodehouse remembers needing money, but loving his time at the Earle Hotel, where he was staying. 'I was very hard up in my Greenwich Village days, but was always very happy. There were trees and grass and, if you wanted to celebrate the sale of a story, two wonderful old restaurants, the Bevoort and the Lafayette [...] everything such as food and hotel bills was inexpensive: one could live on practically nothing, which was fortunate for me because I had to.'*

Hotel Earle
103 WAVERLY PLACE
NEW YORK

May 5. 1910

Dear Bradshaw.

Thanks awfully for your letter. You are a bear-cat. Whether the story goes through or not, I shall be equally grateful. Nobody could have done more than you have. I think it's ripping of you.

Just had a letter from England, to say that I have sold two more stories to the *Strand* for £50. That makes 6 they have taken altogether.[1]

[...]

I've just discovered a hole in my trousers. These are Life's Tragedies.

Billy Watt[2] promised me 6 copies of *Jimmy* today.[3] If they arrive I'll send one up to you. Do you mind if I keep the vol of the *Captain* for a day or two? I may need it. I'm sending May *Captain* with this in case you haven't seen it. I like 'Sanctuary', though I guessed the end. did you?[4]

The *Express* don't want me to go to the Jeffries–Johnson fight,[5] so I shall almost certainly be in England when you are. Great stuff.

Yours ever

P.G.W.

Ps. I won't come up & see you, as I must avoid office till story is decided on.

1 In 1910, *The Strand* published PGW's 'The Good Angel' (February); 'The Man Upstairs' (March); 'Archibald's Benefit' (April), 'Rough-Hew Them How We Will' (April); 'Deep Waters' (June)' and 'Love Me, Love My Dog' (July).
2 Billy Watt, a maverick New York publisher, founder of W. J. Watt & Co.
3 PGW's latest novel, *The Intrusion of Jimmy*, drew on his growing knowledge of turn-of-the-century Manhattan, as well as English country life. Following its publication in England, it was published in book form in America in May 1910 as *A Gentleman of Leisure*. The book had numerous variant titles in stage, serial and book versions, including *The Gem Collector* and *A Thief for a Night*.
4 R. S. Warren Bell's short story in the May 1910 *Captain*, 'Sanctuary', tells 'Of a Greyhouse Half-Back and of How his nimbleness helped him at a Certain Crisis in his "old boy" Days'.
5 A match had been scheduled for 4 July 1910, between James J. Jeffries and Jack Johnson. Jeffries, the former undefeated heavyweight boxing champion, had come out of retirement,

declaring his motive to be that of 'proving that a white man is better than a Negro'. Johnson won the fight, silencing Jeffries, but triggering race riots.

Hotel Earle
103 Waverly Place
New York

Monday

Dear Bradshaw.

Are you game to put a little snaky work for me? As follows. Will you show enclosed to Brubaker, just saying that I sent it to you to read & that everyone who has read it says it is my strongest story.[1] If he says (a) 'I don't think much of it', bow & retire gracefully but if (b) he says 'this is hot stuff', then say casually 'Wodehouse wants $600 for it. He told me he was going to keep it by him till he could get that for it.'

Now, at dese crool woids, Brubaker will either say (a) 'Let him wait' or (b) 'My God, we must have this if it breaks the firm.'[2]

Everybody tells me I mustn't let this story go at my usual rates, so I'm out to get something big for it. You catch the idea, don't you? I don't actually offer the MS to *Success*. They merely see it by accident, & if they want to buy at $600, all right.

I've decided to abandon *Psmith* for the time being, but I shall be full up with the play, I think all this week, so let's have our meeting later. Thinking things over, I doubt if you'd better bring the phonograph when you come. There's a woman next door who has been kicking at the piano. She'll turn fits at the 'graph. Send down serial (inst today, can you? I should like to read it).

I've got a short story in May *Captain*.[3]

Yrs

P.G.W.

P.S. Great idea. Tell Brubaker I've particularly asked you to send story back tomorrow as I want to send it to *Collier's*, though I have told *Collier's* nothing about it. Thus will he give it quick reading & we shall win through. Add that I have just sold *Collier's* another for $300. (I did this last Monday. Did I tell you? Baseball story.)[4]

1 Howard Brubaker, editor of *Success* and *Liberator* magazine, among the many magazines for which Bradshaw worked.
2 PGW's phrase 'dese crool woids' is taken from his own fictional character, Spike, the Brooklyn housebreaker in *The Intrusion of Jimmy*, which was published that month in America.
3 PGW's tale of a schoolboy caught smoking, and attempting to avoid being punished, appeared in the 'School Yarns' section of *The Captain* (May 1910), under the title 'Stone and the Weed'.
4 The baseball story 'The Pitcher and the Plutocrat' (*Collier's Weekly*, 24 September 1910), rewritten as 'The Goalkeeper and the Plutocrat' for *The Strand* in January 1912.

Wodehouse returned to London at the end of 1910, renewed the lease on his cottage at Emsworth, and began work again at the Globe.

TO LESLIE HAVERGAL BRADSHAW

Constit. Club
WC.

January 19. 1911

Dear Bradshaw.

Thanks for the very timely tip about Seth![1] I shall certainly be out of town. I wonder what brings him this side.

[...]

By the way, I have started my new novel, which merges about ¹/₂ way into the plot (with variations) of *Psmith, Journalist*.[2] (Psmith doesn't appear). It's going to be a corker – good love interest – rapid action from first chapter – length about 100,000 words. Watt is bringing it out in the Fall. Will you be spying out the land meanwhile for serial publication. How about *Success*? I know you would place it for me for nothing, but I hope you will take 10%. I could get it done by the middle of February, I think, as the last half will come easy. The people you might sound (after *Success*) are Billy Taylor, of the *Associated Sundays*; Stone, of the *Metropolitan*; and the *Cosmo*; & any others you can think of. All the characters are Americans. The scene is laid for the first 7 chapters on an island in the Mediterranean, after that in New York. The title is *A Prince at Large.*

[...]

My next Black's book is on rather different lines.[3] It is a serial I wrote for *Chums* 3 years ago rather in the Andrew Home vein! But there is such a lot of good stuff in it that I have decided to let it go through with the others. I am v. pleased with the sales of my Black's books. The royalties come to over £60 this year.

[...]

Yrs.

P.G.W.

1 Seth Moyle, PGW's second literary agent in the USA, had, PGW recalls, 'this extraordinary knack of fast-talking an editor into taking a story' (Jasen, p. 44).
2 PGW's 'new novel' referred to as *The Prince at Large* was to become *The Prince and Betty* (1912).
3 PGW's 'next Black's book' was meant to be the *Chums* serial *The Luck Stone*. This never appeared, and *The Luck Stone* found posthumous publication in 1997.

TO LESLIE HAVERGAL BRADSHAW

Emsworth, Hants

May 21. 1912

Dear Bradshaw.

I haven't had a moment to write before. A million congratulations on the serial.[1] It is perfectly wonderful to have placed one at your age. This has certainly been a big year for you so far. At the rate you work you'll probably have another ready before the winter. Considering how you have been worked at the office, it's simply wonderful your having done a long story so quickly. I am plugging away at mine. I reached $^1/_2$ way a few days ago. It is giving me a lot of trouble, but the results are good so far.[2]

[...]

I am having a great time now the *The Pink Lady* is over here. I have met nearly all the principals except Hazel Dawn. Louise Kelley, the girl who plays the Countess, is a very good sort, & Alice Dovey, of course, is the nicest girl I ever met.[3]

Tell friend Chas Buck that I'm writing to him very soon.[4] I had a friendly letter from Douglas Fairbanks yesterday in answer to mine of July last![5] American hustle!

Westbrook is going to be married on the 28th!!! Ella King-Hall. I don't think you ever met her.[6]

Good notices of *Betty* this side. I don't know how it's selling. Its shortness is rather against it.

Well, so long,

Yours ever

P.G.W. (Chickens)

1 Bradshaw's five-part serial *Before the Dark* had been placed in *The Argosy* – America's first 'pulp fiction' magazine – running in December 1912.

2 PGW's 'long story', probably *The Little Nugget*, published as a one-shot by *Munsey's Magazine* in August 1913, and in three parts, with the love story excluded, in *The Captain* in January to March 1913.

3 Alice Dovey, one of the leading ladies in Ivan Caryll's Broadway musical *The Pink Lady*. Born in Plattsmouth, Nebraska, the Dovey sisters (Alice and Ethel) had been well-known child stars, renowned for their precocious talent.

4 Charles Neville Buck (1879–1930), short story writer, whose work appeared alongside PGW's *The White Hope* in *Munsey's Magazine* in May 1914.

5 Douglas Fairbanks (1883–1939), later famous for his roles in silent movies such as *Robin Hood* and *The Mask of Zorro*, played the hero, Jimmy Pitt, in the Broadway theatrical adaptation of PGW's novel. *The Intrusion of Jimmy*, entitled *A Gentleman of Leisure*.

6 Ella's brother recorded that the couple had 'been devoted for 10 years and were married in Paris [...] they will live in a small flat near the Temple' (*The Diary of George King-Hall*, 17 June 1912) (private archive).

Wodehouse and Arthur Conan Doyle had often played cricket together in matches such as the Authors v. Actors, alongside other literary men of the time, such as E. W. Hornung and A. A. Milne. Both also played for J. M. Barrie's cricket team, the 'Allahakbarries'. In 1912, Wodehouse was playing regularly throughout the season, including at Lord's. When not playing cricket, Wodehouse was busy finishing his latest novel. The Little Nugget *drew on his knowledge of Emsworth House School, mixing the English school story with an American gangster plot.*

Constitutional Club
Northumberland Avenue, W.C.

Aug 9. 1912

Dear Comrade Doyle.[1]

Will you stand by me in a crisis? A New York lady journalist, a friend of mine, is over here gunning for you. She said 'You know Conan Doyle, don't you?'. I said, 'I do. It is my only claim to fame'. She then insisted on my taking her to see you at Crowborough, and mentioned next Sunday, the 11th. Can you stand this invasion? If so, we will arrive in the afternoon. (Rather like Malone going to see Challenger!)[2] I enclose a telegraph-form and hope that all will be well. (I have traded so much in America on my friendship with you that my reputation will get a severe jolt if you refuse it!)

I am absorbed in *The Lost World*! I have just finished a novel of my own for an American magazine, but I had to write it so quick that I am afraid it is pretty bad. I shall revise it later.[3]

I was glad to see you on form with the bat the other day. I hope we shall smash the publishers.

Yours ever

P. G. Wodehouse

1 PGW's joking, notionally socialist mode of address – 'Comrade' – echoes that of his character Psmith.
2 PGW refers to characters in Doyle's serial *The Lost World*, in which the journalist Edward Malone sets out to interview the fearsome Professor Challenger as part of his quest to impress the woman he loves, and ends up on an expedition to the Amazon basin. The tale, which featured dinosaurs and vicious ape-like creatures, was serialised in *The Strand Magazine*, alongside Wodehouse's *The Prince and Betty*, from 1912 to 1913.
3 *The Little Nugget* (1913).

Bradshaw was having a degree of success as a writer of school stories. His latest book, The Right Sort, *was dedicated to Wodehouse. Bradshaw needed Wodehouse's encouragement. He was moving locations frequently, working as an editor on various magazines, and as a private secretary to wealthy men, all the time desperately trying to make a living. At the point of writing, he had just landed a job working for Thomas W. Lawson, a broker and author. This was especially fortuitous as Bradshaw, despite familial disapproval, had fallen in love and was trying to establish himself so that he might be in a position to marry.*

TO LESLIE HAVERGAL BRADSHAW

Emsworth

September 9. 1912

Dear Brad.

I am afraid I have left your letter a long time unanswered. Congratulations on the Lawson business. You seem to go ahead every day. It's wonderful.

I have just heard from Seth that Bob Davis likes *The Little Nugget!* Thank goodness.[1]

I am coming over on the *Olympic*, either Oct 9 or 30. I hope the bally boat doesn't go down.[2] The uncertainty as to date is because I am coming with my friend Thwaites, of the N.Y. *World*, & I don't quite know when he can get away.

[...]

The weather here has been simply infernal. I made 27 in 7 minutes for the Authors at Lord's before being stumped, & then rain stopped play. Last Sat'y I got 50 for our village & took 7 wickets. We had to run everything out & it nearly killed me. With boundaries I should have made a century.

Are you back in N.Y. yet? If so, go & pal up with *The Pink Lady* crowd, espec'y Alice Dovey, the Hegemans & Louise Kelley. You'll like them.

Tell me all about Olive when you write.[3]

So long

Yours ever

Chickens.

1 Bob Davis, editor of *Munsey's Magazine*, was seen by many writers as the 'literary godfather'. See Q. D. Leavis, *Fiction and the Reading Public* (Harmondsworth: Penguin, 1979), p. 221. PGW described him as 'a fellow who would give you a plot and then buy the story you had written for his magazine', Jasen, p. 50.
2 PGW's reference to the 'bally boat' going 'down' alludes to the sinking of RMS *Titanic* on 14 April 1912.
3 Bradshaw's girlfriend, Olive Marie Barrows, from Philadelphia.

TO LESLIE HAVERGAL BRADSHAW

Hotel Algonquin
59 to 65 West Forty-Fourth Street
New York

May 6. 1913

Dear Brad.

Yes, here I am, & sorry not to find you in N.Y. I didn't expect to, as I knew your visits now were rare. When can we meet? Can't you get Lawson to send you in here?

I have started in already on a new novel for Bob Davis. I haven't mapped it out properly yet, but it is coming, I think. He asked me if I could have it finished by July 1. I said 'Oh, yes.' I don't know how many thousand words a day these guys think I can write!

This place suits me a lot better than the Earle. Owing to Fairbanks & Megrue both recommending me, the management can't do enough for me.¹ I asked for a chair, & they gave me so many that I haven't room to move about!

[...]

Brother Alfred alas was a <u>ghastly</u> frost!! Grossmith made me write & re-write 'till all the punch was lost, & it ran just a fortnight to empty houses. I never saw such notices, all thoroughly well deserved.²

[...]

Alice Dovey & Louise Kelley welcomed me with open arms. I have got over my little trouble re first-named & we are the best of friends. She is too devoted to Hamilton King for me to form a wedge & break up the combination, so I gracefully retire.³

Isn't it hot! I sweat off a pound a day. They are building a sky-scraper next door, & that keeps me on the jump. How New York has blossomed out since I was here last. It's quite a city now.

Well, so long

Come here soon

Yours ever

Chickens

1 Roi Cooper Megrue (1883–1927), popular Broadway playwright during the years 1912–21. PGW alludes to Megrue's 1914 farce It Pays to Advertise in A Damsel in Distress (1919).
2 British actor, Lawrence Grossmith (1887–1944), son of comedian and writer George Grossmith Sr and brother of George Grossmith Jr, had commissioned PGW to write Brother Alfred, a one-act play, based on his Reggie Pepper story, 'Rallying round Old George'. It was co-written with Herbert Westbrook. It limped through fourteen performances at the Savoy Theatre, before folding.
3 Hamilton King (1871–1952), American illustrator famous for his pictures of 'cigarette girls'. King had probably met Alice Dovey while working on the publicity posters for The Pink Lady.

Back in London in the spring of 1914, Wodehouse 'was engaged to write a revue [Nuts and Wine] *(at £7 a week) for the Empire Theatre', in collaboration with his friend, C. H. Bovill. 'We spent some of the time', he recalls, 'working out the plots of the Bleke stories', which appeared in* The Strand *and the* Pictorial Review. *A few months later, he was packing to return to New York. Wodehouse found some comfort in London after Alice Dovey's refusal. Lillian Armstrong, a London widow, claimed his affections. Wodehouse visited Mrs Armstrong frequently when in London, and was fond of her daughter, Olive (known as 'Bubbles'). His proposals of marriage to Mrs Armstrong were not accepted.*

TO OLIVE ARMSTRONG

Emsworth
Hants.

July 13. 1914

My darling Bubbles.
I am dreadfully sorry, but I cannot possibly come & see you before I sail.

I shall be so busy packing and getting ready. I will come and see you directly I get back.

Mind you have learned to swim by then. I want you to be a really good swimmer, and then we will go away together to the sea-side and swim all day.

I am sending you a little present. It doesn't look very nice, but it means quite a lot of money. It will buy you all sorts of nice things. Give it to Mrs Pennington and tell her what you specially want to buy, and she will get it for you. Let me know some of the things you buy. You might get another doll if you wanted one.

Love and kisses
from
P.G.

A few weeks after the declaration of the First World War, Wodehouse was back in New York, and once again staying in his friend Norman Thwaites' New York apartment.

TO LESLIE HAVERGAL BRADSHAW

43 East 27th Street
New York

Sept 1. 1914

Dear Brad.
Thanks very much for the clippings and the story. I liked the latter very much, but what a little there is in it, when you come to analyse it. That is what I've always wanted to be able to do, to interest the reader for about five thousand words without having any real story. At present, I have to have an author-proof plot, or I'm no good. I expect one has to be about ten years older than I am to do it properly.

[...]

This is in a way a crucial week, for I have a story out with the *Metropolitan* and another with the *Saturday Evening Post*. If either of them lands, I shall ask a big price, and then we'll see what Honble

Ruddy Mackenzie has got to say about getting first refusal on all stuff at $300 per![1] I feel it in my bones that the *Post* will take that yarn. It is really one of the very best I have ever done. Of course, it will mean that they will refuse the next dozen or so as not up to the same standard, but that can't be helped. I want to get into the *Post* – we are asking $500 for the story – in order to beat hell out of these other guys. Mackenzie at present is far too much the Heavy Editor to please me. The whole purport of my campaign is to shift the burden of obligation, and make it jolly decent of me to let *McClure's* have my stuff, instead of jolly decent of them to want it.

My position is fine and strong now, for Mrs Wilkening has sold the *Man Upstairs* book of short stories to the Famous Players Movie people.[2] I don't know how much they are giving, but it can't be less than $100 a story, and as there are nineteen stories, I ought to clear in the neighbourhood of $2000. This will put me in shape to treat editors like so many tripe-hounds, especially with the *Nugget* coming on. My ambition is to inaugurate a regular reign of terror. I hope nothing goes wrong with the works!

Meanwhile, I simply can't get another idea for a short story. My record till now has been great, – three in just over a month; but I never can keep it up. It will probably be another six weeks before I get going again.

In this crisis I am trying to get the 'Squidge' going again, but the enthusiasm has gone.[3] This war and everything makes me feel too jumpy for steady work on a serial. I am in the mood when I want to turn out short story after short story and get quick results. Besides, I am just at the most infernal part of the book, when I am introducing the characters and don't feel certain of them yet.

[...]

The state of the War is as follows. I have driven Seth back and I think annihilated him. Billy Watt, however, has taken the offensive in the centre, and is threatening my communications.

I had an agitated phone call from Mrs Wilkening the other day, asking me to come up. It seems that Billy had been calling her down good and hard about me. He said that he ought to have been informed of all that she was doing. What was more sinister was that he was claiming 25% of all movie rights on some stuff which Thompson Buchanan had published with him![4] His ground was that he had introduced Thompson to Mrs Wilkening!! Aren't these men perfect death-traps over here. I'm getting scared whenever anyone – except you – gives me a pleasant word. It seems to follow almost automatically that they claim ten per cent on some of one's money.

[...]

[H]is behaviour has been so sinister that I have signed all sorts of papers making Mrs Wilkening my sole agent. I bank on her. If she lets me down, my faith in human nature is done for. She is the only professional agent I have met yet who seems honest. I like her, too, which is an enormous asset.

Billy has not sent the check yet! It is now twenty-two days since he promised to send it in ten days. I suppose he wants me to write to him again, and then he can denounce me [...] I shall just let him take his time, – up to a month or so, that is to say. Then I shall mobilise the legal brigade.

You would think I was the most quarrelsome chap in the world to look at my list of enemies! My real trouble with all these people is that I don't really like them. We are only bound together by business, and when anything goes wrong with that everything snaps.

Which reminds me of Pinkie! Not a word from her yet! The other day I was hurrying down 34th street, and I passed her and Peggy. We passed within four feet of each other, but she didn't make a sign.[5] Whether it was a deliberate cut I don't know. It's quite possible, if you're thinking of something else, to brush past a person without seeing him, but it looks suspicious. The funny part is that I hardly miss her at all. I really believe that, unless you're in love with her, you can dispense with any woman, – in other words one's real friendships are never with them. Pink was pleasant to have around, but, if she's not there, I don't notice it.

My kick against life at present is that it's so infernally monotonous. I get up, try to work, feed, and go to bed again day after day. As long as I'm working I feel all right, but in between stories it's rotten. That's why I have always enjoyed Emsworth. There was never a day without something breaking loose, if it was only the dog rolling or one of the kids breaking a window.

[...]

My brother passes through tomorrow on his way to Hong-Kong. It will be nice seeing him.[6] I wish you could get to town again soon.

Well, so long. Do you want those clippings back?

Yours ever

Chickens

---

1 Cameron MacKenzie, editor of *McClure's*, a monthly periodical with a 600,000 circulation, specialising in 'strong clean stories, vital and well told'.

2 PGW was still struggling to find a good literary agent. His relationship with Cora Wilkening did not last long, and he later refers to her as a 'hopeless incompetent'. Wilkening made a habit of suing her clients for large sums if deals were made without her consultation. The Famous Players film company (eventually Paramount Pictures) was one of the new companies formed in 1912.

3 'Squidge' – probably a reference to *Something Fresh*, the serial PGW published in 1915.

4 Thompson Buchanan (1837–1937), writer and director.

5 PGW's spat with 'Pinkie', the actress and silent movie star Hazel Dawn, famous for her role in *The Pink Lady*, seems to have had no further repercussions. Hazel Dawn's younger sister, Margaret Romaine ('Peggy'), was also in New York, starring in musical comedies.

6 PGW's brother Peveril was on his way to join the Hong Kong police.

The following letter survives as an extract transcribed by Bradshaw and sent to his fiancée, Olive. Bradshaw and Olive Barrows were engaged, and the wedding had been set for a month earlier – 22 August. Bradshaw's family were strongly opposed to the marriage. His father threatened to kill him, and his mother claimed to be dangerously ill just before the date. The wedding was postponed, leading to a tempestuous correspondence between the couple and Bradshaw's family. Bradshaw notes that 'if my mother had her choice I would not be married until I was 30'. Tension was increased by Bradshaw's peripatetic existence – he divided his time between Boston, where he worked as a private secretary for Thomas W. Lawson, a stock-broker and author, and New York, where he stayed with Wodehouse and freelanced for various magazines, including Everybody's *and* The Delineator.

Bradshaw reports that Wodehouse was in good spirits at this time, treating his friends to champagne at his flat. Wodehouse 'had a date' on 23 September, the day before he wrote this letter. His companion was called Ethel May Wayman.

September 24. 1914

[...]

I really meant what I said about your writing. I know it must be deadly dull for you all alone in Boston. But you ought to buckle to and try and do something in the writing line. Why don't you write about something which has to do with your present life? You are in a position most writers would love to get. You can surely work out something connected with the unique Lawson atmosphere.

You tell those anecdotes of Lawson's mannerisms so vividly that you must be able to make fiction out of him.[1]

I think myself that you would be perfectly justified in marrying now, if you want to. The present state of things is idiotic and absolutely unfair to you. Nobody would blame you if you refused to endure it.

Well cheerio.

Yours ever,

Chickens

1 Lawson kept a 1,000-acre estate in Scituate, Massachusetts, called 'Dreamwold', where he bred and raised spaniels. Bradshaw had given a spaniel to Olive as a token and proof of his love. It seems that Bradshaw's 'unique Lawson atmosphere', along with many aspects of his life, finds its way into Wodehouse's fiction, in the shape of wealthy eccentric Americans, henpecked British secretaries, and canine love-tokens. Lawson specialised in shares in the copper-mining industry, and seems to have provided the inspiration for Wodehouse's T. Patterson Frisby, the dyspeptic millionaire in *Big Money* (1931).

CHAPTER FIVE

Love on Long Island

Wodehouse and Ethel had only known each other a few weeks when they were married in the Little Church Round the Corner, off Madison Square on East 29th Street. Their courtship was shot through with comedy. An early date was cut short because Wodehouse had toothache; a fit of sneezing overcame him at the moment he tried to propose; and the marriage ceremony itself was delayed because the minister was busy making a killing on the stock market. But their feelings for each other were serious. Ethel was, for Wodehouse, an 'angel in human form'.[1] This unlikely union, between two lonely English people, could be put down to 'what the unthinking call coincidence'.[2] But while chance played a part, there was more to it than that. Four years younger than Wodehouse, Ethel Rowley Wayman was an astute and clever woman. Described as a 'mixture of Mistress Quickly and Florence Nightingale with a touch of Lady Macbeth thrown in', she always worked to turn contingency to opportunity.[3] Handsome, long-legged, glamorous and intensely sociable, she was in many ways Wodehouse's opposite – but she understood him well.

Ethel's spirited nature proved to be a triumph of sorts [see plate 21]. She had not had a straightforward life. Born in Norfolk, with the given name Ethel Newton, she was the illegitimate daughter of a farmer and a milliner. She disliked her mother, who was an alcoholic, and was looked after partly in care, and partly by her maternal grandmother. In her teens, she began to earn her living as a dancer, and it was in 1903, while she was working in Blackpool for the summer season, that she became pregnant. The father, Leonard Rowley, was a university student studying engineering. To avoid scandal, the pair swiftly married. A year later, while Wodehouse was still making his way in the world of London journalism, the Rowleys – and their daughter, Leonora – set off for Mysore in India, where Leonard was to work as an engineer. He died in 1910, in obscure circumstances, believed to be due to drinking infected water.

Left to provide for her seven-year-old daughter, Ethel returned to England. By January of the following year, she married again. She was soon to be twice-widowed. Her second husband, a London tailor called John Wayman, became bankrupt after a failed business venture, and committed suicide. Ethel returned to the career she knew best – the stage. Placing Leonora in a boarding school, she began a series of trips to America, appearing as an 'artiste' in various repertory and variety productions under the stage-name 'Ethel Milton' [see plate 16].

If not a socialist, Wodehouse had always been, in his own way, an emancipated novelist. So many of his novels would go on to show the butler commanding the aristocrat, the chorus-girl triumphing over the debutante. Much of this came from Wodehouse's own innate sense of justice and equality. Part of the attraction of America, for him, was its real sense of 'knockabout' democracy, in which a college professor and a barman could laugh at the same thing. In 1915, he gave an interview in which he passionately argued that British comic writing was hampered by its class-bound nature. The best humour, he commented, 'is universal'.⁴ The force of this must have been felt all the more once he had met Ethel. For though she was only to speak of this privately, she – like the inimitable Sue Brown and the intrepid Jill Mariner – was a chorus-girl who came from nowhere.

In marrying Ethel, Wodehouse not only gained a wife. He also 'inherited' Leonora, her daughter [see plate 17]. He first met his new step-daughter in the spring of 1915, when she was eleven years old. They immediately became close, and he formally adopted her that year.

Leonora soon joined the Wodehouses in Long Island, went to school in America for a time, and spent her holidays riding her bicycle around the local roads. Wodehouse adored Leonora. The early US edition of *Piccadilly Jim* is dedicated 'To my step-daughter Lenora [*sic*], conservatively speaking the most wonderful child on earth', while *Leave It to Psmith* is 'For my daughter, Leonora, Queen of her Species'. Indeed, Wodehouse's 1914 satire on the fashion for eugenic family planning (*The White Hope*) was oddly prescient. Family, for Wodehouse, was forged through love, not genetics. Leonora – or 'Snorky' – as she soon became, was far more precious to Wodehouse than any of his biological relations.

Wodehouse and Ethel had little money when they married. She 'had seventy dollars' and 'I had managed to save fifty', he recalls – but the letters record them being all the happier for their makeshift existence together. This was an intensely productive time for Wodehouse. He was appointed drama critic for *Vanity Fair*, wrote numerous feature articles, and sold many of his stories to top magazines.

Crucially – in 1915 – a serial was bought by the top 'slick' paper, the *Saturday Evening Post. Something Fresh* (published in America as *Something New*), the tale of hard-up Ashe Marson and the enterprising Joan Valentine, marked Wodehouse's arrival as a major writer in America. The first of his Blandings Castle saga, this was just the beginning of many more appearances by the absent-minded Earl of Emsworth and the dread Lady Constance Keeble. The writing of this was, Wodehouse recalls, 'a turning point': 'It gave me confidence and I suddenly began to write much better.'[5]

The year 1915 was also important for Wodehouse as it saw the first appearance of two of his most memorable characters. The *Saturday Evening Post* story 'Extricating Young Gussie' features a 'drone', Bertie Wooster, making 'his formal bow, not very forcefully assisted by Jeeves, whose potential was yet to be realised'.[6] Writing fifty years later, Wodehouse commented that 'I find it curious, now that I have written so much about him, to recall how softly and undramatically Jeeves first entered my little world. Characteristically he did not thrust himself forward.'[7]

But Wodehouse was thrusting forward at quite a rate. His greatest opportunity came not in the field of novel writing, but in that of musical theatre. While he had already had some small success, writing occasional lyrics for musicals in London, the years from 1916 to 1918 were in a different league. This was his great period of collaboration with the British-American librettist Guy Bolton (1884–1979) and the New York composer Jerome Kern (1885–1945). Kern, who was at this point a rising star, would go on to write such songs as 'Ol' Man River', 'All the Things You Are' and 'Smoke Gets in Your Eyes'. Wodehouse later recalled that 'Guy and I clicked from the start like Damon and Pythias.'[8] The 'trio of musical fame' collaborated on a series of hits known as the 'Princess' musicals that included *Miss Springtime* (1916), *Have a Heart* (New York, 1917), *Oh, Boy!* (New York, 1917), *Leave It to Jane* (New York, 1917), and *Oh, Lady! Lady!!* (New York, 1918) [see plate 20]. They toured these musicals across the eastern states of America –

testing their success with audiences and refining the music and lyrics – before opening in New York.

The cover of the sheet music for Wodehouse and Kern's song 'Bill', first performed in 1918.

Wodehouse was an extraordinarily talented lyricist. 'Ten years of training in repression, and the worship of good form at public school', as he admitted, beat sentiment out of a man.[9] But the presence of music allowed him to capture moments of feeling with great tenderness, as shown in perhaps his best-known lyric, 'Bill'.

Despite his new-found personal happiness and success, Wodehouse knew all too well the daily devastation that was taking place in Europe.

The darkness leaves no trace in the fiction of this period – save, perhaps, for the comic figure of Willie Partridge, the enthusiastic bomb-maker in *Piccadilly Jim*. Wodehouse's letters touch on war from time to time. He considers the Zeppelin threat; there is a mention of his friend, Thwaites, who had been shot through the neck; he worries about the old Dulwich boys who were still on the front; he frets that his friend Lily will not get enough to eat. But, characteristically, Wodehouse can never bear to brood on pain for long.

1 'Preface' (1969), *Something Fresh* (1915).
2 *Something Fresh*, Chapter 4.
3 Malcolm Muggeridge, *Chronicles of Wasted Time*, quoted in Phelps, p. 104.
4 Interview with Joyce Kilmer, *The New York Times*, 7 November 1915.
5 PGW to Richard Usborne, 21 May 1956 (Wodehouse Archive).
6 Jasen, p. 56.
7 *The World of Jeeves* (London: Jenkins, 1967), p. viii.
8 *Performing Flea* (London: Jenkins, 1953), p. 14.
9 Kilmer.

1914–1918:
'Something Fresh'

TO LESLIE HAVERGAL BRADSHAW

TO LESLIE HAVERGAL BRADSHAW

Hotel Astor
New York

Oct 1. 1914

Dear Brad.

Excuse delay in answering letter. Been busy getting married to Ethel Milton! We are here for tonight, then tomorrow to Melrose Grange, Bellport, Long Island.[1]

I'll write again from there. This is just a note to tell you of the marriage.

Yours ever,

Chickens

1 Melrose Grange, the Wodehouses' destination, seemed to be a special place to the couple. The US edition of *Vanity Fair* for 15 August includes a story entitled 'The Eighteenth Hole', written under the pen-name 'Melrose Grainger' – a private joke, or tribute, perhaps, to the woman he had just met, and whom he was soon to marry.

Wodehouse and Ethel May Wayman were married on 30 September 1914. In writing to Bradshaw to tell him of their marriage, Wodehouse uses her stage name – Ethel Milton. Bradshaw reports to Olive that the letter was 'A complete surprise. [...] She is the girl we took down to Long Beach about a month ago. She has been married before, I believe. She is rather English, has fair hair, and talks very well. I knew he was keen about her, but didn't think it went to this length. I didn't see him this last time because I had seen him so recently and knew he was busy.' He adds that 'Ethel Milton is very nice – I don't mean to imply anything about her – but I can't picture him married to anyone. He must have found the very person he wanted or he wouldn't have done it, for he has had about 11 years in which to look over all the girls of his acquaintance. I remember vividly his telling me recently that he thinks the main thing in marriage is to be pals with a girl, rather than to be continually in a fervent passion of love.'

The newlyweds rented a bungalow in Bellport, Long Island – a quiet town by the edge of the ocean.

TO LESLIE HAVERGAL BRADSHAW

Box 478
Bellport
Long Island

Oct 10. 1914

Dear Brad.

I've been feeling an awful worm not having written to you as I said I would, but really the fevered rush of life has been such down here that I haven't had a moment, especially as we have not yet been able to get a maid, and have had to do all the house-work ourselves since we arrived! Golly, I don't know what they mean by saying the country is dull. It's one long round of excitement. Yesterday I was bitten by a dog!

Can't you take a day off and come down and see us, when we get settled? You can have your choice of about six spare bedrooms, and there are fifty acres of ground to wander about in. It's perfect down here at present, but I fear we are going to cop it in the matter of cold later on.

Married life really is the greatest institution that ever was. When I look back and think of the rotten time I have been having all my life, compared with this, it makes me sick. And when I think that I was once actually opposed to the idea of your getting married, I am amazed at myself. My latest and final pronouncement on the Brad–Olive situation is, Get married at once, and don't care a blow about anyone, because it is borne in on me very strongly that this business of marriage is so exclusively one's own business that it is ridiculous to let even one's mother have a say in it. The only point to be considered is finance. Do you feel that you can undertake the contract from a financial point of view? The idea of my talking prudence is pretty thick, seeing that I have at this moment $70 in the bank! But I am hoping for more eftsoones or right speedily. If you can manage it on your salary, as I feel certain you can, I should charge in, if I were you.

Speaking as an old married man (ten days!), I think the main question about marriage is not so much whether you are in love with each other as whether you have the essential points in common which enable you to live with each other without getting on each other's nerves. I know you and Olive have, so I don't see what is to keep you apart. It seems to me, brooding on your situation, that you are at present getting all the disadvantages of being married i.e. sickness at headquarters and general civil war, without any of the advantages, and that you can't make things much worse at home by going the whole thing. It's a difficult thing to advise anyone about, but in your case it isn't so much advising as ceasing to advise. You made up your mind long ago on the essentials of the situation, and were only kept from marrying by a sort of tidal wave of advice from all quarters. If you are certain that Mr Lawson will stand by you and continue to weigh out the plunks per week, I think you should go ahead and risk the consequences. It's a ghastly position for you, with your mater taking this curious stand, but, as the Bible says, a man shall cleave to his wife and all that sort of thing.

I can only argue, of course, taking a line through my own case. All I know is that for the first time in my life I am absolutely happy. It is a curious thing about it that the anxieties seem to add to the happiness. The knowledge that it is up to one to support someone else has a stimulating effect.

You were the first person I told about it, but since then I have notified others – mostly bad men like Billy from whom I hope to get dough. I sent a story to *Ainslee's* the other day, and told the editor – whom I have never met – that he should send a check as a wedding-present irrespective of the merits of the story. No answer yet!

Before I forget. Certainly go ahead with 'Alcala', if you think you can make anything of it.[1]

The financial situation continues moderately thick. I sent Billy a peremptory telegram yesterday, and, if the check doesn't come soon, I shall startle the life out of his greasy body by putting the Authors' League onto him. One thing married life does for you, – it removes that shyness about savaging people who have worked that 'friendship in business' gag on you to the extent of keeping your hard-earned for themselves. I am sorry for Billy, but we need all the Wodehouse money exclusively for the upkeep of the Wodehouse home, and cannot afford to keep the Watt family going as well!

[...]

The peace of this place is wonderful. It is very primitive of course. There is no postal delivery, and one has to walk a mile to get mail. Also at any moment the water supply is apt to fail. Still, we both love it.

Ethel sends her love. She liked you tremendously. She says you must come down when you can manage it, but says not until she has got a maid. However, that only means another day or two. Apparently maids are plentiful in these parts after the middle of this month.

How is the writing going? I didn't mean to hint that you had cracked under the strain, as Boston didn't. I know what you have had to go through. Still, I hope you will get going soon. Good luck.

Yours ever

Chickens

1 Bradshaw was planning to dramatise PGW's 'In Alcala'.

TO LESLIE HAVERGAL BRADSHAW

Box 478
Bellport
Long Island

Oct 14. 1914

Dear Brad.

I took your letter to Friend Wife, who was cooking the family dinner, and, having read it, she laid it absently down on a large sheet of fly-paper, so I shall have to answer it from memory.

First, in the matter of the present. It is tremendously decent of you to want to give us one, and we shall certainly appreciate it. The first ballot resulted in Ethel voting for a bottle of scent and myself for a box of cigars; but the second and final showed us both solid on a photograph-frame to take my photograph. It is a fairly large one, but most of it is margin, so if you can secure something – <u>not too expensive</u> – about the same size as this sheet of type-paper, that will be just what we want, and thanks awfully for thinking of it.

Lots of news. Thank goodness, the ice-pack has at last broken. Ella King-Hall has cabled me over a hundred and nineteen quid, the proceeds of the English rights of some short stories, and Mrs Wilkening writes to say that Doty – Douglas Z.,[1] as you rightly remark – has taken the last story *McClure's* refused and will make an offer for it directly he returns to town. Also, with a nasty hacking sound which you could hear for miles, Billy coughed up $50 yesterday, and promises another $88 tomorrow. He only parted after I had sent him a frightfully abrupt telegram, and in his letter he is very very stiff and formal, and concludes with a postscript to the effect that he 'resented the tone of my telegram'. Not a word of congratulation about my marriage! And incidentally I believe he is doing me in for a small sum of money, for *The Intrusion of Jimmy* is running in the *Evening World*, and Mrs W. says she didn't sell it to them, so evidently Billy has and has pouched the proceeds. I shall have to hound him for that. He really is too maddening for words. One has to beg for one's money as if it were a loan, instead of being one's rightful earnings long overdue. Never again!

I don't know why I called *Brother Fans, The Man Upstairs*.[2] Just a slip. I enclose a letter I received from Barry, which looks promising. If it goes well at the Palace, it ought to be a cert for a long booking. We could do with forty weeks at $25 per.

We are still without a maid, and today we are blowing thirty cents on an advertisement in the local paper.

Must stop now and get down to the village for my morning visit to collect mail and buy things. That is the big event in the day here. There might be good news from Mrs Wilkening, as she sent a story of mine to the *Saturday Evening Post* last week, and they read stuff very quick. But I have a feeling that I shall never land with the *Saturday*.

So long

Yours ever

Chickens

---

1 Douglas Zabriskie Doty (1874–1935), editor of *The Century Illustrated Monthly Magazine*.
2 *Brother Fans*, a PGW short story about baseball (*McClure's*, August 1914) that had been

Bradshaw felt that the Wodehouses' request for a wedding present 'was too modest, so I sent them the other articles they mentioned; to her a small bottle of Coty's L'Effleurt Essence, and to him a box of cigars'. The requested photograph frame was, he told Olive, 'hand-carved wooden, with a dull bronze finish, with a very quiet and unobtrusive Egyptian design on the border'.

TO LESLIE HAVERGAL BRADSHAW

Oct 19. 1914

Dear Brad.

Thanks awfully for the cigars and the scent. They are splendid. The cigars came precisely as I had smoked my last. I am afraid they are going to spoil me for the twofers which I usually smoke (at three cents per), but that can't be helped.

[...]

Mrs Wilkening's confounded optimism has again caused me a disappointment. Apparently Doty has not taken that story after all, though from the enclosed letter he does not seem absolutely to have rejected it. He appears to have sent it back, though, for Mrs. W. writes that it is under consideration elsewhere. I can't remember the occasion to which Doty refers. I didn't know he had ever seen my stuff officially before.

I wish she wouldn't do this German-official-news stunt. It's maddening to whoop over a victory and then find that it was only a near-victory after all.

However, it hasn't made as much difference as it might have done, for the financial situation is pretty good.

[...]

Billy has coughed up $88 more, so, deducting the $275 which I have had to pay as first instalment on the $550, I have about $425 in the bank, besides my London savings, so, living being so cheap down here, I am pretty well ahead.[1]

[...]

I may have to run up to New York tomorrow. I don't want to a bit, as it is the dickens of a business getting to the station now that the road is all up. It means a two and a half mile walk. This makes it hard for Ethel to come up with me. On the other hand, if I leave her, I shall have to get back by an early train, for a night alone in this place would give her the Willies. I don't quite see how I can manage to see the sketch. I suppose it has had its first production by now. I hope it has gone well.

Are you reading the Sherlock Holmes story in the *Sunday Tribune*? I guessed the solution with ridiculous ease a week ago. I call it a low down trick of Doyle to ring in one of those Part Two acts, like in *The Study in Scarlet* [sic], where the action is suddenly shoved back twenty years and Holmes put into the background.[2]

[...]

We are still without a maid, though one is promised for the first of the month. It really is the devil of a business trying to get on without one. You feel it in all sorts of little ways. The washing-up is the worst. It is not so much the labour of it, as the fact that it comes after meals, just when you want to be peaceful and unemployed.

A powerful odour of scent tells me that Ethel is near. She has just come in and sends her love, and thanks you awfully for the scent. She hasn't been able to write herself so far, as she is always being interrupted, just as she is settling down, by our landlord, who pays at least ten visits a day and drools on about a stove he is going to put in for the winter.

So long

Yours ever

Chickens

1 PGW's agent, Billy Watt, had placed *The Intrusion of Jimmy* in the *Evening World Magazine*, and had not yet passed on the proceeds.
2 Doyle's *The Valley of Fear* ran in *The Strand* from September 1914 to May 1915.

Bellport

Long Island

Oct 24. 1914

Dear Brad.

Thanks most awfully for the photograph frame. It looks splendid in spite of the gargoyle in the middle of it.

Since I wrote to you I have made two hasty dashes up to New York, and, believe me, it takes some doing from here. The first day I walked two and a half miles to Bellport Station to catch the 9.50, and found they had taken it off last Sunday, and had to walk four miles in just under the hour to catch the next train at Patchogue. Coming back, I caught the 5.29, and found that it stopped at Bellport on Saturdays only. So I had to walk out from Patchogue!

Things seem brisking up a bit. I sent a much-refused story to *Ainslee's*, and they have taken it for $125, which, down here, means about two months keep.[1] Also Lawrence Grossmith has come over from England, and is making himself very busy about *Brother Alfred*. William Collier wants a play in a hurry, and there is a very good chance that a version of *B.A.*, revised by some big pot, may suit him. It would be corking if we managed to extract some bones from that frost after all.[2]

[...]

Ethel has come out very strong with three fine plots! I am working on them now. If she can keep this up, the maintenance of the home is a cinch!

I never appreciated married life so much as last night. I came home, tired and hungry, after having walked out from Patchogue and having had nothing to eat for hours, and there was a fine dinner and a blazing fire, and E. fussing over me, and all sorts of good things. It was perfectly ripping. Incidentally there were twelve letters waiting for me. A record!

We are still without a maid, but I have developed a wonderful liking for washing dishes. I find it stimulates thought, and is generally soothing. So I am going to take on that department till we get a maid.

We have two kittens and a puppy now. The puppy kept us awake the night before last from two-thirty onwards.

I haven't heard yet who is going to do the rest of the *Nugget*. I hope Frohmann [*sic*] gets some good man.[3]

So long

Yours ever

Chickens

1 'The Romance of the Ugly Policeman' appeared in *Ainslee's* in April 1915, and earlier in *The Strand* in January 1915.
2 After PGW's *Brother Alfred* had flopped in London in 1913, Grossmith was planning a revival in New York.
3 Arrangements for a theatrical production of *The Little Nugget* continued, but were never realised. Charles Frohman, an American theatrical producer, died the following year.

Lillian 'Lily' Barnett (née Hill) was Wodehouse's housekeeper at Threepwood and a life-long friend. Wodehouse's letter shows his desire to keep in touch with Emsworth, and with his English counterparts. By December 1914, coverage of the war in the American press reflected the gravity of the situation, but there was still a sense that the conflict could be ended relatively quickly.

TO LILLIAN BARNETT

Box 478
Bellport
Long Island
U.S.A.

Dec 2. 1914

Dear Lily.

I expect you have heard that I am married, and have been wondering why I did not write and tell you about it. The fact is, things have been in such a rush that, every time I have tried to settle down, I have had to start in and do something else. We have only just been able to get a maid, and for the first six weeks my wife did all the cooking and I washed the dishes and did the house-work. It has increased the admiration I have always had for you! How on earth you managed to look after me and your own home and the two children I can't understand. I don't wonder you used to get up at four in the morning or whatever it was. My only wonder is that you were ever able to go to bed at all. What an awful lot there is to do about a house. I also realise more than ever what a lot you used to do for me with the animals. We have two cats, a dog, and a puppy here, and however many of them we turn out of the dining room at meal times, there always seems to be one left, shouting for food. I gather them up in armfuls and hurl them into the kitchen.

I'm afraid I shan't see Emsworth for another year. We have taken this place for the whole of 1915. But at the end of that time I hope to settle down for good in England. This place rather reminds me of Emsworth. There is the same sort of shallow bay, with an island like Hayling stretched across the mouth of it. I believe it is perfectly splendid in Summer, but the cold is very bad in January and February. I hope by working hard to make enough to spend January at least somewhere where it is warmer. I get frightfully home-sick at times, but the war has cut my English money all to pieces, and I have to stay in America and try and sell some stories here.

[...]

I am sending you a little present, to buy something with at Christmas, and to make up for the fact that I shall have to stop the money from Mant.[1]

[...]

I wish you would ask somebody who knows about sending things over here, and see if it would be possible to let me have some of my things. What I think you might do is buy a suit-case (get the money from Mant), and pack some of my things in it and send it off to me here. Get a case which doesn't lock, and then the Customs people will be able to open it.

The things I want particularly are my sweater, my heavy boots, and that woollen waistcoat. I don't think there's anything much else, but you might shove in anything that looks worth having. A thing I want, or shall want, very much is my bicycle, but I don't know whether it would be worth the expense of getting it over. Will you ask about it? If it isn't too expensive to send, I should like to have it for use in the Spring. You simply can't get a decent bicycle this side. Hardly any of them have free wheels and none of them have a step at the back. Besides which, they all seem to be built for midgets.

I nearly forgot to say that it didn't matter a bit about that contract I asked you to find, after all. The whole thing is so tremendously complicated that no one knows what is happening. The whole trouble is that the moving pictures have only just come into popularity. When we drew up that contract, no one thought anything about cinema rights, and so they weren't mentioned in the contract. The consequence is that it has not been decided yet whether a theatrical contract covers the moving picture production.

[...]

Well, married life is suiting me splendidly. It is certainly the only life, if you're suited to each other, as we are. My wife is an English woman who has spent several years in America, so she can sympathise with the English and American sides of my life. She is a widow, about five years younger than me, and I have a little step-daughter! I have not seen her yet, but I hear she is delightful.[2]

Knowing me, you will understand the importance of my marrying somebody who was fond of animals. Thank goodness, she is almost fonder of them than I am. We keep open house for all the dogs in the neighbourhood. She is very anxious to meet Nancy. Our puppy is awfully nice, but no dog will ever be like Nance.

How is the war affecting you all? I get such different accounts of the state of things in England. My mother writes as if Cheltenham were an armed camp, but my friend Bovill, in London, wrote as if there were no war on at all, and Mr King-Hall didn't seem very disturbed about it.[3] Anyhow, it looks very much as if the Germans had shot their bolt. Over here, people are drawing parallels between this war and the American Civil War, and showing that the position of Germany now is very much the same as that of the South after the Battle of Gettysburg. If it is, the war ought to be over by the middle of next year.[4] I don't believe in these Zeppelins.[5] If they ever got to London, they couldn't do so very much damage.

Well, write and tell me all the news,

Yours ever

P. G. Wodehouse

1 J. R. Mant & Sons was an Emsworth company which had two businesses (a butcher's and a cycle works). Mant paid Lily a form of retainer on PGW's behalf, and gained a literary

mention in return, in the shape of PGW's Colonel Horace Mant in *Something Fresh*.

2 Leonora was being educated in England. The events of the war meant that it was difficult for her to travel to be reunited with her mother and new stepfather, but they were soon to meet.

3 PGW's parents had moved to Cheltenham in 1902; Charles Bovill, a former colleague at the *Globe*, lived in Battersea, South London. King-Hall was owner of the Emsworth House School, and Westbrook's brother-in-law.

4 The defeat of the Confederate troops at the Battle of Gettysburg was often considered a turning point in the American Civil War, so the comparison suggests that Germany was in a position similar to that of the Southern Confederate states – approaching defeat.

5 PGW writes a little over a month before the first Zeppelin airships were sent from Germany to England, when there was much speculation in the press about their potential threat.

Bradshaw had broken off relations with his family, and planned a wedding for 20 February 1915.

TO LESLIE HAVERGAL BRADSHAW

Bellport

Dec 15. 1914

Dear Brad.

We shall both be delighted to see you & Olive, if you don't think the double journey will be too much for her. As a matter of fact, acc'd to my time-table, the Sunday trains, though few, are good. There is a 9.02 which gets here at 11.02, and a 5.15 from here which reaches N.Y. at 6.54. You had better verify them.

On arriving at Bellport, you get into the stage & tell the man to drive to Axtell North Cottage – I think they call it. Another name it has is Melrose Grange.

Of course, you understand that it <u>will</u> practically be camping-out? I know <u>you</u> do, but does Olive? I mean, will she be appalled at our tin salt-cellars? I think you had better see what she thinks about the trip, as it is considerable Arctic exploration at this time of year, and the delicately-nurtured feminine might kick at it.

[...]

Yours,

Chickens

Bellport
Long Island

January 20. 1915

Dear Brad.

Sorry for delay in writing. I have been trying to get my novel finished before coming to N.Y., which I propose to do next Monday. Address at present uncertain.

[...]

I have been working like a navvy for about two weeks, in which time I must have written very nearly forty thousand of my novel. It seems to me the best long thing I have done, and I have great hopes of landing it somewhere good. I have got about another ten thousand to do, and then there will be some revision. I am divided between the desire to get action on it right away and a wish to keep it back and polish it up to the limit. I have adapted the Boot incident from *The Lost Lambs* and it fits in splendidly, but of course I shall have to cut it out for England.[1] There is some of the funniest knockabout stuff in this book that I have ever written. It is just the sort of book Billy Watt would like, but not a line of it shall he see! I wonder if the conversation turned on me when you dined there?

I found Reynolds a very good sort indeed.[2] He was pleasantly different from Seth and Mrs Wilkening, and didn't make one windy promise of selling my stuff for millions. He just said that he hoped that he would make good on it, and declined to prophesy. I am bound to say, though experience has made me wary of rejoicing prematurely, that he seems to be just the man I need. He is a man of a certain position, thank goodness. What I mean is that he belongs to decent clubs, where he presumably does not get tight, and that is a great thing. One always felt about Seth that at any moment he might disappear into nowhere with a lot of one's money and never appear again. Reynolds seems to be one of the aristocrats of the profession. The first man we met in the club was Scribner, and his attitude towards Reynolds was a sort of respectful chumminess.[3] Horrid Thought: Was it a 'property' Scribner, a pal of Reynolds simply engaged to pretend to be Scribner so as to impress me!

[...]

I got the *Windsor* and the *London* magazines the other day and was horrified to see the effect the war had had on them. The *London* had, I think four pages of advertisements and the *Windsor* about the same. I suppose they are just hanging on and publishing at a loss until better times come. Mrs Westbrook writes to say that the *Strand*'s advertisements have fallen off a lot, but I expect they are doing better than most of the others. Westbrook expects to be off for the front very soon now.

Have you ever read *The Guest of Quesnay* by Booth Tarkington? It is one of the best books I have read lately. I thought of writing to congratulate him, but prudence intervened. I want to crib his heroine, and it is imperative that, if denounced, I shall be able to say 'I never read any *Guest of Quesnay*. Who is this Booth Tarkington of whom you speak?'⁴

Thwaites writes that he has been given an extra month's leave to go to Bath and take the waters for his tummy. I am afraid he will have to go back to the war later on. I don't think he is a bit keen now, poor chap. I don't wonder.⁵

[...]

Mrs Westbrook wrote to say that she has a big deal on with the movie rights of my stories, and a few days ago cabled to ask me to suggest prices as a basis for her to work on, so it really looks as if there were something doing, though I don't want to be too sanguine after the Wilkening fiasco. But it seems to me that she would hardly have sent a long cable unless there was something practical in the air.

Well, so long. See you early next week.

Regards to Olive

Yours ever

Chickens

---

1 PGW was working on *Something New* (published in the UK as *Something Fresh*). The novel features a scene in which a character finds a paint-splashed lady's shoe in the library after a theft, and attempts to identify its owner. This scene was omitted from *Something Fresh*. PGW had previously used the same sub-plot, involving a boot, in the second part of the school novel *Mike* (*The Lost Lambs*).

2 Paul Reynolds was the first full-time literary agent in the USA. His clients included William James, Jack London, George Bernard Shaw and Winston Churchill.

3 Charles Scribner II (1854–1930), president of the publishing house Charles Scribner's Sons.

4 Booth Tarkington (1869–1946), Pulitzer Prize-winning American novelist and dramatist, was among PGW's favourite writers – and gains a mention in *A Damsel in Distress*. Tarkington's *The Guest of Quesnay* first appeared in 1907.

5 PGW's friend, the journalist Norman Thwaites (formerly of the *New York World*), was now a Captain in the Dragoon Guards. He had been fighting on the front in Northern France, and had survived being shot through the neck and chin in November 1914.

TO GEORGE WILSON (A. & C. BLACK)

> Bellport
> Long Island
> USA

March 28. 1915

Dear Mr Wilson.

Splendid. I should be delighted if you would publish *Psmith, Journalist* on the same terms as the other books.

Go right ahead. I don't want to add or alter anything. It seems to be one of those masterpieces you can't alter a comma of.

Yours sincerely,

P. G. Wodehouse

Wodehouse had made a research visit to Bustanoby's Café on 1845 Broadway – the famous New York restaurant and the place where the high-society public dancing competition craze took off. The result was Wodehouse's 'corker' 'At Geisenheimer's', an O. Henry-style tale of an estranged couple whose troubles are solved by a canny professional dancer.

TO LESLIE HAVERGAL BRADSHAW

June 3. 1915

[...]

Do you remember coming to Bustanoby's one night, while I took notes for a story? That is the story I have just sold to the *Post* for $500.

It is a corker, quite one of the best I have done, with a touch of the 'In Alcala' stuff in it. I wish I could get some more plots like it. The funny thing is that it was refused by the *Pictorial Review*, and the one I put over with *The Ladies' Home Journal* was refused by the *Post*, so there is no knowing exactly what editors want.

Just at present I am very barren of ideas. I have a few sketchy outlines of plots for serials, but nothing that I can start on yet, and the short-story plant is temporarily out of action. The worst of getting into the $500 class is that one has to be careful what one sends out. I don't want to slip back again, now that I have at last got up to ten cents a word. It is better to produce nothing for a time than to send out bad stuff.

[...]

The car is going perfectly splendidly now. Ethel is a magnificent driver, and she has to be on the roads round here, the same being the filthiest on record. We went out to East Moriches the other day, and the roads weren't roads at all, just tracks through the woods, feet deep in sand. They are building state roads all over the place, and you have to make long detours across country to get anywhere.

I have just had a budget of school magazines from England. I revelled in them. Dulwich seem to have had a magnificent football team last year. They beat Bedford and Haileybury by thirty odd points each, an unheard of thing. They have got a freak wing three-quarter, who got into the team two years ago at the age of fourteen, he being then six foot tall and weighing eleven and a half stone. He has two more years at school. He scored four times against Bedford, four against Haileybury, and twice or three times against each of the other schools. In the return match against St Paul's he scored seven times. I see my way to writing another *Mike*, with the hero a footballer instead of a cricketer.

[...]

I have just bought *Empty Pockets* by Rupert Hughes, to try to get a line on what the magazines do want as serials. He writes good safe stuff that would sell anywhere. He seems to know New York pretty thoroughly.[1]

Well, so long. See you soon, I hope. I suppose I shall be hard at it over this darned play for some weeks to come. I hope it really is going to end in something good.

Yours ever

Chickens

1 *Empty Pockets*, New York-based 1915 novel by Rupert Hughes (1872–1956). Hughes kept pace with current events, sending his heroine overseas as a war nurse. It had been serialised in *The Red Book Magazine*.

By 1915, Wodehouse was producing a great deal of non-fiction, alongside his serials. He 'used to write about half' of Vanity Fair *'each month under a number of names – P.G. Wodehouse, Pelham Grenville, J. Plum, C.P. West, P. Brooke-Haven and so on [...] I also became the V.F. dramatic critic'.*

TO LESLIE HAVERGAL BRADSHAW

Bellport

L.I.

June 25. 1915

Dear Brad.

[...]

I was interested to hear that you had met Fairbanks. I was only in town for a short time, & was kept so busy doing *Vanity Fair* stuff that I couldn't get round to you. I had to go to Coney, the Eden Musee,[1] & the Castles in the Air.[2] All very dull except Coney, which I liked.[3] Fairbanks is a good sort. I wish I could do another play for him.

Do you know when Watt gets back to N. Y.? The swine owes me $360!

Did I tell you that Mizzie had had kittens? Four of them. They are just beginning to walk.

We are seeing a lot of the Mackenzies down here. They lent us their apartment on 24th St when we went to town.

Fancy Hilder being married. Were you best man?[4]

Doesn't the cover of the *Saturday Evening Post* look good this week! [see plate 18][5]

Cheerio. Just off to revise Act 2 of the *Nugget*. It's coming out well.

Yours ever

Chickens

P.S. I should like to see the movie scenario.

1 The Eden Musee of waxworks moved from New York City to Coney Island in 1915.
2 'Castles in the Air' was a cabaret on the roof of the 44th Street Theatre, opened by ballroom dancers Vernon and Irene Castle. PGW went on to write a lyric entitled 'My Castle in the Air' (1916) for the show *Miss Springtime*.
3 The results of his visits were published in the August 1915 edition of *Vanity Fair*: 'The So-Called Pleasures of Coney Island, with a Few Undignified Sketches by Ethel Plummer', by P. Brooke-Haven; 'The Expulsion from Eden, a Long and Sad Farewell to the Many Waxworks at the Eden Musee', by Pelham Grenville, drawing by Thelma Cudlipp'; and 'Cabarabian Nights, a Little Tour of Cabarets, by P. G. Wodehouse' (vol. IV, no. 6), pp. 51, 63, 45.
4 John Chapman (Jack) Hilder, writer, author and former editor. Thwaites, Bradshaw, PGW and Hilder often spent time together in New York, hosting late-night parties.
5 The cover of the *Saturday Evening Post* for 26 June 1915 billed '*Something New* by Pelham Grenville Wodehouse' on its front cover. Lorimer had bought the story for 'a hotsy $3500'.

Between 1915 and 1918, PGW's career took off in many directions. In 1915, Jeeves first made an appearance in the short story 'Extricating Young Gussie', published in the Saturday Evening Post. Uneasy Money *was published in 1916, and the same year saw him writing* Piccadilly Jim. *This was also the period when his career as a lyricist was at its height.*

The 'Princess' musicals toured the eastern states of America, testing their success with the audiences and refining the music and lyrics, before opening in New York. In terms of musical history, these were pioneering works. Bolton, Wodehouse and Kern were the first to 'move away from the fractured structure of variety, focusing on music that developed out of mood and situation [...] to present a coherent world picture on stage'.

At the time of writing the following letter, Wodehouse had just been 'out on the road' working with Bolton on a show called See You Later, *starring Roy Barnes, Charlie Ruggles and Victor Moore. In fact, the show did not survive the try-outs and folded. He had returned to the new Wodehouse residence, which was just outside the village of Great Neck. 'Scott Fitzgerald and his crowd lived about three miles from us. There were a lot of actors there. Ed Wynn [...] Roy Barnes, Donald Brain and Ernest Truex [...] That's the place where I wrote about the Oldest Member and all my golfing stories.' Bradshaw's letters to Olive give regular, slightly envious updates on the increasing luxury of the Wodehouses' accommodation, noting that in 1916 they possessed three white-tiled bathrooms. By 1918, they had 'three acres of grounds including a tennis court' and 'a Stearns-Knight car with a Victorian top'.*

Arrandale Road
Great Neck
Long Island
U.S.A.

June 20. 1918

Dear Lily.

I have been meaning to write to you for ages, but something has always interfered. I have been terribly busy for a long while, having been out on the road with a new piece. We tried it out in Baltimore and it was all wrong, so we set to and rewrote the entire play in a week!! We threw away all the music and got a new lot written and then started out again. The piece now looks like a big success. It did very well in Washington and for three weeks in Philadelphia. It will come on in New York in the Autumn.

As you see, we have also been moving again. This time we have <u>bought</u> a house! It is a very nice place, with three acres, including a tennis court and a garage. I only wish you and Bert were here to look after us.[1] Why don't you come out after the war and settle down here? There are splendid schools for the children. This place is about fourteen miles from New York, but is right out in the country and on the seashore. I haven't done much bathing yet, but I have taken up golf and am having a fine time.

We had a Swiss couple here, looking after us, but the man smashed up our car and the woman took two hours cooking an egg, so we didn't get on, and a week ago they suddenly announced that they had got another job, so now we are doing our own cooking and so on just as we used to do down at Bellport.

You really must come out here after the war. You and Bert together, he as chauffeur-gardener and you to cook, would get twenty pounds a month at least and probably twenty-five. I know we would give you that to get you. And Hugh would have such a splendid chance in this country. We should have to teach Norah to sing and dance, and then I could give her a part in one of my plays! I suppose the children are getting enormous now? I always forget how old they are, but Hugh must be getting very big.

[...]

I am working away just as hard as ever. I shall have five plays running in New York in the Autumn, possibly six. I find I can do a lot of work here, as it is so quiet, and there are no distractions. I go about all day in flannels, just like at Emsworth. We have three dogs, two parrots, and a canary! Only one of the three dogs really belongs to us. The other two are a French bull-dog and an Irish terrier. The bull-dog is rather a responsibility. It belonged to a friend of ours who lives in New York and wanted a country home for the dog. It is a prize dog, and they have refused a hundred pounds for him! So you can imagine how we feel when he rushes out and attacks motor-cars in the road. It is like seeing a bank-note fluttering away on the wind. I must say I prefer dogs that aren't quite so valuable. These high-bred dogs never seem to have any sense. Of course, I shall never have a dog that I can love as much as Nancy. When you write, tell me if old Pat is still going strong. I'm afraid it is a hard time for dogs nowadays in England. I don't see how anyone can manage to keep them.

Are things very bad? Of course everything is terribly expensive. It's like that over here. I'm told that in a week or two we shan't be able to buy a chicken. Everything has gone up to about three times its usual price.

[...]

I am sending you three pounds, which I hope will come in useful. Would you mind doing something for me. Write to the Editor, *The Alleynian*, Dulwich College, Dulwich, S.E. and ask him to send you copies of *The Alleynian* from 1915 onwards. Then will you send them on to me. It will be safer than telling him to send them direct to me. It's the school magazine, and I haven't seen a copy for three years. Oh, and ask him to send a copy of the Register of Old Alleynians at the Front. I don't know how much this will all come to, but I should think something under a pound.

Well, goodbye for the present.

Do write soon and tell me all the news. Nothing is too small to be interesting. Love to Bert and the children.

Yours ever

P. G. Wodehouse

---

1 Lily was married to the local postman in Emsworth, Bert Barnett.

CHAPTER SIX

The Roaring Twenties

For Wodehouse, the 1920s were a period of continual movement. As soon as he settled down to write a novel or a short story, he was interrupted to plan a musical with Guy Bolton and Jerome Kern, or summoned to America to rescue a flagging show. Life was full of partings at Paddington, and parties in Palm Beach, punctuated by frenzied periods of writing on the top deck of ocean liners. Even the Wodehouses' London residence appeared to change almost annually, as Ethel moved her household around a variety of stylish addresses. It was a time in which Wodehouse could not help but catch something of the atmosphere of the 'Roaring Twenties'. At times exhilarating, it often felt more like 'one damned bit of work after another'.[1] 'Everybody', Wodehouse writes, 'wanted me to do a play' – and the demands were hard to refuse.[2] Theatrical impresario Florenz Ziegfeld was known to send ten-page telegrams press-ganging his favoured authors into service, while the producer 'Colonel' Savage had a reputation for working authors and composers intensely hard – and trying to take more than his fair share of the profits. 'He walked with a slight limp, having probably in the course of his career been bitten in the leg by some indignant author', as Wodehouse recalls.[3] Wodehouse would find himself frantically trying to keep all demands at bay – attempting to complete one novel, twenty-eight short stories and a musical over the course of just a few months.

Wodehouse's literary work was energised by his experience of musical theatre. As he writes to Bill Townend, 'In musical comedy you gain so tremendously in Act One if you can give your principal characters a *dramatic* entrance instead of just walking on.'[4] The theatrical work was, however, particularly time-consuming; weeks were spent not simply writing, but rehearsing the plays, and rewriting them in 'try-outs' on tour in America, before the shows hit Broadway. By the end of the 1920s, he claimed that he would do anything to 'escape musical theatre'.

Wodehouse's fiction of the time summons the frantic atmosphere of city life, as he conjures 'New York's vast body', with its '[h]urrying mortals, released from a thousand offices. [...] Candy-selling aliens jostling newsboys' and men popping 'in and out of the subway entrances like rabbits'.[5] It is not surprising to find him drawn back, nostalgically, to the stability of his Edwardian fictional world.

With the publication of the short-story collections *My Man Jeeves* in 1919 and *The Inimitable Jeeves* in 1923, the 1920s could be seen as the point at which Wodehouse's long-standing relationship with Reginald Jeeves and his negligibly intelligent employer, Bertie Wooster, took a firmer shape. The sources for the character of Jeeves are manifold. Named after a Warwickshire cricket player, the gentleman's gentleman had made his first appearance in a 1915 short story, taking aspects of his character from manservants that Wodehouse had encountered in art, as well as in life. Bertie was slower to find a definite personality – emerging from the model of the Edwardian 'knut' – the younger son of an aristocratic family – 'he was a trifle on the superfluous side': blessed with an allowance, a tailor and a club, he flits between dinners at the Savoy Grill, the Goodwood races and the country, the only shadow on the horizon the presence of a match-making aunt, or a debutante with an entrancing profile and a copy of Nietzsche in her hand.[6] After all, every aspect of the Woosterian equilibrium depends on the continuation of bachelor life.

Wooster's ideal might have been an all-male preserve, but the world of Wodehouse was anything but. The 1920s were a period in which Wodehouse created some of his strongest and most likable female characters, marking the appearance of the dauntless Jill Mariner in *Jill the Reckless*, Sally Nicholas in *The Adventures of Sally*, and Sue Brown in *Summer Lightning*. Wodehouse's fictional world was Edwardian, but his sense of women, influenced by the changes that had come about since both the Suffragist movement and the First World War, was a decidedly emancipated one. Wodehouse encountered numerous beautiful and intelligent actresses during this time, from the dazzling blonde dancer Marilyn Miller, to the devastating Scandinavian, Justine Johnstone. But his ideal model for his fictional heroines came in the shape of his step-daughter, Leonora. Charming, talented and kind, 'Snorky' was just sixteen in 1920, and finishing her education first at boarding school in England and then in Paris. In her twenties, she often holidayed with Wodehouse, or kept him company on his travels. She became for Wodehouse part confidante, part muse. Most of all, though, Leonora was his adored daughter, someone on whom he could lavish love and affection, and who would indulge his 'lingering boyishness' as they shared the comic supplement of the Sunday papers.[7]

As Wodehouse worried about lyrics and plot-lines, wayward directors and pressing deadlines, much else was happening on the world's stage. This was the age of the rise of mass movements – as the forces of communism, fascism and socialism jostled for power. There were strikes on both sides of the Atlantic – and the prohibition of alcohol in America added to the social tension. Wodehouse's tongue-in-cheek attitude to the political scene appears in the likes of his short story 'Comrade Bingo', in which the unfortunate Bingo Little finds himself caught up with the 'Red Dawn' communist league, who 'yearn for the Revolution' in Marble Arch.[8] Wodehouse's own sense of class unrest in these letters seems less committed. His complaint about the 'nuisance' of the national coal strike of 1921 is that of a wearied citizen – 'if it isn't something it's something else or something'.[9] For Wodehouse, political events were marginal to his imaginative life – the imperative was to avoid disturbance of any kind.

Indeed, one of the overriding themes of the letters of this period is his attempt to find peace from the world around him, and space and time in which to write. The continual interruptions to his creative flow explain, in part, why this was a period in which he produced so many short stories. 'You have to live with a novel', he confided to Bill Townend, 'if I drop my characters they go cold and I forget what they are like'.[10] Nevertheless, this was a period in which Wodehouse produced a series of highly successful novels, culminating in the outstanding Blandings tale *Summer Lightning*, in 1928. Some of these interruptions were the call of musical work. Others were caused by the frenzy of social activity that inevitably occurred whenever Ethel was around. For Wodehouse, as for many of his henpecked fictional counterparts, home was not necessarily a safe place: 'intruders lurked behind every door'.[11] One visitor, Robert J. Denby, became something of a fixture during the 1920s. A particular friend of Ethel's, Denby also acted as a literary agent for Wodehouse, sometimes taking more than his fair share. It was for this reason that Wodehouse often took refuge elsewhere – staying as a houseguest at the crumbling Hunstanton Hall in Norfolk, hiding at Emsworth or at Impney Spa Hotel, or holed up in what Ethel referred to as 'that awful club in Northumberland Avenue', the Constitutional. 'I just', Wodehouse writes wistfully, 'want to be left alone with my novel.'[12]

In terms of literature, this was a period that was to mark the appearance of some of the most radical and groundbreaking works of the century. The year 1922 brought not just *The Waste Land* but *Ulysses* and *Jacob's Room*. Later years saw the publication of *The Trial*, *Crome Yellow* and the final volume of *À la recherche du temps perdu*. Wodehouse's own literary confidence was at a high during this time, but he kept his contemporary interests more mainstream, praising works by writers such as Booth Tarkington, Sinclair Lewis and Michael Arlen. Wodehouse's literary circle was small – and his only regular literary correspondence was with the novelists Denis Mackail and William Townend. By 1922, Conrad was beginning to wear thin for Wodehouse, while the plotlessness and 'intellectual pallor' of the Bloomsbury novelists find themselves subject to a certain degree of satire.[13] Throughout his life, Wodehouse would return, in his reading, to Shakespeare and the Romantic poets.

Wodehouse had his share of personal concerns. There are repeated exchanges with his schoolfriend William Townend, who was struggling as a writer, offering both advice and stealthy transfers of cash. 'I feel sort of responsible for him, as I egged him on to be a writer', he confesses to his agent, Paul Reynolds.[14] He disliked being apart from Ethel and Leonora, and worried about illness. And there is, among these letters, an air of more existential worry; he writes of his 'periodical fits of depression'.[15] There was, as Wodehouse put it, 'something dead and depressing about London' in the 1920s; the Riviera was 'loathsome' and New York 'appalling'.

It was Wodehouse's contemporary, Ernest Hemingway, who saw those who came of age in the 1920s as a 'lost generation' – a generation who were suffering from the aftershocks of the loss of war as well as from a certain loss of direction. Writers in this period – from Evelyn Waugh to Samuel Beckett – touch both on the urge for meaningless escapism and on the wistful spirituality of the age. Individuals toyed with séances, spiritualism and horoscopes, as attempts to both ward off and assuage the gloom. Wodehouse, like many of his contemporaries, made joking references to these practices, and the devotion of his brother Armine to theosophy gains a number of mocking mentions in his fiction of this period. But Wodehouse was not entirely sceptical. He had his own spiritualist leanings: 'I think it's the goods', he wrote to Townend in 1925, after reading H. Dennis Bradley's introduction to the spirit world, *The Wisdom of the Gods*.[16] Wodehouse had a large collection of spiritualist books in his library, and attended a number of séances with Leonora.

Glimpses of Wodehouse in mystical mood apart, throughout these letters, one sees little of Wodehouse's emotional side. Even the death of his father in 1929 seemed not to stop his frenzied pace of work. A set of lyrics that he proudly transcribed for Leonora in 1924 – 'Put all your troubles in a great big box / And lock it with a great big key' – could stand as the motto for his correspondence at this time.[17] For Wodehouse, as for his favourite hero Lord Emsworth, the deepest feelings remain unspoken. Some of the most poignant moments in his fiction at this time – such as the short story in which the East End child, Gladys, steals Lord Emsworth's heart as she slips 'a small, hot hand into his' – have something of the quality of the silent movie about them. Contained and nostalgic, there is a reserve about this 'mute vote of confidence' that borders on tragi-comedy.[18]

In 1925, Wodehouse writes to Leonora of his desire to escape to the sort of rural idyll that his fiction repeatedly describes – a world full of 'dogs and cats and cows and meadow-land'.[19] Such a desire for a familiar landscape is no surprise. His own world was changing almost daily. One of his staples – musical theatre – was finding new competition. Near the close of the 1920s, Wodehouse began negotiations with film producer Sam Goldwyn. The talkies had arrived, and Hollywood beckoned.

1 PGW to William Townend, 16 December 1922 (Wodehouse Archive).
2 PGW to Leonora Wodehouse, 1 May 1921 (Wodehouse Archive).
3 *Bring on the Girls*, p. 36.
4 PGW to William Townend, 29 December 1922 (Dulwich).
5 *Piccadilly Jim* (1917), Chapter 8.
6 PGW, 'Preface' (1974) to *Joy in the Morning* (London: Barrie & Jenkins, 1974).

7 *Piccadilly Jim*, Chapter 1.

8 'Comrade Bingo', first published in the UK in *The Strand* and in the US in *Cosmopolitan* (May 1922). Repr. in *The Inimitable Jeeves* (1923).

9 PGW to Leonora Cazalet, 1 May 1921 (Wodehouse Archive).

10 PGW to William Townend, 12 November 1924 (Dulwich).

11 *Piccadilly Jim*, Chapter 1.

12 Ethel Wodehouse to Denis Mackail, 8 October 1931 (Wodehouse Archive); PGW to William Townend, 8 January 1930 (Dulwich).

13 See the description of Blair Eggleston in *Hot Water* (1932).

14 PGW to Paul Reynolds, 9 September 1920 (Columbia).

15 PGW to William Townend, 23 July 1923 (Dulwich).

16 PGW to William Townend, 14 December 1925 (Dulwich).

17 PGW to Leonora Wodehouse, 23 November 1923 (Wodehouse Archive).

18 'Lord Emsworth and the Girl Friend', first published in 1926 in the US in *Liberty* (January) and in *The Strand* (February) in the UK. Reprinted in *Blandings Castle and Elsewhere* (1935).

19 PGW to Leonora Wodehouse, 30 March 1925 (Wodehouse Archive).

1919–1930:
'This, I need scarcely point out to you, is jolly old Fame'

In 1920, Wodehouse renewed his correspondence with his old Dulwich school friend, William Townend, who had been demobilised from the army the previous year. Wodehouse's joking discussion of wartime activities reveals some self-consciousness about the fact that he had been unable to see active service.

Though the Wodehouses had just taken a house on Walton Street as their London base, Wodehouse was soon to set off for a visit to Palm Beach to discuss a new show with Florenz Ziegfeld. Wodehouse found life in America exhausting. To escape from the constant socialising of the theatrical scene, he took up golf at the Sound View Golf Club, Long Island. Golf was, he wrote, 'the infallible test. The man who can go into a patch of rough alone, with the knowledge that only God is watching him, and play his ball where it lies, is the man who will serve you faithfully and well.'

TO WILLIAM TOWNEND

Great Neck

Feb 28. 1920

Dear Bill.

Thanks awfully for your letters and the clippings. The Jenkins advertisement took my breath away.[1] I've been waiting all these years for a publisher who didn't shove my book down among the 'and other readable stories' in small print at the foot of the column! That is something like what you might call a gentlemanly advertisement.

I say, before I forget. By every post these days I get piteous letters from Comrade Hoffman,[2] of which I enclose samples. What about all this pessimism? Your letters read fine. Not a care in the world and all that sort of thing. [...] I didn't see where he could say that a story like 'Missing' was gloomy. But perhaps you've been firing in others that I haven't seen. I see you announced for next month, and I am going to rush and get it.

I suppose, as a matter of fact, that it was humanly impossible to go through the war as you did and not come out feeling that things were a bit off. I have been seeing something of a chap called Hamilton Gibbs,[3] brother of Philip Gibbs and author of *The Grey Wave* (I think it's called. It's called *Gun Fodder* over here. A corking book. Do get it.), and he says it's the hardest thing in the world for him to write a story that's cheerful.

I'll buck you up when I get home. That's to say, if I'm not arrested and shoved in chokey for not helping to slug Honble Kaiser. How <u>does</u> the law stand in that respect? I registered in the draft over here – age sixty-three, sole support of wife and nine children, totally blind, and all the rest of it, but ought I to have done anything as regards registering in England? I thought not, as I was out the country when the war started, and anyway wouldn't have been a dam bit of good, as my only pair of spectacles would have bust in the first charge.

Ethel and I are looking forward to seeing you both tremendously. I don't suppose you are either of you much altered since the day we met. I am much the same, except that the trousers I was wearing then have at last given out and had to be chucked away.

Business of looking up your letter to see what questions you asked.

(1) I now write short stories at a terrific speed. I've started a habit of rushing them through and then copying them out carefully, instead of trying to get the first draft exactly right. I have just finished an eight thousand word golf story in two days!![4] Darned good, too. It just came pouring out. I think this is a record that will stand for a long time, though. It nearly slew me. As a rule, I find the inside of a week long enough, if I have got the plot well thought out.

(2) On a novel I generally average about eight pages a day, i.e. about 2500 words. On the other hand, I've just done 100,000 words of a new novel[5] in exactly two months. But I don't know what's come over me lately. I've been simply churning out the stuff. I think it was due to knocking off stories for a year or so and doing plays.

(3) Lately I have had a great time with my work. We have been snowed up here, and nobody has been able to get at us for over two months. As a rule I like to start work in the mornings, knock off for a breather,

and do a bit before dinner. I hate working after dinner. Yet in the old days that was my only time for work. I don't know why I've changed.

(4) Plots. Dam hard to get, but they've been coming along fine of late. Sometimes I run absolutely dry.

(5) I think a good agent is the finest invention in the world. I use Paul Reynolds, an excellent man. [...]

(6) There's no moral or legal necessity to inform an agent you want to work for yourself. You just go and do it. Unless, of course, you have signed anything. I got had that way. I was working in 1914 with a hopeless incompetent called Mrs Wilkening (she sued Mary Pickford the other day for alleged commission and tried to get $100,000)[6]. I had signed a paper making her my agent, and two years afterwards, when I sold the *Post Something New* off my own bat, she swooped down and sued me for 10 per cent commish, and I had to give her 5% to avoid a lawsuit.

(7) I am doing quite a lot now with the picture people. Not original stuff, but selling them my novels. There's a lot of money in it. I got $8000 for *Piccadilly Jim*, – only to have to disgorge 6000 of it to Comstock,[7] who claimed that it belonged to him because he had commissioned a play on the novel.[8]

(8) Yes, I drive my own car. Very hot stuff. In all sorts of traffic.

(9) I play nothing but golf. Greatest game on earth. You must take it up. It beats everything else.

[...]

I got a letter from Greenwood the other day. He says he is very busy. He's a chartered accountant. Did you know that Tid Lowe was in partnership with Cumberlege (old Cambridge scrum half) in a motor garage?[9]

[...] Oh, by the way, you asked me about Armine. Married surreptitiously a year ago and is now about to have a baby. At least, Mrs Armine is. He's living at Bexhill, and my father says he is as keen on Theosophy as ever, but devours vast quantities of meat and all the drink he can get! Bang against the rules, of course.[10]

Old Brook[11] has been out in India. He is not yet demobbed, but is returning to England shortly. He has been sub-editing the *Pioneer* out there. Mrs Westbrook is doing well with the agency. Why don't you send her your stuff? She handles all mine in England, and does awfully well with it. She is very keen, and gives you individual attention which these blighters like Watt don't, they being on too large a scale.

I must get hold of Waugh's book.[12] I have heard a lot about it. He must be a pretty warm writer to be able to do anything at seventeen.

The serial ought to start in about a month in *Collier's*. I'll send you copies. We sail on the *Adriatic* on April 24, as follows: – Ethel, carrying black kitten, followed by self, with parrot in cage, and Loretta our maid with any other animals we may acquire in the meantime. We shall have to leave the bull-dog behind, worse luck, owing to the quarantine laws.

Well, so long. Do write again. I read all your letters a dozen times. I've got a large budget of them which you wrote in 1915.

Love to Rene from us both

Yours ever

P.G.W.

1 Wodehouse had a close relationship with his British publisher, Herbert Jenkins, which would continue until Jenkins' death.

2 Arthur Sullivant Hoffman, chief editor of *Adventure* magazine, which featured Townend's writing.

3 Hamilton Gibbs also wrote for *Munsey's Magazine*. His war memoir, *The Grey Wave*, or *Gun Fodder*, was published in 1920. PGW had worked with his brother, Cosmo, in musical theatre.

4 The 8,000-word golf story was 'The Clicking of Cuthbert', published in *The Strand* in 1921 and *Elk's Magazine* in the US in 1922, repr. in *The Clicking of Cuthbert* (1922).

5 His 'new novel' was published in the UK as a serial in *Woman's Home Companion* in 1921, in book form the following year under the title *The Girl on the Boat* in the UK, and as *Three Men and a Maid* in the USA. The 'new serial' would be become *The Little Warrior*, first published in serial and book form in America in 1920, and in the UK as *Jill the Reckless* the following year.

6 The suit remained contested, and Wilkening renewed it in 1920.

7 Ray Comstock (1880–1949), manager of the Princess Theatre, had produced the musical comedies *Oh, Boy!* (1917), *Oh, Lady! Lady!!* (1918) and *Oh, My Dear!* (1919), for which Wodehouse wrote the lyrics. Comstock was 'a thin, rangy individual', who spent his time 'perpetually telephoning' and calling everyone 'honey' (*Bring on the Girls*, p. 45).

8 The film of *Piccadilly Jim* was made in 1919, featuring Owen Moore.

9 Old Alleynians. John Eric Greenwood left Dulwich in 1910 and went on to captain Cambridge University at rugby, and played for England in 1919–20. Cyril Nelson (Tid) Lowe left Dulwich in 1911, was a Cambridge rugby Blue, capped twenty-five times for England, and a British flying ace. Lowe, who had featured in an early PGW poem, became the inspiration for W. E. Johns' character Biggles. Barry Cumberlege was not a Dulwich boy, but played rugby at Cambridge alongside Lowe.

10 Wodehouse's brother Armine had returned from India. He had become interested in theosophy, a doctrine of religious teaching and mysticism, founded by Helena Blavatsky and others, and had been teaching at the college of a prominent theosophist, Annie Besant, in India.

11 'Old Brook' – Herbert Wotton Westbrook – who was working for *The Pioneer*, an Indian newspaper founded in 1865.

12 PGW refers to Alec Waugh's controversial account of boarding school life, *The Loom of Youth*, written in 1917, when he was only seventeen. Alec was the elder brother of Evelyn.

After the whirl of American social life, the Wodehouses were spending a summer break on the Suffolk coast, enabling them to be closer to Leonora, who was now at boarding school.

TO LEONORA WODEHOUSE

Quinton Farm
Felixstowe

Aug 7. 1920

My darling angel Snorkles.

At last I'm able to write to you! I finished the novel yesterday,[1] and I wish you were here to read it, as I think it's the best comic one I've done. It's not meant to be in the same class as *The Little Warrior*, but as a farce I think it's pretty well all to the mustard. I've done it in such a hurry, though, that there may be things wrong with it. Still, I'm going to keep it by me for at least two weeks before sending it off to America, so perhaps you'll be able to see it after all before it goes. If not, you can read the original M.S.

[...]

I really am becoming rather a blood these days. In a review of *Wedding Bells*[2] at the *Playhouse*, the critic says 'So-and-so is good as a sort of P. G. Wodehouse character.' And in a review of a book in the *Times*, they say 'The author at times reverts to the P. G. Wodehouse manner.' This, I need scarcely point out to you, is jolly old Fame. Once they begin to refer to you in that casual way as if everybody must know who you are all is well. It does my old heart good.

[...]

I'm glad you liked *The Little White Bird*. One of my favourite books.[3]

Georgie O'Ramey is singing 'Galahad' in Cochran's new revue.[4] Isn't it darned cheek! I want heavy damages and all that sort of thing.

What scares me is that she has probably pinched 'Cleopatra', 'Very Good Girl On Sunday', and 'Blood' from *Springtime* as well. It begins to look like a pretty thin sort of world if tons of hams unfit for human consumption are going to lift one's best things out of shows and use them themselves without even a kind smile.[5]

Well, pip pip and good-bye-ee and so forth

Your loving

Plummie

1 *The Girl on the Boat*.

2 *Wedding Bells*, a comedy by Edward Salisbury Field.

3 *The Little White Bird* by J. M. Barrie.

4 Charles B. Cochran, the British theatrical manager, staged many revues in London in the 1920s, and was often referred to as 'the British Ziegfeld'.

5 'Sir Galahad' and 'Cleopatterer' were lyrics that PGW wrote for *Leave It to Jane*. 'A Very Good Girl on Sunday' and 'Melodrama Burlesque (The Old Fashioned Drama)' shortened to 'Blood') came from *Miss Springtime*, Bolton and Wodehouse's 1917 musical comedy.

Though business-related, Wodehouse's correspondence with his agent, Paul Reynolds, is often revealing. In the following letter, he mentions the physical exercises that remained crucial to him throughout his life. Any Wodehouse character found doing physical jerks (especially in the morning) usually turns out to be a hero. See, for example, the discussion that surrounds Ashe Marson in Something New: *'A gentleman named Lieutenant Larsen, of the Danish Army, as the result of much study of the human anatomy, some time ago evolved a series of Exercises. All over the world at the present moment his apostles are twisting themselves into knots in accordance with the dotted lines in the illustrative plates of his admirable book. From Peebles to Baffin's Bay arms and legs are being swung in daily thousands from point A to point B, and flaccid muscles are gaining the consistency of India-rubber. Larsen's Exercises are the last word in exercises. They bring into play every sinew of the body. They promote a brisk circulation. They enable you, if you persevere, to fell oxen, if desired, with a single blow.' Larsen was fictitious, but Wodehouse probably drew his inspiration for Marson's daily regime from the popular daily systematic exercises of the Swede Pehr Ling, or those of Lieutenant Muller of the Danish Army.*

Constitutional Club
London W.C.

Sept 9. 1920

Dear Reynolds.

I finished the novel two or three days ago, and I think it is good.[1] It is certainly full enough of situations, and if we were selling it to the *Post*, I would say it was one of the best I'd done. Whether it's not a little too farcical for a woman's magazine I don't know. Still, the editress told me to forget I was writing for women and just do my usual stuff. The story is rather on the lines of *Something New*, the first one you sold of mine. Not in plot, but in tone. Anyway, it's darned funny. I'll inform the universe!

[...]

I'm awfully bucked that you will handle the Townend story. I know from experience what being handled by you means! I am keeping a rigid eye on Townend and getting him to write the sort of story I sent you, with a real plot and a punch at the end, instead of the gloomy studies he has done lately. [...] He is an awfully good chap, and I would rather see him land in some big market than sell my next serial for forty thousand. We were at school together and have been friends since 1897. I feel sort of responsible for him, as I egged him on to be a writer. He used to be an artist before that.

[...]

Did you read that article in *Collier's* by Walter Camp the other day, giving a new set of physical exercises warranted to cure all ills? I have been doing them for a month and they are simply terrific. [...] They really are the most marvellous things. You get out of bed feeling a wreck, and you do these exercises and feel as if you were in training for the Olympic Games.

Yours ever

P. G. Wodehouse

1 *The Girl on the Boat.*

The Daily Dozen

THE *following directions are reprinted, for your convenience, from Collier's of June 5. The first three exercises are intended for use wherever the Daily Dozen is taken in groups with a leader. They are to improve the carriage and poise, and especially to develop quick coordination. The men are sent through the motions upon orders of the leader, who will sometimes make a false motion to see if the men are following orders or merely watching him. This practice can also be followed even where there are only two taking the exercises together, each acting alternately as leader for the other. The remaining nine exercises are for use individually or in groups:*

1 HANDS : Stand erect, arms hanging at sides, heels slightly separated, feet pointing straight ahead.
2 HIPS : As before, but with hands on hips.
3 HEAD : Arms up, hands meet with fingers just touching each other at back of head.
4 GRIND : Arms outstretched straight from shoulders—called the "cross" position. Turn palms upward ; make six-inch circles with hands, five times forward, five backward ; keep arms stiff.
5 GRATE : Arms at "cross" position ; palms down. Lift arms very slowly to angle of about forty-five degrees, inhaling ; bring them down slowly to shoulder position, exhaling. Repeat ten times.
6 GRASP : Let fingers of both hands meet at back of neck. Bend neck back. Bend body forward very slowly from waist, keeping head up, neck bent back ; eyes fixed on object height of man's eyes. Come back slowly to first position ; then bend backward. Repeat ten times.
7 CRAWL : Stand at "cross" position. Raise right arm ; let left drop at side. Then let left crawl slowly down toward the knee, at same time curving right arm over head until fingers touch left side of neck. Return to "cross" position and let right hand crawl and left curl over head. Five times with each hand.
8 CURL : Stand at "cross" position. Clench fists. Begin to inhale deeply while lowering arms and bringing them slowly forward, bent at elbow ; curl arms around until fists come under armpits. Bend head and shoulders backward as inhalation is completed. Loosen hands and push straight

forward, beginning to exhale. Bend forward from waist, exhaling, and letting hands come back across hips ; continue movement until, as you remain bent, the arms are raised behind you. Begin to inhale again as you return to "cross" position, ready to repeat. Ten times.
9 CROUCH : "Cross" position, feet 18 inches apart. Raise on toes ; keep arms out. Squat slowly down as far as you can, inhaling. Come up slowly, exhaling, and letting heels touch floor as you rise. Five times.
10 WAVE : "Cross" position. Raise arms, bending wrists until fingers touch above head. Bring both arms against head with snap movement. Moving *only from waist*, bend forward slightly, then to right, then backward, then to left, and continue until you are making a circle with your clasped hands extended above head. Repeat five times in each direction, reversing circle after first five.
11 WEAVE : "Cross" position, feet apart. Raise right arm, keeping eyes on it as it goes up ; bend left knee and lower left arm until fingers touch floor between feet. Back slowly to "cross" position and reverse. Five times for each hand.
12 WING : "Cross" position. Exhale, bringing arms straight out before you. Continuing exhalation, swing arms down and back, bending forward slowly from waist. Continue bending forward, pushing arms back and letting breath out as movement is completed. Keep head up and eyes forward. Now inhale as you go back slowly to "cross" position. Repeat ten times.

Walter Camp's 'Daily Dozen', *Collier's Magazine*, 17 July 1920.

TO LEONORA WODEHOUSE

Constitutional Club
Northumberland Avenue
London W.C.

Sept 27. 1920

My precious darling Snorky.

Here is a letter from one of the Ely Court nibs which Mummie gave me to send on to you. Opened in error and all that sort of thing.[1]

I've been living at the club for the last two weeks, trying to do some work. Mummie has been at Chingford, which isn't a bad place in itself but is too near the East End of London to be really nice. I was out there yesterday, and the place was overrun with motor buses and picnic parties. Still, in another few days we move into the house, thank goodness. I am so sick of having my meals in restaurants and at the club that I don't know what to do.

[...]

The novel is being typed, and must also be finished by now, I should think.[2] I'll send you on the original manuscript, and you can read it in the train. I am now trying to get a central idea for a new serial for *Collier's*. The editor keeps writing to me to say that *The Little Warrior* was the best thing that ever happened, so I feel I must do something special next shot. The trouble is, unless I write a sequel and bring Freddie Rooke in again, I don't see how I can introduce a dude character, and without a dude character where am I? Among the ribstons.

I've just had a letter from a man in California who wants me to buy an interest in a gold mine for five hundred pounds. He says 'I happened to pick up the Sept *Cosmopolitan* and on one of the front pages I see a list of authors and artists and I said to myself that bunch could put this over and I have a hunch they will and your name is in the list and I'm writing you along with the others to send me your check for twenty-five hundred dollars and write on the check that it is for a one-thirtieth interest in the eight-year lease of the Kid Gold Mine and then after a while I will send you a check for your share of a million or a letter of regret telling you I have spent the money digging through the mountain and my hunch was a bum one, but anyway I expect your check.' Sanguine sort of johnny, what? I'm going to put the letter in a story.[3]

Well, cheerio, old bean.

Lots of love

From Plummie.

P.S. Oh, by the way, you must stop pinching Mummie's clothes. It worries her frightfully, and you know how nervous she is.

1 Leonora's school, Ely Court.
2 *The Girl on the Boat*.
3 Wodehouse went on to use the anecdote about the gold mine speculator in *Big Money* (1931).

After a family stay in the area, the Wodehouses decided to send Leonora to a new boarding school in Felixstowe. Wodehouse was also busy turning his stories about the Drone, Archie Moffam, into a novel, The Indiscretions of Archie *(1921).*

TO LEONORA WODEHOUSE

16 Walton St
London S.W.

Nov 24. 1920

Darling Snorkles.

We were so glad to get your letters and to hear that you are having a good time. I thought you would like Felixstowe. I'm so glad you've started riding.

The Haileybury match was a disaster, darn it. We were without Addison, and with him we should have won easily, but still they had a couple of good men away. Still, we ought to have won anyhow, only the blighters started the game scared, because Haileybury had beaten Bedford so easily, and they let them score twice in the first five minutes. It wasn't till after half time that we woke up, and then we simply put it all over them. But it was too late then, and we couldn't catch up. They scored four times and we scored three. We ought to have scored half a dozen times. Murtrie played a splendid game, and your little friend Mills, the fly-half, was brilliant at times, only he spoiled it by making one or two bad mistakes. He made one splendid run nearly the whole length of the field. On Saturday we finish up by playing Sherborne.

Great excitement last night. Mummie came into my room at half-past two and woke me out of the dreamless to say that mice had been snootering her. She said one had run across her bed. To soothe her I went to her room to spend the rest of the night, thinking that there may have been mice in the room but that she had simply imagined that they had got on the bed. We had hardly turned off the light when — zip! one ran right across the pillow!!! So then we hoofed it back to my room and tried to sleep there, but the bed was too small, so I gave up my room to Mummie and went back to the mice room. And for some reason or other Mister Mouse made no further demonstration, and I wasn't disturbed. But the result is that we are both very sleepy today. I have been trying to work, but can't rouse the old bean.

I am at present moulding the Archie stories into a book. The publisher very wisely says that short stories don't sell, so I am hacking the things about, putting the first half of one story at the beginning of the book and putting the finish of it about a hundred pages later, and the result looks very good. For instance, I blend the Sausage Chappie Story and 'Paving the Way for Mabel' rather cunningly. You remember that the blow-out of the latter takes place in the grill-room. Well, directly it has happened there is a row at the other end of the grill-room, which is the Sausage Chappie having the finish of his story. Rather ingenious, what!

[...]

Mummie came out of the nursing home rather tired, as it was one of those places where they wake you up for breakfast at seven-thirty. She has been resting a lot since coming out, and seems much better now. We have got Ian Hay[1] coming to dinner tonight.

The house is very still and quiet without our Snorky.

[...]

I have to go for my walks by myself.

We listened to the Palladium on the electrophone the night before last.[2] The chap who sings 'Smith, Jones, Robinson, and Brown' had another good song, as a naval officer. [...]

It sounds wonderful when I sing it. You must hear me some time. Well, cheerio, old fright. Write again soon.

Your loving

Plummie

1 Ian Hay (John Hay Beith) (1876–1952), a Scottish novelist and playwright, who later collaborated with PGW, dramatising *A Damsel in Distress*.
2 A precursor to the wireless, the 'electrophone' was an audio system, licensed through the Post Office, which relayed live concerts and church sermons to individual homes, via specialised head-sets. Around 2,000 Londoners were subscribing to its services in the early 1920s.

Wodehouse now began work on another Ziegfeld production – Sally – although the news that Ziegfeld had hired further lyricists prompted a long-distance row.

TO LEONORA WODEHOUSE

16 Walton Street
London S.W.

Nov 28. 1920

Darling Snorkles.

[...]

We[1] beat Sherborne yesterday after a very hot game, so that we have wound up the season with five wins and one defeat. Pretty hot!

I forgot to tell you in my last letter the tale of the laughable imbroglio – or mix-up – which has occurred with Jerry Kern. You remember I sent my lyrics over, and then read in *Variety* that some other cove was doing the lyrics and wrote to everybody in New York to retrieve my lyrics. Then that cable came asking me if I would let them have 'Joan of Arc' and 'Church Round Corner', which, after a family council, I answered in the affir.[2] Well, just after I had cabled saying all right, I got a furious cable from Jerry – the sort of cable the Kaiser might have sent to an underling – saying my letter withdrawing the lyrics was 'extremely offensive' and ending 'You have offended me for the last time'! Upon which, the manly spirit of the Wodehouses (descended from the sister of Anne Boleyn)[3] boiled in my veins – when you get back I'll show you the very veins it boiled in – and I cabled over 'Cancel permission to use lyrics'. I now hear that Jerry is bringing an action against me for royalties on *Miss Springtime* and *Riviera Girl*, to which he contributed tunes. The loony seems to think that a lyrist is responsible for the composer's royalties. Of course, he hasn't an earthly, and I don't suppose the action will ever come to anything, but doesn't it show how blighted some blighters can be when they decide to be blighters.

[...]

Well, cheerio.

Mummie sends her love. She is washing her hair or something this morning.

Your loving

Plummie

1 Dulwich College rugby team.
2 'Joan of Arc' – aka 'You Can't Keep a Good Girl Down' – and 'Church Round the Corner', lyrics for *Sally*.
3 Wodehouse's claim to illustrious ancestry was true – he was descended from Lady Mary Boleyn, sister of Anne Boleyn.

Wodehouse made his peace with Ziegfeld and Kern, his lyrics were kept, and Sally *was a smash hit in New York, opening in December 1920. By March 1921, he was heading to America to investigate options for musical shows. He was also working on a number of contracts:* The Golden Moth, *with music by Ivor Novello, on which he was to collaborate with English playwright Fred Thompson, and also a follow-up to* Sally *called* The Cabaret Girl. *Thompson, the 'cheery old bean', worked occasionally with Wodehouse and Guy Bolton, and makes an appearance in Chapter 5 of* The Inimitable Jeeves.

TO LEONORA WODEHOUSE

S.S. Adriatic

Southampton

March 23. 1921

Darling precious angel Snorklet.

I have written to mother about your going down. You might drop a line, too.

I think the jolly old boat is just starting. I shall mail this at Cherbourg. It begins to look like a jolly voyage, if we don't cop any rough weather. This cabin is a snorter. About the size of my den, with a lounge, a chair, two windows, and a closet and a chest of drawers. In fact, if only there was that bit of lawn and shrubbery we discussed the other day, I would settle down here for life and grow honey-coloured whiskers. As it is, I shall probably keep fowls during the voyage.

Only blot is, the table they have given me is one of those ones that sway in the breeze and wobble violently if you touch them. What it will be like out in the open ocean heaven knows. If all goes well, I ought to be able to do quite a chunk of work.

I have already been interviewed by the representative of the White Star Publicity for publication in N.Y., and Mummie is running round in circles breathing smoke because I didn't lug her into it. I tell her that I will feature her when the reporters arrive at N.Y.

We had a very jolly journey down, talking of this and that. (First this, then that.) Thompson is going to be a very cheery old bean to have around on the trip, and altogether everything looks pretty well all right. But I haven't managed yet to get into the George Drexel Steel class, if you know what I mean, and it's generally felt throughout the ship that I shan't work it till tomorrow.[1]

It's wonderful what a difference it makes having a decent cabin. This one is more like a room than a cabin. All very jolly.

Mummie was saying such sweet things about you in the cab. We wept in company on each other's shoulders at the thought that we had to leave you.

The engines have just started going pretty hard, so I can now tell what it will be like trying to work during the voyage. All right, I think.

I'll write and tell you how New York looks. Goodbye, my queen of all possible Snorkles.

Lots of love

Your

Plummie

1 George Drexel Steel was a New York socialite and financier.

The Wodehouses arrived in New York and settled themselves into the Hotel Biltmore on Madison Avenue, between 43rd and 44th Streets. Built in 1912, the huge twenty-storey building was considered to be the last word in modern hotel construction. The Astor Hotel, which made the Wodehouses 'sick to look at', was a more architecturally elaborate building, with a selection of decorative features from Chinese to German Volk to Native American. Wodehouse's comment is surprising, not least because the Astor had been the site of their two-day honeymoon in 1914.

New York in the early twenties was subject to Prohibition. Since April 1920, the consumption of alcohol had been illegal in most states. The 'noble experiment', Wodehouse recalls, created the '"Hooch Age", and the same spirit that made bath-tub gin [...] was the same devil may care quality that accounted for flagpole sitters, marathon dancing, and the bull market'.

TO LEONORA WODEHOUSE

Hotel Biltmore
New York

April 2. 1921

Prcious (or, rather, precious) angel Snork.

Well, we blew in yesterday morning and are all feeling rather wrecks after a strenuous day yesterday. In their usual blighted fussy way they got us up at six when there was no earthly need to get up before nine or ten, and it seemed hours before we could get past the passport people. It bucked us up a bit when the photographers buzzed round us and took all sorts of pictures including some movies. The only trouble is that I can't find that any paper has printed them. Maybe they'll be in the Sunday papers. One was supposed to be for *Town and Country*, a weekly paper.

Mummie hunted all round New York for a hotel. The Astor made us sick to look at it, and we very soon gave that the go-by, after having a very bad lunch there. We finally settled on this at fourteen seeds a day, which won't do a thing to the old bank-balance. Fortunately, this morning I got a good idea for a short story, and hope to write it while I'm here. We've got a very nice room, looking down onto the roof garden and three pigeons (which are thrown in free).

Our first act was to summon a bell-boy and give him the Sinister Whisper, to which he replied with a conspiratorial nod and buzzed off, returning later with a bottle of whisky – at the nominal price of seventeen dollars!!! I suppose if you tried to get champagne here you would have to throw in your Sunday trousers as well. Apparently you can still get the stuff, but you have to be darned rich.

Mummie was frightfully tired. Our cabin was on the promenade deck, and we were kept awake most of the last night by the row made by lugging trunks out of the hold just outside our window. Still, we got – or climbed – into our respective evening suits and went off to *Mary*, not being able to get seats for *Sally*, which was sold out.[1]

They are bringing *Mary* to London, where it will die the death, I predict (or prognosticate). It is a weird show. Imagine a typical rowdy American musical comedy like *Listen Lester*, with everything in it exaggerated a dozen times. Every number was plugged with dances and stunts, and the chorus men were too frightful for words. Fred Thompson, who had never seen anything like them before, sat and goggled at them. They came on number after number flapping their hands in front of them like seals. I sent round word to the management that they could have 'em, as I didn't want them.

Today we rang up all sorts of people, and I had lunch with Paul Reynolds, who talked of this and that. Mummie wandered off to Rickson's, and is now lying down, very worn out.[2] I am going to make her go to bed and dine in bed. This is a ripping hostelry, and we have a very nice waiter on our floor.

One of the first things I did was to get a *Journal* and cut out a Crazy Cat [*sic*] for you.[3] And another today. Both good.

[...]

We both keep saying what chumps we were not to have brought our Snorky with us. You must certainly come next time.

We had an awfully nice trip. Fred Thompson was a wonderful chap to have with us. Full of funny stories and a most awfully good sort. We are all tremendous pals. The journey didn't seem a bit long, though it took nine days. I sweated like blazes at the novel, and wrote and revised another 12,000 words, so that I now have about 70,000 words of good stuff, and am going to shoot it in without waiting to finish the thing.[4] I shall finish it bit by bit while I am here. I'll keep a copy for you. The scene at the boxer's training-camp came out splendidly, though it was very hard to write. I had a wobbly table, which I had to prop up with trunks, and writing wasn't easy. I generally worked every afternoon from three to half-past six. I did a good scene for Sally and Ginger.[5] There are some fairly difficult bits still to do, but I hope I shall polish them off all right. It ought to be easier doing them in New York.

I hope you are getting on all right. This darned coal-strike is a nuisance.[6] Did you have much trouble clearing up and getting out of Walton Street?

Mummie sends her love and hopes everything is all right – or all correct-o, if you prefer it.

We haven't got in touch with Loretta or Sammy yet.[7] I find that ocean-travelling dogs go with the ship's butcher, and live in dark rooms lighted with electric light some of the time. I don't suppose old Sam will mind it much, as he will be asleep all the time, but it must be rotten for a lively dog. One of the passengers brought over a Sealyham puppy. We saw it at the dock, and it looked very subdued, but that may have been just because he found everything strange.

Well, cheerio, old scream. We're thinking of you all the time.

Oceans of love

Your loving

Plummie

---

1 PGW's references to 1920s musical comedy include *Mary* by Harbach and Mandel, the 'rollocking' New York smash *Listen Lester*, and *Sally*, written by Guy Bolton and Jerome Kern, with two lyrics by PGW.

2 Rickson's was a gentleman's outfitters.

3 George Herriman's 'Krazy Kat' daily cartoon strip appeared in the *New York Evening Journal*.

4 PGW refers to *The Adventures of Sally*, published in the UK in 1922. It first appeared in the US as a serial in *Collier's Weekly* from October to December 1921, and in *Grand* magazine in England. It was published in America under the title *Mostly Sally* in 1923.

5 The hero and heroine of *The Adventures of Sally*.

6 A state of emergency had been declared in England on 31 March due to a coal miners' strike.

7 Sammy the bulldog had been a gift from one of the girls who performed in PGW's revue *Miss 1917* (*Performing Flea*, p. 16).

With The Cabaret Girl *over, Wodehouse returned to England and spent time at his beloved Emsworth, and at his club in London. Wodehouse's letter to the younger writer Denis Mackail [see plate 19] marked the beginning of a lifelong friendship and correspondence.*

Constitutional Club,
Northumberland Avenue
W.C.2.

May 13. 1921

Dear Mr Mackail,

I feel I must write a line to say how much I enjoyed your *What Next*. It is simply terrific. If it is your first book, as I believe I read somewhere, I call it a marvellous effort.

Hoping you will produce something of the same sort every few months,

Yours sincerely

P. G. Wodehouse

In 1921, Leonora was sent to a new school, the Old Palace in Bromley, Kent. A school friend remembered that it consisted of 'about thirty girls [...] taught by completely unqualified teachers. The owner was Belgian, and the school professed to specialise in French. The girls were instructed to speak French to each other all day long, which led to a good deal of "Passez-moi the salt, s'il vous plaît". When Wodehouse visited Leonora he hid in the shrubbery on the drive and she went out to meet him because he was frightened of meeting the headmistress.' Wodehouse's letter here offers a rare mention of his immediate family. Philip Peveril John Wodehouse (or 'Pev'), Wodehouse's eldest brother (1877–1951), was then Deputy Superintendent of the Hong Kong Police, and had been made Companion of the Order of the Indian Empire in 1919. Wodehouse's youngest brother, 'Dick', was Richard Lancelot Deane Wodehouse (1892–1940).

8 Launceston Place
Gloucester Road
W.8

May 20. 1921

Darling precious angel Snorkles.

You will be thinking me a f.i.h.s. (fiend in human shape) for not having written to you before, but, gosh ding it, four separate jobs collided and I was sunk in the whirlpool. Old Savage[1] arrived and I had to buckle to on the Lehar piece; Fred Thompson came back and I had to pop onto the Adelphi piece; Reynolds cabled and I had to revise *The Girl on the Boat*; and he also said that *Collier's* wanted the rest of *Sally*. My impulse in these circumstances was to go to bed with a hot-water bottle and a book, but I decided to have a dash at tackling the jobs, so I started by cutting twenty thousand words out of *The Girl on the Boat*, after which I wrote a scene of the Lehar piece and a scene of the Adelphi piece. I haven't touched *Sally* yet. They will have to wait a bit for that.

On Wednesday afternoon I had an interview with Savage, who read and liked my lyrics and then calmly told me that, for purposes of copyright, he would have to have the remaining two lyrics by today (Friday) at four!!! I hadn't even got ideas for them. By great good luck I managed to get two good ideas, and now – at 2 o'clock – I have just finished them both. So I have now done all the lyrics, thank goodness. He wants the book completed by two weeks from tomorrow. I think I can manage it all right, but it will be a sweat, and I would like to be out in this fine weather. Still, if I <u>am</u> so much in demand it can't be helped.

[...]

Mummie has biffed off to Lingfield,[2] previously touching me for two pounds.

I am so glad that you like the jolly old school. It sounds ripping – or, as you would say now, <u>épatant</u>. How do you like talking French all the time?

I say, Snorky, old Pev blew in from Hong-Kong two weeks ago, and, though it sounds like exaggeration, he's a worse ass than Dick. (Now don't go leaving this letter about or letting the family see it!). But a singular and sinister thing has happened. Mother passed through town on the Friday, and Mummie and I asked Pev and his wife to lunch. Pev turned up but the wife not, on the plea that she was tired. This would be nothing in itself, but we have seen neither of them since then!!! It looks as if we had got the go-by, what?

[...]

Must stop now as the bell is ringing.*

Lots of love

Your

Plummie

* telephone-bell next door.

1 Henry Wilson Savage, theatrical producer. Wodehouse was working for Savage on *The Blue Mazurka*. Music was originally to be by Jerome Kern and Franz Lehár, but it opened in London in 1927 with music by Lehár alone.
2 A racecourse in Surrey.

TO LEONORA WODEHOUSE

9 Launceston Place
Gloucester Road
W.8

June 15. 1921

My poor precious angel,

We were frightfully sorry to hear of your accident, you poor old thing. What an awful shame having this happen to you right in the middle of the summer term when you want to be playing tennis and swimming. You do have the most rotten luck. Never mind, we shall have to make up for it in the holidays.

Does it hurt very much? I hope not. Do you remember when you came such a smash bicycling near the bungalow at Bellport?

I will come down and see you the very first moment I can manage. I simply must take a day to clean up the Savage play, as he wants it by Saturday. But after that down I come with bells on.

[...]

Father came up yesterday, and he is downstairs now waiting for his bites. He looks very fit.

All sorts of exciting things have been happening. Courtneidge wants to put on the Archie play – to my acute disgust as I think it's rotten.[1] I am trying to double-cross the gang and get him to put on *Piccadilly Jim* instead. Also Dillingham[2] has cabled to Guy asking him to rush through the play which he and I and Vecsey[3] are doing, so I have promised, as Guy is busy, to dialogue it. More work! If I can stall off this Adelphi piece, I shall win through, but I am losing weight. Quite the jolly old sylph these days, and getting sylphier all the time.

Bobby Denby has gone off to Ascot, and we have undertaken to pay one-tenth of his losses or take one-tenth of his winnings. I hope the lad bets wisely! He's got a nice day for it, anyway.[4]

Father wants to know if you would like to do a bit of Cheltenham in the holidays. How about it? If you think well of the schema we might put in a week there together. But something more in the nature of the vast rolling prairie was my idea, or the little cottage by the sea.

[...]

Jolly old Armine writes from India hinting that he is tired of his job before he has started it, and rather thinks of branching out on his own as an advertising specialist – or, presumably, anything else that requires no work. One of the things that buoys me up when I am toiling away on these hot afternoons is the thought that I am putting by money for Armine to touch me for later on. I wonder when he will next have the hateful task of asking me for a thousand quid to buy a collar-stud.

[...]

I am persping violently as I write. I envy you that garden of yours. Guy Bolton has just come back from staying with the Carylls at Deauville.[5] They have a house twice as large as their one at Great Neck, with stables and, I think, a private race-course and polo ground. Old Felix has eaten himself into such a state that he trembles, Guy tells me, like a jelly and his eyes are popping out of his head. He said they used to gorge a vast lunch and then sit around talking of what they were going to have for dinner.

Well, cheerio, old scream. You mustn't let this arm-breaking become a habit and take up time which might be devoted to the more serious issues of life.

Oceans of love
From your
Plummie

P.S. Darling thing, your letter has just come. I'm heartbroken that you're having such pain. I'll be right down and darn the Savage play. He'll have to wait.

1 Robert Courtneidge, father of the musical comedy actress Cicely Courtneidge, was one of the last London actor-managers. Neither the 'Archie' play, nor a play of *Piccadilly Jim*, was produced.
2 PGW had worked with the manager Charlie Dillingham for many years. He recalls that Dillingham 'alone was capable – for there never was a more genial man – of luring an author into anything' (*Bring on the Girls*, p. 74).
3 The composer Armand Vecsey. The show was *The Hotel Mouse*, which eventually opened without contributions from Wodehouse.
4 R. J. B. ('Bobby') Denby was 'a charming, recently demobbed US Army Captain [...] became an acknowledged part of the household for the next few years'. He socialised and stayed with the Wodehouses, and conducted literary business deals for PGW (McCrum, p. 148).
5 Ivan Caryll (Felix Tilkin), composer of *The Pink Lady*.

TO LEONORA WODEHOUSE

9, Launceston Place,
Gloucester Road
W.8.

July 3. 1921

Darling angel Snork,

How I have neglected you! I've been in a state of coma since I saw you last, unable to get up enough energy to do anything, even write a letter. The old bean went right back on me, but I'm all right again now.

I hope the arm is getting better. I wonder if you'll be able to do any swimming in August. We are still undecided where to go. Mummie speaks of Le Touquet (in France), but I have an idea it's an overcrowded sort of place, and I'd rather go somewhere where we could biff about in old clothes.

[...]

Mother writes to say that Pev is going to pay Nella's fare over to India, but strikes a jarring note when she adds something to the effect of his not being quite sure he can manage all of it.[1] Does or does not this look as if the old dad were going to get it right in the ribs again? Now if it were a question of paying <u>Pev's</u> fare to India or some other distant spot. . . However, these are idle dreams.

[...]

Mummie gets back from Folkestone tomorrow, and I shall be darned glad to see her again. I have been very sad and lonesome since she went away. But I think the change will have done her good.

I went down to Dulwich yesterday to see the Sherborne match. It was thrilling. We just won when there were only three more minutes to play. I never thought we should do it. I very nearly went about the place scattering pound-notes to the lads. Wiser counsels, however, fortunately prevailed, and I still retain doubloons in the left trouser-pocket.

Love Among the Chickens is out in the cheap edition. I'll send you a copy. Townend told me it was on sale at the Charing Cross bookstall, so I rolled round and found they had sold out. Thence to Piccadilly Circus bookstall. Sold out again. Pretty good in the first two days. Both men offered to sell me 'other Wodehouse books', but I smiled gently on them and legged it.

I have got four new freckles on the top of my head. Where will this end? I think I shall buy a parasol.

[...]

Well cheerio. I'll pop down and see you pretty soon.

Your loving

Plummie

---

1 Nella (Helen) Wodehouse was Armine's wife.

11 King St
St James' S.W.

December 21. 1921

Darling angel Snork.

The Wodehouse home is en fête and considerably above itself this p.m. Deep-throated cheers ring out in Flat 43, and every now and then I have to go out on the balcony to address the seething crowds in St James Street. And why? I'll tell you. (I'm glad you asked me).[1] This afternoon at Hurst Park dear jolly old Front Line romped home in the Hurdle Handicap in spite of having to carry about three tons weight. The handicappers crammed an extra ten pounds on him after his last win, so he had to carry thirteen stone three pounds, and it seemed so impossible that he could win that I went off and played golf instead of going to Hurst Park. It is an absolute record, – the *Evening Standard* says there has never been a case before of a horse winning a good race under such a weight.

We get four hundred quid in stakes – minus fifty quid which we have to cough up to the second horse and twenty-five to the third. Rot, I call it, having to pay them, and I am in favour of seeing if they won't be satisfied with seats for *The Golden Moth* or copies of my books, but apparently it can't be done. We also have to give the trainer a present of fifty quid, and a few extra tips to various varlets and lackeys, not omitting one or two scurvy knaves. Still, with what Mummie (The well-known gambler) got on at six to one, we clear five hundred quid on the afternoon, which, as you justly remark, is not so worse.

In addition to this, Mummie's judgement in buying the horse is boosted to the skies, and everybody looks on her now as the wisest guy in town. If we sold the horse today we could make a profit of a thousand pounds probably, – certainly seven hundred.* But we aren't going to sell.

My first remark on hearing the news was 'Snork will expect something out of this!' It seemed to me that the thing must infallibly bring on a severe attack of the gimmes in the little darling one. Mummie says that when you come back you shall collect in the shape of a rich present. (Box of candy or a fountain-pen or something lavish like that. Or maybe a string of pearls. Maybe, on the other hand, not.)

Well, that's that. So Mummie has started her career as the Curse of the Turf in great style.

I have been spending the last two days in a rush of ideas for a new novel. It will be on the lines of *Something New* and *Piccadilly Jim,* and it is coming out amazingly.[2]

I have also played golf today and yesterday, swinging a mean spoon.

Cheerio, old cake

Oceans of love

Your Plummie

* P. S. No. Wrong. It would fetch <u>two</u> thousand more now than when we bought it.

1 See *The Girl on the Boat*: 'Was this Mrs Hignett *the* Mrs Hignett [...] I'm glad you asked me' (Chapter 1).
2 PGW had begun *Leave It to Psmith* (1923), his second Blandings novel.

TO LEONORA WODEHOUSE

Constitutional Club,
Northumberland Avenue,
W.C.2.

Jan 24. 1922

Darling Snorky.

How's everything? Darned cold, what? So 'm I.

I say, I've got out the plot of a Jeeves story where Bertie visits a girls' school & is very shy and snootered by the girls & the head-mistress. Can you give me any useful details? What would be likely to happen to a chap who was seeing over a school? Do you remember – was it at Ely? – the girls used to sing a song of welcome. Can you give me the words of the song & when it would be sung? And anything else of that sort that would be likely to rattle Bertie.[1]

[...]

Must stop now, as I don't hear the bell ringing.

Love

from Plummie

1 The story that Wodehouse refers to was to become 'Bertie Changes His Mind', in *Carry On, Jeeves* (1925) – the only Jeeves and Wooster story narrated by Jeeves – first published in *The Strand* and *Cosmopolitan* in August 1922.

TO WILLIAM TOWNEND

4, Onslow Square,
S.W.7.

June 27. 1922

Dear Bill.

Sorry I haven't written before. I went away of Thursday for a motor-tour, Ethel and Nora being in France. I took in Stonehenge and finished up at Emsworth for the sports, – a ghastly ordeal. The only time I can stand Emsworth now is when Bud is there alone.[1] All sorts of terrible creatures buttonholed me, who were kids there in the eighties. I find that Ella K-H (or rather W.) is more than I can manage unless I'm feeling very strong. She gasses about old Brook all the time, as if we were bosom friends.

I've just wired to say that I think the story is great. [...] Listen, laddie. Any more humorous plots you can think out will be heartily welcomed. I've got to start another dam series in the *Strand* Feb number, and haven't got any ideas except that I think I'll do a series about Ukridge this time. I have one good plot, where he steals a chap's trousers in order to go to a garden party and all that sort of thing. At the date of the series he is still unmarried and you can make him always in love with girls, like Bingo, if necessary. The keynote of the series is that he and all his pals are devilish hard-up – sort of Leonard Merrick Bohemian stuff, only London[2] – and a plot which has as a punch Ukridge just missing touching a man for two bob would be quite in order.

[...]

Am off to Dinard on July 15.[3] Probably only for a fortnight or three weeks, as rehearsals of Winter Garden show begin in Aug.[4]

I am now contracted to finish a novel, 28 short stories, and a musical show by the end of October. I have no ideas and don't expect to get any. All right, what!

Love to Rene.

Yours ever

Plum

1 Baldwin King-Hall ('Bud'), proprietor and headmaster of Emsworth House School.
2 Leonard Merrick's stylistically dense short stories focused on the fate of artists in the bohemian quarter of Paris.
3 Dinard, a popular holiday resort in Brittany, which provided the inspiration for St Roque, the setting for *Hot Water* (1932).
4 The 'Winter Garden' show was *The Cabaret Girl*, with music by Kern and lyrics by Wodehouse and George Grossmith Jr, a rags to riches showbusiness tale which played on the same formula as *Sally*.

TO LEONORA WODEHOUSE

4, Onslow Square,
S.W.7.

Sept 20. 1922

Darling angel Snorky.

Well, Bill, maybe we didn't do a thing to the customers last p.m. Wake me up in the night and ask me! Honestly, old egg, you never saw such a first night. The audience were enthusiastic all through the first and second acts, and they never stopped applauding during the cabaret scene in act three, – you know, the scene with no dialogue but all music and spectacle. I knew that scene would go big, because the same thing happened at the dress rehearsal.[1]

I take it from your wire this morning [...] that you have seen the notices. They are all very good, but I'm a bit sick that they don't even refer to the lyrics! I haven't seen the evening papers yet. I hope they will continue the good work.

Leslie Henson was up in the gallery through the show!!! It must have been rotten for him, for Griffin made a tremendous hit and there wasn't a moment when the show dropped because of him. Grossmith was immense, so was Heather Thatcher. As for Dorothy Dickson, she came right out and knocked 'em cold.[2]

This morning Mummie and I are not our usual bright selves, as we didn't get to bed till six and woke up at nine! William Boosey gave a party at the Metropole and we didn't leave till 5.30. It was rather funny, – we had the Oppenheims, Justine and Walter, and Beith with us at the show, so they (the Opps) gave us supper at Ciro's, then went on to the Metropole at one o'clock and sat right down to another supper. Even I began to feel as if I had tasted food recently when they brought on oysters and grouse just after I had surrounded a mess of lobster and lamb (with veg.).[3]

[...] There isn't any doubt that we've got an enormous hit. The libraries have taken a lot of seats for three months, the same number they took for *Sally*, and everybody I met last night said the show was splendid. Jerry's music was magnificent. Every number went wonderfully, especially 'Dancing Time'.

Snorky darling, isn't it a nuisance, I've got to sail for New York on Saturday. I hope I shan't be away more than about three months, but I hate being away from Mummie and you. This year I seem to have been separated from you all the time. I do hope Mummie will be able to come over and join me very soon, as I know I shall be lonely. But this Ziegfeld show is sure to be a big thing and I mustn't miss it as I missed *Sally*. All these dramas go to help buy the baby new footwear.

[...]

Your loving

Plummie

PS Do write Bobby a line, precious. He wrote you such a long letter and must be feeling blue all alone at Dinard.

---

1 Though *The Cabaret Girl* was a great hit, running for nearly a year, the run-up to the first production had not gone smoothly. The original star, Leslie Henson, had been taken ill on the morning of the opening. The show was postponed for five days, then opened with Norman Griffin as the lead.
2 A former Follies star, Dorothy Dickson had played the lead in the first London production of *Sally*.

3 PGW's dinner companions included bestselling novelist E. Phillips Oppenheim and Justine Johnstone, one of the Ziegfeld Follies girls who had initially been 'brought on' by PGW and Guy Bolton to appear in *Oh, Boy!*. Johnstone, PGW recalls, was a Norwegian beauty, with the looks and carriage likely to 'provoke the long, low whistle' (*Bring on the Girls*, p. 56). She was married to the film producer Walter Wanger. The other dinner guest, Beith, was the author Ian Hay, who would later collaborate with PGW on three plays.

After the success of The Cabaret Girl, *Wodehouse headed to the USA (under Ziegfeld's urgent instructions) to work on the musical* Pat, *another attempt to work the same Cinderella formula that had been so successful with* Sally *and* The Cabaret Girl. *Wodehouse was also developing a musical called* Sitting Pretty *for two vaudeville comediennes, the Duncan Sisters: 'two small girls who created the impression of being about twelve years old.' – 'They looked like something left over from a defunct kindergarten. [...] Their names were Rosetta and Vivian. [...] Their forte was the delivery of numbers [...] in close harmony, and they were – there is no other word – terrific'.*

TO WILLIAM TOWNEND

17 North Drive
Kensington, Great Neck
Long Island N.Y.
U.S.A.

Dec 16. 1922

Dear Bill.

[...]

Life has been one damned bit of work after another ever since I landed. First, Bolton and I settled down and wrote a musical comedy in two weeks for Ziegfeld. (It has been lying in a drawer ever since. Ziegfeld has been busy over another play, and this one doesn't look like getting put on this year! This, I should mention, is the play Ziegfeld was cabling about with such boyish excitement, – the one I came over to do. You never heard the fuss they made when I announced that I couldn't make the Wednesday boat but would sail on the Saturday. They gave me to understand that my loitering would ruin everything.)

I then sat down to finish *Leave It to Psmith*, for the *Saturday Evening Post*. I wrote 40,000 words in three weeks.

Since then I have been working with Bolton on a musical comedy for the Duncan Sisters, music by Irving Berlin. This is complicated by the fact that Bolton's new comedy has just started rehearsals and he is up to his neck in it. So the work is proceeding by jerks. We were supposed to go into rehearsal tomorrow, but shall not till tomorrow fortnight. All in all, it looks as if I should be here till the Spring.

The good old *Satevepost* have done me proud. Although they never commission anything, they liked the first 60,000 words of my serial so much that they announced it in the papers before I sent in the remainder.[1] I mailed them the last part on a Wednesday and got a cheque for $18,000 (my record) on the following Tuesday!!! That's the way to do business.

[...]

Well, I must ship this screed off now or I shall miss the mail.

Cheerio

Yours ever

Plum

1 *Leave It to Psmith.*

By May, Ethel had joined Wodehouse in Easthampton, where he had been 'working like a beaver' to finish his latest novel, Leave It to Psmith.

TO DENIS MACKAIL

Easthampton
Long Island
USA

May 20. 1923

Dear Denis.

I am bathed in confusion and remorse. Goodness knows why I haven't written to you all this time. [...] I came over here on Sept 23 in response to an urgent cable saying that my presence was needed to put on a show. I have been here ever since, but no show yet! [...] Still, I have had a good time and have improved my golf beyond my wildest dreams. You will scarcely credit it, but I now go round almost habitually in the 80s – generally 85 – and once did a 79. This was at Aiken, down in what is technically known as Dear Old Dixie-Land, where I spent three months of the winter and played eighteen holes every day. [...] We are now down by the sea for the summer and I am getting a taste of seaside links in the wind.[1]

[...]

I think I shall be over in England in August, for the rehearsals of the new Winter Garden piece.[2] George Grossmith is coming here the week after next to work on it with me. He is going to quail when he sees the only bed we have to offer him. As hard as nails and full of small mountains. This is a typical American seashore furnished house, and we have only just got all the china dogs and other horrors hidden away. Still, we Wodehouses can rough it.

[...]

Yours ever

P.G.

---

1 PGW and Ethel had spent some time at Aiken, South Carolina, where PGW won his first and only golfing trophy. 'Playing to a handicap of sixteen', he recalls, 'I went through a field consisting of some of the fattest retired business-men in America like a devouring flame' ('Preface', *The Heart of a Goof* (1926)).
2 The musical *The Beauty Prize*, with music by Jerome Kern, which opened in September 1923.

TO WILLIAM TOWNEND

Easthampton
Long Island, USA

July 23. 1923

Dear Bill.

Have you ever been knocked over by a car? If not, don't. There's nothing in it. I was strolling along yesterday evening to meet Nora who had gone down to the station in our Buick, and half way to the village she sighted me and pulled in to the pavement. The roads here are cement, with a sort of No-Man's Land of dirt between pavement and road. I had just got onto this when I saw a Ford behind our car. Naturally I thought it would pull up when it saw that Nora had stopped, but it must have been going about forty miles an hour, for I suddenly observed with interest that it couldn't stop and was swinging in straight for me on the wrong side of the road to avoid colliding with the Buick. I gave one gazelle-like spring sideways and the dam thing's right wheel caught my left leg squarely and I thought the world had ended. I took the most awful toss and came down on the side of my face. Broke honble glasses and skinned my nose, my left leg, and right arm. Otherwise pretty sound. This morning all sort of unsuspected muscles and bones are aching, and I can hardly move my right arm. But, my gosh, doesn't it just show that we are here today and gone tomorrow! If I had been a trifle less fit and active I should have got the entire car in the wishbone. Oh well, it's all in a lifetime.

Last night I went to bed early and read *Peter the Greek*.[1] For the first half I thought it was the best thing you had ever done, full of action and suspense. But, honestly, as you seem to think yourself from your letter, it does drop a bit after that. [...] Mogger, whom you have established as a sinister menace, gets his teeth drawn too quickly. In the first place he is weakened by that scene with Teame where Teame swats him. Error, I think, ever to have your villain manhandled by a minor character. Just imagine Doctor Moriarty punched by Watson.

A villain ought, until the very end of the story, to be a sort of scarcely human invulnerable figure. The reader ought to be in a constant state of panic, saying to himself 'How the devil <u>is</u> this superman to be foiled?'. The only person capable of hurting him should be the hero. [...] Taking Moriarty as the pattern villain, don't you see how much stronger he is by being an inscrutable figure and how much he would have been weakened if old Conan had switched off to a chapter showing his thoughts?

[...]

I say, laddie, you'll never guess. Reconciliation with Old Brook!!!! I came to the conclusion that it was silly to let a quarrel go on for ten years, so I wrote him an amiable letter, in reply to which I got enclosed!!![2] He doesn't seem to have altered much, what? The only difficulty is that I don't in the least want to see him again, and now I suppose I shall have to.

[...]

Jenkins' death was a great shock to me. I was very fond of him. I always had an idea that he would not last very long. He simply worked himself to death. He was just a fragile thing with a terrific driving mind and no physique at all, one of those fellows who look transparent and seem always tired. I actually had a clause in my contract that, if he should die, the contract lapsed. One used to wonder how long he could possibly last. He shirked his meals and exercise and concentrated entirely on work. You can't do it.

[...] I've given Conrad one more trial and find he is not for me.[3] His leisureliness gets on my nerves. [...]

I wish I could have a couple of hours with you now. I am undergoing one of my periodical fits of depression about my work. I don't seem to have the vim I used to have. But it's probably due to the hot summer and the fact that I have just been working rather hard on a musical comedy which didn't interest me.

So long. Love to Rene. I hope she is getting better every day and that you'll soon be able to come back to England. Do write me a line at the Constitutional.

Yours ever

Plum

1 Townend's story, later published in *Adventure*, April 1924.
2 No 'enclosure' survives.
3 PGW had earlier questioned why 'this bird' (Conrad) 'is such a wonder. Granted, I've only read about three lines he has written! Is he a marvel? I hate his way of telling a story, when you have to think back and add up to see who is speaking' (PGW to William Townend, 28 May 1923 (Dulwich)).

Wodehouse had sailed back to London for three weeks, to rehearse the Winter Garden show, The Beauty Prize. *Although he managed to meet up with Denis Mackail for a curry at the Prince's Grill Room, he never managed to see Townend. Wodehouse refers, in this letter, to the Prince of Wales, who was then twenty-nine years old and was the centre of attention of the British Press. Every new item of clothing he wore became the fashion overnight, and the Embassy Club in Bond Street, which the Prince attended, had become the smartest night-spot in London. The Prince was attracted to the stage and was often to be seen in Adele Astaire's dressing room, when she and her brother Fred were appearing in London. In the following letter, it appears that one of the leading ladies in* The Beauty Prize *had caught the Prince's eye.*

TO WILLIAM TOWNEND

11 King St
St James'
London S.W.

Aug 24. 1923

Dear Bill.

[...]

You've no notion what a ruddy blank London is without you. What a difference it would make if only you were here to yarn with me. I arrived on Aug 6 for the rehearsals of the new Winter Garden piece, and ever since have been in a perfect agony of boredom. What is the matter with London and England generally? A year ago, when I was at Onslow Square and you were just round the corner, I liked being here, but now I am counting the days till I can get away and have decided from now on to live in America. I suppose a lot of this is due to Ethel not being here. I miss her terribly. But, even apart from that, there seems something dead and depressing about London. I don't know what it is. I've suddenly discovered that I don't care any more for watching first-class cricket, and of course that knocks the scheme of things endways, as last year I used to spend all my spare time at the Oval. Oh well, there it is, anyway. [...]

[...]

Bill, my lad, I'm thoroughly fed up with the British aristocracy – don't know why – and also with our old pal the Prince of Wales. He seems to spend all his time hanging round the stage-door of the Winter Garden. I think the press-campaign people have overdone their boosting of him, don't you?

[...]
Yours ever
Plum

Despite the letterhead, Wodehouse writes from Guy Bolton's house in Great Neck.

TO WILLIAM TOWNEND

c/o Guaranty Trust Co
44th St and 5th Ave
New York

November 4. 1923

Dear Bill.

What a shame that we missed each other by a day! Never mind. I have completely given up my idea of settling in America and intend to return to England directly I have cleared up things here.

[...]

Ethel is in Paris, putting Nora at a finishing school. She cables that she likes the place, so maybe we shall give Paris a shot next. I think I would like to potter around Europe a bit. I'm afraid America is only for visits. New York is appalling. All noise and smell. Bracing for an occasional day, but no good for living in.

[...]

I have been meaning to write to you for some time about 'The Talking Doll'. I was awfully sorry when I got Hoffman's letter saying he couldn't use it.

[...]

I seemed to see [...] a story of the same genre as Kipling's 'At the End of the Passage'. It should have ended with a real creepy situation.

[...]

I think you have made a mistake in starting interesting stuff and then dropping it. The beachcomber in chapter one is so intriguing and novel that it is a dull shock to find that he only makes that one appearance.

[...]

The principle I always go on in writing a long story is to think of the characters in terms of actors in a play. I say to myself, when I invent a good character for an early scene, 'If this were a play, we should have to get somebody darned good to play this part, and if he found he had only a short scene in act one he would walk out. How therefore can I twist the story about so as to give him more to do and keep him alive till the fall of the curtain?'

This generally works well and improves the story. A good instance of this was Baxter in *Leave It to Psmith*. It became plain to me as I constructed the story that Baxter was such an important character that he simply had to have a good scene somewhere in what would correspond to the latter part of act two.

I was hoping, till you killed him off, that the beachcomber was going to have a big share in the plot. He was such a new and arresting figure. Did you ever read Ian Hay's *A Knight on Wheels*? He made the same mistake there. He created a wonderful figure, the uncle of a hero, who wrote begging-letters for charitable purposes, and dropped him out of the story one-third of the way through the book. Killing off that beachcomber is almost as bad as if in *Love Among the Chickens* I had dropped Ukridge after chapter one.

[...]

Cheerio,

Yours ever

Plum

TO LEONORA WODEHOUSE

17 Beverly Road
Great Neck
L.I.

Nov 14. 1923

Well, ma belle, how goes it? You like the – how is it you Americans say? – the Gay City, hein?

Over here, figure to yourself how it is triste. One gets through the time somehow, but we miss the delicately nurtured. Life has lost its savour. The world is dull and grey. The only bright spot is Jack, the Cat Supreme.

[...]

Did Mummie tell you I was working on the new novel[1] in a new way, – viz. making a very elaborate scenario, so that when the time came to write the story it would be more like copying out and revising than actual composition. It is panning out splendidly, but is, of course, the dickens of a sweat, because I can't persuade myself that I am really accomplishing any actual work besides just mapping the story out. I have reached about half-way now, and it has taken 30 pages, – each containing 600 words as they are typed close like this letter. That is to say, I have written 18,000 words of scenario, the equivalent of about three short stories!

I must say I think, when it is all finished, I shall be surprised at the speed at which I shall be able to polish off the story. There are whole scenes practically complete with dialogue and everything, and I am getting the beginnings of each chapter right, which is what always holds me up. I often spend a whole morning trying to think of the best way of starting a chapter, and now I shall be able to go right ahead.

I wish you were here to discuss the plot with. I think it is a corker. Certainly it is as good as *Psmith* up to the point where I have got to, and I think the rest will hold up. I have got the plot more or less complete, and am cleaning it up bit by bit.

We are anxiously awaiting letters from our Byng [sic] Girls In Paris.[2] Mummie's first one arrived about a week ago. What a rotten time you must have had at first. C'est toujours ça, what?

Since you left I have met a lot of people you would have liked. Donald Ogden Stewart is about the best candidate for your hand that we have dug up as yet. A very cheery bird. Very ugly, but what of that? We have also seen quite a lot of Elsie Ferguson, who is very nice. Mummie would like her.[3] Guy is doing a play for her, and she lives about two hundred yards away in North Drive.

[...]

I am wondering if you and Mummie have decided that Paris is a good spot for the family to take up its headquarters. I must say I shouldn't mind trying it for a bit. I have got very tired of America.

Great Neck seems quite different this year. Last winter, with the good old loved ones around me, I enjoyed it tremendously, but it makes me restless now. I suppose it is simply because I miss you and Mummie. This bachelor life is no good for me at all.

Oh yes, I was forgetting. I have also met Scott Fitzgerald.[4] In fact, I met him again this morning. He was off to New York with Truex, who is doing his play, *The Vegetable*.[5] I believe those stories you hear about his drinking are exaggerated. He seems quite normal, and is a very nice chap indeed. You would like him. The only thing is, he goes into New York with a scrubby chin, looking perfectly foul. I suppose he gets a shave when he arrives there, but it doesn't show him at his best in Great Neck. I would like to see more of him.

[...]

Denis Mackail has a splendid story in the *Strand* this month.[6] I wish you were here. I should like to discuss him with you. Is he a menace or simply a young fellow trying to get along? I'll tell you one thing, his mind either runs on very similar lines to mine or else he pinches my stuff. The plot of this story is based on an idea exactly like 'The Man with Two Left Feet'.

Well, cheerio, old sort. Je vous Embrasse.

Your

Plummie

1 *Bill the Conqueror* (1924).
2 Wodehouse alludes to *The Bing Boys Are Here* – the hugely successful London show of 1916 featuring the hit song 'If You Were the Only Girl in the World'.
3 Donald Ogden Stewart was a noted 1920s playwright; Elsie Ferguson, a famous Broadway and silent movie actress.
4 The novelist F. Scott Fitzgerald had become famous with *This Side of Paradise* (1920) and *The Beautiful and Damned* (1922).
5 Ernest Truex (1889–1973), Broadway actor, and PGW's Long Island acquaintance.
6 Mackail's new story was 'At Mr Besley's'.

17 Beverly Rd
Great Neck,
L.I.
U.S.A.

December 23. 1923

[...]

Tonight we are all going to the opening of Oscar Hammerstein's play *Mary Jane McKane*. He is doing a terrific amount of work now. [...] Mrs Hammerstein is coming to lunch today. We are having our dinner in the middle of the day.

Oh, by the way. Mummie tells me that you have taken to wine in your old age. I wish you wouldn't. I have always pointed with pride to you as the one female in the world who can subsist on water. I should preserve the record, if I were you.

We had quite a scare at the Customs when Mummie returned. The poor boobs knew that she had brought in a lot of jewelry, and they thought we still had a residence at Great Neck, especially as all her baggage was labelled for there. So a detective stopped us as we were leaving and wanted to know where we thought we got off. I told him we had sold our house in 1920, and he retired, bathed in confusion.

Jack the cat has got a red ribbon round his neck today. Looks an awful ass.

That's all. Cheerio.

Bolton and Wodehouse were at Bolton's house, working on the lyrics for Sitting Pretty. *Irving Berlin and his partner, Sam Harris, had lost interest in the piece, as the Duncan sisters no longer wished to star in the musical. It was rescued by Ray Comstock, who had been the producer of Wodehouse, Bolton and Kern's 'Princess' musicals.*

17 Beverly Rd
Great Neck, L.I.
U.S.A.

Christmas Morning
(or, putting it another way,
Dec 25. 1923)

My precious angel Snorky.

Your lovely letter (*billet le plus charmant*) arrived this morning while I was at breakfast (*déjeuner*) champing (filling *le visage avec*) about half a pound of sausages (*saussisons*) [*sic*]. It caused great fun and laughter among both young and old.

I have been working so darned hard these last few weeks that I hadn't even time for a letter to you. Did Mummie tell you I had sold the novel to the *Sat Eve Post* for $20,000?[1] (Of course, they haven't actually accepted it in so many words, but they read the scenario and said it was just what they wanted and agreed to the price, so it is all o.k.). I have now had a cable from England saying the *Strand* will publish it in England and pay twelve hundred and fifty quid. So it looks like a white Christmas, what?

I am enclosing the original scenario. I can't send one of the typed copies, as two are out and I have to keep the third to work with. Still, you'll be able to read this one all right. I want you to tell me frankly if it isn't a pippin. It seems to me quite as good a story as *Psmith*, though of course I shall miss Psmith when it comes to dialogue, – though I think Judson will be a good comedian.[2]

[...]

Thanks awfully for the handkerchiefs. As nifty a lot as I have ever had. Dashed good of you to send them. Mummie is having them marked, and I shall treasure them.

[...]

Well, Snorky, old lad, a million blessings. ('Peace on thy head!' 'Two pieces on yours!') I'll write again very anon.

Your loving
Plummie

1 *Bill the Conqueror*.

2 The novel's hero, Bill, is required to keep an eye on his best friend Judson Coker, a 'devout drinker'. Judson consequently causes much trouble for Bill.

TO WILLIAM TOWNEND

17 Beverly Road
Great Neck
Long Island, U.S.A.
(Permanent address till I leave America)

Jan 26. 1924

Dear Bill.

I'm awfully sorry I haven't written for so long. I have had a great drive of work against time, having completed 55,000 words of a new novel in a month!

[...]

I say, listen, old horse. Is this a crazy idea? 'The Haunting of the Hyacinth' or some such title. I suddenly thought the other day, there are always rats on board ship, so why shouldn't one rat, starting by being a bit bigger than the others, gradually grow and grow, feeding on his little playmates, till he became about the size of an Airedale terrier. Then there begin to be mysterious happenings on the ship. Men are found dead etc. End with big scene where your hero discovers and is attacked by Honble Rat in the dark of the hold or somewhere. Big fight and so on.

Is this any good to you? It certainly isn't to me. I should have to put the rat in an eyeglass and have the hero trip over a tub of potatoes. But you might see something in it. Anyway, I give it you with my blessing.

[...] At present, it seems to me that your stuff is too psychological for the low-brow magazines. It's good because you make one interested in your people. But can't you do something that would be interesting absolutely independent of who it happened to, – e.g. a fight with a giant rat. (I defy anyone not to be interested in a fight with a giant rat. Personally I would run a mile to avoid unpleasantness with a small one).[1]

[...]
Cheerio. Must stop now. Write again soon.
Yours ever
Plum

1 Townend did indeed use the idea that PGW suggested here in a 1934 *Harper's* magazine story, forgetting that PGW had given it to him (*Performing Flea*, p. 24).

TO LEONORA WODEHOUSE

> 17 Beverly Road
> Great Neck
> U.S.A.

Feb 4. 1924

Darling angel Snorky.

Your long letter made a big hit in the home. We weren't so keen, though, on this fainting business. Where do you get that stuff? I hope your cold is all right again now, and that you are once more settled down to the gaieties of that dear Paris.

Well, say, listen, kid, lemme tell ya sum'fin. I sent the first 70,000 words of *Bill the Conqueror* off to the typist (*la sténographie*) yesterday, and believe me or believe me not, it's <u>good</u>. I'm taking a day off today and tomorrow [to] plunge into the remaining 25,000, which ought to be pie. This is certainly one swell story, as good as the old man has ever done, and, thank God, I have been able to work in that line about 'I know it's paraffin, but what have they put in it?'. Judson has worked out immense, and Flick, the heroine, is so like you that the cognoscenti cannot help but be charmed.

[...]

I've never worked so well on a novel before. I must have done over 50,000 words in a month. Oh yes, and I forgot to say that Ray has now gone cold on *Pat*, so we shall have to try and place it elsewhere. Ziegfeld wired from Palm Beach asking if it would do for Leon Errol, but that only evoked from us a faint, sad smile. We know these Ziegfeld commissions.

Talking of Palm Beach, this place has closely resembled it this winter. Thermometer never below forty, and last Sunday up to fifty-six. Gorgeous Spring weather, in which I have revelled.

Mummie is going great guns. She has developed into a regular athlete. She comes out for long walks with me and <u>runs</u> half the way. She is the nearest thing to the untamed jack-rabbit of the Californian prairie you ever saw.

[...]

We loved the photographs. You looked very beautiful. Though, while on the subject of looking beautiful, you ought to see the Light of the Home in her Paris dresses. A pip, believe me. She flashed the blue one with the white fur collar on me the other day and I keeled over. Nor is the beige to be despised. Mummie simply is sylph-like now, as slim as anything.

[...]

Well, cheerio. Will write again very soon, if I can take an hour off from finishing *Bill*. I must get it finished this month, as the *Post* won't start it till it is complete and they have to have the stuff six weeks in advance.

Your loving
Plummie

Wodehouse travelled from America to Paris (where Ethel bought a new wardrobe) before moving on to London, then Emsworth, and finally Harrogate, with the aim of sampling the spa waters. Wodehouse used his visits to Harrogate (and later Droitwich) to inform the background of a number of short stories – most notably his 1937 story 'Romance at Droitgate Spa'.

TO LEONORA WODEHOUSE

Sept 12. 1924

Darling Snorky.

We are so awfully worried about your cold, darling. You simply must make a real business of taking care of yourself, because you are evidently not any too strong – good opening for joke here, but I can hear you saying 'Obvious!'. Do please wrap up warmly, especially when you come back to England, as the climate is so rotten.

[...]

Harrogate isn't such a bad old spot. I played golf today for the first time and feel fine. The waters taste quite ordinary now, though the first two times I took them it was too awful for words. Exactly like rotten eggs.

[...]

Mummie is the belle of the hotel, and dances like a breeze. Oh, by the way, there's no holding her now. A woman wrote to the *Tatler*, asking the editor to settle a bet by telling her which was Mrs Wodehouse and which Miss Wodehouse in that photo of us [see plate 22]. The side Mummie has been sticking on ever since has been something awful, – only equalled by mine when a letter turned up the other day addressed to 'P. G. Wodehouse, London'. I am going to write to myself and address it 'P. G. Wodehouse, England' and see if it arrives. The next step will be to send one addressed simply 'P. G. Wodehouse'.

I do a lot of reading here, and have added three new Edgar Wallaces to my collection! Unfortunately, the last, which I got this morning, is a dud and not worth reading.

The Winter Garden show opened last night (unless it was postponed).[1] We have heard no news of it. The morning papers never contain the notices, as I suppose they start from London too early. There will be something in the Sunday papers, though.

Cheerio.

Your

Plummie

1 *Primrose*, book by Bolton and Grossmith, music by George Gershwin and lyrics by Desmond Carter and Ira Gershwin.

Grand Hotel
Harrogate
Yorks

Sept 23. 1924

Dear Bill.

Awfully sorry I haven't written for long. I've been dashed busy. I've done a couple of short stories since I got here and also practically completed scenario of a new novel.

By the way, can you possibly let me use that idea of yours about a fellow getting engaged to three girls, two of them in Cardiff? It would be a godsend. I just want it to establish a character.

[...]

I say, do you like the title: – SAM IN THE SUBURBS

I have got a good central idea. Hero takes semi-detached house at Dulwich next door to heroine, who has told him she never wants to see him again, and they scrap across the wall. Hero's dog assaults heroine's kitten and so on. Meanwhile, crooks are trying to get at stolen bonds which a former crook has buried somewhere in hero's house. See? It's working out fine.

[...]

Did I ever tell you I met Brook again? !!!! Went to dinner at his house. He's awful! All his old affectations increased to the nth power. He gives me the heebie-jeebies.

[...]

Cheerio. Love to Rene.

Yours ever

Plum

While in Harrogate, Wodehouse reported a 'rather odd' experience in which he 'got the idea for a short story, "Honeysuckle Cottage", absolutely complete one morning [...] and wrote it practically at a sitting. Some time after I went out to a séance and a spirit spoke, saying among other things that he had been with me at Harrogate and had helped me. Curious, wasn't it.

That was the séance where Leonora and I, who were sitting well apart from each other, heard a voice say "Loretta Wodehouse". Loretta was the name of a little girl who worked for us at Great Neck when Snorky was a kid, and she and Snorky were inseparable. She was devoted to us and died a few years later. Her surname was Ninesling, but both Snorky and I heard the words "Loretta Wodehouse". I have never known what to make of it.'

TO WILLIAM TOWNEND

Harrogate

Oct 1. 1924

Dear Bill.

[...]

Thanks awfully about the three men and girl. Also about the atmosphere stuff for the ship. I haven't been able to give a thought to my novel for ten days, having in that time written two short stories, both dam good. This may not be much of a place to live one's life in, but it's a great spot for work. I leave here on Friday and settle down for nine months at 23 Gilbert St, Grosvenor Square, where we have a butler who is a V.C. (Either that or a D.S.O.) What does one say to a V.C. butler if one wasn't in the war oneself? I think I shall start, 'Well, Meadowes, and what is that medal for? Saving life at sea?'.[1]

The short story I have just finished, entitled 'Honeysuckle Cottage', is the damnedest funniest idea I've ever had.[2] A young writer of detective stories gets left five thousand quid and a house by his aunt, who was Leila May Pinckney, the famous writer of sentimental stories. He finds that her vibrations have set up a sort of miasma of sentimentalism in the place, so that all who come within its radius get soppy and maudlin. He then finds to his horror that he is ... but it will be simpler to send you the story, so I am doing so. I polished it up a good bit in typing it out.

[...]

How splendid that Rene is getting better. Talking of getting better, there was no earthly need for us to come to Harrogate at all. Ethel did not drink the waters, and only had massage treatment which she could have got equally well in London. I, on the other hand, who thought I had nothing the matter with me was ordered sulphur water twice a day.

[...]

Did you read Wells' *The Dream?* Pretty good. But what asses his Utopians are.[3]

Well, cheerio. I do hope we can meet soon.

Yours ever

Plum

1 The reference to 'Meadowes' relates to Jeeves's predecessor as Bertie Wooster's valet, who was fired for stealing Bertie's silk socks in 'Jeeves Takes Charge' (1916), repr. in *Carry On, Jeeves* (1925). The name would later be used for Archibald Mulliner's valet in 'The Reverent Wooing of Archibald' (1928, repr. in *Mr Mulliner Speaking*, 1929), and 'Archibald and the Masses' (1935, repr. in *Young Men in Spats*, 1936). By way of contrast, in *The Mating Season* (1949), Bertie Wooster (using the pseudonym Gussie Fink-Nottle) pretends to have a valet named Meadowes, who is actually his friend, Catsmeat Potter-Pirbright.
2 PGW's 'Honeysuckle Cottage' (1925, repr. in *Mr Mulliner Speaking*, 1927), a brilliant parody of the 1920s romantic novelette, also sheds light on his interest at this time in matters occult. This was a period in which he attended at least three séances at the home of H. Dennis Bradley, a popular writer on spiritualist matters (see McCrum, p. 163).
3 H. G. Wells' *The Dream*, a novel about a man from a utopian future who dreams the life of a twentieth-century man, was published in 1924.

TO WILLIAM TOWNEND

23 Gilbert St.
Mayfair, W.

Nov 12. 1924

Dear Bill.

[...]

I enclose a sheet of questions, which you will save my life by answering. They come in chapter three,[1] the chapter I ought to be working on now. Owing to lack of technical atmosphere I have had to skip and start writing chapter twelve!

[...]

Chapter Three starts as follows:

Sam Shotter stood outside the galley of the tramp steamer *Araminta* in pleasant conversation with Clarence – ('Soup') Todhunter, – the vessel's popular and energetic cook.

Now then:

(A) How was Sam dressed? (All his luggage had come over on the *Mauretania* and he had sea-clothes on. This is very important, as in next chapter it is essential that Sam shall look like a dead-beat and be taken for a burglar.)

(B) What did Sam see, hear and smell, as he stood outside the galley?

(C) Sam is the stepson of a millionaire and has a penchant for travelling on tramps. He must have had at least one voyage on the *Araminta* before, because it is essential that he knows the skipper well. Therefore, in what capacity did he sail? Would it be ship's etiquette for him to chum up with the skipper as well as the cook?

(D) On the voyage the only thing Sam has to look at has been a photograph of a girl cut out of the *Tatler*. Could he have a cabin to himself? And do you call it a cabin or a state-room?

(E) The *Araminta* is sailing from America to England. How long would the voyage take? Also, where would she start from, and where dock? Could she dock at Port of London, and be going on to Cardiff?

(F) I particularly want Sam to be in London when Chapter starts so that he has an easy trip to the West End, which is the setting of the next chapter. Please give me some atmosphere for Port of London, or wherever it is, i.e. something for Sam to see from the deck of the ship.

(G) Can you possibly write me a description of Soup Todhunter from your knowledge of ship's cooks? It is immaterial what he looks like, of course, but it will help.

[...]

Well, that's all I can think of at present... I do hope you're not busy on anything just now, as I don't want to interrupt you... I can skip the sea stuff and go on working on the shore scenes till you are ready.

1 *Sam the Sudden* (1925) – US title *Sam in the Suburbs*. Townend replied in detail, but in the end few of his suggestions were used.

In 1925, Wodehouse spent some time on the French Riviera, having his 'usual struggle' to get new ideas. A letter written to Townend in April

*mentions 'a luncheon with old Sir Coning' (Conan Doyle). 'He has written
a spiritualistic novel (!!).'*

In early December, the Times Literary Supplement *published a brief
and fairly cursory review of Wodehouse's latest novel,* Bill the Conqueror:
'Bill West, the nephew of Mr Paradene, an American millionaire, though
he knows nothing whatever about his uncle's business is sent over to investigate a marked falling-off in the profits of the London branch. In a midnight
escapade he comes across pretty Flick Sheridan just as she is running away
from home rather than marry a weak-kneed son of a newspaper peer. Bill
and a friend take her under their wing, and she obtains a stenographer's
situation with Slingsby, Mr. Paradene's London manager. True, she only
stays there one morning, but that suffices for her to discover that Slingsby
is a crook, so that when, after a great many more equally improbable
episodes, Bill and Flick are at last married and Mr. Paradene appears on
the scene, Bill is able to inform him that he has succeeded in his mission
and is thereupon made manager himself, though he still knows nothing
whatever about the business, at any salary he cares to name.'*

TO DENIS MACKAIL

23 Gilbert Street
Mayfair

Dec 4. 1924

Dear Denis.

Your letter was like the well-known balm in Gilead. I was sitting in a
corner, muttering to myself and licking my wounds, when it arrived,
and it cheered me up.

The bitter part of the whole affair is that, while I usually read the
Times Lit Sup at the club, this time I went out and bought a copy, so
that in addition to having my finest feelings gashed I am threepence
out of pocket, with no hope in sight of getting back at them.

I have been analysing my feelings towards reviews, and my position
is this. I don't mind the review which says 'Why the devil this ass
sells a single copy, we cannot understand, but there is no getting away
from the fact that he sells thousands', but a notice like this, which

might have been that of the first book of an amateur, cuts deep. It is particularly maddening because in a sense it is all perfectly true. She – I agree with you that it was written by a governess – simply omits to mention that I have gone to great pains to cover each of the points she raises, so that in the book they are quite plausible. But what's the use? I feel as if someone had flung an egg at me from a bomb-proof shelter. But your letter has made me feel ever so much better, and I am holding my head up again.

I should love to see *Patricia* next week.[1] The only thing is that the Boss insists on seeing it, too, which rather dishes the Athenaeum dinner.[2] I think the best plan would be for you to come and dine here. We can then discuss all sorts of matters before going on. By this system you get a glass (or more) of the Wodehouse port, which you would otherwise miss.

Cheerio. Death to the *Times.*

Yours ever

Plum

1 A comedy in three acts by Denis Mackail, Arthur Stanley and Austin Melford, with music by Geoffrey Gwyther.
2 Though he dined there from time to time, Wodehouse was not a member of the Athenaeum (a club known as 'that morgue' by Wodehouse's Galahad Threepwood).

Wodehouse, Ethel and Leonora were frequent visitors to Hunstanton Hall in Norfolk, both together and separately [see plate 23]. Hunstanton was, Wodehouse wrote, 'one of those enormous houses, about two-thirds of which are derelict. There is a whole wing which has not been lived in for half a century [...] thousands of acres, park, gardens, moat, etc., and priceless heirlooms, but not a penny of ready money.' In practical terms, Hunstanton provided a writing refuge away from the constant socialising of Mayfair life. The house, an eclectic mix of rambling carrstone and pebble, with its surrounding grounds, also acted as an imagined stage set for much of his fiction, providing rose-gardens in which to find romance, stout downspouts by which to escape it, and moats into which characters might fall and be duly rescued. Its atmosphere of genteel poverty, with its dusty heirlooms and brooding butlers, informs so much of his fiction. Aunt Agatha's house at Woollam Chertsey, with its 'miles of what they call rolling parkland, trees in considerable profusion well provided with doves and what-not cooing in no uncertain voice' has its roots in Hunstanton, along with the crumbling Rudge Hall in Money for Nothing. *The owner of Hunstanton, Charles Le Strange, was a 'keen breeder of jersey cows', and Wodehouse bestowed elements of his host's interest in livestock on his hero Lord Emsworth. As Norman Murphy notes, Hunstanton's pig-sty was likely to have been the inspiration for the most impressive of all Wodehouse's characters, the Empress of Blandings.*

TO WILLIAM TOWNEND

23 Gilbert St.
Mayfair, W.

December 22. 1924

Dear Bill.

[...]

We are off to Norfolk for Christmas. Back in about a week, I imagine. Hunstanton Hall, Hunstanton is the address, c/o Charles L'Estrange. (Who is, between ourselves, a weird bird, but he has the most wonderful house.)

I'm awfully glad you liked *Sally*. I don't remember the *Times* review of it, but they seem to loathe my stuff. They gave *Bill the Conqueror* a rotten notice. However, it doesn't seem to make much difference.[1]

Do you find you work easily these days? I've been having a deuce of a job on my new story. The stuff, when I've done it, is all right but I don't seem able to write more than about three or four pages a day. I found that over *Sally*, which I wrote in London, so I suppose it's something to do with being in London. Of course, I have had a lot of interruptions in the shape of dinners and things. I don't know why it should affect my work if I am going out to dinner, but it does. It always makes me stop an hour before I need.

[...]

Yours ever

Plum

P.S. Merry Christmas and all that. Though I'm always glad when it's over, aren't you?

1 Despite 'rotten notices', *Bill the Conqueror* 'sold 10,000 copies on the day of publication. Hot stuff' (PGW to Townend, 17 November 1924 (Dulwich)).

Missing the American sunshine, the Wodehouses set off for the South of France.

TO LEONORA WODEHOUSE

Gallia Hotel,
Cannes*
(*Famous Pleasure Resort – Ha, ha!)

March 30. 1925

Darling Snorkles.

I am now at last in a position to give you the low-down on the Riviera, as based on the observations of self and egg-scrambler. Two days ago, I was gloomy and pessimistic on the subject of the entire Cote D'Azur, especially featuring Cannes, and Mummie reproached me, saying that Cannes was really a delightful spot. Next day, I was all chirpiness and joie de vivre and went about pointing out villas which we could buy and live in for the rest of our lives, while Mummie maintained a strange silence. Today, suddenly, we both exclaimed together that we thought Cannes the most loathly hole in the known world and that, once we got out of this damned Riviera, nothing short of armed troops would induce us to return.

Of all the poisonous, foul, ghastly places, Cannes takes the biscuit with absurd ease. Until we came here, I was thinking Monte Carlo not all it might be, but now I look back to those dear old Monte Carlo days with an absolute pang.

Mummie says in her letter that we have done nothing here but stay in the hotel and walk on the front, but this, with the exception of going to the Casino, is all there is to do. The only tolerable thing about

Cannes is the hotel garden, which contains ornamental water with ducks, water-rats etc, and forms an oasis in this bloodsome desert. Mummie and I have come to the conclusion that we loathe foreign countries. We hate their ways, their architecture, their looks, their language and their food. So we must simply buckle to and get a house for you in England somewhere. I am all for the Chippenham neighbourhood. We both want dogs and cats and cows and meadow-land. Directly you get out of England you get nothing but spiky palms and other beastly shrubs. I asked someone yesterday who was recommending St Juan les Pins as a spot where you might obtain rustic comfort within reach of the gay (Ha!) Cannes life if we could buy plenty of ground there. She said Oo yes! Certainly enough for a tennis lawn. That's their idea of a rolling estate, these poor damned souls out here. If they have a stucco villa with another stucco villa adjoining it and two more stucco villas on each side and a back yard with a potted cactus, they expand their chests and say 'Gosh! This rural solitude is the stuff!'. Blast, if I may use the expression, them.

Of course, in many ways Cannes is most delightful. (I mention this because I am leaving this letter on the machine while I go down to dinner, and I think the maid can read English.)

To resume. March 31st.

Good news today. Cable from America saying that the script of *Sam in the Suburbs* has arrived safely.

On the other hand, ghastly shock. The editor of the Newnes magazine which is running *Sam* serially wants to change the title and have [*sic*] decided on SUNSHINE SAM!!!!! I have written anguished letters of protest to Mrs Westbrook and also to E. V. Lucas of Methuen. Can you imagine such a foul title? Isn't it pure Ruby M. Ayres? The only thing it could be except Ruby M. Ayres is Harold Bell Wright, in which case Sunshine Sam would be a quaint, drawling old Westerner, who cheers up the other cowboys with his homely philosophy, showing that you can be happy though poor, provided you do as the good book says.[1]

I thought that terrific about the Nevada accident and Thank God this wasn't you. Also the nifty about April.

Mummie's cold doesn't seem to get any better. How can it in this plague-spot?

We are now dickering with the idea of a little flat in Paris as our official address and a country house in England for you. How long ago it seems that I was writing home roasting Paris. I hadn't seen the Riviera then.

Do you know anything about Chantilly? That might be a solution. Near Paris and on a golf-links. I went there once, and thought it fairly decent, but don't remember it very well.

[...]

I've been sitting out in the garden all afternoon, and, by Jove, Cannes doesn't seem so bad after all. I think the solution is never to go into it. I propose to spend all my time in the garden from now on.

Cheerio

Your

Plummie

P.S. April 1. Not such a bad place, Cannes! We went to the Casino last night & I won 500 francs, which makes me feel a bit benevolent. Also, Italian musicians have been singing under our window this morning, all very jolly.

---

1 Wodehouse's alarm about the branding of his current novel was unwarranted. In the end, the UK edition bore the title *Sam the Sudden*. The romantic novelist Ruby M. Ayres (1883–1955) gains a sneer from Wodehouse here, but she was not without her uses. Ayres is often seen as the model for Wodehouse's fictional character Rosie M. Banks, author of works such as *Madcap Myrtle* and *Only a Factory Girl*, who marries Bingo Little. Harold Bell Wright (1872–1944) was a bestselling American writer who outsold any other writer in the first quarter of the twentieth century.

TO DENIS MACKAIL

23 Gilbert Street, Mayfair, W.

June 18. 1925

Dear Denis.

I started the sale of *Greenery Street* off with a bang this afternoon by rushing into Hatchard's and insisting on a copy.¹ They pretended it wasn't out. I said I had seen it mentioned among 'Books Received' in my morning paper. They said in a superior sort of way that the papers got their copies early. I then began to scream and kick, and they at once produced it.

When I had got to page 42, I had to break off to write this letter. No longer able to hold enthusiasm in check. It is simply terrific, miles the best thing you have ever done – or anyone else, for that matter. It's so good that it makes one feel that it's the only possible way of writing a book, to take an ordinary couple and just tell the reader about them. It's the sort of book one wishes would go on for ever. That scene where Ian comes to dinner is pure genius.

The only possible criticism I would make is that it is not the sort of book which should be put into the hands of one who ought to be working on a short story. Ethel got skinned to the bone at Ascot yesterday – myself present, incidentally, in a grey tophat and white spats – and I promised her I would work all day today at something that would put us square. So far I have done nothing but read *Greenery Street*.

[...]

Yours ever

P. G. Wodehouse

1 *Greenery Street*, a tale of domestic life in Chelsea, was based on Mackail's early experiences of married life on Walpole Street – which, coincidentally, was Wodehouse's address for much of 1901 to 1908.

Wodehouse had planned to spend the summer of 1925 at Hunstanton Hall, but instead accepted what he referred to as a 'ghastly task' – to work on The Nightingale, *a musical about the life of the Victorian artiste Jenny Lind – and ended up spending the latter part of 1925 in America, including a few weeks on Ziegfeld's yacht. Wodehouse had also been making a few new publication deals, and switched his American serial publication allegiance from the* Saturday Evening Post *to* Liberty *magazine.* Liberty *would be publishing his latest novel,* The Small Bachelor, *in the autumn of 1926. Reynolds discovered that the editor of the* Post, *Mr Lorimer, 'was rather angry about Wodehouse [...] but he thought at the end of next year he would be ready to take him back'.*

In the summer of 1926, Wodehouse spent a dutiful fortnight with his parents at their home in Bexhill-on-Sea, on the Sussex coast. 'The spot which God forgot' was to become the model for many of Wodehouse's 'bracing' fictional seaside resorts, disguised, variously, as 'Bramley' or 'Bingley-on-Sea'.

TO WILLIAM TOWNEND

Hunstanton Hall
Norfolk

June 26. 1926

[...]

I have been spending two weeks at Bexhill, the spot which God forgot, but am now in my beloved Hunstanton and am writing this sitting in a punt on the moat with my typewriter on a bed-table balanced on one of the seats. There is a duck close by which makes occasional quacks that sound just like a man with an unpleasant voice saying nasty things in an undertone.

When I was at Bexhill, I thought to myself 'I'll just pop round the corner and see old Bill', having got a sort of idea that Cliftonville was just beyond Hastings. I then looked at a map and found that the journey was about a hundred miles, so that was off.

I am trembling on the verge of making another trip to America. I have had a cable from Guy Bolton asking me to sail on July 8th and do a show with him.[1] I am trying to put it off till the 24th. I am torn between a loathing of leaving Ethel for a couple of months and a desire not to let a good thing get by me.

[...]

1 Guy Bolton's planned show was to become the hit musical *Oh, Kay!*, featuring Gertrude Lawrence. Wodehouse had drawn on a 1923 anecdote from his Easthampton days for this 'light-hearted Prohibition frolic', recalling one of Ethel's more unusual evenings out, when she, Leonora and George Grossmith found themselves driven, in full evening dress, from the dinner table to the shore, to unload a stash of rum.

Wodehouse sailed back to America on 24 July, and recalls spending the summer in the American heat: 'it is not too much to say that I played like one of those fountains at Versailles, taking off some fourteen pounds in weight. [...] Gertie was angelic to work with'. The following fan letter suggests that Wodehouse considered working in Hollywood at this point, but there is no record as to whether any film work took place.

TO MR DAVIES

17 North Drive
Great Neck N.Y.
USA

August 17. 1926

[...]

In November I am going to California to write some moving-pictures. It ought to be very interesting seeing them made and meeting all the picture stars. I have known Douglas Fairbanks for a good many years & like him very much. I suppose I shall meet Charlie Chaplin this time.

The man I am going to write pictures for is Raymond Griffith. Have you ever seen him on the screen? I haven't, but they tell me he is very good.

[...]

Back in London after the success of Oh, Kay!, Wodehouse left Bobby Denby to organise some of his business matters. In early January, Denby negotiated a settlement with the Famous Players film company to cancel one of Wodehouse's contracts, earning Wodehouse the settlement sum of $7,500. Denby cabled Wodehouse that he had settled for $5,500, regarding the rest as commission. Denby's letter of explanation to Wodehouse, which crossed with the outraged telegram below, stated that 'your $5,500, of course, is absolutely pure velvet which comes to you, to a great extent, through our initiative in suggesting the business. Is that all right old man?'

Western Union Cablegram,
Received at 40 Broad Street,
New York

Jan 22. 1927

CANNOT UNDERSTAND YOU CABLING THAT YOU HAVE SETTLED
FOR FIVE-THOUSAND FIVEHUNDRED DOLLARS WHEN THE SUM
WAS REALLY SEVENTHOUSAND FIVEHUNDRED DOLLARS STOP I
WILL NOT CONSENT FOR A MOMENT TO YOU AND PUTNEY [sic]
TAKING ONE THOUSAND APIECE AS COMMISSION AND YOU MUST
HAVE KNOWN IT WHEN YOU SENT YOUR CABLE STOP PLEASE
DEPOSIT THE FULL SUM MINUS TEN PERCENT COMMISSION IN
GUARANTY TRUST

WODEHOUSE.

In 1927, Wodehouse had just completed arguably his finest work to date,
Summer Lightning. *Reynolds was negotiating for a $40,000 serialisation*
with Collier's Weekly. *Wodehouse writes from a new rented sixteen-room*
house, just off Park Lane in Mayfair, which seemed to match the scale of
his latest success. 'The [...] running of the establishment called for a retinue
of servants such as the Wodehouses had never before required. There was
a morning secretary to keep the household-expenses books, an afternoon
secretary [...] a cook, a butler, a kitchen maid, two housemaids, one lady's
maid, one odd-job man, and a chauffeur for the new Rolls Royce.'

17, Norfolk Street,
Park Lane. W.1.

Feb 5. 1927

Dear Reynolds.

Thanks very much for the *Vanity Fair* articles, which arrived safely.

[...]

In re Denby. I am rather at the outs with that man of wrath. He cabled me that the Famous Players wanted to cancel that contract of mine and would I leave it to him to make the best terms. I said yes, and he then cabled 'Have settled for $5500'.

Naturally, thinking the money so much velvet, I cabled back Yes. I then get a letter from him saying that the price the F.P. actually paid was $7500, but, in consideration of the trouble they had taken, he assumed I would have no objection to him and Putnam taking $1000 each commission, as I had already cabled that $5500 was satisfactory to me!!!

[...] I cabled back to him at great expense that I wanted the entire sum minus the customary 10%, and I have also written to Putnam to that effect.

Denby has paid in $5500 to my account, and there is another $1250 to come. If there is any hesitation on his part in paying this in, will you send me the 5% you pay him on my stories till the sum is made up?

Don't let this make any difference to you in your dealings with Denby. I think he is a very useful man provided you keep a sharp eye on him and don't let him have the handling of the money. I should be quite willing for him to handle movie deals for me <u>through you</u>, but never again through Putnam.

The whole thing reminds me of the time when Abe Baerman asked me if I would take $75 for the first story he sold for me, to which I agreed eagerly and then found that the editor had paid $100. Considering that Denby owes me nearly two thousand five hundred pounds, I think the thing was a bit thick.

Mind you, I don't suppose he deliberately thought he was doing anything dishonest. Like all those smart, hustling devils, his mind works in a peculiar way. He argued 'Wodehouse will be pleased with $5500, therefore why give him more?'. It is just the same as if you have told me that *Collier's* would give me $32,500 for this next serial. I should have said to myself 'Ah! A nice advance in price. Grab it.'

But doesn't it make your mouth water, as an agent, – this idea of scooping in $2000 on a $7500 deal!!!

I am in great shape with the writing these days. I have finished two more short stories and am three parts of the way though two more, with about ten plots up my sleeve in addition to the plot of a serial. I am going to try and work off half a dozen short stories before starting the serial.

I have just been asked to write the next show for the Astaires, so I shall be over in New York again towards the middle of July.

Yours ever

P. G. Wodehouse

TO WILLIAM TOWNEND

17. Norfolk Street,
Park Lane. W.1.

Feb 12. 1927

Dear Bill.

A long time since we communicated, laddie. How is everything with you? I hope old Hoffer is doing his bit.

I have been sweating away with incredible vim since I saw you last. I had a cable from Gilbert Miller asking me to rush through an adaptation of a French piece, which I had thought was a November job.[1] I got this shipped off, and now I read in the papers that his play *The Captive* in New York has been pulled by the police and everybody connected with it arrested![2] I'm afraid this is liable to take his mind off my piece. His last cable said that they were going into rehearsal last Monday. Since then I have heard nothing.

I have also written three short stories since I got back from Hunstanton on Jan 8.

It is an infernal nuisance your being so far away. I wish you could settle for awhile in London. I miss our walks and talks. Isn't it curious how few people there are in the world whom one wants to see. Yesterday, I looked in at the Garrick at lunch time, took one glance of loathing at the mob, and went off to lunch by myself at the Cheshire Cheese.

This house is still in an awful mess, with workmen all over the place, and Ethel says she loathes it. As a matter of fact, when it is finished I think she will like it. It's going to be pretty hot. My library is magnificent, if a bit too much like 'Mr Wodehouse among his books'. It is lined from floor to ceiling with old books and it is only on closer inspection that you find that these are absolutely unreadable. They are what is known in the trade as 'book furniture', – i.e. old encyclopaedias etc, bunged in to act as background. To think that I, who always swore that I would never have a book in the house which was not one of my favourites, should have sunk to this![3]

[...]

I have now achieved the ambition of a lifetime and, possess two typewriters! Both Monarchs. One I keep in the library, the other in my bedroom. It is a darned good investment, as my work can now be continuous. While one is being fixed, I work on the other.

Did you see Fust on the films? V.g. Or, rather, Faust.[4]

[...]

Cheerio

Yours ever

Plum

---

1 Wodehouse's French piece was *The Cardboard Lover*, an adaptation by Valerie Wyngate of an original play by Jacques Deval. Set to star Laurette Taylor and Leslie Howard, the play looked promising, and was to be produced by Gilbert Miller and Al Woods, who had produced PGW's smash hit, *The Play's the Thing*, earlier that year, but it needed to be completely rewritten. As it was due to open on Broadway on 21 March, PGW had fewer than eight weeks to turn it around.

2 *The Captive*, a pioneering three-act drama about lesbianism, adapted from Bourdet's *French*, was produced by Charles Frohman and staged by Gilbert Miller. It was closed by the New York Police Department as part of a New York 'morality campaign'.

3 Wodehouse did not embrace his new study, and ended up working on a small deal table and chair in his bedroom (Jasen, p. 107).

4 Murnau's silent film *Faust* had been produced the previous year.

Wodehouse was familiar with The Hotel Impney at Droitwich, as he had spent time there with Guy Bolton, pacing the terraces as they worked on Oh, Kay! He now returned, so that Ethel could sample the brine baths. The hotel was an extremely grand Victorian building, which was based on the style of a French chateau, set in 155 acres of parkland, lakes and tropical gardens. It was also, Wodehouse wrote, 'the quietest place under the sun'. Wodehouse's letters from the Impney are written on the architecturally resplendent hotel stationery. As Norman Murphy notes, the images of the building have a strong resemblance to Buckstone Abbott's 'Victorian monstrosity', Walsingford Hall, in Summer Moonshine: *'a vast edifice constructed of glazed red brick, in some respects resembling a French château, but, on the whole, perhaps, having more the appearance of one of those model dwellings in which a certain number of working-class families are assured of a certain number of cubic feet of air. It had a huge leaden roof, tapering to a point and topped by a weathervane, and from one side of it, like some unpleasant growth, there protruded a large conservatory. There were also a dome and some minarets.'*

TO WILLIAM TOWNEND

Hotel Impney,
Droitwich,
Worcestershire

March 15. 1927

Dear Bill.

Ripping getting your letter. I didn't go to Cannes after all, as Ethel, who had been talking of going to Droitwich for years, at last decided to come here. It has been a great success. She has a long way to go yet before she is right, but the treatment is doing her good, I think, and I am feeling fine as a result of the brine swimming-bath and Phospherine!!

I felt so damned run down and stale in London that I thought I would try the stuff. It has picked me up wonderfully, and I am now full of beans. You ought to try it. Very easy to take and just gives the brain that flick which it needs when one is stale.

[...]

That was rather queer about the planchette and Kate Overy.[1] Do you remember she and her brother both committed suicide. I knew her fairly well. Have you had any more results?

We have got a new Peke, not as nice as Dinah but quite all right. She had a bad home before she came to us and is very timid except with us.

Must stop now. Will write again soon.

Love to Rene. Yours ever

Plum

---

1 Wodehouse's long-standing interest in spiritualism again shows here. A planchette, otherwise known as a ouija board, moves to spell out messages in a séance.

TO WILLIAM TOWNEND

Hotel Impney,
Droitwich,
Worcestershire.

May 5. 1927

Dear Bill.

Returning to London today.

[...]

Isn't that publicity stuff the devil. You ought to let me write yours and you write mine. I simply can't put the arty thing they want down on paper. What they want is 'When you meet Mr Townend, you are struck at once by a look in his eyes – it is the look of a man who has communed with his soul in the teeth of nor'-eastern. The writer not many years ago, on a tramp steamer in the Atlantic – etc.'

It's hopeless to try to do that sort of thing yourself. If I were you, I'd just give a suitable record of your war-service voyage etc.

(Why do they show the picture here, and at top of page?!)[1]

Fancy anyone turning down 'Distinguished Service'. I really believe the *S.E.P.* have hit it when they say 'the dialect is too weighty'. You know, in the 'Disting. Service' one does rather have to dig the story out of a difficult mass of dialect. Scotch is particularly hard for the

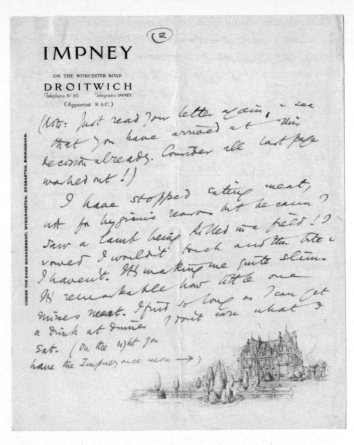

P. G. Wodehouse to William Townend, 5 May 1927.

ordinary reader. I believe you would do better to go through every story of this kind after it's written and take out every bit of dialect you can manage without hurting the atmosphere. I know in some of your stories which you've shown me you have people saying 'yuh' for 'you' every time they speak. I don't think this is necessary. You might say, of course, if this bird says 'yuh' here why should he say 'you' elsewhere?, but in practice it doesn't work out that way, as the reader doesn't notice. Whereas each 'yuh' you put in trips up the eye for an instant.

(Note: just read your letter again, and see that you have arrived at this decision already. Consider all last page washed out!)

I have stopped eating meat, not for hygienic reasons but because I saw a lamb being killed in a field! I vowed I wouldn't touch another bite and I haven't. It's making me quite slim. Its remarkable how little one misses meat. I find so long as I can get a drink at dinner I don't care what I eat.[2]

(On the right you have the Impney once more →)

[...]

Well, cheerio. Write to me soon at Norfolk St.

Yours ever

Plum

---

1 PGW refers to the illustrated writing paper, decorated with pictures of the hotel.
2 Vegetarianism was increasingly popular in the 1920s, but Wodehouse's own attempt at it was short-lived. Any sort of dietary limitation in his fiction is usually seen as a cruel and unusual form of torture – see, for example, Madeline Bassett's unsuccessful attempt to convert Gussie Fink-Nottle to vegetarian ideals in *Stiff Upper Lip, Jeeves* (1963), which results in his eloping with the cook.

TO WILLIAM TOWNEND

Hunstanton Hall,
Norfolk

July 27. 1927

Dear Bill.

I am here till Friday, then London for a few days, and then back here, I think. Send me your address, if you leave Fairlight as you were going to do.

I've just read your story in the *Strand*. It's perfectly magnificent, – in its way as good a thing as you have ever done. You have the most extraordinary knack of making your minor characters live – e.g. Rhoda and the kid. But listen, laddie, you were saying you wished you could find a character to write about. Well, why on earth not Captain Crupper? You could make a second Captain Kettle out of him. He is absolutely alive, and I could sit right down and think out half a dozen adventures for him.

[...] Already I can see that he has the finest stamp collection on the Western Ocean and will go anywhere and brave any perils to get a new rare stamp (Chance of working off that old stamp story of yours). Also he would like to be taller and is apt to try patent medicines which he thinks may make him grow. He is very respectable at heart and has a rowdy, drinking brother of whom he is much ashamed but whose life he saves in order to keep his name out of some provincial paper for getting tight and assaulting the Mayor. Gosh! There's a million stories in him.

Listen, laddie. Have you read 'Pig-Hoo-o-o-o-ey'? I have a sort of idea you once wrote a story constructed on those lines – i.e. some perfectly trivial thing which is important to a man and the story is apparently about how he gets it. But in the process of getting it he gets entangled in somebody else's love story and all sorts of things happen but he pays no attention to them, being wholly concentrated on his small thing. If you never did a yarn on these lines, try one with Cap Crupper. It's an awfully good formula.

Lord Emsworth is wholly indifferent to the fact that the happiness of two lives is at stake. The important thing to him is that his pig starts feeding again. Can't you see a Crupper story on these lines?

Anyway, bung-oh! I'm sweating blood over a novel, and have just finished 53,000 of it. Meanwhile, I have to Anglicize *Oh, Kay!* (our American mus. comedy) by Aug 9, attend rehearsals, adapt a French play, write a new musical comedy and do the rest of this novel – all, as far as I can see, by about Sept 1.

Love to Rene. Any more planchette news.

Yours ever

Plum

Wodehouse recalls that in the period 1926 to 1928 'every day seems to have been given to either writing or rehearsing. The protracted tours of the 'Princess' days had given place to a more or less standard two weeks try-out. This was a period of intensive effort, of re-writing, or early and late rehearsals [...]. The chief intervals of rest were those spent on an ocean liner – though even there you would most likely have found the team, rug-wrapped in adjoining deck-chairs, busy with pad and pencil.' In late 1927, Wodehouse had rushed over to America with George Grossmith, at Ziegfeld's request, to work on the lyrics for the new musical, The Three Musketeers, *as they travelled. As he describes to Townend, he had also been co-opted into working on a number of other shows, including Ziegfeld's musical* Rosalie – *a vehicle for Ziegfeld's mistress, Marilyn Miller. Although Wodehouse did not like* Rosalie, *the musical was to continue to haunt him, as he was later commissioned to turn it into a motion picture.*

TO WILLIAM TOWNEND

14 East 60 St.
New York

Nov 28. 1927

[...]

I would have written to you long before this, but ever since I landed Hell's foundations have been quivering like a jelly. I came over here to do the *Musketeers* for Ziegfeld, and we finished a rough version on the boat. But like all work that is done quickly it needed a terrible lot of fixing, which was left to me, as Grossmith went home. [...] I was working gaily on it when a fuse blew in the Marilyn Miller show [...] ever since then have been sweating away [...]. Meanwhile Gilbert Miller wanted a show in a hurry for Irene Bordoni, so I started on that, too, – fixing the *Musketeers* with my left hand the while. By writing the entire second act in one day I managed to deliver the Gilbert Miller show on time and I have now finished the lyrics and the *Musketeers*, and all is well till Ziegfeld wants all the lyrics rewritten as I believe he is sure to do.

[...]

Just at present I feel as if I would never get another idea for a story. I suppose I shall eventually. But this theatrical work certainly saps one's energies.

[...]

New York is noisier than ever. I found my only way of getting any work done was to take a room out at the Great Neck golf club and work there. So I am the only man on record who commutes the wrong way. I catch the twelve o'clock train from New York most days and return after dinner.

[...]
Cheerio
Yours ever
Plum.

TO WILLIAM TOWNEND

Impney
Droitwich

April 30. 1928

Dear Bill.

So sorry not to have written before. I have been much tied up with a very difficult story.[1] I wish to goodness you were here to help me with it. It's one of those maddening yarns where you've got beginning and end and only want a bit in middle. The idea is that Lord Emsworth has been landed with a niece at the castle, niece having got engaged to man her family disapproves of. Freddie has seen a film where the same thing happened and the man disguised himself with false whiskers, went and sucked up to the family, and then, when they all loved him, tore off the whiskers and asked for their blessing.

So he sends this young man to stay at Blandings, telling Lord E. he is a pal of his named Robinson. He tells the young man to strain every nerve to ingratiate himself with Lord E.

Now, you see what happens. The young man spends his whole time hanging round Lord E. helping him up out of chairs, asking him questions about the garden etc etc, and it simply maddens Lord E., who feels he has never loathed a young man more.

See the idea? Well, what is bothering me is the getting of the cumulative details which lead up to Lord E. loathing the young man. Can you think of any? What would a young man in that position do, thinking he was making a big hit with the old man and really driving him off his head? It all leads up to my big scene, where Lord E., having at last, as he thinks, eluded the young man, goes and bathes in the lake and is so delighted at being away from him that he starts to sing and kick his feet from sheer joy. Which causes the young man, who is lurking in the bushes, to think he is drowning and dive in and save him.

[...]

I've done the first 2500 words, up to the moment of the young man's arrival at the castle, and it is great stuff. I now have to think of some detailed stuff to fill in before the big scene. Gosh, I wish you were here. It's lovely down here, but rather lonely all by myself. I am hoping Ethel will be fit enough to come down on Saturday. Then I shall spend another week here before returning. If you are in London at all, do let me know, as I will run up for the night. I have endless things to talk about.

Love to Rene

Yours ever

Plum

1 'Company for Gertrude', *The Strand*, September 1928, was included in the collection *Blandings Castle and Elsewhere* (1935; US title, *Blandings Castle*).

This is Wodehouse's earliest surviving letter to Ira Gershwin, by now a hugely successful lyricist, living in New York and married to Leonore (Lee). This letter hints that Wodehouse was to provide the impetus for one of the Gershwins' next hit shows, a stage version of Show Girl.

TO IRA GERSHWIN

17 Norfolk Street,
Park Lane, W.1.

Nov 8. 1928

Dear Ira.

Your letter with the checks just arrived. Thanks ever so much. I don't feel as if I had any right to them but they will come in very useful.

I was most awfully sorry to miss you when you were on this side. I only heard quite casually that you were in London two days before you sailed, and those two days I was absolutely tied up. I was frightfully sick about it, as there's no-one I would leap more nimbly to buy a fat lunch for than you and Lee. I always look back wistfully to those meals of ours at Boston. What a shame it is that there's always something to worry one on the road and prevent one enjoying the cheery side of a tour. Every time we had dinner together, a voice seemed to be saying in my ear all the while 'Sa-a-y! How about that Ex-Kings number?'. Still, even taking those blasted ex-kings into account, we did have a great time.

Is there any chance of your coming over to see *Funnyface*?[1] Everything points to a record-breaking success. Not an empty seat on the road – I know, because I was staying near Birmingham and made three unsuccessful tries to get in. [...] You really ought to come over and enjoy it.

Have you read *Show Girl*? Gosh! What a story! I wish I knew McEvoy. He must be a great chap. I never read anything better in my life. If you haven't read it, get it and read the account of the dress rehearsal at Atlantic City.[2]

I take it you have another hit with the Gertie Lawrence show. It seems to be gooling them in Phila.[3]

[...]

I have just signed a contract with the *Cosmopolitan* for eighteen short stories at $6500 each (including English rights).[4] Also a serial for *Collier*'s for $40,000.[5] So I am on velvet as regards my story work, except a ghastly difficulty in getting plots. If you come across anybody with a funny plot for a story, make him sell it to me.

[...]

So long. I'll send you a cable about *Funnyface* when it opens. I am told Henson is wonderful and the other comedian, Howard, almost as good.

Love to Lee and George

Yours ever

Plum

---

1 *Funnyface*, with George Gershwin's music and Ira's lyrics, was a New York hit in 1927, moving to London in 1928 – 'the best produced in London for many years' (*Gramophone*, February 1929). Both casts featured Fred and Adele Astaire.

2 The novel *Show Girl*, by American writer Joseph Patrick McEvoy, revolves around Dixie Dugan, 'an aspiring eighteen-year-old singer whose involvements with four suitors [...] catapult her, through a madcap sequence of events, to stardom on the Broadway stage', Howard Pollack, *George Gershwin: His Life and Work* (London: UCP, 2006), p. 451.

3 The 'Gertie Lawrence show' was *Treasure Girl*, a 1928 musical with book by Fred
Thompson and Vincent Lawrence, music by George Gershwin and lyrics by Ira
Gershwin and, when it opened, starring Gertrude Lawrence. *Treasure Girl* had its try-out
in Philadelphia, beginning on 15 October 1928, and the musical opened on Broadway
at the Alvin Theatre on 8 November 1928, the date of PGW's letter.
4 Wodehouse's eighteen short stories included 'Jeeves and the Song of Songs',
'The Indian Summer of an Uncle', 'The Ordeal of Young Tuppy' and 'Gala Night'.
5 *Summer Lightning*.

TO LEONORA WODEHOUSE

Feb 10. 1929

Darling Poots.

Thanks awfully for your letter. It cheered me up. I had been feeling
very weak and feeble. Have you ever had flu? It leaves you a terrible
wreck. Today for the first time I am feeling pretty good again.

Mummie has gone off for the week-end to Loxwood. I drove down
with her yesterday, and came back in the car. What a nice place it is.
But what exactly do you feel about old Pop Frankland? I love Ma
Zouche, but he seems to me rather a facetious old son of a Bishop, a
good deal too full of small jokes. I rather think somebody must have
told him as a boy that he was bright.[1]

[...]

I haven't read *Gen. Crack* yet.[2] But when I was in bed I read *The
Ugly Duchess*, and liked it very much. I am now heading for *Jew Suss*.[3]

Mummie is very busy interviewing an architect who seems about
fifteen years old. She is planning all sorts of improvements in the
house. She thinks you ought to come back and join in the discussions.

We miss you at every turn. I had to send off the serial without your
seeing it. But I can make any changes you want for book form. I am
not quite satisfied with it, but I don't know just what is wrong. It gets
by all right on its situations, but I feel it is too hurried and needs some
more stuff shoved in. Did Mummie tell you of the bad time we had,
when *Collier's* threatened to cancel their contract if the story started
in the *Pall Mall* before they could use it? After a lot of anxiety and
cabling, everything was settled, but things looked very black for a
while.

[...]

Must end now darling, as I am off to dine with Ian.

Your loving

Plummie

P.S. I lost ten pounds in the five days I was in bed! I am quite slim and willowy now. I liked your bed. It was nice being so near to Mummie. We had the doors open occasionally and chatted.

1 Loxwood Hall, a Georgian mansion in West Sussex, which was built for the King family, then passed to the ownership of Baroness Zouche. The 17th Baroness Zouche (1875–1965), Mary Cecil Frankland, is the 'Ma Zouche' to whom PGW refers (her husband, Sir Frederick W. F. G. Frankland, would have been the 'Pop Frankland' of the letter).

2 *General Crack*, a 1928 novel by the British author Gabrielle Margaret Vere Long (née Campbell), writing under the pseudonym George R. Preedy.

3 PGW's reading offers some insight into his political views at the time – he seems to have been focusing on historical fiction with an anti-Nazi bent. *The Ugly Duchess* and *Jew Suss* were both written by the German-Jewish novelist and playwright Lion Feuchtwanger (pseudonym J. L. Wetcheek; 1884–1958). Feuchtwanger was a fierce critic of the Nazi Party years before it assumed power, and he became a target of persecution after Hitler's appointment as Chancellor of Germany in 1933. *Jew Suss* (*Jud Süß*) (1925) tells the story of Jewish businessman Joseph Süß Oppenheimer's rise and fall. Feuchtwanger's story was cruelly distorted and made into a Nazi propaganda film in 1940.

TO WILLIAM TOWNEND

Hunstanton Hall
Norfolk

May 12. 1929

Dear Bill.

I would have written before but I have had a hell of a week. On Sunday I had to condense *Good Morning, Bill* into a sketch for Heather Thatcher (She opens at Coliseum on Whit Monday).

[...]

I'm here till after Whitsun. Isn't it a gorgeous place. I spend all my time in a boat on the moat. This is the place where the scene of *Money for Nothing* is laid. Things are not so frightfully cheery just at the moment, as host has had a row with butler, who has given notice. The butler is a cheery soul who used to join in the conversation at meals and laugh heartily if one made a joke, but now he hovers like a spectre. Still, I'm hoping peace will be declared soon.

[...]

Cheerio

Yours ever

Plum.

Wodehouse's father Ernest died on 27 May 1929, leaving Eleanor a widow. There is no reference to his death in any of Wodehouse's surviving correspondence.

TO WILLIAM TOWNEND

Hunstanton Hall
Norfolk

July 26. 1929

Dear Bill.

[...]

I've come to the conclusion that what I want for my next novel is a real Ruby M. Ayres basis – you know, the sort of plot that, treated seriously, would be a mushy love story. Then I can turn it into a comedy.

[...]

I'll tell you something I have discovered.

[...]

The actual core of a story must be intelligible to the reader. That is to say, there are some things, for instance, which everybody knows are valuable and haven't merely a value for the occasional crank, – e.g. jewels, pictures, and in this case china. Make the thing stamps and you are in the position of having to convince the reader that it is really valuable. That is why the absolutely primitive things like hunger and death – as in 'Bolshevik' – are sure fire. I don't believe I'm making this a bit clear, but what I mean is that even in my stuff the basis has to be solid. That is why *Leave It to Psmith*, where there was a necklace at stake, was so much easier to write than *Summer Lightning*, where I had to try to convince the reader that a man could get all worked up about a pig.

(Re-reading this, it seems to me a bit delirious. But do you see what I mean?)

Must end now. Got a lot of letters to write.

See you soon. Love to Rene.

Yours ever

Plum

In the letter that follows, Wodehouse is sketching a description of a rugby match, through the eyes of Bertie Wooster, which resulted in the following passage in his 1930 story 'The Ordeal of Young Tuppy': 'I know that the main scheme is to work the ball down the field somehow and deposit it over the line at the other end, and that, in order to squelch this programme, each side is allowed to put in a certain amount of assault and battery and do things to its fellow man which, if done elsewhere, would result in fourteen days without the option, coupled with some strong remarks from the Bench.'

TO WILLIAM TOWNEND

Nov 11. 1929

[...]

I'm longing to come down and see you all, but I'm in the middle of a story, which I must finish before I can make any move. I've gone and let myself in for one of those stories which lead up to a big comic scene and now I'm faced with writing the scene and it looks as if it is going to be hard to make it funny. It's a village Rugger match, where everybody tries to slay everybody else, described by Bertie Wooster who, of course, knows nothing about Rugger. It's damned hard to describe a game you know backwards through the eyes of somebody who doesn't know it. However, I suppose it will come. These things always do. But it isn't easy to get the comic high spots.

[...]

Constitutional Club
Northumberland Avenue

Nov 11. 1929

[...]

I'm afraid it's going to be difficult to work that Townend story on the lines we laid out. I don't mean the writing of the story, which I'll start soon, but the payment end of it. My wife is very jumpy about money just now, as she was rather badly caught in that slump, and if I suggest that I give Townend $5000 for helping me with a story she will have a fit. The only plan is for you to detach the money on the side somehow. There is such a lot coming in these days that it should not be hard.

[...]

TO WILLIAM TOWNEND

Park Lane W.1.

Jan 8. 1930

Dear Bill.

What do you mean? This story is absolutely all right. I think you have got it running nicely now, and I'm sure it will sell. I have made one or two suggestions for cuts. Not important.

[...]

My novel is coming out terrifically so far.[1] I am very nearly half way through. The aunt has been eliminated altogether, and so has the hero's father – after four distinct and separate versions scrapped. I may be able to get in that stuff you sent me, but at present it looks as if detective stuff would suit the story better, as the hero pretends to be a secret service man.

My main trouble is that my heroine refuses to come alive, and, what makes it worse is that the second girl is a pippin. I'm afraid the reader will skip all the stuff dealing with the hero and heroine and concentrate on the scenes between the dude and the second girl.

It looks as if Hollywood was off. I had some nerve-racking sessions with Goldwyn, but he wouldn't meet my price. The poor chump seemed to think he was doing me a favour offering about half what I get for a serial for doing a job which would be a most ghastly sweat. My one ambition is to get out of ever doing a musical piece again. He said, when he sailed today, that he would think things over and let me know, but I'm hoping I have made the price too stiff for him. I don't want to go to Hollywood just now a bit. Later on, in the Spring, I should like it. But I feel now that I just want to be left alone with my novel.

Isn't it great to think that Christmas is over! I am resolved to spend next Christmas on a liner. I came in for the New Year festivities at Hunstanton, and had to wear a white waistcoat every night.

Susan and Winks are both well. I hope the pups are flourishing.

What a ripping atmosphere the suburbs is to write about. I feel very much at home with this novel. I've just written the chapter where Lord Hoddesdon goes down to Dulwich in a grey top hat, which excites the citizenry a good deal. I've got one good line. He asks a loafer outside the Alleyn's Head the way to Mulberry Grove. 'I want to go to Mulberry Grove.' he says. The man gives him a look and nods curtly. 'Awright.' he says. 'Don't be long'.

Cheerio

Yours ever

Plum

1 *Big Money* (1931) was serialised in *Collier's* in 1930 and *The Strand* in 1930–1.

CHAPTER SEVEN

Wodehouse in Hollywood

With the arrival of the Talkies, numerous possibilities opened up for the film industry. The 1927 sound sensation caused by Al Jolson's performance in *The Jazz Singer* was swiftly followed by the first all-talking feature, *Lights of New York* (1928), which grossed over a million dollars. Studio heads were keen to cash in. The 'advent of sound', as Wodehouse recalls, 'had made the manufacture of motion pictures an infinitely more complex affair than it had been. It was no longer possible to just put on a toga, have someone press a button, and call the result *The Grandeur That was Rome* or *In the Days of Nero*. A whole new organization was required. You had to have a studio Boss to boss the Producer, a Producer to produce the Supervisor, a Supervisor to supervise the Sub-Supervisor. [...] And above all, you had to get hold of someone to supply the words'. It was a new gold rush for writers, and the slogan was 'Come one, come all, and the more the merrier.' The late thirties were, Wodehouse recalls, 'an era when only a man of exceptional ability and determination could keep from getting signed up by a studio in some capacity or other'.[1]

The Wodehouse finances had taken a number of severe blows in the Wall Street Crash, and income tax liabilities were an ongoing worry, so Wodehouse was keen to increase his income. But he could never have predicted the sort of figures that would be on offer. In 1929, Wodehouse accepted a staggering deal with Metro-Goldwyn-Mayer – he was to be paid over $2,000 dollars a week, for six months, with a further option of six months.

As he rolled into Pasadena station, he encountered a new and strange atmosphere. Hollywood seemed, to Wodehouse, something like Alice's Wonderland, with its '[t]all eucalyptus. . . blue-flowered jacarandas, feathery pepper trees dotted with red. . . And what looked like a thousand shiny new cars'.[2] Wodehouse settled with Ethel into a rented house belonging to the Hollywood screenwriter and actress Elsie Janis, and set to work as an MGM employee. Leonora, too, joined the payroll for a while, while Ethel visited the local resort spas, and mingled with Hollywood society. Maureen O'Sullivan, the Irish beauty catapulted to fame by MGM, and soon to star in *Tarzan the Ape Man*, lived nearby [see plate 26]. Other members of their circle included the glamorous actress Norma Shearer, their old friend and former Broadway star Edward G. Robinson, and Boris Karloff, famed for his role as Frankenstein's monster. Wodehouse later became friends with many of the English expatriates in Hollywood, including C. Aubrey Smith, the elderly actor and former Test cricketer. When Smith founded the Hollywood Cricket Club, Wodehouse acted as Secretary at their inaugural meeting.

Despite these new friends, letters were particularly important to Wodehouse at this time, as he felt the isolation of life in Los Angeles deeply. A sprawling city, 'some thirty miles long', in a huge state, within a vast country, Hollywood was quite removed from the rest of the world in both geographical and cultural terms.[3]

Wodehouse's job was not a demanding one, but it was utterly different from what he had experienced in his writing life to date. He was 'set [...] on to dialogue' movies alongside eight or more collaborators, with the result that the script was continually changing, often beyond recognition. Wodehouse was called on to add moments of authentic English charm – the 'Earls and butlers', as he put it: 'the system is', he explained, 'that A. gets the original idea, B. comes in to work with him on it, C. makes a scenario, D. does preliminary dialogue, and then they send for me to insert Class and what-not. Then E. and F., scenario writers, alter the plot and off we go again' [see plate 25].[4]

A few years later, Wodehouse would go on to produce a series of satirical writings about the Hollywood he had known, as well as the novels *Laughing Gas* and *The Old Reliable*. In stories such as 'Monkey Business' and 'The Rise of Minna Nordstrom', Wodehouse skilfully caught what he saw as the ludicrous emptiness of this world of mass-produced 'culture' and grasping short-termism. In one story, Wodehouse takes a swipe at the mindless consensus that he saw powering the film industry, encapsulated in the figure of the 'Nodder':

It is not easy to explain [...] the extremely intricate ramifications of the personnel of a Hollywood motion-picture organization.

Putting it as briefly as possible, a Nodder is something like a Yes-Man, only lower in the social scale. [...] The chief executive throws out some statement of opinion, and looks about him expectantly. This is the cue for the senior Yes-Man to say yes. He is followed, in order of precedence, by the second Yes-Man – or Vice-Yesser, as he is sometimes called – and the junior Yes-Man. Only when all the Yes-Men have yessed, do the Nodders begin to function. They nod.[5]

While never a 'nodder', Wodehouse's criticisms of studio life are initially tempered by a sense of loyalty to the studio. Gradually, his dislike for Hollywood ('this place is [...] loathsome', he reports), and his longing for home emerge.[6]

As an Englishman in Beverly Hills, Wodehouse was not really an outsider. Hollywood, after all, was a place inhabited by displaced individuals. As Norman Murphy points out, 'all the studio heads, except one, were Jewish immigrants from Europe' for whom English was a second language.[7] Nobody in Hollywood was really at home. Where Wodehouse stood out was in his wry indifference to the whirl of activity. For most of Hollywood's inhabitants, such as ex-glove salesman Sam Goldwyn and ex-pool hustler Harry Cohn, this was a place of ultimate opportunity. Hollywood was 'a place of despots', all of them vying for attention.[8] Neither needing nor wanting this sort of fame or approval, Wodehouse looked on at this 'dream world' – a 'combination of Santa Claus and Good-Time Charlie' – with a raised eyebrow.[9]

Indeed, in this era of cultural pronouncements, one can see a touch of the cultural critic about Wodehouse. Throughout these letters, one can see his repeated concern with a sense of slipping values. Some of his scorn was directed towards what he saw as the emptiness of modern culture. Elsewhere, his focus is on the lowering of standards. While his later letters show a certain prurient interest in the seamier side of Hollywood, in the late twenties and early thirties this sort of moral atmosphere was anathema. His daily swims, frequently mentioned in his letters, seem like so many subconscious efforts to ward off the American sloth. He clings to his boarding school regime of regular exercise, and prides himself on looking 'like something out of Sapper', the archetypal British bulldog.[10]

Wodehouse disliked much of the work that he was asked to do. 'It needs', he told Townend, 'a definitely unoriginal mind', but there was one notable bugbear in this period at the studio.[11] *Rosalie*, a musical comedy set in an imaginary kingdom, had been bought by MGM for Hearst's mistress, the movie star Marion Davies, and numerous writers had been charged with the task of rewriting it. Wodehouse had originally had a part in the creation of *Rosalie* as a musical comedy at the Amsterdam Theatre in 1928. He was now given what he saw as a particularly tiresome job: recasting the newly plotted film scenario of *Rosalie* as a novelette, which would then be sold as a spin-off product. Much of Wodehouse's other work hit the cutting-room floor, as ideas changed and writers rotated – and the novelette, once completed, was also deemed to be surplus to requirements.

Reflecting in an interview on his time spent working on *Rosalie*, Wodehouse recalls that 'it wasn't my story. But it was a pleasant light little thing, and no one wanted me to hurry. When it was finished they thanked me politely and remarked that as musicals didn't seem to be going so well, they guessed they would not use it.'[12]

Soon, he began to see his role as almost entirely redundant, and focused his energy on his novels and short stories. As he wrote to Denis Mackail, work for Goldwyn 'cut[s] into my short-story-writing. It's odd how soon one comes to look on every minute as wasted that is given to earning one's salary.'[13] Throughout the letters, one sees a sense that the role of the writer, in Hollywood, had diminished to that of an insignificant bit-part. Showered with money, Hollywood scriptwriters were almost entirely expendable, forced to write in 'little hutches' like so many battery-farmed animals, while their product was regarded with some contempt.[14] Jack Warner of Warner Bros and Columbia's Harry Cohn were 'famous for their refusal to read a book or a play'.[15] Wodehouse was not alone in his critique. While Evelyn Waugh condemned the 'Californian Savages', Raymond Chandler soon tired of this 'showman's paradise':

> To me the interesting point about Hollywood's writers of talent is not how few or how many they are, but how little of worth their talent is allowed to achieve.
>
> [...]

It makes very little difference how a writer feels towards his producer as a man; the fact that the producer can change and destroy and disregard his work can only operate to diminish that work in its conception and to make it mechanical and indifferent in execution.[16]

As Wodehouse's Hollywood years unfold, one sees, increasingly, his sense of the place as one of mirages and illusions. With its child stars and gorilla impersonators, Hollywood was nearer to a zoo or a circus than a recognisable world – 'so unreal', as Wodehouse put it, as to make one feel 'removed from ordinary life'.[17] Nothing in Hollywood 'is what it affects to be': 'What looks like a tree is really a slab of wood backed with barrels. What appears on the screen as the towering palace of Haroun al-Rashid is actually a cardboard model occupying four feet by three of space. The languorous lagoon is simply a smelly tank with a stagehand named Ed wading around it in bathing trunks.'[18] Nathanael West captured the same sense of illusion:

> The fat lady in the yachting cap was going shopping, not boating; the man in the Norfolk jacket and Tyrolean hat was returning, not from a mountain, but an insurance office; and the girl in slacks and sneakers with a bandanna around her head had just left a switchboard, not a tennis court.[19]

In the end, it was Wodehouse's inability to keep the conventional mask up that led to the end of this period of his Hollywood career. Interviewed about his work, Wodehouse spoke to the journalist Alma Whitaker of the *Los Angeles Times*, and was candid about the way in which writers were treated and paid. 'I have', he claimed, been paid '$104,000 for loafing'. 'I feel as if I have cheated' the studios, he added cheerfully.[20] Wodehouse's interview made the front page of the Sunday edition of the paper, and outraged both studio and readers. His services, he soon found out, were no longer required – and Hollywood studios began to make massive cutbacks. As the financial situation in America became increasingly unstable, his comments seemed particularly insensitive. 'I am a sort of Ogre to the studio now', he confessed.[21]

Wodehouse, in fact, never worked as little as he claimed in Hollywood. His snipe at the studio was, in part, revenge for the never-used *Rosalie* novelette, but there was, as McCrum notes, a certain delicious bravado in claiming that his time on the MGM payroll had been spent writing 'a novel and nine short stories [...] brushing up my golf, getting an attractive suntan and perfecting my Australian crawl'.[22] As they prepared to leave Hollywood in November 1931, Ethel made elaborate plans for a world cruise, in which she imagined 'Plum riding camels and elephants and taking pot shots at anything he may see'.[23] The plan, in the end, was rejected, and the Wodehouses made their way to France.

1 P. G. Wodehouse, 'The Girl in the Pink Bathing Suit', *Hollywood Omnibus* (London: Hutchinson, 1985), p. 9 (first published as 'Slaves of Hollywood', *SEP*, 1929).

2 *Bring on the Girls*, p. 234.

3 PGW to William Townend, 16 January 1931 (Dulwich).

4 PGW to Denis Mackail, 26 June 1930 (Wodehouse Archive).

5 'The Nodder', first published in January 1933 in *The Strand*, and in the same month in *The American* as 'Love Birds'. Repr. in *Blandings Castle and Elsewhere* (1935).

6 PGW to Denis Mackail, 28 December 1930 (Wodehouse Archive).

7 Murphy, p. 312.

8 Salman Rushdie, 'Debrett Goes to Hollywood', *Imaginary Homelands* (London: Granta, 1991), p. 326.

9 'The Girl in the Pink Bathing Suit', p. 9.

10 PGW to Denis Mackail, 26 June 1930 (Wodehouse Archive).

11 PGW to William Townend, 26 August 1931 (Dulwich).

12 Interview, *Los Angeles Times*, quoted in Robert McCrum, 'A Lotus Eater in Hollywood', *Observer*, 29 August 2004.

13 PGW to Denis Mackail, 26 June 1930 (Wodehouse Archive).

14 P. G. Wodehouse, 'The Hollywood Scandal' (1932), *Louder and Funnier* (London: Vintage, 1997), p. 16.

15 Murphy, p. 313.

16 Evelyn Waugh to A. D. Peters, 21 November 1946 (Austin, Texas); Raymond Chandler, 'Writers in Hollywood', *Atlantic Monthly* 176 (Nov. 1945), p. 52.

17 PGW to Denis Mackail, 26 June 1930 (Wodehouse Archive).

18 'The Hollywood Scandal', p. 15.

19 Nathanael West, *The Day of the Locust* (London: Grey Walls Press, 1951), pp. 6–7.

20 Interview, *Los Angeles Times*, 7 June 1931.

21 PGW to William Townend, 26 August 1931 (Dulwich).

22 McCrum, 'A Lotus Eater'.

23 Ethel Wodehouse to Denis Mackail, 8 October 1931 (Wodehouse Archive).

1930–1931:
'this place is loathsome'

Metro Goldwyn Mayer Studios
Culver City
California

June 26. 1930

Dear Denis.

Frightfully sorry I haven't written before. I have been in a whirl of work. After three months absolute deadness, my brain began to whirr like a dynamo. So you see one does recover from these blank periods. I hope yours is gone. I have written three short stories, an act of a play, and the dialogue for a picture in three weeks, and have got six brand new plots for short stories!!! I believe our rotten brains have to go through those ghastly periods of inertness before getting a second wind.

[...]

Susan is dead.[1] Did Ethel tell you? Apparently she just toppled over quite quietly in the Park, and it was all over in a minute. She had no pain, thank goodness. It's just like losing part of oneself. The only thing is that everything is so unreal out here and I feel so removed from ordinary life that I haven't yet quite realized it.

Mrs Patrick Campbell came to dinner the other night and talked a lot about you. It made me feel I wasn't so far from civilization, after all.[2] This is the weirdest place. We have taken Elsie Janis's house.[3] It has a small but very pretty garden, with a big pool. I have arranged with the studio to work at home, so I sometimes don't go out of the garden for three or four days on end. If you asked me, I would say I loved Hollywood. Then I would reflect and have to admit that Hollywood is about the most loathsome place on the map but that, never going near it, I enjoy being out here.

My days follow each other in a regular procession. I get up, swim, breakfast, work till two, swim again, work till seven, swim for the third time, then dinner and the day is over. When I get a summons from the studio, I motor over there, stay there a couple of hours and come back. Add incessant sunshine, and it's really rather jolly. It is only occasionally that one feels as if one were serving a term on Devil's Island.

We go out very little. Just an occasional dinner at the house of some other exile – e.g. some New York theatrical friend. Except for one party at Marion Davies's place, I have not met any movie stars.[4]

The second day out on the liner I developed a terrific attack of neuritis, and spent the rest of the voyage in bed. I managed to get rid of it about two weeks later. One of the rules, when you have neuritis, is that you must knock off drink, so I got a flying start with that two weeks and kept on the wagon for another six. Then I had to go to a party, and I couldn't go through it without cocktails. They have the damnable practice here of inviting you to dine at seven-fifteen. If you are a novice, as I was, you arrive at seven-fifteen. You then stand round drinking cocktails till nine-thirty, when the last guest arrives. Then you go in to dinner. At Marion Davies's, I refused all drinks and it nearly killed me. By dinner time I was dying on my feet. Poor old Snorky had to talk to the same man from seven-fifteen till 9.30 and then found she was sitting next to him at dinner!! Fortunately, it was such a big party that we were able to sneak off without saying goodbye directly dinner was over. Gosh, what an experience.

On the other hand, teetotalism certainly makes one frightfully fit. Also slim. I have become a lean-jawed, keen-eyed exhibit, like something out of Sapper.[5]

The actual work is negligible. They set me on to dialogue for a picture for Jack Buchanan. I altered all the characters to Earls and butlers, with such success that, when I had finished, they called a conference and changed the entire plot, starring the earl and the butler. So I am still working on it. So far, I have had eight collaborators. The system is that A. gets the original idea, B. comes in to work with him on it, C. makes a scenario, D. does preliminary dialogue, and then they send for me to insert Class and what-not. Then E. and F., scenario writers, alter the plot and off we go again.

I could have done all my part of it in a morning, but they took it for granted I should need six weeks. The latest news is that they are going to start shooting quite soon. In fact, there are ugly rumours that I am to be set to work soon on something else. I resent this, as it will cut into my short-story-writing. It's odd how soon one comes to look on every minute as wasted that is given to earning one's salary. (Now, don't go making a comic article out of this and queering me with the bosses!!)

Let's have a line soon. Tell me all the news. I hear nothing out here. Have you resigned from the pest house yet?[6]

Yours ever

Plum

1 Wodehouse's beloved Pekingese dog.

2 Mrs Patrick Campbell (1865–1940), British stage actress, born Beatrice Stella Tanner, who appeared in several motion pictures, best remembered today as being the original Eliza Doolittle in *Pygmalion* (1914).

3 Elsie Janis, stage and film actress and writer, who had starred in *Miss 1917* and *Oh, Kay!*

4 Marion Davies (1897–1961), American film actress, known for her relationship with newspaper tycoon William Randolph Hearst. She made a number of comedies and musicals during the 1930s, and had appeared in PGW's *Oh, Boy!* (1917) and *Miss 1917*. She maintained a long relationship with Hearst, though the two were never married.

5 Herman Cyril McNeile (1888–1937), British author, who published under the name of 'Sapper', best known for creating hearty, sportsman-like characters such as Bulldog Drummond – a former officer of the First World War who spends his post-war leisure time as a private detective.

6 The Garrick Club. PGW was persuaded to join it in 1922, but soon came to dislike it and had resigned his membership.

TO ARNOLD BENNETT

724 Linden Drive
Beverly Hills, California

Aug 16. 1930

Dear A.B.

How awfully nice of you to write to me about Jeeves.[1] I am so delighted that you liked him. I would rather have a card from you than a column from anybody else.

I can never see why printers should do their job so slackly. I had to leave England without seeing page proofs, but I went to enormous trouble over the galleys. In one place I had written 'festive s.', meaning 'festive season', & they printed it 'festives'. So I wrote on the margin of the galley as follows: – 'Not 'festives'. Please print this as two words 'festive s.', – 'festive' one word, 's' another. Bertie occasionally clips his words, so that when he means 'festive season' he says 'festive s.' This is quite clear, isn't it? 'Festive' one word, 's' another?" And so the book has come out with the thing printed as 'festives'. I see now that I didn't make it clear enough.[2]

I am having a very pleasant time out here. I do nothing but work and swim in the pool in the garden. It is a great place for work.

Yours ever

P. G. Wodehouse

1 *Very Good, Jeeves* (1930).
2 To add to the confusion, Doubleday Doran printed it in the American edition as 'the festivities'. In the 1931 *Jeeves Omnibus*, Herbert Jenkins changed it to 'Christmas'.

TO WILLIAM TOWNEND

Metro-Goldwyn Studios
Culver City
California

Oct 28. 1930

Dear Bill.

[...]

Well, laddie, it begins to look as if it would be some time before I returned to England. The Metro people have taken up my option and I am with them for another six months. And Ethel has just taken a new house for a year! Which means that I shall probably stay that long.

I only wish you could come out here. Would you be able to if I got you a job?

[...]

Anyway, I think I have definitely got a pull with these people now, so write and tell me how you stand on the subj. California would suit Rene, wouldn't it.

If you came over here and settled down, I think I would spend at least six months in every year here. I like the place. I think Californian scenery is the most loathsome on earth, – a cross between Coney

Island and the Riviera, but by sticking in one's garden all the time and shutting one's eyes when one goes out, it is possible to get by.

Listen, laddie, as life goes on, don't you find that all you need is about two real friends, a regular supply of books, and a Peke?

They have rather done the dirty on me at the moment. There was a musical comedy called *Rosalie* – imaginary kingdom stuff – which was bought for Marion Davies. Everyone had a go at it, including myself. The big boss has now worked out a story on his own, which isn't at all bad, and he has told me [to go] off to do it. But – and here is the catch – he wants me to write it as a novelette, – which is about eight times as much sweat as just doing dialogue. I wrote my first version of *Rosalie* – in dialogue form – between Sunday and Thursday of one week. This is going to take me a couple of months and is a ghastly fag. However, I don't suppose they will hurry me.

[...]

Snorky is on the payroll of Metro Goldwyn at fifty dollars a week, and has worked out quite a good picture. If they like it, she ought to strike for more.

We move into our new house Nov 16. I shall absent myself for a couple of days during the moving. [...]

I am still bathing vigorously three times a day, though in the early morning the water is pretty chilly. They tell me that with care you can bathe all through the winter. The swim I enjoy most is before dinner. I have a red hot bath and get absolutely boiled, and then race down the back stairs with nothing on and plunge in. Rather like the Turkish bath system. [...]

Winks is barking like blazes in the garden. I think it must be the Japanese gardener, whom she hasn't accepted even after seeing him every other day for six months.

Last night Maureen O'Sullivan (screen actress) brought her new Peke round here, and Winks was very austere.[1] Do you remember the day you and Rene and Bimmy arrived in Norfolk St? I had been looking forward sentimentally to the reunion of the two sisters, and as I came down stairs I heard the most frightful snarling and yapping, and there was Winks trying to eat Bimmy. Odd, too, how the row all stopped directly we took them out on the steps. Apparently a Peke only resents visitors in the actual house.

Leave It to Psmith seems to have got over very big.[2] Thanks for the notices. Of course no-one else ever thought of sending me any. (Aren't people funny about that? They write and tell you there was something awfully nice about you in the Phoenix (Arizona) *Intelligencer*, and take it for granted that you must have seen it yourself.)

Psmith did twenty-four hundred quid at Golders Green and two thousand and seventeen first week at Shaftesbury, during which week, of course, a lot of free seats had to be begivne – or, rather – given – away. (By the way, have you ever thought what wonderful names you could invent for characters simply by misspelling words on the typewriter. I can see 'Begivney', for instance, as a rather sinister butler.) *Damsel in Distress* only did sixteen hundred in its first week in London.

What rot most pictures are. I haven't seen more than one decent one since I came here.

I had a wild idea of dashing over to England, seeing you, watching the Haileybury match and dashing back after ten days in England. But then the thought of the distance appalled me. That's the trouble about being here. You say to yourself you'll dash away when so disposed, but you don't.

[...]

There is great business depression over here. Movies are doing terribly badly and miniature golf-courses have bust up altogether. Magazines are at a very low ebb, except for the big ones, and even they have lost twenty five per cent of their ads.

I'm afraid it will be another year or so before things get easy again. And before that Mussolini will have started another war, I suppose![3]

Write again soon.

[...]

Yours ever

Plum

1 Maureen O'Sullivan was the screen actress famous for her role as Jane in *Tarzan and the Apes*. She was later married to the writer John Farrow. She and PGW became great friends. PGW dedicated *Hot Water* to her in 1932.
2 *Leave It to Psmith* had been dramatised by PGW and Ian Hay, and opened in London in 1930.
3 The Italian dictator was then arousing comment. His invasion of Ethiopia in 1935 confirmed many people's fears.

1005 Benedict Canyon
Beverly Hills
California

Dec 28. 1930

Dear Denis.

I feel an awful worm, not having written to you for so long, but a genuine pressure of work stopped me. The studio wished an awful job on me – viz. They made me write a perfectly rotten picture <u>as a novel</u>!! Exactly eight times as much sweat as doing an ordinary picture. What the idea was, I don't know, unless they thought that, writing it in that form, I would put in a lot of business which they could use. It ran to 45,000 words, and I was writing a little thing of my own at the same time against the clock. It shows what a great climate this is, that I didn't succumb.

Asked to what he attributed his success, Mr Wodehouse replied that he thought, on the whole, that it could be attributed to cold water. Have you ever taken a cold bath? I bet you haven't. Well, listen. Every morning before breakfast – and I mean every morning, not once a month – I put on a bathing suit, do my exercises, and then plunge into our swimming-pool, the water of which is now exactly fifty degrees. And, what is more, I like it. I can't think what has come over me since I've been here. I used to loathe anything but the hottest water, and now, even if I do have a hot bath, I take a cold shower after it. The result is that I have lost seven pounds in weight and am almost unbelievably beautiful.

The great advantage of this place is that it is so loathsome the moment you get outside the garden that there is no temptation to do anything but sit at home and work. I am turning out incredible quantities. I don't get any more ideas than I used to, but – give me an idea – and I can deliver in a couple of days.

[...]

I say, laddie, a significant thing showing what will happen to you and me later on. *Strand* Christmas number. Story by Conan Doyle inside. On the cover no mention of him. Could you have foreseen that twenty years ago?

Snorky is still in New York. Having a wonderful time, by all accounts. She proposes to return some time or other via Cuba, Palm Beach, New Orleans etc. I rather hope she doesn't return here till the Spring. We get torrential rains soon, I believe, and she is having much more fun in New York than she could get here.

Ethel and I were discussing what to give her for Christmas. Ethel had a cocktail and suggested two hundred and fifty dollars. Then she had another cocktail and raised it to five hundred. Finally, after a liqueur brandy, she said sentimentally that one was only young once and so on, with the result that Snorky got a cheque for one thousand bones. I suppose she's spent it by now.

[...]

Well, so long. Send me more news soon.

Yours ever

Plum

P.S. The maddening thing about this place is that I haven't been able to get a single story out of it yet. I suppose there are plots to be found in Hollywood, but I can't see them. For the moment, then, our old line of Dukes and Earls will continue as in the past.

The next letter to Townend marks the beginning of Wodehouse's problems with MGM. That week, the show business magazine, Variety, *had published the following note: 'Following* Variety's *report of the ludicrous writer talent situation, eastern executives interrogated the studios as to instances such as concerned one English playwright and author who has been collecting $2,500 a week at one of the major studios for eleven months, without contributing anything really worthwhile to the screen.' The note foreshadows the indignation in Hollywood when, a few months later, in an interview with Alma Whitaker of the* Los Angeles Times, *Wodehouse spoke about how much he liked Hollywood, and how much he had enjoyed his stay – his one regret being 'that he had been paid such an enormous amount of money without having done anything to earn it'.*

M-G-M Studios
Culver City
California

March 14. 1931

[...]

Does the Spring make you restless? I have been feeling rotten for some days, but today have been fine. I have a hunch that the studio won't engage me again after May. I shall spend the summer here and return in the Autumn, I think. I have a lot of work to do in the way of stories.

If you have a moment of leisure, here is a bit of a story that is bothering me. I want a tough burglar to break into a country-house and there to have such a series of mishaps that his nerve breaks and he retires from the profession. The conditions can be anything you like, – e.g. Pekinese on the floor who bite his ankle etc. It ought to be one of my big comic scenes like the flower-pot scene in *Leave It to Psmith*. Don't bother about it if you're busy, but if anything occurs to you send it along.

I am doing a picture version of *By Candlelight* now for John Gilbert.[1] This looks as if it might really come to something. Everything else I have done so far has been scrapped, – not my fault, mostly.

But I doubt if they will give me another contract. The enclosed par from *Variety* can only refer to me, and it looks to me darn sinister. My only hope is that I have made myself so pleasant to everyone here that by now I may count as a relative. The studio is full of relatives of the big bosses who do no work and draw enormous salaries.

I must stop now, as I have to go out to dinner. (Corinne Griffith, as a matter of fact. She is a ripper).[2]

[...]

Cheerio

Yours ever

Plum

---

1 The play *By Candlelight*, adapted from Siegfried Geyer's original by Harry Graham, had been very successful in London.

Wodehouse's friendship with the comic writer Will Cuppy was to last for many years.

TO WILL CUPPY

1005 Benedict Canyon
Beverly Hills
Cal.

April 29. 1931

Dear Mr Cuppy.

Thanks most awfully for sending me the two books. I immediately fell upon the Dorothy Sayers one, and loved it. It is extraordinary how much better she is than almost all other mystery writers. I started the Hammett one last night, as I find you have to be feeling pretty robust for him. [...]

Hammett is out here now, by the way, but I have not met him. They tell me he gets tight pretty often and is rather tough when under the influence.[1]

[...]

In re *The Hermit*, which I have just read right through once again.[2] Apart from its gorgeous humor, what fascinates me about it is the atmosphere. I used to live on the south shore of Long Island, and I always felt what a wonderful retreat that sand bar across the Great South Bay would make. I don't know exactly where Jones Island is, but it must be somewhere near Bellport, where I settled in 1914.

Before the war, I had a cottage on the Hampshire coast in England, just like your place. I just put in a bed and a few deal tables and chairs and let the furnishing go at that.

[...]

How are you feeling now? I have just passed through one of those Byronic spells, caused principally by two days rain. In England, I love rain, but here it is an outrage. I brooded somberly until yesterday, when I went for a seven mile walk at top speed in hot sunshine and sweated off about three pounds and had a swim in my pool and felt marvellous. I just sat down and dashed off the last fifteen hundred words of a short story, and then immediately wrote a thousand words of a new one. Pure intellect – that was me.

Of course, if you have to read twenty-four detective stories at a stretch, I can see how life may seem a bit of a wash-out to you occasionally. I think there ought to be a law that all mystery stories should have an English setting. As soon as I come on the words 'precinct' or 'district attorney', all my interest goes. Murders ought to take place only in old English country-houses.

I see Dorothy Sayers has got a new one out in England, – *The Five Red Herrings*. If you want to get rid of your copy, shoot it along.

Well, so long. Do write again soon. I find I get far too few letters out here.

Yours ever

P. G. Wodehouse

---

1 Dashiell Hammett (1894–1961), American author of hard-boiled detective novels and short stories, including the quintessential detective, Sam Spade.
2 Cuppy's book, *How to Be a Hermit, or, How a Bachelor Keeps House*, was published in 1929.

TO DENIS MACKAIL

1005 Benedict Canyon Drive
Beverly Hills
California

May 10. 1931

Dear Denis.

Your letter arrived yesterday, and I am answering it today. You will note the improved efficiency.

[...]

My contract with MGM ended yesterday, and they have shown no sign whatever of wanting to renew it. My plans are to stay out here till September and then dash over to England if only for a short visit. I say, why don't you come over here and stay with us in August? Could Diana spare you? The trip would pay for itself over and over again, as I know you would get a novel out of Hollywood. Think this over and let me know. You could do all the writing you wanted in this house.

I haven't been able to get much out of Hollywood so far, but then I have been restraining myself from satire out of love and loyalty for dear old M-G-M. Now that the pay envelope has ceased, maybe I shall be able to write some stuff knocking them good.

This place has certain definite advantages which make up for it being so far from home. I love breakfasting in the garden in a dressing-gown after a swim in the pool. There's no doubt that perpetual sunshine has its points. I've never been able to stay more than a few months in one place before, let alone a year. And the people here are quite fun. I find I enjoy going out to dinner.

[...]

I have done a twenty thousand word scenario of a new novel, and shall be starting it soon. I find that if one has the energy to make a long scenario, it makes the actual writing much easier.

I have written eleven short stories since the first of June last, which is better than I have done for years.[1] I have also written a play and made a novel out of it and novelized that *Good Morning, Bill* thing I wrote some years ago.[2] I find this a good place for work.

[...]

The movies are getting hard up and the spirit of economy is rife. I was lucky to get mine while the going was good. It is rather like having tolerated some awful bounder for his good dinners to go to his house and find the menu cut down to nothing and no drinks. The only thing that excused the existence of the Talkies was a sort of bounderish openhandedness.

Do think over the idea of visiting us. It would be a wonderful change for you and would fill you with new ideas.

Yours ever
Plum

1 PGW had been working on his Mulliner stories, along with *Laughing Gas* (1936).
2 *Who's Who*, a play co-written with Guy Bolton, ran for nineteen performances in 1934;

this became the novel *If I Were You* (1931). The 'novelized' version of *Good Morning, Bill* was *The Medicine Girl* (US title), serialised in *Collier's Weekly* in 1931. The UK title was *Doctor Sally* (1932).

TO WILLIAM TOWNEND

May 19. 1931

Dear Bill.

[...]

How have you been doing lately? I'm afraid things must have been bad, with your illness. The world seems to have taken a sort of nose-dive, doesn't it. The movies are in a rotten state, and MGM showed no desire whatever to re-engage me when my contract lapsed last week. (Keep writing there still, as I go and fetch my letters. I like having an object for a walk.)

[...]

Have you noticed how everybody is writing like Hemmingway [*sic*] nowadays? I read a book called *Iron Man* the other day, and it might have been written by him. It seems to me a darned easy way of writing, – just short, breathless sentences.

I have started another novel, and it is coming out fine.[1] The only trouble is that it is really a sort of carbon copy of *Leave It to Psmith*. I hope people won't notice it.

Well, cheerio. Love to Rene.

Yours ever

Plum

P.S. Don't mention the enclosure when you write.[2]

1 *Hot Water* (1932).
2 This is PGW's usual method of mentioning that he is sending a cheque. He was always anxious that Ethel should not know about these regular subsidies.

1005 Benedict Canyon Drive
Beverly Hills
California

Aug 17. 1931

Dear Cuppy.

Thanks most awfully for the books. I want a serious word with you about our old pal, Dorothy Sayers. She writes so darned well that one gets the illusion for a while that this last one of hers is a good story. Laddie, it's a <u>lousy</u> story.[1] It drools on and on and round and round, and oh, God! those time-tables with their 'arrive Peebles 4.32 unless you go round by Loch Katrine and take the 6.27 boat for McCockle, stopping at Wulliewuakie'.

Tick her off and make her get back to the old snappy stuff.

[...]

I've just sweated for three solid months in a roasting temperature and finished my masterpiece. It really is the best thing I've done, I believe, the only trouble being that it's a little like some of the others.

Cheerio

Yours ever

P. G. Wodehouse

P.S. I shall be here another three months, so bung some more books along.

1 PGW refers to Sayers' *Five Red Herrings*.

1005 Benedict Canyon Drive
Beverly Hills
Cal.

Aug 26. 1931

Dear Bill.

I was thrilled by your description of battle with Pop Grimsdick.[1] I'm awfully glad the thing has been settled and they are going to publish

We Sailors. (Wouldn't there be someone who would suggest *In the Blood* as a title!). I hope the Book Society people take the book, as it means a big boost. I had no notion they got their books quite so cheap, though.

[...]

I have never been able to concentrate so on a novel before. This is a marvellous place for work, as the life is perfect monotony. Except for an occasional dinner I have been able to give every day up to the story for three and a half months.

Our plans have clarified to the extent that we are definitely going to be back in London at the end of next April. We leave here in November and are still doubtful as to how to fill the gap. I want to go round the world on the *Empress of Britain* – you know the sort of thing, one day at Naples, two in Egypt, snatch and sandwich [*sic*] and race through the Holy Land etc. I thought I might get a novel out of the cruise, but the family are afraid we might get terribly fed up with our fellow passengers, so the latest scheme is to sail from San Francisco and visit the Far East. I'm not so keen on this, as I can't see myself getting any material out of Japan and India. I suppose we shall settle something eventually.

Of course, my career as a movie-writer has been killed dead by that interview. I am a sort of Ogre to the studios now. I don't care personally, as I don't think I could ever do picture writing. It needs a definitely unoriginal mind. Apparently all pictures have to be cast in a mould. [...]

We are becoming gradually infatuated with Maureen O'Sullivan's Peke, Johnnie (female in spite of the name). This was the one which was run over and lost an eye. We sent her to the vet and the eye has been neatly treated so that now it looks all right. The vet also clipped her. Have you ever seen a clipped Peke? She looks weird, but very attractive.

Isn't it odd how short dogs' memories are. Do you remember the historic meeting between Winks and Bimmy which ended in the sort of scene you have in your stories, – real waterfront saloon stuff. Exactly the same thing happened when Johnnie returned. She and Winks had been the greatest friends when she left a week before, but the moment she entered the house Winks flew at her. An hour later all was well and they are now inseparable again.

Golly, it's been hot here this summer. Nothing like it last year. It was 97 in shade yesterday, hottest day of year, and I spent two hours in the pool in the morning and another hour in the afternoon. You're right about this climate. I think it would get me in the end. Still, it has had a wonderful effect on my figure. I weighed myself yesterday and I was exactly thirteen stone. When I left England I was fifteen stone in my clothes, so presumably I have lost about seventeen pounds.

[...]

Love to Rene. I'll write again soon.

Yours ever

Plum

1 Derek Grimsdick was the chief editor of Herbert Jenkins Ltd who took over the company after Herbert Jenkins' death.

TO WILLIAM TOWNEND

Sept 14. 1931

Dear Bill.

This business of writing to you has taken on a graver aspect, the authorities here having raised the ante to five cents per letter. I can bear it bravely as far as you are concerned, but, darn it, I do grudge having to spend five cents on a letter to some female in East Grinstead who wants to know if I pronounce my name Wood-house or Wode-house.

Have you seen the *Cosmopolitan* yet? 'Sport!' is prominently featured and magnificently illustrated, and I am boiling with fury at the thought that they only paid you $250 for such a masterpiece. Also, how in the name of everything infernal did a story like that go begging all that time? I can only suppose that most American editors sheered off it because of its intensely English atmosphere. Honestly, it is the best thing you have done for years.

I have had exactly a month of nerve-wracking idleness. I have thought of one or two plots, but don't seem to get them into just the shape where I can start writing. I have three more stories to do for the *American*, and the editor has put me right out of my stride by asking me to write about American characters. My difficulty is that Americans aren't funny. If they were, there would be more than about three American humorous writers. I've a darned good mind to tell him that if he insists on non-Wodehouse stuff, I'll do it but he can't expect it to be funny. But nowadays one can't alienate an editor. I suppose I shall work out something.

We dined last night with Douglas Fairbanks and Mary Pickford. She is a most intelligent woman, quite unlike the usual movie star. I talked to her all the evening.[1]

We are still debating what to do to fill in between November and April, when we return to England. We talk of a trip round the world, but the more I think of it the less I feel I want to see foreign countries. I wouldn't be surprised if we didn't stay on here. It's great here in the winter, and I have become very keen on tennis, we having a court. Ethel plays, too, so we have lots of it. But I feel a bit unsettled, and my brain doesn't seem to work properly. Isn't it ghastly when you have finished a novel and have to turn to something else. For three and a half months I had the most marvellous time, not a dull moment. I feel now as if I couldn't write at all.

The news from England is pretty depressing. Snorky had a letter this morning from Charles le Strange, saying that he has got to clear out of Hunstanton as he can't afford to live there. I don't know how I shall get on without Hunstanton to go to. It was the most wonderful place of refuge.

We have just had four friends of Snorky's staying here for a week. Quite nice, but gosh how it congested the place.

Did you read Milne's serial in the *Mail*? I thought it good. Nothing happened in it, but his characters were so real. I wonder how a book like that sells. Do people want a story or not?

Miss Winks kept Ethel awake the whole of one night by scratching and was bundled off to the vet, who said she had been overfed. She came back full of beans and smelling like rotten eggs from a sulphur bath.

[...]

Well, laddie, write again soon.

Yours ever

Plum

1 Known as 'Hollywood royalty' (Fairbanks was often called 'the King of Hollywood'), silent film stars Douglas Fairbanks and Mary Pickford married in 1920. Both were instrumental in forming United Artists in 1919, along with Charlie Chaplin and D. W. Griffith, 'to avoid being controlled by the studios and to protect their independence'. The two famously entertained at their Beverly Hills estate, 'Pickfair', but parted in 1933. Before moving to Hollywood and becoming a film star, Fairbanks had been on Broadway, and starred in the first theatrical adaptation of Wodehouse's work in August 1911, when he played Jimmy Pitt in *A Gentleman of Leisure*.

1. Eleanor Wodehouse with Pelham Grenville aged 2 months and 3 weeks, January 1882.

2. Peveril, Armine and Pelham Wodehouse in 1887, taken when Pelham (on the right) was five years old.

3. Ernest Wodehouse in Hong Kong, front row, third from the left, *c.* 1885.

5. William Townend at Dulwich, *c.* 1898.

4. The cover of one of Wodehouse's childhood favourites, *The Boy's Own Paper*, 11 April 1891.

6. The HongKong and Shanghai Bank rugby football team *c.* 1901. Wodehouse sits in the second row, second from the right.

7. P. G. Wodehouse's Mike Jackson at the New Asiatic Bank, visited by Psmith.
When working at the bank, Wodehouse, like Mike, was 'appalled' by the monotony of this
'desert of ink and ledgers'. Illustration from *The New Fold* (*Psmith in the City*),
which appeared in *The Captain*, October 1908, p. 84.

8. Ernestine Bowes-Lyon, or 'Teenie', *c.* 1902.

9. Herbert Wotton Westbrook, *c.* 1914.

10. Ella King-Hall *c.* 1910. Wodehouse's UK literary agent for many years. Admired by Wodehouse, Ella was later to marry Herbert Westbrook.

11. The cover of *Chums* magazine, 7 October 1908, featuring Wodehouse's serial *The Luck Stone*.

12. George Grossmith Jr in *The Girls of Gottenberg*, a 1907 musical containing lyrics by Wodehouse. Grossmith, in such roles, was one of the models for Wodehouse's Bertie Wooster.

13. Lillian Barnett, Wodehouse's housekeeper at Emsworth, with her daughter Norah, *c.* 1912.

14. Leslie Havergal Bradshaw, 1912.

15. Alice Dovey, *c.* 1912.

16. The passenger list for the *Sicilian* liner, which travelled from London to Quebec in August 1912. Ethel 'Milton' is billed as an 'artiste', part of a troupe of performers that included a conductor and a comedian.

17. Leonora Rowley, *c.* 1915.

18. The cover of the *Saturday Evening Post* for 26 June 1915, featuring Wodehouse's serial, *Something New*.

19. Denis Mackail with his Pekinese, Topsy, *c.* 1923.

20. The chorus line of *Oh, Lady! Lady!!*, Wodehouse's 1918 musical comedy, written with Jerome Kern and Guy Bolton.

21. Lady Ethel Newton Wodehouse by Bassano (whole-plate glass negative, 1 June 1922).

CHAPTER EIGHT

Wodehouse in the Thirties

The 'dream of every redblooded man', Wodehouse wrote in 1957, is to do 'down the income tax authorities'.[1] It could be said that trying to make practical sense of the emerging swathe of tax legislation in England and America was one of Wodehouse's main concerns in the 1930s. He was one of the highest-earning authors in the world, making large sums in each country, on which he was, quite reasonably, required to pay income tax. As with Osbert Mulliner, income tax assessors might have 'screamed with joy when forwarding Schedule D to his address'.[2] However, the international agreements which prevented two sets of tax authorities from trying to tax the same income in full were not to be negotiated until the late 1940s. Throughout his career, Wodehouse dealt with the requirements of income tax, but he only wanted to do so once.

His judgement had undoubtedly been at fault in appointing John Rumsey, a play-broker, to handle aspects of his American tax affairs in the 1920s, for Rumsey had responded to this act of faith by failing to file any tax returns on Wodehouse's behalf for five years. Rather than ask his literary agent, Reynolds, to pick up the pieces and bring his tax affairs up to date, he delegated the task to Bobby Denby, a family friend. Denby also did nothing, and the situation remained unresolved in 1932. At this point he turned to professional advisers. But the meaning of several new tax laws enacted in each country was unclear, and their correct interpretation by the courts lagged many years behind. Therefore, as Wodehouse was one of the very first transatlantic commuters with substantial income on both sides of the Atlantic, he and his advisers had a number of disagreements with each set of revenue authorities as to their correct interpretation, and he had to endure a number of court hearings to obtain rulings on several matters.

In England, he won the only case that came to court, which resulted in the assessments made on him being revoked in 1934. The technical disputes in America were more numerous, and the American Internal Revenue Service raised huge assessments, some plausible, some bizarre. Disputes and tax hearings in America punctuated the 1930s, with the IRS claiming over $250,000 in 1934, as well as freezing his American assets and future American earnings. All the technical disputes were then settled for the lesser sum of $83,000 two years later. Further disputes arose in America during the 1940s, and after a series of court cases (including some which reached the Supreme Court), Wodehouse won on all substantive points.

The tax situation had emotional as well as financial consequences. The Wodehouses had already spent much of the twenties moving between locations to avoid tax liabilities. After their time in Hollywood, just as Ethel felt herself to be tired of living abroad and Wodehouse was looking forward to catching up on the cricket with Bill Townend, they realised that they had to be even more careful about residency. They shifted to the South of France, renting a house in Auribeau, near the French Riviera, where their neighbours were H. G. Wells and the mystery writer E. Phillips Oppenheim.

Despite all their tax issues, the Wodehouses were never in any danger of being badly off. From the start of his career, with his careful log of *Money Received for Literary Work*, Wodehouse was financially realistic, and guarded the 'family sock' with care; what Bertie would term 'the oof', the 'moolah' or the 'spondulicks' was, in many ways, the driving force behind both his plots and his life. Wodehouse turned fifty in 1931, and, despite the inconvenience caused by the financial uncertainty, his letters also show a certain sense of excitement at the prospect of existing, for a while, on the edge. He confesses to feeling pleased at having something to assuage life's monotony. 'Everything was so easy for me', he notes, 'I was getting a bit bored.'[3] The only cloud was the continued financial responsibility that he felt towards his friend William Townend. Some thirty years after their time at Dulwich, Wodehouse was still offering to rewrite Townend's work to make it more saleable, and canvassing publishers on his behalf. 'If only you were making a couple of thousand a year steady', he told Bill, 'I shouldn't have a worry in the world.'[4]

Wodehouse's own writing was seeing widescale success, with the publication of some of his greatest novels, including *Thank You, Jeeves*

(1934), *Right Ho, Jeeves* (1934) and *The Code of the Woosters* (1938). With his new British agent, A. P. Watt, operating alongside Reynolds in the States, Wodehouse was established not simply as a writer, but as an international brand. Notes from his agents show that an 'option' on Jeeves had been sold to promote '"Sir" shaving requisites'; 'The Pipe and Tobacco Guild' requested Wodehouse's contributions in a book to promote smoking; the *Daily Mail* commissioned a series of feature articles from Wodehouse to increase circulation; and Wodehouse investigated options for a spin-off Jeeves cartoon, with a butler called 'Keggs'.

In 1934, Wodehouse was also surprised to receive an offer from Paramount Studios to return to Hollywood. For tax reasons, he had to decline. He was, in his words, 'Public Enemy Number One in America', but found the offer 'rather gratifying after the way Hollywood took a solemn vow three years ago never to mention my name again'.[5] Wodehouse's Hollywood scandal had obviously been swiftly forgotten: in 1936 he was offered, and accepted, a six-month contract with MGM to work on various scripts, including the seemingly never-ending musical *Rosalie*. A return to Hollywood allowed him to renew his friendship with the movie star Maureen O'Sullivan, and her husband, John Farrow.

Among the highlights of 1932 was the announcement of Leonora's engagement. Leonora had met her fiancé, Peter Cazalet, in the late 1920s. A leading amateur steeplechase jockey and trainer, Peter was the youngest son of four, and was later to take over the management of the family estate. Wodehouse had known the Cazalet family for a number of years through Leonora's friendship with Peter's sister, Thelma. He had stayed at Fairlawne, the family home in Kent, where he met writers and artists such as Rudyard Kipling and Hugh Walpole. He also accompanied Leonora and Thelma to Lord's cricket ground in 1926, when Peter scored a century for Eton against Harrow. Wodehouse instantly approved, writing with delight about the engagement. Part of his pleasure came from a sense of relief. Wodehouse had been worried by some of Leonora's admirers. The prospect of having to welcome a sensitive new-age twenties man as a son-in-law (a Percy Gorringe type from *Jeeves and the Feudal Spirit*) had filled him with dread. The unidentified figure of 'Dennis Freeman' stands, in these letters, as a cipher for the sort of man Wodehouse detested, the sort who, as he put it elsewhere, would spend his time 'twittering all over the place, screaming: "Oh, Lionel!"'[6]

After returning to London for the wedding, Ethel and Wodehouse spent 1933 and 1934 in France, living in both Auribeau and Paris, and summering at Hunstanton. During this period, there was a new collaboration for Wodehouse, as he joined Guy Bolton and Cole Porter on what was to be the hit musical *Anything Goes*. Bolton detested Paris, so Wodehouse's French headquarters moved to the small holiday resort of Le Touquet, on the northern coast of France. Wodehouse soon grew to 'love the place'. There is 'nothing to do but work', he told Denis Mackail, 'we really are leading the most hermit existence here'.[7]

Le Touquet, resort of choice for the Drones' annual weekend away, had a history of welcoming the English.[8] In 1904, a British linoleum tycoon, John Whitley, had bought up land in the area, with the aim of selling it on to members of the British upper classes. Hundreds of individually designed Art Deco villas were built, as well as a huge casino. Sports facilities, a sea-front pool, a racecourse, a golf course and a cricket ground made Le Touquet into a luxury playground for England's wealthy elite, attracting visitors such as Noel Coward, H. G. Wells and the then Prince of Wales. Before renting a house, the Wodehouses enjoyed staying at the brand-new Royal Picardy Hotel, famous for its nine-room suites, each with its own pool. Geographically, Le Touquet suited the Wodehouses well. Within easy reach of England, they were able to make visits to England to see Leonora and the growing Cazalet family: a daughter (Sheran) and a son (Edward) were born in 1934 and 1936.

After Wodehouse's return from Hollywood, he and Ethel spent a brief spell in London, before deciding to make Le Touquet their permanent base. The latter part of the decade was to bring considerable recognition for Wodehouse. In 1939, Oxford University awarded him an honorary doctorate. After the crushing disappointment of being denied an Oxford education this was, for Wodehouse, a particular triumph.

Although the situation in Europe was becoming increasingly unsettled, Wodehouse resisted acknowledging the reality of impending conflict. His comments to Bill Townend at this time demonstrate his belief that this was a war that would never happen. In the months following 1 September 1939, there was – at first – little to disturb the equilibrium of their life in northern France. Wodehouse continued to attend steadfastly to his novels – and his growing brood of animals.

1 *Over Seventy*, p. 107.
2 'The Ordeal of Osbert Mulliner', published in *Liberty* and *The Strand* in 1928. Repr. in *Mr Mulliner Speaking* (1929).
3 PGW to William Townend, 1 December 1932 (Dulwich).
4 Ibid.
5 PGW to William Townend, 11 June 1934 (Dulwich).
6 See *Performing Flea*, p. 71. 'Dennis' or 'Denis' Freeman occurs occasionally in PGW's correspondence as an unwanted house guest who borrowed money, and repaid the Wodehouses with bouncing cheques. See PGW to William Townend, 10 October 1932 (Dulwich).
7 PGW to Denis Mackail, 6 April 1932 (Wodehouse Archive).
8 See *Uncle Fred in the Springtime* (1939), Chapter 4.

1932–1940:
'A jolly strong position'

Domaine de la Frayère
Auribeau
Alpes Maritimes

March 6. 1932

Dear Bill.

The above is our new address. We move in on Thursday. We have taken it for a year. It is a sort of Provencal country-house, with a hundred acres of hillside and large grounds and a huge swimming-pool. It ought to be lovely in summer. Just at the moment it is a bit bleak.

[...]

I have been having rather a rotten time with my work. *The American Magazine* editor did not like my last two stories, and played me rather a dirty trick by going and seeing Ethel in N.Y. and asking her to make me change them.[1] The result is that she keeps after me about them, and I can't change the damn things – it means inventing entirely different plots. So whenever I try to start a new story Ethel comes up and asks me what I have done about these two, which puts me right off my stroke.

[...]

You're absolutely right about Kip. Gosh, what a rotten story that pig story was.[2] As a matter of fact, Kip was the outstanding case of the Infant Prodigy. His stuff done in the early twenties was great, but he lost that terrific zest and got married and settled down and made his stuff too long and it's only the remnants of the old fire that make his later work readable.

[...]

I bought Aldous Huxley's book, but simply can't read it. Aren't these stories of the future a bore. The whole point of Huxley is that he can write better about modern life than anybody else, so of course he goes and writes about the future.[3]

[...]

I'm wondering a little if this move of living in the south of France is going to work. Cannes itself is a most demoralising place. One wants to be at the Casino all the time. But this place we have taken is twenty minutes away in a car, so perhaps one will be out of the temptation zone. But the atmosphere of the Riviera – the moral atmosphere, I mean, – is very unhealthy.

There is one advantage about living here. One can get to England very easily. I doubt if I shall be able to be over much this summer, but I shall certainly take in next year's footer. We must see the Bedford match together. At Bedford next year, isn't it? We ought to have a good team.

[...]

We all dined at the Casino last night. I played chemmy after dinner, won four thousand francs, and legged it home with the loot at half past one. Ethel stayed on till 8 a.m. and lost about as much!! I can't understand women. I mean, their vitality. Ethel is always complaining of not being fit, but she can stay up all night without suffering from it. I collapse hours before she has begun feeling tired.

[...]

Cheerio

Yours ever

Plum

1 The stories that Wodehouse had published in *The American* in 1932 were the *Mulliner* stories: 'The Bishop's Cat' (February), 'The Bishop's Folly' (March), 'Open House' (April). The editor's dissatisfaction presumably arose over Wodehouse's 'Hollywood' stories, published in late 1932 and 1933, which included 'A Cagey Gorilla' (December), 'Love Birds' (January), 'Love on a Diet' (February), and 'A Star Is Born' (March).
2 Rudyard Kipling's 'Beauty Spots', a story which features an enormous semi-tame white sow, was published in *The Strand Magazine* in January 1932.
3 Huxley's *Brave New World* had been published earlier that year.

The Wodehouses' companions on the Riviera included the writers Michael Arlen, E. Phillips Oppenheim and H. G. Wells. Wodehouse found Wells 'an odd bird'.

TO WILLIAM TOWNEND

[u.d.] 1932

[...]

I like Wells, but the trouble with him is that you can never see him alone. He is accompanied wherever he goes by the woman he's living with. When they came to lunch, we were all set to listen to his brilliant table talk, and she wouldn't let him get a word in edgeways, monopolizing the conversation while he sat looking like a crushed rabbit. I did manage to get him away in a corner after lunch long enough for him to tell me that he had an arrangement with her that when he went to London, he went by himself, and he added, his face lighting up, that he was going to London next week. Then she yelled for him, and he trotted off.

By the way, when you go to his residence, the first thing you see is an enormous fireplace, and round it are carved in huge letters the words: TWO LOVERS BUILT THIS HOUSE.

Her idea, I imagine. I can't believe Wells would have thought of that himself.[1]

[...]

1 H. G. Wells and his lover, Odette Keun, had designed their own villa, Lou Pidou, in Malbosc, on the French Riviera. PGW adapts this real-life anecdote for *The Code of the Woosters* (1938): Bertie recalls that he 'once stayed at the residence of a newly married pal of mine, and his bride had had carved in large letters over the fireplace in the drawing-room, where it was impossible to miss it, the legend "Two Lovers Built This Nest", and I can still recall the look of dumb anguish in the other half of the sketch's eyes every time he came in and saw it' (Chapter 3).

In the following letter, Wodehouse shows the genesis of the plot for Thank You, Jeeves, *in which Bertie disguises himself as a banjo-playing minstrel [see plate 27]. Wodehouse was writing this novel when 'blackface' performers were the height of fashion. Al Jolson, Bing Crosby and Shirley Temple were among many actors who performed blacked up during this period.*

Domaine de la Frayère
Auribeau
Alpes Maritimes
France

April 1. 1932

Dear Bill.

Thanks for long letter. Good, selling that story. Also thanks for the material for the short story. I haven't had time to brood on it yet, but I think it will be a great help.

Now, one other S.O.S., if you have time. Don't bother if you haven't.

Do you remember, when I was writing my last novel, I asked you for comic stuff about a chap burgling a house, and you came back with a magnificent wad. It didn't fit in to that novel, but it will come in fine in the one I am writing now, a Jeeves novel where Bertie, who is blacked up like a nigger minstrel, is scouring the countryside for butter to remove his blacking. To get it, he breaks into a house.

Your stuff, you remember, was as follows: – House is owned by animal breeder. Burglar falls foul of monkey in red coat, sixteen Pekes (puppies), an older Peke, and a quantity of white mice. Can you think of anything else?

The house is a country house. It can have anything you like in it, and anything you like can happen to Bertie in it. Incidentally, I wonder if it would be funnier to scrap the animals – or keep only a few of them – and have it [in] a girls' school? Can you see Bertie chivvied by a Games Mistress? [...] Of course, he cannot be arrested. He gets away. But I can see dimly a scene where he hides in a dormitory, the kids welcoming him enthusiastically because he seems to be a nigger minstrel.

NOTE: I see a way to keep your stuff in toto, as well. With Bertie on this occasion is Sir Roderick Glossop, also blacked up. They could break into different houses and compare notes on meeting again. Sir R. could do the animal house stuff.

I really think this would be better, as for the Bertie scene one would be able to have a dialogue scene, – B. under bed, mistress coming in and questioning the girls etc. Will you give it a moment's thought some time, but don't let it interfere with your own work. But you have a genius for thinking of comic details, and I feel you might dig up some with luck. Anyway, if you brood, brood on the girls' school idea.

[...]

The scenery here is marvellous. But I haven't yet got used to being away from England or America. I can't see any stuff for stories in this locality, though you would probably get a dozen out of the Cannes crowd.

We have a German butler, an Alsatian footman, a Serbian cook, a French chauffeur, an Italian maid, and an English odd-job man. Good material for the next war. But they all seem to get on well together.

Well, so long.

Yours ever

Plum

TO DENIS MACKAIL

Domaine de la Frayère
Auribeau
Alpes-Maritimes

April 8. 1932

[...]

I'm so glad you liked Snorky's story. I thought it was marvellous.[1] It's such a pity that she writes with such difficulty. Have you ever seen a Snorky MS.? She sits in bed with a very thin-paper pad and one of those pencils that make the faintest possible mark, and in about four hours produces a page. Then she writes another page next day and puts ring round it and a hieroglyphic on page one, – that is to show that part of page two goes on page one, then you read the rest of page one and go back to page two, in the meantime inserting a bit of page four. All in that filthy, obscene handwriting of hers. Still, the results are good. Do egg her on to writing some more. I'm so afraid this beastly dress business of hers will absorb her.

[...]

Yours ever

Plum

TO WILLIAM TOWNEND

> Domaine de la Frayère
> Auribeau
> Alpes-Maritimes

Aug 13. 1932

Dear Bill.

[...]

I am hoping that this rise in the American stock market means the beginning of better times out there. There is no doubt that the magazines are in awful straits in New York [...]

Hell's foundations are quivering a bit at the moment on account of vast sums to be paid out soon for both English and American income tax. The trouble about this income tax business is that if you simply pay you get soaked much too much, while if you engage a hired bravo to fight them on every point and contest every claim, you save a lot in the end but it means that you are suddenly informed that your income tax affairs dating from the year 1896 are now settled and will you kindly forward a cheque for about three thousand quid.

In America it's even worse. God knows how much I shall be made to pay there. Fortunately, in America you can keep a thing like that dragging on for ever and pay in installments.

It wouldn't matter, of course, only I can't sell any of my stocks to pay taxes, as I bought Honble stocks at about 260 and they now stand at around 27!

However, thank Gawd I have now eight short stories in my drawer, besides the serial which *Cosmop* have started to pay for.[1] So no need to sell Miss Winks.

[...]

We have been seeing a lot of Maurice Chevalier.[2] Not a bad chap, but rather a ham. I can't ever really like actors, can you?

We now have Mrs. Barney in our midst! I haven't seen her, but I am told she haunts low bars in red pyjamas and talks to everybody at the top of her voice. I can't see what it matters whether she actually slew the young drug fiend or not, – they ought to have hung a woman like that on principle.[3]

Well, cheerio. Dashed hot here, but I see it is in England, too. I'm writing like blazes. A novel and eight short stories in seven and a half months.

Yours ever

Plum

1 The serial was *Thank You, Jeeves*, which was not published as a serial until 1934. The short stories include 'The Amazing Hat Mystery' (*Cosmopolitan*, August 1933, and *The Strand*, June 1934), 'The Luck of the Stiffhams' (*The Strand*, March 1934, and *Cosmopolitan*, November 1935) and 'The Fiery Wooing of Mordred' (*Cosmopolitan*, December 1934, and *The Strand*, February 1935).
2 French actor, singer and vaudeville performer, now best known for his later role in *Gigi* (1958).
3 Mrs Elvira Dolores Barney, married to an American singer, was accused of murdering her lover, after a cocktail party, in her London flat. In 1932, she was fully acquitted and moved to the Auribeau region of France.

TO DENIS MACKAIL

Domaine de la Frayère
Auribeau
Alpes-Maritimes

Oct 9. 1932

Dear Denis.

I'm awfully glad you liked *Hot Water*. Wonderful reviews from everybody except a blighter named Frank Kendon in *John O' London's Weekly*, of all papers, and a moderate stinker from someone called Dilys Powell. I must say I thought the editor of *J O' L* might have restrained Frankie, considering that the offices of the paper are on the same floor as the *Strand* and blood is supposed to be thicker than water.

Priestley, however, was the worst of all, because he analysed me, blast him, and called attention to the thing I try to hush up, – viz. that

I have only got one plot and produce it once a year with variations. I wish to goodness novelists wouldn't review novels.

In re. *Ian and F.* I ordered it weeks ago, but from sheer kindheartedness, not wishing our local postman to have to lug a parcel up all these hills, I did it through the Cannes Library.[1] [...]

I always envy you being able to hold the reader with real life stuff. I have to have jewels, comic lovers, and about a dozen American crooks before I can move. My great trouble is that I have to have rapid action for serial purposes, and how can one get rapid action without there being something at least half the characters want to steal.

[...]

I have now got out a sequel to *Summer Lightning*,[2] but I am very dubious about it. I can't kid myself that it's as good as *S.L.*, – principally because the hero and heroine are already engaged, which deprives me of the good old light comedy love scenes. Also, I can't get a decent part for Galahad, who was the best character in *Summer Lightning*. Altogether, I am glad that I am so far ahead with my work, because this one will want a lot of thinking over.

According to present plans, Ethel and I dash over to London at the end of the month for a week or two. This, of course, involves leaving Miss Winks here, and I doubt if, when the time comes, we shall be capable of it. What a curse that quarantine law is. It seems so damned silly to extend it to Pekes, who couldn't possibly give rabies to anyone. Oh, by the way. Charlotte. Masterly. The best Peke in fiction.

After visiting England, there is some idea of a trip to New York. Ethel wants to open Norfolk Street again, and I am all for it. But once more one comes up against the Winks problem. Our latest scheme is to buy her a cat-skin and bring her in disguised as a cat.

[...]

Yours ever

Plum

1 Mackail's latest novel was *Ian and Felicity, or Peninsula Place*, which featured a Peke called Charlotte.
2 *Heavy Weather* (1933).

Domaine de la Frayère
Auribeau. AM. France

Nov 6. 1932

Darling Snorky.

You may well imagine (pens bien figurer) the excitement your letter caused in the house. Mummie was having a bath when she got it and rushed out with a towel round her shrieking for me. Winks barked, I shouted, and a scene of indescribable confusion eventuated.

It certainly was wonderful news. You know me on the subject of Peter. Thumbs up, old boy. Not only a sound egg but probably <u>the</u> only sound egg left in this beastly era of young Bloomsbury novelists and Denis Freemans. He really has got everything. It is wonderful that you should be marrying a man who is not only the nicest chap I know but likes exactly the sort of life you like. You're bound to be happy.

And isn't it marvellous that you're so fond of Molly & such a friend of Thelma's, so that there's no awkwardness of taking on a strange family.[1] I mean, if you were marrying – say, the Prince of Wales, there would be all that business of getting acquainted with the rest of them. Personally, I think any girl would be wise in marrying Peter simply to get Molly for a mother-in-law.

Peter really is ideal. What a ripper. Have you ever met anyone who didn't like him? I don't suppose there is anybody who doesn't. He's the most charming, unaffected fellow in the world, and he will make the most wonderful husband.

What fun you're going to have! You never could have been really happy with a London life. You need the country, and I can't imagine the country under more perfect conditions. Peter, apart from being Peter, has got such an interesting job. You'll love it.

The only flaw in the whole thing is that we can't go yelling the news all over the place. I'm so happy about it that I want to tell everyone I meet. I want to stop French peasants on the road and say 'Figurez-vous, mon brave, ma fille est fiancée à M. Pierre Cazalet, le jeune homme le plus admirable de l'Angleterre!'

Well, you will have gathered from all this that you have sold the idea to the old folks.

All my love, darling, and tell Peter that he is just as lucky as you are, because there's no one like my Snorky.

Your

Plummie 🐷

P.S. Winks and Boo must be bridesmaids, carrying your train in their mouths.

---

1 Leonora's future mother-in-law, 'Molly', was Maud Lucia Cazalet (née Heron-Maxwell).

TO WILLIAM TOWNEND

Dorchester Hotel
Park Lane
W.1.

Dec. 1. 1932

Dear Bill.

Thanks for your letter. I have been hoping that I could get down to see you, but it has been impossible. Hell's foundations have been quivering, and I have been tied up all the time with income tax agents.

A very nasty wallop has recently hit the home. Denby wrote to us some months ago from America saying that the income tax authorities there had started to make enquiries and told us that the only thing to do was to put everything in the hands of a firm who would manage things for us. Then we were told that the head of this firm must come over – at our expense! – to confer with our English man.

Well, he arrived [...] and the first thing he did was to inform us that we owed the dear old Amer. Govt. $187,000!!!

After this shock he rather gave us to hope that he could reduce this to about $70,000.

Anyway, the devil of it is that we have had to sell at an average of about 30 all those shares we bought for about $300. When the smoke has cleared away, I shall have lost around a hundred and fifty thousand quid since 1929.

The position now seems to be that we shall have a capital of forty thousand quick, plus whatever we can save from the wreck in America. [...]

Anyway, we always did have too much money, and a nest egg of about fifty thousand quid in gilt edged securities is as much as anybody could want. [...]

[...]

As a matter of fact, in some ways I am not sorry this income tax business has happened. Everything was so easy for me before that I was getting a bit bored. I now can spit on my hands and start sweating again, feeling that it really matters when I make a bit of money.

[...]

Snorky seems to be on velvet. She is very much in love with Peter, and he is one of the few decent chaps left nowadays. The financial end of the thing is a bit muddled [...] what Peter actually gets, I don't know, but he and Snorky will be pretty rich.

Don't you find, as you get on in life, that the actual things you really want cost about two hundred a year? I have examined my soul, and I find that my needs are a *Times* Library subscription and tobacco money, plus an extra bit for holidays. If only you were making a couple of thousand a year steady, I shouldn't have a worry in the world.

[...]

Well cheerio. Don't refer to any of this in your next letter.

Yours ever

Plum.

TO WILLIAM TOWNEND

Domaine de la Frayère
Auribeau. AM. France

Jan 4. 1933

Dear Bill.
Happy New Year and what not.

I was frightfully sorry not to be able to come down and see you while I was in London. It simply wasn't possible. Every day we had conferences with our English income tax man, and I couldn't get away. It ended in our sending him over to America! (Incidentally, he travelled on the *Majestic* and ran into the worst storm on record, and must be cursing us.)

The final score is as follows:– I have had to sell out at about twenty a million stocks. I bought at 250 and higher. The money has been transferred from America to England and is now in an English bank, where the American authorities can't touch it. It amounts to about seventy thousand quid. A nice sum in itself, but the American income-tax people at present are demanding about fifty thousand!

My scheme is to imitate dear old France – the only sensible country on earth – and sit tight. If they will settle at a reasonable figure, o.k. If not, not a penny do they touch. A jolly strong position. I am hoping they will settle for about six thousand quid.

Anyway, there it is.

Meanwhile, am getting on splendidly with a new novel. I hope to have it finished before I return to England. If I put off my return till March, that is to say. At present, we plan to come back at end of Jan and open Norfolk St.

I shall be glad to be settled in England again. This country is fine, but we are too far away from everything. And if one lives in Cannes, there is the constant temptation of the Casino. London is the best spot, all round.

How have you been doing? Any luck? I'm afraid it is still a bad time for the magazines. I wish America would buck up and get itself in hand.

[...]

The wedding went off splendidly and is turning out an enormous success. Snorky reports that she has never been happier. They had a three days honeymoon in Paris and then legged it back! It's wonderful that she loves just the sort of life she will have to lead, – quiet country existence. At present they are at Fairlawne with Mrs. Cazalet, whom Snorky loves, but I'm afraid Fairlawne is too big to be kept up after those death duties.

Did you see the photograph of me in topper? [See plate 29.] V. hot stuff.

[...]
Yours ever
Plum

TO WILLIAM TOWNEND

Domaine de la Frayère
Auribeau, A.M.

Feb 9. 1933

Dear Bill.

[...]

These last four days have been rather trying. I am alone in the house with the caretaker and his wife, who cooks for me. I take my meals on trays. It's funny, I used to think it the ideal life. I remember when Ethel left me in America when she went to fetch Snorky and I was at our shack at Bellport without even a servant, doing my own cooking and working on *Something New*, I had the time of my life. But then I had the village to go to and American papers to get, and that filled the day. Up here I am absolutely isolated.

[...]

I remember Grinlinton at school. He was just before your time. (In case you've forgotten, I mean the chap Jimmy George wrote to you about.) He created a terrific sensation by having a fight with Jack Treadgold and beating him up badly. Grinlinton was coming out of Gilkes' room, where he had just been whacked for smoking, and Jack Treadgold kidded him and G. flew at him and half killed him.[1]

Isn't Life rummy. I mean, the effect of time. Evidently he is now a typical ex-soldier crank. I really believe you and I and Slacker are the only people who have remained like they were at school.[2] I sometimes feel as if I were a case of infantilism. I seem mentally so exactly as I was then. I haven't developed mentally at all since my last year at school. All my ideas and ideals are the same. I still think the Bedford match the most important thing in the world.

I want to have a talk with you about money matters when I return. The outlook is dashed good. Even after a disastrous visit to the Casino last Saturday, I am two thousand quid ahead on my year's gambling, so I'll be able to ease the situation a bit at Fairlawn. My idea is to guarantee an overdraft, so that you will feel safe. If you don't need it, then it's still there. But if you want to take six months off to write a novel, that will be at the back of you. [...]

[...]
Cheerio
Yours ever
Plum

P.S. Better not write to me here, unless I let you know that I am staying on. In any case, of course, no mention of money.

1 Jack Treadgold was the son of Wodehouse's housemaster at Dulwich. Grinlinton, another Dulwich boy, left the school in 1897.
2 McCulloch 'Slacker' Christison, a former Dulwich College boy.

TO PAUL REYNOLDS

NAIII 25 CABLE VIA FRENCH
GRASSE NFT FEB 15 1933
LCD CARBONATO

SEVENTY THOUSAND WORDS OF NOVEL WRITTEN WILL MAIL DIRECTLY TYPED IDEAL SATURDAY POST SERIAL TELL COSTAIN BEST I HAVE EVER DONE[1]

WODEHOUSE.

1 *Heavy Weather*, Wodehouse's latest Blandings novel, was published in the *Saturday Evening Post* from May to July 1933. Thomas B. Costain was the *Post*'s fiction editor.

On April 11, Reynolds sent the following telegram to Wodehouse: 'FEDERAL TAX AUDITOR IN ANNUAL AUDIT OUR BOOKS FOUND LARGE PAYMENTS TO YOU AND LATER INFORMED US YOU HAD PAID NO TAXES HERE [...] SITUATION VERY SERIOUS ALL FUTURE INCOME IN JEOPARDY'

TO PAUL REYNOLDS

1 Norfolk Street
Park Lane W.1.

April 12. 1933

Dear Reynolds.

Your cable was a bombshell. I simply cannot understand what it means. You speak of the authorities informing you of our non-payment of taxes as if it were a new discovery. Surely the whole point of all this trouble we have been to for the last year or so – sending Wiltshire over to N. Y. etc. – has been due to the fact that we knew we had not paid taxes & the authorities knew we had not paid taxes and that we wanted to pay them & get the thing settled.

[...]

Do write & explain fully.

[...]

With best wishes

Yours ever

P. G. Wodehouse

TO PAUL REYNOLDS

Constitutional Club
London W.C.

April 18. 1933

Dear Reynolds.

[...]

My wife is frightfully worried about this Income Tax thing, but,

242

personally, I can't see that it will be so bad, as my Stock Exchange losses were so big that, if – as is presumably the case – I am allowed to deduct these, there should be very little tax to pay. And, anyway, surely I can make an arrangement to work it off by giving the Tax people – say half of whatever I make in America till further notice.

[...]

Yours ever

P. G. Wodehouse

TO DENIS MACKAIL

Hunstanton Hall
Norfolk *
*(till Sept 30)

Sept 10. 1933

Dear Denis. (Bluff old Squire Mackail, we used to call him, and many is the time I have seen him striding over the fields in his gaiters, chewing a straw.)

Sorry I haven't written before. You know how it is. One's Art. I was on the last chapters and couldn't leave them. Finished yesterday, making three novels and 10 short stories in 18 months, which, as Variety would say, is nice sugar.

[...]

Burglary o.k. Nothing of importance taken. In her childhood Snorky – in her imbecile way – used to collect empty jewel cases. These were stacked in a cupboard and must have made the burglars feel they were on to something hot. [...]

They pinched my field glasses and some of my winter underclothing. Also a packet of shares in a company which went bust in 1915.

They seem to have had a good time otherwise, playing the gramophone and so on. The police, presumably, listening outside and occasionally going in to ask them to play 'Stormy Weather' again.

We are getting thoroughly fed up with rural life and are counting the days till we can get back to Norfolk St. What a dull place the country is, really. And, oh my God, these county families. They turn up in gangs of twenty for tea, and talk about somebody who was a Wapping and whose mother married a Sigabee.

[...]

See you soon.

[...]

Yours ever

Plum

Leonora's first child, a daughter, Sheran Cazalet, was born on 31 March 1934.

TO OLIVE GRILLS (NÉE ARMSTRONG)

Carlton Hotel, Cannes

April 26. 1934

Dear Bubbles,

You will think me crazy, addressing the envelope like this, but I've clean forgotten your married name! I have it down in a book, & of course I lost the book in my removal to Cannes. Sorry!

The Leonora baby arrived in scenes of terrific excitement. We went down to spend Easter with her, & on Good Friday night there were symptoms which made my wife send for the doctor. He said no prospect of anything happening for two weeks. And at 4.30 that morning it all started. She was hurried in an ambulance from Tonbridge to a London nursing home and the baby was born at 8 a.m. on March 31. I slept through the whole thing & woke to find everyone gone, & then the telephone rang & I was told!

The baby is sweet – A girl.

By the way, did you think your baby was hideous when it was born? Leonora did. She was expecting something with curly golden hair. But she is devoted to it now.

I am so glad it is all over.

I am down here for a few more days, when I go to Paris. If you write to me here, it will be forwarded.

I have to be out of England for a year, owing to some income tax technicality. It's a great nuisance, but can't be helped.

I am working hard on a new novel, which is coming out splendidly. But I shall be glad to see my wife & Pekingese again. I join them in Paris.

Best wishes

Yours ever

P. G.

Wodehouse was now working simultaneously on his novel, The Luck of the Bodkins, *and, with Guy Bolton and composer Cole Porter, on the book of what was eventually to become the musical* Anything Goes, *starring Ethel Merman. Porter's extravagant party-going lifestyle meant that he was not the most reliable colleague. Bolton found it impossible to work in Paris, so Le Touquet was chosen as a writing base.*

TO WILLIAM TOWNEND

Royal Picardy
Le Touquet-Paris-Plage

Aug 2. 1934

Dear Bill.

Thanks for yours. I'm glad the novel is coming out well. What a sweat all that sea stuff must be.

[...]

I'm having a devil of a time with this musical comedy Guy Bolton and I are writing. I can't get hold of Guy or the composer, so have been plugging along by myself. Still, Guy says he will be here on Saturday. What has become of the composer, heaven knows. Last heard of at Heidelberg and probably one of the unnamed three hundred shot by Hitler.[1]

Bill, do you realize that in 1914 just about a tenth of what has been happening in Austria would have caused a world war? I think the world's reaction to the Dolfuss [*sic*] thing is a very healthy sign.[2] It seems quite evident that nobody wants war nowadays. I would much rather have all this modern unrest than that sort of feeling of swollen simmering of 1914. The great thing nowadays is that you can't just say to the populace 'Hoy! The Peruvians have invaded Antigua. Pitch in and attack France.' They want to be told exactly what is in it for them before they start.

[...]

Yours ever

Plum.

1 The key to this rather morbid aside is the fact that Cole Porter was a known homosexual. Wodehouse had presumably been reading, throughout July 1934, of Hitler's coup, in which a number of prominent Nazi SA leaders ('Brownshirts') were arrested and shot; the SA leaders were accused of insurrection, 'degrading conduct' and homosexual practices. Some two hundred or more SA officers in Berlin were also shot as part of Hitler's 'clean-up' campaign. Articles about the 'abnormal proclivities' of the victims continued throughout July in the British press ('Herr Hitler's Defence', *The Times*, 14 July 1934), along with leader articles expressing concerns about the Nazi party's principles.
2 Austrian statesman and dictator, Engelbert Dollfuss, was assassinated by a group of Austrian Nazis on 25 July 1934.

TO WILLIAM TOWNEND

Royal Picardy Hotel
Le Touquet

Aug 16. 1934.

Dear Bill.

Thanks awfully for your letter.

[...]

Things aren't so bad as they seem at first sight, always provided that the English income tax people don't reopen that case which I won before the Commissioners in January. If they do, and win it, I may be soaked for a pretty good sum.

[...]

[...] In a way, the excitement of the thing rather dims the financial loss, though I'm afraid Ethel is worried. I feel as if I were starting a new life. I can now send stuff to America without having to make it exactly like all my other stories. It will be rather fun seeing if I can build up another name.[1]

Of course, we have not yet gone into all the possible ways of beating the game. [...]

I feel very vicious against them, as they have behaved like bandits. They fined me 25% for not making a return and on top of that 75% for making a false return. Now, how anyone can make a false return without making a return at all is a thing that seems to me to need explaining.

[...]

Have you ever considered how difficult it is to select a pseudonym. Now that I may have to, I can think of no name that sounds like anything. My mind dwells on things like Eustace Trevelyan (Old Brook has just written a story under the name of Batt Rimes!!). I think the thing is to combine two actual names – such as Reeves Grimsdick.

A slight contretemps is caused by the fact that I am now writing with Guy Bolton a musical comedy for New York which ought to be the biggest thing of the season, as it will be the only one with three cast-iron stars and Cole Porter is doing the music. It seems very moot whether I shall be able to cash in on this. However, we shall see.

[...]

Cheerio. Write soon.

Yours ever.

Plum

1 To avoid the consequences of a tax lien, Wodehouse very briefly experimented with the practice of submitting a story under a pseudonym.

TO LEONORA CAZALET

Royal Picardy
Le Touquet
Paris-Plage

Aug 24. 1934

Darling Snorky.

We are simply enraptured by the photographs of Sheran. I never saw such a beautiful baby. What a change from the old Chinese gangster who leered at us on your bed in April, fingering her gat under the swaddling clothes. You must have her photographed every year.

We dined the other night with Mrs Somerset Maugham.[1] Diana Churchill was there and talked a lot about you. She is an awfully nice girl.[2]

[...]

My relations with U.S. Government continue distant. I am now rather in the stage of hitching my shoulder petulantly and saying nasty things about them in a falsetto voice.

Washburn went to Washington the day before yesterday with our latest offer, and Mummie and I watched the clock all day, calculating how soon we could get a cable.

[...]

Eventually Washburn's cable came [...] and read 'Offer submitted. Decision within a month'. So there we are!

[...]

Winky and Boo have just been washed, preparatory to being exhibited with Mummie in the 'Madame de 1934 et son chien' event in the local dog show. As far as I can gather, this is decided partly by how the Madame is dressed and partly by personal influence with the judges. We have one of them in our pocket and are full of confidence.

[...]

The other night I went to the Casino, had a shot at Roulette, won three mille in two minutes and came home. At seven a.m. Winky was restless, so I took her out, and we had been out about ten minutes when Mummie arrived, having been at the Casino all night and lost three mille. So we took the dogs for a walk and went in and had breakfast.

Love to all

Plummie.

---

1 Syrie and Somerset Maugham had divorced in 1928. Syrie Maugham was a renowned interior decorator and her Le Touquet salon, furnished entirely in shades of beige, was widely admired.
2 Diana, the eldest daughter of the MP, and later Prime Minister, Winston Churchill.

Low Wood
Le Touquet

Nov 12. 1934

Darling Snorky.

Just been reading your letter to Mummie. How splendid that you have taken up riding and enjoy it so much. Rather, as one might say, you than me, but I'm awfully glad you're doing it.

BOOKS. Yes, do send me the two Claudius books.[1] I'd love to have them.

I had a letter from Denis Mackail, laughing heartily at me for saying I liked *Goodbye, Mr Chips*. I still stick to it that it's a jolly good book. I was on the eve of getting the author's last one, *Lost Horizon*, but mercifully found out in time it was a tender, wistful story of Thibet. Gosh darn these writers who leap from one spot to another.[2]

Have you read Evelyn Waugh's *Handful of Dust*? Excellent in spots, but he ought to have you to read over his stuff before he publishes it. You would have told him (a) that he couldn't have a sort of Mr Mulliner farce chapter about the man going to Brighton if he wanted the story to be taken seriously and (b) for goodness sake to keep away from Brazil.

What a snare this travelling business is to the young writer. He goes to some blasted jungle or other and imagines that everybody will be interested in it.

Also that Dickens stuff. Marvellous in a short story, but too much dragged in.

[...]

Our N.Y. lawyer cabled us that he was having a conference with the income tax people last Saturday, but we have heard nothing since.

[...]

Love to all

Your

Plummie.

---

1 Robert Graves' *I, Claudius* and *Claudius the God and His Wife Messalina* were both published in 1934.
2 *Good-bye, Mr Chips*, by James Hilton, was serialised in *The Atlantic*.

Low Wood
Le Touquet
France

March 20. 1935

Dear Mr Watt.

A letter from Miss Ella King-Hall, my literary agent in England, informs me that owing to ill health she is closing her agency on April the 5th. And I am wondering if you would care to take on my work.

There are one or two complications. The first is that I know your commission is 10% and I would not want to pay more than 5%.

[...]

My reason for paying only 5% is that there is so little work involved in handling my stuff.

[...]

I am particularly anxious to centralize all my work in England in your hands, as I shall be doing a good deal of theatrical work and movie work from now on, and I should like a big organization like yours behind me. I see that Cochran is to produce the American musical comedy, *Anything Goes*, after all, and I am part author of this.

[...]

Well, will you think it over and let me know?

[...]

With best wishes

Yours sincerely

P. G. Wodehouse

P.S. While I was writing this, a telegram arrived from Miss King-Hall saying that Westbrook was willing to go on handling my work. [...]

Now, this is a thing I am particularly anxious to avoid. [...] A literary agent's is a highly specialized job, and can't be done by an amateur. Also, strictly between ourselves, the brains of the firm was always Mrs Westbrook. [...]

Low Wood
Le Touquet

March 28. 1935

Dear Bill.

I'm so glad the cutting of *Voyage Without End* has come out so well. [...]
I forgot to tell you. Raymond Needham says I ought not to come over
to England for another two months. This case is pending with the
income tax people and he thinks he would have a much better chance
of getting them to shelve it if he could prove that I wasn't in the country
and hadn't been for more than a year and was, so to speak, off the map.

It's a damned disappointment, as I was hoping to see you in a week
or so. But there's over twelve thousand quid at stake, so I mustn't run
any risks. [...]

[...]

I have been writing a farce, and you've no idea what a sweat it is
doing it by oneself.[1] When I work with Guy Bolton it is all so easy [...]

Playwrighting is like what Kipling says in *The Light That Failed*
about line-work for an artist. You are up against it and can't fake.

[...]

Another bit of news is that owing to ill health Ella King-Hall has
closed down the agency, and I have now gone to Watt. [...] I must say
I'm glad in a way. I can't help feeling that a big organization like Watt
must increase one's earnings. [...]

Listen, laddie, do you realize what a much more wholesome frame
of mind the world is in now. Can you imagine a situation like this
German one not leading to war twenty years ago? Things seem to me
to look promising. I don't believe you could get this country into a war
for another thirty years

[...]

Cheerio. Love to Rene and Bim.

Yours ever

Plum

1 *The Inside Stand*, Wodehouse's adaptation of his own novel, *Hot Water*.

Wodehouse's correspondence with S. C. 'Billy' Griffith CBE., the former Alleynian, began in the 1920s. Griffith was an outstanding cricketer who joined Dulwich Prep School in 1922, long after Wodehouse had left, and went up to Cambridge in 1933. Letters were exchanged between the pair, based on their interest in sport and in Dulwich. At this point, Wodehouse congratulates Griffith for receiving his Cambridge Blue.

TO S. C. 'BILLY' GRIFFITH

Shipbourne Grange
Tonbridge
Kent

May 17. 1935

Dear Billy.

I have just read the great news in the *Evening Standard*. I can't tell you how bucked I am. You had made yourself a certainty, of course, but it's wonderful to get your Blue in the middle of May. You must be the only case on record of a man doing it with snowstorms going on all over England!

I wish I could be at Cambridge tonight to celebrate your Blue and Hugh's great century.[1]

Yours ever

P. G. Wodehouse

1 Hugh Bartlett, another talented cricketer and former Alleynian, who went on to play for Surrey and Sussex.

TO LEONORA CAZALET

Low Wood
Le Touquet

June 4. 1935

Darling Snorky.

[...]

Sensational news. Yesterday we bought Low Wood!!! We have been changing our minds every day since we got back, and as late as yesterday morning had made an offer for another house. But it was refused, and then Mummie suddenly switched back to Low Wood.

I must say I am delighted. I have grown very fond of the house, and with the alterations we are going to make it will be fine [see plate 31]. We came to the conclusion that we wanted to live in Le Touquet and that Low Wood was the best bet on account of the position.

[...]

Armine and I went down to Bexhill and saw Mother.[1] She seemed a bit frail, but not too bad. I say, what an enormous size Armine is. I made him walk from the Dorchester to Victoria, and three times en route he pleaded for a cab. And when we got to Bexhill he had a fat lunch at half-past one, a big tea with some friends of his at Cooden at three-thirty, and another tea at Mother's at four-fifteen. He told me he thought he had put on a little weight in front – did I notice it? I said I thought he had, a little.

Must stop now. Lunch.

So long. Love to all.

Your

Plummie.

---

1 Armine had recently retired from his role as Professor of English at the Deccan College in India. He later returned to Poona, where he acted as a tutor to the young Prince of Sangli.

TO A. P. WATT

Low Wood
Le Touquet

June 21. 1935

Dear Mr Watt.

I have so much work on hand that will have to come ahead of *Daily Mail* articles that I would prefer not to tie myself down to a contract at present. [...]

[...]

Newspaper articles are always a difficult proposition. What editors want is 'What are you going to laugh at this Whitsun?' or 'Should the Modern Girl use lipstick?', whereas my ideals are very soaring and I won't write that [*sic*] isn't good enough to appear simultaneously in the *New Yorker*. [...]

I have an idea for a thoughtful thesis on the subject of Literary Criticism entitled 'Back To Whiskers' – my argument being that the soppiness and over-enthusiasm of modern literary criticism is due to the fact that critics are now clean shaven instead of wearing full-size whiskers, as in the brave old days when authors and critics used to come to blows. What we need is a return to the old foliage and acid reviews. [...]

Yours sincerely,

P. G. Wodehouse

TO LEONORA CAZALET

Low Wood
Le Touquet
Pas-de-Calais

Sept 8. 1935

Darling Snorky.

Just caught boat, and found that about two thousand of the proletariat had decided to catch it, too. [...]

I loved my visit, as always, and wish I could have stayed longer. ('The hell you do', you mutter. 'It seemed quite long enough to <u>me</u>.') I carried away with me sentiments of the liveliest gratitude for your refined hosp.

I arrived back to find my *Daily Mail* article the talk of Le Touquet. Everybody seems to think it is my masterpiece! There's one thing about writing for the *D.M.* – you do get read.

Mummie is very fit and longing to see Sheran.

[...]

Bill and Rene sent their love. Poor little Bim wasn't well. V. pathetic. Winks and Boo, on the other hand, bursting with health. I got a great reception.

All my love, darling. Love to the Puss and Nanny etc.

Your

Plummie

September 15. 1935

[...]

If Hunt can give me a reasonable time for the Haggis article I think I could do it. My difficulty is that I know nothing about Haggis and must have some facts in order to be funny about it. Do you know of a good Haggis reference book?

[...]

TO WILLIAM TOWNEND

Low Wood
Le Touquet

Jan 20. 1936

Dear Bill.

Just off to Carlton Hotel, St Moritz, where I expect to stay for a few weeks. I don't know how I shall like it. I've always avoided Switzerland up to now, but I hear there is wonderful sunshine there and it is a very good place for getting material for my sort of story.

Doesn't Kipling's death give you a sort of stunned feeling?[1] He seems to leave such a gap. I didn't feel the same about Doyle or Bennett or Galsworthy. I suppose it is because he is so associated with one's boyhood. It has made me feel much older all of a sudden.

I went to Snorky's for Christmas, but hadn't a chance of getting over to see you. It was one of those visits where you have to be around all the time. [...] Armine and Co. have left Bexhill for Cheltenham. Much better for them all, I think. They have managed to sell the house.

[...]

Low Wood is in a hideous mess now, but will emerge as a very nice house when it is finished. [...]

Love to R and B. Write to me at St Moritz.

Yours ever

Plum.

---

1 Kipling died of a perforated duodenal ulcer on 18 January 1936.

TO LEONORA CAZALET

Feb 26. 1936

Darling Snorky,

Your fat letter to Mummie arrived by this afternoon's post. I'm so glad you're feeling better. Jolly sensible taking that three weeks in bed. Nothing like it.

Stephanie. Oke with me, though Mummie says it reminds her of the Rector of Stiffkey.[1] I once knew a girl named Stephanie Bell. I like the name. The thing that is breaking me all up is this idea of Edward if offspring is a son. I suppose Mollie is all for it, but I can't see where it comes in. Pete can't have been old enough to have known Edward Cazalet very well, so I don't see why he and I – two of the best fellows in the world – should be exposed to the risk of being related to someone who, unless steps are taken through the proper channels, will be called Teddy. Why not William, after Mr Cazalet? Then we should have a good honest Bill, which would be great.

Alternatives

(a) 'I see old Bill Cazalet, the Rugger blue, won the Grand National yesterday!'

(b) 'They tell me Teddy Cazalet is on the Riviera with Dennis Freeman, getting brown absolutely all over.'

No comparison.

[...]

Your loving

Plummy

P.S. Teddy would take to ski-ing like a bird.

1 Harold Francis Davidson (1875–1937), Rector of Stiffkey in Norfolk, was a press sensation in the early thirties. Known as 'the Prostitutes' Padre' for his work ministering to streetwalkers, he was banished from the Church in 1932, accused of immoral practices.

TO ARMINE WODEHOUSE

March 17. 1936

Dear Armine.

I was awfully glad to hear from you. I hope you are feeling fitter now.

[...]

I worked for six weeks solid on a novel after coming back from Switzerland and ran over to Snorky's last week for a few days. I hadn't a chance of getting down to see you, as my time was so occupied with going to London on business. Snorky was looking extraordinarily well, I thought, considering that the event is only a few weeks off. She takes great care of herself.

I feel in tremendous form with the typewriter just now. My holiday did me good. I don't seem to get ideas quite as readily as I should like, but the ones I do get are good, and the novel is coming out well. I don't know if you saw it in *Pearson's Magazine* as a short serial, – about 20,000 words? It is called *Laughing Gas* and the central idea is a shameless crib of *Vice Versa*.[1] My hero goes to Hollywood and he and a child star have teeth out under gas simultaneously and their souls get into the wrong bodies. Since writing it in short form I have had a lot of further ideas, so I am now making it a full length novel. I'm afraid those who remember *Vice Versa* may raise their eyebrows a bit, but I don't believe the reading public remembers the book at all and the theme may seem quite new. Anyway, the setting and plot are original.

We didn't like Switzerland at all, but I am glad I went, as it gives me a new atmosphere. I expect I shall get some stories out of it later on.

We would love to have you and Nella over here, but I fear it will be a long time before we can move into the renovated Low Wood. The Norfolk Street house won't be free till next February, so that we can't get our furniture till then. I suppose next May is about the time when we shall settle in. You must come then. I think you would like Le Touquet. I like it far better than England to live in, though of course there are a lot of things in England that I miss. Still, I can always get over for any cricket match I want to see.

Peter took me down to Eton on Sunday, and I lunched at one of the houses. I am rather dubious about Eton. I admire it in a great many ways, but Etonians as a class always strike me as a bit weedy. Perhaps it is those awful clothes they wear.

I think that idea of a family reunion is an excellent one. I am all for it and will turn up when you say the word. Pev seems likely to be the difficulty. He apparently goes nowhere now and sees nobody. Still, I imagine he would roll up for a thing of that sort. We must certainly go and have a look at Ham Hill. Also Stableford, which is an easy motor ride.[2]

I found Ethel much better when I got back last night. Before I left, she had been a bit down and had been having a lot of pain, but most of it seems to have gone, thank goodness. This is a bad place for her in the winter, but now Spring seems on the way. Today was simply gorgeous, – as good as Cannes.

I must stop now, as I have rather a lot of letters to write. If I can get over to London fairly soon I'll let you know, and you might come up for the night.

Love to all

Yours ever

Plum

1 *Vice Versa: A Lesson to Fathers*, an 1882 novel by F. Anstey about a father–son body swap caused by an Indian magic stone.
2 'For two weeks every summer the three Wodehouse boys would go to stay at Grandmother Wodehouse's home', Ham Hill in Powick, Worcestershire, which overlooked the river Teme. For PGW, 'it was always the great event of the year' (Jasen, p. 7). The Wodehouse family lived in Stableford, Shropshire, during PGW's last years at Dulwich.

April 2. 1936

Dear Bill.

I'm sorry you are going through a mistrustful phase in your book, but I am pretty certain it is only because you have been working so hard at it. I have had just the same experience with the one I am doing, – a novel length version of a short serial which came out in *Pearson's* last year – did you see it – about the man whose soul goes into the body of a child film star. A few days ago, it all seemed absolutely idiotic, but it looks quite all right again now.[1]

[...]

Listen. Extract from a book by Arnold Bennett called *How to Become an Author*.

'He should take care to produce books at regular short intervals. He may continue this process for years without any really striking result in fame or money, and he may pessimistically imagine that his prolonged labours are fruitless. And then newspapers will begin to refer to him as a known author, as an author the mention of whose name is sufficient to recall his productions, and he will discover that all the while the building of his reputation has been going on like a coral reef.

Even mediocre talent, when combined with fixity of purpose and regular industry, will infallibly result in a gratifying success.

But it must never be forgotten that while the reputation is being formed, the excellent and amiable public needs continuous diplomatic treatment. It must not be permitted to ignore his existence. At least once a year, and oftener if possible, a good solid well made book should be flung into the libraries.'

He also advises against frittering away energy on a lot of small things, – e.g. short stories.

That seems to me to sum up your position, except that you certainly can't call yours a 'mediocre talent'. Really good stuff like yours is bound to succeed if you keep turning it out. I think this plan of yours of doing a lot of novels is the right one. What you've got to remember is that, in a sense, you really started with *Voyage Without End,* because the other books were buried.

I believe you're going to see a big improvement when Chapman and Hall have published three or four.

Arnold Bennett's own case was just the same. His early books didn't sell. But gradually one began to see his name about.

[...]

I'm awfully sorry poor old Bim is bad again. What a tragedy. I do hope she gets all right.

More later. Love to Rene.

Yours ever

Plum

1 *Laughing Gas* (1936).

TO LEONORA CAZALET

Low Wood
Le Touquet

April 16. 1936

My darling angel Snorky,
This is just a line to tell you how much I love you and how much I am thinking of you. I am praying that you won't have too bad a time, because you're very precious to me.

I am bucking myself up by thinking of the lovely summer you will have when it's all over. What a fuss we shall make of you.

I shall come over directly you are able to see people. What a long time ago it seems that I saw you with Sheran at the nursing home and you said she was like a Chinese gangster! And do you remember Lord Somebody's baby being brought in from next door, and we agreed that Sheran looked prettier than that, anyway.

I can't bear the thought of you being in pain. I do hope things will be as easy as last time. Thank God there won't be that awful rush and confusion. I'm glad Mummie will be with you.

It's a lovely sunshiny day, and I shall stroll about with the dogs and think of you. And tonight I shall take out all your old letters and read them.

I hope this reaches you before the great day. I want you to know how much I admire you for the way you have gone through all this beastly time of waiting. Everybody thinks you have been wonderful.

Bless you, darling,

Your

Plummie

Leonora gave birth to a son in April. 'Everybody is very pleased about it', Wodehouse wrote. 'She had hardly any trouble about it. [...] I dashed over and saw her, and she was looking splendid.' Despite Wodehouse's protestations and prognostications, the child was named Edward Stephen.

In June 1936, Wodehouse received a letter offering him 'the Mark Twain Medal', in recognition of his 'outstanding and lasting contribution to the happiness of the world'.

TO WILLIAM TOWNEND

Golf Hotel
Le Touquet

July 23. 1936

Dear Bill.

I've just returned from a hurried visit to England, but simply couldn't get a moment to get in touch with you. I had a phone call from Ethel saying that Guy Bolton had been rushed into hospital at Worthing with acute appendicitis and nearly died, and I had to spend my time travelling up and down. He seems to be all right now, thank goodness, but it was a near thing.

[...]

Enclosed will give you a laugh. Me and Mussolini!¹

[...]

Yours ever

Plum

TO NELLA WODEHOUSE

The Beverly Wilshire
Beverly Hills, California

Oct 10. 1936

My dear Nella.

Your cable came as a stunning blow to us, and I really hardly know how to write. I can only say how deeply Ethel and I are feeling for you and wishing that we could be with you. I hate to think what you must be going through.

I feel quite humbled by the shock of it. I always felt so near to poor Armine and looked up to him so enormously. He was a man whom everybody loved, and he and I had always seemed so particularly close to one another. Ours was one of those attachments which are not dependent on close contact. I always felt that we could pick up the thread even after not seeing each other for years.

It is awful to think that he has gone. He will leave a gap in my life which can never be filled.

I shall always treasure the letter which I got from him when I sailed. (When your cable arrived, I was just about to write in answer to it, telling him how much I appreciated all he had said and how absolutely right he was in his criticisms of my work.)

It must be a consolation for you at this awful time to feel how tremendously happy you made him. I can't imagine a more ideal marriage than yours. You have been wonderful.

I feel so far away here, and I am worrying whether you are all right. If there is anything I can do, will you let me know.

Bless you

Yours

Plum

The Wodehouses' return to Hollywood in October 1936 offered Ethel the chance to socialise on a grand scale. 'Parties were very easy to do', she recalled, 'if you had the money. We did, because Plum was getting $2,500 a week. I would go down to the supermarkets and buy a big saddle of lamb, vegetables, turkey, ham and chicken livers. We would have seven cases of champagne. Our butler Arthur would handle the floral arrangements. [...] Then we hired a caterer and barman.' Wodehouse was less comfortable in the celebrity set, but enjoyed spotting the movie stars in town. 'I saw Clark Gable the other day,' he wrote to Bill Townend, 'also Fred Astaire, wearing horn-rimmed spectacles and looking about a hundred.' Wodehouse was working hard, and still found Hollywood difficult to like.'[E]verything', he reflected, 'seems flat.'

TO LEONORA CAZALET

> 1315 Angelo Drive
> Beverly Hills,
> California

Dec 28. 1936

Darling Snorky.

I had just settled down to work off my correspondence – owing to my having ignored all letters for about a month in order to concentrate on work, I have quite thirty letters to write – when Mummie brought me your letter, so the rest of them will have to wait.

[...]

Yes, I am back on *Rosalie* again, just as in the dear old days, but this time, thank goodness, it really is a solid proposition. [...] [T]hey are planning it for their big musical of 1937 and if I can pose as the saviour of the thing – the man who converted a half-million dollar loss into a five-million profit I shall be in very strong at the studio.

[...]

Thanks for the page from *Express* about the recent Edward.[1] Over here, the Hearst papers, of course, took a very yelling attitude about the thing, trying to stir up feeling on the ground that wasn't a pure, sweet American girl a fitting mate for the highest in the land: but the others were all right, and Mencken wrote a very good article, putting the thing very sanely and showing what an ass Edward was.

A significant thing, I thought, was that when I went to the pictures the other night and Mrs Simpson came on the news reel there wasn't a sound. Nobody clapped. It shows once more how futile the Hearst papers are when it comes to influencing the public. He roasted Roosevelt day after day for months, and look what <u>he</u> done! What people buy the Hearst papers for is the comic strips.

I agree with you that England has come darned well out of this. By God, sir, I'm proud of the boys. Can you imagine any other country in which a king's abdication would have been received with a sort of universal 'Oh, yes?' and just left at that?

[...]

Must stop now. Love to you all.

Your

Plummy

1 In December 1936, Edward VIII, who had been King for less than a year, announced his intention to marry an American socialite and divorcée, Mrs Wallis Simpson. This created a constitutional crisis, resulting in his abdication on 10 December.

By April, Wodehouse's time with MGM was drawing to a close. The Hollywood studio RKO had bought the rights to Wodehouse's 1919 novel A Damsel in Distress, *and contracted Wodehouse to work on the script. The film would feature Fred Astaire and Joan Fontaine [see plate 30].*

TO LEONORA CAZALET

1315 Angelo Drive
Beverly Hills
Cal.

April 10. 1937

Darling Snorky.

Your marvellous letter arrived this morning. The best I have ever had from you. [...]

The home is passing through a bad time just now. Poor Mummie is in great trouble. She had her teeth X-rayed the other day, and it appeared that they were in terrible condition. Last Tuesday she had gas and had about four taken out, on Thursday four more, and now she has gone to the dentist to have another lot out. Also one of the bones in her face had got poisoned and had to be curetted. It has been unbelievably ghastly for her, but she has been heroic over it, and what we are all hoping is that the cause of her arthritis has at last been discovered and that she will now get all right.

Apart from the pain, it means that she will have to lie low for two or three months, till the new set can be put in, and see nobody. Fortunately, she has never been keen on parties and dinners, so maybe it won't be so bad. We shall be able to go to the movies. It will be the same sort of hermit life which we led in Le Touquet during the winter, and we were both very happy then.

The only trouble about that is that we haven't the walks we had there. Our favourite walk on the mountain is now barred, owing to rattlesnakes. This place is rather like La Frayère, – when you go out, you have to go either up a hill or down one, so that you can't stroll as we used to do on the golf links at Le T.

I must say the thought of another six months out here appals me a bit. It puzzles me why I should have liked it so much last time and dislike it so much now. It may be the weather. Just after I started swimming again, it has suddenly got icy. And, of course, I am having one of my in-between books times. I finished the novel I had been working on since last May, and haven't managed to get another plot going yet. I am beginning to get glimmerings of one now, so I expect I shall be all right soon.

I think you're quite right about only coming out here for three or four months. The place isn't really fit for human habitation after that.

Helen Wills is here now, having tests at Fox. What on earth they think she can do on the screen, I can't imagine. I gave her lunch yesterday. I have an idea she has more or less split up with Pop Moody.[1] At least, she never mentioned him, and she seems to spend all her time away from him.

Your letter made me very homesick! What an ideal life you lead. We were thrilled by your hunting feats. [...]

I do hope that idea of going to live at Fairlawne comes off. It would be perfect. I don't see how you're going to be able to put Anthony[2] and me up at the Grange much longer, with She-She wanting a room of her own soon and Edward throwing his weight about. My objective is a cosy suite at Fairlawne, with use of swimming-bath.

[...]

The situation as regards the movies is as follows: – It seems to be pretty certain that I shall do a four weeks job on *Damsel in Distress* for Fred Astaire, unless some other job comes up before that. There is talk of my doing *Robin Hood* for Warner's and also a new Grace Moore picture for Columbia. Meanwhile, my new novel is being shown round the studios, and that may click. I think the obstacle in the way of my getting work is the fact that my agent is demanding $2000 a week, while there seems to be a strong feeling that I'm damned lucky if I get $1750. Personally, I think I'm worth about $500. When you reflect that horny-handed directors, with dozens of successes behind them, are only getting $1500, what have I done to deserve $2000? On the other hand, I'm such a good chap that I feel my yessing alone is worth a good stiff salary.[3]

[...]

1 Helen Wills Moody, American tennis player, eight times Wimbledon champion. Wills was the former girlfriend of Victor Cazalet, Leonora's brother-in-law. She had since married Frederick Moody.
2 Anthony Mildmay, 2nd Baron Mildmay of Flete, a gifted amateur steeplechase jockey.
3 PGW refers to his satirical short story about Hollywood, 'The Nodder'.

TO LEONORA CAZALET

1315 Angelo Drive
Beverly Hills
California

July 13. 1937

Darling Snorky.

Your fat letter arrived this morning and cheered me up a lot at a time of depression, owing to the fact that poor Mummie is having a very bad time. She was taken off to the hospital last Saturday.

It started on Friday night. All through Friday she had been wonderfully well. At five in the evening she had a rather heavy massage, and then went and did a lot of exercises, so that she tired herself out. I was in my room, reading with the communicating door open, and she called out to me that she had overtired herself. I was feeling rather tired myself after a heavy day's work, so I said that this was obviously the moment for us to split half a bottle of champagne. So I brought it up to her, ice cold, and we drank it, and in about half an hour she suddenly became terribly sick and went on being sick all through the night. In the morning the doctor came and she was taken off to the hospital – which isn't quite what it sounds but is more like going to a nursing home. (They don't have nursing homes here, but you take a private room at a hospital.)

On Sunday and yesterday she was very bad, but I went to see her this morning and found her a lot better, though terribly weak and having pain. The doctor was there, and said he was delighted with her progress. I don't understand the first thing about 'blood count', but apparently it ought to be around 8000, and that was what hers is today – after being 18,000 a couple of days ago.

It seems that the trouble is in her kidneys principally. But there is also the possibility that she has eaten vegetables which have been sprayed by the gardeners with arsenic. Do you remember how bad you were after that grape diet, probably through grapes that had arsenic on them. What amazes me is the calmness with which people here accept the idea that these Filipino market-gardeners spray the vegetables with too much arsenic to kill the insects. According to one man, there are a thousand people at the moment down with this poisoning around here, and yet nobody seems to consider making any protest.

The unfortunate thing is that Mummie's imagination is always so active, and there is no doubt that her symptoms are very like those of Jean Harlow.[1] Also, it didn't help when the news reached her that George Gershwin had just died in the same hospital.

Still, she did seem ever so much better today. She was very weak, but she seemed to be improving. The nausea has stopped. The doctor absolutely assured me that her recovery was now only a matter of days. Yesterday I was horribly anxious, but tonight I feel everything is going to be all right.

That was a shocking tragedy about Gershwin, wasn't it. The grue-some thing about it is that everybody treated the thing so lightly. I mean, at first. We had asked him to our party, and he couldn't come and Mrs Ira Gershwin said that it was 'simply something psycho-logical' – in other words, rather suggesting that he had had a fit of temperament because Sam Goldwyn didn't like a couple of his songs. On the night of our party, too, Mrs Edward G. Robinson (the wife of the film star)[2] invited us to a party she was giving for George Gershwin on July 14. I said we should love to come, but wasn't he supposed to be ill? She smiled in a sort of indulgent, knowing way and said 'Oh, <u>he</u>'s all right. He'll be there', – again suggesting that he was doing a sort of prima donna act. Then last Sunday in the paper was the news that he had been operated on for a tumor in the brain, and a few hours later he was dead.[3]

Well, let's get on to something more cheerful!

Your account of Ascot made me very homesick. I do hope I don't get entangled into staying out here longer than my one year. I rather shudder when my agent talks to me about what he is going to do, once the *Damsel in Distress* is produced and I get a big screen credit. If I do make a hit with it and get offers at enormous salary, I shall do like Sherriff and come over here for visits of no longer than three months. I wouldn't take on another salaried job like the last one for anything.

I must say it is altogether different working at R.K.O. on a picture based on my own novel from being on salary at M-G-M and sweating away at *Rosalie*! I like my boss, Pandro Berman, very much. He is the first really intelligent man I have come across here – bar Thalberg, whom he rather resembles. Everything is made very pleasant for me, and I like the man I am working with – a chap named Pagano. The way we work is, we map out a sequence together, then I go home and write the dialogue, merely indicating business, and he takes what I have done and puts it into screen play shape. Thus relieving me of all that 'truck shot' 'wipe dissolve' stuff!

It is also pleasant to be working on something that you know is a real live proposition and not something that may be produced or may be put away in a drawer for years! As far as I can gather, we are going to start shooting this picture in about a week. We have actually completed about sixty pages out of probably a hundred and fifty, but this isn't as bad as it sounds, because we can write twenty pages while they are shooting two. There is a whole sequence laid in London which will take them at least ten days to shoot, I imagine, and they can be getting on with that while we are finishing the script.

Helen Wills is getting a divorce !! I thought she would.

Did Mummie tell you that I went on the air with Hedda Hopper the other day.[4] She does a weekly talk about Hollywood, and she asked if she could interview me. I wrote a comic interview, full of good lines, (which I gave mostly to her – nothing small about me), and it was a great success, – in spite of the fact that she killed my gags by laughing in front of each one and putting 'Well' at the head of each line. (I find I am a real ham at heart. I go about now with my hat on the side of my head, saying 'Say, lissen, if that dame hadn't of stepped on my laffs, I'd have had 'em rolling in the aisles'.)

My God! What a hell the home must be, with old Pete boiling pig's urine in the study! When I get back, you and I must get together and dope out a plot, using all Pete's stuff. Chemistry in the study is exactly the sort of thing Lord Emsworth would do.

[...] The Henry Daniels [*sic*] had asked us to dine the night Mummie was taken ill.[5] His wife smokes cigars, – the only woman I have seen do it except Mrs Patrick Campbell. And not just ordinary cigars, but those huge five-bob things that Basil Rathbone gives his guests.

[...]

Johnny and Maureen remain our greatest friends here. We go down to their house at Malibu from time to time. It is lovely there for a day, but I think I would get sick of it. There is talk of Maureen going to England to do a picture with Robert Taylor. I hope she does, though we shall miss her, as it will be a big thing for her. She is sweeter than ever. Also prettier. Her marriage seems a terrific success. Johnny is very sedate, and absolutely devoted to her.[6] [...]

[...]

Winky is in marvellous shape. Nine years and two months old and brought up from infancy on cheese, sugar, cake, milk chocolate and ham, and the fittest dog in California!

Love to everybody

Your

Plummie

1 The movie star Jean Harlow was hospitalised with kidney failure in 1937, and died in early June.
2 A Romanian-born American actor, famous for his 1931 movie, *Little Caesar*.
3 George Gershwin had been diagnosed with a brain tumour and died at the Cedars of Lebanon Hospital, Los Angeles, following surgery.
4 Hedda Hopper (1885–1966), American actress, radio presenter and gossip columnist.
5 Henry Daniell, an English actor, living in Hollywood.
6 Maureen O'Sullivan had married the writer John Farrow in 1936.

TO PETER CAZALET

1315 Angelo Drive
Beverly Hills
California

May 7. 1937

Dear Pete.

A letter from Snorky arrived this morning, in which she said that your wrist was healing well. I'm awfully glad. Rotten luck getting crocked like that.

[...]

I have been seeing a lot of Gubby Allen, who came back from Australia via Hollywood. A very good chap. I met him two years ago at Le Touquet. He was extraordinarily interesting about body-line, and the picture he drew of conditions during the Jardine–Larwood tour were almost exactly like an eyewitness's description of the Spanish War.¹ Larwood, apparently, was going about saying that he did not intend to return to England without having killed at least a couple of Australian batsmen, and Jardine threatened to leave Gubby out of the team if he would not promise to start bowling at the batsmen's heads immediately he was put on.

This tour seems to have been almost as bad in a quieter way. Apparently the Australians never cease trying to slip something over on the English captain. [...]

[...]

There is a big strike on in the studios now, which may quite easily develop and close down the picture industry indefinitely. I get a big laugh out of it. 'So you wouldn't take up my option, eh?' is the way

I feel. 'Well, now see what's happened to you.'

In addition to this, our butler is still, at the moment of writing, soused to the gills. Over here, the domestic staff takes every Thursday off, and apparently our man went and got badly pickled. I got down this morning at nine, to find all the blinds still drawn and no preparations for breakfast. It is now nearly lunch time, and he is still sleeping it off.

I liked Snorky's description of your Coronation orgies.[2] Free beer for the village is going to set you back a bit. I wish I could be with you. We made a bad mistake in taking this house on for a year instead of six months.

Love to all

Yours ever

Plum

1 Sir George Oswald Browning ('Gubby') Allen was an Australian-born England cricketer. 'Bodyline': a tactic first used by the English cricket team on the 1932–3 Ashes tour of Australia, aimed at curbing the runmaking of the new star, Don Bradman. The ball bowled at great pace was aimed at or wide of the leg stump, pitched short to rise towards the batsman's body. If he played a defensive shot, he could be caught by one of several close legside fielders; if he hit out, he could be caught by fieldsmen deep on the legside. Australian crowds and the media were bitterly hostile to the tactics, leading to a protest by the Australian Board of Control, and a controversy which extended into the diplomatic arena. But the England authorities backed MCC captain Douglas Jardine, who led his team to victory by four Tests to one. The laws of cricket were later changed to prevent this tactic being repeated. Harold Larwood was one of the English bowlers.
2 The Coronation of King George VI (and Queen Elizabeth, later the Queen Mother) took place at Westminster Abbey on 12 May 1937, in the wake of Edward VIII's abdication. This was the first coronation to be transmitted on television, and there were celebrations throughout the country.

TO LEONORA CAZALET

1315 Angelo Drive
Beverly Hills
California

Aug 13. 1937

Darling Snorky.

How clever of you to write to me direct about that money. It would have spoiled Mummie's day! There is no need for her to know anything about it, as I have written to the Hongkong Bank to send old Pete a cheque, which you ought to get soon after you get this letter. What a damned nuisance these income tax people are. Have you noticed that there's always some sum like eighty pounds to be paid, however much you shell out.

It's much better recouping Pete on the quiet like this, as Mummie is so keen to get back to what we had before we paid out that twenty thousand to the American tax people. I shan't miss it from my Hongkong account, as it was all gambling winnings, anyway, so what the hell!

I loved the snap shots. Sheran is becoming a regular beauty.

[...]

Mummie is all right again now and going strong. We had a domestic upheaval a week ago, when she fired the staff. I really think the average servant here is the scum of the earth. We found out later that these two had worked for the Frank Morgans and, when thrown out, wrote dirty cracks about them on all the walls of the kitchen premises. They had a Scotch terrier with them, which used their bedroom as a Gents Toilet, and it took us two days cleaning up.

We went to a party at the Edward G. Robinsons the night before yesterday. Very nice, but I do hate getting to bed late. Heather was there. She starts a small part in a picture today, I think. She isn't doing badly, really, – three pictures this year – but I doubt if she will ever really make much of it out here. She looks too young for 'Aunt Caroline' parts and not young enough for heroines or comic sisters.[1]

Scandal about Henry Daniel [sic] and wife. Apparently they go down to Los Angeles and either (a) indulge in or (b) witness orgies – probably both. Though don't you think there's something rather pleasantly domestic about a husband and wife sitting side by side with their eyes glued to peepholes, watching the baser elements whoop it up? All it needs is the kiddies at their peepholes. And what I want to know is – where are these orgies? I feel I've been missing something.

Dirty story for Pete. Two men pick up two women in the street and take them home. Shortly after they have retired, one man knocks at the other man's door and says he's afraid they will have to change girls, as the one he's got turns out to be an aunt of his. (Not so very funny, really. I suppose it wants telling. Reggie Gardiner told it to me at the studio yesterday, and took about ten minutes over it, working it up with dialogue and business.)

We were thrilled by the book of photographs of Low Wood. How you must have worked over it. It looks as if you had made the place marvellous.

Met a rattlesnake just outside our front gate a few days ago. Fortunately the puppy wasn't with me, or she would have started playing with it.

I had a letter from Victor a couple of days ago, saying that he would be out here on Sept 7. It will be great seeing him again. What we are wondering is if he has come out to marry Helen Wills!! Do you think there is any chance of it? She is an awfully nice girl. What a mug she was to marry that man.

Love to all

Your

Plummie

1 Heather Thatcher, English actress, who had appeared in Wodehouse's *Sally*, *The Cabaret Girl* and *The Beauty Prize*, as well as in a specially written abridgement of *Good Morning, Bill*, condensed into one act for the London Coliseum in 1929.

TO PAUL REYNOLDS

1315 Angelo Drive
Beverly Hills
California

Aug 19. 1937

Dear Reynolds,

I enclose a letter from Mr Leff, with whom I have been having some correspondence about a proposed comic strip based on one of my butlers. I have told him to use the name 'Keggs' instead of 'Jeeves'.

The idea is, I gather, that I shall simply lend my name. I believe J. P. McEvoy has done this with a comic strip.[1] A bit undignified, of course, but I don't see that it can hurt me, and there ought to be quite a lot of money in it, if it catches on.

Will you get in touch with Mr Leff and fix up the contract. The terms he names are quite agreeable to me.

Best wishes

Yours ever

P. G. Wodehouse

1 The writer J. P. McEvoy had turned his 1928 novel *Show Girl* into a comic strip, *Dixie Dugan*, which was syndicated to a number of American newspapers.

TO WILLIAM TOWNEND

Low Wood
Le Touquet
Pas-de-Calais

Nov 22. 1937

Dear Bill,

[...]

Did you ever read a book called *Helen's Babies* about a young bachelor getting saddled with some kids?[1] The *Ladies' Home Journal* editor has got a fixed idea that a splendid modern version could be done, and he has actually offered me $45,000 if I will do it. And here's the tragedy. I can't think of a single idea towards it. When *Helen's Babies* was published, all you had to do was to get the central idea and then have a monotonous stream of incidents where the kids caused trouble. Nobody seemed to mind in those days that you were being repetitious. But surely that sort of thing wouldn't go now. In any case, I can't work it. But isn't it tragic, getting an offer like that and not being able to accept it.

Maybe you can dig up a fine plot on those lines?

I'm dying to see you. Millions of things to talk about.

Love to Rene

Yours ever

Plum

1 John Habberton's *Helen's Babies* (1876).

The 'Jeeves novel' Wodehouse mentions here is The Code of the Woosters *(1938), in which the villainous Roderick Spode makes his first appearance. A man who looks 'as if Nature had intended to make a gorilla then changed its mind at the last moment', Spode is modelled on the politician Sir Oswald Mosley. Wodehouse's fictional 'amateur dictator', and leader of the 'Black Shorts', mocks Mosley and his British Union of Fascists, which, by the mid-thirties, was becoming increasingly aligned with the Nazi party.*

TO WILLIAM TOWNEND

Low Wood
Le Touquet
Pas-de-Calais

January 4. 1938

Dear Bill.

[...]

I am finding finishing my Jeeves novel a ghastly sweat. I don't seem to have the drive and command of words that I used to. [...] Still, the stuff seems good enough when I get it down.

[...]

We had quite a nice time at Snorky's, but I hate Christmas and all the overeating. Sheran (granddaughter) is a nice kid. She took a great fancy to me and hauled me off for long walks.

[...]

Love to Rene

Yours ever

Plum

40 Berkeley Square
W. 1. *
(Good address. Ca fait riche)

Jan 4. 1939.

Darling Snorky.

I can't get over the awed feeling of having been lushed up at the Grange for a solid month. Nobody but the iron Cazalets could have stuck it out. But, grim though the experience may have been for you, always remember that I enjoyed it. Nay, loved it. I was feeling so emotional about it yesterday that I came within an ace of buying Pete two shillings' worth of halfpenny stamps, to replace those I pinched. Wiser feelings prevailed, however, and he doesn't get them. (I have used the word 'feeling' three times in above. Flaubert would have something to say about that.)

We are frightfully snug here. The last word in luxury.

[...]

We ran into Randolph Churchill on Sunday and lunched with him at his flat yesterday.[1] I have misjudged him. Very good chap.

Love to all.

Yours ever

Plum.

1 The son of Sir Winston Churchill, and also a Conservative MP from 1940 to 1945.

TO LILLIAN BARNETT

Low Wood
Le Touquet
Pas-De-Calais

April 5. 1939

Dear Lily.

It was so nice to hear from you again. I'm sorry Bert is not well.

I hope Norah will be very happy. I enclose a cheque. Will you buy her a wedding present. I'm afraid it is a bit late, but I couldn't write before.

How exciting the news from England is these days. My wife is rather pessimistic, but I have a feeling that things are soon going to be all right. I don't think Germany would dare to do anything that would bring England and France down on them.

It was very sinister here in September. Everything was quite quiet in Paris Plage, which is the little seaside town near Le Touquet, but every day, when I went to buy things, I would find that the man of the shop had slipped away to the Maginot Line.[1] This time I haven't noticed this. My tobacconist is still there, and so are the others, as far as I can make out. So let's hope that all will be well.

[...]

Best wishes to you all

Yours ever

P. G. Wodehouse

1 The French defence line of concrete fortifications, tank obstacles and machine-gun posts that ran along the borders with Germany and Italy.

TO WILLIAM TOWNEND

Low Wood
Le Touquet
Pas-de-Calais

April 23. 1939

Dear Bill.

[...]

I am coming over – unless there is a gale – next Sunday (today week). Mind you're in, and I will get a car and drive over for tea.

I'm sorry you are finding it difficult to write short stories. It was just the same with me. Those first hot days of Spring bowled me over. I have now managed to get out two plots, with a third almost completed. I think you have earned a rest. I'd take it easy for a bit.

Do you know, a feeling is gradually stealing over me that the world has never been farther from a war than it is at present. It has just dawned on the civilians of all countries that the good old days of seeing the boys off in the troop ship are over and that the elderly sportsmen who used to talk about giving sons to the country will now jolly well have to give themselves. I think if Hitler really thought there was any chance of a war, he would have nervous prostration.

Incidentally, doesn't all this alliance-forming remind you of the form matches at school, when you used to say to yourself that the Upper Fifth had a couple of first fifteen forwards, but you'd got the fly half of the second, the full back of the third and three forwards who would get their colours before the season was over. I can't realise that all this is affecting millions of men. I think of Hitler and Mussolini as two halves, and Stalin as a useful wing forward.

Anyway, no war in our lifetime is my feeling. I don't think wars start with months of preparation in the way of slanging matches. When you get a sort of brooding peace, as in 1914, when a spark lights the p. magazine, that's when you get a war.[1] Nowadays, I feel that the nations just take it out in blowing off steam. (I shall look silly if war starts on Saturday, after Hitler's speech!)

The ghastly thing is that it's all so frightfully funny. I mean, Hitler asking the little nations if they think they are in danger of being attacked. I wish one of them would come right out and say 'Yes, we jolly well do!'.

Wonder and the pup are now great friends, and play together all the time. Ethel keeps saying that three dogs are too much of a nuisance, and she's about right. But I think that if we can get into Low Wood, where they will be able to run about in the garden, all will be well. At Northwood we have a small front garden opening on the street – or road – and there is no way of preventing the dogs getting out. The Low Wood garden is wired all round, so as to form a pen.

Love to Rene

Yours ever

Plum

1 Powder magazine – a place where gunpowder is stored.

After Oxford University decided to award Wodehouse an honorary doctorate, Douglas Veale, the University's Registrar, had some difficulty in getting in touch with him. The initial letter was sent to the Constitutional Club and not forwarded, so it was some months before Wodehouse received any communication from Oxford. He immediately telegraphed his acceptance.

TO DOUGLAS VEALE

May 16. 1939

HONOURED TO ACCEPT WRITING
P G WODEHOUSE

TO DOUGLAS VEALE

Golf-Hotel Du Touquet
Sur les Links
Le Touquet – Paris – Plage P de C

May 17. 1939

Dear Mr Veale.

I am so sorry I did not receive your first communication. I generally look in at the Constitutional for letters pretty regularly, but I have not been in England for some time.

I am tremendously flattered that I have been chosen for this honour. I wonder if you can give me some idea of the nature of the ceremony?

Does it involve making a speech? I ask this in trepidation, as I have never made a speech in all my life, though well stricken in years, and I have a sort of complex about it. If you can relieve my mind by telling me that I can preserve a dignified silence, I shall be most grateful.

Yours sincerely

P. G. Wodehouse

Veale was delighted to receive Wodehouse's response, declaring himself 'an ardent devotee'. He noted that 'the only place at which you are exposed to the risk of having to make a speech is at the dinner' at Christ Church 'and I think the risk is not very great there'.

Golf-Hotel Du Touquet
Sur les Links
Le Touquet – Paris – Plage P de C

May 24. 1939

Dear Mr Veale.

Thanks most awfully for your letter and its reassuring contents.

I propose to present myself in a dark grey suit with black bootings. I take it this will be all right? If not, I have a dark blue suit. If really pushed, I could dig out my morning suit, but as you say there is no need for it, I would much rather not.

I'm afraid I can't claim the credit of having taught you Latin. I was never a schoolmaster. When I left school, they put me into a bank, from which I escaped after two years to start doing the 'By the Way' column on the old *Globe*. I wonder if it could have been my brother E.A.

Best wishes

Yours sincerely

P. G. Wodehouse

Golf-Hotel du Touquet
Le Touquet
Paris-Plage
Pas-de-Calais

June 3. 1939

Dear Reynolds.

So glad the short stories are selling.

[...]

Great excitement here. The University of Oxford is making me a Doctor of Letters, which is apparently a biggish honor. Mark Twain appears to be the only man who has got it, outside of the dull, stodgy birds whose names are quite unknown to the public but who seem to get honors showered on them. I go to Oxford on the 20th, stay two nights with the Vice-Chancellor, and wear a cap and gown throughout!

For the last three weeks I have been trying to get out a plot for a novel. It is in a frightfully chaotic state, as usual, but in the last two days has begun to clarify a little, and I am hoping that something definite will shortly emerge. I find that infinite patience is the only thing that really does it, and I cheer myself by remembering that every story I have ever written has been through this stage. *Uncle Fred* was the worst of them all. It wasn't till I had written three hundred pages of notes that I got the idea of putting Uncle Fred into the story at all! So maybe this one will come out all right.

Yours ever

P. G. Wodehouse

Despite reassurances from Mr Veale that a speech would not be required at Wodehouse's doctoral award, the students of Christ Church did call upon him to speak at dinner that night – banging the tables, with cries of 'Speech!' Wodehouse 'rose awkwardly to his feet [...] mumbled "Thank you", and sat down in confusion'.

TO MARY GORDON

Hotel Splendide and Green Park Restaurant
105 Piccadilly
London, W.1

June 23. 1939

Dear Mrs Gordon.
I wonder if anybody has ever enjoyed a visit to the President's Lodging as much as I did.[1] Henry the Seventh, possibly, but nobody else. I shall never forget how kind you all were to me. It was wonderful of you to give me such a good time.

My only complaint is that that bedroom has spoiled me for the sort of thing I shall have to put up with for the rest of my life. I shall feel like a sardine in the one I have at Le Touquet.

I forgot to tell you that I achieved a complete triumph over the geyser. I had it eating out of my hand before I left.

I hope you are not feeling too tired after your Encaenia exertions.[2] I thought the Garden Party was a tremendous success.

With best wishes

Yours sincerely

P. G. Wodehouse

P.S. Love to Simon.

1 Wodehouse stayed with George and Mary Gordon. George Stuart Gordon was the Vice-Chancellor of Oxford University from 1938 to 1941, and President of Magdalen College.
2 An academic ceremony at the University of Oxford in which honorary degrees are conferred.

TO MOLLIE CAZALET

Low Wood
Le Touquet
Pas de Calais

July 10. 1939

My dear Mollie

Thanks most awfully for your letter.

I had a great time at Oxford. I stayed with the Vice-Chancellor, who is a splendid chap, and enjoyed every minute of it. Did Victor tell you that I rolled up to the Christ Church dinner in a black tie, to find four hundred gorgeous beings in white ties and decorations? It never occurred to me that an all-men dinner would be white tie. However, the robes hid my shame quite a bit. They were dove grey and scarlet – very dressy. I had to wear them all day, and was sorry I couldn't go around in them in private life. They certainly do give one an air!

[...]

I ran over to London for three days last week to see the Gentlemen and Players match, but the visit was spoiled by the weather.[1] Most of the people I met seemed a bit nervy, but Ian Hay was comforting. He seemed to think that things would be all right. The thing I noticed chiefly was that plays were doing badly and books not selling. I suppose nobody feels like reading nowadays. Thank goodness, my last book has had a record sale (for me – well over twenty thousand in England), but I am wondering what will happen to the new one, which comes out in August. Personally, I am optimistic. I don't think Germany will dare risk a war.

Love from us both

Yours ever

Plum

1 The Gentlemen v. Players match, played annually between teams consisting of amateurs (the Gentlemen) and professionals (the Players). The 1939 match was played on 5 July at Lord's, and was won by the Players. PGW went over to see Billy Griffith play.

TO WILLIAM TOWNEND

Low Wood
Le Touquet
Pas-de-Calais

Oct 3. 1939

Dear Bill.

When this war started, I suddenly found myself totally unable to write letters. I don't know why. I suppose I had the feeling that they would never get to their destination. But now the post does seem to be working, if a bit spasmodically. I expect you'll get this in about ten days.

I'm wondering a lot how you are getting on. They all say that there is going to be a big boom in books, and I suppose that will include magazines, so maybe we shall be all right. I should think a book like *And Now England* – what a pity they didn't call it *The Hun*, as they were thinking of doing, – ought to take on a new life if it is pushed properly.[1]

Are you doing any war work? Mine is confined to running a doss house for French officers. We have three, though the only one I see anything of is the one actually in our part of the house. Owing to the war catching Low Wood half furnished, we had only one guest room and the others have had to sleep in the staff wing. (Which sounds as if L.W. were about the size of Blandings Castle!)

When was your silver wedding? Weren't you married just before me? Ours was last Saturday, and we gave a party for the whole of Le Touquet, including fifteen non-English-speaking French officers, who of course arrived early, before we could muster our linguists. Still, after a rather sticky ten minutes, everything went triumphantly. The officers lined up in front of us and sang an old Flemish chant, which involved two of them holding a towel over our heads. Rather impressive.

How is your part of the world for living in these days? Le Touquet is fine. One slight drawback is that the war has caused almost all the villas to be occupied, so that I don't get that desert island feeling which I love. Still, if we are going to be marooned here for three years, perhaps a few neighbours will be a good thing.

We black out, of course, which is a nuisance. But the worst nuisance is that we are not allowed to 'circulate'. That is to say, the only place we can go is Paris Plage. Ethel was talking airily about running into Boulogne for a bite of lunch today, and we found it couldn't be done even with fifty-five passes and cards of identity. I don't mind very much, as I never do want to go anywhere.

How is the work? I am well on in a new novel, and enjoying writing it tremendously, as I feel I can take my time.[2] My only qualms are about how to get more typewriter ribbons. I suppose I shall be able to get some from London or Paris after a bit of delay. My other qualm is that I am wondering if the m.s. will get to America all right. I suppose boats are running. Qualm three is the feeling what a blank it will leave in my life when I have finished the book. (By the way, the S.E.P. insist on serials with instalments not over 8000 words – presumably seven of them, which makes it necessary to add a colossal amount for book form. It's a great handicap to one's ease of writing, as I keep feeling that I can't let myself go.)

I keep getting letters from A. P. Watt, asking if I will consent to accept three and sixpence for Latvian rights of something. I have told him he's got to decide for the duration.

Didn't you think that was a fine speech of Churchill's on the wireless? Just what was needed, I thought. I can't help feeling that we're being a bit too gentlemanly. Someone ought to get up in Parliament and call Hitler a swine.

Must stop now, as our only link with the post office is leaving and I must get this off.

Love to Rene

Yours ever

Plum

1 Townend's novel, *And Now England*, was published in 1939.
2 This was almost certainly *Joy in the Morning*.

TO FRANK SULLIVAN

October 6. 1939

Dear F.S.

I'm so sorry I've been all this time answering your letter. C'est la guerre!

I do hope *S. at Bay* is going strong.[1] It ought to sell terrifically both on its merits and because everybody wants some cheerful stuff.

Everything is very quiet & peaceful here. I was just about to come over to America when all this started, and now I suppose I shall have to wait till it's over. When I do come, do let's meet.

Yours ever.

P. G. Wodehouse.

1 *Sullivan at Bay* (1939).

TO WILLIAM TOWNEND

Low Wood
Le Touquet
Pas-de-Calais

Dec 8. 1939

Dear Bill.

Long time since I wrote. Sorry. How is everything with you?

Things have been very gloomy with us this last week. Our Boxer suddenly got ill, and we took it for granted it was tick fever and he had two injections. Then a vet came from Boulogne and said the trouble was with his kidneys. Today, after being a bit better, he has started walking very stiffly, which looks as if it had been tick fever after all, and we are very anxious. He is the most angelic dog, and we love him. Of course, he may still recover, but I'm afraid it is doubtful. It does seem a shame that a place like this, so perfect in every other respect, should be spoiled by these ticks. One lives from day to day, wondering if the dogs will get through all right.

The outline of the novel you sent me sounds very good. How is it getting on? I finished mine, and it should be on its way to America by now. (It is being typed in Paris.) I am now in the dismal state of trying to think out another and having no ideas. One always goes through this stage, of course, but one never seems to get used to it. What I would like to do would be a Jeeves story. But it is so hard to get a good menace for Bertie – I mean the doom which is hanging over him which Jeeves averts.

In addition to the *Windsor*, *Pearson's* has stopped publication, also the *Cornhill*. I'm afraid the day of the magazine is pretty nearly over.

[...]

I have been reading all Churchill's books – i.e. the World Crisis series. Have you read them? They are terrific. What strikes me most about them is what mugs the Germans were to take us on again. You would have thought they must have known that we should wipe them out at sea and that there never has been a war that hasn't been won by sea power. It's very curious to see how the same old thing is happening all over again, with the difference that we are avoiding all the mistakes we made last time. I never realized before I read Churchill that the French started off in 1914 by losing four hundred thousand men in the first two weeks. Also, what perfect asses the Germans made of themselves. There was a moment when all they had to do was strike East and they needn't have worried about the blockade. Instead of which, they went for Verdun, which wouldn't have done them any good if they had got it.

[...]

I see in your first letter you asked me about Peter. He started as a second in command of an anti aircraft unit and proved to be so good that he has now been singled out for all sorts of weird courses etc, and looks like being something quite big. He really is a splendid chap, he throws himself into everything he takes up and is on his toes all the time.

Snorky is another marvel. I forget if I told you that they had moved into Fairlawne? Anyway, they had scarcely got in when she was allotted eighty-six children, plus about twenty adults!! She assimilated them all without turning a hair. She and her crowd live in one wing of the house, and the other is given up to the children, and apparently everything works absolutely smoothly. She now says she is giving a party on Christmas Eve for the children, the teachers and all the children's parents, and she says it won't be any trouble. Of course, she has got a lot of space. Fairlawne was built at a time when you didn't look on a home as a home unless you had about thirty spare bedrooms. I was there for a day or two last Spring, and I used to get lost in the place. Miles of passages, rambling all over the countryside.

When this war is over, you must get another Peke. The puppy we had and gave to a girl who lives here has turned out the most angelic thing you ever saw. It comes up to spend the day about four times a week and brightens the whole place up. Its name is Mrs Miffen, and it is one of those rowdy Pekes who bound about and think nothing of a seven mile walk. It reminds me of Bimmy a little, though different colour.

Wonder is in great form.

Love to Rene

Yours ever

Plum

Low Wood
Le Touquet
France

Jan 23. 1940

Dear Bill,

[...]

Your description of the writing of the novel took my breath away. As far as I can make out, you thought out and wrote the thing in a month! It sounds good.

Thank goodness the *S.E.P.* have taken my serial.[1] At a time when it is so difficult to get money out of England, a bit over in America will be useful. I have also managed to get out four short story plots this year, which is a record for me.

I agree with you about the weariness of war. I find the only thing to do is to get into a routine and live entirely by the day. I work in the morning, take the dogs out before tea, do a bit of mild work after tea, and then read after dinner. It is wonderful how the days pass. One nuisance of living here is that we get today's papers tomorrow, and not always then. The *Continental Daily Mail* is regular enough, but a touch of fog in the Channel is often enough to stop the English papers.

[...]

I liked Churchill's speech the other night, didn't you? When he had finished, we switched off the radio and discussed it, not knowing that the next item on the programme was a Ukridge story. Still, I don't imagine I missed much.

[...]

I can't make out what is going to happen. Do you think everything will break loose in the Spring? I don't see how it can, as surely by that time we shall be too strong. My only fear is that Germany will be able to go on for years on their present rations. Apparently a German is able to live on stinging nettles and wood fibre indefinitely.

[...]

Love to Rene.

Yours ever

Plum

1 *Quick Service* (1940).

Elmer Flaccus was an admirer of Wodehouse's work and collected his books.

Low Wood
Le Touquet
Pas-de-Calais

Feb 3. 1940

Dear Mr Flaccus,
Thank you so much for your letter. It was very nice to hear from you again. Congratulations on your marriage.

Everything is very quiet here. This place is within a few miles of Boulogne, so we are not touched by the war except in so far as seeing people we know go off to it. Our gardener has left, also the postman, who was a great friend of mine. They both came back on leave the other day, looking very fit. Life on the Maginot Line seems to be healthy.

We are also putting up one or two French officers, very nice fellows but they don't talk English and my French is in a very elementary state. We also see a lot of the R.A.F. boys, who come over here on short leave. We had a great party at Christmas.

Nobody seems to know what is going to happen, if anything is. To me, knowing nothing about it, it seems that if Germany were really going to do anything big, they would have had to do it long ago. Chamberlain in his last speech said that England already had a million and a half men under arms, and I believe our air defences are now such that it would be ruinous for Hitler to try to attack England. I suppose he could do some damage, but at a cost which would not make it worth it.

[...]
Best wishes to you both
Yours sincerely
P. G. Wodehouse

Low Wood
Le Touquet
Pas-de-Calais

April 6. 1940

Dear Bill.

I keep looking out in the papers for your new book. When does it come out?

[...]

Also, how did the novel go in America? I wrote four short stories at the beginning of the year, and have now discovered that one of them will have to be chucked away because I need the plot for a novel. Does that ever happen to you? It's agony, as the short story was really good. But it contains a solution for a Jeeves novel, so I am trying to work out a plot. Listen, is it possible for a hard-up young peer to become a <u>country</u> policeman? A London one, yes, but this must be country. Could such a man start in as a village cop, with the idea of later on, if in luck, getting into Scotland Yard? Would a village policeman have any future? I wish you would buttonhole the next policeman who passes your door and ask him if it would be possible for him to soar to the heights. (My chap has got to be a policeman, because Bertie pinches his uniform in order to go to a fancy dress dance, at which it is vital for him to be present as he has no other costume).[1]

The other day Lady Dudley's[2] parrot (now living with us) was outside on the terrace and Wonder, the Peke, inside the sitting room. The French window was shut, and they suddenly fell foul of one another and started a desperate fight with the glass of the window in between them. Honble parrot beat at the glass with his beak and Wonder leaped at it, yelling. Eventually the parrot moved off, so I suppose Wonder won.

We now go out in the afternoon with seven dogs, – our two, the visiting Peke and four belonging to a neighbour.

[...]

We alternate here between a sort of cook-general life and a staff of servants such as you would find at Blenheim or somewhere. This is due to the fact that all the men we have ever employed come and work for us when they get leave. This last week we have had a marvellous butler (husband of the cook) and two extra gardeners. In a day or two they will have disappeared. I do think the French are marvellous. They just take a war in their stride. They toddle off and fight and come back and work and then go and fight again.

Everyone seems to expect great things of Reynaud. And I am glad that Churchill now seems to be running things in England.[3] But I wish, when they have a Cabinet shuffle, they wouldn't just make A. and B. swap jobs. I would like to see something entirely fresh, like Nuffield being made Minister of Air or something. Incidentally, don't you feel you would make a good Chancellor of the Duchy of Lancaster? It sounds the sort of job I could do on my head.

I am having a very pleasant time, except that I can't get enough to read.

Love to Rene

Yours ever

Plum

1 This character is to become G. D'Arcy 'Stilton' Cheesewright, an old Etonian and Oxford man, who becomes a village policeman in *Joy in the Morning* (1946).
2 The actress Gertie Millar, a successful variety actress and singer, originally from Yorkshire, had married the Earl of Dudley in the mid-twenties. She now lived in Le Touquet.
3 Paul Reynaud had been elected Prime Minister of France in March 1940. Winston Churchill had been appointed First Lord of the Admiralty, and was then made Chairman of the Military Coordinating Committee in April. He became Prime Minister the following month.

TO PAUL REYNOLDS

Low Wood
Le Touquet
Pas-de-Calais

April 25. 1940

Dear Reynolds.

I'm afraid I have changed my plans about coming over for the moment. It is such a business getting started, what with permits and so on, and then having to sail from Genoa. (I suppose any day now Genoa will be barred, too!). So I am sitting tight here and writing a new Jeeves novel, of which I have just finished the first four chapters.

I was tremendously pleased that you got the same price for *Quick Service*. I think they must have liked it, as they are giving me eight instalments, and in the proofs not a line has been cut.

[...]

I wish I could get over to have another of those lunches with you, but I doubt if I shall be able to manage it till the Fall.

Yours ever

P. G. Wodehouse

CHAPTER NINE

Internment

Among the scant correspondence from Wodehouse's war years, a small white postcard has survived, the message bluntly pencilled in slanted capitals. 'GOODNESS KNOWS WHEN YOU WILL GET THIS', he begins. The handwriting pales against the bold institutional typeface, which reads '*Kriegsgefangenenpost*' – or 'Prisoner of War Post'. It was October 1940, and Wodehouse was being held captive by the Germans. His complex journey through Nazi-occupied Europe to the camp in Tost, Upper Silesia, had begun five months earlier, at a critical point during the war.

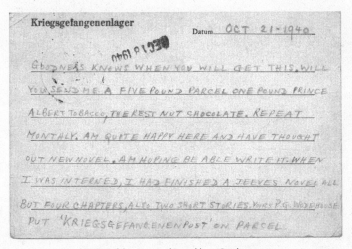

P. G. Wodehouse to Paul Reynolds, 21 October 1940.

In the initial months of 1940, a move from Le Touquet seemed unnecessary. They lived, Wodehouse wrote in February 1940, 'in an odd sort of backwater'.[1] As Ethel described, the early part of 1940 was 'a very delightful time, with our beloved R.A.F. squadron dropping in at all moments for tea. [...] We would turn up the rugs after dinner, and dance to "My Heart Belongs to Daddy". We would listen to the radio and hear that there was a slight bulge but nothing serious, we believed that the Germans were beaten already [...] didn't think they had a kick in them, because we treated the B.B.C. as our Bible. Then the Germans really got a move on, and our R.A.F. disappeared. [...] We became a little anxious, but not seriously so.'[2]

As time went on, the Wodehouses were among a number of expat families in Le Touquet who stood firm. This was partly a practical decision. They were reluctant to leave their house, and their beloved animals, before it seemed absolutely necessary. It was also a sign of their faith in the British troops, and of their sense of the importance of 'morale'. They, like their neighbours, hoped that the German invasion of France could be halted by the Allied Forces. They were wrong. The speed of the Germans' advance took everyone, including British Intelligence, by surprise.

In the spring of 1940, a massive panzer tank attack was planned on France. On 9 May, the German troops stormed into Belgium and the Low Countries. British troops raced to the aid of the Belgians, leaving the Germans free to burst through the Ardennes Forest in the south, aided by Luftwaffe bombers in close support. By 15 May, the panzers were advancing virtually unopposed. On 20 May, Ethel set off for the local military hospital to seek advice as to the timing of their departure. The Commanding Officer reassured her that they were in no imminent danger, but the rest of the day was spent packing.

A fortnight later, France would see evacuation on a huge scale, as the Allied forces were carried to safety from the encircling German army by a hastily assembled flotilla of boats. While Churchill was praising Dunkirk's 'miracle of deliverance', a catalogue of snags, errors and mechanical problems was unfolding back in Le Touquet. From daybreak, nothing went smoothly. Less than two miles from home, the Wodehouses' car broke down, forcing a return to Low Wood. On their next attempt, they were separated from their neighbours, the Grants, who were also trying to escape. The Wodehouses loyally returned to search for them, and found that the Grants' car had also broken down. A second night in Le Touquet proved to be decisive. As Ruth Grant recorded, 'before the dew was off the rosemary bushes edging the lawn, through the green forest they rolled. First, the motorcycles, noisy, brutal and fast, then car after car in which the grey-green officers seemed to sit in tiers, all facing forwards, two or three on the folded hood.'³ The Germans had arrived.

Le Touquet under occupation was a strange, tense place. Ethel recalls that 'a German sergeant and soldiers, marched in the house, and asked to see all our food supplies'. They 'took practically everything', and frequently returned to the house.⁴ Wodehouse was later to make light of the fact that, at any moment, he might find a German officer using his bathroom, or occupying his front garden. In reality, one imagines that he was appalled and fearful. As an 'enemy alien', Wodehouse was under continual surveillance, forced to report on a daily basis to a *Kommandant* with a glass eye in the Hôtel de Ville.⁵

In July, the Nazis feared sabotage, and decided that it was unsafe to leave British civilians free in France. All enemy males under sixty were to be taken into captivity. Wodehouse was fifty-eight years old, thereby failing to avoid internment by some fifteen months. When the summons came, he was given little time to prepare. Ethel remembers one lunchtime in the garden when Wodehouse appeared 'and told me there was a German soldier in the Garden [...]. He only had ten minutes to pack a suitcase. I was nearly insane, couldn't find the keys of the room for the suitcase, and Plum went off with a copy of Shakespeare, a pair of pajamas, and a mutton chop.'⁶

Arrangements for civilian prisoners were makeshift and often primitive, and the Le Touquet group experienced the full force of this chaos. First the Germans took them to a former prison in Loos. Sitting in his cell, Wodehouse describes the 'whitewashed walls, bed in corner under window. Large window about 5 foot by 3, air quite fresh. Granite floor. Table and chair chained to it – toilet in corner near door.' Despite the objective air, panic creeps in. Even the fixtures and fittings have a malevolent edge. He notes the 'two staples' over the bed 'for chaining dangerous prisoners', only to correct himself jokingly in the margins: 'No. Merely for fastening bed up'. For Wodehouse, it was imperative to resist looking at the dark side of things. The cold, the hunger, the endless marches – all are refracted through comedy. 'Amazing how soon one gets used to this', he notes.⁷

The prisoners were soon moved on to a former Belgian army barracks in Liège. By August they were held in a citadel in Huy, before transfer to an *Internierungslager*, or *Ilag*, in the town of Tost, Upper Silesia – in a former lunatic asylum. Conditions during Wodehouse's earlier internment were sometimes almost intolerable. At times, he was transported from one camp to another in crowded cattle trucks full of human excrement. For many nights, he was sleeping on a thin straw mattress and no blanket, with twenty other men in the same room. There were weeks when he had very little food, relying on stale bread to get through, and during his time in internment, he lost over sixty pounds in weight, leaving him 'looking like something the carrion crow had brought in'.[8]

But the camp at Tost was quite different. While sometimes bleakly monotonous – it was, Wodehouse remembered, 'an enormous place with bars on all the windows and a general air of gloom' – the camp itself was never unbearable.[9] As McCrum describes, many internees 'were in regular contact with the outside world, following events with patriotic interest, and having a highly motivated attitude to self-improvement. There was an internees' newspaper, the *Tost Times*, for which Wodehouse abridged a story.'[10] The internees seemed to have adequate food, attended chapel, and played cricket. 'I found', Wodehouse wrote, 'I could still skittle the rabble out, but was helpless when I came up against a decent bat. [...] We used to play in the yard with a string ball, but towards the end of my stay they let us out once a week to the sports field, where we had a real ball.'[11]

Wodehouse also had access to books and paper, and, eventually, a place in which to write and even a borrowed typewriter. Indeed, throughout his time, Wodehouse kept a diary and, as an extraordinary testament to his determination, continued to write fiction: his tale of aristocrats and small-time crooks, *Money in the Bank*, was completed in captivity.

Indeed, it was through the act of writing that Wodehouse managed to 'get used' to camp life, reimagining his world with so many fictional analogies. His fellow inmates, 'Jocky', 'Algy', 'Arthur' and 'Scharny' feature in his diary like motley schoolboys in 'a junior dormitory at school'; a German officer is the 'equivalent of the Colonel living at Cheltenham or Bexhill'; prison camp is 'rather like being on the road with a theatrical company' and 'also like being at Hollywood' – 'a smile from a German Sergeant is as if you were smiled at by Capra'.[12]

Wodehouse knew that such fictions could only take him so far. A snatch from *Don Quixote*, recalled and inscribed in his diary, suggests a longing for a more complete escape – 'Blessings on him that first invented sleep. It wraps a man all round like a cloak.' Repeatedly, Wodehouse's diary records his fear and anxiety. 'Monotony terrible', he notes. 'One man was taken away from 9 children with no mother. Another's mother died of shock when he was taken away, and his wife was in hospital having a child.' The 'great drawback' he notes, 'is apprehension – one feels we are alright so far, but what about when it rains at food time, or if sickness breaks out'. The absence of news from Ethel, he notes, 'stabs me like a knife sometimes'.[13]

Ethel was, in fact, displaced from Low Wood soon after Wodehouse left. She recalls that 'a German major came with a General and said he wanted to look over the house. He sat on the terrace the entire afternoon enjoying the view, then looked over the villa, and announced he wasn't going to move, and his soldiers brought over everything and put them in Plummie's bedroom. I could have killed him!' Clutching an address of a trout farm some fifty kilometres away, which had been given to her by a French officer, Ethel was ordered to leave her home, and was driven away by a German soldier. She was only allowed a few personal possessions, but managed to take Wonder, their beloved dog, and Coco the parrot, who belonged to their friend, Gertie Dudley. Her arrival at the trout farm was a bleak moment: 'My hostess met me at the door at a rather dreary house in a neglected field, and I was shown into a small back bed-room, there I sat for an hour or so, wondering how I should keep up my courage, and nearly out of my mind about Plummie.'[14]

Wodehouse was equally troubled by his separation from Ethel. Indeed, of all the hardships of Wodehouse's time in internment, the worst, for him, was the fact that he felt he was writing into a void. Nevertheless, while it was extremely difficult for the pair to communicate, they did, after a while, manage to send each other letters. Correspondence with those in Britain was impossible, but America's neutral position meant that Wodehouse could also write to his agent, Paul Reynolds. However, the unreliability of the Red Cross postal system, and the hand of the censor, meant that Wodehouse had little faith in his letters getting to their destination.

After three months at the trout farm, Ethel managed to get a permit to go to Lille, but she found it extremely difficult to find anywhere to stay: 'everything requisitioned, not a hotel anywhere. At 8-0 clock I gave it up and went to a restaurant, sat in the corner, and shed a few tears.'[15] A kindly cashier took pity on Ethel, and temporary accommodation was found. Later, she found a bed-sitting room in Lille, where she stayed for three months, before moving back to the countryside.

Wodehouse, meanwhile, remained at Tost.

1 PGW to S. C. 'Billy' Griffith, 2 February 1940 (private archive).

2 Ethel Wodehouse to Denis and Diana Mackail, 26 June 1945 (Wodehouse Archive).

3 Ruth Grant, 'Diary', p. 12 (Wodehouse Archive).

4 Ethel Wodehouse to Denis and Diana Mackail, 26 June 1945 (Wodehouse Archive).

5 P. G. Wodehouse, 'Apologia' (Berg).

6 Ethel Wodehouse to Denis and Diana Mackail, 26 June 1945 (Wodehouse Archive).

7 *The Camp Notebook* (Wodehouse Archive).

8 See McCrum, p. 285. McCrum quotes Max Enke's *Tost Diary* (Wodehouse Archive).

9 PGW to Raven von Barnikow, 26 July 1942 (Wodehouse Archive).

10 McCrum, p. 293.

11 PGW to S. C. 'Billy' Griffith, 17 July 1945 (private archive).

12 *The Camp Notebook*.

13 Ibid.

14 Ethel Wodehouse to Denis and Diana Mackail, 26 June 1945 (Wodehouse Archive).

15 Ibid.

1940–1941:
'Am quite happy here'

Postcard from P. G. Wodehouse to Paul Reynolds, reverse side.

TO PAUL REYNOLDS

Ilag Tost

Oct. 21. 1940

GOODNESS KNOWS WHEN YOU WILL GET THIS. WILL YOU SEND ME A
FIVE POUND PARCEL ONE POUND PRINCE ALBERT TOBACCO, THE REST
NUT CHOCOLATE. REPEAT MONTHLY. AM QUITE HAPPY HERE AND
HAVE THOUGHT OUT NEW NOVEL. AM HOPING BE ABLE WRITE IT.
WHEN I WAS INTERNED, I HAD FINISHED A JEEVES NOVEL ALL BUT
FOUR CHAPTERS, ALSO TWO SHORT STORIES. YOURS P. G. WODEHOUSE
PUT 'KRIEGSGEFANGENENPOST' ON PARCEL.

*Had Wodehouse written a few months earlier, the news of his capture would
have been a terrible shock. Just before he was interned, Leonora was reassuring*

Wodehouse's agent that he was 'in no immediate danger'. In fact, the postcard came as a great relief. By August, rumours of Wodehouse's internment had reached Britain, and in October Reynolds and an anxious Leonora had written to each other about Wodehouse's whereabouts, and Reynolds referred to his being held in a 'concentration camp'. It is clear from contemporary correspondence that nobody in Britain or America actually knew what a 'concentration camp' was: one of Wodehouse's fans cheerfully notes that 'I doubt if a stay in a concentration camp bears any resemblance to an Eagles' picnic'.

Nevertheless, Wodehouse's reference to his 'Jeeves novel' (Joy in the Morning), and to what was to become Money in the Bank, was a clear signal that conditions could not be as bad as Leonora and Reynolds had feared. Indeed, in many ways, Wodehouse later wrote, 'camp was really great fun'. He had secured permission to use a typewriter, entertained his fellow internees with accounts of life at Tost, and enjoyed contributing to the Camp newspaper, the Tost Times:

As part of a campaign for his release, Reynolds made a decision to publish Wodehouse's postcard in the December issue of Time *magazine. It prompted a surge of fan mail. The P. J. Reynolds Tobacco Company sent a one-pound tin of Prince Albert Tobacco 'with best wishes for his early release', while an 'admirer of P. G. Wodehouse' and 'student of biochemistry' suggested sending 'special nut chocolate, containing vitamins which are probably deficient in German prison diet'. Reynolds thanked the correspondent for her 'suggestions', although he pointed out that it might be 'difficult to carry out practically'.*

Wodehouse's second postcard is more heroic than it would first appear. Given his public profile, he guessed that a message from him might act as a coded point of orientation for others, allowing the families of his friends to establish the whereabouts of their loved ones. Max Enke was a fellow internee, known by Wodehouse as the camp 'linguist' and 'chess champion', and used as the model for Lord Uffenham in Money in the Bank *and* Something Fishy. *Enke's daughter wrote to Reynolds to thank him for cabling the money, adding that 'It's very good of Mr Wodehouse to have used the space on his limited letters to send the message'.*

TO PAUL REYNOLDS

Ilag Tost

Nov. 1. 1940

WOULD YOU MIND SENDING FIVE DOLLARS TO MRS RUTH CHAMBERS 4TH AVE R.R.2. LADYSMITH BRIT. COLUMBIA AND FIFTEEN TO STEPHEN ENKE 700 POWER ST HELENA MONTANA — OR RATHER THE OTHER WAY ABOUT, FIVE TO ENKE AND FIFTEEN TO CHAMBERS. I BORROWED FROM A MAN HERE AND HE WANTS IT PAID AS ABOVE. REGARDS P. G. WODEHOUSE

Left: Described as the first 'Souvenir Number' of the *Tost Times*, 1 June 1941, which contains an abridged version of Chapter 1 of Wodehouse's 'All's Well with Bingo'.

CHAPTER TEN

The Broadcasts

Opening their copies of *The New York Times* just after Christmas, American readers would have discovered an update on one of their favourite British writers:

'Wodehouse Works at New Book in Padded Cell at German Camp – Held at Former Asylum, Writer Is in Good Spirits – Diet Develops "Admiration" for the Potato – He Declines Favors'.[1] Despite the cheerful tone of this piece, conditions in Tost were never easy. From the photograph accompanying the article, it was clear that Wodehouse had lost a great deal of weight. He looked frail and ill [see plate 32]. The winter in Silesia had been extremely harsh, driving some to suicide.[2] But as the newspaper report account suggests, Wodehouse remained stoical, acting as a sort of father figure to those who were struggling, cheering them through the winter months with the thought that they would be 'Home Before Christmas'.[3] Wodehouse's own Christmas gifts – baked beans and tobacco – arrived early, in the hands of this article's author, an American journalist, Angus Thuermer.

Thuermer had been working on a special report about conditions in prisoner-of-war camps, and the publicity generated by the publication of Wodehouse's postcard to Reynolds led him to Tost. The consequences of the meeting were, from Wodehouse's perspective, disastrous. Thuermer's aim had been to express his admiration for Wodehouse's bravery and camaraderie. Although the headline was 'He *Declines* Favors' – the word 'Favors' worked suggestively, planting the idea that Wodehouse was being singled out for special treatment. The black comedy of the piece, in which Wodehouse noted his growing fondness for the 'German potato', might also have struck readers as ill-judged, or blithe to the realities of war.

The tone, in fact, was typically Wodehousean. From Dulwich days onwards, the notion of mentioning hardship was, for him, the ultimate in 'bad form'. In times of crisis, cheerfulness was seen as a vital, even patriotic, virtue. This was further demonstrated in Wodehouse's growing body of comic writings about camp life, material for which he was keen to find an audience. In this sense, Thuermer's appearance seemed, to Wodehouse, particularly well timed. Coupling friendship with business, Wodehouse persuaded the journalist to act as both a courier and literary agent for an article about his wartime experiences, and began to work up sections of his camp notebooks in readiness for publication.

Spurred on by the publicity that Wodehouse was receiving from this *New York Times* piece, the attention of officials in the German Foreign Office began to focus on Prisoner Number 796, and the possibility of his release was discussed. A critical factor for the Germans was the fact that the US had not yet joined the war, although public opinion was very much on the side of the Allies. Given Wodehouse's status in America, the German Foreign Office foresaw that his public release might be of potential benefit to Germany. In showing clemency towards a 'British-American', there was the hope that the Germans would be able to claw back some ground from the swelling of American support for the Allied cause. Wodehouse's release, George Orwell noted, was 'a minor move, but it was not a bad sop to throw to the American isolationists'.[4] When, however, the Gestapo overruled the Foreign Office's recommendations for Wodehouse, a plan of almost baroque complexity was devised. This began with the suggestion that Wodehouse could broadcast some of his writings to his fans in America. The initial idea for such broadcasts may have been proposed by the camp's Commandant, Lagerführer Buchelt.

As far as Wodehouse was concerned, the notion of broadcasting was simply another assignment, rather like the interview he had given to Thuermer. The broadcasts, from his perspective, would give him the opportunity to respond to many letters from his admirers in America, which he had not been allowed to answer. While Wodehouse saw no relationship between the prospect of being released from internment and speaking on the radio, as McCrum notes, 'his responsiveness to the Lagerführer Buchelt's idea of a broadcast to America had the desired effect [...] from the point of view of the German Foreign Office. Once Buchelt reported that Wodehouse was willing to go to the microphone to broadcast to the USA, the Gestapo withdrew its objection to his release.'[5]

On 21 June in the early evening, Wodehouse was playing cricket with his fellow prisoners, when two men from the Gestapo arrived. He was given ten minutes to pack, and was told that he had to leave his near-complete manuscript, *Joy in the Morning*, behind. Wodehouse made the assumption that this summons was a release from the camp. The timing of his departure from Tost was unexpected – but given that he was only a few months from his sixtieth birthday (the age when internees were generally released) he claimed that, overall, he 'felt no surprise'.[6] A night train took him to Berlin, and after trying several hotels the Gestapo found accommodation for him at the Adlon, on Unter den Linden, directly opposite the Brandenburg Gate.

Later that morning, tired, lonely and in need of a new set of clothes, Wodehouse was glad of the apparently chance encounter with two acquaintances whom the Wodehouses had known from their time in New York and Hollywood, Raven von Barnikow and Werner Plack. Although the meeting seemed accidental, both men were already well aware of Wodehouse's presence in Berlin. A Luftwaffe officer and Prussian aristocrat, Barnikow had been part of the Beverly Hills circle in the 1930s, and had once been engaged to the Warner Bros. movie star, Kay Francis. He had been attempting to obtain Wodehouse's release, in exchange for a German businessman interned in England. Plack, meanwhile, had been planted by the German Foreign Office, to stage-manage Wodehouse's radio appearance. Wodehouse remembered the encounter in a letter to Guy Bolton. 'After I was released and taken to Berlin [...] I was dumped down at the Adlon and there I ran into a man named Barnikow, one of my oldest friends. [...] I had never looked on him as a German at all, as he was so entirely American.'[7] As Wodehouse recalls, Barnikow left, and Wodehouse and Plack continued talking. 'Plack asked me if I was tired after my journey and how I liked Camp. It was in the course of this conversation that I mentioned the number of letters I'd received from American readers, and said it was maddening not being able to answer them [...] Plack asked me if I would like to broadcast to America. I said "Yes", and he said he could have me brought to his office next day to arrange details.'[8] By the end of the day, Wodehouse was sitting in a Berlin hotel room, typing up his broadcasts on a borrowed typewriter. Designed to entertain his American audience, the broadcasts were based on the humorous vicissitudes of life as an internee, and almost identical in content to a series of satirical talks that Wodehouse had given to entertain his fellow prisoners at Tost.

Wodehouse was also under siege by reporters, who were eager for interviews. Just three days after his release from prison camp, Wodehouse was at the microphone, recording the broadcasts onto wax discs. Accepting a fee of 250 marks (about £20) from Werner Plack 'not realizing the implications' he then cabled his American friend the movie star Maureen O'Sullivan, to make sure that she listened in.[9]

TO MAUREEN O'SULLIVAN

Berlin

27 June. 1941

LOVE TO YOU BOTH LISTEN IN TONIGHT FRIDAY JUNE 27TH OVER STATION DJD 25.49 MTS DJB 19.74 MTS DZD 28.43 MTS 6.00 PM PACIFIC TIME [10]

When reflecting on his broadcasts, Wodehouse said that 'it never occurred to me that there could be anything harmful about such statements as that when in camp I read Shakespeare, that the Commandant at Huy Citadel had short legs and did not like walking uphill, that men who had no tobacco smoked tea and that there was an unpleasant smell in my cell at Loos Prison'.[11] Numerous historians and critics have discussed Wodehouse's 1941 texts, focusing on the substance of what he said. The real political import of the broadcasts, however, is in their tone. In the abstract, Wodehouse's particular form of comic resistance was anything but harmful to the Allied cause. His narrative, which moves from the whimsical to the absurd, and bordering on tragedy, takes its place in a body of wartime literature that responds to international politics not through clear opposition, but with resistant satire – standing alongside classics such as Hašek's *The Good Soldier Švejk* or Vonnegut's *Slaughterhouse-Five*.[12]

However, what Wodehouse failed to realise was the relationship between the medium and message. Wodehouse's experience of radio had, to date, been confined to the discussion of radio rights for his stories and a small number of face-to-face radio interviews and feature-style programmes. He had little sense that there was a war taking place 'in the ether' as well as one on the ground – and in the air. The implications of broadcasting on Nazi short-wave radio – the fact that wireless communication was, for the Nazis, a 'sharp and reliable weapon' – was lost on this author.[13] For, by 1941, the propaganda war was in full flow. Driven by Hitler's conviction in the power of the 'spoken word', the German Ministry of Propaganda formed a special Radio Department. 'All that happens in and through radio today', claimed Nazi radio director Eugen Hadamovsky, ensures that 'entire nations will be drenched through and through with our philosophy'.[14] Wartime radio, as W. H. Auden wrote just a few years later, created, and signified, solidarity and consensus – 'suddenly breaking in with its banal noises' and compelling its listeners to 'pay attention to a common world'.[15] Nazi radio was not 'just news', a British-born Nazi broadcaster recalls. It was 'a huge performance'.[16]

In time, Wodehouse was to write that becoming part of this perfor-mance had been 'criminally foolish'.[17] But, in June 1941, Wodehouse had few people to advise him and, without advice, made the worst possible choices. Leonora and Ethel were entirely unable to commu-nicate with him. His agent, Paul Reynolds, was laissez-faire, even encouraging, wiring the message 'HOPE BROADCASTS WILL BE OF SUCH NATURE AS TO PROMOTE VALUE OF NOVEL'.[18]

Just before the first broadcast was aired, Wodehouse delivered an interview with the CBS journalist Harry Flannery. The entire wording of the interview was scripted by Flannery in advance, and struck American listeners as blithe about current events, too friendly with the Germans, and ambivalent about the war's outcome. In dealing with the question of how his books might sell after the war, Wodehouse declared, through Flannery's text, that his concern was not with 'the war', but with 'whether the kind of England I write about will live after the war – whether England wins or not, I mean'.[19]

The German Foreign Office, keen that Wodehouse's broadcasts should appeal to the American listener, would have been unhappy with this interview. It was important that Wodehouse was perceived as being a neutral party, rather than pro-German, in order to make his release seem like an act of kindness on their part. It was therefore decided that Wodehouse's removal from Berlin would prevent further damage. At this point, Raven von Barnikow stepped in, and offered Wodehouse a refuge – a retreat in the German countryside. Though Barnikow's plans fitted the German Foreign Office's needs, and were approved by the Reich, his actions were, in fact, motivated by genuine concern. A secret but fervent anti-Nazi, Barnikow wished to save Wodehouse from himself. He telephoned his fiancée, Baroness Anga von Bodenhausen, and begged her to take Wodehouse in [see plate 34].

Meanwhile, after assessing the adverse Allied press coverage surrounding Wodehouse, the Ministry of Propaganda decided that it would be more useful to portray Wodehouse as a Nazi sympathiser, and began to leak false information to this effect. They also arranged to compound this impression by having Wodehouse's broadcasts aired to Great Britain. Oblivious to the import of his actions, Wodehouse recorded a brief preface for his English audience, emphasising what he felt was the innocuous nature of the talks.[20]

In replaying the broadcasts – originally intended solely for America – to Britain, the Nazis were hoping to weaken British morale. The sound of an English voice on Nazi radio waves had a peculiar power to disturb, as the Germans had already proved with their use of the infamous 'Lord Haw-Haw' (William Joyce), the English-speaking announcer who broadcast on the Nazi programme *Germany Calling*. It could only be helpful to the German cause that Wodehouse was known to sound peculiarly similar to Joyce – so much so that the British War Office had, in 1939, thought of using Wodehouse as a foil to caricature Haw-Haw on air, to boost the spirits of the British.[21]

Once aired, the broadcasts met with an outcry of horror, and Wodehouse was branded, by many, as a traitor. As the talks had been recorded on wax, the Germans had the opportunity to play them repeatedly to the British, on different wavelengths, and at varying times of the day and night.

Conscious that Wodehouse was by now embroiled in a scenario far larger than he realised, a number of Wodehouse's friends, both in England and in America, attempted to find out what was going on, and to prevent Wodehouse from appearing on the radio again. Reynolds, realising that he had been remiss in his duties, telephoned and cabled repeatedly. Such messages either were not received or were misunderstood by Wodehouse.

By the end of his week in Berlin, Wodehouse was pleased to escape. He might have been oblivious to the import of his actions but, in spite of his polite on-the-record remarks, the atmosphere of Nazi Berlin 'gave him the pips [*sic*]'.[22] On 28 June 1941, just a week after Wodehouse's release from internment, the Baroness von Bodenhausen made her way to Berlin to collect Wodehouse, and bring him home to her country estate in the Harz Mountains. 'I wore my blue coat from Florence', the Baronness recalls, 'and was pleased about the beautiful colour and even more pleased [...] that this nice Englishman emerged at my side amongst the crowds of the Adlon Hotel.'[23]

The Baroness knew that Wodehouse was still, by the terms of his agreement, required to go back to Berlin to record two further broadcasts, and she was hoping to stop these from going ahead. Bodenhausen's daughter, Reinhild, was only ten at the time, and recalls the moment when Wodehouse began to understand the import of what he had done:

> It was a perfect balmy summer's day when uncle Plummie started to play his record. We all listened. We felt the tension between my mother and uncle Plummie rising. She looked at the script he had read on the radio. The letter heading was stroked out with a dark blue pencil. 'Reinhild', she called, 'bring me an India rubber from the study.' [...] She took hold of uncle Plummie's manuscript and rubbed out the dark blue pencil mark. Something incredibly ghastly seemed to emerge. [...] I think what she read was '*Deutsches Propaganda Ministerium, Berlin*'. Goebbels, and not [the] Foreign Office, as she had thought.

A heated exchange ensued between the Baroness and Wodehouse, but one in which Wodehouse still failed to understand what the headed paper indicated – that his broadcasts, now the sole property of the German Ministry for Propaganda, rather than the German Foreign Office, were going to be used against the Allied cause. But in the coming weeks, things changed. Reinhild recalls that particular summer as a time in which Wodehouse 'replayed his records over and over again on the verandah. [...] Sometimes he stopped to lift the record needle to place it back and to listen again to certain phrases. He was clearly in anguish.'[24]

The remaining recordings, Reinhild remembers, 'turned out to be a nightmare for him'. 'He could just brace himself to reach the car to leave Degenershausen', the Baroness wrote in her diary. After his third visit to Berlin, the Baroness informed the Ministry that Wodehouse was too unwell to continue broadcasting. Wodehouse received the news that his broadcasts were over 'like a drowning man' being 'rescued'.[25]

She was right to fear for Wodehouse. As the broadcasts were aired in series by the Nazis, the transmissions gave the misleading impression to British listeners that Wodehouse was continuing to make his comments on a weekly basis, despite British disapproval – and long after he had realised his own mistake. Edison's dream for the phonograph, '[t]he captivation of sounds, with or without the knowledge or consent of the source of their origin', was to hold Wodehouse captive for years to come.[26]

Despite the shadow of the broadcasts, the early autumn of 1941 seemed to have its share of happiness for Wodehouse. Protected from the barrage of press abuse, he spent his sixtieth birthday surrounded by children, dogs and the German countryside, discussing 'not solely the war' but 'the life of leeches, of ticks [...] wild geese, spiritualism' and Conan Doyle.[27] Above all, he was reunited with Ethel, who joined Wodehouse at Degenershausen – before having to return to Berlin for urgent dental treatment.

But Wodehouse was still 'worried and uncertain' about his future, confiding to Anga von Bodenhausen that, 'being an enemy', he was reluctant to return to Berlin. 'How grim the Germans are', he reflected.[28] As winter drew in, the massive house became too expensive to heat. Reinhild and her mother went to stay with relatives. Wodehouse returned to Berlin, to Ethel – and his beloved Pekingese, Wonder.

1 Angus Thuermer, 'Wodehouse Works on New Book', *The New York Times*, 27 December 1940.
2 See McCrum, p. 291.
3 Ibid.
4 George Orwell, 'In Defence of P. G. Wodehouse', in Peter Davidson (ed.), *The Complete Words of George Orwell* (London: Secker and Warburg, 1998), vol. XVII, p. 60.

5 McCrum, p. 298.

6 P. G. Wodehouse, 'Now That I've Turned Both Cheeks', p. 10 (Wodehouse Archive).

7 PGW to Guy Bolton, 1 September 1945 (Wodehouse Archive).

8 See P. G. Wodehouse's statement in Major Cussen's 'Report on the Case of P. G. Wodehouse', 3 October 1940, HO 45/22385–66279 (PRO), repr. in Ian Sproat, *Wodehouse at War* (New Haven and New York: Ticknor & Fields, 1969), p. 69.

9 See Cussen, p.12. For transcripts of the broadcasts, see http://www.pgwodehousesociety.org.uk/controversy.html.

10 PGW to Maureen O'Sullivan, 27 June 1941 (Columbia).

11 This was PGW's introductory remark to his broadcast on 9 August 1941. See Sproat, p. 161.

12 This aspect of the broadcasts was recognised by the American military – see the letter from PGW to Evelyn Waugh, 31 May 1947.

13 E. T. Lean, *Voices in the Darkness: The Story of European Radio War* (London: Secker and Warburg, 1943), p. 19.

14 Ibid.

15 W. H. Auden, *The Age of Anxiety* (1947), repr. in *Collected Poems*, ed. Edward Mendelson (London: Faber, 2007), p. 452.

16 James Clark, broadcaster for Nazi radio, interviewed in *Germany Calling: The Voice of the Nazi*, Radio 4, 16 May 1991.

17 PGW to the Home Secretary, 4 September 1944 (Wodehouse Archive).

18 Paul Reynolds to PGW, 26 June 1941 (Columbia).

19 Harry Flannery, *Assignment to Berlin* (London: Michael Joseph, 1942), pp. 246–7.

20 Sproat, p. 161.

21 Lieutenant-Colonel Aylmer Vaillance to Frederick Ogilvie, BBC Director General, 11 December 1939 (BBC Archive) http://www.bbc.co.uk/archive/hawhaw/8924.shtml.

22 *The Unknown Years*, p. 10.

23 *Diaries of Anga von Bodenhausen* (private archive).

24 *Unknown Years*, p. 15, p. 24.

25 Ibid., p. 25.

26 Thomas Edison's article, 'The Phonograph and Its Future', *North American Review* (Jan–Feb 1878); pp. 527–36, at p. 530.

27 *Diaries of Anga von Bodenhausen* (private archive).

28 Ibid.

CHAPTER ELEVEN

Berlin

The news, in June 1941, that Wodehouse was to broadcast from Germany led to outraged correspondence in the press. The letters page of the *Daily Telegraph* included attacks on Wodehouse from fellow writers such as A. A. Milne and Storm Jameson.[1] Comments were biting and personal, and parallels with Charles Lindbergh and William Joyce were drawn. Even friends and colleagues, such as his long-time collaborator Ian Hay, turned on him. 'We are', Hay wrote, 'horrified':

> No broadcast from Berlin by a world-famous Englishman, however 'neutral' in tone, can serve as anything but an advertise-ment for Hitler [...] an ingenious dose [...] of soothing syrup for America, designed to divert American thoughts from the horrors which are being perpetrated in German prison camps today.[2]

Other correspondents were more measured, arguing that Wodehouse might have been put under considerable pressure by the Germans ('the Hun has means of persuasion', one noted).[3] Wodehouse's friend, the novelist Dorothy L. Sayers, perceptively pointed out that Wodehouse might well have had 'not the slightest realization' of current events:

> At the time of the Battle of France, when he fell into enemy hands, English people had scarcely begun to realize the military and political importance of the German propaganda weapon. Since then we have learned much. We know something of why and how France fell; we have seen disintegration at work in the Balkans; we have watched the slow recovery of American opinion from the influence of the Nazi hypnotic.
>
> But how much of all this can possibly be known or appreci-ated from inside a German concentration camp – or even from the Adlon Hotel?[4]

Following Wodehouse's broadcasts, the journalist William N. Connor – known as 'Cassandra' – was encouraged by the Cabinet Minister, Duff Cooper, to make an 'indictment' of Wodehouse on the BBC airwaves. Further letters followed. This time, a number of correspondents were outraged at the seemingly partisan 'invective' and 'personal abuse' that Cassandra had seen fit to broadcast, especially as he had no knowledge of the background to Wodehouse's talks. Nevertheless, anti-Wodehouse feeling ran high throughout the country, with the writer becoming labelled as a 'Nazi stooge'. His novels were banned in Northern Ireland, and removed from the shelves of some British libraries and pulped.

Those closest to Wodehouse – Leonora, Reynolds, Thelma Cazalet-Keir and William Townend – were desperately trying to find a way to prevent him causing further damage to himself, and were only able to glean his activities from unreliable newspaper reports. All William Townend's letters to Wodehouse were, at this point, returned to him marked 'undelivered'. For them, there was no question about Wodehouse's motives. As Leonora wrote, 'I am completely and utterly certain that he is completely unconscious of any wrongdoing. However it isn't exactly helping our war effort so he is very naturally judged accordingly.'[5] Reynolds noted that 'I am perfectly certain that your father is just as anti-Nazi as any of us are but he is about the world's worst person with newspaper reporters. He also seems to have very little idea of the feeling or point of view of this country or of England due to the fact that things have changed so and he's been out of touch with newspapers. He could ruin himself for years in this country in half an hour's interview with newspaper reporters [...]. He wouldn't mean to but he is too honest and too naïve.'[6] Leonora, as she wrote to Mackail, felt 'a bit like a mother with an idiot child that she anyway loves better than all the rest'.[7]

Wodehouse was protected from the worst of the press coverage, especially at Degenershausen, deep in the German countryside. But, in November 1941, the Baroness von Bodenhausen closed her house for the winter, and the Wodehouses moved back to Berlin, taking up residence, once again, in the Adlon Hotel. Wodehouse was familiar with the Adlon from his previous stay in June, and as an English-speaker in Berlin he had plenty of company. A number of American journalists also took refuge there; in the bitter Berlin winter, the Adlon was the only place where one could guarantee a supply of hot water. The Wodehouses may have enjoyed this aspect of relative luxury, but in truth they were 'not allowed to stay anywhere else', and would much rather have been elsewhere. 'We made several attempts to move to less conspicuous hotels and we also tried a number of pensions, but without success. At our first visit to these hotels and pensions we were always informed that we could have accommodation, at our second, that they were full up.'[8]

Staying at the prestigious Adlon only compounded the abuse levelled against Wodehouse. This grand building, within walking distance of the German Foreign Office and the Reich Chancellery, was the favoured hotel of the Nazis. This was a place where Hitler's speeches were broadcast nightly to the entire dining-room and, unbeknownst to the Wodehouses, where German spies haunted the public rooms, and telegrams concerning the Final Solution were received.

Berlin in 1941 was gripped with tension. By October, the Chief of Police signed the order to begin the deportation of the city's Jews. Over a thousand citizens were loaded onto the first train, which left Berlin for Łódź, in eastern Poland. Later, they would be moved on to Auschwitz, Treblinka and other concentration camps. Thousands more were to follow. Rumours of mass killings echoed round Berlin, though few knew the truth. It is likely that little or nothing of this reached the Wodehouses in their protected Adlon world.

The visible signs of war were, however, impossible to miss. Hulking flak towers loomed over the city to counter the Allied air-raids which were increasing in frequency and ferocity. Citizens were demoralised by the poor food and shortage of coal. Even the Adlon was forced to observe a weekly 'Eintopf Day', when vegetable stew was the only dish on the menu – an idea enforced by government edict to promote solidarity and austerity. Nevertheless, luxuries were still available for those who could afford them. Restaurants, bars and cafés continued to trade – although the price of a meal out would cost the average Berliner their weekly wage. Champagne and lobster remained unrationed, and the few racy cabaret sites and jazz clubs to survive the Nazi clampdown gave an atmosphere of frenzied cheerfulness to night-time Berlin.

Wodehouse was retrospectively guarded about his time in Berlin. '[T]here is', he wrote 'so little to tell':

> Naturally everyone would suppose that an Englishman in Germany in war time would have a thrilling tale to relate, but I am a creature of habit and as the result of forty years of incessant literary composition have become a mere writing machine. Wherever I am, I sit down and write, or, if I have nothing to write about, I walk up and down and think out plots.
>
> When I was in Berlin at the Adlon, this was my life day after day. Get up, do my Daily Dozen, bathe, shave, breakfast, take dog for saunter, start work. Work till lunch. After lunch the exercise walk, resuming work at five. Work from five till eight. Go down to dinner and from dinner back to my room to read or else walk round and round the corridors of my floor, thinking. Except when we went to lunch with an English or American friend, this programme never varied. I seldom spoke to a German. Occasionally one would come up to our table and say he had liked my books and I would be civil, but that was all.[9]

Many of Wodehouse's Berlin letters dwell on practicalities of daily life in wartime Berlin: the exercising of his Peke, Wonder, in the Tiergarten; the difficulties of finding enough food; and, of course, his main preoccupation – his work. It seems extraordinary that, during this time in Tost, Berlin and Paris, Wodehouse managed to complete four novels. *Money in the Bank* – a tale of gangsters and jewel-pilfering in a large country house – was written during his time in internment; *Joy in the Morning*, the story of Bertie's entanglement with the fearsome Florence Craye, featuring the wrathful constable Stilton Cheesewright, had been plotted and partly written before his capture. He completed it in his first winter in Berlin. *Full Moon*, his sixth Blandings novel, had also been left behind, in manuscript, when the Germans invaded Le Touquet. This most English of novels was completed in the leafy peace of Degenershausen. *Uncle Dynamite*, the return of the incorrigible and chaotic Frederick Altamont Cornwallis Twistleton, fifth Earl of Ickenham, was written, in part, in a Paris maternity home, under detention by the French police.[10]

Wodehouse's claim that he 'seldom spoke to a German' is, however, not entirely true. From the first, the Wodehouses had frequent contact with their friend Werner Plack, whom they had met in Hollywood. A flamboyant former actor and wine merchant turned civil servant, he was suspected of working as a German spy in America in the 1930s. His work for the German Foreign Office was punctuated by travel, partygoing in Berlin and illicit entanglements with women. Plack was, as McCrum describes, 'the self-styled English-speaking go-between with foreigners the Nazis hoped to exploit for propaganda purposes', and frequently found time to visit the Wodehouses at the Adlon, visiting their rooms to collect letters to deliver abroad.[11] Subsequent events indicate that Plack also did his best to support the Wodehouses, making concerted, though unsuccessful, attempts for the couple to be released to some neutral country.

At this time, the Wodehouses were also worried about their finances. A prolonged stay in an expensive hotel meant that additional sources of income had to be found. They relied, in part, on such royalties as could be collected from neutral countries. Wodehouse also negotiated a contract with a German film company, to augment their income. Ethel attempted to help, socialising with Germany's top directors and actors in the Adlon bar and dining-room, and speculating on future film contracts.[12]

Wodehouse and Ethel were also 'great friends' with Johann 'Jonny' Jebsen [see plate 33]. Jebsen was part of the German Military Intelligence organisation, the Abwehr, but he openly despised the Nazi regime. He cut a rather sinister figure: blond, with a monocle, 'very bad black teeth' and an occasional limp – but he was a loyal, humorous and daring man, who helped the Wodehouses financially 'from time to time'. By 1943, Jebsen had become a double agent, joining MI5 under the code-name 'Artist'. As part of his mission, he reported to the Home Office that the Wodehouses were in 'close touch' with Paul Schmidt, Hitler's interpreter, who had often spoken to Ethel about conversations he had interpreted for Hitler. Despite these German friendships, Jebsen recorded that Ethel was 'very pro-British' and was 'inclined to be rude to anyone who dares to address her in German. She has on occasion said loudly in public places "If you cannot address me in English, don't speak at all: you had better learn it as you will have to speak it after the war, anyway."' Wodehouse, Jebsen noted, 'was entirely childlike and pacifist'.[13]

Initially, the German authorities would not allow the Wodehouses to leave, despite Wodehouse's attempts to return to England, with the aim of 'reaffirming his loyalty'.[14] Under such circumstances, Ethel contented herself with enjoying what social life there was in Berlin. Wodehouse much preferred the peace of Degenershausen, and returned there in the summer of 1942, to be with Anga and Reinhild. By the autumn, Allied raids on Berlin had intensified. Life was becoming increasingly dangerous, with night after night spent in the Adlon's air-raid shelter. In 1943, after some difficulty, the Wodehouses were finally granted permission to leave Berlin for the relative safety of occupied Paris, where they were to remain 'under supervision'.[15]

1 *Daily Telegraph*, 1–13 July 1941.
2 Repr. in Sproat, p. 16.
3 Ibid., p. 21.
4 Ibid., p. 23.
5 Leonora Cazalet to Paul Reynolds, 16 July 1941 (Columbia).
6 Paul Reynolds to Leonora Cazalet, 27 August 1942 (Columbia).
7 Leonora Cazalet to Denis Mackail, 21 July 1941 (Wodehouse Archive).
8 Major Cussen's 'Report on the Case of P. G. Wodehouse', 3 October 1940, HO 45/22385–66279, pp. 8–9 (PRO).
9 PGW to H. D. Ziman, 26 September 1945 (private archive).
10 *Money in the Bank* (US 1942; UK 1946); *Joy in the Morning* (US 1946; UK 1947); *Full Moon* (US 1947; UK 1947); *Uncle Dynamite* (UK and US 1948).
11 McCrum, p. 298.
12 See Ethel Wodehouse to PGW, 8 August 1942. 'A film actor [...] insisted on my sitting at his table [...]. He had with him a Director, I think quite a famous one [...]. Very interested in your work, wanted to get hold of you' (Wodehouse Archive).
13 Included in a report about the wartime activities of the double agent Dusko Popov ('Agent Tricycle'), KV 2/856 (PRO).
14 Sproat, p. 84.
15 Ibid.

1941–1943:
'so little to tell'

As America remained neutral until 8 December 1941, Wodehouse was able to send brief communications to his family through his agent, Reynolds.

TO PAUL REYNOLDS

Berlin
RCA Radiogram Telegram

Nov 18. 1941

TELL LEONORA ETHEL WELL GIVE HER OUR LOVE
PLEASE CABLE AMERICAN REACTION TO MY SERIAL[1]
HOPE WELL RECEIVED REGARDS
WODEHOUSE

1 *Money in the Bank* had just been serialised in the *Saturday Evening Post*.

TO PAUL R. REYNOLDS

Adlon Hotel
Berlin

Nov 27. 1941

Dear Reynolds.

Thanks so much for your cable, telling me that the reaction to the serial had been favourable. I had visions of people writing to Stout asking him how he dared print a story by the outcast Wodehouse.[1] It really looks as if all that fuss that happened in the summer has subsided. You know, I still cannot fathom the mystery of that article of mine in the *S.E.P.* You said in your letter of June 17, 1941 'The *Post* was very

317

pleased with your article', and I got a cable from Stout not more than a month later, which ended 'Your article strongly resented by many'. Why anyone should resent a harmless humorous article about men in camp growing beards and servers at meals hitting the bowl with the fish stew four times out of five, it is beyond me to imagine. Evidently the *Post* people didn't on June 17. Amazing that an article which pleased them at the end of June should have roused indignation at the end of July. It seemed to me, when I wrote it, that I was doing something mildly courageous and praiseworthy in showing that it was possible, even though in a prison camp, to keep one's end up and not bellyache.

It is a great relief to learn that *Money in the Bank* has gone well. Things are looking very bright as regards my Art. My wife, when she joined me in July, brought along the Jeeves novel which I was working on when I was interned, and I have now finished it and, if I can manage it, will ship it over to you [...]. I have also written half of a new novel about Lord Emsworth and his pig, called *Full Moon*. This I have shelved for the time being in order to work on a book of Camp reminiscences. This will be good, but shortish. Could you let me know the minimum length for a book of this type.

[...]

Also, do you think it ought to be published while the war is still on? If people in America resented that article in the *S.E. Post*, they would presumably resent a book of the same tone. It is very funny, a little vulgar in spots, and contains a chapter where I state my case to my English critics and – I hope – make them feel pretty foolish. [...]

(A man from Tauchnitz has just phoned up from the lobby and wants to see me, so must stop for the moment.)

The man from Tauchnitz turned out to be a charming girl.[2]

Do you know Berlin at all? It is a very attractive city and just suits me because I am fond of walking and the sidewalks are very wide and not too many cross-streets. We have the Tiergarten, a park rather like the Bois du Boulogne, just outside the hotel, – invaluable for exercising the Peke.

Best wishes to you all

Yours ever

P. G. Wodehouse

P.S. Will you please on receipt of this send to the Reilly and Lee Co, 325 West Huron Street, Chicago, the sum of One Thousand dollars and chalk it up to me on the slate. Tell them to hold it for Edward Delaney. Important.[3]

P.P.S. The chocolates and tobacco arrived very intermittently, presumably owing to difficulties of transport. I received two pounds of tobacco at intervals and, I think, four lots of chocolate. By the way, don't slacken off on these parcels because I am now out of camp. I need them just as much as ever.

[...]

1 Wesley Stout, editor of the *Saturday Evening Post*.
2 Tauchnitz was a publishing firm based in Leipzig, producing English-language versions of books for the Continental market. Wodehouse had been working with them since 1924.
3 Edward Delaney, also staying in the Adlon at this time, was an American who was employed by the Germans to broadcast Nazi propaganda to the US, under the pseudonym 'E. D. Ward'. He was indicted for treason in 1943, but released due to a lack of evidence. Reynolds, in fact, did not transfer PGW's funds, noting that Delaney was a 'prisoner of the enemy', and was subsequently informed by the FBI that Delaney was a Nazi representative. Reynolds' son later noted that 'presumably the Nazis gave Wodehouse $1000 in German marks and asked him to have us send $1000 to Delaney in Chicago. Wodehouse had no reason to believe that he was asking us to do something that might be harmful to the United States or to England' (Reynolds Jr, *Diary of a Middle Man* (New York: William Morrow & Company, Inc., 1972), p. 112).

By July 1, Wodehouse's broadcasts were under discussion in the House of Commons, and the question was aired as to whether he could be subject to prosecution under the Treachery Act. Wesley Stout, editor of the Saturday Evening Post, *had sent an appalled telegram to Wodehouse:* 'MONEY IN BANK GOOD. EAGER TO BUY BUT CAN ONLY ON YOUR EXPLICIT ASSURANCE THAT YOU WILL NOT BROADCAST FROM GERMANY EUROPE OR OTHERWISE ACT PUBLICLY IN MANNER WHICH CAN BE CONSTRUED AS SERVING NAZI ENDS [...]'. *Stout had also written to Paul Reynolds noting that Wodehouse had 'alienated' his readers and that he felt he would be 'a liability to* The Post', *adding in a later letter: 'Our own belief is that he traded himself out of prison camp with his eyes open.'*

Adlon Hotel
Berlin

Nov 29. 1941

My Dear Stout.

I have just had a cable from Reynolds, saying that the reaction in America to *Money in the Bank* has been 'extremely favorable', which is a great weight off my mind, as I have naturally been worrying since your cables of July.

I am still bewildered about that article of mine in the *Post*. You cabled me that it had been 'strongly resented by many', and I can't understand what there was in it that could have offended people. I read it as a paper in the camp to an audience of several hundred, all rabid patriots, and had them rolling in the aisles. And they not only laughed, but applauded and cheered. So what <u>can</u> have been wrong with it? I must say that when I wrote it I felt a little complacently that I was keeping my end up by being humorous about camp life and not beefing, but from what you say people in America must have resented this tone. But surely all that stuff about growing beards and the servers dishing out the fish stew was harmless. I wish you would write and tell me exactly why it was resented.

The great joy of being out of the camp is that I am now able to see an occasional *Post*. I get them only in driblets, when somebody happens to have one, and I have to make what I can of the serials by reading installments two, six and seven – the last I saw of Budington Kelland's Silver Spoon hero was him facing a peeved gangster (to be concluded), and I suppose I never shall get around to knowing how it all came out. Still, even an occasional *Post* is a godsend after an abstinence of nearly two years.

My Art is flourishing like the family of an Australian rabbit. I have in my desk, complete to the last comma, a Jeeves novel called *Joy in the Morning*, – and when I say <u>a</u> Jeeves novel, I mean <u>the</u> supreme Jeeves novel of all time. This is the one I was writing when I was interned, and I have now been able to finish it. In addition to this, I have written half of a Blandings Castle novel called *Full Moon*, so funny that it will be almost dangerous to publish it. The rest is all scenarioed out, and I can finish it in a month or so. I don't know why it was, but having to write in pencil in camp seemed to inspire me.

Best wishes,

Yours sincerely,

P. G. Wodehouse

The Baroness von Bodenhausen was engaged to her cousin, Raven von Barnikow, whom Wodehouse had known in Hollywood and met in Berlin. Although he served in the Luftwaffe, Barnikow was fervently anti-Nazi. As he became aware of the German treatment of the Jews, Barnikow became deeply depressed. He had refused to fight on the Western Front, had taken to drinking heavily, and was briefly sent for rehabilitation in various hospitals in Berlin.

TO ANGA VON BODENHAUSEN

Adlon Hotel
Berlin

Dec 24. 1941

Dearest Anga.

Just a line to let you know we are thinking of you all and hoping you will have a happy Christmas. I don't suppose the children have learned enough English to read enclosed, so will you read them and give them our love and a lot of kisses.

It must be heavenly on Rügen Island.[1] Everything is very quiet at the Adlon now, which I enjoy. Ethel went to see Raven yesterday, and thinks he seems ever so much better. He is very quiet, of course, and not in his usual spirits, but that is only to be expected. The great thing is that his health seems good again and I feel sure he has got over his bad time. We were going to see him the day before, but he was off to the pictures, which seems a good sign that he is better and taking an interest in things. When you consider the terrible shock he has had, I think he has made splendid progress.

[...]

Werner has at last got us a radio, but we can only get Breslau on it! Still, that is better than nothing.

Ethel is busy dressing for our luncheon party, and has just shouted through the door to give you her love. So here it is, with lots of love from me and Wonder, and a hope that 1942 may see us all happy and you back on Holland Estates shooting rhinoceroses![2]

Yours ever

Plummie

1 The Baroness's father had a castle on Rügen Island in the Baltic.
2 'Holland Estates' – the Baroness's two farms in Tanganyika, Africa, which she and her late husband had bought in 1932.

By March 1942, Wodehouse was longing to return to the peace of Degeners-hausen. The following letter gives the first mention of Wodehouse's work for the Berliner Film Company, in which he speaks of a year's tie-in contract. Later, writing about this decision to Major Cussen, Wodehouse notes that the company decided to develop his novel Heavy Weather. *Wodehouse 'insisted on the insertion in the contract of a clause' which gave assurance that his work would 'not be twisted for propaganda purposes', and he was 'given to understand that the picture would not be released until after the war. [...] The scene of the story would be changed from Shropshire to Pomerania and [...] all the characters would be German'. He received 40,000 marks as an advance.*

TO ANGA VON BODENHAUSEN

Hotel Adlon
Berlin

March 30. 1942

My dearest Anga.

What a lovely fat letter from you! It was wonderful to get it and to know that you are preparing the old home for my arrival. I can hardly wait to get to dear Degenershausen. I feel that when I am there I can just settle down and forget what horrible times we are living in. It is a little haven of peace in this awful world. I shall stroll in the park and think out wonderful stories.

[...]

I think the best plan will be for me to stay on here till something definite is settled about the picture I am going to do, and then I shall not have to break my stay at Degenershausen by coming up to Berlin. What has happened so far is that they have paid me a sum of money which binds me to sell my novels for pictures to them alone for a year. The next step is for them to decide which of my books they want made into a picture. When this is done, they pay me some more money and then I retire into the country and write the picture. Werner says that Theo Lingen, who will probably star in whatever picture I do, arrives here tomorrow, when I suppose there will be a meeting and I shall know how I stand.[1] But I feel sure I shall be able to go with you when you go back to Degenershausen.

How wonderful the place must be looking now, and how angelic it is of you to say we can come to you for the whole summer. Are you really sure you can stand us for so long? We talk of you and your sweetness all the time. Words can't express our gratitude for all you have done.

[...]

I must stop now, as I have to go down to dinner and the slightest delay means that one does not get a table! Oceans of love, dearest Anga, and bless you for all your sweetness.

Yours

Plummie

1 Theo Lingen (1903–78) was a successful German film actor. Lingen's wife, Marianne Zoff, was of Jewish descent, but due to Lingen's popularity, Goebbels granted him a special permit enabling him to keep performing and protecting his wife.

May 11. 1942

Dear Bill.

At last I am able to write to you!! This is being taken to Lisbon by my Hollywood friend, Werner Plack, who is escorting the U.S. Embassy boys to freedom tomorrow. He will mail it there, and I hope it will eventually arrive.

You really have been wonderful, Bill, writing to me so regularly. I got all your letters and loved them.

[...]

I'm so glad you liked *Money in the Bank*. It was written at the rate of about a page a day in a room with fifty other men playing darts and ping-pong and talking and singing. It just shows how one can concentrate when one has to. After I had finished it, I started a Blandings Castle novel called *Full Moon* and had done about a third of it when I was released. Ethel then joined me in the country, bringing with her about two thirds of a Jeeves novel called *Joy in the Morning*, which I had been writing at Le Touquet during the occupation. I finished this, and then I tackled *Full Moon* again and finished that. I have also written a book about life in camp – very funny, but a bit on the short side. I shall not publish that till after the war.

Camp was really great fun. Those letters in the *Daily Telegraph* about my having found internment so awful that I bought my release by making a bargain with the German Government made me laugh. I was released because I was on the verge of sixty. The Germans don't intern people after sixty. When I was in Loos Prison the first week, a dozen of us were released because they were sixty, including my cellmate William Cartmell, the Etaples piano tuner.[1] Of course, he may have made a bargain with the German Government by offering, if set free, to tune its piano half price, but I don't think so. And even if he did, what about the other eleven? One of them was a man who eked out a livelihood by standing on Boulogne pier and spitting into the water. You can't bribe a Government just by promising that if set at liberty you will stand on piers and spit. No, I think that all these men were released for the reason stated, because they were sixty, and so was I. Though I admit that it doesn't make nearly such a good story.

Camp was fine. The first few weeks, at Loos Prison, Liege Barracks and the Citadel of Huy, were on the tough side, but once we got to Tost everything was great. I played cricket again after twenty-seven years, and played havoc with the opposition with slow leg-breaks. I was in the middle of an over when they came and told me to pack. (What happens in a cricket match when the bowler is suddenly snatched away in the middle of an over? Can you play a sub? And, if so, is he allowed to bowl?) We used to play with a string ball (string wound round a nut) which our sailors manufactured.

I remember you saying to me once how much you liked the men in the last war. It was the same with me. I really do think that there is nothing on earth to compare with the Englishman in the cloth cap and muffler. I had friends at Tost in every imaginable walk of life, from Calais dock touts upwards, and there wasn't one I didn't like.

[...]

I got very religious in camp. There was a Salvation Army colonel there who held services every Sunday. There is something about the atmosphere of a camp which does something to you in that way.

I shall have to stop now, as the deadline for writing is approaching. Werner is due here to pick up our letters in about five minutes.

Love to Rene

Yours ever

Plum

1 Described in his broadcasts as 'courteous and popular', William Cartmell shared a cell with PGW and 'Algy', the resident clown from a local bar in Le Touquet. Cartmell was the 'senior member' of the cell. 'He used to talk to us of pianos he had tuned in the past, and sometimes he would speak easily and well of pianos he hoped to tune in the future, but it was not the same. You could see that what the man wanted was a piano *now*. Either that, or something to take his mind off the thing' ('Second Berlin Broadcast', repr. in Donaldson, *P. G. Wodehouse*, p. 333).

In the summer of 1942, Wodehouse gladly made his way back to Degeners-
hausen. Ethel, who enjoyed the quiet of the countryside less, needed dental
treatment, and remained at the Adlon.

TO RAVEN VON BARNIKOW

Degenershausen

July 26. 1942

Dear Raven.
The sweater arrived yesterday. Thanks most awfully for taking all that
trouble to get it for me. It is a magnificent sweater, very thick with a
collar and is just what I want.

[...]

We think and talk of you all the time here, and it was a terrible
disappointment when we heard that you were not able to come to
Degenershausen after all. I do hope you will be able to get leave in
August. I suppose with all this talk of a second front leave is out of
the question for a bit. What a shame. I was looking forward so much
to seeing you again.

Anga will have told you that at the moment we are in a state of siege
owing to a Bolshie prisoner having escaped from Ermsleben. He is
supposed to be hiding in the cherry orchard, and this afternoon, Anga,
Count Rantzow, Bwana and the children are going there heavily armed,
to have a look around. I may go, but am feeling very lazy these days
and prefer just strolling in the park.

Degenershausen is looking lovely now, and it only needs you here,
to make it perfect. We lead a quiet life. Anga and the children milk
the cows and the goat and I sweep out the stable.

[...]

Ethel as you probably know stayed on in Berlin and seems to be
having quite a good time. She is very fond of the Tiergarten and she
has Wonder the peke to keep her company. [...] Ethel says Werner is
back again from Africa and got a big laugh from everyone at a party
by putting on his African kit. How that man does get about. It seems
only yesterday that he was in Greece.

[...]

I'm afraid life must be pretty awful for you just now. That telephone work you have to do must be very wearing. Let's hope it won't last much longer.

Sometimes I feel very optimistic and at other times I wonder if the thing will ever end.

[...] It's curious that you too should be quartered in a lunatic asylum. I wonder if it is anything like Tost.

[...]

Well all our best Raven, old man and I'm hoping to see you here in August.

Yours ever

Plummie

TO THE FOREIGN OFFICE

Via the Swiss Representatives in Berlin

November 21. 1942

Sir,

In the hope that by doing so I shall be able to re-establish myself in the eyes of the British Government and people and to remove the bad impression created by my unfortunate broadcasts over the German short wave system in July 1941, may I be allowed to put before you the circumstances connected with those? I am not attempting to minimise the blunder, which I realise was inexcusable, but I feel that I can place certain facts before His Majesty's Government which will show that I am guilty of nothing more than a blunder.

In the press and on the radio of Great Britain it has been stated that I bought my release from internment by making a bargain with the German Government, whereby they on their side were to set me free and I on mine undertook to broadcast German propaganda to the United States.

This I can emphatically deny. I was released, as were all the internees who had reached that age, because I was sixty years old. In the first week of my internment, at Loos Prison, a dozen men were sent home because they were sixty or over. I left the camp a year later in company with another internee of that age, who was released at the same time and for the same reason. I mention this to show that no special consideration was extended to me, and that there was never any suggestion at any time that the German Government were expecting a quid pro quo.

Nor did the suggestion that I should broadcast come from the German Government. It happened that the first man I met on arriving in Berlin was an old Hollywood friend of mine, who had returned to Germany at the beginning of the war to work in the Foreign Office. And after we had talked for a while and the conversation had turned to my plans for the future, I said that the thing I was anxious to do as soon as possible was to make a few broadcasts to the United States, to let my correspondents there know how I had been getting along.

In the last thirty weeks of my captivity, I should mention, I had received a great number of letters from American readers of my books, full of sympathy and kindness and all very curious for details of the life I was living, and none of these had I been able to answer. For in camp internees are allowed to write only to near relatives.

Those letters had been preying on my mind. I felt that their writers, having no means of knowing the circumstances, must be thinking me ungrateful and ungracious in ignoring them. I still could not reply to them individually, but I thought that if I were to speak on the radio, describing my adventures, it would at least be an interim acknowledgement. Next day I arranged to do five talks, covering the five phases of my imprisonment – the start at Le Touquet; the first week in Loos Prison; the second week in Liege Barracks; the third, fourth, fifth, sixth and seventh weeks at the Citadel of Huy; and the last forty-two weeks in Tost Lunatic Asylum.

I can now, of course, see that this was an insane thing to do, and I regret it sincerely. My only excuse is that I was in an emotional frame of mind, and the desire to make some return for all those letters had become an obsession, causing me to overlook the enormity of my action.

It seemed to me at the time that there would be no harm in reading over the radio a short series of purely humorous and frivolous reminiscences which, if I had been in England, would have appeared in *Punch*. I had written those talks while in camp and had read them to an audience of fellow-internees, who were amused by them, which would not have been the case had they contained the slightest suggestion of German propaganda.

All this, I realise, does not condone the fact that I used the German short wave system as a means of communication with my American public, but I hope it puts my conduct in a better light.

With regard to my life since I left camp, I have been living during the spring, summer and autumn at the house of the family of another Hollywood friend. In the winter, when the house is closed, I have been obliged to stay at the Adlon Hotel, as I do not speak German and the difficulties in the way of living anywhere else would have been insuperable. All my expenses are paid by myself, partly with borrowed money and partly from the proceeds of the sale of my wife's jewellery. If the impression in England is that I am being maintained by the German Government, I should like to deny it totally.

I should like to conclude by expressing my sincere regret that a well-meant but ill-considered action on my part should have given the impression that I am anything but a loyal subject of His Majesty.

I am, sir, your obedient servant,

P. G. Wodehouse

By December 1942, in the face of another bitterly cold German winter, the Wodehouses began 'working on getting out of Germany'. Conditions worsened in the new year. By early February, Field Marshal Paulus and the German troops at Stalingrad had been forced to surrender to the Russians. Almost no German family was untouched by the massive loss of life. A radio announcement on 3 February informed the German people that the struggle for Stalingrad had ended in defeat. Three days of national mourning followed, and theatres, cinemas, vaudeville halls and cafés were shut to mark the sombre occasion. By March, Berlin was sustaining heavy damage from Allied bombing. Ethel and Wodehouse moved from the Adlon to the Bristol, another hotel on Unter den Linden, probably in the hope of escaping some of the worst of the air raids.

On the night of 1 March, there was a particularly heavy raid on Berlin, when nearly 300 aircraft bombed the city, causing more damage than on any previous raid. 191 people were killed, and much damage occurred on

Unter den Linden, near to the Wodehouses. Anga von Bodenhausen had her own anxieties. She had broken off her engagement to Raven von Barnikow but remained close to him. In late 1942, he committed suicide. His despair had been prompted by the suicide of a friend who had been helping German Jews escape the Nazis, by the death of his father – and by the thought of 'the frightful future ahead'.

TO ANGA VON BODENHAUSEN

Bristol Hotel
Berlin

March 5. 1943

Dearest Anga.

Ethel and I were so excited by your news yesterday. I couldn't hear very well, as I was speaking from the telephone room on the fourth floor with all sorts of noises going on, but I gathered enough to understand that you think the prospects of our going to Sweden are good. It's wonderful of you taking all this trouble.

The raid was pretty bad. The only good thing was that this time we had had dinner, so the waiting was not so tiring. After the All Clear had been blown, we went out into the Unter den Linden, and it was an extraordinary sight. Large fires seemed to be blazing everywhere. At first I thought that one of them was some little distance beyond the Bristol, and then I discovered that the Bristol was on fire. So I rushed up to my room and threw half my things into a suitcase and took them over to the Adlon, then came back and fetched the rest. I managed to get a room at the Adlon for the night, and came back here the next night, as the fire was only on the top storey of a part quite a distance from my room.

A great deal of damage seems to have been done, though you can't notice anything hardly as you walk about the town. We have met so many people who have been burned out. The big Roman Catholic church has been destroyed. But really it does seem silly making these raids, as you can't possibly do any real harm to a city the size of Berlin.

[...]

Ethel took the raid splendidly, and did not seem a bit nervous at the time and has had no bad after effects. Wonder remained perfectly calm throughout. We had put her in her little bag, so that she should not be seen, and she stayed there quite happily all the time. But she must have been disturbed, as quite early next morning she clamoured to go out, and I took her into the Tiergarten and she put up a performance which even Bwana has never equalled in the middle of the path!

[...]

One good result of the raid is that two dinner engagements which we had have been cancelled! I do hate going out at night in times like this. I like to be within reach of the Adlon cellar. And it is so difficult getting about at night. Lunch and tea are the only possible meals in war time.

We were so delighted to get the photographs of our dear Raven. They are so exactly like him. But how sad his face looks, doesn't it. It's terrible to think of how he must have been suffering all that time when he was on the coast. I look at the photograph and think how different he was at Hollywood, where he was always happy. It's one of the ghastly tragedies of the war that a man like him should have been sacrificed. It does seem such a pity that he felt it his duty to join up again, because at his age he could so easily have stayed in America.

Lots of love from us both. We are so looking forward to seeing you again.

Yours ever
Plummie

TO ANGA VON BODENHAUSEN

Hotel Bristol
Berlin

April 15. 1943

Dearest Anga.

I have been trying to write to you for days, but what with being kennel maid to Wonder I never seem to have a moment. Ethel has now moved back to the Adlon, so that she can get on with her packing, and I am here with Wonder, and whenever I want to sit down at my desk she has to be taken for a walk. I've just got back from an hour's stroll in the Tiergarten, and it was so warm I could scarcely drag myself along. How wonderful it must be at Degenershausen now. It makes me so sad to think of my pine wood and to feel that wounded officers will be walking there instead of me this summer. It would be splendid if I could come down for a week or two when I get back from Schlesien in September.

Yesterday I had a telephone call from the Ministry of Propaganda, asking me if I would join a party of writers who were being taken down to Smolensk to look at the corpses of those unfortunate Polish soldiers who were murdered by the Bolsheviks in 1940.[1] I had to refuse, because of what would have been said in England, but I was very regretful that I couldn't go, as it would have been a great experience. When I heard the offer, I said to myself 'Ah, they're starting to ask me to do things', but I believe it was just a detached thing and does not mean anything. The man who rang me up came to see me later in the day and we had a chat, and he turned out to be the son of Baroness von Hutten, the novelist, and he had lived a great deal of his life in England and was very charming.

[...] We are all on edge these days. [...] What with these air raids and everything else, nobody is quite normal. Thank goodness they have kept away since March the 29th, but one expects them all the time, and the worst of it is that the last raid started at a quarter past one in the morning, so one never knows when one is safe for the night. I find that one develops a sort of philosophy and becomes a fatalist.

We had a guest to lunch at the Adlon yesterday, and the food was simply garbage. I can't think why they can't take more trouble. Here at the Bristol the food is wonderful, but the nuisance is that you can only occasionally get wine, whereas at the Adlon, whatever its other defects, there is always plenty.

[...]

I have been thinking so much lately of our dear Raven. How sad life has become since that day I met him in the Adlon and thought how marvellous he looked. But one has moods in which one rather envies him for being out of it all. Isn't it extraordinary, when every nation must be feeling the strain almost intolerable, that they can't get together and make peace.

Will you tell Reinhild how much I loved the photographs of my precious Bwana. I will write to her very soon. I suppose Ortrud will be with you in a day or two. How she will enjoy it after Berlin. I suppose you are feeling a bit apprehensive about the wounded officers. I hope they will send you some nice ones.

All our love

Yours ever

Plummie

1 In 1940, the Soviet secret police had massacred approximately 22,000 Poles. The victims included officers, policemen, intellectuals and civilian prisoners-of-war. Many of the victims were murdered in the Katyn Forest in Russia. By 1941, Nazi Germany was at war with Russia, and the discovery of the mass graves in the Katyn Forest in 1943 was a useful tool for the anti-Russian arm of Goebbels' propaganda machine.

To escape the bombing, Wodehouse and Ethel travelled to Lobris, in Lower Silesia, and were taken in as paying guests by some Anglophile acquaintances, the Count and Countess von Wolkenstein. Wodehouse recalls that 'my upper [sic] *Silesian host was a man who had lived a great part of his life in England, and you can imagine my joy when I found in his library five years of* Punch *and the* Saturday Review *and also great masses of the* Cornhill'.

TO ANGA VON BODENHAUSEN

Lobris

Kr Jauer

Schlesien

June 11. 1943

Dearest Anga.

I suppose you will get this at lunch time when you are out on the verandah looking at my lime tree! And Mister Bwana will be there wondering where I am. Do the parachutists have lunch with you, or have you given them a mess room downstairs?

Ethel turned up here two weeks ago, giving me a big thrill, as I had not expected her till two days later. She made the journey all by herself! I came with Frau von Wulfing a month earlier, bringing Wonder with me. I was expecting that objections would be made to her travelling in the compartment, but nobody said anything and she was as good as gold.

This is a very big place with enormous rooms. It is built round an inner courtyard and the rooms on the other side of the courtyard are not used. The country round is very different from Degenershausen. Practically no woods, just corn fields and beet fields. Everything is farming here. Ethel and I go for walks and read a lot, and I have started a new novel and am getting on very well with it. The time goes by quite quickly.

[...]

Ethel found her last week in Berlin very trying, as there was an alerte [sic] every night, generally at about one in the morning, and she had to get up and dress and go to the cellar, and then nothing happened! It is a great comfort to feel that one can go to bed for the rest of the summer knowing that one won't be routed out.

I saw in a paper the other day that the English in East Africa have started forced labour for the natives, so I suppose all your friends are hard at it. I wonder if this includes the Masai. It will do them good to do a bit of honest work instead of wasting their time jumping up and down.[1]

[...]

Yours ever

Plummie

1 While at Degenershausen, Wodehouse had enjoyed watching a film of Anga's former life in Africa, 'A day on my farm in Holland Estate in Tanganyika'. He was particularly delighted by the 'scene of the Masai jumping up and down during their welcome dance' when the Baroness returned from Germany (*The Unknown Years*, p. 95).

Lobris,

Schlesien

Sept 1. 1943

Dearest Anga.

We were so delighted to get your letter yesterday, but so sad to hear of the upheavals which have been taking place at the old home. At first we got the impression that about twenty officials had come to stay with you, but then we read the letter again and realized that it was only their baggage. Still, it must be bad enough having to give up the whole lower floor. I simply can't imagine where you are putting everybody on the first floor. I suppose you must be using the room at the end, but even so what a squash! Poor Anga, we are so sorry! I expect you to dig yourself in in your room and never come out.

Unless plans are altered at the last moment, we leave for Paris on Tuesday, Sept __th. We shall have to stay one night in Berlin, as we have to get our English passports renewed, so we leave here on Monday the __th,¹ arriving in Berlin about six-thirty in the evening and go to the Bristol. We are praying that there won't be a raid that night. In Paris we stay at the Bristol, but I am hoping that we shall be allowed to go to Hesdin, where Ethel lived before she came to Germany.

[...]

I feel terribly sad about leaving Germany and all our friends. We shall never forget how wonderful you were to us. It is very melancholy to feel that we may not see Degenershausen for years. [...] I wonder if you are right in being so optimistic about peace coming soon. How marvellous it would be if it did. I remember all your prophecies!

[...]

Ethel is very well, but gets rather frequent touches of toothache. I am hoping that we shall find a good dentist in Paris who will put her right. Wonder is in tremendous form, and has never been happier. I am very well, but I find the war beginning to weigh upon me more than it used to. The horrible senselessness of it all oppresses me. I can't see how any sort of a world can be left after it is over. How is England to pay the bill? Already, as far as I can work it out, they have a National Debt on which they will have to pay about seven hundred million pounds a year, and where is the money coming from?

Goodbye, Anga dear. You will know that we are thinking of you all the time, even though we are in France. Ethel sends loads of love.

Yours ever

Plummie

1 The dates on this letter appear to have been censored.

CHAPTER TWELVE

Paris

For the Wodehouses, as for many Parisians, life in an occupied city was, more often than not, reduced to a daily struggle for survival. Food was still in very short supply, and accommodation hard to find. The Germans kept tight control over both print and broadcast media, as determined collaborationists and equally determined resistance fighters struggled to gain ground.

Wodehouse spent much of his time looking for ways to redeem his reputation in England. Alongside his novels, he was working on a book of reminiscences about camp life, entitled *Wodehouse in Wonderland*. His urge to publish the book demonstrated both his inability to waste what he saw as good material and his determination to explain his actions. Indeed, the tone of these letters is, for the most part, defiant. In the opening stages, Wodehouse is oblivious to what he was to call the 'global howl' surrounding his actions.[1] As the gravity of the situation emerges, he remains indignant, but also shows himself to be anxious about his portrayal in America, England – and, on a smaller scale, at his beloved Dulwich. Indeed, there is a growing sense in these letters of vulnerability – a fear of being both out of touch and out of date. Wodehouse repeatedly wonders whether there will be a place for his sort of writing in a post-war world. 'It seems a waste of time', he frets, 'to write about butlers and country houses if both are obsolete. [...] I can't see what future there is for Blandings Castle.'[2]

Once Paris was liberated from the Germans, Wodehouse encountered more pressing fears. As Herbert Lottman writes, 'when the Free French led by Charles de Gaulle returned to the mainland [...] a symbol of the enemy remained on French soil in the hard core of collaborationists. To identify and punish them was the order of the day.'[3] In the months after August 1944, the French *épuration*, or purges, ensued – the punishment of people known, or suspected, to have assisted the enemy. Traumatic, brutal and often horrifying, the purges ranged from courtroom prosecutions to street executions, summarised by daily lists in *Le Figaro* under the headline 'ARRESTS AND PURGING'. Once again, Ethel and Wodehouse found themselves in danger, as the Comité Parisien de Libération considered whether Wodehouse could, given the broadcasts in Germany, be seen as dangerous to the cause of French liberty.

The Wodehouses remained isolated for the majority of these war years and communications continued to be unreliable. Information that reached them, both on a national and on a personal level, came slowly – and was subject to censorship. When he was interned in Tost, it was some months before Wodehouse learnt that his mother, Eleanor, had died in a nursing home. The news that their beloved daughter, Leonora, had died in May 1944 was even more delayed. Leonora was, in an unusual way, a casualty of war. Admitted to hospital for a routine operation, she suffered a post-operative haemorrhage, but a bombing raid in the night meant that her call for assistance was not heard, and she was left to die. 'Nothing seemed to matter after such dreadful news', wrote Ethel. 'Nothing can hurt us as much as that has done.'[4]

As their time in Paris drew to a close, and plans were made to move to America, it is not surprising to find a sense of darkness pervading the letters. 'What a hell the last few years has been', Ethel reflected, near the end of the war. 'Do you remember [...] those happy days at Le Touquet, when our darling Leonora was with us, how happy we all were, and didn't realize what we had in the near future to face.'[5] Wodehouse, characteristically, is more reticent. The years of war, the loss of Leonora and the furore surrounding the broadcasts cast a sort of 'black out' over their lives.[6]

After the liberation of Paris, Major Cussen, a British barrister and MI5 interrogator, was sent to interview Wodehouse, and to produce a report on the events surrounding his broadcasts. The report found that Wodehouse, while foolish, had done nothing that was either criminal or that could be seen as aiming to help the Nazi cause. A brief statement was made, to this effect, in the House of Commons in 1944. The statement was important, but without reading Cussen's report it meant little to the national press. Cussen followed his report with further investigations after the war, all of which were to corroborate his initial conclusions: that Wodehouse was exonerated of any crime. Two years later, Wodehouse was under scrutiny again, when the

Director of Public Prosecutions considered whether the mere act of speaking on German radio, regardless of intent, was a criminal offence. Documents show that by 1947 Wodehouse's MI5 security file was considered closed, and Wodehouse cleared.[7] However, it was not until 1965 that Wodehouse was told that if he were to come to England there would be no question of any proceedings being taken against him.[8]

Wodehouse meanwhile was conscious that he was at the mercy of the media, and that he had been repeatedly manipulated by journalists. He particularly disliked Harry Flannery, the journalist who had interviewed him in 1941, and who had discussed the broadcasts in his book, *Assignment to Berlin*. Flannery's account had, Wodehouse wrote, 'not a word of truth in it', but was read by MI5 investigators, and, at one point, used as evidence in Wodehouse's security file.[9] 'The hostility to Wodehouse', as McCrum argues, 'was derived partly from ideological conviction':

> As George Orwell pointed out, Wodehouse became associated in the public mind with the wealthy, idle, aristocratic nincompoops he often wrote about, and made an 'ideal whipping boy' for the left.[10]

Wodehouse's own handling of his public profile continued to do him no real favours in this respect. His first extended interview with *Illustrated*, in 1946, shows him smiling broadly, pipe in hand, alongside the caption 'I've Been a Silly Ass' [see plate 35]. But the interview itself casts a more serious note. Wodehouse speaks of his 'ghastly blunder'.[11] Elsewhere, he was to write of the 'mental pain' that he felt in the face of the events of the previous six years, and of the mistakes he had made.[12]

Tragically for Wodehouse, Cussen's report and his further investigations were, despite persistent requests for disclosure, not released until 1980 – five years after Wodehouse's death. Until then, the press and the general public were unaware that his name had been formally cleared. The broadcasts were to cast a shadow over his remaining years.

---

1 PGW to William Townend, 13 September 1945 (Dulwich).
2 PGW to Frances Donaldson, 2 June 1945 (Wodehouse Archive).

3 Herbert R. Lottman, *The People's Anger: Justice and Liberation in Post-War France* (London: Hutchinson, 1986), pp. 13–14.

4 Ethel Wodehouse to Denis Mackail, note appended to PGW to Denis Mackail, 4 January 1945 (Wodehouse Archive).

5 Ethel Wodehouse to Thelma Cazalet-Keir, 5 April 1945 (Wodehouse Archive).

6 See Ethel Wodehouse to Bea Davis, 20 August 1945 (Wodehouse Archive).

7 See G. E. Wakefield to G. C. Allchin, 25 July 1947, FO 369/3509 (PRO).

8 This was an informal communication. While an official memo notes that 'no Attorney General can say authoritatively whether any individual will or will not be prosecuted at any given moment of time in the future', another note states that should Wodehouse return 'he would be admitted without any difficulty'. See F Elwyn Jones to The Right Hon. Sir John Hobson, 23 March 1965 and F. Elwyn Jones, Memo, 23 March 1965, LO 2/1166 (PRO).

9 PGW to William Townend, 30 December 1944 (Dulwich); see memo of 31 August 1944, KV/2/3550 (PRO).

10 McCrum, p. 319.

11 *Illustrated*, 7 December 1944, p. 9.

12 Cussen Report, p. 12.

1943–1947:
'under surveillance'

*On their arrival in France, Werner Plack organised a room for the Wode-
houses at the Hôtel Le Bristol in Paris. This, again, was an ill-advised move.
As McCrum notes, 'Wodehouse may have been oblivious to the fact ... but
the Bristol was the Nazi hotel in occupied Paris'.*

TO ANGA VON BODENHAUSEN

Hôtel Le Bristol
Rue du Faubourg Saint-Honoré
Paris

Nov 21. 1943

Dearest Anga.

What a long time since I wrote to you. (Il est longtemps que je vous
n'ai pas écrit.). I wonder if you are still at Degenershausen. If I
remember, you generally go off for your cure about this time. Il doit
être assez froid chez vous actuellement.

We are having a very pleasant time in Paris. I must say I prefer the
city in its present calm state with no roar of traffic. We have started
using the Metro and it has enlarged my scope of movement very much.
Ethel is very busy going round the shops and seeing collections, and
I am trying hard to learn French. (When you write to me, write in
French, if it comes easier to you, as I now read French with complete
facility.) I went for a couple of weeks to the Berlitz school, but now I
have a private teacher who comes three times a week, and in between
her visits I read Colette's novels and am translating my last novel into
French. I can understand all that is said to me, but I don't seem to
make much progress in speaking.

Ethel got pinched the other night for being out without her papers.
She arrived back at the hotel with five military policemen, but the

leader of them turned out to be a reader of my books, so all ended well. It was a very unpleasant experience for her, though.

We have had one bit of luck. The manager of this hotel has been charming and has given us splendid rooms at a nominal rate. We shall pay him the difference after the war. This is very fortunate, as everything is terribly expensive here. We were taken to dinner at Maxim's the other night, and the sight of the bill nearly made me sick. You could have got a good dinner before the war for less than what they charged for one portion of fish. There seems to be a great deal of money in Paris. The theatres and cinemas are packed at every performance. But the average restaurant is pretty bad. We take all our meals at the hotel. [...] We have also run into one or two of our Le Touquet friends, which has been very pleasant. We have got to know a few very nice people, so we have a little circle.

I had a very nice letter from Schmidt the other day.[1] He said he had been talking to an English officer who had been taken prisoner and the English officer had said about me that although the British Government might be angry with me they couldn't do anything and couldn't even start a campaign in the British press, because if they did the British public would at once come forward to defend me. Schmidt said 'He added that the Britons are missing you very much, as they consider you an English institution.' That was nice, wasn't it? Schmidt said that he had read in an American paper that I was the favourite author of Princess Elizabeth. So things are looking up![2]

Love from us both. Ethel sends all sorts of messages. I wonder when we shall meet again. However long it may be, we shall always be thinking of you, Anga darling.

Yours ever

Plummie

1 Paul Schmidt, Hitler's interpreter.
2 In 1941, the Royal Librarian reported that the Queen Mother had ordered eighteen new books for Princess Elizabeth, all of which were by P. G. Wodehouse (William Shawcross, *Queen Elizabeth, the Queen Mother* (London: Macmillan, 2009), p. 335).

Hôtel Le Bristol
Rue du Faubourg Saint-Honoré
Paris

May 3. 1944

Dearest Anga.

[...]

We continue to lead a quiet life, though a good deal disturbed just at present by continual alertes and a general atmosphere of strained nerves owing to everyone wondering when the invasion is going to come and what will happen when it does! People tell us we ought to lay in a stock of food enough for three weeks in case of trouble, but it is difficult to do that, as tinned stuff is almost impossible to get. So we are simply hoping that things will be all right.

[...] We generally get an alerte round about midnight, which means not getting to bed till about half past one, and then it often happens that planes which have been to Germany come back past Paris and the flac [sic] fires at them and wakes us up at four in the morning. The only consolation we have is that it is unlikely that they would deliberately bomb the centre of Paris, though Montmartre got it rather badly the other night and there is always the chance of a stray plane coming down on one's head!

What a terrible time Berlin has had since we left it. A man here went to stay at the Bristol the night it was destroyed, but had the good luck to have a business appointment at Wansee [sic] that night, so escaped. But I am afraid that all the maids and waiters we used to like so much were killed. Mr Vetter, the manager of the dining room, and the manager of the hotel, the man who had the dog, are both safe.

[...]

Our main worry just now, apart from the danger of being bombed, is that our money is running rather short. We have plenty in Berlin, and Schmidt was arranging to have it sent to us, but I suppose his accident will prevent this. Still, we have got our furniture up from Le Touquet and it is now in storage here, so that we shall be able to raise a bit by selling it. Unfortunately, in the four years since we left Le

Touquet, a good many things have disappeared.

It is awful being so out of touch with you. I always think of Degeners-hausen as the peaceful place I knew and loved so much, but for all I know you may be overrun now with refugees. I hope not. I like to think of you all alone there with Reinhild and possibly Heinrich, wandering round the drive after dinner and listening to the radio – the German radio, of course, – in the library.[1]

All our love, Anga dearest. Remember me to everyone at Degeners-hausen, and do write, if you can, and tell me all that is happening to you.

Yours ever

Plummie

1 A concealed and light-hearted reference to the BBC World Service, which they listened to regularly, in breach of strict German rules and regulations.

6 June 1944 – 'D-Day' – marked the beginning of the bloodiest stage of the conflict for occupied France. Coded messages were sent from the BBC alerting the French resistance to set their plans into action. By 31 July, the Allies had broken out of Normandy. On 17 August, French Communist resistance fighters launched an uprising in and around Paris. The days before liberation saw heavy conflict in the Latin Quarter and around the Gare de la Villette. Over the next week, some 1,500 resistance fighters were killed. The French Second Armoured Division brought about the German surrender of the city on 25 August. Wodehouse later remembered the scenes of celebration, and of violence.

Hotel Lincoln
Rue Bayard
Paris

December 30. 1944

[...]

The afternoon of the big parade down the Champs Elysées, Ethel and I and Wonder went to the part near the Marigny Theatre and Ethel managed to wriggle into the front rank of the crowd, leaving me with Wonder. I was just starting to give Wonder a run on the grass near one of the restaurants which are in the gardens when I saw a policeman coming, so edged away. At that moment a brisk burst of firing came from the restaurant, which would have outed me if I had been on the grass. The guns began to go off all over the place, and I was in a panic because I thought Ethel was still in the crowd. I rushed about looking for her, and was swept into the Marigny with the crowd. A dead girl was brought in on a stretcher and laid down beside me. It was all rather ghastly. Eventually the firing stopped, and I was able to get back to the Hotel Bristol, where we were staying then, and found Ethel there. She had gone back before the firing began, but had run into another battle outside and inside the hotel. It was all very exciting, but no good to me from a writing point of view. [...]

With Paris under Allied control, the British Government sent over an MI5 officer and barrister, Major Cussen, to interview Wodehouse. Wodehouse recalls feeling most alarmed by this 'flinty-eyed Home Office official' who listened to his evidence – and by the fact of 'not knowing if he believed a word of it and wondering, even if he did, whether I hadn't been technically guilty of crimes punishable by death'. He wrote the following letter in advance of the interview.

Hôtel Le Bristol
Rue du Faubourg Saint-Honoré
Paris

Sept 4. 1944

Sir,

In view of the fact that on numerous occasions, through official and other channels, charges of great seriousness have been brought against me, I am hastening to report to you my presence here.

This is not the occasion for me to make a detailed statement, but may I be allowed to say that the reports in the Press that I obtained my release from internment by agreeing to broadcast on the German radio are entirely without foundation. The five talks which I delivered were arranged for after my release, and were made at my own suggestion.

That it was criminally foolish of me to speak on the German radio, I admit. But my only motive in doing so was to give my American readers a humorous description of my adventures, as some response to the great number of letters which I had received from them while I was in camp. The five talks covered the five phases of my imprisonment, were purely comic in tone and were designed to show to American listeners a group of English keeping up their spirits and courage under difficult conditions.

You will understand that my present position is a highly embarrassing one, and I am most anxious to do everything possible to clear it up. I should be most grateful if you would let me know when I may have the opportunity of doing so.

Meanwhile, unless you desire my presence in England, I will remain at the above address and keep in touch with the British authorities here.

I am, Sir,
Yours obediently,
P. G. Wodehouse

In anticipation of Cussen's visit, the British Government decided that Wodehouse should be kept under surveillance, and so a young MI6 officer, Malcolm Muggeridge, who was already in Paris, was sent to meet him and to report back. Muggeridge was a British liaison officer with the Services Spéciaux, and took on the task of a preliminary 'investigation' of the Wodehouse case. In due course, Muggeridge and the Wodehouses became friends and, once Major Cussen had arrived, Muggeridge continued to keep in touch with them.

Muggeridge discovered that the Wodehouses were out of touch with events in England. Most poignantly, they were unaware that their daughter, Leonora, had died. Given that Ethel was 'in an extremely hysterical state' as a result of Cussen's interrogation, the British Government was urged by Thelma Cazalet-Keir (Leonora's sister-in-law) to allow Muggeridge to deliver the news of the family's loss personally. The following message from Thelma was delivered:

'Only just found your address. Greatly fear Red Cross message sent by Peter in May can never have reached you. Our most beloved Leonora died suddenly of heart failure on May 16th. Gloriously well and happy until peaceful end. Peter and children wonderfully brave. Peter now in France with his regiment. Very glad to hear you are safe. All our dear love and may we meet soon. Communicate with me at Fairlawne about your plans.'

Ethel and Wodehouse were devastated.

Writing to Muggeridge later, Wodehouse noted that 'Ethel has had a terrible time, but is more herself now'. The following message was forwarded via the Foreign Office for Thelma Cazalet-Keir.

TO THELMA CAZALET-KEIR

September 27. 1944

Thank you dear Thelma for your message. Your sad news came as a terrible shock and has stunned us. Poor Ethel is prostrated. We still cannot realise we shall not see our darling Leonora and Victor again in this life.[1] Our love to Molly and yourself and deepest sympathy. We remain this address [sic] indefinitely. Longing to see Sheran and Edward. Terribly anxious about Peter.[2] Can you get news of him.

Plum

1 Thelma's brother, Victor Cazalet M.C., MP, had been killed on active service during the war.

2 Peter Cazalet, Leonora's widower, was a Major in the Guards Armoured Division and had come over to France as part of the D-Day landings force.

TO WILLIAM TOWNEND

Oct 24. 1944

Dear Bill.

At last I am able to write and thank you for all the letters you wrote me, which were a great comfort. We were so glad to hear from Rene. It's nice to think of you settled again in a home, and thank goodness you are both of you all right after these last five years. When you write, be sure to tell me what books you have written since the war started and what sort of sales you are having now. I have had several very nice postcards from friends in England. Everything is going quite well with us, but we are quite crushed by the dreadful news about Leonora. I really feel that nothing matters much now.

    Love to Rene

    Yours ever

    Plum

Cussen's verdict on Wodehouse's 'unwise' behaviour was that 'a jury would find difficulty in convicting him of an intention to assist the enemy'. Nevertheless, the French authorities were still suspicious of the Wodehouses' motives, and arrested them. They had been staying at the Lincoln Hotel, to avoid reporters in the wake of Cussen's interview, when the arrest took place. Ethel recalls that Plum was staying on the floor above her, and at 12.30 a.m. she 'suddenly woke up and saw a sinister man leaning over my bed with his hat on and his coat collar turned up exactly like a movie. I produced my British passport. Useless. I was told if I didn't dress at once I would be taken in my night gown!!'

November 22. 1944

Dear Malcolm.

Ethel and I were arrested last night at one in the morning by the French police. We passed the night on hard chairs and we now learn (6 p.m.) that we have another night of it before us, before we are taken to Drancy, the charge being 'making German propaganda', – IE those five talks of mine, nothing else.[1]

We have not tasted food all day. I believe the bearer of this is going to get us some, if he can, but what can he get and where? Can you supply anything. We are absolutely fainting with hunger, & Ethel is on the verge of collapse. Do try to send us something.

I understand the Embassy has heard of our arrest and is enquiring into it, but unfortunately the Prefet de Police had left before the Embassy inspecteur arrived.

There seems to be absolutely nothing against us except the five talks, so I feel sure the Embassy won't let us be taken to Drancy because of those.

Is there any chance of your coming to see us tonight?

Yours ever

P.G.

This is absolute hell, old man. We have spent the day sitting on hard chairs in a draughty passage – nothing to eat, not even a glass of water to drink. I can't wash and my face is a foul mass of beard!

---

1 Drancy was a transit camp, just outside Paris, which had been used to hold thousands of Parisian Jews. It was now used to hold suspected collaborators. Conditions were extremely harsh.

Wodehouse was still not popular in England, but given the ferocity of the French purges, there was concern over his arrest. Churchill wrote that 'it seems to me that the French are overdoing things about P. G. Wodehouse. Is he a British subject? If not, we have no interest. But if he is, I think we ought to know what he is accused of doing.' By December, the Wodehouse question remained, for Churchill, 'rather a poser'. 'Would it be too much to ask the French to let him live under mild surveillance out of the way as long as he can find the money to do so. [...] We would prefer not ever to hear about him again and this would be best in the general interest. His name stinks here, but he would not be sent to prison. However, if there is no other resort, he should be sent over here and if there is no charge against him, he can live secluded in some place or go to hell as soon as there is a vacant passage.'

The French authorities released Ethel, but kept Wodehouse in custody while they decided how they would proceed. After a few days, the French decided that while it was not deemed safe to release Wodehouse, an improvement in living conditions for him could be achieved by stating that he was suffering from ill-health, and moving him to a hospital where he would be kept under guard. But all hospitals in Paris were already full, so Wodehouse found himself billeted to a maternity home. Conditions there were not at all bad. Ethel noted that 'Plummie was on velvet in the hospital, about the only place heated in Paris. I was frozen at the Lincoln, no heat whatever or hot water, and Plummie had both.'

TO ETHEL WODEHOUSE

Nov 25. 1944

My own darling.

How lovely to hear from you & thanks awfully for the parcel. There is so much to tell you, but I can't make this very long, as your nice friend who brought it has to leave.

The first person I met here was Mrs Sholto Douglas! She is charming – leaving tonight, I believe, & I am to have her room, which is ever so much nicer than mine.

Everything is <u>absolutely all</u> right with me, except that I miss my darling so terribly. Once I can start to write I shall be fine. Meals quite good, but can you send me the big thermos and a pound of tea. Then I shall be ok. Also some red wine or brandy, but this is not too important. What a time we're having! Thank God you are all right – they can't possibly touch you. I don't know how long I shall be here. The cop told me this morning that I was being released soon, but it may be just a ruse. I think it would be well to get in touch with the de Rocquignys and see if they can have us, so that if I do get out on that 50 miles from Paris scheme we can start straight off there without any delay.

Darling, you're all I'm worrying about. Keep your courage up and don't be too sad. Always remember that I'm quite comfortable here. Everyone, including the cops, are friendliness itself. One of the doctors gave me tobacco today and sent that letter to you. I am great friends with M. de Castellane. Do you remember once an old gentleman stopping us in the gardens and admiring Wonder? That was M. de C.

I wouldn't worry too much about the publicity. It's more likely to get me sympathy in England than otherwise.

Anyway all this prejudice will pass away in time. But what a time you must have had with those two reporters, curse them. I think they will leave you alone in a day or two.

This is such a hurried letter, sweetheart, and I feel I'm leaving out all I really want to say. I think of you all the time and love you more than ever. Every minute! I can't believe that two people who love each other as we do can be separated long.

My, damn it, I've got to hurry and finish. God bless you, darling.

Your

Plummie

My day is – get breakfast in bed at about 8 then all sixty nurses, cops, etc. come in and chat – then we go for an hours walk in the garden, then lunch – then stroll in corridor, read and so on – dinner at 6 – bed at 9 – suite all right and will be okay when I start work. Send all the papers in the drawer in writing table where script of *Uncle Dynamite* is, as some of them are scenario. Keep me well supplied with baccy, and as soon as reporters have died away and won't follow you come and see me. Better bring Francie to help you find the way.

Keep your spirits up, angel. I am fine.

TEA & THERMOS!!!

Hotel Lincoln
Rue Bayard,
Paris

Dec 30. 1944

[...]

I wish there was some means of getting to know just how I stand now in England. I had resigned myself to being an outcast with no friends except you and Rene, but since the liberation we have had the nicest possible cards from all our friends in England, and now you say that Christison, Rees, Paddy Millar etc have been asking after me.[1] It gives me the pleasant feeling that I have lost none of my friends, and I am hoping that eventually things will straighten themselves out. The unfortunate thing was not being able to contradict lies told about me at the time.

[...]

My arrest by the French came as a complete surprise! I had gone to bed at about twelve on the night of November the twenty-first, and at one o'clock woke to find two inspectors in my room. They took Ethel and me to the Palais de Justice, and we spent sixteen hours without food in a draughty corridor. Next day they released Ethel, and I spent four days in the inspectors' office. I was then brought to this hospital, where I have been ever since.

The original idea was to put me in the camp at Drancy, but thank goodness that was changed. I believe Drancy is very tough, not at all like my beloved Tost, where life was one long round of cricket, lectures, entertainments and Red Cross parcels. Here in the hospital I am sitting pretty, though naturally it is pretty foul to be cooped up. I have a room to myself, quite good food, plenty of tobacco and drinks, and Ethel is allowed to come and see me. I also had a marvellous five days visit from Peter. He used to bring champagne every day and we had great times.

I generally wake up at four a.m., lie in bed till six, then get up and boil water on a boiler lent me by one of the doctors and have breakfast. The concierge arrives with the *Paris Daily Mail* at nine, and after my room has been cleaned, that is by half past nine, I start writing. Lunch at half past twelve. At four I get my walk in the garden with an inspector, the only time I am allowed out of doors. I walk up and down on the landing from six-thirty to eight, and then go to bed. Light out at nine-thirty. The nurses and inspectors are very friendly, and I am improving my French. When I get visitors, they usually come at three. It isn't a bad sort of life at all, if you have a novel to write. The only point in the day when the time drags a bit is between half-past one and four. The mornings are taken up with work, and after five, when I come in for my walk, I always feel all right.

[...]

Wonder is in terrific form. Ethel, poor darling, is having a rotten time just now, as Paris is entirely without heating and her hotel is icy. It was bad enough when I was there, but since then the weather has turned really cold and she suffers a lot. She tells me this place is a Paradise in comparison, and I suppose it is, as we have hot water and the rooms are warmed.

Well, I must be stopping now. I hope this reaches you safely.

Love to Rene.

Yours ever

Plum

1 Old Alleynians.

TO DENIS MACKAIL

Hotel Lincoln
Rue Bayard
Paris

Jan 4. 1945

Dear Denis.

The above address is where letters should be sent, as they will always be forwarded. At the moment, however, I am in the hospital where I was taken six weeks ago, to live under the surveillance of an inspecteur.

[...]

A few days ago I got your card, which was very welcome. Peter came to see me about a month ago, and was speaking about your words in the *Times* about our darling Leonora, telling me how much they had touched him. What a horrible, bleak feeling it gives one, to think that we shall never see her again. It just sets the seal on all the ghastliness of life these days.

[...] I can imagine how you must be hating this present state of things, and I am afraid that 'Swan Court' must mean that Church Street is no more. Low Wood, I believe, is a ruin, like everything else in Le Touquet. I don't suppose we shall ever go back there again. As far as I can gather, the whole place is a mass of bomb craters and the forest is destroyed, so it is hardly worth while rebuilding the house after the war. [...] Do write to me if it is possible to send letters from England. Love to Diana.

Yours ever

Plum

Back in Paris, Ethel noted that 'the food situation is simply terrible'. The cook 'has been pinching our bread tickets [...]. I go to bed with about four sweaters on, and skiing drawers, scarves etc, and I am frozen and so is Plummie.' 'We don't', Ethel confided, 'want to go into any of the black market shops as we don't want to be arrested again. Can you imagine what the headlines would be. "WODEHOUSES SWILLING CHAMPAGNE IN BLACK MARKET RESTAURANTS WHILE PARIS STARVES!"'

TO WILLIAM TOWNEND

Hotel Lincoln
Rue Bayard
Paris

Feb 15. 1945

Dear Bill.

[...]

I was in the clinic when I wrote to you last. (I hope you got the letter all right). I spent eight weeks there, and then Malcolm Muggeridge drove Ethel and Wonder and me down to Barbizon, about thirty miles from Paris, in the most awful blizzard. We lunched at a marvellous restaurant in Fontainebleau forest in front of a great log fire and thought things were going to be wonderful. But when we got to the hotel at Barbizon we found it was a strictly summer hotel, no carpets, no heating and no running water owing to the frost freezing the pipes. However, we settled down and had a very good time for three weeks, and then the hotel was requisitioned, so now we are back in Paris. I think eventually we shall go to Ethel's friends the De Rocquignys at their house near Hesdin, but in the meantime Paris is very pleasant, though living conditions are getting tougher every day and I don't like the look of the Seine, which may burst its banks at any moment. Still, Paris is always Paris, and we are quite happy.

I was thrilled by what you told me about Dulwich winning all its school matches last cricket season, including Harrow and Malvern. It's odd, but I don't find that world cataclysms and my own personal troubles make any difference to my feelings about Dulwich. To win the Bedford match seems just as important to me as it ever did. I wonder how I am regarded at Dulwich. Have you any means of finding out? Perhaps Slacker could give you some idea. Mine is a curious position, as I meet nobody but friends and keep getting encouraging letters, so that I sometimes get the illusion that everything is all right. I have to remind myself that there must still be an enormous body of public opinion which is against me. (I was just writing this, when an air raid warning sounded. I thought all that sort of thing was over in Paris. I can't imagine the Germans having planes to spare to send here. Still, there it is. I will let you know how the matter develops.) Where was I? Oh, yes. Enormous body of public opinion. Or is there? It's so difficult to find out. I meet English and American soldiers, and when they discover who I am they are perfectly friendly. And yet unpleasant things still appear from time to time in the papers. By the way, what was it that the *Times* said about me – you referred to it in your last card – which you said was nice? It's fine if the papers are beginning to change their attitude. But I'm afraid there is a long way to go before things can come right, but I haven't a twinge of self-pity. I made an ass of myself, and must pay the penalty. One thing these troubles have driven home to me and that is what wonderful friends I have. When everything goes right, one rather tends to take one's friends for granted, but being in a position like mine makes one realize how splendid they are. (Hon'ble air raid still apparently in progress, as there has been no All Clear, but nothing seems to be happening. We got a scare one night at Barbizon when terrific explosions suddenly shook the hotel. I believe it was some Allied plane which had to jettison its bombs in the neighbourhood.)

Do tell me, when you write, about your work since the war started. You mention books you are writing but don't tell me how you are selling these days. I am longing to know the figures. You must have built up a large public by now. Is the *Strand* still going? Have you read (All Clear just gone) Hesketh Pearson's life of Conan Doyle? Very interesting. [...]

I have been plugging away at my latest novel. I managed to get a hundred pages done while in the clinic, in spite of constant interruptions. I would start writing at nine in the morning and would get a paragraph done when the nurse would come in and sluice water all over the floor. Then the concierge arrived with the morning paper, then the nurse with bread for lunch, then another nurse with wine, then a doctor and finally a couple of inspecteurs. All the inspecteurs were very interested in my writing. It was the same thing in camp, where I used to sit on my typewriter case with the machine balanced on a suitcase and work away with two German soldiers standing behind me with guns, breathing down the back of my neck. They seemed fascinated by this glimpse into the life literary.

[...]

So long. Yours ever

Plum

TO WILLIAM TOWNEND

Feb 24. 1945

[...]

What you say about the book you want me to write is very valuable. The posish at present is this. In 1941, when I was in the Harz Mountains, I wrote a comic book about my adventures at Le Touquet and my camp experiences, but I'm not sure whether it is the sort of thing that is needed. At that time I saw the situation thus: – There had been a terrific outcry in England about the talks, but it had all happened before I made the talks. They were then relayed to England, and I supposed that everybody there had now heard them and realized that they were harmless, so I took rather an airy tone in my book, – all having a good laugh together over the whole amusing misunderstanding sort of thing. And now it seems that practically nobody heard the talks, so that the bulk of the populace are under the impression that I did propaganda. In other words, instead of writing for a friendly public, I shall have to assume that ninety per cent of my readers will be hostile. In which case, a humorous treatment might be resented. It is all very difficult. But Malcolm Muggeridge insists that I shall be making a mistake if I try to write differently from my usual style, and I feel he is right.

One thing against a serious treatment is the fact that everybody in England has been through such hell these last years that it seems to me that it would be simply ludicrous if I were to try to make heavy weather over the really quite trivial things that happened to me. It isn't pleasant to travel for three days and nights in a third class compartment with wooden seats and four aside and almost nothing to eat and drink, but I don't see how I can attempt to make a tragedy of it when writing for an audience which has been under fire from V-bombs for months. There was a picture in *Punch* during the last war, showing a woman talking to a soldier just back from Paschendael [*sic*] and telling him about an air raid on London. She says 'A bomb fell quite close to us. It was terrible. <u>You simply can't imagine what it was like</u>.' That's the sort of attitude I must avoid at all costs.

[...]

A thing I particularly want to clear up is this Adlon business. We had to stay at the Adlon, we had no option. We tried several times to go elsewhere, but were foiled, – or, when I say foiled, I mean that always at the last moment there was some hitch and we were told that it couldn't be managed owing to one thing or another. But I doubt if I shall ever be able to drive it into the nut of the public that I wasn't living a riotous life there, having nightly parties with all the leading Nazis.

That story you told me in your letter about Mowat saying that while I was in camp the German officers talked to me in German is amusing.

I wonder why people invent these things. All the German I know is 'Es ist schonus [sic] wetter'. As a matter of fact, they didn't even talk to me in English. It's extraordinary how things get twisted. When I was making my statement in Paris after the liberation to the Foreign Office representative, he started by questioning me keenly as to whether I had written for a German paper (in English) called *The Camp*, which was circulated among British prisoners. It seemed that somebody had denounced me as having done so, and all that had happened really was that in one number there was a parody of my Jeeves stuff under the title of 'Bertie at the War' or something like that, signed 'P. G. Roadhouse' or some such name. A damned bad parody, too. I was rather surprised that nobody brought up that article I wrote for the *Saturday Evening Post* when I was in camp, which ended with an offer to make a separate peace with Germany, they to give me a loaf of bread and direct the gentleman with the musket at the front door to look the other way for a few moments, while I agreed to hand over India, an autographed set of my books and a recipe for cooking potatoes on the radiator, known at present only to Internee Arthur Grant (the Le Touquet golf pro) and myself.

Of course, the thing that really gets my goat is that statement of Flannery's that Werner Plack came to Tost and arranged with me about my release. I never saw the chap, and I don't suppose he ever came within miles of the camp. It's just that these blighters have to try to sell their books by inventing sensational things. And all that rot about Ethel and the evening dresses. She happened to mention to Flannery that she had lost a trunk and that it contained her evening dresses, and he went on from there. You would think that anyone would know that one doesn't dress for dinner in war time. The nearest I ever came to it was putting on a dressing gown when I lined up with my bowl.

Talking of Mowat, I can't place him, but I had the most tremendous liking and admiration for the War Graves Commission men. They really are the salt of the earth. With one of them, Bert Haskins, I formed a friendship which will last all our lives. He was pure gold, and we kept up a correspondence all the time after I left Tost until, a few weeks before the liberation, his letters suddenly ceased and I assumed that he had been repatriated. I hope so. Bert was the chap who, when we were spending that eight hours in the cattle trucks before leaving Loos, suddenly appeared at my side with half a loaf of bread, butter, radishes, wine and potted meat. He didn't know me, but out of sheer goodness of heart he came and gave me the stuff. He was a splendid chap, and all the other War Graves men I met were fine, too. I was always so sorry that Bert was not in my dormitory, as when in camp you don't see much of people who aren't in your dormitory. It's like being in a house at school. Did I tell you that Lord Uffenham in *Money in the Bank* was drawn from a man in my dormitory?[1] It isn't often one has the luck to be in daily contact with the model for one's principal character.

[...]

This new push in the West makes me uneasy. I hope to God Peter and Anthony [Mildmay] will be all right. Did I tell you that Anthony had a very narrow escape some time ago? He happened for some reason to be sitting on the floor of his tank and a shell came along and smashed the upper half, so that if he had been in the seat he would have been killed. Peter's wound was a slight one in the forearm, which he got while standing by someone else's tank. He was terrifically fit when he came to the clinic, and just the same as ever. He wants us to come and live at Fairlawne for the rest of our lives.

[...]

Well, so long. I've probably left out a dozen things I wanted to say, but I will put them in my next.

Yours ever

Plum

1 Max Enke.

In December 1944, Sir Donald Somervell, the Attorney-General, had stated in the House of Commons that Wodehouse was cleared of all charges of collaboration. 'There is not enough evidence of intent to assist the enemy which would justify proceedings', he commented. It follows from this that the contents of the Cussen Report, although not disclosed for another thirty-six years, had been accepted, bringing much relief to the Wodehouses. In February 1945, the question of Wodehouse's broadcasts was once again raised in the House of Commons. There were no grounds for the renewal of this question, but without the publication of the Cussen Report, Thelma Cazalet-Keir reported to Wodehouse that 'the publicity the next day was bad'.

Hotel Lincoln.
Rue Bayard, Paris.

March 1. 1945

Dearest Thelma.

[...]

Do write us all the news and give the letter to Malcolm to bring back with him. We are longing to hear how you all are, and particularly if there is any improvement in poor little Edward's condition.[1] I can't bear to think of him being on his back like that week after week. It must be terrible at his age. [...]

Paris is having a bad time just now, as food is very scarce. We manage to get along, though life is frightfully expensive. All the black market places have been closed, and all the others except the Ritz and Claridge's taken over by the troops, so what people do I can't imagine. Gertie Dudley sent us some packets of powdered soup some time ago, and we have been dining off that for a week.[2]

We were so sorry to see in the papers about Lloyd George's illness. It must be a very anxious time for Megan and for you, too.[3] I do hope he will soon be better.

[...]

Would it be possible for you to get hold of a copy of *Hansard* containing that debate in the House when the Attorney-General made that statement about me? If so, I wish you would give it to Malcolm to bring back with him. [...]

Love to Mollie and the children, and all our good wishes to you. We think of you all the time.

Yours ever

Plum

We are dining tonight with the only man in Paris who is able to get a bit of fish! How he does it, I don't know. Turbot, egad! I can scarcely wait.

In the spring of 1945, Muggeridge brought George Orwell to meet Wodehouse.

TO MALCOLM MUGGERIDGE

Hotel Lincoln
Rue Bayard
Paris

April 16. 1945

Dear Malcolm.

The anguish caused by your departure in your circle of admirers here shows no signs of abating. You can do without Paris, but can Paris do without you? The answer is no. Our lives creep along on a crippled wing, as Tennyson says, and we miss you all the time. It is a frightful thing to have to realize that you aren't round the corner, waiting to cheer us all up.

So far, no major problems have arisen calling for the Muggeridge touch, and it is Muggeridge the Man whom we miss, rather than Muggeridge the Diplomat. We sip our cognac (last bottle) and wish that you were there to sip too. Our only consolation is reading *The Thirties*, which came as a delightful surprise.[1] I never dreamed that you would be able to lay your hands on a copy. A masterly work, which I devoured at a sitting and am now re-reading at intervals. Ethel loved it too. It is a book one can always dip into after the first reading.

[...]

I had a long letter from Watt the other day. [...] He has heard from the Jenkins people, who come out strongly in favour of publication of my 'camp' book as a starter. But since writing the above Mrs Cazalet-Keir rang me up and we had a long talk about you and your affairs. Thelma seems to think that 'the publication of a new book, either a defence or a novel, would be inadvisable for some time'. So I suppose the best plan is to wait a bit. I must say, though, that it seems to me that no harm could be done by publishing a defence.

[...]

We do miss you terribly, Malcolm. We have tried at times to express all we feel about your wonderfulness to us, but we feel we made a poor job of it. It is ghastly, having to try to get on without you. It wasn't only the definite things you did, it was the way you always bucked us up. In our moments of despondency we used to feel 'Oh, it will be all right when Malcolm comes round.' And now you are in London, where they can't possibly need you as you are needed here. We try to picture you in London, but it seems all wrong. Surely a word from you to the men up top would be enough to bring you back here.

Ethel sends her love. We talk of you all the time. Do drop us a line to let us know how you are doing.

Yours ever

Plummie

1 Muggeridge's *The Thirties: 1930 to 1940 in Great Britain*, published in 1940, surveyed the events of the last decade, especially those leading up to the war.

During this period, the Wodehouses had trouble finding accommodation. The authorities still would not allow Wodehouse to leave France, but after the liberation of Paris the Americans requisitioned large numbers of hotel rooms, so it was difficult to know where they could live. Ethel was allowed to keep her room at the Bristol hotel, but Wodehouse was asked to leave, and went to stay in a friend's apartment at Neuilly. Even if a departure to England had been allowed, Ethel would have found it hard to countenance the idea: 'I have my beloved Leonora's photograph by my side as I write, and I can hardly bear the thought of ever returning [...] and she won't be there to meet me. It's knocked me all to bits, and I feel I shall

never be able to cope with life again. I feel in a dream most of the time,
and it seems so strange to see people laughing in the streets and doing this
and that.'

TO WILLIAM TOWNEND

78 Avenue Paul Doumer
Paris

April 22. 1945

Dear Bill.

[...]

I had a long letter from Watt the other day, the contents of which
were quite encouraging. [...] The bad period was at the end of 1942,
when the sales dropped to about 6 copies of each book. In the first
half of 1943 they rose to about 100 per book, and in the first half of
1944 they were up to as much as 900. I haven't had the returns for
the last half of 1944. But in all the cheap editions seem to have sold
about half a million in three years, which looks as if people had had
a change of heart. Of course, they may be buying my books with one
hand and hating my insides with the other, but I hope not.

Somebody, presumably Slacker, sent me the Dulwich Year book for
1943 and 1944, which I was delighted to have, though it was saddening
to see the Roll of Honour. Most of the names I did not know, but quite
a few were of chaps I knew slightly as members of the cricket and
football teams. I see Doulton's son and D. G. Donald's have both been
killed, and also R. H. Spenser, who played half, and a fellow named
Darby who was in the cricket team of 1935 and wrote to thank me for
a notice I gave him in my report of the Tonbridge match.

[...]

You never told me if H. T. Bartlett was all right. He got through
Arnhem with Billy Griffith, and then I heard a rumour that he had
been blown up by a mine. I do hope it wasn't true. And I hope to
goodness that Billy is all right. I had a message through an R.A.F.
man in September from A. C. Shirreff, so he was all right then, but
you never know from one day to another, worse luck. At last reports

Peter and Anthony Mildmay were all right, but they must be down near Bremen, and somebody was telling me that it was pretty nasty there. There is nothing one can do but hope and wait for the end, which surely can't be far away now. I was told today that the Russians were four miles from the centre of Berlin, but of course it may be just a story. Still, they can't be very far away, I imagine. Gosh, won't it be wonderful when it's all over. I am hoping that the Russians will establish General Paulus in authority and that he will be able to surrender for Germany. It only needs someone who is in a position to speak for Germany against the Nazis.

I hope my letters are reaching you all right. Love to Rene. I have reluctantly come to the conclusion that I really am 63 and a half. I can't go on kidding myself that though that may be my official age I am really about 40. I tire rather easily now and feel pretty weak sometimes, though that may be just a hangover from a bad cold which I have had plus this extraordinary hot spell.

Yours ever
Plum

P.S. I have been reading Mark Twain's letters. Very interesting.

TO MALCOLM MUGGERIDGE

78 Ave Paul Doumer
Paris

May 19. 1945

[...]

We had a marvellous letter from Peter the other day. Thank God he has come through all right. He says the toughest time of all was just before the finish. They took a town and cleared out all the Germans, as they thought, and fixed themselves up in a headquarters and were just settling down to lunch when a Guardsman poked his head in at the door and said 'You'll excuse me troubling you, gentlemen,' or words to that effect, 'but the house is surrounded and the Germans are coming through the garden.' Then followed a terrific battle with shooting through the windows, and then suddenly Peter's great friend, Anthony Mildmay, arrived with a lot of tanks and saved them all, just like the United States Marines in a film. Anthony got his head phones shot off and one of his ears chipped by a bullet, but he has come through, too, so all is well.

[...]

Frances Donaldson, later Wodehouse's biographer, had been Leonora's best friend.

TO FRANCES DONALDSON

78 Avenue Paul Doumer
Paris
France

June 2. 1945

Dear Frankie.

[...]

I wonder what England is like after six years of war. All our correspondents there speak of London as being very dirty and shabby, which it might well be after what it has gone through.

[...]

I have had a long spell of inaction since finishing a novel at the end of March. I suppose I shall get another plot some day, but nothing seems to stir as yet. [...] My trouble is that I already have five novels waiting to be published in England, so that anything I write now will presumably appear round about 1950, and I find it very hard to imagine what the world will be like then. I mean, it seems a waste of time to write about butlers and country houses if both are obsolete, as I suppose they will be. I can't see what future there is for Blandings Castle, and I doubt if Bertie Wooster will be able to afford a personal attendant with the income tax at ten shillings in the pound. It looks to me as if the only one of my characters who will be able to carry on is Ukridge. His need for making a quick touch will be all the greater in an impoverished world, though I don't see who is going to be in a position to lend him the ten bob he is always wanting.

Love to you and the family from us both. Do drop me a line if you have time and let me know how things are going.

Yours ever

Plum

TO WILLIAM TOWNEND

78 Avenue Paul Doumer
Paris

June 30. 1945

Dear Bill.

[...] In one of your letters you asked me if I had ever read anything by Trollope. At that time I hadn't, but the other day, reading in Edward Marsh's *A Number of People* that Barrie had been fascinated by a book of his called *Is He Popenjoy?* I took it out of the American Library. I found it almost intolerably slow at first, and then suddenly it gripped me, and now I am devouring it. It is rather like listening to somebody who is a little long-winded telling you a story about real people. The characters live in the most extraordinary way and you feel that the whole thing is true. Of course I read Trollope's *Autobiography* and found it very interesting. But I still don't understand his methods of work. Did he sit down each morning and write exactly fifteen hundred words without knowing when he sat down how the story was going to develop, or had he a careful scenario on paper? I can't believe that an intricate story like *Popenjoy* could have been written without very minute planning. Of course, if he did plan the whole thing out first, there is nothing so very bizarre in the idea of writing so many hundred words of it each day. After all, it is more or less what one does oneself. One sits down to work each morning irrespective of whether one feels bright or lethargic and before one gets up a certain amount of stuff, generally about fifteen hundred words, has emerged. But to sit down before a blank sheet of paper without an idea of how the story is to proceed seems to me impossible. Anyway, I think Trollope is damned

22. Wodehouse, Ethel and Leonora in France, photographed by *Tatler*, August 1924. The magazine caption reads 'a recent snapshot at Le Touquet, where the famous author and writer of so many excellent lyrics for musical comedy is having a bit of well-earned relaxation'.

23. Wodehouse at Hunstanton Hall, *c.* 1929.

24. Leonora Wodehouse, 1929.

25. A still from *Those Three French Girls*
(1930), one of the films for which
Wodehouse provided dialogue.

26. Wodehouse's friend, Maureen
O'Sullivan, with Johnny Weissmuller
in *Tarzan the Ape Man* (1932).

So I stayed where I was, letting "I dare not" wait upon "I would," like the poor cat i' th' adage. That's not my own, by the way. It's Jeeves'. He said it about young Pongo Twistleton-Twistleton of the Drones' once, and it's always stuck in my memory. Pongo had been invited for the week-end to his uncle's place in Hampshire, and couldn't make up his mind whether to go or not.

On the one hand, there was the fact that his cousin Wilfred would be there, which meant that at a conservative estimate a couple of quid in his pocket, Wilfred having the mistaken idea that he could beat Pongo at billiards. On the other hand, he would have to go to church twice on the Sunday. And when I told Jeeves about the poor chap's inward debates, he said the Pongo was letting "I dare not" wait upon "I would," like the poor cat i' th' adage. And I remember thinking, as I had often thought before, how well Jeeves put these things.

79

27. The first page of *Thank You, Jeeves* in *Cosmopolitan* magazine (May 1934), with an illustration by James Montgomery Flagg.

28. The marriage of Leonora and Peter Cazalet, December 1932.

29. Wodehouse, Bea Davis (centre) and Ethel, at Leonora's wedding.

30. The composer Ray Noble, actress Constance Collier, P. G. Wodehouse, Fred Astaire, and actor Reginald Gardiner, during the filming of *A Damsel in Distress* (1937).

31. A 1938 magazine spread about the Wodehouses' renovated villa, Low Wood, in Le Touquet.

The Wodehouse Villa

A Novelist's Home at Le Touquet

It has been said that from the first two decades of this century only two fictitious characters will live : Forsyte and Jeeves. Immortal or not, the immense present popularity of the latter and his book-fellows has assured their creator a comfortable position in life, a house in Park Lane, and a villa at Le Touquet. The bright and shining residence illustrated on this page was bought by P. G. Wodehouse two years ago, shortly before leaving for Hollywood. He made additions to it, had in Mrs. Marie Louise Arnold to decorate, stocked the shelves with novels and hung some restrained modern paintings on the walls. It is a contrast to the Park Lane house, which is furnished in strict classical style, antiques, old masters, and so on. The grounds of the villa are right next door to the Le Touquet golf-course.

Maximum daylight is a feature of all the rooms in the villa. There are no ceiling-lamps or picture-rails.

The spring sun shone down on Mr. and Mrs. Wodehouse on the terrace with Winkie and the Pug.

32. Wodehouse in the Kommandant's Office, Civil Internment Camp, Tost, Boxing Day, 1940.

33. The Wodehouses' friend, Johann Jebsen (Agent Artist).

34. Anga von Bodenhausen and Raven von Barnikow.

35. Wodehouse's first post-war feature interview with *Illustrated* magazine, 7 December 1946.

LITTLE LULU

"Okay, Jeeves, you may pass the Kleenex!"

— *Little Lulu says...* Compare tissues—compare boxes—and you'll see why 7 out of 10 tissue users like Kleenex* best! Soft! Strong! Pops Up! It's America's favorite tissue.

© International Cellunotion Products Co.   *T. M. Reg. U. S. Pat. Off.

36. Advertisement for Kleenex, *Life* magazine, 15 September 1947.

37. Wodehouse's old friend, Ellaline Terriss in *The Beauty of Bath*, 1906.

THE BRINKMANSHIP OF GALAHAD THREEPWOOD
A BLANDINGS CASTLE NOVEL BY
P.G. WODEHOUSE

38. Cover of *The Brinkmanship of Galahad Threepwood* (Simon and Schuster, 1964). Wodehouse disliked the jacket design, in which, he felt, Galahad looked too young and resembled 'one of the Beatles'.

39. Wodehouse with a model maker from Madame Tussauds, 1974.

good and I mean to read as much of him as I can get hold of.

[...]

I'm sorry the short story didn't get over with the *S.E.P.* How extraordinary that they should be so against war stories. It is a complete change of policy since the last number I read, which was only about a year ago. At that time the synopsis of a *S.E.P.* serial would be something like 'Major Dwight van Renssaeller, a young American officer in the F.G.I. has fallen in love with a mysterious veiled woman who turns out to be Irma Kraus, assistant Gauleiter of the Gestapo, who is in New York disguised as a Flight Lieutenant of the R.A.F. in order to secure the plans of the P.B.O. One night at a meeting of the X.T.D. he meets 'Spud' Murphy, in reality a Colonel in the T.H.B., who is posing as Himmler in the hope of getting a free lunch at a German restaurant on 44th St. They decide to merge the Y.F.S. with the P.X.Q., thus facilitating the operations of W.G.C. Go on from here.'

[...]

Peter is back at Fairlawne and expects to be demobbed in September. Ethel is well, but very tired today after an awful night with Wonder, who had some medicine and kept her up all night. We still manage to get along with the housekeeping. Something like a chicken or a bit of veal keeps turning up. The French bread is very good now. I am very fit, ever so much more than I was when feeding at the Bristol. I have resumed my daily five-mile walks.

Love to Rene.

Yours ever

Plum

While Wodehouse's letters continue to be fairly optimistic, Ethel's were decidedly depressed: 'if only our Leonora could be here', she wrote, 'it comes over me sometimes like a heavy black out, just suddenly, as it did last night, and I broke down for hours, but Plummie was so sweet and understanding.' Wodehouse's sympathies also extended to George Orwell, whose wife had just died. Orwell's loss was especially tragic, as the couple had only recently adopted a baby boy.

78 Avenue Paul Doumer
Paris (16)

Aug 1. 1945

Dear Orwell.

I wrote to you a few days before your letter arrived to thank you for *The Windmill*, and I am writing again to tell you how terribly sorry I am to hear of your sad loss. I am afraid there is nothing much one can say at a time like this that will be any good, but my wife and I are feeling for you with all our hearts, the more so as a year ago we lost our daughter and so can understand what it must be for you. I am so glad you have got a nurse for your little boy and that he is all right. If you come to Paris again, do let us know. We should both so much like to see you again.

I want to thank you again for that article.[1] It was extraordinarily kind of you to write like that when you did not know me, and I shall never forget it. [...]

[...] It was a masterly bit of work and I agree with every word of it.
With best wishes
P. G. Wodehouse

1 George Orwell had written an article, 'In Defence of P. G. Wodehouse', published in *The Windmill* in July 1945.

---

78 Avenue Paul Doumer
Paris (16)

Sept 1. 1945

Dear Guy.

[...] As far as we are concerned, things are beginning to stir faintly, like the blood beginning to circulate in a frozen Alpine traveller who has met a St Bernard dog and been given a shot from the brandy flask. Some weeks ago we were told by our London bank that by a new arrangement 'French' accounts had been started for us, whereby we could touch a certain amount of our cash, and today I read in the paper that residents in France now enter into full possession of what stuff they have in England. This relieves the financial situation. We have also started to set matters in train for a dash to America.

[...]

I was awfully pleased and grateful for what you said in your letter about getting up that petition for me.[1] How sweet of Virginia to sweat round with it. You say it did no earthly good, but I'm not sure. I think it was that and the agitation made by the *Saturday Evening Post* that induced the Germans to release me three months before I was sixty. Certainly something happened to make them do it, and it certainly wasn't anything to do with my broadcasting, because the idea of broadcasting did not come up till after I had been released. Isn't it the damnedest thing how Fate lurks to sock you with the stuffed eelskin.[2] [...] Do write again soon and tell me all you are doing. I hope you are busy with rehearsals.

Yours ever

Plum

1 In 1940, a petition, canvassing for Wodehouse's release from internment, had been arranged by Guy Bolton and signed by a large number of writers and well-known individuals in the US. The petition gained the attention of the *Saturday Evening Post*.
2 Stuffed eelskins were an old favourite of Wodehouse's when it came to metaphors and similes: 'What is life but a series of sharp corners, round each of which Fate lies in wait for us with a stuffed eel-skin?' (*Uneasy Money* (1916), Chapter 13); 'He resembled a minor prophet who had been hit behind the ear with a stuffed eel-skin' ('Ukridge's Dog College', *Ukridge*, 1924); 'I didn't want to get there and find Aunt Agatha waiting on the quay for me with a stuffed eelskin' ('Jeeves and the Unbidden Guest', *My Man Jeeves* (1919)).

TO WILLIAM TOWNEND

78 Avenue Paul Doumer
Paris (16)

Sept 13. 1945

Dear Bill.

[...]

It looks to me as if my position in America was swaying in the balance. An American newspaper woman (on *News Review*) who came to lunch yesterday told me that except for the extreme leftists everyone over there was pro-me, and I have had a letter today from Paul Reynolds Jr which suggests that things are coming right. But Ben Hibbs, the new editor of the *S.E.P.*, uncompromisingly refuses to consider publishing anything of mine in the *Post*, saying that if he did there would be a storm of protest. So I really don't know what to think. Anyway, the camp book will settle it. If it goes, then everything will be well.

[...] My trouble has been to get the right tone. You know how one's moods change from day to day. I go for a walk and work up a spirit of defiance and come home and write a belligerent page or two indicating that I don't give a damn whether the public takes a more favourable view or not, because all my friends have stuck to me and it's only my friends I care about. Then I sleep on it and wonder if this is quite judicious! Also, comedy will keep creeping in at the most solemn moments. I wrote this yesterday –

> The global howl which went up as the result of my indiscretion exceeded in volume and intensity anything I had experienced since the time in my boyhood when I broke the curate's umbrella and my aunts started writing letters to one another about it.

I showed the script to Ethel, making sure that she would swoon on reading the above and insist on it coming out, and she thought it marvellous and said that whatever I cut it mustn't be that. What do you think? Will the reaction be 'Ha, ha. I don't care what this chap has done. He makes me laugh' or 'Mr Wodehouse appears to imagine that his abominable action is a subject for flippancy.' You see. It might go either way, and I can't tell in advance.

[...]

Ethel is rather tired [...] these days, as Wonder, who sleeps on her bed, has taken to scratching in the night and waking her up. She is full of pep, however, and goes off daily to see one of Peter's friends, a Captain in the Welsh Guards, who has had flu and is in a small hotel which has been turned into a hospital.

[...]

I must stop now and take Wonder for a walk.

Love to Rene

Yours ever

Plum

H. D. Ziman, an English literary journalist, was introduced to Wodehouse by Malcolm Muggeridge. Wodehouse had sent him the manuscript of his book of camp reminiscences. The extract from the following letter shows his response to Ziman's feedback.

TO H. D. ZIMAN

78 Avenue Paul Doumer

Paris (16)

Sept 26. 1945

[...]

8. 'Admit candidly that I made a mistake'.

Yes. I agree with that. What has hampered me is the difficulty of writing the stuff – what is called 'expressing contrition' – without grovelling. It seems to me that anything would be better than grovelling. Surely, if I do, people will rank me with all the Germans who now go about saying how much they disliked the Nazis. Won't it seem that I am simply trying to curry favour? I would much rather be thought a Benedict Arnold than a Uriah Heep.

But there must be a way of doing it, if one could only find a method of avoiding servility. I have felt all along that the tone of the book was too flippant, but I couldn't find the mean between flippancy and grovelling.

[...] Best wishes from us both

Yours ever

Plum

P.S. I have been greatly cheered by a letter from a very big American theatrical manager, to whom I wrote to ask if he would care to read a play I was writing. I said in my letter that I was quite prepared to have him reply that it would be impossible to put on a play by me on account of anti-Wodehouse feeling in the States, but he writes that he doesn't feel that way.

He says: –

'I think you will find that your German troubles are pretty well forgotten in this country. As your personal spy, I will tell you that the general consensus of opinion is that you did a foolish thing but not a malicious thing. In any case, I can assure you that it would have no effect whatever on the public reaction to anything that you might write.'

This has naturally bucked me up more than somewhat, and I am hoping that the feeling in England will eventually be the same.

All well here. We now have the Duke and Duchess of Windsor as comparatively near neighbours.

Do come back to Paris as soon as you can.

TO DENIS MACKAIL

78 Avenue Paul Doumer
Paris (16)

Oct 14. 1945

Dear Denis.

[...]

I wish we were together and could have a talk, for I would like to discuss with you the subject of the Nude on the stage. Peter got tickets for the Casino de Paris and I sat brooding on the Nude and wondering how it can always come as a fresh surprise to the French audience. Revues must have been going for well over a century in Paris and every one of them not only relies for its big first act curtain on *Nudes Through the Ages* but one spots Nudes at intervals all the way through, and yet no-one ever seems to get tired of it. If you want a subject for another essay, I would suggest one on chorus girls, featuring the Paris chorus girl. Their utter lack of interest in their job is what amazes me.

They just walk through the show without a smile. As for dancing, they never attempt it.

I must say *Ho!* gave a pretty grim picture of what life in London must have been like during the war.[1] But I always think London is depressing and wonder at your devotion to it, considering that your aim, like mine, is to avoid your species. Now that I am 64 (tomorrow) I want to settle down in some quiet nook and turn into a vegetable.

[...]

Yours ever

Plum

1 Denis Mackail's wartime reminiscences, *Ho! Or How It All Strikes Me*, were published in 1944.

TO DENIS MACKAIL

36 Boulevard Suchet
Paris (16)

Nov 7. 1945

Dear Denis.

First of all, observe and jot down in your tablets the above address. It is a new flat into which we move as soon as we can get our packing done. Very posh, being right on the Bois (wonderful facilities for Peke exercising) and two doors from neighbour Windsor, who lives at No 24 and will no doubt be dropping in all the time. We got it through Bea Davis, the owner being a friend of hers, and the price is almost the same as we are paying for the Paul Doumer hovel. I think we shall have a good time there, as it is beautifully light and, as I say, with vastly superior facilities for promenading the petit chien. If we feel in sporting mood, Auteuil race course is only a hundred yards away. One excellent feature is that I have a very good work room. The only drawback, which can easily be remedied by taking the dam thing down and hiding it in a spare room, is an enormous picture of a nude which dominates the living room. I have already expressed to you my views on nudes. I want no piece of them.

[...]

Talking of books, as we so often do when we get together, ought I to be ashamed of confessing to you a furtive fondness for Angela Thirkell?[1] You told me once that she bullied you when you were a child, and for years I refused austerely to read her. But recently *Wild Strawberries* and *Pomfret Towers* have weakened me. I do think she's good, though if we are roasting her I will add that *August Folly* was rotten and I couldn't get through it.

[...]

Keep me supplied with news about the pug, in whom I am very interested.

Yours ever

Plum

I'm so glad you like Malcolm Muggeridge. Words can't tell what a friend he has been to us.

1 The novelist Angela Thirkell was Denis's sister. The pair were not close, and Wodehouse learned later that Mackail did not appreciate hearing compliments about her.

TO WILLIAM TOWNEND

36 Boulevard Suchet
Paris

Nov 8. 1945

Dear Bill.

[...]

Yielding to the overwhelming pressure from Watt etc, I have decided to postpone publication of the camp book. I still agree with you about it, but everybody else is so insistent that it should be held back till this Belsen business has become a thing of the past that I am pigeonholing it for the time being.[1]

[...]

Love to Rene

Yours ever

Plum

1 The concentration camp Bergen–Belsen had been liberated by the British in April 1945. Over a hundred thousand people had died within its walls – and some twenty thousand more were too ill to survive, even after liberation came. Between August and November 1945, the Commandant of the camp, and forty-four others, were tried in a British war crimes court at Lüneburg. Thirty were found guilty, and twelve were sentenced to death.

Ethel, meanwhile, recovering from the shock of her daughter's death, was starting to enjoy life in Paris more. 'I had a very nice cocktail party the other day. [...] I thought it was about time I paid back to a few people who had been so nice to us. I couldn't begin to find anything to eat or drink, but a friend of mine, an American girl and her Mother came to the rescue [...] and she found everything [...]. Lots of decorative young officers came, and it was a great success.'

TO DENIS MACKAIL

36 Boulevard Suchet,
Paris (16)

Nov 27. 1945

Dear Denis,

[...]

I find that my personal animosity against a writer never affects my opinion of what he writes. Nobody could be more anxious than myself, for instance, that Alan Alexander Milne should trip over a loose boot lace and break his bloody neck, yet I re-read his early stuff at regular intervals with all the old enjoyment and still maintain that in *The Dover Road* he produced about the best comedy in English.

It was awfully good of you to write to Iddon in my defence, and I think it must have done good, as he appears to have been impressed.[1] You know, I can hardly blame anyone in America for being hostile to me after the weird things that have been printed there about me. Yesterday Ethel got a letter from an old friend of hers in Boston, in which the latter mentioned an article which said that we used to lie in bed in Berlin feeding our dog with pork chops!! How on earth the writer was supposed to have got his facts, I don't know. Actually we used to victual Wonder just as you in similar circumstances would have victualled Tan, – we had an ounce of meat each daily and we gave this to Wonder and ate vegetables ourselves. I don't think I ever saw a pork chop when I was in Germany.

The new flat is a stupendous success. It is like living in the country with all the conveniences of town. We are right on the edge of the Bois, and every morning I put on plus fours and a sweater and go and do my Daily Dozen under the trees before breakfast. The improvement in my health has been immediate. I am now very fit, and my eyes, which had been troubling me owing to the bad lighting at 78 Paul Doumer, are now all right again. One thing I love about the French is that they are not hicks, – I mean that if they see anything unusual they accept it politely and don't guffaw. Not a single pedestrian who has passed me during my morning exercises has even turned his head. They see a man in a white sweater and golf bags bending and stretching and they say to themselves 'Ah, a man in a white sweater and golf bags bending and stretching. No doubt he has excellent motives, and in any case it has nothing to do with me'. [...]

Love to Diana and Tan and all

Yours ever

Plum

1 Don Iddon, a British journalist, had written an unfavourable article about PGW.

TO DENIS MACKAIL

36 Boulevard Suchet,
Paris (16)

Dec 23. 1945

Dear Denis.

[...]

You're quite right about my books being early Edwardian. I look on myself as a historical novelist. I read a book about Dickens the other day which pointed out that D. was still writing gaily about stage coaches etc long after railways had come in. I don't believe it matters and I intend to go on hewing to the butler line, let the chips fall where they may. By the way, I was vastly encouraged, when reading in the paper about Viscount Selby and his lady friend, to see that at one point 'the butler' entered and spoke a line or two. So they still exist.

More later. Send news of pug.

Yours ever

Plum

TO WILLIAM TOWNEND

36 Boulevard Suchet
Paris (16)

Jan 11. 1946

Dear Bill.

[...]

Life here continues very pleasant. I am getting fonder and fonder of Paris. It was a blow when they started rationing bread again, but in actual practice it doesn't affect us much. We now have a cook who buys the stuff and there always seems enough. There is some sort of row on just now between the wholesale and retail butchers, which has resulted in no meat for the populace for about two weeks. But something always seems to turn up. There is a mysterious Arab gentleman who calls from time to time with offerings. He has just come and fixed us up with a great chunk of mutton. And a rabbit! Also a Dane (unknown to me) has sent us an enormous parcel, the only trouble being that all the contents are labeled in Danish, so we don't know what they are. There are three large tins which I hold contain bacon, but Ethel, who is in a pessimistic mood today owing to a bad night, says that they are stuff for cleaning floors. But surely even the most erratic Dane wouldn't send us stuff for cleaning floors. The only way I can think of of solving the mystery is to ring up our Danish friend at Neuilly and spell the labels over the phone to him and ask him to translate. (N.B. We did very well at Christmas, managing to buy two chickens and a turkey, and our ex-lodger of the Low Wood 1939 days, who is in the fish business, sent us a large box of fish.)

[...]

Who do you think I heard from a couple of days ago? Old Brook. A shortish letter written on filthy paper. He seems to be getting along still and says that somebody has bought an option on a dramatization he made of *A Diary of a Nobody*.

[...]

Love to Rene.

Yours ever

Plum

Wodehouse's lyric 'Bill', with music by Jerome Kern, had been imported into the 1927 musical Show Boat. *In 1945, Kern and Hammerstein revived the show, and made sure they gave Wodehouse a writing credit on the programme.*

TO DENIS MACKAIL

Paris

Jan 26. 1946

Dear Denis.

[...]

'Bill'. I am enclosing a sheet from the programme of *Show Boat* which has just been revived in N.Y. Don't you think it was extraordinarily decent of O. Hammerstein to go out of his way to print a thing like that? He is one of the few men of whom I have never heard anyone say a bad word. Everybody likes him, and I don't wonder. Years ago, I remember, Oscar lent me his script of *Show Boat* to read some time before the original production. I read it in a kindly spirit, liking him so much, but was quite convinced it hadn't a chance of success. I came to the same conclusion about *On the Spot* when Edgar Wallace gave it to me to read.[1] So I seem to be a good picker.

Ethel is yowling in the passage that my cocktail is ready, so no more for the present.

Yours ever

Plum

1 The detective novel *On the Spot* is regarded as Wallace's masterpiece.

In February 1946, Wodehouse wrote to Townend about a 'visit from the Home Office bloke who came to Paris after the Liberation to take my statement'. Although Cussen was 'terrifically friendly' he raised a 'snag': this related to the recent trial and execution of William Joyce ('Lord Haw-Haw'). In stark contrast to Wodehouse, Joyce actively collaborated for many years with the Nazi regime and had regularly broadcast Nazi propaganda to Britain. The Director of Public Prosecutions had noted that Wodehouse 'was in an altogether different category' and 'made only isolated unpolitical broadcasts'. Nevertheless, Wodehouse writes, '[i]n the Joyce trial the Judge laid it down that it was an offence to speak on the German radio, irrespective of what one said. This means that I have been technically guilty of an offence and that if I came to England the authorities would presumably take some action. This man said that the case against me had been completely and entirely dropped, but that if I came to England it might have to be re-opened.'

TO MAJOR EDWARD CUSSEN

36 Boulevard Suchet
Paris (16)

Feb 1. 1946

My dear Cussen.

It was such a joy to us to see you again, looking so fit (and much thinner!). [...]

[...]

I wish you had not had to leave in such a hurry, as there were a number of questions I wanted to ask you about my position as regards England. That pronouncement of the Judge in the Joyce case bars me from coming to England. Right. But for how long? Indefinitely? For ever?

If for ever, how do I live? The present regulations of the Bank of England seem to make it impossible for me to touch my money over there. [...]

In these circumstances, how do I manage? [...] If they are going to go on for ever refusing to allow me to receive my literary earnings and won't let me touch my capital, it looks as if I would either have to starve or else buy a gun and a black mask and go about Paris holding up the fortunate people who have a bit of the stuff on them. And I don't know enough French to stick natives up.

With best wishes from us both

Yours sincerely

P. G. Wodehouse

TO WILLIAM TOWNEND

36 Blvd Suchet
Paris

March 7. 1946

Dear Bill.

[...] I am wondering, with some mild amusement, what the result is going to be of the impact of a book like *Money in the Bank* on the world of 1946! It is so absolutely archaic. It assumes a state of affairs which is as out of date as *Three Men in a Boat*. It will be very interesting to see how it goes. I believe that people will jump at something that takes them away from modern conditions. The same applies to the impending publication of my Jeeves novel in America.[1] But of course my stuff has been out of date since 1914, and nobody has seemed to mind.

[...]

Yours ever

Plum

1 *Joy in the Morning.*

Wodehouse was writing to his granddaughter, Sheran, just before her twelfth birthday.

36 Boulevard Suchet

Paris

March 27. 1946

My darling Sheran.

If I post this tonight, it ought to reach you on the 31st, so many happy returns and I hope you will have a lovely birthday and get all the presents you most want. We shall be thinking of you on Sunday and will drink your health.

[...]

I am working very hard trying to plan out a story about Bertie Wooster and Jeeves which I began to work at in 1942 and couldn't get on with because I couldn't think what could happen.[1] Yesterday and this morning it suddenly began to come out, and now I really think it is going to be funny. Bertie has a friend called Stilton Cheesewright – at least, his name is really D'Arcy Cheesewright, but everybody calls him Stilton – and they are both going to stay at a house in the country with some people they have never met. Well, the night before they are supposed to go Stilton (who is rather quick-tempered) has a fight with someone in the street and is arrested by the police and the magistrate says he will have to go to prison for two weeks. And if he does not go to the house for this visit of his[,] his family will find out that he is in prison and will be very angry with him, so Bertie asks Jeeves what is to be done, and Jeeves says the only thing to do is for Bertie to go to the house pretending to be Stilton. So Bertie goes, and the first thing he finds is that the man who owns the house is a great enemy of Stilton's, though they have never met. (This sounds odd, but it is all explained in the story.) This makes things very awkward for Bertie, because he can't say he isn't Stilton.

Meanwhile, the magistrate thinks it over and decides that he was too hard on Stilton, so he says Stilton can pay a fine instead of going to prison. So Stilton comes to the house because he is going to marry a girl and she will expect to get letters from him every day written from the house, and he can't go as himself because Bertie is pretending to be him, so he comes there pretending to be Bertie. So everybody thinks Bertie is Stilton and Stilton is Bertie and all sorts of funny things happen. I haven't got the middle of the story yet, but I have thought out the end of it, which is always the most important part, and I believe it is going to be good. But just fancy having to take four years to think out a story!

[...]

You would like this flat, as you are so fond of horses, for it is within a hundred yards of Auteuil race course, so when I want to go to the races all I have to do is just stroll round the corner. I meant to go last Sunday, but it rained very hard all day and I thought it would be nicer indoors.

Lots and lots of love to you and Daddy and Buddy and Nitty and everybody.[2]

Your

Plummie

1 *The Mating Season.*
2 'Buddy' is Edward, Sheran's brother; 'Nitty' is Anthony Mildmay.

TO DENIS MACKAIL

36 Blvd Suchet
Paris

March 28. 1946

Dear Denis.

[...]

Not much news from the Paris front. The other night, having run out of Murine,[1] Ethel squirted some stuff into her eyes which the vet prescribed for Wonder, and a quarter of an hour later complained of violent pains in the head and said that the room was all dark and she couldn't read the print of her *Saturday Evening Post*. Instead of regarding this as a bit of luck, as anyone should do who knows the present *Saturday Evening Post*, she got very alarmed and remained so till next morning, when all was clear again. It just shows what a dog has to endure. Though, as a matter of fact, I believe dogs' eyes are absolutely insensitive. I don't think dogs bother about their eyes at all, relying entirely on their noses.

[....]

Well, lunch now. More later.

Yours ever

Plum

I have been looking through my diary and I realize that I must be one of the world's great correspondents. This is the 43rd letter I have written this month, and my monthly average for the last year has been over thirty. Do you write a lot of letters? I love getting letters, so I get a reward for my large output.

1 Eye drops.

TO IRA GERSHWIN

36 Blvd Suchet

Paris

April 5. 1946

Dear Ira,

That bit in your letter of March 14 about Leonore sending us parcels stirred me like a bugle. Parcels are what we don't want anything except. Before I send off this letter I will consult Ethel, who is out at the moment, and ask her what we particularly need. It really would be frightfully good of her to send us something, if it isn't too much trouble, as the food situation, though better, is still a long way from being what it should be.

[...]

I have now written eleven lyrics, and I really think they are good. But how difficult it is to write lyrics without the melody. I could never make out how you and George worked. Somebody told me once that George sat down at the piano and doped out a tune and that you stood alongside working out the lyric at the same time, but it sounded impossible. Don't you have to sit down all by yourself somewhere and hold your head and gradually chisel the thing out? Jerry[1] set quite a number of my lyrics, but I always worked best when he gave me the completed melody. That old devil Friml used to drive me off my nut because he would never finish a tune. He would tell me he had got one ready for me and then play about four bars on the piano and wander off into nothing and say 'Of course, it's just a sketch.' I live in hopes of one day doing a show with Romberg. He gave me the impression during the *Rosalie* time of being a wonderful composer to work with.

Love to Leonore

Yours ever

Plum

Ethel has now come in and says that what we need most are the following: –

> Sardines (or any tinned fish)
>
> A cake
>
> Jam (with which is incorporated anything
>
> to spread on bread – e.g. honey)
>
> Canned Meats to be spread on bread
>
> Candy
>
> Cheese

But anything Leonore picks will be okay with us. Ethel says Thank you both ever so much. It really is wonderful of you.

1 Jerome Kern.

In early 1946, in the wake of William Joyce's execution, the Attorney-General, Hartley Shawcross ('an Old Alleynian, blast him!', noted Wodehouse), spoke about Wodehouse in the House of Commons. He declared that 'the question of taking proceedings against Mr. Wodehouse would be reconsidered if and when he came within the jurisdiction of the British courts'.

36 Boulevard Suchet
Paris

April 10. 1946

Dear Monty.

Thelma Cazalet-Keir came over here a couple of days ago and told me of the marvellous way you had been sticking up for me in England. I can't tell you how grateful I am. It makes the whole situation seem different when I know that friends like you are still with me.

The recent remarks of the Attorney-General in the House of Commons came as rather a shock after the attitude taken by the previous Attorney-General, making my position difficult again. Apparently the view taken now, as the result of what the Judge said in the Joyce trial, is that the mere act of speaking on the German Radio is regarded as a crime, irrespective of what was said. My five talks were simply a humorous description of life in camp, designed purely to amuse American readers of my books and made because I wanted to do something to show my gratitude for letters and parcels they had sent me, but that, it seems, does not let me out. The Government seem to be standing firmly on a technicality, against which of course I have no defence. So I can only hope that time will eventually straighten things out.

[...]

My own position is rather like that of the mild man with the small voice who sits in a corner making remarks that nobody listens to. I keep on writing, and the books have been piling up for five years or so, but I am the only person who reads them. However, the dam shows signs of bursting. Doubleday are bringing out my Jeeves novel in the Autumn, and I suppose after that the others will follow. They will be definitely historical novels now, as they all deal with a life in which country houses flourish and butlers flit to and fro. I'm hoping that people, in America at any rate, will overlook the fact that they are completely out of date and accept them for their entertainment value. I think they're all pretty funny, but, my gosh, how obsolete!

[...]

A few days ago I received a formal notification from the French Government that I was no longer considered 'dangereux' to the safety of the Republic. Up till now the Republic has been ducking down side streets when it saw me coming and shouting 'Save yourselves, boys! Here comes Wodehouse!', but now all is well and me and them are just like that. I am glad of this, because I have always considered them one of the nicest Republics I have ever met, my great trouble being that I simply can't master the language. My instructor at the Berlitz was strong on pencils. She would keep saying 'Un crayon. Le crayon est jaune. Le crayon est bleu' and so on till I really got good on pencils. But in actual conversation I found that it didn't carry me very far. I was sunk unless I could work the talk round to pencils, and nobody seemed really interested in them. I now leave everything to my wife who can't speak a word of French but somehow manages to make herself understood.

I do hope you will some day be coming over to Paris, so that we can meet again. I haven't gone at length into what I think of your wonderful loyalty to me, because I know you know how I feel. God bless you!

Yours ever

Plum

Wodehouse was writing to his grandson Edward, just before his tenth birthday.

TO EDWARD CAZALET

35 Boulevard Suchet
Paris

April 23. 1946

My darling Buddy.

Many happy returns of the day. What splendid news that you are so much better and can go out in the car. I hope by the time your next birthday comes you will be quite well and riding again and that it won't be long before you are playing cricket. I do think it's wonderful how brave you have been.

[...]

I wonder what you have been reading lately. I found a book in the American Library which I am sure you would like. It is called *The Sword in the Stone* and it is about the childhood of King Arthur – you know, the Round Table chap. It is very exciting and very funny because all the characters talk like people of today. There is a king called King Pellorin who spends all his time chasing the Questing Beast with a hound that keeps getting its leash entangled in his legs. I don't know if it has been published in England, but if it has do ask Daddy to get it for you as a present from me.

[...]

It was lovely seeing your Daddy and your aunt Thelma, and I wish they could have stayed longer. Did they tell you about the funny little man with the white beard in the restaurant? He told us what he wanted us to eat and wouldn't let us eat anything else. Poor Bunny wanted fish, but he said she mustn't have fish because the rest of us were having duck and we must all have the same, and when she asked for a salad he said she couldn't have salad with duck. By the way, a friend of ours in America sent us a parcel of chocolates the other day. They were good! You can't get chocolates in Paris unless you are a growing child, which I'm not. I am thinking of putting on a sailor suit and having a try, but I doubt if it will work.

Well, I wish I could be with you for your birthday, and I hope this will arrive on or about the right day.

Oceans of love

Plummie

TO WILLIAM TOWNEND

36 Blvd Suchet
Paris

April 29. 1946

[...]

George Orwell. I wish I could get hold of that book of his, as it's just the sort of thing I like reading nowadays. He is a friend of my friend Malcolm Muggeridge and about a year ago or more came over to Paris and gave us a very good lunch at a dingy place down by Les Halles (the markets to you). He then sent me that article about me, which appeared in *The Windmill* and later in his book. I liked him very much indeed. Odd him being an old Etonian. He wrote a book once called *Down and Out in Paris* [*sic*] and gave me the impression of somebody out of your novels, a sort of gentleman beach-comber. I thought that criticism he did of my stuff was masterly. I was tremendously impressed by his fairmindedness in writing such an article at a time when it was taking a very unpopular view. He really is a good chap. I wonder, though, how many people read a book of essays. I should think that article ought to help me with writing people, but I'm afraid the general public will miss it.

[...]

Yours ever

Plum

Ever since Wodehouse's broadcasts, the Cazalet family had felt strongly that Wodehouse should keep as low a public profile as possible, stop publishing – and remain away from England. The book of camp reminiscences was seen as a particularly dangerous publication. Thelma Cazalet-Keir was generally against any of Wodehouse's work appearing in print at this time, in order to protect Wodehouse from doing further damage to himself. She frequently wrote to Wodehouse's publishers, Herbert Jenkins, on this subject. The continuing lack of information from official sources surrounding what had actually taken place in Berlin explains Thelma Cazalet-Keir's caution, but Wodehouse found it difficult to comprehend.

36 Blvd Suchet
Paris

May 7. 1946

Dear Denis,

[...]

How right you are in the passage at the foot of page one of your letter of April 24. (May as well be discreet, even to a trusted friend like you.) Every word you say about the party of whom you said the words you said is true to the last drop. The party of whom you said the words you said is thinking solely of the interests of the said party and not of mine. I have felt all along that the Camp book should have been published right away and that it was only the sinister influence of the party that made all the jelly-backboned people who gave their opinions (no names) take the stand they did. I'll tell you one thing. If *Money in the Bank* (you should be receiving your copy shortly) gets over, I intend to do a bit of Russian expansionism and throw my weight about. And by 'gets over' I mean if it sells. Slams from the baser element don't matter a damn so long as the heart of the Public is sound.

[...]

Hectic visit, just finished, from Gertrude, Countess of Dudley, bless her. Just the same as ever and very sound on the party to whom I alluded earlier. In fact, after a champagne dinner topped off with brandy she dictated a specimen letter which she wanted me to send to the party which would infallibly have led to severing relations for ever. (Cruel Sports of the Past, – Severing the Relation.)

What a shame Treasure is no longer with you. Wonder is in great form, but let the side down on our walk this morning by squatting down and then changing her mind.

Yours ever
Plum

36 Boulevard Suchet,

Paris

May 31. 1946

Dear Ira.

A perspiring Frenchman, sagging badly at the knees, has just staggered
to our back door drooping under the weight of Leonore's two magnificent
parcels. I never saw such enormous ones in my life, and Ethel and I
are overcome and really don't know how to thank Leonore enough.
Contents exactly what we wanted, too, – all those little delicacies which
you can spread on bread. There was a good story in the *New Yorker*
some time ago about an Englishwoman writing to an American friend
about parcels and saying 'For heaven's sake send something that tastes
of something.' I know exactly what she meant. We opened a can of
roast beef last night, and while it was filling it just meant nothing.
How different with your effort! That fruit cake alone would have made
us happy.

By this time, I imagine, you are up to your eyes in the new show
and wondering what on earth induced you to become a lyrist.[1] I love
all the preliminaries to doing a show, – the invitation to join the gang,
the meetings with the rest of the crowd, the diving in and out of
managers' offices, but what a sweat it is when you really have to get
down to the work. I shall always remember Boston and *Rosalie*,
particularly those testing days when you and I hammered out 'Say so'
with George [...].

The other day I was asked to do book and lyrics for a show from
Vienna in which Grace Moore is to star, Hassard Short directing, –
about Madame Pompadour, and I was torn between the desire to get
in on what will presumably be a big production and a hit, especially
as I was an old beach-comber trying to make a come back after thirty
years, and the desire to put on a false beard and hide somewhere till
the thing had blown over. I imagine you probably feel the same as I
do when asked to work on a 'period' musical show, – a sort of deadly
feeling that you are going into a fight with one arm strapped to your
side and hobbles around your ankles, because you won't be able to

use anything in the nature of modern comedy lines or ideas and so are robbed of your best stuff. When I write a lyric I want to be able to work in Clark Gable and Grover Whalen's moustache and corned beef hash, and you can't when you are dealing with La Pompadour.

[...]

However, I rather think the thing has fallen through, as I gather the offer was contingent on my coming to America immediately, and I don't believe I can manage it. I am hoping to be able to get over towards the end of the summer, but a flying start is impossible. I expect to hear more definitely tomorrow, but I have already made up my mind that the deal is off.

Still I was – and continue to be – very bucked at having received the offer after all that has occurred. Compare the story of the old gentleman of eighty who was accosted by a tart one dark night in Piccadilly and said with a good deal of feeling 'Madam, I thank you for the compliment.'

[...]

Love from us both and again a thousand thanks for the parcels.

Yours ever

Plum

1 Gershwin's new show, *Park Avenue*, about marriage and divorce in the smart New York set, opened on Broadway in 1946, with book by Kaufman and Johnson, music co-written with Schwartz, and lyrics by Ira Gershwin. It was not a success.

TO COMPTON MACKENZIE

36 Boulevard Suchet
Paris

June 4. 1946

My dear Monty.

It was wonderful getting your letter. Send me more!

I asked Watt to send you a copy of *Money in the Bank*. I hope this reaches you safely and that you will like it. I haven't seen any reviews of it yet, but imagine that if there are any they will be stinkers. [...]

Whisky Galore sounds promising.[1] I hope it comes out without any of those awful hitches in the middle which whiten an author's hair. Why is it that even if you prepare the most detailed scenario you always seem to strike a snag somewhere in a book? I have just got out the plot of a new Jeeves novel and it looks as if it would write itself, but difficulties are sure to crop up.

Yes, the Duke of Windsor is practically next door to us. There is only a derelict barracks in between. Oddly enough I haven't seen him yet.

[...]

Yours ever

Plum

1 Mackenzie's *Whisky Galore*, a novel about a shipwrecked cargo of whisky off the coast of a small Scottish island, was published in 1947.

TO V. S. PRITCHETT

36 Boulevard Suchet
Paris

June 15. 1946

Dear Mr Pritchett.

A friend of mine has just written to tell me of the kind way in which you spoke of my *Money in the Bank* on the Home Service on the night of the 12th, and I am kicking myself for having missed it. I really don't know how to thank you enough. It will mean everything to the book, and I am tremendously grateful.

Apart from the <u>réclame</u> (as we call it over here) it is a joy to know that a critic of your standing liked the story. I am particularly pleased that Lord Uffenham amused you. I had great luck with him. There was a man in camp with me who was Uffenham to the life, except for the murky past and the conviction that he was irresistible to women. All the Uffenham obiter dicta were thrown off by this man from time to time in the dormitory. I simply had to drink the stuff in and write it down.

The whole story was thought out and written while I was in camp. I had to do it in pencil in a room where a hundred men were playing darts and ping-pong, with generally a lecture on Beowulf going on in the background, but oddly enough it came out quite easily, though a bit slowly. Until I tried, I wouldn't have thought it possible for me to write a story by hand, as I have worked on the typewriter since 1911, but it turned out to be perfectly simple. It just meant being satisfied with doing a page a day instead of my usual eight.

You can probably imagine how I felt when I heard of your talk, for it was not without diffidence that I agreed to the publication of the book. I saw myself rather in the position of a red-nosed comedian who has got the bird at the first house on Monday and is having the temerity to go on and do his stuff at the second house, outwardly breezy and cheerful but feeling inside as if he had swallowed a heaping tablespoonful of butterflies and with a wary eye out for demonstrations from the gallery. And now comes this applause from the stalls, thank God! Bless you.

Best wishes

Yours sincerely

P. G. Wodehouse

TO DENIS MACKAIL

36 Boulevard Suchet
Paris

July 4. 1946

Dear Denis.

I saw that stinker in the *Observer* and for a couple of moments reeled beneath the coarse abuse, but it wasn't long before I was saying 'What the hell?' and realizing that the fact that a man who obviously hated my guts couldn't refrain from praising the book was all to the good. (In their advertisement ye Jenkinses have boiled the review down to the words 'Eminently readable', bless them!). Anyway, a few days later my spies inform me that the B.B.C. of all people gave the book a terrific boost per V. S. Pritchett in his *Book Talk*, and the sales have been absolutely all right, – 21,000 up to the morning of June 12 [...]. The *Times Lit. Supp.* also gave me quite a decent notice, and the heart of the *Yorkshire Post* and others seems to have been sound. So, as I say, what the hell!

But I agree with you that the Camp book must be published.

I am still trying to get a visa for America, and feeling that the only thing to be done was to get as many people as possible to assail the U.S. Embassy in London.

[...]

Too hot to write any more now. Love to all.

Yours ever

Plum

Oh, I was forgetting. A <u>most</u> satisfactory review of A.A.M.'s *Chloe Marr* in the *Daily Mail*. In case you missed it, it said that it was the silliest book of the year. I must say from the notices I have seen it sounds pretty bad drip.

Yes, you were right. I lifted Pennefather out of *Happy Thoughts*.[1] I had no idea that even you with your encyclopaedic knowledge of Eng. literature would remember *Happy Thoughts*. By the way, in another opus entitled *Uncle Dynamite* the names of the girl's publishers are Popgood and Grooly [*sic*].

1 Wodehouse's character Ernest Pennefather is a cab-driver who appears in *Money in the Bank*. He is modelled on George Cornelius Pennefather, a character in Francis Cowley Bernand's *Happy Thoughts*, published in *Punch* in 1863–4. Popgood and Groolley feature as the hero's publishers.

TO WILLIAM TOWNEND

36 Boulevard Suchet
Paris

Aug 27. 1946

Dear Bill.

Thanks for your letters. I would have written to you a long time ago, but have been tensely occupied with a rush job which started on Aug 8 and finished last night, – viz. the dramatization of *Leave It to Psmith* for America. Did I tell you about that? An American manager named Montgomery Ford apparently thinks it is the finest book in the language, and we corresponded and eventually decided that he was to construct the thing and I would dialogue it. His effort reached me on the 7th, together with a letter saying that he was on the verge of getting backing for it to the tune of $75,000. In New York now it apparently costs that to put on an ordinary comedy. A musical show on a biggish scale costs $200,000. It beats me how anybody continues in the theatre business.

[...]

The position at the moment, I gather from this Joint Opinion,[1] is that they think it would be unwise for me to go to England for a while. They say there is no question of a trial for Treason, but I might get caught on Section 2, Sub-section A of the Defence Regulations or something of that sort, – for which, they say, the penalty is two months in chokey (though, they add, it is possible to get imprisonment for life!).

They say the Prosecution would try to convince the jury that my object in making the broadcasts was to attract listeners to the German radio, and that it is no answer to this to say that as they were made at four in the morning the number of listeners who got up at that hour to hear them must have been very small. A thing I've noticed in these legal Opinions is that nothing that would convince an ordinary sensible man ever is an 'answer'. I haven't suggested it yet to any of my advisers, but I should have thought the best proof that I had no desire to have Germany triumph and ruin England was that my entire life savings are invested in British Government securities, which in such circs would inevitably have gone phut.

So I am off to Switzerland probably on Sept 2, and expect to return about Sept 4. I shall then start making arrangements for going to America, as Ford is anxious that I shall be with him when the show goes into rehearsal. This, like the trip to Switzerland, will be a hell of a business. I don't want to fly, and if one goes by boat it means sharing a cabin with about thirty other men on a 10,000 ton Liberty ship. Though I am not sure if on the Liberty ships the number of passengers isn't limited. Are they really cargo boats? What I would like would be to get a passage on one of your tramp steamers, but how is this managed? Anyway, I expect I shall leave somehow towards the middle of September. We have to give up this flat on Oct 15, and Ethel wants me out of the way during the move. I am hoping that she will clean everything up and join me in N.Y. in about a month.

[...]

Since I wrote last, we have had a short holiday at Le Touquet, where I ran into several men from my camp and was relieved to find them all very friendly. I went several times to see Low Wood. It isn't in such bad shape as I had feared. The walls, ceilings, staircases and mantelpieces are still there. It would apparently cost about two thousand quid to put right, and Ethel has given a man an option till next Monday to buy at four thousand. Our trouble is that, until they relax this rule about not being able to touch our English capital, we simply can't raise two thousand, and four thousand paid over in cash would be the salvation of us. At present we are living on driblets from America and England, just enough to keep us going. But I am hoping that in a year or so things will be normal.

[...]

I must stop now, as I have to go to the Swiss Embassy to get my visa.

Love to Rene

Yours ever

Plum

You say you tend to get tired nowadays. Me, too. But I am really very fit, and I find that though I write slower these days I turn out just as good stuff.

---

1 Wodehouse had asked the advice of his London solicitor, who engaged a Junior Counsel and a KC to advise further.

TO WILLIAM TOWNEND

36 Blvd Suchet
Paris

Aug 30. 1946

Dear Bill.

I simply must write and tell you the good news. This morning there arrived from a newspaper friend in Virginia a review of *Joy in the Morning* from the *New York Times Book Review*, Sunday last, raving about the book and concluding with this:

Maybe Wodehouse uses the same plot over and over again. Whatever he does, it's moderately wonderful, a ray of pale English sunshine in a gray world... There is, of course, the question of Mr Wodehouse's 'war guilt'. Upon mature post-war reflection, it turned out to be about equal to the war guilt of the dachshunds which were stoned by super-heated patriots during World War I.

Terrific, isn't it? The one paper that matters is the *N.Y. Times*.

I sent you a copy of *Joy in the Morning* yesterday. I hope you will like it. I don't think it's bad, considering that it was written during the German occupation of Le Touquet, with German soldiers prowling about under my window, plus necessity of having to walk to Paris Plage every morning to report to a German Kommandant with a glass eye, which made him even more formidable than the ordinary German Kommandant.

[...]

When you say you liked Priestley's book, do you mean *Bright Day*? I read that and liked it, and I also liked *Daylight on Saturday*. I haven't seen any others by him. Yes, I think he's a bit pompous, but he writes very well and is always readable. I am now reading Evelyn Waugh's *Put Out More Flags*, and am absolutely stunned by his brilliance. I think you said you didn't like *Brideshead Revisited*, which I haven't read, and I imagine it's different from his usual work. But I do think that as a comic, satiric writer he stands alone. That interview between Basil Seal and the Guards Colonel is simply marvellous.

Love to Rene

Yours ever

Plum

By December 1946, the Wodehouses were settled in 'a couple of rather chilly hotel rooms' in a village just outside Paris. A long feature interview appeared in the British paper, Illustrated; *the first complete interview that Wodehouse had given to any British journal since the broadcasts.*

Pavilion Henri Quatre
St Germain en Laye
France

Dec 2. 1946

Dear Mr Shively.

[...] I have read the reviews of *Joy in the Morning* with great interest. They are a good deal better than I expected but I note rather a sinister anti-Jeeves tone! The *New Yorker* frankly said he had become a bore. [...] My own opinion is that critics get fed up with a character years before the general public. After all, the *Katzenjammer Kids* still seem popular after about half a century![2] And the great thing is that *Joy in the Morning* has sold well. By the way, do keep me posted regularly about the sales. I was delighted with that October jump to 19,950, and I am hoping that by now we are well over the 20,000. What sort of a final total do you anticipate? And do you feel that Jeeves ought to be shelved after thirty years of service? I am now about two-thirds of the way through the Jeeves novel I am working on, and hope to finish it fairly soon.

Best wishes
Yours sincerely
P. G. Wodehouse

1 Shively was one of the editors at Nelson Doubleday, his American publishers.
2 An American comic strip which ran from 1897 to 1912 in the *New York Journal*.

TO WILLIAM TOWNEND

Pavillon Henri Quatre
St Germain-en-Laye
France

Dec 24. 1946

Dear Bill.

[...]

It's curious how life nowadays has got down to simplicities. I mean,

Fame and all that doesn't seem to matter a damn, all that matters is the three square meals a day and light and warmth. Here we are all right for food, in fact extremely well off, though the stuff is very expensive. But every Monday and Tuesday there is no electric light till six in the evening, which means that the heating subsides to nothing, as the apparatus relies on electric current. I have come to the conclusion that the greatest thing in life is gin and Italian vermouth. Every day at 12.30 Ethel mixes me a large bumper and it sends a glow all over my system. I very seldom drink anything else all day, but I do love the moment when the first sip trickles down my throat and I begin to warm up. [...]

I return the Rich and Cowan letter.[1] Of course, the man's dotty. These publishers do think up the darnedest objections to an author's work. [...]

My publisher is not so dotty as yours, but I, too, have had my troubles. In *Joy in the Morning* Bertie speaks of himself as eating a steak and Boko is described as having fried eggs for breakfast, and Grimsdick of Jenkins is very agitated about this, because he says the English public is so touchy about food nowadays that stuff like this will probably cause an uproar. I have changed the fried egg to a sardine and cut out the steak, so I hope all will now be well. But I was reading Agatha Christie's *The Hollow* just now, and the people in it simply gorge roast duck and soufflés and caramel cream and so on, besides having a butler, several parlourmaids, a kitchen maid and a cook. I must say it encouraged me to read *The Hollow* and to see that Agatha was ignoring present conditions in England.

[...]

The interview in *Illustrated* has apparently appeared, as I have had one or two letters about it. I don't want to see it, though, as these interviews always make me sick and upset me for days. So if you come across it, don't send it over!

[...]

Must stop now. Ethel has just come in and wants tea.

Love to Rene

Yours ever

Plum

1 Townend's London publishers.

Pavillon Henri Quatre
St Germain-en-Laye
France

March 29. 1947

My darling Sheran.

Many happy returns of the day. I hope this will reach you on Monday, but you never know nowadays how long letters are going to take. And I hope you have a very happy birthday. I wish I could be with you.

Wonder and I are very lonely without our Bunny. Since she left, I have been going to bed at nine at night! Now that I am alone, I find meals an awful nuisance. [...]

Bunny and I are very excited about getting Low Wood rebuilt. Won't it be lovely when it is fit to live in again and you and Buddy can come over and stay with us. You would love it at Le Touquet. It is an absolute Paradise except that there are ticks in the grass, and some of them are poisonous and kill the dogs. [...]

Tell Bunny that I went to the shop opposite the Bristol Hotel yesterday to have my clothes fitted and they had to take the trousers in an inch and a half because I had got so much thinner since I was last there!! I was very proud of myself. Do you find you have any special temptation in the way of food, which you know you ought not to eat so much of but can't resist? Mine is bread. If it didn't make me fat, I could live on bread. But I am very strong-minded and make myself eat what the French call biscottes, which taste like sawdust but are very good for the figure.

All my love, darling.

Your

Plummie

CHAPTER THIRTEEN

Return to America

On 26 April 1947, *The New York Times* noted the arrival of a 'bald, ruddy-faced author': 'WODEHOUSE HERE, ADMITS MISTAKE', the headline reads. Wodehouse had made his nine-day journey with Ethel on the luxury liner, the *SS America*. Fellow passengers included the musical star Mary Martin, Fred Astaire's mother and 'a thirty-six bell carrillon', a gift for a Presbyterian church in New York.

Back in northern France, a 'circle of ruined houses' surrounded the remains of their Le Touquet home. Bombs had damaged the roof, and scavengers had removed the doors, staircases and baths, 'leaving us just the walls'. The whole of Le Touquet had been badly damaged by bombing, and 'the ruins of the Golf Hotel made me shudder', Wodehouse wrote.[1] The Wodehouses had every reason to move on. But their actual departure from Paris was painfully drawn out. Their passage was initially planned for the autumn of 1946, but once strikes had pushed their journey towards Christmas, Wodehouse decided to settle back down in Paris and attempt to finish *The Mating Season*. In December, it was Ethel's turn to stall. 'My wife', Wodehouse reported to his publisher, 'refuses to sail till she has got some clothes.'[2]

Wodehouse had been extremely worried about his reception in America for some time. He had written to his publishers, Doubleday, earlier in the year, noting that he was 'very uneasy' about the publication of *Joy in the Morning*, and hoped that they 'would take time out to hold my hand'. I 'have the feeling', he wrote, '[i]t will be said that here is a man who is well known to be a Nazi collaborator, and now that the war is over he thinks he can quietly slip back into his former position in America'. 'I am full', he said 'of forebodings.'[3]

To their great relief, the American press were extremely welcoming, and the early months in New York were, for Wodehouse, cheered by a wave of publicity and media attention. Wodehouse had built up a backlog of unpublished novels in his time in Berlin and Paris, and Doubleday began by publicising his sixth Blandings novel, *Full Moon*, with a major press conference and cocktail party. *Spring Fever, Uncle Dynamite* and *The Mating Season* were to follow.

Nevertheless, Wodehouse soon began to feel ill at ease in New York. Despite some initial success with *Cosmopolitan* and *This Week*, he found, for the first time in many years, that his particular brand of short story was being met with rejection. Wodehouse's lawyer tactfully concealed one particular letter from the editor of the *Saturday Evening Post*, which described his writing as 'dated and out of place'.[4] But Wodehouse knew enough to recognise that he was out of step with the current commercial and artistic climate. 'I don't seem able to get the remotest flicker of an idea for any sort of story these days, long or short,' he complained.[5] Magazines rejected his 'English dudes' in favour of 'stodgy grey stuff about life in the swamps of the Deep South'.[6] 'Isn't it extraordinary how the public taste has changed in books and plays', he wrote to Townend. 'At the moment I am exactly in the position of Ukridge, expecting to cash in on my vision and broad outlook, but always with the prospect that the bottom will drop out of everything. I have more or less given up hope of making any money with short stories'.[7]

Although his novels continued to sell well in England, Wodehouse needed the emotional boost of theatrical work. Plans for a production of *Leave It to Psmith* came to nothing, so he turned to his friend Guy Bolton for support. By 1948, he was working with Bolton on three simultaneous productions. The first, *Sally*, was the revival of the 1920 smash hit written with Bolton and Kern. The second, *The Play's the Thing*, was another revival – this time, of Wodehouse's own adaptation of a comedy by Molnár, which had been a hit in 1926. The third, *Don't Listen, Ladies!*, was a translation from a French play by the writer Sacha Guitry. The year 1948 saw him on tour with a straight play, *The House on the Cliff*, starring the actress Fay Bainter. Reliving something of the pace of his writing life in the 1920s, Wodehouse found himself in the far reaches of Skowhegan, Maine, working late into the night on rewrites. By 1949 he was struggling with the script of *Keep Your Head* – an unlikely murder-mystery affair about Burmese headhunters in an English country inn. While *Don't Listen, Ladies!* was a hit in England, none of these works found a widespread success in America, and Wodehouse continued to feel ill at ease in the New York theatrical climate, 'bewildered by the disappearance of the old-time manager'.[8] As he wrote to Townend:

> Over here there is a great demand for gloom and tragedy, which has invaded even the musical play field. Two musicals have just opened and both might have been written by Ibsen in one of his gloomier moods. In the old days we used to worry because 'they' 'hadn't seen the girls' since page twenty of the script, and we would have to twist the plot round so as to bring in a number showing the chorus. In the modern musical show – in America – they don't have any girls. The big moment in one of these musicals is where the heroine – I suppose you would call her – watches her husband die of heart disease, when she could have saved him, because she wants to cash in on his money. It beats me. And look at the terrific success of *Death of a Salesman* and *Streetcar Named Desire*.[9]

Health problems lowered the Wodehouses' mood further. Ethel was becoming exceedingly delicate – and spent a period in hospital with 'bronchial pneumonia'. Wodehouse, meanwhile, experienced mysterious spells of dizziness. Though no serious cause was found, his symptoms concerned doctors and, for a while, a brain tumour was suspected.

Gradually, Wodehouse became accustomed to his New York life and, by 1951, another Blandings novel, *Pigs Have Wings*, was ready for publication. The Wodehouses also enjoyed summer trips to Guy Bolton's house in Remsenburg, Long Island. In 1952, Ethel, with her characteristic impulsiveness, bought a house in Remsenburg that was to provide Wodehouse with a welcome refuge.

This period, for Wodehouse, was one of consolidation rather than intense creativity. Collaboration with Bolton was one way of finding the confidence to keep writing. Adaptation and recycling was another. He turned his friend George Kaufman's 1925 play *The Butter and Egg Man*, into the Broadway novel *Barmy in Wonderland* (1951). An attempt to convert his novel *Spring Fever* into a play was in his words 'a wash out', so he used the drafted play, now changed beyond recognition, to create a new novel, *The Old Reliable*.[10] More consolidation came in the shape of a series of memoirs. *Bring on the Girls*, written with Guy Bolton, was a narrative of reminiscences focusing on his work in the musical theatre of the 1920s. Crucially, 1953 also saw the publication of *Performing Flea*, a collection of Wodehouse's correspondence with William Townend, including extracts from Wodehouse's diaries during internment. The book allowed Wodehouse to explain the issue of the broadcasts – and it was not without success. Critics in England received it well, and the positive reviews of the book were, for Wodehouse, a vindication of sorts, and yet he remained suspicious of the press, and deeply sensitive to criticism. 'My vicissitudes', he reflected, 'must have soured a once sunny nature.'[11]

1 See PGW to Thelma Cazalet-Keir, 18 December 1947 (Wodehouse Archive) and PGW to Billy Griffith, 17 July 1945 (private archive).

2 PGW to Nelson Doubleday, 2 December 1946, quoted in Jasen, p. 205.

3 PGW to Nelson Doubleday, 11 March 1946 (Library of Congress).

4 Ben Hibbs to Watson Washburn, 25 January 1950 (Wodehouse Archive).

5 PGW to Townend, 4 July 1947 (Dulwich).

6 PGW to Hesketh Pearson, 13 December 1947 (Wodehouse Archive).

7 PGW to William Townend, 24 February 1948 (Dulwich).

8 PGW to Elmer Flaccus, 29 June 1947 (private archive).

9 PGW to William Townend, 5 November 1949 (Dulwich).

10 PGW to William Townend, 11 March 1949 (Dulwich).

11 PGW to Thelma Cazalet-Keir, 18 December 1947 (Wodehouse Archive).

1947–1954:
'New York is overwhelming'

BENOÎT DE FONSCOLOMBE[1]

Care of Messrs Doubleday and Co
14 West 49 Street
Rockefeller Center
New York City

May 11. 1947

My dear Fonscolombe.

The above is the best address to give you, as letters sent there will be forwarded to me without delay. (At the moment – till June 1 – we are at the Hotel Weylin, 54 Street and Madison Avenue, but we are trying to get an apartment.)

We had a very nice voyage, though the weather was terrible the first four days and we were two days late. I was besieged by reporters on arrival at Quarantine, but fortunately they liked me and were quite kind in what they wrote, particularly the representative of the evening paper *P.M.* which is strongly Leftist and the paper I was most afraid of. I got on so well with the *P.M.* man that he kept coming round to the hotel for a chat and last Monday gave a big dinner for my wife and me at his home!! He wrote a most friendly article about me, and the whole Press has been excellent, which is a great relief.

[...]

New York is overwhelming. It seems twice the size it used to be. Living conditions here are fantastically luxurious. Mountains of food everywhere. It is as if there had never been a war. And everything, of course, terribly expensive. [. . .] Fortunately, owing to the fact that the U. S. Government are refunding most of the $40,000 which they seized when they were suing me for unpaid income tax, we have plenty to be going on with, and no doubt we shall get something cheaper later on.

All good wishes to you and Madame and the family

Yours sincerely
P. G. Wodehouse

1 Fonscolombe was Wodehouse's French translator and friend.

TO WILLIAM TOWNEND

Hotel Weylin
54 St and Madison Avenue
New York City

May 11. 1947

Dear Bill.

[...]

Well, sir, my visit to N.Y. has proved a sensational triumph. [...]

On the second morning in N.Y. I held a formal 'Press Conference' – no less! – at the Doubleday offices, with a candid camera man taking surreptitious photographs all the time. (I hadn't a notion that I had ever looked as I did in the one I enclose, but I suppose I must have done.) Everybody was wonderfully cordial – they were the literary columnists this time – and I am going to a cocktail party at the house of one of them next week.

On Wednesday I was interviewed on the radio, reaching three hundred and fifty stations. I wrote the interview myself and made it as funny as I could, and it was a terrific success, so they tell me. I confined myself to funny cracks about New York and my books, making no mention of the broadcasts (which nobody seems a dam bit interested in here). It really was rather good. Several big laughs. Ethel was listening in the control room and was quivering with nervousness, but she was delighted with the thing and told me I had been fine. So that was all right.

[...]

I'm writing a devil of a lot about myself, but I know you will want to hear how it all came out. Final Score – everything in the garden lovely [...] New York is simply incredible. About five times larger than it was when I last saw it, and more bustling than ever. I said in my radio talk that every time I came back to New York, it was like meeting an old sweetheart and finding she has put on a lot of weight.

[...] I really must stop. Love to Rene.

Yours ever

Plum

---

53 East 66 Street
New York City

May 31. 1947

My dear Waugh.

I can't tell you how much I appreciated your letter. It really was good of you to write as you did.

I never see the London papers and don't subscribe to a press clipping agency, so I knew nothing of what had been appearing over there. I gather from what you say that brickbats have been flying about once more, though I had hoped that the brickbat season was over. But I don't care what the papers say, so long as people like you are on my side.

[...]

An amusing thing has just happened. I find that the War Department here were using my broadcasts as samples of <u>anti-Nazi propaganda</u> throughout the war at the U.S. Army Intelligence School at Camp Ritchie[1]. This would seem to show that there was nothing subversive in them.

One of the horrors of war, as far as I was concerned, was that until now I was unable to get hold of *Brideshead Revisited*. I have now got it, and am looking forward to the joy I always get from your books. I do hope you are busy on another. If you aren't... well, I can always re-read the old ones, which I do about once every six months, enjoying them just as much as the first time.

Best wishes, and again thank you a thousand times for your letter.

Yours ever

P. G. Wodehouse

1 On hearing that Wodehouse was making this 'suggestion', MI5 investigated, and claimed that 'the truth is precisely the opposite'. See letter of 29 August 1947, names of correspondents redacted, LO 2/1166 (PRO).

53 East 66 Street
New York City

June 6. 1947

Dear Bill.

[...]

Both Ethel and I have been depressed lately and wondering how long we can go on living in New York. I am hoping this will pass off and we shall settle down. One thing is, it ought to be nice and cool in the apartment. We have a roof and have bought roof furniture. It certainly seems quite cool up here when it is hot down in the street. I think I shall be all right when I get working again. My trouble is a lack of ideas. A woman's magazine turned down one of my golf stories but sent a gushing letter saying that they were dying to have a story from me, so I want to think out a comic love story. But nothing stirring yet. I have also got to do an article for *Town and Country* on any subject I like, and so far have been unable to think of anything.[1] But I imagine all this will clear up soon. The nuisance is that my mornings are so broken. Wonder always wants to go for her walk at about eleven, which makes it impossible to get any work done.

Another thing which is rather preying on my nerves is the theatrical situation. I miss the old-time manager, who seems to have completely disappeared. In the old days I would pop in on Flo Ziegfeld and find that he wanted lyrics for a new show, and then call on Dillingham and get a contract for a musical comedy, but all that is over now. As far as I can make out, you have to write your show and then go about trying to interest people with money in it. *Leave It to Psmith* seems all set for a Fall production, but I believe my manager has only got $50,000 so far of the $85,000 which he needs. But he seems confident of getting the rest.

[...]

Must stop now. Lunch. Love to Rene. Send me cricket news when you write.

Yours ever

Plum

1 *Town and Country* for October 1947 carried PGW's article 'They'll Go No More a' Buttling'

Wodehouse was scrupulous about answering all his fan mail. Mr Summers,
Wodehouse's correspondent in the following letter, was a fan who wrote, as
so many did, asking about sources of inspiration for his fiction.

TO MR SUMMERS

53 East 66 Street
New York City

Aug 12. 1947

Dear Mr Summers.

With most of my stories your question 'How did you come to write
it?' would be a hard one to answer, but it so happens that 'All's Well
With Bingo' was based on an experience of my own and I can remember
the various steps which led to the assembling of the material.[1] I was
in the Casino at Le Touquet one night, wandering about and occasionally risking a small sum at one of the tables, and zero came up when
I was backing Black, and at the same moment I happened to get into
conversation with someone, and it was only some time later that I
observed a pile of counters on Black and realized that they were mine.
My gratification at scooping in the stuff was heightened by the immediate realization that I had got the core of a story.

Obviously, the hero's gambling would have to be on a larger and
more important scale than mine, so I started hunting around for a
means of heightening the drama. This soon led me to Bingo Little
and Mrs Bingo, and everything fell into shape without any trouble.
Feeling that the drama could stand still another shot in the arm, I
tried to think of something that would make the winning of the money
vital to Bingo, and hit on the bookie stuff. And so on.

My stories don't usually come out that way. As a rule, I start by
saying to myself that I will write a story about one of my characters
and then sit and hold my head till I have found what happened to

him. But this one started with a scene and I worked from that. That way of composition is much easier, but the trouble is you have to have the 'scene', and it is not often that 'scenes' drop out of a blue sky. In fact, the only other one I can remember in my books is the bit in *A Damsel in Distress* (if anyone remembers *A Damsel in Distress*, which I doubt) where the girl jumps into the hero's taxi and he has to hide her.

The thing that makes writers of humorous stories pick at the coverlet is the haunting fear that they have overlooked something and laid themselves open to the question 'Well, if your hero was in this jam, why didn't he do so-and-so?', the inference being that, if he had, there would have been no story. But in 'All's Well With Bingo' I think that, given that Bingo could not simply draw himself to his full height and defy his wife, the thing hangs together.

Best wishes

Yours sincerely

P. G. Wodehouse

1 'All's Well with Bingo' was published in the *S.E.P.* on 30 January 1937 and in the *Strand* issue of April 1937. It was included in the short-story collection *Eggs, Beans and Crumpets* in the UK and in *Crime Wave at Blandings* in America.

Following the death of his long-standing American agent, Paul Reynolds, Wodehouse instructed Scott Meredith, an American who had supported him during the war, to be his agent.

TO WILLIAM TOWNEND

53 East 66 St
New York City

Sept 22. 1947

Dear Bill.

[...]

Scott Meredith hasn't reported anything yet about your stories (nor about mine, incidentally). I rather gather there is a temporary slump in the magazine world – in fact, a man told me last night that *Collier's* might fold up at any moment and the *S.E.P.* wasn't doing any too well!! – and this makes stuff hard to sell. My only immediate source of income seems to be the Kleenex people. They used Jeeves in several of their advertisements, and my lawyer is convinced that we can sting them for at least $1000! [See plate 36.]

[...]

I think that Jew novel you are planning sounds awfully good. Aren't the Jews extraordinary people. They seem to infuriate all nations, as nations, and yet almost every individual has a number of Jewish friends. I was totting up the other day and found that, apart from my real inner circle of friends (numbering about three) most of the men I like best are Jews – e.g. Scott Meredith, Ira Gershwin, Lengyel, Molnar, Oscar Hammerstein, Irving Berlin... and a lot more. But, my gosh, what idiots the British Government are. At the very moment when it is vital to have good relations with America they go and pull that Exodus stuff and club Jews and put them behind barbed wire and so on. I should have thought it would have been infinitely better to let the poor devils into Palestine. That trouble at Hamburg has simply played into the hands of the anti-English here. But officials in every country are always dumb bricks.[1]

[...]

The book trade here is in a bad way. When you look at the things they publish, it seems quite natural that it should be. I haven't come across anything good yet. All the novels seem to be about negroes or drunkards. No good to me.

I was very interested in the clipping about Bailey.[2] He seems to be the coming man. A good fast bowler who is also a fine bat ought to walk into any English side. How extraordinary about that 20,000 crowd being shut out of Lord's. [...] By the way, how many old colours will Dulwich have at footer this year? Reading the characters in the *Alleynian*, I totted it up at thirteen survivors of last season's unbeaten side. Can this be right? If so, we ought to slay the opposition.

I think you certainly ought to have that operation on your legs. It sounds as if it would put you right. I am enclosing a cheque which will cover it, with love to you both.

Must stop now. Lunch.

Yours ever

Plum

1 The *Exodus 1947* sailed from France in July 1947 bound for British-controlled Palestine, with over 4,500 Jewish passengers, most of whom were Holocaust survivors. Many were without legal immigration certificates. The British Navy intercepted the ship off the coast of Palestine and boarded it forcefully; two passengers and one of the crew were killed and others injured. The British Government then deported the passengers to Europe – first to France and then to Hamburg (which was then in the British occupation zone), where they were placed in a number of camps.

2 Trevor Bailey (1923–2011), England Test cricketer, writer and broadcaster, deemed to have been 'one of England's most outstanding post-war all-rounders'. Bailey attended Dulwich College from 1937 to 1942 and began playing for the 1st XI aged fourteen, going on to captain the 1st XI side of 1941–2. He had recently (in July) played for the Gentlemen at Lord's, in the Gentlemen v. Players match.

TO WILLIAM TOWNEND

Hotel Adams
2 East 86 Street
New York City

Nov. 15. 1947

Dear Bill.

[...]

First about this place. It has turned out a terrific success. Before we moved in, Ethel said that my bedroom was too small for me to work in. I don't know what gave her that impression, as it is quite large, so much so that I have at last got a decent size desk. [...] We are on the 17th floor, so we get a magnificent view. [...]

[...] [T]here has been an annoying lull in my activities. I have three plays going the rounds, one of my own and two adaptations, but nothing has clicked yet. And I can't get going with the magazines. I am in the extraordinary position that New York is full of editors who want my stuff, but they are all editors of women's magazines and my stories lack the 'woman angle', whereas editors of magazines like *Collier's* and the *Post*, for which my stories would be suitable, object to me personally and won't have any dealings with me. [...]

As a matter of fact, I doubt if *Collier's* and *Post* editors would take my work even if they were friendly, as their whole policy seems to have changed. To me the change seems to consist of the fact that they now print nothing but tripe. [...]

Yours

Plum

TO WILLIAM TOWNEND

2 East 86 Street

New York

Feb 24. 1948

Dear Bill.

The *Strand*s and your letter with the Billy Griffith clippings arrived this morning. Thanks so much for sending them. It was the first I had heard of Billy's triumph and I was delighted. I can't imagine anything that would please him more and, as they say over here, it couldn't have happened to a nicer guy.[1]

But listen. What <u>has</u> happened to English cricket? I had to read that line about 'his captain, Gubby Allen' twice before I could realize that I hadn't misread it. It was almost as if it had been C. J. Kortright or N. A. Knox.[2] Gubby Allen's last year at Eton was 1920, so he must have been at least 18 then. If the man isn't 46, my arithmetic is at fault. Is my Motherland trying to tell me that it can't dig out a fast bowler who isn't on his way to fifty? It's appalling. What on earth is going to happen next year when the Australians come over with a team including at least nine men capable of making double centuries? The second clipping, with the West Indies score of 160 or whatever it was for no wickets, made me shudder. If the West Indies can murder us like that, the Australians will have to play lefthanded. It's awful. The only bright spot is that it looks as if they would have to play Billy as first wicket-keeper now.

[...]

I haven't seen Lucille Ball, though of course I know her name well.[3] I loved Cynthia [*sic*] Johnson in *Brief Encounter*.[4] But the girl I love is June Allyson.[5] Have you seen *Good News*? She's charming.

[...]
Must stop now. Got to take Wonder for a walk.

Love to Rene

Yours ever

Plum

1 'Billy' Griffith had been selected as wicketkeeper on the tour of West Indies over the winter of 1947/48. In the test match at Port of Spain, he also played as makeshift opening batsman and became the first (and only) England player to make his first century in first-class cricket on his Test debut, making 140 in the first innings.

2 G. O. B. ('Gubby') Allen had played for England from 1930 onwards, and captained England for the last time against the West Indies at the age of forty-five. Kortright had captained Essex in 1903 and Knox, a contemporary of Wodehouse's at Dulwich, played for England in 1907.

3 Lucille Ball (1911–89), American actress, comedian and television star. Ball began acting in the 1930s, earning the nickname Queen of the Bs for her roles in B-movies in the 1940s, and going on to star in the popular TV series I Love Lucy in the 1950s.

4 Celia Johnson (1908–82), British actress who starred in the 1945 film Brief Encounter.

5 June Allyson (1917–2006), American actress who had been in the 1946 film Till the Clouds Roll By, the supposed biography of Jerome Kern.

TO SHERAN CAZALET

2 East 86 Street
New York.

March 28. 1948

Darling Sheran,

Many happy returns of the day. Bunny sent you some chocolates not long ago. I hope they arrive on your birthday. [...]

I am very busy these days, as I have two shows in rehearsal. One, *The Play's the Thing*, is a straight show and opens next Thursday at New Haven. The other, *Sally*, which is a musical, ought to have opened months ago, but we have a loony management and it has been one long muddle. However, we have at last started rehearsing with quite a good cast, though quite different from the one we were supposed to have and we are supposed to open in New Haven on April 22. (It says in the papers April 16, but we can't possibly get ready by then.) It's very funny going from one rehearsal to the other. At *The Play's the*

Thing everything is very hushed and quiet and then I look in at the *Sally* rehearsal and find eight boys and twenty girls dancing their heads off with those metal things on the soles of their shoes which make such a noise. I was there for three hours yesterday and came away exhausted. Both shows look as if they might be successes, and of course they ought to be, because they both <u>were</u> years ago. *Sally* ran for seven hundred performances in New York in 1921 and *The Play's the Thing* for 300 in 1926. So I am hoping for the best!

[...] I can't read any of the magazines except the *New Yorker*, and that has suddenly got deadly dull. I am reduced to English mystery stories and my own stuff. I was reading *Blandings Castle* again yesterday and was lost in admiration for the brilliance of the author. I'm so glad Buddy is reading *Leave It to Psmith*.

[...]

Lots of love to you all

Yours ever

Plummie

TO GUY BOLTON

2 East 86 St
New York

May 15. 1948

Dear Guy.

[...]

Sally. I have just been to the matinee. Upstairs packed. Downstairs sold out except for the last couple of rows. (Incidentally, I looked in at *The Play's the Thing* and their downstairs wasn't as good as *Sally*'s). I think business is a bit quiet everywhere just now and complete sell-outs confined to *Mr. Roberts* and *Streetcar*.[1] I went to the Martin Beck for the Wednesday matinee and the Thursday night show. Wednesday matinee was about two-thirds full. Thursday almost sold out downstairs, but thin upstairs. This, I think, was due to the fact that it had pelted with rain all day. (Miss Nicholson told me that our Thursday house was as good as any other show in town.)

The encouraging thing on all these occasions was the reception. They yelled every time Willie Howard opened his mouth. [...]

[...]

Love to Virginia.

Yours ever

Plum

1 *A Streetcar Named Desire* (1947), by American playwright Tennessee Williams. Williams received the Pulitzer Prize for Drama in 1948 for *Streetcar*. The play opened on Broadway in December 1947 and ran for 855 performances, closing in December 1949. *Mister Roberts*, a 1948 hit play based on a 1946 novel of the same name by Thomas Heggan, was adapted by Heggan and Joshua Logan.

A great Wodehouse admirer, the novelist Lawrence Durrell went on to model his Antrobus stories on the Mulliner series.

TO LAWRENCE DURRELL

2 East 86 St
New York

May 19. 1948

Dear Mr. Durrell.

Thank you so much for your letter. [...]

Yes, Jeeves certainly came quite by accident. His first appearance was in a Bertie Wooster story called 'Disentangling Old Duggie' and all he did was to appear in the doorway and announce 'Mrs Travers, sir'. It never occurred to me at the time that he would ever do anything except appear at doors and announce people. Then – I don't think it was the next Bertie story but the one after that – I had got Bertie's friend into a bad tangle of some sort and I saw how to solve the problem but my artistic soul revolted at the idea of having Bertie suggest the solution. It would have been absolutely out of character. Then who? For a long time I was baffled, and then I suddenly thought 'Why not make Jeeves a man of brains and ingenuity and have him do it?' After that, of course, it was all simple and the stories just rolled out one after the other.

I only once did an actual Jeeves series. The earlier stories were dotted at long intervals over about five years. I now find it more congenial to use the long novel form. It gives so much more scope than the short story.

I couldn't say that Jeeves ever had an actual model. I suppose I had the stage butler type in my mind when I started, and then, as always happens, he began to develop individuality.

Yes, I had always heard that Doyle grew to loathe Holmes. I have never had any feeling of that sort about Jeeves. I love him and all I ask is for a constant supply of 'Jeeves' ideas. Actually, I prefer my Blandings Castle stories to the Jeeves stories, but I have a very good time writing the latter. I think Lord Emsworth is my favourite character. But Jeeves runs him very close.

I wish you would send me one of your books. I am an old Faber and Faber man myself. (*Louder and Funnier*, published by them ages ago and now so emphatically out of print that I had to pay £5 to get a copy the other day.)

Best wishes

Yours sincerely

P. G. Wodehouse

TO WILLIAM TOWNEND

2 East 86 Street
New York

June 5. 1948

[...]

What a shame you should have got such a bad jacket for *The Fingal's Passenger*. I haven't seen any of the Jenkins copies of my post-war books, but the Doubleday *Spring Fever* jacket is awful and the illustrations even worse. The whole plot you might say turns on Lord Shortlands looking like a butler, and this blighter has drawn him with a walrus moustache.

I am getting about as fed up with Doubleday as you are with Rich and Cowan, who do seem to be a weird crowd.[1] Can't Watt do something to stir them up? [...] Which brings me to the subject of the Jews. Bill, what is the matter with those birds over in England, the Cabinet, I mean? America is simply seething with fury at their attitude about Israel. I can understand that there must be very bitter feeling against the Jews after those outrages in Palestine, but to chuck away Anglo-American friendship as they are doing seems to me simply cuckoo. [2] All the influential writers here like Winchell are Jewish, and they are pouring out poison every day against England.[3] There are probably twenty million Americans who think just as Winchell tells them to think. I believe there is quite a serious boycott of English goods now, and heaven knows where it will end. Just a spot of tact on the part of Bevin and Co would have solved everything, but this damned Labour Government just goes ahead and alienates everybody. Oh, well.

Personally, I have always got on splendidly with Jews. I like them. Of course, in the New York theatre world I meet the nicest ones. You couldn't want better chaps than fellows like Irving Berlin, Oscar Hammerstein, Ira Gershwin, Arthur Schwartz etc.

What a wretched thing failure in the theatre is. There isn't a single dramatist from Shakespeare downwards who hasn't had the most ghastly flops, but one never gets over that feeling of pollution you get when you are associated with a bad failure. Poor old *Sally* is on the rocks and I shouldn't be surprised to find that it doesn't open on Monday. Everything went wrong with it. Idiotic management, actors without personality etc. [...] It's a great consolation to have *The Play's the Thing* such a success.

I do hope Rene is all right again now. Ethel's knee seems almost well again, thank goodness.

Yours ever

Plum

1 Townend's London publishers.
2 In 1947, a UN Partition Plan had been instituted, rejecting the idea of a divided Israel and declaring that 'Jew shall not dominate Arab and Arab shall not dominate Jew in Palestine'. Truman, and the American Government, refused to support this statement, instead wanting the Jewish communities in Palestine to have more protection. In response to this conflict with America, the British Government declared its desire to withdraw from the Mandate of Palestine, which had included certain provisions for the protection of Jewish rights in Palestine, and the situation was handed over to the United Nations. The UN voted in favour of creating independent Arab and Jewish nations.

The British Government accepted the plan, but refused to enforce it, and withdrew its Mandate earlier than expected, leaving the region in a position of instability.
3 Walter Winchell, American journalist and radio commentator.

By June, Wodehouse and Bolton began to feel uneasy about potential bad publicity concerning their forthcoming London production of Don't Listen, Ladies! *The play's original author, Sacha Guitry, was a known Nazi collaborator.*

TO GUY BOLTON

2 East 86 St
New York

June 17. 1948

Dear Guy.

[...]

[T]he Paramount guy, didn't think there would be any trouble about putting on a play by Guitry. On the other hand, there <u>is</u> a strong anti-Guitry feeling in many quarters.

[...]

Did I tell you in my last letter that Ethel was in a stick-up? I don't think I did. She was being fitted at her dressmaker's on Madison Avenue and a young man came in with a knife and threw his weight about, collecting fifteen bucks from Ethel and twenty from Francie de Moreuil. The big laugh was that Ethel had put her diamond clips on the table and Francie officiously had taken them and put them in Ethel's bag. So when Ethel gaily produced her bag, thinking it contained only $15, she nearly fainted when she saw the clips. Luckily the man overlooked them, so all was well. But really life isn't safe in this city.

[...]

Must stop now, Lunch.

Love to Virginia

Yours ever

Plum

2 East 86 Street
New York

July 17. 1948

[...]

[A] couple of good stories: –

(a) Clergyman doing crossword puzzle. Clue 'Appertaining to the female sex'. He has got the last letters all right . . . u. n. t. He consults another clergyman, who says the word is 'aunt'. 'Ah, yes, of course', says the first clergyman. 'Would you mind lending me your eraser for a moment, my dear fellow.'

(b) Big advertising firm is approached to handle a suppository. They like the prospect of the business, but their policy has always been to have a slogan for everything they handle. How to get a slogan for this depository [*sic*]? They offer a prize in the office and the office boy wins it with

Jones's Suppository
YOU KNOW WHAT YOU CAN DO WITH IT

[...]

Yours ever
Plum

In August, Ethel sailed for Europe to visit her grandchildren, and to investigate the sale of Low Wood in Le Touquet. Wodehouse had planned to go with her, but by August he had decided against it, arguing that the pressure of work seemed too great: 'things are hotting up too much here', he wrote to Guy Bolton. Ethel was to spend the winter months in Paris, 'wrestling with our furniture'. Wodehouse, meanwhile, felt 'very lost without her'.

2 East 86 St
New York

Sept 4. 1948

Dear Guy.

[...]

I can hardly wait to hear about the opening. Have the libraries made a deal? Was there any booing of Guitry? It must have been nervous work watching the show.

No more now. Love to Virginia

Yours ever

Plum

---

2 East 86 St
New York

Sept 17. 1948

Dear Guy.

[...]

A film by Sacha Guitry has just been produced here.[1] The notices were mixed, but the cheering thing is that not one of them referred to his war record. They accepted him as a pre-war Guitry.

[...]

1 *The Lame Devil.*

2 East 86 Street
New York

Oct 24. 1948

[...]

In about four hours from now I shall be going through a ghastly ordeal, – viz. being televised. The man who is running it got hold of me just after my broadcast from Sardi's Restaurant, when I was feeling so happy that that was over that I was willing to agree to anything. He swears that it won't really be an ordeal. There is a very well known artist here named Rube Goldberg and he apparently draws pictures and we – the guests – have to guess what they are. I shan't be alone, thank goodness. There will be four guests including me, one of them Gypsy Rose Lee, the famous stripteaser!!! One good thing is that I can bring Wonder.

[...]

TO GUY BOLTON

2 East 86 St
New York

Nov 11. 1948

Dear Guy
[...]
I've discovered another gem in Keats. As follows: –

When wedding fiddles are a-playing
Huzza for folly O!
And when maidens go a-maying
Huzza etc
When Sir Snap is with his lawyer
Huzza etc
And Miss Chip has kissed the sawyer,
Huzza etc.[1]

Well John, I'll tell you. It's got the mucus, but it needs a lot of work.[2]

Love to Va.

Yours ever

Plum

1 John Keats, 'Extracts from an Opera' (1818).
2 During his time in Hollywood, working for MGM, PGW had come to know the
Polish-born Sam Goldwyn, whose many linguistic errors were infamous. Goldwyn
had reportedly said of a show starring Jessica Tandy, 'with Tandy in it, that play's got
the mucus'. PGW used the line in 'The Castaways' (*The Strand*, June 1933), where
Mr Schnellenhamer says of *Scented Sinners*: 'It has the mucus of a good story.'

TO GUY BOLTON

2 East 86 St
New York

Nov 24. 1948

Dear Guy.

Your letter of Nov 16, written at rehearsal, was full of good cheer. The company sounds splendid. [...]

The thing that is worrying me stiff now is the possibility of you all not being able to sail on Dec 9 because of this damned dock strike. I never know the rights or wrongs of these blasted strikes. All I know is that the blighters are bitching everything up and probably ruining the Marshall Plan.[1] I can't understand why somebody doesn't do something and settle it. I'll bet you or I could fix it in ten minutes. I am torn between a feeling that anyone who works shifting baggage around on a pier deserves all the money he can get and a sort of growing bias in favour of slavery. What this country wants is about five million robots (Good title for a play – *Mister Robots*), who would do all the dirty jobs.[2]

[...]

I'm thrilled about all the shows you have got lined up for us and the tame managements. I am sweating like blazes to clear up all outstanding work, so as to be ready when you want to start. I am rewriting that *Spring Fever* play of mine for the fourth time, and this time it looks as if it might turn out reasonably good. I test everything by your maxim 'Never give the audience too much to think about at one time', and it's extraordinary what a touchstone it is.

I take it you will come back with the company. I shall meet you at the pier and immediately start to discuss Shelley with you. Entirely on account of the many plugs you have given Percy Bysshe, I went out and blew three dollars on a book containing all his poems and Keats's, and I want you to tip me off as to which are his winners. I have always liked 'Epipsychidion' and 'Ozymandias', but last night I tackled 'The Revolt of Islam' and it was like being beaten over the head with a sandbag. I'm afraid I have got one of those second rate minds, because, while I realize that Shelley is in the Shakespeare and Milton class, I much prefer Tennyson, who isn't.

Incidentally, what lousy prose Shelley wrote. I do hate the way people wrote in those days. 'It is an experiment on the temper of the public mind, as to how far a thirst for a happier condition of moral and political society survives, among the enlightened and refined, the tempests which have shaken the age in which we live. I have sought to enlist the harmony of metrical language, the ethereal combinations of the fancy, the rapid and subtle transitions of human passion, all those elements which essentially compose a Poem, in the cause of a liberal and comprehensive morality.' Block those double adjectives, Perce!

Why will people collect ALL a poet's work into a volume instead of burying the bad stuff? It's a nasty jar, after reading 'The Nightingale', to come on the following little effort of Keats: –

There was a naughty boy,
And a naughty boy was he,
He kept little fishes
In washing tubs three
In spite
Of the might
Of the maid
Nor afraid
Of his Granny-good –
He often would

Hurly burly
Get up early. . .[3]

I can see Keats shoving that one away in a drawer and saying to himself 'Thank God no one will ever see <u>that</u> baby!'. And then along comes some damned fool and publishes it.

So long. Love to Virginia.

Yours ever

Plum

1 PGW refers to an eighteen-day strike of longshoremen along the Atlantic seaboard. The strike – the first in the history of the American Federation of Labor dock union – began unofficially on 10 November and ended later that month.
2 Wodehouse here puns on the Broadway success, *Mister Roberts*.
3 Keats' 'A Song about Myself', probably written for his sister in 1818.

TO SHERAN CAZALET

2 E. 86 St
New York

Jan 13. 1949

My darling Sheran.

How clever you are! The day before your parcel came I was in a tobacco shop on Madison Avenue saying to the shop girl that the only tobacco I really liked was Bondman and couldn't she get me some. And then your tins arrived! Thank you ever so much. I am smoking some of it now as I write.

You will probably have heard that *Don't Listen, Ladies!* was a terrible flop in New York. Everything was against it and the management put the lid on it by raising the curtain twenty minutes late on the opening night, thus putting the audience in a mood where they wouldn't have liked it if it had been *Oklahoma* and *Annie Get Your Gun* rolled into one. The only bright spot is that we would have had to close the London production because Francis Lister is down with double pneumonia and we couldn't get anybody good in his place, and now Jack Buchanan is flying to London and will open on Monday. I believe your Daddy doesn't think much of Jack, but he is a tremendous draw in London, so business will probably boom.

I have just finished the fourth version of a play I started in 1946, and I really do think it's good now.[1] I have sent it to the man who starred in *The Play's the Thing* over here. If he likes it, any management will put it on. Meanwhile, Guy Bolton has arrived with plans for three London shows! So I shall be kept busy.

[...]

Bunny sails back on the Queen Mary on the 19th. She will have been away exactly five months. It will be a great day when we have her back. I don't believe Wonder has missed her at all. I don't think dogs can count, and so long as one of [us] is with her it is the same as if we both were. But she will go mad when she does see her mother. She and I have been inseparable all these months. I have never left her alone for a minute. It has meant that I have never been able to go out at night, but it has been worth it to keep her happy.

Love to everybody and thank you again for the lovely tobacco.

Yours ever

Plummie

1 This was the play that began as the novel *Spring Fever*, and was to become the novel *The Old Reliable* (1951; serialised in *Collier's* from June to July 1950 as *Phipps to the Rescue*).

TO WILLIAM TOWNEND

2 East 86 St
New York

Jan 15. 1949

Dear Bill.

I am looking forward to getting *Fool's Gold*. I wonder how it is doing. Well, I hope. Meanwhile, I have sent you – at enormous expense. Four dollars, no less – a book that has headed the American best seller lists for months, *The Naked and the Dead*. I can't give you a better idea of how things have changed over here than by submitting that book to your notice. It's good, mind you, – in fact, I found it absorbing – but isn't it incredible that you can print in a book nowadays stuff which when we were young was found only on the walls of public lavatories. [...]

The running mate of this book is a thing called *The Young Lions*, about the war in Germany, and I found it dull.[1] A curious thing about American books these days is that so many of them are Jewish propaganda. Notice in *The Naked and the Dead* how the only decent character is Goldstein. *The Young Lions* is the same. It is a curious trend. The Jews have suddenly become terrifically vocal. Did you see that picture, *Gentleman's Agreement*? I am wondering if that book of yours about Jews might not do well over here. If you will send me a script, I will see what I can do with it.

Incidentally, do you think old Pop Bevin has the remotest idea of the storm he is kicking up here with his anti-Israelism?[2]

[...]

Poor little Wonder woke me up the night before last at one-thirty, crying and restless, and kept me up all the rest of the night. So yesterday I took her to the vet, where she will be till at least Monday. The vet says her teeth want seeing to again. It's awful being without her, and she does loathe going to the vet's so much, though the vet assures me she has settled down and is not fretting. She had been constipated for two days, and she is getting a thorough cleaning out, which ought to put her right. But she's twelve and a half, and I have the feeling that she can't last much longer.

Talking of age, do you feel that your trouble is that you aren't so <u>keen</u> as you used to be? That is what is wrong with me. I simply can't make myself sit down and write a short story, because I have lost all my zest for it. I am still keen on novels and plays, which is a comfort. But there seems something so silly in writing a short story for a magazine. *Uncle Dynamite* is doing very well over here. Marvellous reviews. (I don't know how much they matter.)

[...]

I'm terribly sorry to hear poor Rene has been having trouble with her eyes. I do hope she is better now.

Yours ever

Plum

1 *The Young Lions*, a 1948 novel by American writer Irwin Shaw (1913–84), which follows the lives of three soldiers in the Second World War. Shaw was born Irwin Gilbert Shamforoff to Russian-Jewish immigrants, and one of the three main characters in *The Young Lions* is also Jewish. *The Young Lions*, seen as a rival to Mailer's *The Naked and the Dead*, quickly became a bestseller.

2 Ernest Bevin (1881–1951), a British Labour politician who became Foreign Secretary in 1945. Bevin was criticised for his handling of the situation in the Middle East at this time, particularly for some perceived anti-Semitism.

TO WILLIAM TOWNEND

1000 Park Avenue
New York

Nov 5. 1949

Dear Bill.

[...]

I often brood on your position as a writer as compared with what it ought to be. I can't see, for instance, why Conrad is looked on as a sort of magician while you don't get reviewed. And I believe it's because you have never sought publicity in any form. Do you realize that you have written thirty-odd books without... as far as I know... your photograph ever having appeared in a paper? And you have never mixed with the literary gang. These writers who get reviewed are fellows who hang around the Authors Club and all that sort of thing. I think that in the long run your method is the best. Though of course a sedulous pusher can boost himself quite a bit. I always look on Hugh Walpole as the supreme pusher of all time. Of course he had the goods to a certain extent, but two thirds of his position in the world of letters was due to his never letting up for an instant in the great push. You have to be a certain – rather loathsome – type of man to conduct a lifelong campaign of that sort. I wouldn't do it for anything. But then I couldn't make a speech, and making speeches is the principal factor in boosting yourself. If you were a different sort of man – thank goodness you aren't! – you would be racing all over the country addressing women's clubs and so on and lecturing on life at sea. I don't see how these chaps ever find time to write anything, and as a matter of fact they don't. Look at Ian Hay. He would have done much better to sit on his bot and turn out the stuff instead of wasting his time giving the prizes at a school in Devonshire on Monday and dashing off to lecture in Edinburgh on Tuesday and so on.

[...]

I join you in gasping over the 75,000 sale of Nancy Mitford's *Love in a Cold Climate*. It is selling enormously here as well, and I can't understand why. It's dirty, of course, and the modern public, especially in America, loves dirt, but I thought it was dull. Wasn't that house party ghastly! Of course, Nancy Mitford probably knows everybody, and I should imagine that a lot of her characters are real people, and that always boosts sales. But, my gosh, what a book!

[...]

Must stop now. Lunch.

Love to Rene

Yours ever

Plum

TO WILLIAM TOWNEND

1000 Park Avenue
New York

Nov 16. 1949

Dear Bill.

Sorry to trouble you again, but just cast an eye on enclosed. If you don't swoon when you read it, you're a better man than I am, Gunga Din.[1]

The first thing that attracts our attention is that old Brook[2] is marrying an Earl's daughter: the second, that neither he nor the bride (nor, I suppose, the Earl) have a bean. We then go on to the fact that old Brook seems to expect to earn a living on the stage, never – so far as know – having appeared on the boards, even in a Number 3 touring company.[3] Finally, we get the ages. Brook must be 67, and she is 30. It absolutely beats me. What on earth does a man of sixty-seven want to marry for? And what is the attraction in old Brook? If he were even fifty, I could understand it, because he always had lots of sex appeal, but, my God, at his present age!![4]

Still, there it is. What a weird life he has had. You could make a novel out of it, but it is beyond me. Incidentally, if the Oil can afford to run Naworth Castle, surely he can support old Brook.

I shall look forward to getting your comments on this strange affair. By the way, do you gather from his letter that he proposes to come to America? I hope to God not. I can just manage to get by with only Ethel, Wonder and Squeaky to support. I simply can't finance old Brook and Lady Caroline Westbrook.

[...]

This isn't supposed to be a letter. I just wanted to send you Brook's dossier.

Love to Rene.

Yours ever

Plum

1 Rudyard Kipling's 1892 poem 'Gunga Din' finds frequent mention in Wodehouse's work. See *Three Men and a Maid*, *The Clicking of Cuthbert* and *Jeeves and the Feudal Spirit*.
2 Herbert Westbrook.
3 A company that mainly played at theatres in small market towns and the suburbs.
4 Westbrook had announced his engagement to Lady Carolyn Bridget Dacre Howard. She was, at thirty-one years old, forty years his junior. A marriage was not forthcoming.

TO DENIS MACKAIL

1000 Park Avenue
New York

Nov 18. 1949

Dear Denis.
I wish to God I could be with you. I feel so utterly helpless all these miles away.

Your letter arrived this morning, and my heart sank when I read that the doctor held out no hope, but I tried to make myself believe that he was mistaken and this afternoon a letter came from Townend saying that our darling Diana was dead.

I don't know how to go on. Words seem so futile and I am afraid that nothing I can say can be much good, but I do think it helps a little when you have had an awful blow to know that the people who love you are thinking of you.

Ethel is upstairs writing to you now. She is heartbroken. She loved Diana as much as I did. You two were always our dearest friends. I can hardly realize even now that I shall never see Diana again. She was always so wonderful. I can remember little things about her and things she said all through the years since we first met.

I'm afraid this ghastly thing will have knocked you out completely, and I imagine you are feeling that you will never be able to write again or want to write. But you have always had such wonderful courage that I am sure you come through even this.

I won't say any more. It's hopeless to try to put down on paper what one is feeling. This is just to tell you that we are thinking of you all the time.

Yours ever

Plum

TO WILLIAM TOWNEND

1000 Park Avenue
New York

June 22. 1950

Dear Bill.

I feel very remorseful, not having written to you for so long. I have been tied up with a gruelling job of work, the rewriting of that show, *The House on the Cliff*, which I have spoken of in my letters. [...] Fay Bainter herself is a darling. Have you seen her on the screen? She played Danny Kaye's mother in 'Mr Mitty'. She has been married to the same husband, a naval man, for twenty-nine years, which is always a thing that makes a strong appeal to me.

[...]

I was very interested by your account of the visit to Dulwich and all the news about everybody. I knew Sherlock played in that 1898 Bedford match, but I didn't know Jimmy George did. I often wonder why Jimmy G. didn't make more of a success at his job. He was a natural comedian but took himself too seriously. Isn't it odd how often it happens that a man with a gift for comic stuff thinks it beneath him and does third rate serious stuff. Jimmy was really a comic artist.

I can't make up my mind about the Dulwich of today, whether to say 'Ichabod' or not.[1] I read the *Alleynian* and am appalled at the way it is edited now. Pages and pages of ghastly amateur poetry, which who wants to read? And a thing like the report of the Bedford match disposed of in about ten lines with no list of the team and sometimes not even the score. I remember one Haileybury match which began: – 'Played at Dulwich. Dulwich (–), Haileybury (–)', and it wasn't a pointless draw, either. If I remember, we won. All these debates and political meetings and poetry societies they have at Dulwich now shock me, I being the original moss-grown diehard. Incidentally, wouldn't you hate to be starting your eighteenth year now, with the prospect of having to do two years in the army and then try to get a job? I don't know how the beginner breaks in at writing these days. I used to pick up ten bob here and ten bob there with verses and so on, and I imagine all that is a thing of the past.

[...]

1 See Robert Browning's poem 'Waring': 'Ichabod, Ichabod / The glory is departed! / Travels Waring East away'.

TO GUY BOLTON

1000 Park Avenue

July 17. 1950

Dear Guy.
First, thanks for that wonderful photograph of Vicky. What an angel! I have stuck it into the frame of the photograph of you and look at it daily.

[...]

[...] Tonight I go to Skowhegan, Maine, to open – or rather to start ten days rehearsals of – the Fay Bainter show, for which we have now got Ian Keith, who ought to be fine. It has come out very well. Rather funny, I lifted a couple of gags from *Oh, Kay!* (the play being all about bootleggers) and one or two from *Candlelight*, and my agent, Bertha Case of Lyons, took it on herself to go through the script like a school-mistress, making notes like 'Get better line here', 'Weak' and so on, and she censored all the *Candlelight* stuff and all but one of the *Oh, Kay!* lines, all of which were big laughs in New York twenty years ago.[1]

[...]

Love to Virginia.

Yours ever

Plum

Squeaks in terrific form. I take her round the reservoir every afternoon, and only have to carry her about a third of the way.

1 The A. S. Lyons Agency in Hollywood.

TO WILLIAM TOWNEND

1000 Park Avenue

July 17. 1950

Dear Bill.

[...]

I have at last got the Horton play into final shape, and I am hoping this week to hear that Audrey Christie will play in it.[1] (Do you know her?) She is absolutely perfect for the part I want her for, and when I met her last week, she was very enthusiastic. If I can get her <u>and</u> Horton tied up, the thing's in the bag. Any manager will put it on.

The catch about plays is that, while I love writing them, I hate all the business connected with them, like going on the road. I would like to sit at my desk and write play after play and have a partner to do the rest of it. Still, I think a few weeks out of N.Y. will buck me up. The weather here has been awful lately. Deluges of rain and sticky heat next day. Fortunately, our roof is always reasonably cool.

I loved *The Show Must Go On* and am re-reading it now.[2] But, as you say, what a welter of sex. Funny how they love it over here. All you have to do in order to write a best seller is to bung in loads of risky scenes. But *The Show* is absolutely true to New York theatrical life, as it ought to be, Elmer Rice being a very successful playwright.

[...]

I hate to send you a skimpy letter like this, but needs must. If I can find anywhere to write in Skowhegan, I'll send you another from there.

Love to Rene

Yours ever

Plum

1 The play, *Phipps*, was to be a dramatised version of *Spring Fever*.
2 A novel by Elmer Rice.

Hotel Emery Corporation,
Bradford, Pennsylvania

August 14. 1950

Dear Bill.

Don't go writing to the above address, as I expect to be back in New York on Friday.

Talk about Hell's foundations quivering, you ought to go on one of these Summer Theatre tours. I left New York on July 17 and landed at Skowhegan, Maine, at 5-30 a.m. I then had a taxi drive of thirty miles to Lakewood (where I got your letter safely). Lakewood is five miles from Skowhegan, so one is absolutely marooned without a car. We had eleven days of rehearsal and then opened and played a week there. Our manager arrived during the week and blandly announced that our next port of call would be Watkins Glen, N.Y., just a nice little motor drive of 580 miles. We did it on the Sunday in two station wagons belonging to Fay Bainter and one of the women in the company. It nearly killed me. I imagine it's roughly equivalent to driving from Land's End to Edinburgh. From Watkins Glen to Bradford is a mere 150 miles, which seemed nothing, but the company go next to Chevy Chase, just outside Chicago, and then on to Easthampton, Long Island, this last jump, as I figure it out, being about 1150 miles. I have stoutly refused to stick with the show after this week. I wouldn't put it past the management to do a quick jump from Easthampton to San Francisco. The only consolation is that I really have been seeing America and ought to be able to get a novel out of it.

Ethel turned up at Watkins Glen with both dogs, but I persuaded her to go back to New York yesterday. She would have been bored stiff here, not that Bradford is a bad little town. It lies in a valley, surrounded by tree-covered hills, and I like it. It is in the oil country and about the richest town of its size in America. So I hope we shall do good business. So far, we have done very well and audiences like the play, but the opinion seems to be that the thing is too slight to be a hit on Broadway. I can't make up my mind about this myself. There are any amount of laughs in the show. I think they may do a tour of Canada before coming to New York, as this would probably make a lot of money.

Meanwhile, I am supposed to be working on a musical, and my agent and my collaborators keep sending me urgent letters, asking how I am getting on.

I have got very soured on theatrical work. It means such a lot of trouble. I took it up primarily because I couldn't sell my stuff to the magazine, but now that I have had a serial accepted by *Collier's*, the situation may have changed.[1]

I would like to sit at home peacefully writing stories and not see anyone. Incidentally, with all these new taxes that are going to be put on, there is not much point in sweating oneself to the bone to make a lot of money, only to have to give it up to the Government.

[...]

Love to Rene

Yours ever

Plum

1 The serial was *The Old Reliable*.

1000 Park Avenue
New York

December 25. 1950

[...]

Last Thursday we had the O.A. New York dinner, ten of us, me in the chair.[1] It was really a joy to get back into an atmosphere where one could discuss whether J. B. Smith was right in passing to his wing in the Haileybury match of 1907 or would he have [been] better advised to try to go through on his own, and was it 56 or 65 that R. J. Jones made against St Paul's in 1911. One of the men there was W. G. Skey, not the one who was in the cricket team with me. Interesting chap. He was three and a half years a prisoner of war with the Japs and his weight went down to 97 pounds. He was rescued the day before he was to have been shot for having a home made radio. Isn't the modern world extraordinary. Skey asked one of the guests if he knew Java, and the guest, a mild-looking young man, said he didn't actually know Java but he had often bombed it.

I agree with you that it's a bit of a shock to think that someone like Jimmy George is seventy. But I believe it's largely because all one's life one has been brought up on the Bible's statement that 70 is the end of all things. I'll swear I'm fitter at 70 than I was when I was living in London in 1926 and used to have eggs and bacon for breakfast, four courses for lunch, tea and toast and cake at five and six courses with port to follow for dinner. Skey told me that I looked much thinner than in 1926. He said I had a pronounced stomach then!

[...]

Must stop now. Going out to an early dinner with some friends. Love to Rene.

Yours ever

Plum

1 The Old Alleynian dinner, a gathering of former Dulwich pupils.

1000 Park Avenue
New York

Jan 23. 1951

Dear Bill.

[...]

Do you brood much about reaching the seventies? I find myself getting a bit down about it sometimes. I feel fine so far, but I can't escape the reflection that in another ten years I shall be eighty. One symptom of advancing age is that I always turn first to the Obituary page when I get my paper in the morning. How people do seem to be dying off these days. [...]

[...]

Curious thing how few novelists now have what I call real technique. [...] Incidentally, why do they worship Scott Fitzgerald over here? *The Great Gatsby* was good, but his short stories, the things he made his name on, are AWFUL. (Did you ever read any of them in the *S.E.P.*?) They are unabashed 'magazine' stories. Frightful!

[...]

Love to Rene

Yours ever

Plum

1000 Park Avenue
New York

Jan 31. 1951

Dear Bill.

Listen. Extract from book I've just read: –

'In any form of activity, greatness is more than skill or immense accomplishment; its touchstone is not to be found even in a highly individual style. The quality of greatness, surely, is most evident when an artist or craftsman so sums up in his work the typical characteristics of his occupation that we readily speak of him as the apogee of his art. Genius of the first order gives us a consummation of its particular study; it leaves no potentialities wasting through lack of cultivation. etc etc

Ah, you say to yourself, another of those thoughtful essays on Shakespeare or possibly Milton. No, it's the start of Neville Cardus's article on the batting of W. Gunn of Notts. Don't you wish you could get as worked up as that about cricket? [...]

Bernard Shaw. Didn't it make you sick when you read about his will? With people starving on every side and doctors needing every penny they can get for cancer research and so on, he leaves his entire fortune to starting a new alphabet. I believe the man was dotty. I met a man who was with him a lot in his last days and all G.B.S. would talk about was his income tax. You would feel that when you got to 94 and had a million or so salted away that you would feel it didn't matter much what the income tax authorities nicked you for.

[...]

A Life of Scott Fitzgerald has just been published.[1] Rather dully written, but interesting. One never ceases to marvel what damned fools people can be. Scott Fitzgerald seems scarcely to have drawn a sober breath from the time he was twenty. The thing that astonishes me about the book is that, though he always made a large income, he was always in debt and his principal creditors were his publisher and his agent. I had no notion that it was possible to touch a publisher, certainly not an agent, but Scribner's and Harold Ober apparently coughed up another ten thousand dollars every time S.F. asked for it. It beats me how these fellows do it. Edgar Wallace died owing £140,000 and Ziegfeld died owing a million dollars. Wouldn't you have thought that when the score got to – say – £100,000, somebody would have made a feeble bleat about a little on account? Can you imagine popping in on Watt and saying 'Hey, W.P., I find I've come out without my wallet this morning. Slip me a couple of thousand quid, would you mind, as I'm taking a man out to lunch.' But Harold Ober seems to have parted without a murmur.

Well, sir, it seems that the United Nations have decided that the Chinese Reds are aggressors, but what they're going to do about it nobody knows. Why is it that nations are so naive and childish? I mean, approximately a million Chinese invade Korea, and we say 'Hey! What are you making war on us for?', and they raise their eyebrows and say 'What, us? We're not making <u>war</u>. These million Chinese are simply a million independent individuals who thought they'd like to volunteer, and they just happened to have a lot of tanks and jet planes stored away in the attic. Absolutely nothing to do with <u>us</u>, old boy. We can't help it if they want to volunteer.'[2]

[...]

[...] Everything here is horribly expensive, and Ethel curses freely when she spends two dollars on a bit of steak for Squeaky and Squeaky sniffs at it and walks away. Squeaky's idea of a decent lunch is: –

Sugar

Asparagus au Beurre

Chocolate

Fried potatoes

Cake

She really is a heavenly dog.

[...]

Love to Rene.

Yours ever

Plum

1 *The Far Side of Paradise* by Arthur Mizener.
2 China had just intervened in the Korean War.

In March, Wodehouse 'collapsed in the street', and the diagnosis was worrying. As Ethel writes, 'two doctors broke the news to me that my darling Plummy had a tumour near the brain, and would have to be operated on'. After further tests Wodehouse was found to be in good health.

1000 Park Avenue

March 8. 1951

Dear Bill.

Do you remember a year or so ago my telling you about a giddy attack
I had? I got all right in a day and had no more trouble. But about three
weeks ago I suddenly got another. This was on a Sunday. On the
Monday I felt fine, went for a five mile walk and went to the dentist
and so on. Then on the Tuesday, after lunch, still feeling all right, I
started to walk down town to change my library books and I had got
to 82nd Street and Park Avenue when without any warning I suddenly
felt giddy again. (At least, it's not exactly giddiness. The scenery doesn't
get blurred or jump about. It's just that I lose control of my legs.) Well,
Park Avenue fortunately is full of doctors, and I groped my way to the
nearest, about half a dozen yards. I had great luck, as I happened to
hit on one of the best doctors in New York, quite a celebrated man
who attends Gertrude Lawrence, Oscar Hammerstein and other nibs.
A great admirer of my books, by the way.

Since then I have been having every known form of test, including
that ghastly job of taking fluid out of the spine, and I seem to be in great
shape except for trouble in the left ear. My personal opinion is that the
whole trouble is stomach. I had been eating much too much and smoking
too much. I have had to knock off smoking entirely – today is the
seventeenth day without tobacco – and am on a not too strict diet. Today
is the first day I have been conscious of a really marked improvement,
and I am hoping it will last. But the point of all this is that one has
simply got to be one's age and to recognise that one is seventy. I had been
going along as if I were in the forties, eating and drinking and smoking
much too much. I had always looked on myself as a sort of freak whom
age could not touch. But I shall have to be careful from now on.

I was surprised to find how comparatively easy it was to give up
smoking. After two weeks and a bit I don't miss it much. But the test
will come when I try to work. I wonder if I shall be able to think out
a story without smoking.

[...]

More later. Got to stop for lunch. Love to Rene.

Yours ever

Plum

Wodehouse was collaborating with Ellsworth Conkle on the murder-mystery play about Burmese headhunters, Keep Your Head. *This was his rewrite of* Don't Lose Your Head *(Saville Theatre), which had been a flop in London the year before. A reviewer had noted that 'This is the best play I have seen about Oriental headhunters at large in an English pub. But I have seen no previous play on this surprising theme and, after this adventure, I ask for no other.'*

TO ELLSWORTH PROUTY CONKLE

1000 Park Avenue

New York

March 12. 1951

Dear Mr. Conkle.

[...]

The script is in very good shape, but there is one small hole in it. I start off with the High Priest haranguing the Rajah and this has to be done in native dialect. Have you any friend at the University who could supply any sort of dialogue, however meaningless, which would sound <u>native</u>? If so, will you send some along. I hope you see what I mean? The High Priest is talking the Rajah, against his will, into going to Ireland and getting the head, and for about two minutes we ought to have a longish spiel from the High Priest, followed by some sort of interjection from the Rajah, and then another spiel from High Priest. Then the High Priest exits and the Bose character comes in and that finishes our native dialect until the end of act two, where Bose has to do a sort of chant.

[...]

Yours sincerely

P. G. Wodehouse

In one of his many slightly critical letters, Mackail had accused Wodehouse of misquoting Keats' 'La Belle Dame sans Merci' in The Old Reliable.

TO DENIS MACKAIL

1000 Park Avenue
New York

June 18. 1951

Dear Denis.

I call that a very pleasing conclusion to the great Wight–Knight contro-versy. Both right. You know, I was so sure it was 'knight at arms' that I nearly didn't look it up, and when I did look it up, it was in this weird American volume.[1] But Keats must have been an ass if he thought the wretched wight line was as good as – I mean better than – the other. I think you're right in calling the poem Wardour-Street. I've never really liked it. By the way, do you ever find that you have spells of loathing all poetry and thinking all poets, including Shakespeare, affected fools? I am passing through one now. Prose is the stuff.

[...]

I am feeling a little sobered by the reflection that I have only got another four months to go before becoming seventy. Then I look at Pétain and feel more encouraged. But how on earth does a man who has lived a life like Pétain's – Verdun, sentenced to death (quite a nerve strain, that) and prison – live to 95?[2]

[...]

I had forgotten that you knew Shaw. Everyone says he was charming in private life. But he is the most maddening public character I know. I met him twice, once at lunch at Lady Astor's (another maddening louse) and again on the platform at the Gare whatever that station is – ah yes, du Lyon, when I was off to Cannes and he was starting on his world tour. Ethel, silly ass, gave him an opening by saying 'My daughter is so excited about your world tour', and he said 'The whole world is excited about my world tour.' I nearly said 'I'm not, blast you.'

[...]

Yours ever

Plum

1 See Joe Davenport: 'Whenever I have a spare half-hour, you will generally find me curled up with Keats' latest. "Ah, what can ail thee, wretched wight, alone and palely loitering?" I tell you,' said Joe, 'If that wretched wight were to walk into this restaurant at this moment, beefing about La Belle Dame Sans Merci having him in thrall, I would slap him on the back and tell him I knew just how he felt' (*The Old Reliable*, Chapter 2). Mackail had written to PGW, saying that he had misquoted Keats, and 'wretched wight' should read 'knight-at-arms'. Wodehouse was slightly annoyed at this and said that he would send over the page of Keats on which he had read it. In the first version that Keats wrote in 1819, he had indeed used the phrase 'knight-at-arms' – but a later published version changed this to 'wretched wight'.
2 Philippe Pétain, who had been the French Premier during the Second World War and led the Vichy Government's collaboration with Nazi Germany, turned ninety-five that April. He died a month after PGW wrote this letter.

TO DENIS MACKAIL

1000 Park Avenue

August 11. 1951

Dear Denis.

Sad news to start my letter. Poor little Wonder had to be put to sleep. I had always sworn I would never do this to a dog, but there was nothing else to be done. She was almost totally blind, and she developed some sort of mental trouble – so the vet described it – which made her unable to keep still. She would run about the place, bumping into things, and do this sometimes all night, so that poor Ethel was in terrible shape. Looking back on it now, I see that we did the right thing. We miss her very much, of course, but for the last few months she was so obviously suffering. She wouldn't let anyone touch her, and if you picked her up and put her on your lap, she jumped off again. So now Squeaky is our only dog. She gets more loveable every day.

[...]

Another book I have re-read is George Orwell's *Dickens, Dali and Others*, in which he has a long article entitled 'In Defence of P. G. Wodehouse' which is practically one long roast of your correspondent. Don't you hate the way these critics falsify facts in order to make a point?

It is perfectly all right for him – or any other critic – to say that my stuff is Edwardian and out of date. I know it is. But why try to drive it home by saying that my out-of-touchness with English life is due to the fact that I did not set foot in England for sixteen years before 1939?

If only these blighters would realize that I started writing about Bertie Wooster and comic Earls because I was in America and couldn't write American stories and the only English characters the American public would read about were exaggerated dudes. It's as simple as that.

Another thing I object to in these analyses of one's work is that the writer picks out something one wrote in 1907 to illustrate some tendency. Good Lord! I was barely articulate in 1907.

Orwell gave me lunch in Paris in 1944, and I liked him. Dead now, poor chap.

[...]

Yours ever

Plum

TO WILLIAM TOWNEND

1000 Park Avenue
New York

Oct 16. 1951

Dear Bill.

I think the letters scheme is terrific.[1] Even Ethel, who is usually so critical, approved of it wholeheartedly. I immediately sent your first letter to Ken McCormick, who is the boss of Doubledays now that Nelson Doubleday is dead, and you will see from enclosed letter that he is very interested. I am lunching with him tomorrow.

The great thing, as I see it, is not to feel ourselves confined to the actual letters. I mean, nobody knows what was actually in the letters, so we can fake as much as we like. That is to say, if in a quickly written letter from – say – Hollywood, I just mention that Winston Churchill is there and I have met him, in the book I can think up some amusing anecdote, describing how his trousers split up the back at the big party or something. See what I'm driving at?

You see, all the letters I have written you were written very quickly. I just poured out the stuff as if we were talking to each other. But for the book we need more carefully written stuff.

[...]

The only thing I'm a bit doubtful about is whether to touch on my German troubles (with which are incorporated, of course, my experiences in Paris). I shall talk this over with McCormick. It might be a good way of making some sort of an explanation, but on the other hand it might be better to ignore the whole thing.

[...]

Love to Rene.

Yours ever

Plum

1 The plan for what was to become *Performing Flea*.

Wodehouse completed his latest Blandings Castle story in early 1952 – a tale of romance and fierce pig-rearing rivalry.

In March, the Wodehouses found themselves faced with their own real-life Meadowes. 'We employed a manservant', Ethel reports, who 'was stealing all our money, and got away with $600.' Later that month, they heard by telegram that Wodehouse's eldest brother, Peveril, had recently died. 'It's very sad and quite a shock', Ethel wrote. 'I saw him two years ago when I was in London and he looked as if he would live for years. His wife must be heart broken as although we were not in touch with them I always understood they were a very devoted couple.'

1000 Park Avenue
New York

March 3. 1952

Dear Bill.

Yesterday, after sixteen weeks without a day's let-up, I finished my book – called at the moment *Pigs Have Wings* – and am feeling a bit limp. It has come out extraordinarily well, but only because I kept re-reading it and inking in extra lines. I wonder if you find, as I do, that you never get a thing right first shot these days. When I wrote *Piccadilly Jim* etc, I just bunged the stuff down and there it was, but nowadays writing a book is like building a coral reef. One goes on adding tiny bits. I must say the result is much better. With my stuff it is largely a matter of adding colour and seeing that I don't let anything through that's at all flat. Simple instance: – I had Gally saying to Parsloe, who has accused him and Lord Emsworth of stealing his pig, – 'You can't go making wild charges against people on the strength of etc'. After about twenty re-readings I changed this to 'You can't go making wild charges against the cream of the British aristocracy etc'. Much stronger. I've done that all through, and I'm very pleased with the result.

[...]

Your letters about the progress of the Letters book have been very exciting. I am looking forward to seeing the complete thing. Reading your letters, I do feel a bit dubious as to whether you aren't making it too much of 'J'Accuse' (Zola on Dreyfus case). Is it wise, do you think, to stir up all the mud again? I see what you mean about presenting the thing as wholly by you, my attitude being 'Ah yes, I believe old Bill has published a few of my letters with some comments of his own. No, I haven't seen it yet,' but would you print all those Milne etc letters and the extracts from the books? I don't know. Very moot point.

The trouble is that I can't very well pose as a completely innocent injured person, because I did broadcast from Germany in time of war. True, a lot of fatheads jumped at the conclusion that it was anti-British propaganda and so made asses of themselves, but that does not make me blameless. Of course, I don't know how you have handled it, but one wants to be awfully careful.

[...]

Love to Rene

Yours ever

Plum

TO WILLIAM TOWNEND

1000 Park Avenue
New York

April 15. 1952

Dear Bill.

Your two letters arrived simultaneously.

I have been sweating away at the letter book and am getting it into shape. My first task was to read through it and cut – not actually delete stuff but put brackets round what I thought should come out – and this has resulted in a first cut of 53,000 words!!!

The view I took was that these are not letters, they are <u>extracts</u> from letters. So there is no need for things like 'I'm dying to see you. Millions of things to talk about. Love to Rene. Yours ever'. It's extraordinary how much better the cuts make the letters read. And of course over thirty years there's a lot of repetitious stuff.

[...]

The two things I want to avoid are (a) the slightest hint that I was ever anxious or alarmed or wondering if I should have lost my public and (b) any suggestion that your books have not done so well lately as the earlier ones did.

As regards (a), I naturally poured out my hopes and fears to you, but I don't want the public to know that I ever had a doubt about my future. I want my attitude to be a rather amused aloofness, like Bernard Shaw's when he was attacked so bitterly in the first war. You know what I mean. 'Very silly, all this fuss and indignation, but they can't expect an intelligent man to take it seriously.'

[...]

What a lot there is in it about Pekes and football! I shall probably have to cut the Pekes down a good bit, but I shall leave in a good bit of the footer, as it leads nicely into a part in my 'letter' where I describe a meeting with Lord Birkenhead. It actually happened, as a matter of fact. I sat next to him at dinner one night and asked him how it happened that he didn't get his Rugger blue at Oxford, and he talked on about it for hours. It was the only subject that interested him!

[...]

I was a little anxious lest Ethel should think it a bad thing to rake up all the broadcast stuff and publish the broadcasts, but she is all for it. So that's a weight off my mind. I wonder what the effect will be in England. Will it revive the storm of indignation or will it put me right? Difficult to say.

[...]

Love to Rene

Yours ever

Plum

P.S. Copying my stuff from the camp book has made me realize what a ghastly sweat it must have been typing out all those letters.

On 19 April, William Townend wrote to Wodehouse in 'rather a depressed state of mind' about the letters book. Peter Cazalet had phoned him and said that he was 'horrified and very much against the whole thing'.

TO WILLIAM TOWNEND

1000 Park Avenue
New York

April 24. 1952

Dear Bill.

I don't wonder you were upset by that phone call from Peter. But don't give it another thought. This book is going through, no matter what anybody says. (I delayed writing to you, as I was hoping to get Watt's answer to my letter, but it hasn't come yet.)

[...]

What I ask myself is What have I got to lose? Even if the thing is badly received, I don't suppose the entire population of Great Britain will stop buying my books. If they bought about 450,000 of them when the trouble was at its worst, why should they stop now? And if they do, to hell with them. I don't mind.

I think that in these last ten years public feeling has changed a great deal toward me. If not, why are there so many pleasant references to me in the Press? Why, even Milne the other day said something nice about me! And the B.B.C. have become positively matey.

The publication of the broadcasts ought to do the trick. Of course, it is open to people to condemn them simply because they were made over the German radio, and I suppose a certain section of the critics will do just that. But I feel sure that the average person, reading the book, will think that there is nothing in it to get steamed up about. And, as you very justly remark, if I had listened to Thelma Cazalet, I would never have published *Money in the Bank*. (I would also, if I had taken her advice, gone to live in Switzerland! She was all against my coming to America.)

[...]

TO DENIS MACKAIL

1000 Park Avenue
New York

May 6. 1952

Dear Denis.

[...]

That was wonderful, you liking *Barmy* so much.[1] I think it's the last 'American' book I shall do. The one I finished the other day, *Pigs Have Wings*, – still another Blandings Castle story – has an American heroine but no more. I was very pleased when the editor of *Collier's* not only bought it but made a suggestion which improved the end tremendously.

The first instance on record, I believe, of an editor showing a glimmering of intelligence. I was surprised that he took the story, as English stuff is almost unsaleable over here now.

Well, well, so you have moved and are back in London. I hardly know what to say about it. On the whole, I should think it was a good thing. Hove was never worthy of you, and there are things about London which you will probably like. Of course, if you hate going to the theatre, as I do, it cuts you off a good deal of the London whirl. What you say about preferring a Punch and Judy show is exactly how I feel. The other day a kind friend – equivalent to your Yawx – dragged me off, kicking and screaming, to see Rex Harrison and wife in a bloody thing (by an obviously bloody author, Christopher Fry) called *Venus Observed*, and I never suffered so much in my life. To start with, I dislike Rex Harrison on the stage more than any other actor – I except actresses, as that would include Beatrice Lillie, to avoid seeing whom I would run several miles – and I can't stand Lilli Palmer (Mrs R. H.) and I think Christopher Fry ought to be shot. I tried to go to sleep, but the noise from the stage was too much. [...]

[...]

[...] But talking of television, do you see any future for it? We have a set and I enjoy the fights, but everything else on it is too awful for words. One odd thing about television is the way it shows people up. I always used to think Groucho Marx screamingly funny. I saw him on television the other night, and he was just a middle-aged Jew with no geniality whatever, in fact repulsive.

[...]

Yours ever

Plum

1 PGW's novel *Barmy in Wonderland* (1952), published in the US as *Angel Cake*.

Remsenburg
Long Island, N.Y.

June 18. 1952

My dearest dearest Bill.

Excuse it, please. Sorry. Just the effect of reading the life of Hugh Walpole and his letters to Arnold Bennett. (To do your part of it right, you ought to begin your next 'My sweet Plum'.)

My God, what a book! I feel as if I had been swimming in treacle. I always knew Hugh Walpole was a bit of a louse, but I never knew he was as bad as that. Can you imagine a man keeping that diary of his? (June 1. Met George Smith today and looked into his eyes and asked myself 'Have I met a friend?'. June 2. Sat up late communing with my soul and asking myself 'Am I a real artist?' 3. Lay long in bed musing on the many faults in my character. Was it right of me to have lost my temper and slapped Henry James's hand?)

Another thing that struck me about the book was what asses all these big pots like Henry James seem to have been. His letters are the letters of a dull, pompous chump. Arnold Bennett's aren't much better. How seriously all these fellows took themselves. In contrast I found Rebecca West refreshing. And, golly, what a mess Joseph Conrad was. And what a silly letter that was of Maugham's, the one where he tries to say Alroy Kear in *Cakes and Ale* was not drawn from Hugh W. I mean where he says something to the effect of 'How could you think I meant him for you? Why, I have given him a brown moustache, and yours is pink.' Thank God I never went in for celebrity hunting in my youth. Doesn't it appall you, the relentless way Hugh Walpole forced himself on these people.

[...]

Love to Rene

Yours ever

Plum

Remsenburg
Long Island, N.Y.

August 13. 1952

Dear J.D.

[...]

The stuff from the lawyers and your comments on the letter book arrived safely, and I must say I was a good deal impressed by the thoroughness with which the lawyers had gone into the thing. I agree with everything they say, as I feel it is vital to be on the safe side, and I also agree with everything you say. Townend has been much too vehement and 'protective', and his stuff will need a lot of toning down. But you ought to have seen it in its original form, before I cut out about 50,000 words. [...]

[...]

What I feel about this book is that it is hopeless to stick too closely to what I actually wrote. What I must do is to write a lot of entirely new stuff and to hell with whether it is not word for word what I wrote to Townend on June 6. 1931! That is to say, these letters are simply a vehicle. They make a wonderful oblique form for an autobiography. But we simply can't stick to the actual text. One thing I want to do is to think up a lot of funny stories and jam them in. Our slogan must be Entertainment.

[...]

The new house is a great success. [...] I have got into a very pleasant routine here. I get up much earlier than in New York, and at about eight Guy Bolton drives up with the morning papers and my mail. I work till lunch. Then in the afternoon Guy comes again and we drive over to Westhampton (four miles) and swim in the ocean. Back at about six, just in time for a cocktail. Then dinner. After dinner I fix up what I wrote in the morning and read.

This last week the weather has been bad, twice raining all day, but we have had a great summer apart from that, though blazing hot.

[...]

Best wishes

Yours ever

P.G.

1 J. D. Grimsdick was PGW's publisher who took over after the death of Herbert Jenkins.

In 1952, Wodehouse and Bolton began work on the book of their theatrical reminiscences, Bring on the Girls.

TO GUY BOLTON

1000 Park Avenue

New York

Nov 4. 1952

Dear Guy.

[...]

I think we shall have to let truth go to the wall if it interferes with entertainment. And we must sternly suppress any story that hasn't a snapper at the finish. [...] Even if we have to invent every line of the thing, we must have entertainment.

[...]

You and I ought to be as much as possible Alice in Wonderland, appearing in the story only when we are up against some amusing and eccentric character (except for bits of dialogue between us from time to time). I may be wrong, but I don't think your jumping off the train story is strong enough as it stands. It's a good story, but it ought to be tied in with some other character, – i.e. it should be a story Jerry tells us of somebody. (Jerry is going to be very useful all through as a teller of stories.)

As I say, I may be wrong about this, but that's how I feel.

Up to the end of the 'flop' chapter, everything is fine. We are two eager beavers engaged in making good and having a lot of amusing adventures on the way. But once we are solidly established as successful authors, we simply must have something more than 'Then we wrote *Hamlet*. It was a big hit. After that we wrote *Othello*. It ran for years

453

on the road.' See what I mean? [...] Thus, there is nothing to say about *Oh, Kay!*, for instance, if one sticks to the facts, except that it was a terrific success. What we want is to invent some amusing things that made it look as if it were bound to flop. [...] We must manufacture suspense. [...]

WE MUST BE FUNNY!!!!!!

What we want is a couple of days together, plotting the thing out as if it were a play or a novel. I'll come down as soon as I can.

[...]

Love to Va

Yours ever

Plum

TO DENIS MACKAIL

1000 Park Avenue
New York

Dec 14. 1952

Dear Denis.

PIGS HAVE WINGS. Thanks for kind words and for the notes and corrections. I haven't seen the English edition, but assume that your jottings are accurate. (Though I have been reading all your old letters and you repeatedly chide me for making the distance from New York to Los Angeles 3000 Miles, saying that it is only 2000. But if so why does it take a day to get from N.Y. to Chicago, which is admittedly 1000 miles, and two days to get from Chicago to Los A if it is only 1000 miles? Surely the 'Chief', a notorious flyer, doesn't only go twenty miles an hour? Refresh me on this.)

GALAHAD. Of course you are entitled to your view of him, but if you think him a swine, how do you feel about Falstaff and Mr Micawber and, for the matter of that, Fred Barfield in 'Bradsmith Was Right'? Do you consider Falstaff a drunken lout, Micawber a petty swindler and Barfield a selfish hound? Don't you make <u>any</u> allowances for the fact that a character is supposed to be funny?

[...]

THE HOUND.[1] Would be all right if its bowels didn't act so freely. I take him for a long walk before breakfast, he rears copiously, comes back, and before lunch is doing it all over again on the carpet. Gosh, what a moron he seems compared to Squeaky. One is mad to have anything except a Peke. (Tan, I see by your letters, must be ten now. Isn't it sad that they have to grow old.)

Yours ever

Plum

---

1 Bill the foxhound had turned up as a starving stray at Remsenburg, and was adopted by Ethel.

1000 Park Avenue

New York

Jan 31. 1953

Dear Bill.

[...]

Here's a short story for you. I was reading a book of J. C. Squire's and he mentions that years ago at the British Museum reading room he used to see a seedy man hanging around, and he found out later it was Lenin. Couldn't you do a story about a doctor who is called in to attend to a poor derelict in Bloomsbury and after much sweat saves his life, and it is Lenin and he goes on to upset the whole world entirely owing to the young doctor? I believe there's a good story in that. Or, if you preferred, you could have your doctor travelling in Germany in about 1890 and he meets an agitated woman – my little boy is dying and I can't get hold of a doctor – I am a doctor, madam – Then come at once, hurry and so on. Doctor saves child. What is the little fellow's name? 'Adolf, sir.' 'Well, goodbye, Frau Hitler (or Schiklegruber [sic] I suppose it would have to be). The little chap will be all right now and will grow up to be a credit to you.' It would make a good short-short.[1]

Love to Rene

Yours ever

Plum

Prior to the publication of Performing Flea, *which included copies of the broadcasts Wodehouse made from Berlin, Wodehouse's publisher, J. D. Grimsdick, wrote to him to check whether he was including the broadcasts precisely as he had delivered them.*

TO J. D. GRIMSDICK

1000 Park Avenue
New York

March 28. 1953

Dear J.D.

Before I forget, will you send a copy of each of my books to

Herbert Haskins

160 Knowle Road

Sparkhill

Birmingham

He is the man who was such a pal of mine in camp. [...]

About the Broadcasts. Your letter of March 25 arrived this morning. I certainly agree with you that we ought to print the broadcasts exactly as they were spoken. [...]

What happened was that when I wrote the Camp book, I elaborated the broadcasts and made them separate chapters. That is to say, I added funny material wherever I saw an opportunity. [...]

It was very difficult, when I came to work on the Letter book, to remember what I had actually said and what I had added. I suppose it is safest to be absolutely accurate, though it does seem a pity to cut out funny stuff.

[...]

Cussen sent me a typescript of the fifth talk, so I can't see why he is being so coy about letting you have the other four. [...]

It all turns on whether you think that the authorities, reading this passage:

Algy of Algy's Bar came along and found me gulping.

'Lovely morning,' said Algy. 'The lark's on the wing, the snail's on the thorns, God's in His heaven, all's right with the world, don't you think?'

'No, Algy,' I replied hollowly, 'I do not. Look at Harold.'

'Coo! He's got a suitcase!'

'He's got a suitcase,' I said. 'I fear the worst.'

will publish a manifesto in all the papers saying 'It's a lie! Algy did <u>not</u> say 'The lark's on the wing etc. In the actual broadcast all you said was that you saw a man with a suitcase etc. You never mentioned Algy.'

[...]

Didn't you think Cussen was a priceless ass? But you ought to have seen him in uniform with his little wooden stick![1]

Fox Twentieth Century very interested in *Bring on the Girls*.

Yours ever

P.G.

1 PGW was still frustrated that Cussen's report, and Cussen's subsequent investigations, had not been made public.

TO GUY BOLTON

1000 Park Avenue
New York

June 4. 1953

Dear Guy.

[...]

We saw the Coronation on television.[1] I thought it needed work and should have been fixed up in New Haven.[2] They ought to have cut at least half an hour out of it and brought on the girls in the spot where the Archbishop did the extract from the Gospel.

Brilliant parody of Jeeves in *Punch* May 20. It ought to help the sale of the book.

They did the dirty on us over those Sweep tickets. No horse, not even one of those £100 consolation prizes.

[...]

Love to Va. Yours ever

Plum

1 Queen Elizabeth II was crowned on 2 June 1953, following her accession to the throne in February 1952.

2 Plays were often 'tried out' at New Haven before a Broadway run.

TO WILLIAM TOWNEND

1000 Park Avenue
New York

June 25. 1953

Dear Bill.

I have been meaning to write to you for ages, and this morning your second letter arrived, shaming me into replying at once.

As you will guess, the thing in the *Times Lit Sup* was the only thing my press clipping bureau didn't send me! (It has since arrived). But Watt sent it to me, and I was stunned by it. It really was wonderful. The odd thing is that there was a brilliant parody of my Jeeves stuff in *Punch* the other day, and I wrote to the man saying how much I had liked it, and he tells me he was the chap who wrote the *Times* thing. Fellow named Maclaren-Ross. Do you ever see *Punch*? This thing – 'Good Lord, Jeeves' – was really terrific. Bertie is broke and needs a job, and Jeeves – who has just been given a peerage – takes him on as his valet.[1]

A few days after the *Times Lit Sup* article came another – a whole page and a half – in the *New Statesman*. A wonderful eulogy. So I am feeling pretty bucked, especially as the Penguin people have taken another five books.

I was very relieved that you liked *Ring for Jeeves*.[2] But I think I made a bloomer in using Jeeves without Bertie. It's really Bertie whom people like. What happened was that when Guy and I were doing the play and had given Lord Rowcester a butler named Ponsonby, I got what I thought was an inspiration and said 'Why not make it Jeeves?'. But it would have been better without Jeeves. It's odd about those 'double acts'. You need the stooge. Sherlock Holmes wouldn't have been anything without Watson.

[...] You ask me if your letters bore me. They certainly don't. Don't worry about the things you tell me not being interesting. I devour them all. I was very interested by your account of your Founder's Day visit to Dulwich. I remember Cownley vaguely as a gymnast when I was quite a kid at the school. Do you ever find yourself feeling that 78 is an appalling age, forgetting that we shall be it in another six years!

I suppose I am unusually young and fit for my age. I still walk my five or six miles a day, but I do get tired more easily than I used to, – not exhausted, but more inclined to sit in a chair with my feet on a desk and think instead of working. I wrote a short story the other day and found it a great labour. But I think a lot of that was due to lack of enthusiasm caused by the awfulness of the modern American magazine. It used to stimulate me so much, feeling that whatever I wrote was going to Lorimer. I have lost that feeling altogether. There isn't a single American magazine I am keen on appearing in now.

I do think Television has hurt the magazines. They seem all right on the surface with their circulations of four million and so on, but you get the idea that at any moment they may collapse. *Collier's* – soon to be a twice a month instead of once a week – looks very groggy.

[...] Old Brook and Denis Mackail. Brook keeps writing me these illegible letters. He seems to be plugging along all right, but on what? Where on earth does the money come from? I hear pretty often from Denis. Enclosed is a typical letter from him, though less full of cosmic grievances than some. I simply don't understand what he is driving at with these constant statements that what has made him chuck writing is Angela Thirkell. What on earth has the fact that she is his sister and he doesn't like her or her books have to do with him stopping writing? I don't like to depress him, so I have never hinted in my letters to him that it is rather a silly pose, but that's how I feel. I have an idea that these fellows like Denis and Michael Arlen think that if they stop writing the world will draw a sharp breath and say 'Hullo! What's all this? Something must be done about this.' Whereas nobody of course takes the slightest notice. [...]

Love to Rene

Yours ever

<u>Plum</u>

[...] Oh, by the way, I didn't send Denis a copy of *Ring for Jeeves*. I got fed up with that supercilious attitude of his.

1 J. Maclaren-Ross, 'Good Lord, Jeeves', *Punch*, 20 May 1953, Vol. CCXXIV, No. 5876, pp. 592–3.
2 A 1952 play by Wodehouse and Bolton, later converted into a full-length novel, published in the UK in 1953 and in the USA as *The Return of Jeeves* in 1954.

In this letter, Wodehouse reveals how Marlborough fitted his mental picture of Market Blandings, 'one of those sleepy hamlets which modern progress has failed to touch'. Home of the Emsworth Arms, Market Blandings is a peaceful place: 'The Church is Norman and the intelligence of the majority of the natives paleozoic.'

MR SLATER

1000 Park Avenue

New York

July 2. 1953

Dear Mr Slater.

Thank you so much for your letter. I'm so glad you like my books.

I have never revealed the fact before, but Market Blandings is Marlborough. I passed through it years ago on a motoring tour and was much impressed by it. It seemed to me just the town which ought to be two miles away from Blandings Castle.

I am writing this with persp streaming down me, the temperature being in the middle nineties. Yesterday it was 95 in the shade. (Silly, of course, to stay in the shade.) I have just enough strength left to autograph the enclosed photograph in case you care to have it.

Best wishes

Yours sincerely

P. G. Wodehouse

1000 Park Avenue
New York

July 8. 1953

[...]

Bill, I'm uneasy. The proofs of the Letter book have arrived and I have been shuddering over some of the things I said in the broadcasts. There is one passage in the first talk where I describe myself as 'beaming' at the Germans and I talk about 'fraternizing' with them. I have added a bit to my letter to you, saying that I was trying to be subtle and sarcastic, but I'm afraid the critics will tear me to pieces. I'm wondering if it might not be better to cut the broadcasts altogether. I don't know. Except for that passage and a nasty crack about the Belgians, the stuff is very harmless, but the critics may ignore the harmless stuff and concentrate on the bad bits. It's very worrying, especially as the rest of the book is so good.

This is one of those sweltering New York days, and I find it difficult to think. This is the first year I've noticed the heat much.

Love to Rene

Yours ever

<u>Plum</u>

In 1953, the novelist Arthur Ransome wrote to Wodehouse: 'Ian Hay gave me your address last year and said he thought you might be amused to know that my wife and I have given our boat the name of our favourite female character in fiction, and that LOTTIE BLOSSOM appears in Lloyd's Yacht Register as a five tonner. [...] There are, of course, some ignorant persons who, knowing all the rest of your books, do not know the best of all and ask "Who was Lottie Blossom". We refer them to the book, a copy of which is always aboard [...] and tell them merely that she is a red headed American film star who, to please her publicity agent, travels round with a small alligator in a wicker basket, and, when the Customs came aboard to go through her luggage, asks them to begin with the wicker basket, after which they go no further. [...] You must be tired of being thanked for your books. But I cannot write to you without telling you what lasting *pleasure those orange coloured books have given us both throughout the last thirty years.'*

1000 Park Avenue
New York

November 23. 1953

Dear Arthur Ransome.

Thank you so much for your letter. I am very flattered about the name of the boat. How pleased Lottie would be if she knew! (I am very bucked, too, that you think *The Luck of the Bodkins* my best book, because it is my favourite. The Penguin people are doing another five of mine next year, and I am going to insist on *Bodkins* being one of them.)

[....]

I loved the photographs. That's what I call something like a boat.

We are all wilting over here because of the smog – or the smayse. Nothing like that you had in London a year or two ago, but very unpleasant.

Best wishes
Yours sincerely
P. G. Wodehouse

TO WILLIAM TOWNEND

1000 Park Avenue
New York

November 25. 1953

Dear Bill.

[...]

I see old Pop Churchill is reeling beneath a violent uprising among the Conservatives, who apparently want to get rid of him (and, if you ask me, about time). I never have been able to like Churchill. Every time I've met him he has had a silent grouch on. One of the few really unpleasant personalities I've come across.[1] By the way, it was Churchill, even more than Duff Cooper, who egged Connor on to make that broadcast, so Connor tells me.[2] I can't remember if I told you I gave Connor lunch when he was in New York and we got along together like a couple of sailors on shore leave. We parted on Christian name terms, vowing eternal friendship. [...]

We are up in New York for some months, I think. It is rather sad, but I don't like the apartment as much as I used to, my heart being in Remsenburg. If only we could rely on getting a cook down there, I would never want to leave Remsenburg, always provided I had my books down there. [...]

Terrible strain, the publicity about *Bring On the Girls*. We had to do three radio and three television appearances, plus tea with the Ziegfeld Girls Club! Do you remember Anita Elson? Soubrette in London musical comedies, including one of mine in about 1925. I had a letter from her – she is in California – saying she was at that moment listening to me on the radio. So apparently people do hear these things. But what a sweat!

[...]
Love to Rene
Yours ever
<u>Plum</u>

1 'My relations with Winston consisted of my being introduced to him at intervals and always coming on him as a complete surprise. Seven times in all, I think' (PGW to Denis Mackail, 6 May 1952 (Wodehouse Archive)).
2 William N. Connor, who had spoken vehemently about Wodehouse's broadcasts on the BBC in 1941. They had since become friends.

'I find', Wodehouse wrote, 'in this evening of my life that my principal pleasure is writing stinkers to people who attack me in the press. [...] Don Iddon had one of his sneering allusions to me in the Mail *the other day, and I have just written him a stinker, asking among other things if this is to go on till he dies of fatty degeneration of the brain. I sent Nancy Spain of the* Daily Express *a beauty. No answer, so I suppose it killed her. But*

what fun it is giving up trying to conciliate these lice. It suddenly struck
me that they couldn't possibly do me any harm, so now I am like a roaring
lion. One yip out of any of the bastards and they get a beautifully phrased
page of vitriol which will haunt them for the rest of their lives.'

TO NANCY SPAIN

1000 Park Avenue
New York

December 12. 1953

My poor old girl.
You certainly made a pretty bloody fool of yourself over *Performing*
Flea, didn't you? You should have waited to see what the other fellows
were going to say.

I'll give you a tip which will be useful to you. Always read at least
some of a book before you review it. It makes a tremendous difference,
and you can always find someone to help you with the difficult words.

What the devil was all that bilge about me being 'bewildered'? There
was certainly no suggestion of it in the book. You really must read it
some time.

P. G. Wodehouse

TO WILLIAM TOWNEND

1000 Park Avenue
New York

January 13. 1954
[...]
Gosh, Bill, will one never learn to write? I did a 30,000 word Jeeves
story, the high spot of which was Jeeves suddenly announcing that a
supposedly valuable pearl necklace was really imitation. Okay. Not a
bad situation. But I have rewritten the thing as a full length novel,
and have only this moment spotted the frightful flaw, which was
probably what made the *Ladies' Home Journal* and others refuse the

thing, – i.e. How did Jeeves know the necklace was imitation? I gave no explanation, no build-up earlier in the story to make it plausible, I just shot it at the reader. So however good the story was up to then, it had to flop at the finish. I have just written to a jeweller asking for professional advice on the point. What I want to know is Can <u>anyone</u> be taught to spot imitation jewels, or do you have to have some sort of flair?[1]

[...]

Love to Rene

Yours ever

<u>Plum</u>

1 PGW resolves this plot problem in *Jeeves and the Feudal Spirit* (1954) by making the pearl necklace of cultured rather than natural pearls, and revealing that Jeeves 'knows all about jewellery', having 'studied under' a cousin of his in the profession. 'He knows', Bertie adds, 'as everybody knows, that cultured pearls have a core' (Chapter 21).

TO WILLIAM TOWNEND

1000 Park Avenue
New York

March 10. 1954

Dear Bill.

[...]

Did you see a review in the *Spectator* (of *P. Flea*) by a chap called Kingsley Amis saying how bad my stuff was? He has now published a novel called *Lucky Jim*, which seems to be having a success in England, and the *N.Y. Times*, reviewing it over here, said 'It is funny in something approaching the Wodehouse vein.' Ironical! I should imagine he is one of these clever young men whom I dislike so much. They very seldom amount to anything in the long run.

[...]

Yours ever

<u>Plum</u>

1000 Park Avenue
New York

March 21. 1954

Dear Iddon.

A word for your guidance. Do you realize, you revolting little object, that the copyright of a letter belongs to the writer of it? If you plan to continue your practice of publishing private letters sent to your private address, you are liable to come up against someone who thinks you worth powder and shot – which I don't – and get into trouble.

Of course, only a confirmed cad and bounder would do such a thing, but I suppose your answer to that would be that you <u>are</u> a confirmed cad and bounder.

You say in your column that I am 'angry' with you. Not at all. When I am annoyed by a cockroach, I step on it and demolish it, but I am not angry with it.

You have my permission to publish this one.

P. G. Wodehouse

1 It is not certain whether PGW ever sent this letter.

TO DENIS MACKAIL

1000 Park Avenue
New York

March 21. 1954

[...]

If you want something good, get *People Like You*, I think it's called, by Roald Dahl.[1] I think he is a comer. He had a story in the *New Yorker* a week or two ago so good that I had to turn back and look at the cover to make sure this really was the *New Yorker* I was reading. I always thought a *New Yorker* story had to have no point whatsoever. (I remember now you told me you see the *N. Yorker*, so you may have read it. About the bad husband who gets stuck in the lift and perishes. 'Journey to Heaven' I think it was called).[2]

[...]

1 Dahl's short-story collection, *Someone Like You*, was published in 1953.
2 The story was 'The Way up to Heaven'.

In 1952, A. A. Milne suffered a serious stroke. Wodehouse admired Milne's work and their acquaintance extended back to 1907, when they had played cricket together. The pair had never been close, especially since Milne's attacks on Wodehouse during the war years. But Wodehouse's concern repeatedly extended to his fellow writer. As he wrote to William Townend, 'I don't like him, but I hate the idea of him being so bad.'

TO ALASTAIR WALLACE

[u.d. 1952]

[...]

Poor Milne. I was shocked to hear of his illness. I'm afraid there seems to be little chance of him getting any better. It is ghastly to think of anyone who wrote such gay stuff ending his life like this. He has always been about my favourite author. I have all his books and re-read them regularly.

[...]

TO DENIS MACKAIL

1000 Park Avenue
New York

May 1. 1954

Dear Denis.

[...]

My gosh, it shows how one ought to reserve judgment of one's fellows. Scarcely had I written to you saying that Edward Cazalet had not acknowledged my gift when a long and charming letter arrived from him, thanking me profusely. (Whether owing to his influence – he is Racquets captain and in Pop – or not, I don't know, but I have just been asked by the Eton College Literary Society to address them in July. Can't you see me!! 'Well, boys –'...) [...]

A bastard named Alan Melville says in *Time and Tide* that I have been getting 'steadily unfunnier'. The trouble is that I can't reply 'So are you', because – though obviously a son of a bitch and probably a notorious fairy – he does write darned amusing stuff. I thought of writing him a stinker on general lines but abandoned the idea on picking up the life of Hugh Walpole and finding that he always wrote indignantly to unkind critics. I shall just have to put him on the list as one of those marked for vengeance. But the funny thing is that his review came out in *Time and Tide*, who have just written me a grovelling letter begging me to contribute some articles. 'Not after what has occurred' is about my attitude.

[...]

Ethel has been buying trees like a drunken sailor – if drunken sailors do buy trees – and though we shall have to go on the dole very soon the result is rather wonderful.[1] The garden is beginning to look like something, and as I write hammering comes from the next room, where a squad of workers are putting mirrors on the walls as first step to turning room into a bar, if you'll believe it. I know quite well that when we have our bar Ethel will continue to make the cocktails in the kitchen. But I think the idea is to be prepared in case the Quality come pouring in. Ethel, who loathes seeing a soul except me and the dogs, can't shake off those dreams of being the centre of a rapid social circle. (Good line in my forthcoming Jeeves novel about Bertie's Uncle Tom. 'His face wore the strained, haggard look it wears when he hears that guests are expected for the week end.' Don't you hate having people about the place?)

[...] Are you following the McCarthy business?[2] If so, can you tell me what it's all about? 'You dined with Mr X on Friday the tenth?' 'Yes, sir.' (keenly) 'What did you eat?' 'A chocolate nut sundae, sir.' (Sensation.) It's like Bardell vs Pickwick, which reminds me. Do you hate Dickens's stuff? I can't read it.

Love to Tan

Yours ever
<u>Plum</u>

1 Though written on Park Lane paper, it appears this letter was written from Remsenburg.
2 Fear of Communism in America, in the wake of the Second World War, and fuelled by the Chinese Civil War and the Korean War, was known as the 'Second Red Scare'. Investigations into suspected American Communists were led by Senator Joe McCarthy. In 1954, a conflict arose between McCarthy and the US Army, which was televised in the form of live broadcasts.

CHAPTER FOURTEEN

Final Years

In the early 1950s, the Wodehouses were living between New York and their summer residence in the Long Island area. By 1955, they left New York permanently. Basket Neck Lane in Remsenburg was to be their address for the rest of their lives. The house, near the fashionable resort of Westhampton, was shielded from the road by a hedge, with twelve wooded acres of land behind it. Ethel made numerous alterations to the property and Wodehouse wrote jokingly about their 'show place'. 'Think of Knole or Blenheim and you will get the general idea.'[1] The Wodehouse home was, in fact, a fairly modest affair with four bedrooms, arranged over two floors, a large sitting-dining room and a study.

Living in Remsenburg gave Wodehouse the chance to live and write with very little disturbance. His days would typically begin at eight, with his 'Daily Dozen' exercises, followed by a breakfast of 'toasted black bread, jam, honey and five cups of tea'. After a morning's writing, 'he would join Ethel in her room, where they would watch a soap opera on television; and at one o'clock they would have lunch. Fairly soon after lunch', he wrote, 'I've got to take the dogs out. So I take them to the post office and get the mail. Then I work again from three till about five, when I take my bath. Ethel joins me for cocktails, usually martinis. We have dinner generally at about six or a quarter past six. [...] We used to play double-dummy bridge but we were never very keen on it, so now we generally read. From about eight to about nine, I might go and write letters.'[2] It was, Wodehouse wrote, 'the same routine day after day, and somehow it never gets monotonous.'[3]

One of the main preoccupations for the Wodehouses was their ever-growing brood of pets. Animals had always been an important part of their lives, and a great bond between the couple. Remsenburg gave them even more of an opportunity to tend to numerous cats and dogs, and they became a sort of foster home for strays, or animals left by travelling friends. In the Wodehouses' later years, these included Squeaky the Peke, Jed the dachshund and Poona the cat, as well as Bill the foxhound. Later on, the Wodehouses found themselves the owners, at various times, of Ginger, Blackie, Debbie, Enoch, Minnie, Smoky and Spotty. Ethel also became interested in an animal shelter organisation, the Bide-a-Wee association, and the Wodehouses donated $35,000 for the P. G. Wodehouse Shelter to be built at nearby Westhampton.

One disadvantage of Remsenburg life, for Wodehouse, was the fact that he had to wait until the evening before he could read the daily paper. The house was too far from the local village to get any sort of delivery. But there is a sense in which Wodehouse enjoyed the protection from contemporary events that this distance allowed. 'I detach myself when I'm writing', as he told a television interviewer.[4] Comic writing, was, for Wodehouse, incompatible with what he saw as the increasingly 'tense' atmosphere of contemporary America, with its terrorist threats, political manoeuvrings, and Cold War scares. Wodehouse was also bemused by the increasingly sexualised nature of late-twentieth-century life, full of 'ghastly muck'.[5] He was amused when he did indeed find a place for himself in this market after all – becoming a regular contributor to *Playboy* magazine – sandwiched in between 'photographs of Jayne Mansfield in the nude'. 'It would be great', he jokes, 'if I found myself listed among the dirty writers'.[6]

Wodehouse's attachment to Remsenburg, and America, was confirmed when, in 1955, he became a US citizen. Although his British grandchildren, Sheran and Edward Cazalet, were frequent visitors, Wodehouse was never to return to England. His increasing age and their ever-growing flock of animals were good reasons to avoid a long journey overseas, but the overriding obstacle, for Wodehouse, was the 'fact that there might still be unpleasantness'.[7]

Wodehouse remained very sensitive to the issue of the broadcasts that he had made from Germany – a sensitivity not assuaged by some unfortunately pitched newspaper interviews. In 1954, he accepted Stephen Spender's invitation to publish the original broadcasts in the journal *Encounter*, in an attempt to prove their innocuous nature. Ever the reviser, Wodehouse could not, however, resist making changes to the original script to increase the humour. Wodehouse also had dealings with two biographers in his later life – David Jasen and Richard Usborne. Although he was always charming in person, Wodehouse was naturally reluctant to talk about himself. The following letters reveal that Wodehouse's anxiety about his broadcasts in the 1940s made this experience even more trying.

Nevertheless, he took much comfort from the support that he continued to receive from fellow writers. In 1960, tributes flooded in for Wodehouse's eightieth year – with a notice of birthday greetings placed in *The New York Times* from writers that included W. H. Auden, Nancy Mitford, James Thurber, Lionel Trilling and John Updike. Evelyn Waugh was a regular correspondent and particularly championed Wodehouse – arranging a special tribute for him in 1961 to be aired on the BBC. He finished his account of Wodehouse's work with the following:

> For Mr Wodehouse there has been no Fall of Man; no 'aboriginal calamity'. His characters have never tasted the forbidden fruit. They are still in Eden. The gardens of Blandings Castle are that original garden from which we are all exiled. The chef Anatole prepares the ambrosia for the immortals of high Olympus. Mr Wodehouse's idyllic world can never stale. He will continue to release future generations from captivity that may be more irksome than our own. He has made a world for us to live in and delight in.[8]

After the difficulties that Wodehouse experienced with his writing during the forties and early fifties, this was a period in which he regained much of his confidence. Although he still found difficulty, as he had all his writing life, in inventing plots, he produced a string of successful novels, including *Something Fishy*, *Ice in the Bedroom*, *Do Butlers Burgle Banks?* and *Aunts Aren't Gentlemen*. Another work of reminiscences, drawn from a series of *Punch* articles, *America, I Like You*, was published in 1956,[9] and there were further theatrical collaborations. A revival of one of his 'Princess' musicals, *Leave It to Jane*, was a Broadway success in 1959; 1969 saw him rewriting the lyrics of *Anything Goes* for a London production, while 1973 saw Wodehouse and Bolton working with the composer and lyricist of '*Jesus Christ Superman*' [*sic*] – on a musical based on Jeeves.[10]

Wodehouse dwells, in many of these letters, on how fit and well he is feeling but, as the years go on, it becomes clear that both Ethel and

Wodehouse were growing old. The death of William Townend, Wodehouse's most long-standing and loyal correspondent, was a particular reminder of his own mortality. In the last decade of his life, Wodehouse often began to feel dizzy and short of breath – signs of heart trouble. Ethel had particularly worrying health concerns, and was treated for cancer.

Throughout these letters, Wodehouse's love for his wife, and his reliance on her company, is abundantly clear – especially in the notes he writes whenever hospital visits forced them to spend a few days apart. He could not, he told her, imagine ever having been happy with anyone else.[11]

It was in his final years that Wodehouse received two accolades that brought him great pleasure. The first was a visit from a representative from Madame Tussaud's, as a waxwork model of him had been commissioned for their London exhibition [see plate 39]. The second was the news that he was to receive a knighthood from the Queen. Unable to travel to England, he was knighted in a mock ceremony at Remsenburg. Soon after this, he was admitted to hospital with a painful skin complaint, on the advice of his doctor. A few days later, on the evening of 14 February 1975, Wodehouse died from a heart attack. He had his latest manuscript beside him. Each phrase is crafted with as much care as those in the scores of novels that preceded it, transporting his readers into a world of seemingly effortless comedy. It had been nearly a century of writing, and Wodehouse was working until the end. As he wrote in 1956, 'with each new book of mine I have always the feeling that this time I have picked a lemon in the garden of literature':

> A good thing, really, I suppose. Keeps one up on one's toes and makes one write every sentence ten times. [...] When in due course Charon ferries me across the Styx and everyone is telling everyone else what a rotten writer I am, I hope at least one voice will be heard piping up: 'But he did take trouble'.[12]

1 PGW to Jack Donaldson, quoted in Donaldson, p. 283.
2 Jasen, p. 247.
3 PGW to Denis Mackail, 6 June 1960.
4 Interview with PGW, *Monitor*, BBC, 26 October 1958. Available at http://www.bbc.co.uk/archive/writers/12201.shtml.

5 PGW to Denis Mackail, 8 June 1957.

6 PGW to Denis Mackail, 18 June 1963.

7 PGW to Hesketh Pearson, 24 August 1961.

8 Evelyn Waugh, 'An Act of Homage and Reparation to P. G. Wodehouse', *Sunday Times*, 16 July 1961, repr. in Gallagher, pp. 567–8.

9 Published in the UK with some changes as *Over Seventy* (1957).

10 PGW to Tom Sharpe, 7 October 1974.

11 PGW to Ethel Wodehouse, 3 September 1973.

12 *Over Seventy*, p. 23.

1954–1975:
'he did take trouble'

Remsenburg NY

August 22. 1954

Dear Denis.

[...]

Edward Cazalet is now with us and is a terrific success. Charming chap and just right for the American scene, being completely unaf-fected and democratic. His two great pals down here are the son of the grocer and a college boy who works in the garden at $1.50 per hour. E. flies home next Friday and tomorrow he and Fred Garcia, the grocer's son, drive to New York, where we are putting them up at the Roosevelt Hotel. Ethel and I go up on Tuesday. We thought it would be much better fun for Edward going around N.Y. with a boy of his own age instead of being landed with a septuagenarian like me. Though as a matter of fact Edward and I are very matey. He is very easy to get on with. As you said in an essay, you can't beat a good Etonian, and E. is one of the best specimens I have met.

I have now been at Remsenburg three months and am coming round to Ethel's view that we ought to cut out New York and live here all the year round. There seems very little point in having a New York apartment when we never go to a theatre or to meals at a restaurant. My life in New York is – rise, breakfast, work till lunch, exercise walk from 2.30 to 4 and back home and in for the night. All one needs in life is books, and I can get those down here.

[...]

Were you ever misguided enough to go to the movie of *Gone with the Wind*? Edward lugged me there on Sunday. I left after three and a half hours of it and there was another half hour after that. Isn't it amazing that these movie people have no idea of construction and selection! Anybody could have seen, you would have thought, that there was an hour in the middle of the thing that could have come right out without hurting the story. After an eternity of it Clark Gable and Vivien Leigh fell into the embrace and I was just reaching for my hat, when blowed if they didn't start an entirely new story. I don't believe it was in the book at all. Brooding on this, I have come to the conclusion that Gable saw the rushes of what was supposed to be the complete picture and raised hell because he hardly appeared in it, so they wrote in a lot of new stuff. Significant that Gable refused to come to the original opening and again refused when it was revived.

[...]

Yours ever

Plum

Wodehouse wrote the following letter in response to a number of questions from Usborne, who was writing a biographical account of his work, to be entitled Wodehouse at Work.

TO RICHARD USBORNE

1000 Park Avenue
New York

Jan 14. 1955

Dear Mr Usborne.

So sorry I haven't written before. Great rush of work.

First, it would be fine if you could come over here. But it would have to be in the summer, as we have no visitor's room at 1000 Park, where we spend the winter, whereas at the Remsenburg house there is a swell guest room with private sun parlour.

Now about the questions. I don't know if you are like me and never make a carbon copy, so I am returning your letter in case you want to refer to it.

Heavens! You can't expect me to remember the set books at school after fifty-five years!! We did the usual ones, I suppose, certainly including Homer, and I sweated at Homer then, but I have never read him since. [...] I did reams of Greek and Latin verse, and enjoyed it more than any other work. I was two years in the Sixth – or top – form, never rising to any great eminence – I was about fifteenth of a form of thirty – but I should probably have got a scholarship at Oxford or Cambridge, as several of my inferiors got them. But there was not enough money to send me to the University even with a scholarship. I don't remember much about the English books we read. And I can't remember any examination on English books. I suppose one read a good bit of Shakespeare, and I seem to remember Carlyle ('I, mine Werther, am above it all').[1] Where I got Rem acu tetigisti, I can't say. It just stuck in my mind.[2]

Blandings is purely imaginary, but a composite, I suppose, of a number of country houses I visited as a child. My parents were in Hong Kong most of the time, and I was left in charge of various aunts, many of them vicars' wives who paid occasional calls on the local Great House, taking me with them. Why, I can't imagine, as I had no social gifts. But those visits made me familiar with life in the Servants Hall, as I was usually sent off there in the custody of the butler, to be called for later. So I got a useful insight into the ways of Beach etc. The lake and the bushes and all that I put in as I needed them. Probably my subconscious supplied the lake from Lord Methuen's house at Corsham, Wilts, where I used to go and skate as a child.

No, I was never a tutor. I left Dulwich at the end of July 1900 and by September 1900 was a clerk in the correspondence department of the HongKong and Shanghai Bank.

Ukridge. Actually he was a man named Craxton, whom I never met. W. Townend knew him and gave me all the stuff about him which I put into *Love Among the Chickens* – most of which book, the chicken farm venture and so on, actually happened. But, oddly enough, a friend of mine was also exactly like Ukridge, and I suppose I drew on him for the most part. Man named Westbrook. We used to share digs.

Yes, I did have Ruby M. Ayres in mind for Rosie M. Banks. Not that I ever met her, but I wanted a name that would give a Ruby M. Ayres suggestion.[3]

Do shoot in all the questions you want to. I'll answer them all.

[...]

Aunt Agatha is definitely my Aunt Mary (Mary Deane), who was the scourge of my childhood.

Let's have some more questions. We must make this book a world-beater!

Yours sincerely

P. G. Wodehouse

1 *Sartor Resartus* (1833–4).
2 See, for example, this exchange between Jeeves and Bertie in *Joy in the Morning*:
    'Precisely, sir. Rem acu tetigisti.'
    'Rem – ?'
    'Acu tetigisti. A Latin expression. Literally, it means "you have touched the matter with a needle," but a more idiomatic rendering would be –'
    'Put my finger on the nub?'
    Wodehouse probably remembers the phrase from Plautus, *Rudens* V.II.1.19.
3 For PGW's thoughts on Ayres, see his letter to Leonora Wodehouse, 30 March 1925.

Despite the tone of the following letter, Wodehouse and Christie became frequent correspondents, and she dedicated Hallowe'en *to him in 1969.*

TO DENIS MACKAIL

1000 Park Avenue
New York

March 6. 1955

Dear Denis.

The other afternoon I managed to stir Ethel up and take her for a walk in the park with the dogs, and we met a photographer who took pictures of us. One of these will shortly be on its way to you. Not too good of us, but marvellous of Bill and Squeaky.

[...] I'm seething with fury. Sir Allen Lane of Penguin was over here not long ago and told me that Agatha Christie simply <u>loved</u> my stuff and I must write to her and tell her how much I liked hers. So with infinite sweat I wrote her a long gushing letter, and what comes back? About three lines, the sort of thing you write to an unknown fan. 'So glad you have enjoyed my criminal adventures' – that sort of thing.

The really bitter part was that she said the book of mine she liked best was *The Little Nugget* – 1908 production. And the maddening thing is that one has got to go on reading her, because she is about the only writer today who is readable.

[...]

Yours ever

<u>Plum</u>

Wodehouse is here advising Bolton about his latest musical, Ankles Aweigh, *which opened on Broadway in April 1955.*

TO GUY BOLTON

1000 Park Avenue

March 23. 1955

Dear Guy.

I hope the show is going like a breeze. Brooding on what you said about the laugh line at end of the ship scene not going too well, don't you think it's the showing of the brassiere earlier that hurts the showing of the – no, it's the other way about. The brassiere falls flat because the audience has seen the other feminine garment, the black one (which does get a big laugh). Why not cut one of them out and get a surprise at end of scene?

[...]

Yours ever

Plum

Remsenburg NY

June 3. 1955

Dear Mr Usborne.

Yours of April 25. Here are the answers to the questions.

1. Pronounced Wood-house.[1]

2. No sisters. Three brothers, two older, one younger, all dead now. We all got along very well. Any poisonous small brothers in my books were invented or based on repulsive children I had known.[2]

3. *Mike* is the only book that has been modernized, and I think myself it was a mistake. Not quite as bad as trying to modernize *Tom Brown* but definitely wrong. The whole tone of the story is 1900-odd, and I don't believe anyone could mistake it for a modern school story, however much you change 'Rhodes' to 'Laker'. It was also a pity that *Mike* – though it was originally two stories – should have had to be split up into two six shilling books. It was so much better in one solid chunk. But the price of a book that length today would have been too high.[3]

4. [...]

5. [...]

6. I'm afraid you won't find any busts or portraits of me at Dulwich. (Or anywhere else, for that matter.)

7. When you come over here, I will give you the book in which I kept a record of all the money I earned by writing from the time I started till 1908. (Or I will send it to you, if I can find anyone to do up a parcel.) It's very interesting, though I find it slightly depressing as it shows the depths I used to descend to in order to get an occasional ten-and-six. Gosh, what a lot of slush I wrote! I don't know why I gave up keeping the book in 1908. Probably because early in the following year I went to America and started a new phase.

But I hope you aren't planning to republish any of the stuff I wrote then. What a curse one's early work is. It keeps popping up. I got a nasty shock a month or so ago when I picked up the magazine Charteris (*The Saint*) publishes here and found in it a detective story – yes, a detective story and a perfectly lousy one – which I sold to *Pearson's*

Magazine somewhere around 1910.[4]

Incidentally, have you noticed that all these 'evaluators' like George Orwell always select for examination *Something Fresh*, which I wrote in 1915? Why not something more recent?

8. [...]

9. When was the first number of *Chums*? Was it 1892? Anyway, it contained – in addition to Max Pemberton's *Iron Pirate* – a school story by Barry Pain called 'Two' (published in book form as *Graeme and Cyril*). It made an enormous impression me. It had practically no plot but the atmosphere was wonderful. I was re-reading it only the other day and it's great stuff.[5]

[...] As a child, of course, I read *Eric* and *St Winifred's* and the Talbot Baines Reed stories in the *B.O.P.* I loved them all. I think it is only later that one grows critical of *Eric* and *St W's*. *Tom Brown*, fine. Also *Vice Versa*. But *Acton's Feud* was the best of the lot.

I'm not sure I agree with your prep-school man. The *B.O.P* must have started in the eighties, and *Chums* either in '91 or '92.

10. It's difficult to judge other people's feelings by one's own. I was always so keen on writing that any job not connected with it seemed loathsome to me. I wouldn't have minded the most menial job in a publisher's office, but a bank ...![6] Though, actually, after I had got used to it, I was very happy in the Hongkong Bank. My only fear was that at the end of two years I would be sent abroad, which at that time seemed to me the end of a literary career. It was all pretty exciting. Beach Thomas, who had been a master at Dulwich, had this 'By the Way' job on the *Globe* and when he wanted a day off I would plead illness to the Bank and sneak off and deputize for him and get my ten bob, and then there came the moment when he wanted to take his annual five weeks holiday. Which of course precipitated a crisis. If I was prepared to work on the *Globe* for five weeks, the post awaited me. If I couldn't, he would have to get someone else. So I took a hell of a chance and chucked the bank. I had managed to save about fifty quid and I had five weeks' work assured at three guineas a week, and it seemed to me that – as one could live comfortably in those days on three quid a week – I would be all right for about five months.

It worked out all right, I find, looking at my book, that I made £215.18.1. in my first year as a writer on my own. £411.14.10 the next year, £500 the year after that, and then £505.1.7 and £525.17.1. So I need not have worried. [...]

11. Never! I was a fast bowler and almost a total loss as a bat. I once made a century for the *Globe* printers against the *Evening News* printers and once 97 for the bank against another bank, but the bowling was not so hot.

No, I never got exhausted in the ring. After three rounds I was always willing and anxious to go on and could never understand why the decision went against me, as I couldn't remember the other fellow hitting me at all. This although I was streaming with blood.[7]

12. No, I never had a fight. One didn't. I can't remember a single one in my whole school life. (How different from my literary agent – not Watt, the New York one – who told me he was at a school in Brooklyn for six years, mostly negroes, and had a fight every day during that period).[8]

13. [...]

14. [...]

15. Very very rarely and only for terrific offences.[9]

16. You will find the Wodehouse villa just opposite the fourteenth fairway of the old golf course. It survived the war, though knocked about a bit. In the south of France I lived at a house called Domaine de la Frayère up in the mountains about a dozen miles from Cannes. I was always fond of the Riviera, but till I took La Frayère I stayed at hotels.

Yours ever

P. G. Wodehouse

[...] Orwell. I only met him once. We got on very well and corresponded fairly regularly, but he struck me as one of those warped birds who have never recovered from an unhappy childhood and a miserable school life. He took everything so damned seriously. [...]

1 'You pronounce it "Woodhouse", don't you?'
2 'How many brothers and sisters did you have? Older or younger? Speaking as a man infested with brothers, I note with extra appreciation your remarks on the difficulties of having brothers. (*Mike*, and in at least one of Saint Austin's stories). I also think you are very sound on kid brothers throughout for later books. I wondered if there was any factual source.'
3 'How many of your books have you modernized?'

4 The story was 'The Harmonica Mystery', a partially adapted version of 'The Education of Detective Oakes', which appeared in *Pearson's*, December 1914.

5 'Can you remember which school books and school writers had impressed you most.'

6 'I wonder whether you can tell me a) whether your insistence on a Bank's being equivalent to Dickens' blacking factory was a [...] mild tease of your own bank, where, I guess, you were not wildly happy' or 'b) was the concept general in those days'.

7 'Did you ever make a huge cricket score in good cricket? One of your descriptions (or *Mike*, I think...) suggests that you have personal memories of such wonderful exhaustion. There is a similar description of tiredness in the ring, in one of your stories that suggests you must have been on your last legs in the ring and acutely aware of it. Have you?'

8 'Did you ever have to fight the school bully, or the man who was later going to be your best friend?'

9 'Was there caning at Dulwich when you were there?'

In September 1955, Wodehouse became an American citizen.

TO DENIS MACKAIL

Basket Neck Lane
Remsenburg, New York

Sept 15. 1955

Dear Denis.

This is some new notepaper which Ethel had made for me. Shows up your beastly blue stuff a bit, what? As far as I can make out, I don't actually become a citizen till the middle of November, when I shall have to go over to Riverhead and be addressed by a Judge of sorts, but I gather that that is just a formality and that I am set.

The morning after the proceedings I was rung up on the telephone by the *Mail*, the *Express*, the *Times*, the *Associated Press* and others. They all wanted to know why I had done it, and it was a little difficult to explain without hurting anyone's feelings that, like you, I don't feel it matters a damn what country one belongs to and that what I really wanted was to be able to travel abroad without having to get an exit permit and an entrance permit, plus – I believe – a medical examination. The next day the *Express* rang up again and wanted me to do an article for them. I have done this and it has probably appeared by this time. Quite funny. [...]

If you won't write anything again, at least help a brother-brush. I have got the plot of my next one pretty well fixed, but I want a job that my hero can get.[1] My big comic scene ends with him doing a great service to a young American who has lots of money – this may turn out to be Oofy Prosser of The Drones – and the grateful plutocrat gives him this job, which makes it necessary for him to go to America, which means parting from the heroine. But what job? The plutocrat can be anything – e.g. majority stockholder in a New York store, a chain of papers or anything, but what he is makes the hero what he is. Thus, if hero were an artist, I suppose Pluto could make him head of the store's art department. It ought to be something solid, not a job from which he can be sacked at a moment's notice. The main point is that it has to be in America. Let's have your views.

[...]

Yours ever

Plum

I must call your attention once more to this notepaper.

1 *Something Fishy* (1957), published in the US as *The Butler Did It.*

On 4 July 1955, the Daily Mail*'s René MacColl published a piece about the Wodehouses, ostensibly written in the style of Bertie Wooster. It wrongly gave the impression that Wodehouse was very depressed.*

TO WILLIAM TOWNEND

Basket Neck Lane,
Remsenburg,
New York

July 26. 1955

[...]

[...] About that McColl [*sic*] article. [...]

I frothed with fury, of course. The bastard had rung up saying he was a great friend of M. Muggeridge's and could he come down and have a chat, so we of course laid down the red carpet for him. He tucked into a fat lunch with cocktails and white wine, and was all cheeriness and dear-old-palness, and then he went off, bursting with my meat, and wrote that horrible article. I'm not sure that what didn't wound me most was his thinking he was writing Bertie Wooster dialogue. Very poor stuff, I thought.

[...]

TO WILLIAM TOWNEND

Basket Neck Lane,
Remsenburg,
New York

Feb 21. 1956

Dear Bill.

The trouble about writing to you is that when I do I want to write a long letter, and every day these darned fan letters arrive which I have to answer. I'll tell you the world's worst pest, and that is the fan who writes to say how much he has enjoyed my work. I write back and say Thanks so much etc. Then a couple of days later comes another letter, saying 'On page 31 of your book you say that Bertie Wooster has light hair. Could you tell me if this means that you admire light hair', and I have to write another letter.

Isn't it extraordinary, the wave of filth which is surging over all writing these days. John O'Hara has just got the literary award or whatever they call it for his book *Ten North Frederick*, and it is simply pornography. I wouldn't mind so much if the major characters were dirty, but he lugs in all sorts of minor characters who have nothing to do with the story and just lets himself rip with them. I'll swear you couldn't find anything dirtier in the back streets of Paris.

[...] I find that life of Kip awfully interesting. I'll swear he never asked me that about ending in my stories.[1] I met him once at the Cazalets and again at the Beefsteak Club, but we never discussed writing. [...] I never met Anne Sheridan. She must be a bit of a tick, selling K's conversation – presumably private – to the papers as an interview. But people have no scruples whatever.

485

Love to Rene

Yours ever

Plum

1 PGW was reading Charles Carrington, *Rudyard Kipling: His Life and Work* (London: Macmillan, 1955). Carrington discusses an occasion when 'Rudyard met Wodehouse and challenged him: "Tell me, Wodehouse, how do you finish your stories? I can never think how to end mine"' (p. 490).

On 29 January 1956, the novelist John Wain had reviewed Wodehouse's French Leave *alongside other novels in the* Observer, *concluding that while 'Mr Wodehouse is probably the most endearing author in the world [...] I cannot quite get rid of the feeling that the needle is scratching rather badly and that sooner or later the record will have to be taken off'. Evelyn Waugh wrote to defend Wodehouse in the* Observer, *following it up with his own review in the* Spectator, *entitled 'Dr. Wodehouse and Mr. Wain'.*

TO EVELYN WAUGH

Basket Neck Lane,
Remsenburg,
New York

March 11. 1956

Dear Evelyn.

'At-a-boy! That's the stuff to give 'em. It was really wonderful of you to come to my rescue like that. I suppose John Wain will have some pompous counterattack in next week's *Spectator*, but anybody will be able to see that you have demolished him.

What a curse this new breed of bright young Manchester Grammar School-scholarship at Oxford lads is. Kingsley Amis is another to whom we ought to attend some day. I haven't read his *Lucky Jim* (which I am glad to say was a total flop over here) but his supercilious reviews in the *Spectator* are hard to bear. But how anyone who writes such lousy books as John Wain has the nerve to criticize others beats me.[1]

I have just finished another novel in 30,000 word form (in the hope of a one-shotter sale to some magazine) and am now faced with the prospect of having to expand it to full length. Frightful sweat, but I can take my time.

[...]

Yours ever

P. G. Wodehouse

A book was published here some years ago called *Treasury of British Humour* (I think), containing a large chunk of *Black Mischief*. What wonderful stuff it is. You have eclipsed it since, but it is still one of my favourites of yours.

1 John Wain's first novel, *Hurry On Down*, about a university graduate beginning adult life, had been published in 1953.

TO GUY BOLTON

Basket Neck Lane,
Remsenburg,
New York

July 5. 1956

Dear Guy.

[...] I am still trying without any success to think of a plot for a novel. I want to do another Jeeves one, but am stymied by the fact that Bertie, having a large private income, is so hard to get into trouble. I have used the getting-engaged-to-wrong girl and violence-threatened-by-jealous-rival motifs so often that I don't see how I can use them again. The only other real trouble he can get into would be if he somehow fell foul of the Law, and I am working on that now. I thought that if he could possibly become an accessory after the act (or is it fact?), that might develop into something. However, as Grimsdick is publishing my last one in January, I shan't have to write anything for about a year.

[...]

Raining hard today, much to Ethel's delight, as it will be good for the garden.

Love to V.

Yours ever

Plum

Sept 1. 1956

Dear Mr Usborne.

Yours of August 6.

[...]

My father was never anything of an athlete, though a great walker, a thing I inherited from him. Nor was he anything of a scholar. He went to Repton but I think left fairly young and went to Hong Kong. He was always wonderfully enthusiastic about any athletic triumphs Armine and I happened to achieve, and there was a regular tariff of tips – five shillings for taking six wickets, ten shillings for making fifty and so on.

No, there were no Pekes in my boyhood. Every other sort of dog but not Pekes. It wasn't till 1920 that I became Peke-conscious.

Yours of August 16.

(a) No, there was no Nanny who was a menace. I remember all our nurses as great friends.

(b) No. I have never sung at a village concert.

(c) Heaven knows where I got 'blinding and stiffing'. Isn't it a fairly well-known phrase? I imagine blinding is derived from 'Damn your eyes', but I can't elucidate the stiffing.[1]

(d) With her foot in her hand. I must have picked it up somewhere, but where? I think it's an American expression.

(e) 'Smiling, the boy fell dead'.[2] Mr Usborne, <u>really</u>! I thought everybody knew Robert Browning's poem 'An Incident in the French Camp'. Young lieutenant comes to Napoleon with the news that they have taken Ratisbon. Napoleon quite pleased. He notices that the young man isn't looking quite himself.

'You're wounded!' 'Nay,' the soldier's pride
Touched to the quick, he said:

'I'm killed, Sire!' and his chief beside

Smiling the boy fell dead.

(f) The first time I heard 'The old oil' was when we were writing *Rosalie* for Marilyn Miller and Jack Donahue. Jack spoke the line 'Give him the old oil', and I think he invented it.[3]

I imagine most of my phrases are things I have read or heard. I did invent 'oompus boompus', though. I wanted a synonym for 'ranny-gazoo', which is a well-known American expression. 'Tinkerty-tonk' was knut slang of about 1912.

(g) I was at one time a member of Garrick, Beefsteak, Constitutional, and over here Coffee House. I now belong only to Coffee House and the Lotos of New York. At a very early stage I was a member of a ghastly little bohemian club called the Yorick, and later, of course, the Dramatists Club. But I hated them all and almost never went into them. I loathe clubs. The trouble is, it's so difficult to resign. I have not been inside the Coffee House for three years, though I sometimes lunch at the Lotos when in New York. I think I hated the Garrick more than any of them. All those hearty barristers! I did resign from the Garrick.

The Drones is pure invention. I suppose Buck's would be the nearest thing to it. I never belonged to Buck's but sometimes lunched there with Guy Bolton.[4]

[...] Let me know if there is any further info you want about anything.

Yours sincerely

P. G. Wodehouse.

---

1 Usborne asks about the use of the phrase in a novel such as *Jeeves in the Offing* (1960): 'But I suppose these solid citizens have to learn to curb the tongue. Creates a bad impression, I mean, if they start blinding and stiffing as those more happily placed would be' (Chapter 4).

2 Usborne asked about the provenance of this quotation. (See *The Mating Season*, Chapter 4.) 'My guess is that this is a memorable foolish sentiment from some *Eric or Little by Little* type book of your boyhood. Can you inform me further?'

3 See *Right-Ho, Jeeves* (Chapter 23) when Madeline Bassett compares Bertie Wooster to 'those Knights of the Round Table in *The Idylls of the King*'. 'Dashed difficult, of course, to know what to say when someone is giving you the old oil on a scale like that', Bertie comments. Usborne wrote: 'Giving the old oil' [...] Is that an original PGW coining? [...] Or is it all stuff that you have overheard and grabbed and given a local habitation to? For instance "Oompus boompus", "Tinkerty-tonk", "Rannygazoo".

4 'To which London Clubs did you belong? My vague identification of the Drones is Buck's, perhaps because all of its members appear to be young [...] Did you belong to Buck's?'

Remsenburg, Long Island

Sept 10. 1956

Dear Denis.

[...] Sorry I've been so long writing. Got tied up with my Art. A sort of autobiography lugging in my *Punch* articles.[1] Will probably be called facetious by the eggheads.

We have at last got the workmen out of the house and the place is really looking fine now. At last I have a really spacious workroom with plenty of light. The only trouble is that they have built book shelves to hold about a thousand more books than I possess, so that part of the room looks a bit bare.

[...]

Edward should have been sent out of the army on Sept 3, and I am wondering if this Suez business has led to him being kept on. A dirty trick, if so, but not one I would put beyond the authorities.

Marilyn Monroe Gentile, but Arthur Miller definitely Hebraic. I never heard the name Marilyn before our M. Miller.[2]

I'm still reading Max Beerbohm's dramatic criticism book, as it is in short spasms easy to read at breakfast before the papers arrive. I dislike it more every morning. What lice dramatic critics are, especially if they start off by being lice, like M.B.

Other reading of mine has been the *Daily Express*, large batches of which arrive every other day from a man I was in camp with. What a ghastly loathsome paper! My chief hates are Nancy Spain and Rene McColl [*sic*].

Yours ever

Plum

---

1 *America, I Like You.*

2 The playwright Arthur Miller had married Marilyn Monroe in June 1956. PGW was remembering Marilyn Miller, who had starred in the Wodehouse, Bolton and Kern musical, *Sally*, in 1920.

Remsenburg, Long Island, New York

Dec 10. 1956

Darling Sheran.

[...]

Great excitement on just now. Guy has got the idea of reviving one of our old Princess shows, using all Jerry Kern's best tunes from other shows, and he reports great interest in the idea in New York. We shall probably be lunching next week with Dick Rodgers to discuss it. Of course it would be a cinch if Rodgers and Hammerstein would put it on, but if they don't want it I think it should be easy to get another management. There is a terrific boom in Jerry's music just now, and it would cost something very small to put on an intimate piece with only two sets. I have been working at the lyrics, and they are coming out well.

Love from us both

Yours ever

Plum

Remsenburg, Long Island

Dec 18. 1956

Dear Usborne.

Before I forget. 'Not so but far otherwise' is from Kipling's *Just So Stories.*[1]

So glad the book is getting along. Yes, you're right about *Mike*. I never cared very much for him. He is too straight a character to be really interesting.

Vanity Fair. As far as I can remember, I wrote feverishly for *Vanity Fair* until 1916 when the musical comedies started. (I may have carried on through 1917, though I am not sure.) I wrote under the names of Pelham Grenville, P. Brook-Haven, C. P. West and my own. *V.F.* lingered on till 1936, when it was merged with *Vogue*. According to

Margaret Case Harriman, who was on *V.F.* till she joined the *New Yorker*, it was Claire Booth Luce, the ambassadress to Italy, who killed it. She induced Conde Nast to stuff it full of heavy political articles. Frank Crowninshield, the editor, hated this but could do nothing about it. Of course the loss of Benchley, Parker and Sherwood contributed a lot to the death of the magazine. Nobody seemed to have the knack of doing the right sort of light stuff after they left.

[...] Yours ever

P. G. Wodehouse

1 The phrase appears in Wodehouse's *The Gold Bat*, Chapter 2, and in the 1915 Reggie Pepper story 'The Test Case'.

TO DENIS MACKAIL

Basket Neck Lane,
Remsenburg,
New York

Dec 18. 1956

Dear Denis.

[...] I am now two books ahead and shall not have to publish anything else for about eighteen months, but would like to get a plot of some kind going. So far not a gleam. I see, by the way, that Shaw's *Pygmalion* was lifted from Smollett. Did you know that? I suppose the thing to do is to read all those frightful old books. I inherited from the previous owners of this house a set of Fielding. Maybe I could rewrite *Tom Jones*.

Yours ever

Plum

Collier's has just ceased publication. My only serial market on this side! What a life!

Remsenburg, Long Island

June 8. 1957

Dear Denis.

Nice to hear from you again, but sorry you've been having this gouty-arthritic condition. I always have a feeling that almost anything foul can happen if you live in London. Guy Bolton, who is there now, writes to say it's wonderful, but I don't believe him. For about two years everyone has been telling me that *My Fair Lady* is wonderful, and I had to go to it last Wednesday, a prominent manager having got me house tickets, and I thought it was the dullest lousiest show I had ever seen. Even as *Pygmalion* without Rex Harrison it was pretty bad, but with Rex Harrison it's awful. Who ever started the idea that he has charm? I had always considered Professor Higgins the most loathsome of all stage characters, but I never realized how loathsome he could be till I saw Sexy Rexy playing him. Why everyone raves about the thing I can't imagine. I met a sweet clear-thinking woman the other day who told me she had walked out after the first act, which I would have done if I hadn't had Sheran with me, all dewy-eyed and saying 'Isn't this magical!'.

Sheran came to us for the week end after her return from her eleven thousand mile trip, and was lyrical about Frank Sinatra, whom I have always regarded as the world's premier louse. She was looking very pretty and has lost a lot of weight.

Have you read a book called *Peyton Place*? The filthiest thing ever penned. I wonder if they have toned it down for England. It's worse than *Ten North Frederick*. What ghastly muck they are publishing now. I have almost given up reading modern novels, confining myself entirely to mystery stories and the good old stuff in my shelves – e.g. *The Flower Show* par le maitre Mackail.

I am a third of the way though a new novel. I think *Something Fishy* is going to be made into a musical of all things. Cy Feuer, of Feuer and Martin, who put on *Guys and Dolls* etc, wrote and asked if he could do it as a musical. I shall not have to work on it myself, thank goodness, but just sell him the 'basic rights'.

We are having the usual cook trouble. My typewriter has gone lousy, blast it. Being 85 miles from New York we are out of the cook zone. Otherwise, everything is fine in the house.

Yours ever

Plum

TO DENIS MACKAIL

Remsenburg, Long Island

August 17. 1957

Dear Denis.

[...]

Letter from Sheran reports a visit to you and says you were fit. She certainly seems to move in exalted circles. Intimate little dances at Buckingham Palace and all that sort of thing. Sooner her than me.

How are you on the classics? When we bought this house, a number of books came with it, including all Fielding's works. I have been trying to re-read *Tom Jones*, and my opinion is that it is lousy. Do people really think it's the greatest novel ever written? What I felt after reading a few pages was that if this son of a bishop goes on being arch like this, I'm through. And I was through. Can you stand him?

[...]

Yours ever

Plum

TO DENIS MACKAIL

Remsenburg, Long Island

April 22. 1959

Dear Denis.

Delay in writing due to very strenuous work on new novel, which I finished a few days ago. What a hell of a sweat these things are. I often feel how wise you were to give it up. On the other hand, there's probably nothing so pleasant in life as having got the thing done and being able to do the polishing work without having to wonder if one's going to fall down on the vital scene two chapters ahead. I think this one has come out all right. My agent likes it – not Watt, the American one – which is something.

I wish I could convert you to dachshunds. I used to view them with concern, as you do, but they really are all right. Our new Jed – the first one was killed by a car – is the best company you could imagine. Eccentric, yes, but never a dull moment.

Sheran. We had a letter from her the other day. She seems to be enjoying her new job and will probably end by marrying one of those BBC lads in lavender pull-overs.

[...]

TO GUY BOLTON

Remsenburg NY

October 16. 1959

Dear Guy.

It was a terrific relief to know that Virginia was all right. But you must have gone through a pretty bad time till you heard the verdict.

I have been on the sick list myself, but am better now. Inflamed bladder or chill on the bladder or something, the symptoms being agony when I passed water, as the expression is. It brought back the brave old days when I used to get clap. There is still a certain amount of pain, but nothing to bother me much. The only trouble is that I have to be constantly dashing to the bathroom, which hampers me socially. I wanted to go up to New York to attend a binge Knopf is giving for Ira Gershwin, whose book of lyrics is being published on the 19th, but I didn't dare risk it. Otherwise I'm very fit for an old wreck who was 78 yesterday.

[...]

[...] I have done four good chapters of my novel, but it has taken me a month.[1] I think the going will be brisker after a while. But what I had planned as a minor character has turned into a major character, and I shall have to do some thinking in order to get enough stuff for her. Characters in a novel are just like actors. You engage someone like Alec Guinness and then find that all he has is a good scene in act one. What I need is a smashing block comedy scene. I suppose it will come eventually.

We all miss you both sadly. Edward Cazalet is now with us till early November and is a tremendous success.

Love to Va

Yours ever

Plum

1 *Ice in the Bedroom* (1961).

TO LORD CITRINE[1]

Remsenburg, N.Y.

June 29. 1960

Dear Lord Citrine.

I hope this won't be too much of a bother for you, but you can help me very much if you can spare the time.

After months of brooding I am starting a new Blandings Castle novel starring Lord Ickenham ('Uncle Fred') and Lord Emsworth and his pig, and in chapter two they meet and talk at the House of Lords, and what I want is some local colour.[2] Where would they talk? Is there a smoking room as in the House of Commons? If so, could you give me a brief description of it.

Lord Emsworth is at the House of Lords against his wishes, Lady Constance having ordered him to go there and vote on some bill. I thought at first that he might have gone because the bill was of some interest to himself, but it works better if it is something Lady Constance is interested in, because I want to plant early how she oppresses him. Can you invent some bill which would sound right? (Lord Ickenham, of course, is voting because it gives him a chance to be in London. Lady Ickenham can't object if he goes to London with such public-spirited motives.)

It is a very important chapter, as it introduces Lord Ickenham and gives Lord Emsworth the chance to tell the reader what the book is about. It ends with Lord Emsworth inviting Lord Ickenham to Blandings, because the Duke of Dunstable is staying there and Lord E. feels he needs moral support to help him cope with him.

Did you by any chance see the *Evening Standard* with an interview with me? It was an appalling thing, making me out a sort of gloomy derelict who can't sell a book or an article in America. It appeared, oddly enough, when I had just got a commission from a magazine for a 2500 word article for a price of $2500. I have consulted experts about a libel action, and I am convinced they will tell me I shall be able to soak the *Standard* for thousands.

Best wishes

Yours sincerely

P. G. Wodehouse

1 British trade unionist and politician, and admirer of PGW's work. He was to recommend PGW for a knighthood in 1967.
2 The novel was *Service With a Smile*.

TO LORD CITRINE

Remsenburg, N.Y.

July 23. 1960

Dear Lord Citrine.

How frightfully kind of you to go to all that trouble to help me. I really do appreciate it. Your letter has solved all my difficulties... UNLESS I have got my times wrong, which will be a big disaster.

I start with Lord Emsworth going to London to attend the opening of Parliament next day. Next day I have Lord Ickenham lunching with Pongo Twistleton at the Drones. He has been to the opening of Parliament in the morning.

After lunch he and Pongo go to a registry office to see the hero married (only the bride doesn't turn up). Then on leaving the registry office Lord I. goes with his robes and coronet to return them to Moss

Bros. (Your suggestion.) There he meets Lord Emsworth and the plot thickens.

You see what I mean. I have assumed that the Opening takes place in the morning and that the Peers have some place where they can robe themselves and after the ceremony de-robe themselves and go off in their ordinary clothes to lunch at the Drones. Is this correct? Golly, I hope so, or I shall have a lot of rewriting to do.

In the booklet you sent me I see that Elizabeth the First opened parliament on April 2, 1571, so I am making April the time of the story, though summer would suit me better. Is the opening always in April?

So can you spare a moment to brief me on the following:

1. Is the opening ceremony in the morning?

2. Is it in April?

3. Would Lord Ickenham and Lord Emsworth robe themselves at their hotel or at the House of Lords? And would they after the ceremony get into their ordinary clothes again? (I can't see Lord I. in his robes at the Drones!)

If your answers are favourable, I am home. If not, I shall have to make the Pongo-Lord-I lunch the day following the opening, which won't be so good.

How tricky it always is when one has to keep to known facts. One can't afford to go wrong.

Though I shall not be using the interior of the House of Lords this time, your information is bound to come in handy sooner or later. I am sure to need the Lords atmosphere in some other story.

I think this novel is going to be good, if only I can get the end right. But I usually find that if one gets the thing going, the impetus carries one through.

I had a letter this morning from the Jenkins people saying that my Jeeves book will be out on August 12 and that they are sending me my copies. When they arrive, I will send you one. (I hope the jacket won't be too awful!)

Did I tell you that that *Evening Standard* interview said that I was very rich, very sad and lonely with nothing to spend my money on and depressed all the time because my writing powers were waning and my public had deserted me. (I can't imagine where the man got all that rot.) But the result is that every post brings letters from women in England either asking for a loan or else saying that if I will pay their fare over here they will come and cheer me up. The fact that I have been very happily married for forty-six years and would prefer my wife's company doesn't occur to them.

Yours sincerely

P. G. Wodehouse

TO J. D. GRIMSDICK

Remsenburg, N.Y.

Nov 28. 1960

Dear J.D.

How unerring your judgment always is! And how right you were about Usborne's book. It is quite good, but there is so much rambling off-the-ball stuff that the good parts are smothered.

Of course I cut the 'Internee' chapter right out and also all the references to the broadcasts which I was able to find at a first reading. I am going through the whole book again and ought to be able to return you the script in a few days. As I take it there is no immediate rush, I will send it by sea mail.

I can't make Usborne out. He is supposed to be friendly, but in that Internee chapter and all through the book he was making about as vicious an attack on me as anyone has done so far. And I suppose he will be amazed that I could take any exception to it!

The book is supposed to be an analysis of my work, and references to my private affairs have no part in it. Cut out all the stuff about the broadcasts and you have a neat script, about the right length.

If I had written this letter two days ago, immediately on reading the book, the tone of it would have been much more belligerent. For two days I was absolutely furious with Usborne, but now I have got over it.

He is an extraordinary ass, though. Fancy not realizing – as I suppose he didn't – what the effect of digging up all that old stuff would be. Just as everybody or nearly everybody has forgotten about it.

In your letter you say that you think there should be a factual chapter about the broadcasts at the end. I am against this. Ignore the whole thing, I say. I feel very strongly about this.

I am cutting to the bone in other parts, especially the chapter about the school stories. Who wants three or four pages giving the plot of a thing I wrote for *Chums* in 1905? I am also cutting about five thousand words about my brother Armine and all the stuff about fights at school. He seems to have an obsession about fights.

Well, there it is. I think that what is left will make a very good book.

[...]

Yours ever

P.G.

TO WILLIAM TOWNEND

100 Park Avenue, New York

January 3. 1961

Dear Bill,

The letters arrived yesterday, and I have just finished a first quick perusal.

It gives one an odd feeling reading letters one has written over a period of forty years. Rather like drowning and having one's whole past life flash before one. How few of the people I mention are still alive. Guy Bolton, thank goodness, and Malcolm Muggeridge and Ira Gershwin and Frank Sullivan, also thank goodness, but Flo Ziegfeld, Charlie Dillingham, Ray Comstock, Marilyn Miller, Gertie Lawrence. Jerry Kern, George Gershwin. Lorimer, Wells, Kipling, Molnár... dozens of them, all gone, and you and I in a few months will be eighty.

Solemn thought, that. Makes one revise one's views. I had always supposed that the whole idea of the thing was that others might make the Obituary column but that I was immortal and would go on forever. I see now that I was mistaken, and that I, too, must ere long hand in my dinner pail. I'm not sure I like the new arrangement, but there it is.

It does seem silly that blokes as young and sprightly as you and me should have reached such an age as eighty. However, it has to be faced. I'm slowing up. I still do my before-breakfast exercises every morning, plus touching my toes fifty times without a suspicion of bending my knees, and I can navigate my daily three miles, but I can see I'm not quite the man I was.

Little things tell the story. When on my infrequent visits to New York a taxi driver nearly runs me down, he no longer damns my eyes and wants to know where I think I'm going; he shakes his head indulgently and says, 'Watch it, grandpa!' Furthermore, I am noticeably less nimble when getting after the dog next door if I see him with his head and shoulders in our garbage can. And I note a certain stiffness of the limbs which causes me, when rising from my chair, to remind the beholder, if a man who has travelled in Equatorial Africa, of a hippopotamus heaving itself up from the mud of a riverbank.

[...]

Waugh was to give a talk on Wodehouse on 15 July 1961. It was a preliminary to the later celebration of Wodehouse's eightieth birthday in October.

TO EVELYN WAUGH

Remsenburg N.Y.

Jan 23. 1961

It really was wonderful of you to have fixed up that BBC thing, and I am tremendously grateful. What this world needs is more people like you in it. I can't tell you how I feel about the way you have always championed me against my attackers. I shall never forget it.

We now have one of those latest words in radio where you press a knob and get London, Paris etc, so I shall be able to listen in.

[...]
Yours ever
P. G. Wodehouse

Remsenburg, N.Y.

Jan 31. 1961

Dear J.D.

[...]

About the Usborne book. Sorry, but I destroyed all that broadcasts material. I felt strongly that after you had cut it out of the book there was nothing to prevent Usborne selling the stuff as an article to some magazine, and destroying the stuff would at least compel him to do all his scavenging all over again.

[...]

Yours ever

P.G.

William Connor, the journalist known as 'Cassandra', had condemned Wodehouse on the BBC in 1941. They had since become friends, and Connor wrote in the Daily Mirror *of his desire to 'bury the whole story and to forgive and, where necessary, to hope to be forgiven'.*

TO WILLIAM CONNOR

Remsenburg, New York

May 10. 1961

Dear Walp.

A rather embarrassing situation has arisen. (For me, I mean. I don't suppose you'll turn a hair over it.)

Some time ago I had a letter from Evelyn Waugh, saying (quote) 'I have arranged for the BBC to make an act of homage to you on July 15th, the twentieth anniversary of their attack on you.'

I thought that was fine, but I have just had a letter from Guy Bolton, recently arrived in London, and he says that somebody told him 'that Evelyn Waugh is making a TV appearance which will be an attack on

Cassandra in answer to what he wrote of you'.

Well, dash it, you and I are buddies, and if the above is correct, I don't want you thinking that I had anything to do with this. I value our friendship too much. I'll do what I can to halt the proceedings, though as I say, you probably won't give a damn.

Even before I met you, I had never had any ill-feeling about that BBC talk of yours. All you had to go on was that I had spoken on the German radio, so naturally you let yourself go. And what the hell! It's twenty years ago.

I hope the cats are flourishing. We have just had to add a stray Boxer to the establishment. So now we have two cats (both strays), a dachshund and this Boxer. Fortunately they all get on together like old college chums.

When are you going to make another of your trips to this side?

Yours ever

Plum

TO GUY BOLTON

Remsenburg, New York

Sept 24. 1961

[...]

I suppose you saw in the London papers about Marion Davies's death.[1] I don't know it should upset one, but it does. Maybe it's just because it brings home to one the passage of time. I'm beginning to dislike very much the thought of being eighty in less than a month. It's very hard to get used to it. [...]

1 Marion Davies (1897–1961), the long-term companion of the newspaper magnate William Randolph Hearst, had starred in *Oh, Boy!* in 1917. The Wodehouses had met her again during their stay in Hollywood.

Anything Goes, the hit musical of 1934 with Ethel Merman playing Reno, had been written by Wodehouse, Guy Bolton and Cole Porter, and was then heavily revised by Howard Lindsay and Russell Crouse. It was revived in 1962, and Wodehouse was asked to update the song 'You're the Top'.

Remsenburg, New York

Oct 28. 1961

Dear Guy.

Here is the revised 'You're The Top' lyric. It was a pretty difficult job, as the lines were so short and one was confined to nouns and no chance of using adjectives, plus all those double rhymes. I think it has come out all right, but of course with a lyric like this one will probably get some much better ideas in the course of time. I'm not satisfied with some of the couplets like Cole's 'arrow collar' and 'dollar', which seem flat to me, and the poor devil got very exhausted after doing five refrains. Fancy letting a line like "You're the baby grand of a lady and a gent" get by. Not to mention 'Inferno's Dante'. What the hell does <u>that</u> mean?

Two things about the show disturb me – or, rather, three. I don't like the letter they wrote me saying they thought of making the thing a 1934 opus. WHY? There's nothing in the story that couldn't be 1961, and, as you said in your letter to them, people are sick of those old-style musicals. I think we should insist on making it 1961 and tell them we won't let the show go on as a 1934 piece.

Secondly, I have always disliked *Anything Goes* heartily because the wrongness of the balance offends my artistic soul. Naturally, if you've got Ethel Merman starring, you have to give her something to do, but when the thing becomes non-Ethel-Merman, it's all wrong having Reno do all the three good numbers. It throws everything out of kilter. You feel Why the hell doesn't Billy marry Reno if he thinks so highly of her? Is there no way we can give 'You're The Top' to Hope and Billy? (On second thoughts, no we can't, there's no way of making flip stuff like this suitable for the heroine.)

Thirdly, the score is so thin. Apart from the three song hits we have almost nothing. Even after twenty-seven years I can remember how lousy that 'Gypsy in Me' number was. All we have except for the three big ones are 'All Through the Night' (which is lyrically all wrong for the spot it's in, the love story not having advanced so far) and the comic song by Moon. Apart from those we have four sorts of opening choruses, a reprise and a finale. What we want are two good duets for Hope and Billy.

[...] Summing up, a firm hand with Reno!

Love to Va

Yours ever

Plum

Remsenburg, New York

October 28. 1961

Dear Guy.

[...]

I'm working on the *A. Goes* lyric and have got a masterly couplet, as follows: –

'When the courts decide, as they did latterly,

We could read *Lady Chatterley*

If we chose,

Anything goes.'

(Darned sight better than anything old King Cole ever wrote).

By the way, for London most of my Top lyric will be meaningless. I'll rewrite it. But you will have to collect as many English things to mention as you can. Would they know who Grandma Moses was over there?[1]

I seem to have become the Grand Old Man of English Literature. Grimsdick tells me they have already received more than five hundred inches of press notices of my birthday and more coming in all the time.

[...] Love to Va

Yours ever

Plum

1 Born in 1860, renowned American folk artist Anna Mary Robertson 'Grandma' Moses had turned 100 the previous year.

Remsenburg, New York.

November 1. 1961

Dear Evelyn.

At last I am able to write and thank YOU for your birthday cable. I had over sixty letters to answer from fans and I put off writing to friends till I had disposed of them.

I was stunned by the press I got in England. My publisher wrote me that he had already received over five hundred inches of press stuff and more coming in all the time. Entirely due to that broadcast of yours, for which I can never be sufficiently grateful. It pulverized the opposition.

I hope you are going strong. I feel exactly the same as I did twenty years ago and still do my morning exercises daily. I suppose in due course I shall suddenly fall apart, but as of even date I am in great shape.

I have just been re-reading *Scoop*. What a masterly book! I don't know anyone who can do atmosphere like you. Referring particularly to the home life of the Boot family.

I always feel that you and I lead exactly the same sort of life and enjoy more than anything not having to meet one's fellow men. I have become as attached to this place as William Boot was to Boot Magna Hall. I never leave it except to go to New York for the day about three times a year. The only catch is that I would like to come to England for a visit but can't desert the dachshund, the Boxer and the two cats, who throw a fit if I am away for the inside of a day. Isn't it extraordinary that the country never gets dull. There always seems something to do, if it is only taking out the garbage or exercising the dogs.

I think our old show *Anything Goes* (1934) is going to be revived both here and in London, and I am very busy revising Cole Porter's lyrics, bringing the topical stuff up to date. When I am through with them, I am hoping to start a new Jeeves novel. I have got the scenario all set and it looks pretty good.

Yours ever

P. G. Wodehouse

Remsenburg, N.Y.

November 2. 1961

Dear Guy.

Here is the revised *Anything Goes* lyric. I also enclose another extra refrain for 'You're The Top' (a good one) and Cole's original lyric for 'A. Goes' so that you can see how lousy it was.

The trouble with Cole is that he has no power of self-criticism. He just bungs down anything whether it makes sense or not just because he has thought of what he feels is a good rhyme. Can you imagine turning in stuff like 'So Mrs Roosevelt with all her trimmins (why trimmins?) can broadcast a bed by Simmons, 'Cause Franklin knows anything goes'?

I have rewritten the verse, because Cole's verse seemed to me absolute drivel. What on earth does a line like 'Any shock they should try to stem' mean? and in the first refrain he has 'bare limbs', 'me undressed' and 'nudist parties' one after the other. It shows what a powerful personality Ethel Merman must have, to be able to put that sort of stuff over.

I always feel about Cole's lyrics that he sang them to Elsa Maxwell and Noel Coward in a studio stinking of gin and they said 'Oh, Cole, <u>darling</u>, it's just too marvellous.' Why can't he see that you must have a transition of thought in a lyric just as in dialogue?

Do you remember a lyric of his with a line about 'a burning inside of me', followed by something about something being 'under the hide of me'?[1] No taste!!

[...]

Love to Va

Yours ever

Plum

1 See Cole Porter's 'Night and Day', written for the 1932 musical *Gay Divorce*.

Remsenburg, New York

November 21. 1961

Dear Mr Thuermer.

Awfully nice to hear from you after all these years. How you do get around! I wonder how you are liking it in Ghana.

How well I remember that time you came to Tost. Nor have I forgotten the baked beans and the tobacco. What a curious life that was. I suppose I am one of the few internees who thoroughly enjoyed it. I loved being able to work on my novel without agents and people calling me up to ask how I was getting on and if I could rush the text of it a bit there might be a chance of a movie sale. I used to do about a page a day and never felt I had to do any more.

I'm not so sure I altogether approve of this thing of being eighty. I always thought other people might die but that I was immortal and would go on for ever. I am now beginning to doubt this. Still, I continue wonderfully fit and still do my Daily Dozen every morning, plus touching my toes fifty times without bending the knees. I have done the Daily Dozen every day since 1919 without missing a day even when we were three days on the train going to Tost. [...]

If you ever come to the USA on leave, do give me a ring and we'll foregather.

Yours ever,

P. G. Wodehouse

Remsenburg, New York

December 14. 1961

Dear Evelyn.

I hope this catches you before you start out for the tropics.

It was awfully nice of you to put that charming inscription in *The End of the Battle*, but when I had finished it, which I did ten minutes ago, I felt that I ought to be putting it in a book to you. Yours has always been a high standard, but you have surpassed yourself in this one. It's terrific.

I have been trying to analyse the way you do it, – that unhurried, almost casual, way you tell the story, with no straining for 'punch' scenes, so that for quite a while the reader feels that nothing is happening and then suddenly realizes that you have opened up a whole world to him. (This is rottenly put, but I hope you will get what I mean. I think what I'm driving at is that the whole thing seems so effortless. What an extraordinary gift you have for giving a whole character in a couple of lines or a few words of dialogue.)

[...]

I am now going to read all three books over again. I have been re-reading all yours lately, starting with *Decline and Fall*. I think I told you how much I had enjoyed *Scoop*. I hope *Battle* sells in millions.

[...]

Yours ever

P. G. Wodehouse

TO S. C. 'BILLY' GRIFFITH

Remsenburg
New York

January 30. 1962

Dear Billy.

[...]

How wonderful that Mike has got into Cambridge. It would have been tragic if he had missed. A pity it can't be Pembroke, but if I were you I wouldn't dream of taking the gamble, for, as you say, he might strike a bad day and miss Pembroke after giving up Magdalene. It doesn't really matter what college he goes to, as he is a cert for his cricket, hockey and racquets blues wherever he is.

I do agree with you about the folly of the Cambridge authorities in not paying any attention to 'on the field' excellence. I think they're all wrong making the standards so high. Cambridge ought to be like it was in my young days, a place where you could get in if you could read and write. Bertie Wooster and his pals just walked into their university, presumably purely on charm of manner, and I think that's how it ought to be. Too much of this business of East Salford Secondary Grammar School nowadays.

[...]

Yours ever

P.G.

TO J. D. GRIMSDICK

Remsenburg, New York

February 23. 1962

Dear J.D.

Very sad news today. Bill Townend died last week. I had a letter from his brother. Bill's wife died not long ago, and it completely knocked him out, and on top of that, while alone in their house, he had a bad fall and was not discovered till late next morning. He went to a nursing home and there had two more falls, one of which broke his femur. His brother said he had been in a sort of coma for weeks and had lost the will to live. As you can imagine, it has been a great blow to me.

[...]

The Jeeves novel is coming out fine. I think it will be quite long enough.

Yours ever

P.G.

Writing a few days later, Wodehouse noted that 'Bill Townend's death makes me very sad, but it really was a merciful thing, as his wife, to whom he had been married for forty-seven years and to whom he was devoted, died a few weeks before he did, and he felt he had nothing to live for, especially as he could not do any writing. [...] He would have been a helpless invalid and miserable if he had lived, so I don't feel as badly about it as I might, if things had been different'.

A month later, he was cheered by the appearance of his old friend Ellaline Terriss on the TV show This Is Your Life. *An actress and musical comedy star, Terriss made her stage debut in 1888 and went on to appear in films up until 1939. She was the widow of the famous actor-producer Seymour Hicks, for whom Wodehouse had written lyrics for* The Beauty of Bath *(1906) and* The Gay Gordons *(1907). Terriss had appeared in both shows. It was she who nicknamed Wodehouse 'the Hermit' when he came to stay with them in 1907 and often vanished into the woods for long walks when working out a lyric.*

TO ELLALINE TERRISS

May 20. 1962

My dear Ella.

It was such a joy to me to do my little bit on the tribute to you. I wish I could have come over, but it was impossible. It would have meant leaving Mrs. P.G.W. all alone in the house, and she has just had an operation on her foot and can't walk. (Or couldn't then, but she is much better now and can get around.)

I have had quite a number of letters saying what a success the show was and how sweet you looked! I wonder how many people there are today beside myself who saw you in *His Excellency.*[1] I always remember being taken to that play and loving it. I've always heard that the music was no good, but I thought it fine. Do you remember the 'practical jokes' trio – you and Grossmith and somebody else?

I have never forgotten that Devonshire holiday, nor the Christmas (1906) at your Old Forge house – was it Esher? No, Merstham. How happy those days were.

I am now very cosily settled in this pretty village ninety miles from New York with a wife I adore – we have been married 47 years – two dogs and two cats. I am still writing as hard as ever, but I don't do anything in the theatre now.

> Lots of love
> Yours ever
> The Hermit

1 *His Excellency* opened at the Lyric in 1895.

In 1962, Bolton published a novel on the love affair of Percy Bysshe Shelley and Mary Godwin entitled The Olympians.

TO GUY BOLTON

Remsenburg, New York

July 2. 1962

Dear Guy.

[...]

I came across enclosed in the local paper and wondered if you might not make your next one about Hazlitt. Very interesting character. Did you know that he was a devil of a chap with the women and shocked Wordsworth because when a girl wouldn't yield to his 'lascivious advances' he spanked her? According to a book that's just been published, he was a very unpopular man and only Charles Lamb could stand him.

Yours

Plum

The following letter was written when Ethel had to go into hospital for a cancer check-up.

TO ETHEL WODEHOUSE

Remsenburg, New York

9 p.m. August 21. 1962

My own precious darling Bunny.

I am writing this to tell you how much I love you and how miserable I am when you are not with me. It is about half an hour since we talked on the telephone, and I have just taken round the bird seed – not omitting your brown patches!! – and also filled the bird bowls. So you needn't worry about your pets. No sign of the ducks these last days, but your little red bird has been there, tucking in.

It's odd about the dogs. I know they must miss you, but I think they puzzle it out and say to themselves 'Well, the old man's still here,' and assume that you are bound to turn up soon. They both slept quite happily in the living room last night. I turned in at eleven, and when I hadn't got to sleep by two-thirty I got up and took a pill and went to sleep after that. Due to worrying about you, of course.

It's awful to think of you having to go through all those awful things again. I do hope that after they are through you will get a good rest.

Margie and Lynn are looking after me splendidly. What a nice, cheerful woman Margie is.

I'm worrying if you are getting the right food. Do get the special diet. You ought to eat lots of custards and drink a lot of milk.

[...]

What a sad thing it is being alone. Ordinarily hours pass without my seeing you, but just knowing you're there makes it all right. Now I keep thinking 'I'll go up and see my Bunny', and then I realize that you aren't there. I do miss you so, darling.

I don't suppose you'll get this till Thursday or even Friday, as I shall mail it tomorrow at two in the afternoon. Still, so long as you do get it!

Oceans of love, darling. I'm thinking loving thoughts of you all the time. I love you more and more every day.

Your

Plummie

TO DENIS MACKAIL

Remsenburg
New York

June 18. 1963

Dear Denis.

Thanks for letter and the letter you enclosed. Very gratifying.

[...]

We are lapping up all the Profumo stuff and wondering who the member of the royal family is who is rumoured to have been mixed up with Christine. By the way, am I wrong or is England now a sink of vice and corruption? Viewed from a distance, it gives the impression of a country one is glad no longer to be a citizen of.[1]

Literary note. My last two novels have appeared serially in a magazine called *Playboy* (all other serial markets in the USA having disappeared), and I see in the papers that a warrant for the arrest of the publisher for publishing obscene matter has been issued. Apparently the current number (which I haven't seen) devotes twelve pages to photographs of Jayne Mansfield in the nude (with licentious captions) and so ye Ed is on the run. How will this affect my reputation? It would be great if I found myself listed among the dirty writers. Just what I need to tap another public.

Well, *Cleopatra* has opened, and the *NY Herald-Tribune* says Liz Taylor is a lousy actress.[2] Did you know she was a bosom pal of Sheran's. Sheran, when she was over here, was weighed down with photographs of L.T. and Burton embracing one another, plus some of LT alone, signed 'To Sheran from cousin Elizabeth'. I suppose millions will go to see the ruddy picture, but not me. Can you imagine sitting through a pic that lasts four hours?

[...]

Yours ever

<u>Plum</u>

1 There was a widely publicised scandal in which the British politician John Profumo was exposed as having been involved with Christine Keeler, a prostitute.
2 *Cleopatra*, a 1963 film, directed by Joseph L. Mankiewicz and starring Elizabeth Taylor and Richard Burton. The *New York Herald-Tribune* termed the film 'at best a major disappointment, at worst an extravagant exercise in tedium'.

TO ETHEL WODEHOUSE

P. G. Wodehouse
Remsenburg
New York

October 23. 1963

My own precious darling Bunny.
This is just to tell you how much I am missing you and praying that

you will soon come back safe to me. I love you, darling, more than a million bits.

Oh, how lonely it was without you last night! The house was like a morgue. I buckled down after dinner and wrote thirteen letters and this morning I wrote four more and am now all cleaned up. I wrote long letters to Birdie and Paul Schmidt and told them all about your bad health and how you wanted to write to them but could not.

Gracie turned up this morning with glowing reports of Jed. She said everybody loved him and he was as good as gold. She also said that she would take him if we went away and her sister would love to have Debbie. So if we can fix up Poona and Blackie, we could go somewhere for a change. What companions the animals are! I'm sure they knew that I was blue and missing you last night, for they made a special fuss over me. Poona came and sat on my lap for hours.

I am looking after your birds. I gave them seed and water at lunch time today and at five o'clock yesterday. So they are all right. I gave them the water just now, after taking the dogs for their walk, and every morsel of seed everywhere was eaten! I will give them some more at five. I am being very good and not going out after dark. I just let Debbie out of the kitchen door last night.

Poor darling, you must be having a ghastly time. I do hope they won't exhaust you with those X-rays, but I'm afraid it will be very painful. But I know they will find that everything is all right and you will come back to me in a few days.

Gracie made me a very nice cheese souffle for lunch, and I am looking forward to dinner. How clever you were inviting Guy and Virginia. It will be so nice having them.

All my love, angel, and remember that I never stop thinking of you and how much I love you.

Your

Plummie.

Both dogs and both cats are in my study with me as I write this.

Remsenburg
New York

July 16. 1964

Dear Guy.

[...]

New development in the Wodehouse home. In September my
brother Armine's widow is coming to live with us.[1] She has just spent
a week here and we both like her very much, so I think the new
arrangement will be a success. She will take a lot of work off Ethel's
hands, and one great advantage is that now I shall be able to go to
New York for the night if I want to, which I couldn't do before as I
couldn't leave Ethel alone in the house.

Love to Va

Yours ever

Plum

1 Nella (Helen) Wodehouse.

Remsenburg
New York

August 3. 1964

Dear Guy.

[...]

I have been sticking to my afternoon walk, but it's very dull without
you.[1] I don't often go more than once round. I can't help feeling that
the dogs must get very bored with the same walk every day, but there's
nowhere else to go.

How do you feel about literary classics? I have come to the conclusion that there must be something wrong with me, because I can't
read them. I tried Jane Austen and was bored stiff, and last night I

had a go at Balzac's *Père Goriot* and had to give it up. I couldn't take the least interest in the characters. Give me Patricia Wentworth!

Ethel is convinced that Goldwater will win in November, but I keep telling her he hasn't a hope. The Democrats are the larger party, and I can't see any of them defecting to Goldwater. But it does make one anxious to think there is even a chance of him becoming president. Ethel likes his TV personality, but to me he is a louse. I can't stand him.[2]

Love to Va

Yours ever

Plum

---

1 The Boltons lived about two miles from the Wodehouses. Bolton and Wodehouse developed the habit of taking afternoon walks together.

2 PGW refers to the 1964 presidential election, in which the Republican Senator Barry Goldwater of Arizona ran against the incumbent President, Lyndon B. Johnson, who had come to office the previous year after the assassination of John F. Kennedy. Goldwater was known for his conservative views; the Democrat Johnson, meanwhile, was associated with the popularity of Kennedy, and won the election.

TO MR SCHREYER

Remsenburg
New York

August 13. 1964

Dear Mr. Schreyer,

Thank you so much for your letter. I am delighted that you have enjoyed my books.

When I was your age, my two idols were W. S. Gilbert, the Savoy opera man, and Conan Doyle – with a slight edge in favour of the latter because I knew him through playing cricket with him, whereas Gilbert was a sort of remote godlike character to me. (I did meet him once. A mutual friend took me to lunch at his (Gilbert's) house and I killed one of G's best stories by laughing in the wrong place!)

Yours sincerely

P. G. Wodehouse

P. G. Wodehouse
Remsenburg
New York

Nov 27. 1964

Dear J.D.

The Galahad books arrived after I had written to you.[1] Did you ever see a ghastlier jacket in your life? [See plate 38.] One would have thought that anyone reading the book would have gathered that Gally was a dapper elderly man, considering that he is fully described, and this son of unmarried parents has made him look twenty-five and one of the Beatles at that. Taken in conjunction with the loathsome title, one feels that P. Schwed ought to rent a padded cell in some not too choosy lunatic asylum.[2]

Yours ever

P. G.

1 *The Brinkmanship of Galahad Threepwood* was published in the UK as *Galahad at Blandings*.
2 Peter Schwed, Wodehouse's American publisher at Simon and Schuster.

In 1965, Wodehouse and Ethel's grandson, Edward Cazalet, was to marry Camilla Gage in England.

P. G. Wodehouse
Remsenburg
New York

Jan 27. 1965

Dear Edward.

Thanks so much for the books, which arrived this morning.

I am planning – always provided the Colonel isn't ill[1] – to come over for the wedding, so will you let me know

(a) When it will be

(b) Where

as I shall want to know what boat to sail on.

I suppose morning coat and topper will be of the essence. I shall have to hire them from Moss Bros. I haven't owned them since I attended the wedding of Pop Cazalet and Miss Leonora Wodehouse (and darned attractive I looked, too).

Tell Sheran the *Sunday Times* is arriving regularly.

Yours ever

<u>Plum</u>

P.S. Just sold a short story to *Saturday Evening Post* for $2500. I haven't had anything in the *SEP* since 1940![2]

---

1 'The Colonel' – Edward's nickname for Ethel, often adopted by Ethel herself.
2 'The Battle of Squashy Hollow', *SEP*, 5 June 1965, published along with an article, 'Fifty Years is Practically Half a Century', to celebrate fifty years since his first contribution on 26 June 1915.

TO ETHEL WODEHOUSE

P. G. Wodehouse
Remsenburg
New York

Feb 6. 1965

Darling Angel One.

Life's a terrible blank without my Bunny, but I think you're quite right to stay in NY another week. Dash it, it's about ten years since you were out of Remsenburg and you certainly deserve a change.

Spend money like water, because we are simply rolling in it. The bank statement showed $21,000 odd, and since then I have paid in nearly $6000 from Simon and Schuster royalties, the check for the short story from the *Saturday Evening Post* and a nice little $500 which *Playboy* sent me as a token of their esteem. So go out and buy yourself a diamond tiara.

[...] I am weakening very much on the idea of going to England. It seems silly to take all that trouble and spend all that money just for about ten days there. I think it would be much better to cancel the trip. What do you think? (I thought your voice sounded sad on the phone when you asked me if I was really going.) I told Edward that my sailing was only provisional and depended on how you were feeling, so he won't be disappointed.

It's pretty grim here now with snow and ice all over the place and not a sign of it ever melting. I take the dogs out every afternoon, but it's very unpleasant.

I am making rather good progress with a plot for a new novel, but as always it's slow work.

The kitten is terrifically fit and roams all over the house. She will come and lie on my bed, which infuriates Jed and Debbie.

All my love, darling

Your Plummie

TO GUY BOLTON

P. G. Wodehouse
Remsenburg
New York

August 7. 1965

Dear Guy.

[...]

Edward has arrived with the most charming wife. She is a nice quiet girl with no frills and a sense of humor, – more like the girls of our youth than the modern lot. They are staying till Monday, when they fly to Honolulu, and everything has worked out fine. They are staying as our guests of course at the Patio, and they like it there very much. We have lent Edward the car and they have wangled admission to the tennis at the Golf Club and also have somehow managed to get into the Swordfish, so they are well fixed. They come here for tea and dinner and bridge afterwards, so they are having a good time.

[...]

Love to Va
Yours ever
<u>Plum</u>

In a letter to Sheran Cazalet, Wodehouse described his daily routine. 'I have started a new novel and it seems to be coming out all right, though I have never done one that departed so much from my scenario. There is now nothing left of my original idea and as for the characters all the most important ones have been cut out. Still, it's progressing, though slowly because of the soap operas. I used to watch just Love of Life, *and now I have got hooked to* Edge of Night *and* Secret Storm, *which come on from 3-30 to 4-30, so I have to do my writing after dinner. Also, at 11-30 in the morning I have to watch the* Dick Van Dyke Show. *Have you seen it? It's easily the best thing on TV.'*

TO GUY BOLTON

P. G. Wodehouse
Remsenburg
New York

August 19. 1966

Dear Guy.

[...]

How difficult it is to write stories about a country when you aren't in it. One keeps getting up against facts. I have just got to a point in my novel where a man with a guilty conscience thinks the hero is a private detective trailing him, and they both start for London from somewhere in Sussex which might be Horsham, and of course the guilty conscience man is always looking round and seeing the hero, both of them being headed for the same objective, their mutual bank in Aldwych. Now here's where you can rally round. Do you go to Victoria from Horsham or Hayward's Heath or whatever it is? If so, on arriving at Victoria and wanting to go to Aldwych and not wanting to take a taxi because of the traffic, you take the Tube. What station do you get out at for Aldwych?[1]

Great excitement down here. Yesterday a couple of men got into the house at the end of the lane where Jed barks at the poodle and came out with a lot of silver and a TV set, – and this was early afternoon. Ethel is talking of buying a gun!

Love to Va

Yours ever

<u>Plum</u>

1 See the end of Chapter 5 of *Company for Henry* (1967). In the end, the Hero and the Guilty Conscience end up both going to the Post Office in Ashby Paradene, so the information was not actually required.

TO EDWARD CAZALET

P. G. Wodehouse
Remsenburg
New York

Dec 4. 1966

Dear Edward.

What wonderful news. How happy you must both be feeling, and what a bit of luck for a baby having parents like you and Camilla. He (or she) couldn't have chosen better. We are looking forward eagerly to seeing you and C at Easter. Do stay as long as you can. I'm afraid an Easter visit can't be as long as a summer one, but it will be fine if you can manage a few days. Better still, of course, if you can make it longer.

I don't know if it has arrived yet – probably not at this time of year – but we have shipped off to you a photograph of your mother and me off to Hollywood in 1930. The Colonel hadn't come over yet; she joined us later. It was rather funny – I had two shows in rehearsal, one a straight play starring Gertrude Lawrence, the other a musical for Ziegfeld, and I thought it would be fun to go to Hollywood for a sort of weekend just to get a change, and of course both managements took it for granted that I had skipped off permanently. We had three days in Hollywood and then came back, so all was forgiven. This was the time when we were asked to a party, and Hollywood parties always start with about two hours cocktails, and your mother got stuck with some man before dinner, and as she didn't drink found it a bit much. So when dinner was announced she had found two hours of the man's company about enough and heaved a sigh of relief at the prospect of getting rid of him, only to discover that she was sitting next to him at the meal. I wonder she ever recovered.

[...]
Love to Camilla
Yours ever
<u>Plum</u>

P.S. Here's the old Christmas present

TO ETHEL WODEHOUSE

P. G. Wodehouse
Remsenburg
New York

July 6. 1967

My darling Angel Bunny.
Gosh, how I am missing my loved one! The house is a morgue without you. Do you realize that – except for two nights I spent in NY and the time you were in the hospital – we haven't been separated for a night for twenty years!! This morning Jed waddled into my room at about nine, and I said to myself 'My Bunny's awake early' and was just starting for your room when I remembered. It's too awful being separated like this.

Jed definitely misses you. [...] He is quite cheerful for a while and then he starts wandering round looking for you. Sorry to say Deb hasn't given a sign that she has noticed anything wrong.

I do hope, darling, that you aren't having too bad a time. I'm afraid it's bound to be pretty unpleasant with those X-rays etc. How wonderful it would be if these doctors could get you right.

[...]

Now what else is there? Dogs and cats all well. Jed wouldn't stay on the sofa with Deb and came and slept on Nella's bed last night. Poona is fine. I have fed the birds. I have just come back from my walk with Jed and Debbie and Minnie. How I wish I was coming up to *Edge of Night* and finding you in your room. James is working hard in the garden.

[...] Well, darling, I do hope you are getting along as well as can be expected and getting some sleep at nights. I am counting the days till you can get back to me.

Oceans of love, angel

Your

Plummy

(Can't draw Deb)

July 11. 1967

My darling angel Bunny whom I love so dear.

I am writing this in my chair after dinner. Smoky has at last got out of it after pinching it for the whole day. Poona is asleep on another chair, Jed and Debbie are asleep in the living-room. The Baby is messing around somewhere outside. Blackie and Spotty are out.

I hope Link rang you up and eased your mind about that bond. Apparently it will be quite all right if we attend to it next week.

Oh, darling, I am so depressed about all the pain you have had and the prospect of more with those injections. I am praying that they will make you all right or if not completely cured at least able to walk about without suffering. What a hell of a time you are going through.

The house still seems desolate without my darling one. I think I miss you most after eight o'clock in the evening when I used to go up to your room and watch television. It is very dreary up there all alone. It's wonderful, though, being able to talk to you on the phone.

The Edge of the Night is really terrific. Do take a look at it at ¹/₂ past 3, Channel 2.

Letter from Scott Meredith. Peter Schwed wants to publish in the Spring a book of my humorous articles, but I am doubtful if there are enough of them to make a book. Perhaps there are.

[...] I had to tell *Playboy* I couldn't do the article on 'Royalty – Who Needs It?' (Can you imagine what would happen to me in England if I wrote an article like that!) and they rang up from Chicago to say that they were writing to me, suggesting other subjects. Price $1500, so I hope I shall be able to work out something.

No other letters except wads of junk stuff which I have put on your desk.

I enclose the final version of that lyric you read at the dinner table. It really is good, isn't it? It is just what we need for the end of Act One of the Jeeves musical.

Bless you, angel. Oceans of love. How wonderful to have you back on Saturday.

Your
Plummie

TO GUY-BOLTON

P. G. Wodehouse
Remsenburg
New York

July 17. 1967

Dear Guy.
First, before I forget, the two things you wanted to know. Edward's baby, a boy, was born on June 24, and mother and child in great shape [...] My last social security check was $197. In *Newsweek* this week they said the ante might be raised, which is good, if true.

Ethel got back from hospital on Saturday, very bruised where they had shoved needles into her, but very cheerful, for the X-rays showed that her fears about cancer were without foundation. Also her blood, which used to be not too good, is now fine.

[...]

Love to Va

Yours ever

<u>Plum</u>

TO ANTHONY POWELL[1]

P. G. Wodehouse
Remsenburg
New York

Nov 16. 1967

Dear Mr Powell.

When a book parcel arrived with the name of Edward Cazalet on it, I thought he was sending me the latest Agatha Christie. It was the thrill of a lifetime when I opened it and found *Waring*, the one A. Powell missing from my list. I have been getting them from the British Book Store here and they came through with all the others, but I had lost hope of ever getting *Waring*. My collection is now complete, only marred by the fact that *The Soldier's Art* is the Little Brown edition – long and black and not the neat red Heinemann. Still, it's the contents that matter.

I have always admired your work so much, especially the *Music of Time* series. The early ones are all fine, but what I like, and what I suppose everyone likes, is the feeling that one is living with a group of characters and sharing their adventures, the whole thing lit up by the charm which is your secret. I hope the series is going on for ever. I should hate to feel that I should never meet Widmerpool again.

I finished *Waring* at a sitting and enjoyed every line of it. And had the usual Why-on-earth-didn't-I-think-of-that feeling that I always get when I read your books, – e.g. Captain Plimley's opus pinched by T. T. Waring and the two publishing brothers.

[...]

All the best

Yours ever

P. G. Wodehouse

1 Anthony Powell (1905–2000) was an English writer, particularly known for his twelve-volume opus, *A Dance to the Music of Time*, published between 1951 and 1975. His 1939 novel *What's Become of Waring* is set in a publishing firm.

TO AGATHA CHRISTIE

[...]

I am longing to see the book. I don't think it's out here yet.

I often wonder how you write, – I mean do you sit upright at a desk? I ask because I find these days I can't get out of an arm chair and face my desk and when I write in an arm-chair I have the greatest difficulty in reading what I have written. This may be because I have a deckchair, a Boxer and one of our seven cats sitting on me. But oh, how I have slowed up. It's terrible.

P. G. Wodehouse

TO IRA GERSHWIN

P. G. Wodehouse
Remsenburg
Long Island, New York 11960

Jan 4. 1970

Dear Ira.

Loved your Christmas telegram. It was the nicest Yule thing that happened to me. I find Christmas more of a trial every year. Did I tell you that Ethel and I have started a Shelter for stray dogs and cats in association with Bide-a-Wee? Well, we drafted out an appeal for donations and gave Bide-a-Wee a list of names and addresses which I was supposed to sign, and Ethel thought it would be much better if I signed each letter myself instead of having a what-do-you-call-it-ed signature. Have you ever signed your name 385 times? It's an experience. By the time I had finished I couldn't believe there was such a name as P. G. Wodehouse.

[...]

All love from Ethel and me to you and Lee. I wish we could all meet, but we seem to be tied down here permanently. I am very happy at Remsenburg, but I miss old friends.

Yours always

Plum

P. G. Wodehouse
Remsenburg
New York 11960

March 20. 1971

Dear Henry.

I was just going to write to you when your letter arrived, but was prevented by a tidal wave of fan mail from people who had read that *Times* article. I sent the invitation things off to Freddie Bartholomew.[2]

I am looking forward eagerly to the April 2 binge, and it is awfully good of you to send a car for us. My only qualm is that as I never see *World Turns* I am going to find it awkward meeting its personnel!

Edge of Night gets better and better. I can't imagine how you finish off a terrific sequence and then top it off with one just as good. Friday's curtain was a smash. I wasn't sure you were still doing it, but was reassured the other day when they at last flashed the names on the screen.

I am looking forward to meeting Mrs Henry.

[...]

Yours ever

Plum

1 Henry Slesar (1927–2002), head writer for *The Edge of Night*, a soap opera set in a fictional Midwestern town, between 1956 and 1984.
2 The well-known child filmstar of *David Copperfield* (1935) and *Captains Courageous* (1937), Bartholomew went on to become producer of PGW's favourite TV programme, *The Edge of Night*.

P. G. Wodehouse
Remsenburg
New York

April 22. 1971

Dear Agatha Christie.

How ever did you manage to bear up against that tidal wave of disapproval of *Passenger to Frankfurt*? It must have required a will of iron! The trouble, of course, was that it was so different from your usual. Very fortunate that you were firm. It has been in the middle of the best-seller list over here for months.

I have been reading it again, and like so many of yours it reads even better a second time. It's a pity from a financial point of view that the American magazines have died, but it's a relief not having to read those cut-down-into-three-parts things they used to go in for. I remember reading one of yours in its abbreviated version in *Collier's* and not liking it, but when I got the complete novel, as you had written it, it became one of my favourites. Editors have a gift for cutting out the bits which give personality to a story.

By the way, I was given three copies of *Passenger* for Christmas, having already of course bought one for myself.

I finished my Jeeves novel[1] and my publishers on both sides of the water think it's the best I have done. I enclose a very nice cable I had from Christopher McLehose [*sic*], the man who is now head of Jenkins.

I am now trying to get a plot for a new novel, but so far only incoherent ramblings. But this always happens with me, and so far something has always emerged, so I continue to persevere.

I have just recovered from what I think must have been a bit of heart trouble, brought on by a trying experience. There is a soap opera over here which I am a fan of, and the other day they reached their fifteenth year on TV and gave a big binge in New York to celebrate and insisted on my being there. They said they would send a car to take me to NY and bring me back, but omitted to mention that the car would be picking up and taking back two other celebrants, one of whom lived in a remote spot called Forest Hills. The result was that the journey to New York, normally an hour and a half, took three hours and a half, and owing to the chauffeur losing his way the trip back took over four hours. The result was heart attack as the result of strain. All right again now.

Owing to the postal strike I wasn't able to congratulate you on becoming a Dame. I do so now with a slight shudder at the thought of all the fan mail you must have had to answer!

Yours ever

P. G. Wodehouse

1 *Much Obliged, Jeeves* (1971).

TO GUY BOLTON

P. G. Wodehouse
Remsenburg
New York

June 20. 1971

[...]

[...] I had a letter from Agatha Christie in which she says 'I had a bit of heart trouble two years ago, and I went about puffing and panting and had to prop myself up with pillows every night. Good result, however, was that I lost four of my fourteen stone without chat or bother'. For 'chat' read 'diet'. I am too much of a gentleman to ask her, but I think she must have had the same treatment as me, – i.e. pills to stimulate the kidneys. I sometimes say that it is hardly worth my while to come out of the bathroom, as I have to go in again almost immediately. I am now down to thirteen stone, and I weighed twelve stone six seventy years ago when I was at school. Except for the panting I feel wonderful.

[...]

Yours

Plum

TO NORMAN MURPHY, MURRAY HEDGCOCK AND OTHERS

May 19. 1973

Thinking of you gathered in conference as I sit mumbling over my clay pipe in my inglenook, I feel not only intensely and sincerely grateful for your interest in my oeuvre, but also a little dizzy. Am I really as good as all that, I ask myself, that citizens of sound mind gather in conference on my works. Do I inspire pity and terror, as recommended by Aristotle, or have these splendid fellows been carried away by kindheartedness and a desire to make my nineties, gay nineties? For, let's face it, the world I write about, always a small one, – one of the smallest I ever met, as Bertie Wooster would say, – is now not even small, it is nonexistent. It has gone with the wind and is one with Nineveh and Tyre. In a word, it has had it.

This is pointed out to me every time a new book of mine dealing with the Drones Club and the lads who congregate there is published. 'Edwardian' the critics cry, and I shuffle my feet and blush a good deal and say 'Yes, I suppose you're right.' After all, I tell myself, there has been no generic name for the type of young man who figures in my stories since he used to be called a knut in the pre-first-war days, which certainly seems to suggest that the species has died out like the macaronis of the Regency and the whiskered mashers of the Victorian age.

But sometimes I am in a more defiant mood. Mine, I protest, are historical novels. Nobody objects when an author writes the sort of things that begin 'More skilled though I am at wielding the broadsword than the pen, I will set down for all to read the tale of how I, plain John Blunt, did follow my dear liege to the wars when the fifth Harry sat on our English throne.' So why am I not to be allowed to set down for all to read the tale of how the Hon. J. Blunt got fined five pounds by the beak at Bosher Street Police Court for disorderly conduct on Boat Race night? Unfair discrimination is the phrase that springs to the lips, and it wouldn't hurt if a question or two were asked about it in Parliament.

Two things caused the decline of the drone or knut, the first of which was that hard times hit younger sons. Most knuts were younger sons, and in the reign of good King Edward the position of younger sons in aristocratic families was roughly equivalent to that of the litter of kittens which the household cat produces three times a year. He was always a trifle on the superfluous side.

What generally happened was this. An Earl, let us say, begat an heir. So far, so good. One can always do with an heir. But then – these Earls never knew when to stop – he absentmindedly, as it were, begat a second son, and it was difficult to see how to fit him in.

'Can't let the boy starve,' the Earl said to himself, and forked out a monthly allowance. And there came into being a number of ornamental young men whom the ravens fed. Like the lilies of the field, they toiled not neither did they spin, they just existed beautifully. Their wants were few. Provided they could secure the services of a tailor who was prepared to accept charm of manner as a substitute for ready cash, they were in that blissful condition known as sitting pretty.

Then the economic factor reared its ugly head. Income tax and super tax shot up like rocketing pheasants, and the Earl found himself doing some constructive thinking.

'Why can't I?' he said to his Countess one night as they sat trying to balance the budget.

'Why can't you what?'

'Let him starve'

'It's a thought', the Countess agreed. 'We all eat too much these days, anyway.'

So the ravens were retired from active duty, and Algy had to go to work.

The second thing that led to the elimination of the knut was the passing of the spat. In the brave old days the spat was the hallmark of the young fellow about town, the foundation stone on which his whole policy was based, and it is sad to reflect that a generation has arisen which does not know what spats were.

Spatterdashes was, I believe, their full name, and they were made of white cloth and buttoned round the ankles, partly no doubt to prevent the socks from getting dashed with spatter, but principally because they lent a gay diablerie to the wearer's appearance. The monocle might or might not be worn, according to taste, but spats, like the tightly rolled umbrella, were obligatory. I was never myself by knut standards, dressy as a young man (circa 1905), for a certain anemia of the exchequer compelled me to go about my social duties in my brother's cast-off frock coat and top hat bequeathed to me by an uncle with a head some sizes smaller than mine, but my umbrella was always rolled as tight as a drum and though spats cost money, I had mine all right. There they were, white and gleaming, fascinating the passers-by and causing seedy strangers who hoped for largesse to address me as 'Captain' or sometimes even as 'M'lord'. Many a butler at the turn of the century, opening the door to me and wincing visibly at the sight of my topper, would lower his eyes, see the spats and give a little sigh of relief, as much as to say 'Not quite what we are accustomed to at the northern end, perhaps, but unexceptionable to the south'.

Naturally if you cut off a fellow's allowance, he cannot afford spats, and without them he is a spent force. Deprived of his spats, the knut threw in the towel and called it a day.

But I have not altogether lost hope of a revival of knuttery. At the moment, of course, every member of the Drones Club is an earnest young man immersed in some serious pursuit who would raise his eyebrows coldly if you suggested that he pinch a policeman's helmet on the night of the annual Rugby football contest between the Universities of Oxford and Cambridge, but the heart of Young England is sound. Dangle a consignment of spats before his eyes, and the old fires will be renewed. The knut is not dead, but sleepeth.

When that happens, I shall look my critics in the eye and say 'Edwardian? Where do you get that Edwardian stuff? I write about life as it is lived today.'

P. G. Wodehouse

P. G. Wodehouse
Remsenburg
Long Island, New York

May 25. 1973

Dearest Thelma.

What a wonderful surprise!!!

I feel deeply grateful to all the contributors to the book and even more so to you for all the trouble you must have taken assembling them. And how sweet of Sheran coming all the way over here to bring it to me. It was a joy to see her again, and looking so well and pretty, too.[1]

It really did make me blush – I won't say to the roots of my hair, because I haven't any – to read the marvellous things the writers said of me. I find it hard to believe that I am as good as all that, though, like Jeeves, I have always endeavored to give satisfaction. The book gave my spirits a tremendous lift, badly needed, as I am in the between-books stage when I feel, as I have done for the last sixty-odd years, that I shall never get another plot. I devoured the book at a sitting and shall of course re-read it [at] intervals for the rest of my life.

Who is Richard Ingrams?[2] I think I liked his contribution best of all of them. But they were all terrific.

What appealed to me most, though, was the endless trouble you must have taken. It was just like you. Bless you!

Yours ever

Plummie

1 Wodehouse refers to a book of essays, *A Homage to P. G. Wodehouse*, with contributions by writers such as Sir John Betjeman and Auberon Waugh, which had been conceived and edited by Thelma Cazalet-Keir.
2 Richard Ingrams, then editor of *Private Eye* magazine, wrote a piece on Wodehouse entitled 'Much Obliged, Mr Wodehouse'.

The following extract contains Wodehouse's responses, via his agent, Scott Meredith, to his publisher's comments about his latest novel, Bachelors Anonymous.

July 9. 1973

[...]

1. P. 10. Cut the line about Ethiopian slaves.[1]
2. Shakespeare couldn't even spell his own name, so I don't think we need worry about 'sleaves' and 'sleeves'.[2]
3. Change to black.[3]
4. This money business always worries me. I can't get used to the present inflation. Do you think it ought to be five pounds? It seems a terribly big sum.[4]
5. Yes, I'm right. The song was in one of Cole's flops, so Peter naturally wouldn't know it.[5]
6. The very flat phrase 'the cat brought in' was put there deliberately to balance the very poetic stuff that precedes it. But it could quite well come out if desired.[6]
7. The gag about 'whereabouts' – meaning (a) where one is and (b) under-garments which you wear about you comes from an old London musical comedy. Could it have been *Floradora?* Anyway, it always got a big laugh, so presumably London audiences are exceptionally quick on the uptake. But I'm surprised that Peter didn't get it.[7]
8. [...]
9. Yes, I quite agree. 'Bird' is the right word. 'Doll' would be too American for an Englishman who had never been to America.[8]

1 Schwed wrote: 'I don't think the gag about Ethiopian slaves is that funny and with the climate today being what it is [...] I wish you'd think of something better.'
2 'I don't know why Shakespeare spelled the "ravelled sleave of care" as "sleave" but I'm pretty sure he did.'
3 'A cab in London is referred to as "the yellow one". I never saw a yellow cab in London.'
4 'Do you think that in these inflated times a pound note is big enough to be Miss Priestley's price? Perhaps so, but I would have thought a fiver more likely.'
5 'I would not question your knowledge of Cole Porter but I must admit I never heard of "Mr and Mrs Fitch". Still, I presume that you know what you're writing about.'
6 'You made a pencil change along about the middle of the page when you used the phrase about "looking like something the cat had brought in" [...] I don't think this trite phrase is worthy of P. G. Wodehouse and particularly when it's emphasized by being at the end of the paragraph.'

7 'With respect to the sentence "an old joke about them being at the wash flitted into Joe's mind…" This one completely escapes me and will the reader as well.'
8 'Finally, there are seven references to "popsy" […] I offer as an alternative suggestion a more modern, British term "bird".'

In the following letter, Wodehouse describes his collaboration with Tim Rice and Andrew Lloyd Webber on a potential work based on his novels, which was to become the musical Jeeves. *A year later, Alan Ayckbourn (who took over from Tim Rice) and Lloyd Webber drove to Long Island to meet Wodehouse. 'Our visit', Ayckbourn remembered, 'had to be precisely timed in order to fit in with Plum's current TV viewing habits.'*

TO GUY BOLTON

P. G. Wodehouse
Remsenburg
Long Island, New York

August 15. 1973

Dear Guy.

I'm afraid the difficulty is that the boys regard Jeeves as sacred writ and think that the more of the stuff in the stories they can cram in, the better.[1] I'm sure that CLARITY is the essential thing. Get a clear script and never mind how much good material you have to leave out.

What I would like them to do is jettison all they have done and start again with *Thank You, Jeeves*, which has everything needed for a musical – a clear straightforward story with several good block comedy scenes.

If you remember *Thank You, Jeeves*, it starts with Bertie and Jeeves splitting because Bertie is turned out of his flat because of complaints about his playing the banjo. A pal offers Bertie a cottage on his estate and Jeeves refuses to go there as he is not equal to listening to Bertie's banjo at close quarters. The pal nips in and engages Jeeves.

The pal – Chuffy – is in love with the daughter of an American millionaire to whom B was once engaged. He is there on his yacht. The girl swims ashore to see Chuffy, takes refuge in B's bed and pyjamas and Chuffy finds her there after B, who has been sleeping in the potting shed, comes in, there is a violent quarrel between Chuffy and the girl and they split up. The girl's father finds out that heroine has slept at B's, asks B to dinner on his yacht and says B has got to marry her. The girl's father is giving a negro minstrel party on the boat for his son's birthday, and the only way B can escape is by having Jeeves black him up with boot polish.

B goes back to his cottage and the valet he has engaged in place of Jeeves comes in very drunk, thinks B is the devil, chases him with a carving knife and sets the cottage on fire. B escapes, but he is all blacked up and needs butter to take it off and where is he to get butter? After that the story proceeds quite logically. You've probably read it, so I won't go into detail, but it has a great finish and – which is what we want – clarity all through.

I think we shall have a flop if the boys try to cram in the Spode motif and a lot of other stuff.

[...]

What would be ideal would be if you could rough out a scenario for them.

Must stop now. Dinner just coming up. (Sausages and Mash.)

Love to Va

Yours ever

Plum

1 Tim Rice and Andrew Lloyd Webber.

TO ETHEL WODEHOUSE

Remsenburg
Long Island, New York

Sept 30. 1973

My precious angel Bunny whom I love so dear.

Another anniversary! Isn't it wonderful to think that we have been married for 59 years and still love each other as much as ever except when I spill my tobacco on the floor, which I'll never do again!

It was a miracle finding one another. I know I could never have been happy with anybody else. What a lucky day for me when you agreed with me when I said 'Let's get married'!

The only thing that makes me sad is your health. How I wish there was something I could do. What is so extraordinary is that you come to me in pain and not having slept and you look just as beautiful as you did fifty-nine years ago. But how I wish that you could get a good sleep.

I wish I could say all the things I would like to say, but really they can all be said in one sentence – I LOVE YOU.

Bless you

Your Plummie

TO ETHEL WODEHOUSE

P. G. Wodehouse
Remsenburg
Long Island, New York

March 10. 1974

My precious darling Bunny whom I love so dear.

How I wish this was one of my ordinary love letters for you to read in bed instead of one when you were off to hospital. My only comfort is that they surely must do something to relieve that awful pain. But how I shall miss you!

Isn't it wonderful that after sixty years we love each other more than ever! You sometimes ask me if I love you just as much now that you are ill. Much more! It breaks my heart to see you suffering.

How sad and empty this house will be without you. It's one of the curious things about love that it doesn't matter if you're actually together, so long as I know you're <u>there</u>. How splendid it will be if they only keep you in hospital for a few days.

I shall be thinking of you all the time. I do hope they will make you comfortable. You always get on so well with people that you will probably have half a dozen friends right-away. But they won't love you like I do!

Bless you!
Your

Plummie.

(I can't get all the cats in)

P. G. Wodehouse
Remsenburg
Long Island, New York

July 27. 1974

Dear Tom.

What magnificent news! Your energy is simply incredible. I wrote the last twenty-six pages of *Thank You, Jeeves*, in a day, but I couldn't have done it if it hadn't been the last part of the book. The idea of starting off on a novel and writing six thousand words a day stuns me.

Wonderful news, too, about your new contract. Now you are really set up. Writing as well as you do and with your energy you can't miss. You will always be able to get ideas.

I do admire you for getting that quiet place to write in and getting going at 5 a.m.

How right you are about the importance of the stuff in the middle. That is what is holding my novel up. Fine to the end of Chapter six and the same from about twelve chapters to the end, but I have had to [do] a lot of thinking about the middle part. I think I have got it nearly right, but I don't want to start writing yet, as I keep getting new ideas.

My big news is that they are putting me in Madame Tussaud's, which I have always looked on as the supreme honour. It involves having a sculptor come over here and do me, but I feel it's worth it.

Congratulations again. I think you're a wonder!

Yours ever

Plum

TO J. D. GRIMSDICK

P. G. Wodehouse
Remsenburg
Long Island, New York 11960

Jan 29. 1975

Dear J.D.

I would have written to you long ago, only my typewriter conked out and none of the local vets could restore it to mid-season form. Even now you will see that it refuses to print a or the letter J.

I am trying to decide whether I would advise a young man to become a knight. The warm feeling it gives one in the pit of the stomach is fine, but oh God those interviewers. They came round like flies, and practically all of them half-wits. I was asked by one of them what my latest book was about. 'It's a Jeeves novel', I said. 'And what is a Jeeves novel?' he enquired. Thank goodness they have left me now, including the one who printed 'I don't understand why authors receive knighthoods', when I had said <u>refuse</u> knighthoods. Alters the sense a bit, what?

We are having mild perfect golf weather over here. I hope you are having the same at your end.

All the best

Yours ever

P.G.

Half way through a new Blandings novel. Looks good.[1]

---

1 This was to become the posthumously published *Sunset at Blandings*.

Jeeves's bracer does not contain dynamite as is generally supposed.

It consists of lime juice, a lump of sugar and one teaspoonful of Mulliner's *Buck-U-Uppo*. This, it will be remembered, is the amount of the *Buck-U-Uppo* given to elephants in India to enable them to face tigers on tiger hunts with the necessary nonchalance.

P. G. Wodehouse

1 Godfrey Smith, editor of the *Sunday Times* magazine. This undated manuscript letter, written very late in PGW's life, was probably never posted. Since Buck-U-Uppo is no longer available, it might be wise to follow the more traditional recipe set out in *Carry On, Jeeves*, where we are informed in the opening chapter that the recipe comprises Worcester sauce, raw eggs and red pepper.

This final letter, written less than a fortnight before Wodehouse died, shows him recalling the start of his career. It is likely that Wodehouse had not seen Ernestine, then the Baroness de Longueuil, for sixty-five years. Wodehouse had first met the three Bowes-Lyon girls, Joan (b. 1888), Effie (b. 1889) and Ernestine (b. 1891) around 1898, and came to know them well in London in 1902. He acted as a companion and surrogate elder brother to them, often joining them for tea in the nursery and making up numbers when their mother was short of a spare man for dinner parties. Effie Bowes-Lyon remembered Wodehouse asking them if he should leave the bank and become a full-time writer, and she recalls that they all said he should. Many of his early stories involve young girls, almost certainly based on the three sisters – and his first book, The Pothunters, *was dedicated to them.*

TO ERNESTINE BOWES-LYON

Remsenburg
Long Island
New York

Feb 3. 1975

Dear Teenie.

Wonderful news about Raymond. What a relief it must be to you that he is well again. [...]

This house has been a pandemonium since the knighthood appeared in the papers, a seething mass of interviewers and photographers, all half-wits. And can you imagine it, the BBC, who are doing a series of short stories of mine, suddenly descended on me and I had to do introductions to the stories, which meant writing them, memorizing them and speaking them into the camera. It was alright at first, but after two hours my brain became numbed and I had to repeat the stuff over and over again, to correct mistakes.

Everything is more or less calm now, except that hundreds of fan letters keep coming in. One of them was addressed to 'His Royal Highness PGW'. And talking of Royal Highnesses I got a most charming letter from the Queen Mother. I always remember you and Joan and Effie coming back from Glamis and saying 'Little Elizabeth was sweet.'[1] She still is.

Lots of love

Yours ever

Plum

1 The Bowes-Lyon girls were cousins of Elizabeth Bowes-Lyon, Queen Elizabeth The Queen Mother. As children, all the girls used to meet at their grandfather's home, Glamis Castle, in Scotland.

References

Abbreviations

ARCHIVES

Berg
: The Henry W. and A. Albert Berg Collection of English and American Literature, The New York Public Library

Chapel Hill
: A. P. Watt Records, Louis Wilson Library, General Manuscripts Collection, University of North Carolina at Chapel Hill, North Carolina

Chicago
: Will Cuppy Papers, Special Collections Research Center, University of Chicago Library

Christie
: Agatha Christie Archive, Wales

Columbia
: Reynolds Papers, Rare Book and Manuscript Library, Columbia University in the City of New York

Cornell
: Sullivan Papers, Division of Rare and Manuscript Collections, Cornell University Library

Dulwich
: Dulwich College Archives, Dulwich College, London

Emsworth
: Emsworth Museum, Emsworth Maritime and Historical Trust, Emsworth, Hampshire

LOC
: Manuscript Division, Library of Congress, Washington

Morgan	The Pierpont Morgan Library, Literary and Historical Manuscripts, The Morgan Library and Museum, New York
Muggeridge	Malcolm Muggeridge Papers, Wheaton College Special Collections, Wheaton, Illinois
Oriel	Oriel College Archive, Oxford
Orwell	Orwell Papers, UCL Library Services, Special Collections, London
OUA Oxford	Oxford University Archives, Bodleian Library,
PRO	Public Record Office, The National Archives, Kew
Ransom	Harry Ransom Humanities Research Center, University of Texas at Austin, Texas
Reading	A. & C. Black Papers, University of Reading Special Collections Service, University of Reading
Sharpe	Tom Sharpe Papers, Great Shelford, Cambridge
Southern Illinois	Special Collections Research Center, Southern Illinois University, Carbondale
Waugh	Evelyn Waugh Papers, British Library
Wodehouse Archive	Wodehouse Archive, Shaw Farm, Sussex

TEXTS

Bring on the Girls	P. G. Wodehouse, *Bring on the Girls,* in *Wodehouse on Wodehouse* (Harmondsworth: Penguin Books, 1981)

Cussen	'Major Cussen's Report on the case of P. G. Wodehouse', 3 October 1944, PRO HO 45/22385-66279
Jasen	David Jasen, *P. G. Wodehouse: A Portrait of a Master* (New York: Mason & Lipscomb, 1974)
McCrum	Robert McCrum, *Wodehouse: A Life* (London: Viking, 2004)
Murphy	N. T. P. Murphy, *The Wodehouse Handbook*, Vol. I (London: Popgood & Groolley, 2006)
Over Seventy	P. G. Wodehouse, *Over Seventy*, in *Wodehouse on Wodehouse* (Harmondsworth: Penguin Books, 1981)
Performing Flea	P. G. Wodehouse, *Performing Flea: A Self-Portrait in Letters*, with a Foreword and Notes by W. Townend (London: Herbert Jenkins, 1953)
Phelps	Barry Phelps, *P. G. Wodehouse: Man and Myth* (London: Constable, 1992)
The Unknown Years	Reinhild von Bodenhausen, *P. G. Wodehouse: The Unknown Years* (Sri Lanka: Stamford Lake Publications, 2009)
Yours Plum	Frances Donaldson, *Yours Plum: The Letters of P. G. Wodehouse* (London: Hutchinson, 1990)

(References for the quotations in the commentary are given in normal type. Letters which are reproduced in their full, or fuller form, are in italics)

1899–1900: 'set thy beetle-crusher on the ladder of fame'

p. 40, 'All through my last term', *Over Seventy*, p. 477.

p. 40, *I am badly in need of some funny drorks*, PGW to Eric George (Morgan).

p. 43, *Jeames, friend of me boyhood*, PGW to Eric George, September 1899 (Morgan).

p. 46, *Jeames of me boyhood's hours*, PGW to Eric George (Morgan).

p. 49, 'The Literary Man as Statesman', Scholarship Examination Paper, 1899, (Oriel).

p. 49, '[J]ust as scholarship time was approaching', *Over Seventy*, p. 477.

p. 49, 'A 'Varsity "man"', 'The Fresher at Cambridge', *The Captain*, July 1899, pp. 380–88, at p. 381.

p. 49, 'quaint old coll ... almost like going to Elysium', Fred Swainson, 'The Roden Scholarship', *The Captain*, January 1900, pp. 402–6, at p. 402.

p. 49, *Friend of me boyhood*, PGW to Eric George (Morgan).

1901–1909: 'Got a plot, thanks'

p. 58, *In reply to your letter of today*, PGW to A. & C. Black, 8 December 1902 (Reading).

p. 59, 'drank too much' and 'sponged, more or less on people', William Townend to PGW, 16 February 1957 (Dulwich).

p. 59, *This is great about our Westy*, PGW to William Townend, 3 March 1905 (Dulwich).

p. 61, *I rang you up on the telephone today*, PGW to J. B. Pinker, 16 January 1906 (Berg).

p. 62, *I think the best thing would be*, PGW to J. B. Pinker, 4 May 1906 (Berg).

p. 62, 'a complete shit', PGW to William Townend, 10 June 1907 (Dulwich).

p. 62, 'various houses', PGW to David Jasen, 21 November 1961 (Wodehouse Archive).

p. 63, 'a kind of supercharged', D. J. Taylor, 'Life Before Jeeves', *TLS*, 15 September 2010.

p. 63, *The fact that the preliminary notices*, PGW to Cassell & Co., London, 3 August 1907 (Berg).

p. 63, 'half in love', Richard Perceval-Maxwell, '6925 – The P. G. Wodehouse Connection', *The King-Hall Family and Its Connections*, http://sites.google.com/site/kinghallconnections/Home.

p. 64, *It's all right. Got a plot, thanks*, PGW to William Townend [u.d. 1908] (Dulwich).

p. 65, 'There is no earthly subject', Wilkie Collins, 'The Unknown Public', *Household Words*, 21 August 1858, XVIII, pp. 217–22.

p. 65, 'in house', George Newnes to PGW, 28 October 1908 (Wodehouse Archive).

p. 66, *A Lover's Trials. – CITIZEN's grievance*, PGW and William Townend to various correspondents, *Tit-Bits*, Vol. 54–55, 29 August 1908, p. 567.

p. 68, *Here's a go*, PGW to William Townend, 6 May 1908 (Dulwich).

p. 69, 'Although the plot is excellent', A. & C. Black to PGW, 31 March 1911 (Reading).

p. 69, 'a merry tale, cleverly told', 'Love and Chickens', *The New York Times*, 29 May 1909.

p. 70, *I hadn't time in the hurry*, PGW to J. B. Pinker, 11 May 1909 (Berg).

1909–1914: 'American hustle'

p. 75, *Here I am. As Wilkie Bard was singing*, PGW to L. H. Bradshaw, 7 September 1909 (private archive).

p. 75, *Thanks awfully for your letter*, PGW to L. H. Bradshaw, 9 November 1909 (private archive).

p. 76, *Thanks awfully for mags*, PGW to L. H. Bradshaw [u.d. 1910] (private archive).

p. 77, *The Announcement in the* Argosy, PGW to L. H. Bradshaw, 29 April 1910 (private archive).

p. 77, 'I was very hard up in my Greenwich Village days', 'Preface' to *The Small Bachelor* (London: Barrie and Jenkins, 1970), p. 5.

p. 78, *Thanks awfully for your letter*, PGW to L. H. Bradshaw, 5 May 1910 (private archive).

p. 79, *Are you game to put a little snaky work for me*, PGW to L. H. Bradshaw [u.d. 1910] (private archive).

p. 80, *Thanks for the very timely tip*, PGW to L. H. Bradshaw, 19 January 1911 (private archive).

p. 81, *I haven't had a moment*, PGW to L. H. Bradshaw, 21 May 1912 (private archive).

p. 83, *Will you stand by me in a crisis?*, PGW to Sir Arthur Conan Doyle, 9 August 1912 (private archive).

p. 84, *I am afraid I have left your letter*, PGW to L. H. Bradshaw, 9 September 1912 (private archive).

p. 85, *Yes, here I am*, PGW to L. H. Bradshaw, 6 May 1913 (private archive).

p. 86, 'was engaged to write a review', PGW to Richard Usborne, 21 May 1956 (Wodehouse Archive).

p. 86, *I am dreadfully sorry*, PGW to Olive Armstrong ('Bubbles'), 13 July 1914 (Wodehouse Archive).

p. 87, *Thanks very much for the clippings*, PGW to L. H. Bradshaw, 1 September 1914 (private archive).

p. 90 'If my mother had her choice', L. H. Bradshaw to Olive Marie Barrows, 15 July 1914 (private archive).

p. 90 'had a date', L. H. Bradshaw to Olive Marie Barrows, 23 September 1914 (private archive).

p. 91, *I really meant what I said*, PGW to L. H. Bradshaw, 24 September 1914, quoted in L. H. Bradshaw to Olive Marie Barrows, 26 September 1914 (private archive).

1914–1918: 'Something Fresh'

p. 97, *Excuse delay in answering letter*, PGW to L. H. Bradshaw, 1 October 1914 (private archive).

p. 97, 'A complete surprise', L. H. Bradshaw to Olive Marie Barrows, 2 October 1914 (private archive).

p. 98, *I've been feeling an awful worm*, PGW to L. H. Bradshaw, 10 October 1914 (private archive).

p. 100, *I took your letter to Friend Wife*, PGW to L. H. Bradshaw, 14 October 1914 (private archive).

p. 102 'was too modest, so I sent', L. H. Bradshaw to Olive Marie Barrows, 20 October 1914 (private archive).

p. 102, *Thanks awfully for the cigars*, PGW to L. H. Bradshaw, 19 October 1914 (private archive).

p. 104, *Thanks most awfully for the photograph frame*, PGW to L. H. Bradshaw, 24 October 1914 (private archive).

p. 105, *I expect you have heard*, PGW to Lillian Barnett, 2 December 1914 (Emsworth).

p. 108, *We shall both be delighted*, PGW to L. H. Bradshaw, 15 December 1914 (private archive).

p. 109, PGW to L. H. Bradshaw, 'Sorry for delay in writing', 20 January 1915, (private archive).

p. 111, *Splendid. I should be delighted*, PGW to George Wilson, 28 March 1915 (Reading).

p. 111, *Do you remember coming to Bustanoby's*, PGW to L. H. Bradshaw, 3 June 1915 (private archive).

p. 113, 'used to write about half', *Performing Flea*, p. 13.

p. 113, *I was interested to hear*, PGW to L. H. Bradshaw, 25 June 1915 (private archive).

p. 114, 'move away from the fractured', Judith Flanders, 'Song and Dance', *TLS*, 22 April 2011, p. 3.

p. 114, 'out on the road', PGW to Lillian Barnett, 20 June 1918 (Emsworth).

p. 114, 'Scott Fitzgerald and his crowd', Jasen, p. 77.

p. 114, 'three acres of grounds including a tennis court', L. H. Bradshaw to Olive Marie Barrows, 20 August 1918 (private archive).

p. 115, *I have been meaning to write*, PGW to Lillian Barnett, 20 June 1918 (Emsworth).

1919–1930 'This, I need scarcely point out to you, is jolly old Fame'

p. 123. 'the infallible test', 'The Clicking of Cuthbert', *The Strand Magazine* (October 1921) and *Elk's Magazine* (July 1922), repr. in *The Clicking of Cuthbert* (1922).

p. 123, *Thanks awfully for your letters*, PGW to William Townend, 28 February 1920 (Dulwich).

p. 127, *At last I'm able to write to you!*, PGW to Leonora Wodehouse, 7 August 1920 (Wodehouse Archive).

p. 128, 'A gentleman named Lieutenant Larsen', *Something Fresh* (*Something New*) (1915), Chapter 1.

p. 129, *I finished the novel two or three days ago*, PGW to Paul Reynolds, 9 September 1920 (Columbia).

p. 130, *Here is a letter from one of the Ely Court nibs*, PGW to Leonora Wodehouse, 27 September 1920 (Wodehouse Archive).

p. 132, *We were so glad to get your letters*, PGW to Leonora Wodehouse, 24 November 1920 (Wodehouse Archive).

p. 134, *We beat Sherborne yesterday*, PGW to Leonora Wodehouse, 28 November 1920 (Wodehouse Archive).

p. 135, *I have written to mother*, PGW to Leonora Wodehouse, 23 March 1921 (Wodehouse Archive).

p. 137, 'noble experiment', *Over Seventy*, p. 190.

p. 137, *Well, we blew in yesterday morning*, PGW to Leonora Wodehouse, 2 April 1921 (Wodehouse Archive).

p. 140, *I feel I must write a line*, PGW to Denis Mackail, 13 May 1921 (Wodehouse Archive).

p. 140, 'about thirty girls', *Yours Plum*, p. 17.

p. 141, *You will be thinking me a f.i.h.s.*, PGW to Leonora Wodehouse, 20 May 1921 (Wodehouse Archive).

p. 142, *We were frightfully sorry to hear*, PGW to Leonora Wodehouse, 15 June 1921 (Wodehouse Archive).

p. 144, *How I have neglected you*, PGW to Leonora Wodehouse, 3 July 1921 (Wodehouse Archive).

p. 146, *The Wodehouse home is en fête*, PGW to Leonora Wodehouse, 21 December 1921 (Wodehouse Archive).

p. 147, *How's everything? Darned cold, what?*, PGW to Leonora Wodehouse, 24 January 1922 (Wodehouse Archive).

p. 148, *Sorry I haven't written before*, PGW to William Townend, 27 June 1922 (Dulwich).

p. 149, *Well, Bill, maybe we didn't do a thing*, PGW to Leonora Wodehouse, 20 September 1922 (Wodehouse Archive).

p. 151, 'two small girls who created the impression', *Bring on the Girls*, p. 156.

p. 151, '*Life has been one damned bit of work after another*', PGW to William Townend, 16 December 1922 (Dulwich).

p. 152, 'working like a beaver', PGW to William Townend, 20 May 1923 (Dulwich)

p. 152, '*I am bathed in confusion and remorse*', PGW to Denis Mackail, 20 May 1923 (Wodehouse Archive).

p. 153, *Have you ever been knocked over by a car*, PGW to William Townend, 23 July 1923 (Dulwich).

p. 156, *You've no notion what a ruddy blank*, PGW to William Townend, 24 August 1923 (Dulwich).

p. 157, *What a shame that we missed each other*, PGW to William Townend, 4 November 1923 (Dulwich).

p. 158, *Well, ma belle, how goes it?*, PGW to Leonora Wodehouse, 14 November 1923 (Wodehouse Archive).

p. 161, *Tonight we are all going to the opening*, PGW to Leonora Wodehouse, 23 December 1923 (Wodehouse Archive).

p. 162, *Your lovely letter*, PGW to Leonora Wodehouse, 25 December 1923 (Wodehouse Archive).

p. 163, *I'm awfully sorry I haven't written*, PGW to William Townend, 26 January 1924 (Dulwich).

p. 164, *Your long letter made a big hit*, PGW to Leonora Wodehouse, 4 February 1924 (Wodehouse Archive).

p. 165, *We are so awfully worried*, PGW to Leonora Wodehouse, 12 September 1924 (Wodehouse Archive).

p. 167, *Awfully sorry I haven't written*, PGW to William Townend, 23 September 1924 (Dulwich).

p. 167, 'a "rather odd" experience', PGW to Armine Wodehouse, 17 March 1936 (private archive).

p. 168, *Thanks awfully about the three men and girl*, PGW to William Townend, 1 October 1924 (Dulwich).

p. 169, *I enclose a sheet of questions*, PGW to William Townend, 12 November 1924 (Dulwich). The list of questions is missing in the original letter and they are taken from the version given in *Performing Flea*, pp. 29–30.

p. 170, 'usual struggle' [...] 'a luncheon', PGW to William Townend, 28 April 1925 (Dulwich).

p. 171, 'Bill West, the nephew of Mr Paradene', *TLS*, 4 December 1924, p. 828.

p. 171, *Your letter was like the well-known balm in Gilead*, PGW to Denis Mackail, 4 December 1924 (Wodehouse Archive).

p. 172, 'one of those enormous houses', PGW to William Townend, 12 May 1929 (Dulwich).

p. 172, 'miles of what they call rolling', 'Jeeves and the Impending Doom', *The Strand Magazine* (December 1926) and *Liberty* (January 1927), repr. in *Very Good, Jeeves* (1930).

p. 173, 'keen breeder of Jersey cows', Murphy, p. 350.

p. 173, 'Hunstanton's pig-sty was likely', Murphy, p. 430.

p. 173, *[...] We are off to Norfolk for Christmas*, PGW to William Townend, 22 December 1924 (Dulwich).

p. 174, *I am now at last in a position*, PGW to Leonora Wodehouse, 30 March 1925 (Wodehouse Archive).

p. 176, *I started the sale of* Greenery Street, PGW to Denis Mackail, 18 June 1925 (Wodehouse Archive).

p. 177, 'a ghastly task', PGW to William Townend, 23 July 1925 (Dulwich).

p. 177, 'was rather angry about Wodehouse', Harold Ober to Paul Reynolds, 29 December 1926 (Columbia).

p. 178, *I have been spending two weeks at Bexhill*, PGW to William Townend, 26 June 1926 (Dulwich).

p. 179, 'it is not too much to say that I played', Jasen, p. 104.

p. 179, *In November I am going to California*, PGW to Mr Davies, 17 August 1926 (private archive).

p. 179, 'your $5,500, of course, is absolutely pure velvet', R. J. B. Denby to PGW, 13 January 1927 (Columbia).

p. 180, CANNOT UNDERSTAND YOU CABLING, PGW to R. J. B. Denby, 22 January 1927 (Columbia).

p. 180, 'the running of the establishment', Jasen, p. 107.

p. 181, *Thanks very much for the* Vanity Fair *articles*, PGW to Paul Reynolds, 5 February 1927 (Columbia).

p. 182, *A long time since we communicated, laddie*, PGW to William Townend, 12 February 1927 (Dulwich).

p. 184, 'the quietest place under the sun', *Bring on the Girls*, p. 185.

p. 184, 'Victorian monstrosity', Murphy, pp. 290–91

p. 184, 'a vast edifice constructed of glazed red brick', *Summer Moonshine* (1937), Chapter 2.

p. 184, *Ripping getting your letter*, PGW to William Townend, 15 March 1927 (Dulwich).

p. 185, *Returning to London today*, PGW to William Townend, 5 May 1927 (Dulwich).

p. 187, *I am here till Friday*, PGW to William Townend, 27 July 1927 (Dulwich).

p. 188, 'every day seems to have been given to either writing or rehearsing', *Bring on the Girls*, p. 214.

p. 189, *I would have written to you long before this*, PGW to William Townend, 28 November 1927 (Dulwich).

p. 190, *So sorry not to have written before*, PGW to William Townend, 30 April 1928 (Dulwich).

p. 191, *Your letter with the checks just arrived*, PGW to Ira Gershwin, 8 November 1928 (Wodehouse Archive).

p. 193, *Thanks awfully for your letter*, PGW to Leonora Wodehouse, 10 February 1929 (Wodehouse Archive).

p. 194, *I would have written before but*, PGW to William Townend, 12 May 1929 (Dulwich).

p. 195, *I've come to the conclusion that what*, PGW to William Townend, 26 July 1929 (Dulwich).

p. 196, 'I know that the main scheme', 'The Ordeal of Young Tuppy', *Very Good, Jeeves* (1930).

p. 196, *I'm longing to come down and see you all*, PGW to William Townend, 11 November 1929 (Wodehouse Archive).

p. 197, *I'm afraid it's going to be difficult to work that Townend story*, PGW to Paul Reynolds, 11 November 1929 (Columbia).

p. 197, *What do you mean?*, PGW to William Townend, 8 January 1930 (Dulwich).

1930–1931: 'this place is loathsome'

p. 205, *Frightfully sorry I haven't written before*, PGW to Denis Mackail, 26 June 1930 (Wodehouse Archive).

p. 207, *How awfully nice of you to write to me about Jeeves*, PGW to Arnold Bennett, 16 August 1930 (private archive).

p. 208, *[...] Well, laddie, it begins to look as if*, PGW to William Townend, 28 October 1930 (Dulwich)

p. 211, *I feel an awful worm*, PGW to Denis Mackail, 28 December 1930 (Wodehouse Archive).

p. 212, 'Following *Variety*'s report of the ludicrous writer talent situation', Phelps, p. 170.

p. 212 'that he had been paid such an enormous' see Alma Whitaker, 'Wodehouse Out and Still Dazed', *Los Angeles Times*, 7 June 1951.

p. 213, *Does the Spring make you restless?*, PGW to William Townend, 14 March 1931 (Dulwich).

p. 214, *Thanks most awfully for sending me the two books*, PGW to Will Cuppy, 29 April 1931 (Chicago)

p. 215, *Your letter arrived yesterday*, PGW to Denis Mackail, 10 May 1931 (Wodehouse Archive).

p. 217, *[...] How have you been doing lately?*, PGW to William Townend, 19 May 1931 (Wodehouse Archive).

p. 218, *Thanks most awfully for the books*, PGW to Will Cuppy, 17 August 1931 (Chicago).

p. 218, *I was thrilled by your description of battle with Pop Grimsdick*, PGW to William Townend, 26 August 1931 (Dulwich).

p. 220, *This business of writing to you has taken on a graver aspect*, PGW to William Townend, 14 September 1931 (Dulwich).

1932–1940: 'A jolly strong position'

p. 228, *The above is our new address*, PGW to William Townend, 6 March 1932 (Dulwich).

p. 229, 'an odd bird', PGW to William Townend, 24 August 1932, in *Performing Flea*, p. 66.

p. 230, *I like Wells, but the trouble*, PGW to William Townend [u.d., 1932] (Dulwich).

p. 231, *Thanks for long letter. Good*, PGW to William Townend, 1 April 1932 (Dulwich).

p. 232, *I'm so glad you liked*, PGW to Denis Mackail, 8 April 1932 (Wodehouse Archive).

p. 233, *I am hoping that this rise*, PGW to William Townend, 13 August 1932 (Dulwich).

p. 234, *I'm awfully glad you liked* Hot Water, PGW to Denis Mackail, 9 October 1932 (Wodehouse Archive).

p. 236, *You may well imagine*, PGW to Leonora Wodehouse, 6 November 1932 (Wodehouse Archive).

p. 237, *Thanks for your letter*, PGW to William Townend, 1 December 1932 (Dulwich).

p. 238, *Happy New Year and what not*, PGW to William Townend, 4 January 1933 (Dulwich).

p. 240, *These last four days*, PGW to William Townend, 9 February 1933 (Dulwich).

p. 241, SEVENTY THOUSAND WORDS OF NOVEL, PGW to Paul Reynolds, 15 February 1933 (Columbia).

p. 242, 'FEDERAL TAX AUDITOR IN ANNUAL AUDIT', Paul Reynolds to PGW, 11 April 1933 (Columbia).

p. 242, *Your cable was a bombshell*, PGW to Paul Reynolds, 12 April 1933 (Columbia).

p. 242, *My wife is frightfully worried*, PGW to Paul Reynolds, 18 April 1933 (Columbia).

p. 243, *Dear Denis. (Bluff old Squire ...)*, PGW to Denis Mackail, 10 September 1933 (Wodehouse Archive).

p. 244, *You will think me crazy*, PGW to Olive Grills, 26 April 1934 (Wodehouse Archive).

p. 245, *Thanks for yours. I'm glad*, PGW to William Townend, 2 August 1934 (Dulwich).

p. 246, *Thanks awfully for your letter*, PGW to William Townend, 16 August 1934 (Dulwich).

p. 247, *We are simply enraptured*, PGW to Leonora Cazalet, 24 August 1934 (Wodehouse Archive).

p. 249, *Just been reading your letter*, PGW to Leonora Cazalet, 12 November 1934 (Wodehouse Archive).

p. 250, *A letter from Miss Ella*, PGW to A. P. Watt, 20 March 1935 (Chapel Hill).

p. 251, *I'm so glad the cutting*, PGW to William Townend, 28 March 1935 (Dulwich).

p. 252, *I have just read the great news*, PGW to S. C. 'Billy' Griffith, 17 May 1935 (private archive).

p. 252, *Sensational news. Yesterday*, PGW to Leonora Cazalet, 4 June 1935 (Wodehouse Archive).

p. 253, *I have so much work on hand*, PGW to A. P. Watt, 21 June 1935 (Chapel Hill).

p. 254, *Just caught boat, and found that about*, PGW to Leonora Cazalet, 8 September 1935 (Wodehouse Archive).

p. 255, *If Hunt can give me a reasonable time*, PGW to A. P. Watt, 15 September 1935 (Chapel Hill).

p. 255, *Just off to Carlton Hotel*, PGW to William Townend, 20 January 1936 (Dulwich).

p. 256, *Your fat letter to Mummie arrived*, PGW to Leonora Cazalet, 26 February 1936 (Wodehouse Archive).

p. 257, *I was awfully glad to hear from you*, PGW to Armine Wodehouse, 17 March 1936 (private archive).

p. 259, *I'm sorry you are going*, PGW to William Townend, 2 April 1936 (Dulwich).

p. 260, *This is just a line to tell you how much I love you*, PGW to Leonora Cazalet, 16 April 1936 (Wodehouse Archive).

p. 261 'Everybody is very pleased about it', PGW to William Townend, 5 May 1936 (Dulwich).

p. 261, 'outstanding and lasting contribution to the happiness of the world', Cyril Clemens to PGW, 26 June 1936, quoted in Jasen, p. 149.

p. 261, *I've just returned from a hurried visit*, PGW to William Townend, 23 July 1936 (Wodehouse Archive).

p. 262, *Your cable came as a stunning blow to us*, PGW to Nella Wodehouse, 10 October 1936 (private archive).

p. 263, 'Parties were very easy to do', Jasen, p. 155.

p. 263, 'I saw Clark Gable the other day', PGW to William Townend, 7 November 1936 (Dulwich).

p. 263, '[E]verything seems flat', PGW to S. C. 'Billy' Griffith, 15 March 1937 (private archive).

p. 263, *I had just settled down to work off my correspondence*, PGW to Leonora Cazalet, 28 December 1936 (Wodehouse Archive).

p. 264, *Your marvellous letter arrived this morning*, PGW to Leonora Cazalet, 10 April 1937 (Wodehouse Archive).

p. 266, *Your fat letter arrived this morning*, PGW to Leonora Cazalet, 13 July 1937 (Wodehouse Archive).

p. 270, *A letter from Snorky arrived this morning*, PGW to Peter Cazalet, 7 May 1937 (Wodehouse Archive).

p. 271, *How clever of you to write to me direct about that money*, PGW to Leonora Cazalet, 13 August 1937 (Wodehouse Archive).

p. 273, *I enclose a letter from Mr Leff*, PGW to Paul Reynolds, 19 August 1937 (Columbia).

p. 274, *Did you ever read a book called* Helen's Babies, PGW to William Townend, 22 November 1937 (Dulwich).

p. 275, 'as if Nature had intended to make a gorilla', *The Code of the Woosters*, Chapter 1.

p. 275, *I am finding finishing my Jeeves novel a ghastly sweat*, PGW to William Townend, 4 January 1938 (Dulwich).

p. 276, *I can't get over the awed feeling*, PGW to Leonora Cazalet, 4 January 1939 (Wodehouse Archive).

p. 276, *It was so nice to hear from you again*, PGW to Lillian Barnett, 5 April 1939 (Emsworth).

p. 277, *I am coming over – unless there is a gale*, PGW to William Townend, 23 April 1939 (Dulwich).

p. 279, HONOURED TO ACCEPT, PGW to Douglas Veale, 16 May 1939 (OUA).

p. 279, *I am so sorry I did not receive your first communication*, PGW to Douglas Veale, 17 May 1939 (OUA).

p. 279, 'an ardent devotee', Douglas Veale to PGW, 19 May 1939 (OUA).

p. 280, *Thanks most awfully for your letter and its reassuring contents*, PGW to Douglas Veale, 24 May 1939 (OUA).

p. 280, *So glad the short stories are selling*, PGW to Paul Reynolds, 3 June 1939 (Columbia).

p. 281, '"Speech!"'. Wodehouse "rose awkwardly to his feet"', McCrum, p. 261.

p. 281, *I wonder if anybody has ever enjoyed a visit*, PGW to Mary Gordon, 23 June 1939 (Dulwich).

p. 282, *Thanks most awfully for your letter*, PGW to Mollie Cazalet, 10 July 1939 (Wodehouse Archive).

p. 283, *When this war started*, PGW to William Townend, 3 October 1939 (Dulwich).

p. 285, *I'm so sorry I've been all this time*, PGW to Frank Sullivan, 6 October 1939 (Cornell).

p. 285, *Long time since I wrote*, PGW to William Townend, 8 December 1939 (Dulwich).

p. 288, *Your description of the writing*, PGW to William Townend, 23 January 1940 (Dulwich).

p. 289, *Thank you so much for your letter*, PGW to Elmer Flaccus, 3 February 1940 (private archive).

p. 290, *I keep looking out in the papers for your new book*, PGW to William Townend, 6 April 1940 (Dulwich).

p. 291, *I'm afraid I have changed my plans*, PGW to Paul Reynolds, 25 April 1940 (Columbia).

1940–1941: 'Am quite happy here'

p. 299, GOODNESS KNOWS WHEN YOU WILL GET THIS, PGW to Paul Reynolds, 21 October 1940 (Columbia).

p. 300, 'in no immediate danger', Leonora Cazalet to Paul Reynolds, 31 May 1941 (Columbia).

p. 300, 'concentration camp', Paul Reynolds to L. B. Saunders, 19 September 1940 (Columbia).

p. 300, 'I doubt if a stay', Maerose Barry to Paul Reynolds, 7 October 1940 (Columbia).

p. 300, 'camp was really great fun', PGW to William Townend, 11 May 1942 (Dulwich).

p. 301, 'with best wishes for his early release', P. J. Reynolds Tobacco Company to Paul Reynolds, 13 January 1941 (Columbia)

p. 301, 'admirer of P. G. Wodehouse', Mary Pomeroy to Paul Reynolds, 31 December 1940 (Columbia).

p. 301, 'difficult to carry out practically', Paul Reynolds to Mary Pomeroy, 9 January 1941 (Columbia).

p. 301 'the model for Lord Uffenham', see PGW to William Townend, 24 February 1945 (Dulwich).

p. 301, 'It's very good of Mr Wodehouse', Ruth Chambers to Paul Reynolds, 16 January 1941 (Columbia).

p. 301, WOULD YOU MIND SENDING FIVE DOLLARS, PGW to Paul Reynolds, 1 November 1940 (Columbia).

p. 317, TELL LEONORA ETHEL WELL, PGW to Paul Reynolds, 18 November 1941 (Columbia).

p. 317, *Thanks so much for your cable*, PGW to Paul Reynolds, 27 November 1941 (Columbia).

p. 319, 'MONEY IN BANK GOOD', Wesley Stout to PGW, 23 July 1941 (Columbia).

p. 319, '"alienated" his readers and …would be "a liability"', Wesley Stout to Paul Reynolds, 21 July 1941 (Columbia).

p. 319, 'Our own belief is that he traded', Wesley Stout to Paul Reynolds, 23 July 1941 (Columbia).

p. 320, *I have just had a cable*, PGW to Wesley Stout, 29 November 1941 (Columbia).

p. 321, *Just a line to let you know*, PGW to Anga von Bodenhausen, 24 December 1941 (Wodehouse Archive).

p. 322, 'insisted on the insertion in the contract of a clause', PGW to Major Cussen, 14 September 1944, Cussen, p. 2; PGW statement, Cussen, p. 16.

p. 322, *What a lovely fat letter*, PGW to Anga von Bodenhausen, 30 March 1942 (Wodehouse Archive).

p. 324, *At last I am able to write to you*, PGW to William Townend, 11 May 1942 (Dulwich).

p. 326, *The sweater arrived yesterday*, PGW to Raven von Barnikow, 26 July 1942 (Wodehouse Archive).

p. 327, *In the hope that by doing so*, PGW to the Foreign Office, 21 November 1942 (Wodehouse Archive).

p. 329, 'working on getting out of Germany', PGW to Anga von Bodenhausen, 23 December 1942 (Wodehouse Archive).

p. 330, 'the frightful future ahead', *The Unknown Years*, p. 109.

p. 330, *Ethel and I were so excited*, PGW to Anga von Bodenhausen, 5 March 1943 (Wodehouse Archive).

p. 331, *I have been trying to write to you*, PGW to Anga von Bodenhausen, 15 April 1943 (Wodehouse Archive).

p. 333, 'my upper [*sic*]Silesian host', PGW to William Townend, 30 December 1944 (Dulwich).

p. 333, *I suppose you will get this at lunch time*, PGW to Anga von Bodenhausen, 11 June 1943 (Wodehouse Archive).

p. 335, *We were so delighted to get your letter*, PGW to Anga von Bodenhausen, 1 September 1943 (Wodehouse Archive).

1943–1947: 'under surveillance'

p. 341, 'Wodehouse may have been', McCrum, p.340.

p. 341, *What a long time since I wrote to you*, PGW to Anga von Bodenhausen, 21 November 1943 (Wodehouse Archive).

p. 343, *We continue to lead a quiet life*, PGW to Anga von Bodenhausen, 3 May 1944 (Wodehouse Archive).

p. 345, *The afternoon of the big parade*, PGW to William Townend, 30 December 1944 (Dulwich).

p. 345, 'flinty-eyed Home Office official', PGW to Guy Bolton, 1 September 1945 (Wodehouse Archive).

p. 346, *In view of the fact that on numerous occasions*, PGW to the Home Secretary, 4 September 1944 (Wodehouse Archive).

p. 347, 'in an extremely hysterical state', D. P. Reilly to V. G Lawford, 15 September 1944 (PRO FO/660/229).

p. 347, 'Only just found your address', Thelma Cazalet to PGW and Ethel Wodehouse, transcribed in D. P. Reilly to 'Patrick', 16 September 1944 (PRO FO/660/229).

p. 347, 'Ethel has had a terrible time', PGW to Malcolm Muggeridge, 25 September 1944 (PRO FO/660/229).

p. 347, *Thank you dear Thelma for your message*, PGW to Thelma Cazalet-Keir, 27 September 1944 (PRO FO/660/229).

p. 348, *At last I am able to write*, PGW to William Townend, 24 October 1944 (Dulwich).

p. 348, '"unwise" behaviour', Cussen, p. 15.

p. 348, 'suddenly woke up and saw', Ethel Wodehouse to Denis and Diana Mackail, 26 June 1945 (Wodehouse Archive).

p. 349, *Ethel and I were arrested*, PGW to Malcolm Muggeridge, 22 November 1944 (Muggeridge).

p. 349, 'it seems to me that the French are overdoing things', Winston Churchill to the Foreign Secretary, 28 November 1944 (PRO FO/369/2963).

p. 350, 'rather a poser', Winston Churchill to the Foreign Secretary, 7 December 1944 (PRO FO/369/2963).

p. 350, 'Plummie was on velvet', Ethel Wodehouse to Denis and Diana Mackail, 26 June 1945 (Wodehouse Archive).

p. 350, *How lovely to hear from you*, PGW to Ethel Wodehouse, 25 November 1944 (Wodehouse Archive).

p. 352, *I wish there was some means*, PGW to William Townend, 30 December 1944 (Dulwich).

p. 353, *The above address is where letters*, PGW to Denis Mackail, 4 January 1945 (Wodehouse Archive).

p. 354, 'the food situation is simply terrible', Ethel Wodehouse to Bea Davis, 20 January 1945 (Wodehouse Archive).

p. 354, 'We don't [...] want to go into', Ethel Wodehouse to Bea Davis, 17 April 1945 (Wodehouse Archive).

p. 354, *I was in the clinic when I wrote*, PGW to William Townend, 15 February 1945 (Dulwich).

p. 356, *What you say about the book you want me to write*, PGW to William Townend, 24 February 1945 (Dulwich).

p. 359, 'There is not enough evidence', *Daily Mirror*, 16 December 1944.

p. 360 'the publicity the next day was bad', Thelma Cazalet-Keir to PGW, 8 March 1945 (Wodehouse Archive).

p. 360, *Do write us all the news*, PGW to Thelma Cazalet-Keir, 1 March 1945 (Wodehouse Archive).

p. 361, *The anguish caused by your departure*, PGW to Malcolm Muggeridge, 16 April 1945 (Muggeridge).

p. 362, 'I have my beloved Leonora's photograph', Ethel Wodehouse to Bea Davis, 17 April 1945 (Wodehouse Archive).

p. 363, *I had a long letter from Watt the other day*, PGW to William Townend, 22 April 1945 (Dulwich).

p. 364, *We had a marvellous letter from Peter*, PGW to Malcolm Muggeridge, 19 May 1945 (Muggeridge).

p. 365, *I wonder what England is like*, PGW to Frances Donaldson, 2 June 1945 (Wodehouse Archive).

p. 366, *In one of your letters*, PGW to William Townend, 30 June 1945 (Dulwich).

p. 367, 'if only our Leonora could be here', Ethel Wodehouse to Bea Davis, 20 August 1945 (Wodehouse Archive).

p. 368, *I wrote to you a few days before your letter arrived*, PGW to George Orwell, 1 August 1945 (Orwell).

p. 368, *As far as we are concerned*, PGW to Guy Bolton, 1 September 1945 (Wodehouse Archive).

p. 370, *It looks to me as if my position*, PGW to William Townend, 13 September 1945 (Dulwich).

p. 371, *Admit candidly that I made a mistake*, PGW to H. D. Ziman, 26 September 1945 (private archive).

p. 372, *I wish we were together*, PGW to Denis Mackail, 14 October 1945 (Wodehouse Archive).

p. 373, *First of all, observe*, PGW to Denis Mackail, 7 November 1945 (Wodehouse Archive).

p. 374, *Yielding to the overwhelming pressure*, PGW to William Townend, 8 November 1945 (Dulwich).

p. 375, 'I had a very nice cocktail party', Ethel Wodehouse to Thelma Cazalet-Keir, [u.d. circa 5 July 1945] (Wodehouse Archive).

p. 375, *I find that my personal animosity*, PGW to Denis Mackail, 27 November 1945 (Wodehouse Archive).

p. 376, *You're quite right about my books*, PGW to Denis Mackail, 23 December 1945 (Wodehouse Archive).

p. 377, *Life here continues very pleasant*, PGW to William Townend, 11 January 1946 (Dulwich).

p. 378, 'Bill'. *I am enclosing a sheet*, PGW to Denis Mackail, 26 January 1946 (Wodehouse Archive).

p. 379, 'visit from the Home Office bloke', PGW to William Townend, 3 February 1946 (Dulwich).

p. 379, 'was in an altogether different category', Theobald Mathew to the Home Office, 13 September 1945 (PRO KV/2/3581).

p. 379, *it was such a joy to us*, PGW to Major Edward Cussen, 1 February 1946 (PRO KVZ/75).

p. 380, *I am wondering, with some mild amusement*, PGW to William Townend, 7 March 1946 (Dulwich).

p. 381, *If I post this tonight*, PGW to Sheran Cazalet, 27 March 1946 (Wodehouse Archive).

p. 382, *Not much news from the Paris front*, PGW to Denis Mackail, 28 March 1946 (Wodehouse Archive).

p. 383, *That bit in your letter*, PGW to Ira Gershwin, 5 April 1946 (Wodehouse Archive).

p. 384, 'an Old Alleynian, blast him!', PGW to William Townend, 29 April 1946 (Dulwich).

p. 384 'the question of taking proceedings, PGW to William Townend, 29 April 1946 (Dulwich).

p. 385, *Thelma Cazalet-Keir came over here*, PGW to Compton Mackenzie, 10 April 1946, quoted in Compton Mackenzie, *My Life and Times*, Octave 8, 1939–1941, (London: Chatto & Windus, 1969), pp. 257–8.

p. 386, *Many happy returns of the day*, PGW to Edward Cazalet, 23 April 1946 (Wodehouse Archive).

p. 387, *George Orwell. I wish I could get hold of that book*, PGW to William Townend, 29 April 1946 (Dulwich).

p. 388, *How right you are*, PGW to Denis Mackail, 7 May 1946 (Wodehouse Archive).

p. 389, *A perspiring Frenchman*, PGW to Ira Gershwin, 31 May 1946 (Wodehouse Archive).

p. 391, *It was wonderful getting your letter*, PGW to Compton Mackenzie, 4 June 1946, quoted in Mackenzie, *My Life and Times*, Octave 8, 1939–1941, pp. 259–60.

p. 392, *A friend of mine has just written to tell me*, PGW to V. S. Pritchett, 15 June 1946 (Wodehouse Archive).

p. 393, *I saw that stinker in the* Observer, PGW to Denis Mackail, 4 July 1946 (Wodehouse Archive).

p. 394, *Thanks for your letters*, PGW to William Townend, 27 August 1946 (Dulwich).

p. 396, *I simply must write*, PGW to William Townend, 30 August 1946 (Dulwich).

p. 397, 'a couple of rather chilly hotel rooms', *Illustrated*, 7 December 1944, p. 9.

p. 398, *I have read the reviews*, PGW to George Shively, 2 December 1946 (LOC).

p. 398, *It's curious how life nowadays*, PGW to William Townend, 24 December 1946 (Dulwich).

p. 400, *Many happy returns of the day*, PGW to Sheran Cazalet, 29 March 1947 (Wodehouse Archive).

p. 405, *The above is the best address to give you*, PGW to Benoît de Fonscolombe, 11 May 1947 (Wodehouse Archive).

p. 406, *Well, sir, my visit to N.Y.*, PGW to William Townend, 11 May 1947 (Dulwich).

p. 407, *I can't tell you how much I appreciated*, PGW to Evelyn Waugh, 31 May 1947 (Waugh).

p. 408, *Both Ethel and I have been depressed lately*, PGW to William Townend, 6 June 1947 (Dulwich).

p. 409, *With most of my stories your question*, PGW to Mr Summers, 12 August 1947 (private archive).

p. 410, *Scott Meredith hasn't reported anything*, PGW to William Townend, 22 September 1947 (Dulwich).

p. 412, *First about this place*, PGW to William Townend, 15 November 1947 (Dulwich).

p. 413, *The* Strands *and your letter*, PGW to William Townend, 24 Feburary 1948 (Dulwich).

p. 414, *Many happy returns of the day*, PGW to Sheran Cazalet, 28 March 1948 (Wodehouse Archive).

p. 415, Sally. *I have just been to the matinee*, PGW to Guy Bolton, 15 May 1948 (Wodehouse Archive).

p. 416, *Thank you so much for your letter*, PGW to Lawrence Durrell, 19 May 1948 (Southern Illinois)

p. 417, *What a shame you should have*, PGW to William Townend, 5 June 1948 (Dulwich).

p. 419, *[T]he Paramount guy, didn't think*, PGW to Guy Bolton, 17 June 1948 (Wodehouse Archive).

p. 420, *[A] couple of good stories*, PGW to Guy Bolton, 17 July 1948 (Wodehouse Archive).

p. 420, 'things are hotting up too much here', PGW to Guy Bolton, 7 August 1948 (Wodehouse Archive).

p. 420, 'wrestling with our furniture', PGW to William Townend, 8 December 1946 (Dulwich).

p. 420, 'very lost without her', PGW to William Townend, 7 September 1948 (Dulwich).

p. 421, *I can hardly wait to hear about the opening*, PGW to Guy Bolton, 4 September 1948 (Wodehouse Archive).

p. 421, *A film by Sacha Guitry has just been produced here*, PGW to Guy Bolton, 17 September 1948 (Wodehouse Archive).

p. 422, *In about four hours from now*, PGW to William Townend, 24 October 1948 (Dulwich).

p. 422, *I've discovered another gem in Keats*, PGW to Guy Bolton, 11 November 1948 (Wodehouse Archive).

p. 423, *Your letter of Nov 16, written at rehearsal*, PGW to Guy Bolton, 24 November 1948 (Wodehouse Archive).

p. 425, *How clever you are!*, PGW to Sheran Cazalet, 13 January 1949 (Wodehouse Archive).

p. 426, *I am looking forward to getting* Fool's Gold, PGW to William Townend, 15 January 1949 (Dulwich).

p. 428, *I often brood on your position as a writer*, PGW to William Townend, 5 November 1949 (Dulwich).

p. 429, *Sorry to trouble you again*, PGW to William Townend, 16 November 1949 (Dulwich).

p. 430, *I wish to God I could be with you*, PGW to Denis Mackail, 18 November 1949 (Wodehouse Archive).

p. 431, *I feel very remorseful*, PGW to William Townend, 22 June 1950 (Dulwich).

p. 432, *First, thanks for that wonderful photograph*, PGW to Guy Bolton, 17 July 1950 (Wodehouse Archive).

p. 433, *Only a short letter this time*, PGW to William Townend, 17 July 1950 (Dulwich).

p. 434, *Don't go writing to the above*, PGW to William Townend, 14 August 1950 (Dulwich).

p. 436, *Last Thursday we had the O.A.*, PGW to William Townend, 25 December 1950 (Dulwich).

p. 437, *Do you brood much about*, PGW to William Townend, 23 January 1951 (Dulwich).

p. 437, *Listen. Extract from book*, PGW to William Townend, 31 January 1951 (Dulwich).

p. 439, '"collapsed in the street" [...] "two doctors broke the news"', Ethel Wodehouse to Joyce Wodehouse, 4 April 1951 (private archive).

p. 440, *Do you remember a year or so*, PGW to William Townend, 8 March 1951 (Dulwich).

p. 441, 'This is the best play', *Observer*, 6 August 1950.

p. 441, *The script is in very good*, PGW to Ellsworth Conkle, 12 March 1951 (Ransom).

p. 442, *I call that a very pleasing conclusion*, PGW to Denis Mackail, 18 June 1951 (Wodehouse Archive).

p. 443, *Sad news to start my letter*, PGW to Denis Mackail, 11 August 1951 (Wodehouse Archive).

p. 444, *I think the letters scheme is terrific*, PGW to William Townend, 16 October 1951 (Dulwich).

p. 445, 'We employed a manservant', Ethel Wodehouse to Joyce Wodehouse, 27 March 1951 (private archive).

p. 445, 'It's very sad and quite a shock', Ethel Wodehouse to Joyce Wodehouse, 27 March 1951 (private archive).

p. 446, *Yesterday, after sixteen weeks*, PGW to William Townend, 3 March 1952 (Dulwich).

p. 447, *Your two letters arrived simultaneously*, PGW to William Townend, 15 April 1952 (Dulwich).

p. 448, 'rather a depressed state of mind', William Townend to PGW, 19 April 1952 (Dulwich).

p. 448, *I don't wonder you were upset*, PGW to William Townend, 24 April 1952 (Dulwich).

p. 449, *That was wonderful, you liking*, PGW to Denis Mackail, 6 May 1952 (Wodehouse Archive).

p. 451, *Excuse it, please. Sorry*, PGW to William Townend, 18 June 1952 (Dulwich).

p. 452, *The stuff from the lawyers*, PGW to J. D. Grimsdick, 13 August 1952 (Dulwich).

p. 453, *I think we shall have to let truth*, PGW to Guy Bolton, 4 November 1952 (Wodehouse Archive).

p. 454, *PIGS HAVE WINGS*, PGW to Denis Mackail, 14 December 1952 (Wodehouse Archive).

p. 455, *Here's a short story for you*, PGW to William Townend, 31 January 1953 (Dulwich).

p. 456, *Before I forget, will you send*, PGW to J. D. Grimsdick, 28 March 1953 (private archive).

p. 457, *We saw the Coronation on television*, PGW to Guy Bolton, 4 June 1953 (Wodehouse Archive).

p. 458, *I have been meaning to write*, PGW to William Townend, 25 June 1953 (Dulwich).

p. 460, 'one of those sleepy hamlets', *Something New*, Chapter 5.

p. 460, *Thank you so much for your letter*, PGW to Mr Slater, 2 July 1953 (Wodehouse Archive).

p. 461, *Bill, I'm uneasy. The proofs of the Letter book*, PGW to William Townend, 8 July 1953 (Dulwich).

p. 461, 'Ian Hay gave me your address last year', Arthur Ransome to PGW, [u.d. 1953], *Signalling from Mars: The Letters of Arthur Ransome* (London: Pimlico, 1998), pp. 343–4.

p. 462, *Thank you so much for your letter*, PGW to Arthur Ransome, 23 November 1953 (private archive).

p. 462, *I see old Pop Churchill*, PGW to William Townend, 25 November 1953 (Dulwich).

p. 463, 'I find in this evening of my life', PGW to William Townend, 29 November 1953 (Dulwich).

p. 464, *My poor old girl. You certainly made a pretty bloody fool*, PGW to Nancy Spain, quoted in PGW to William Townend, 12 December 1953 (Dulwich).

p. 464, *Gosh, Bill, will one never learn*, PGW to William Townend, 13 January 1954 (Dulwich).

p. 465, *Did you see a review*, PGW to William Townend, 10 March 1954 (Dulwich).

p. 466, *A word for your guidance*, PGW to Don Iddon, quoted in PGW to Denis Mackail, 21 March 1954 (Wodehouse Archive).

p. 466, *If you want something good*, PGW to Denis Mackail, 21 March 1954 (Wodehouse Archive).

p. 467, 'I don't like him, but I hate the idea', PGW to William Townend, 8 November 1952 (Dulwich).

p. 467, *Poor Milne. I was shocked*, PGW to Alastair Wallace, [u.d.], quoted in Ann Thwaite, *A. A. Milne: His Life* (London: Faber, 1990), p. 483.

p. 467, *My gosh, it shows how*, PGW to Denis Mackail, 1 May 1954 (Wodehouse Archive).

p. 475, *Edward Cazalet is now with us*, PGW to Denis Mackail, 22 August 1954 (Wodehouse Archive).

p. 476, *So sorry I haven't written before*, PGW to Richard Usborne, 14 January 1955 (Wodehouse Archive).

p. 478, *The other afternoon I managed to stir Ethel*, PGW to Denis Mackail, 6 March 1955 (Wodehouse Archive).

p. 479, *I hope the show is going like a breeze*, PGW to Guy Bolton, 23 March 1955 (Wodehouse Archive).

p. 480, *Yours of April 25*, PGW to Richard Usborne, 3 June 1955 (Wodehouse Archive).

p. 483, *This is some new notepaper*, PGW to Denis Mackail, 15 September 1955 (Wodehouse Archive).

p. 484, *About that McColl article*, PGW to William Townend, 26 July 1955 (Dulwich).

p. 485, *The trouble about writing to you*, PGW to William Townend, 21 February 1956 (Dulwich).

p. 486, 'Mr Wodehouse is probably the most endearing', John Wain, 'New Novels', *Observer*, 29 January 1956.

p. 486, 'Evelyn Waugh wrote to defend Wodehouse', *Observer,* 12 February 1956, p. 12; 'his own review of *French Leave*' was 'Dr. Wodehouse and Mr. Wain', *Spectator*, CXCVI (24 February 1956), pp. 243–4.

p. 486, *'At-a-boy! That's the stuff*, PGW to Evelyn Waugh, 11 March 1956 (Waugh).

p. 487, *I am still trying without any success*, PGW to Guy Bolton, 5 July 1956 (Wodehouse Archive).

p. 488, *Yours of August 6*, PGW to Richard Usborne, 1 September 1956 (Wodehouse Archive).

p. 490, *Sorry I've been so long writing*, PGW to Denis Mackail, 10 September 1956 (Wodehouse Archive).

p. 491, *Great excitement on just now*, PGW to Sheran Cazalet, 10 December 1956 (Wodehouse Archive).

p. 491, *Before I forget*, PGW to Richard Usborne, 18 December 1956 (Wodehouse Archive).

p. 492, *I am now two books ahead*, PGW to Denis Mackail, 18 December 1956 (Wodehouse Archive).

p. 493, *Nice to hear from you again*, PGW to Denis Mackail, 8 June 1957 (Wodehouse Archive).

p. 494, *Letter from Sheran reports a visit*, PGW to Denis Mackail, 17 August 1957 (Wodehouse Archive).

p. 494, *Delay in writing due to very strenuous*, PGW to Denis Mackail, 22 April 1959 (Wodehouse Archive).

p. 495, *It was a terrific relief to know*, PGW to Guy Bolton, 16 October 1959 (Wodehouse Archive).

p. 496, *I hope this won't be too much of a bother*, PGW to Lord Citrine, 29 June 1960 (Wodehouse Archive).

p. 497, *How frightfully kind of you*, PGW to Lord Citrine, 23 July 1960 (Wodehouse Archive).

p. 499, *How unerring your judgement always is!*, PGW to J. D. Grimsdick, 28 November 1960 (Dulwich).

p. 500, *The letters arrived yesterday*, PGW to William Townend, 3 January 1961 , repr. in P. G. Wodehouse, *Author! Author!* (New York: Simon and Schuster, 1962), p. 188.

p. 501, *It really was wonderful of you*, PGW to Evelyn Waugh, 23 January 1961 (Waugh).

p. 502, *About the Usborne book*, PGW to J. D. Grimsdick, 31 January 1961 (Dulwich).

p. 502, 'bury the whole story', *Daily Mirror*, 17 July 1961.

p. 502, *A rather embarrassing situation*, PGW to William Connor, 10 May 1961 (Wodehouse Archive).

p. 503, *I suppose you saw in the London papers*, PGW to Guy Bolton, 24 September 1961 (Wodehouse Archive).

p. 504, *Here is the revised 'You're The Top' lyric*, PGW to Guy Bolton, 28 October 1961 (Wodehouse Archive).

p. 505, *I'm working on the* A. Goes *lyric*, PGW to Guy Bolton, 28 October 1961 (Wodehouse Archive).

p. 506, *At last I am able to write*, PGW to Evelyn Waugh, 1 November 1961 (Waugh).

p. 507, *Here is the revised* Anything Goes *lyric*, PGW to Guy Bolton, 2 November 1961 (Wodehouse Archive).

p. 508, *Awfully nice to hear from you after all these years*, PGW to Angus Thuermer, 21 November 1961 (private archive).

p. 508, *I hope this catches you*, PGW to Evelyn Waugh, 14 December 1961 (Waugh).

p. 509, *How wonderful that Mike*, PGW to S. C. 'Billy' Griffith, 30 January 1962 (private archive).

p. 510, *Very sad news today*, PGW to J. D. Grimsdick, 23 February 1962 (Dulwich).

p. 510, 'Bill Townend's death makes me very sad', PGW to Mrs Carroll, 28 February 1962 (Wodehouse Archive).

p. 511, *It was such a joy to me*, PGW to Ellaline Terriss, 20 May 1962 (private archive).

p. 512, *I came across enclosed*, PGW to Guy Bolton, 2 July 1962 (Wodehouse Archive).

p. 512, *I am writing this to tell you*, PGW to Ethel Wodehouse, 21 August 1962 (Wodehouse Archive).

p. 513, *Thanks for letter and the letter*, PGW to Denis Mackail, 18 June 1963 (Wodehouse Archive).

p. 514, *This is just to tell you how much*, PGW to Ethel Wodehouse, 23 October 1963 (Wodehouse Archive).

p. 516, *New development in the Wodehouse home*, PGW to Guy Bolton, 16 July 1964 (Wodehouse Archive).

p. 516, *I have been sticking to my afternoon walk*, PGW to Guy Bolton, 3 August 1964 (Wodehouse Archive).

p. 517, *Thank you so much for your letter*, PGW to Mr Shreyer, 13 August 1964 (Wodehouse Archive).

p. 518, *The Galahad books arrived*, PGW to J. D. Grimsdick, 27 November 1964 (Dulwich).

p. 518, *Thanks so much for the books*, PGW to Edward Cazalet, 27 January 1965 (Wodehouse Archive).

p. 519, *Life's a terrible blank without*, PGW to Ethel Wodehouse, 6 February 1965 (Wodehouse Archive).

p. 520, *Edward has arrived*, PGW to Guy Bolton, 7 August 1965 (Wodehouse Archive).

p. 521, 'I have started a new novel', PGW to Sheran Cazalet, 27 March 1966 (Wodehouse Archive).

p. 521, *How difficult it is to write stories*, PGW to Guy Bolton, 19 August 1966 (Wodehouse Archive).

p. 522, *What wonderful news*, PGW to Edward Cazalet, 4 December 1966 (Wodehouse Archive).

p. 523, *Gosh, how I am missing*, PGW to Ethel Wodehouse, 6 July 1967 (Wodehouse Archive).

p. 524, *I am writing this in my chair*, PGW to Ethel Wodehouse, 11 July 1967 (Wodehouse Archive).

p. 525, *First, before I forget*, PGW to Guy Bolton, 17 July 1967 (Wodehouse Archive).

p. 526, *When a book parcel arrived*, PGW to Anthony Powell, 16 November 1967 (Wodehouse Archive).

p. 527, *I am longing to see the book*, PGW to Agatha Christie, [u.d.] (Christie).

p. 527, *Loved your Christmas telegram*, PGW to Ira Gershwin, 4 January 1970 (Wodehouse Archive).

p. 528, *I was just going to write*, PGW to Henry Slesar, 20 March 1971 (Wodehouse Archive).

p. 529, *How ever did you manage*, PGW to Agatha Christie, 22 April 1971 (Christie)

p. 530, *I had a letter from Agatha Christie*, PGW to Guy Bolton, 20 June 1971 (Wodehouse Archive).

p. 531, *Thinking of you gathered in*, PGW to Norman Murphy et al., 19 May 1973 (private archive).

p. 534, *What a wonderful surprise!!!*, PGW to Thelma Cazalet-Keir, 25 May 1973 (Wodehouse Archive).

p. 535, *P. 10. Cut the line about Ethiopian Slaves*, PGW to Scott Meredith, 9 July 1973 (Wodehouse Archive).

p. 536, 'Our visit [...] had to be precisely timed', Alan Ayckbourn, 'A Meeting with a Living Legend', programme for *By Jeeves*, Stephen Joseph Theatre, Scarborough, 1 May 1996.

p. 536, *I'm afraid the difficulty is*, PGW to Guy Bolton, 15 August 1973 (Wodehouse Archive).

p. 537, *Another anniversary*, PGW to Ethel Wodehouse, 30 September 1973 (Wodehouse Archive).

p. 538, *How I wish this was one*, PGW to Ethel Wodehouse, 10 March 1974 (Wodehouse Archive).

p. 539, *What magnificent news!*, PGW to Tom Sharpe, 27 July 1974 (Sharpe).

p. 540, *I would have written to you long ago*, PGW to J. D. Grimsdick, 29 January 1975 (Dulwich).

p. 540, *Jeeves's bracer*, PGW to Godfrey Smith, [u.d. c.1975] (Wodehouse Archive).

p. 541, *Wonderful news about Raymond*, PGW to Ernestine Bowes-Lyon, 3 February 1975 (Wodehouse Archive).

Select Bibliography

WORKS BY OR ABOUT P. G. WODEHOUSE

Auden, W. H., 'Balaam and His Ass' and 'Dingley Dell and the Fleet', in *The Dyer's Hand and Other Essays* (New York: Random House Inc., 1962).

Bodenhausen, Reinhild von, *P. G. Wodehouse: The Unknown Years* (Sri Lanka: Stamford Lake, 2009).

Cazalet-Keir, Thelma (ed.), *A Homage to P. G. Wodehouse* (London: Barrie & Jenkins, 1973).

Davis, Lee, *Wodehouse and Bolton and Kern: The Men Who Made Musical Comedy* (New York: J. H. Heineman, 1993).

Donaldson, Frances, *P. G. Wodehouse: A Biography* (New York: Knopf, 1982).

Garrison, Daniel H., *Who's Who in Wodehouse* (New York: Peter Lang, 1987).

Green, Benny, *P. G. Wodehouse: A Literary Biography* (New York: Rutledge, 1981).

Hall, R. A., 'The Transferred Epithet in P. G. Wodehouse', *Linguistic Enquiry*, Vol. 4, No. 1, Winter 1973, pp. 92–4.

Jasen, David, *P. G. Wodehouse: A Portrait of a Master* (New York: Mason & Lipscomb, 1974).

McCrum, Robert, *Wodehouse: A Life* (London: Penguin Books, 2005).

McIlvaine, Eileen, James Heineman and Louise S. Sherby (eds.), *P. G. Wodehouse: An Annotated Bibliography and Checklist* (New York: James H. Heineman, 1990).

Medcalf, Stephen, 'The Innocence of P. G. Wodehouse' in *The Modern English Novel: The Reader, the Writer and the Work*, ed. Gabriel Josipovici (New York: Barnes & Noble, 1976, pp. 186–205).

Murphy, N. T. P., *In Search of Blandings* (London: Secker & Warburg, 1986).

——, *The Wodehouse Handbook*, 2 vols. (London: Popgood & Groolley, 2006).

Phelps, Barry, *P. G. Wodehouse: Man and Myth* (Constable: London, 1992).

Quinton, Anthony, *From Wodehouse to Wittgenstein: Essays* (Manchester: Carcanet, 1998).

Ring, Tony, *You Simply Hit Them with an Axe: The Extraordinary True Story of the Tax Turmoils of P. G. Wodehouse* (Maidenhead: Porpoise, 1995).

Sproat, Iain, *Wodehouse at War* (London: Milner and Co. 1981).

Taves, Brian, *P. G. Wodehouse and Hollywood* (McFarland & Co.: North Carolina, 2006).

Thompson, Kristen, *Wooster Proposes, Jeeves Disposes* (New York: Heineman, 1992).

Usborne, Richard, *Wodehouse at Work* (London: Herbert Jenkins, 1961).

Wind, Herbert Warren, *The World of P. G. Wodehouse* (Praeger: New York, 1971).

Wodehouse, P. G., *America, I Like You* (New York: Simon and Schuster, 1956).

——, *Author! Author!* (New York: Simon and Schuster, 1962).

——, *Hollywood Omnibus* (London: Hutchinson, 1985).

——, *Louder and Funnier* (London: Vintage, 1997).

——, *Performing Flea: A Self-Portrait in Letters*, with a Foreword and Notes by W. Townend (London: Herbert Jenkins, 1953).

——, *P. G. Wodehouse: In His Own Words*, eds. Barry Day and Tony Ring (Hutchinson: London, 2001).

——, *The Uncollected Wodehouse*, ed. David Jasen (New York: Seabury Press, 1976).

——, *Wodehouse on Wodehouse* (Harmondsworth: Penguin, 1981).

——, *Yours, Plum: The Letters of P. G. Wodehouse,* ed. Frances Donaldson (London: Hutchinson, 1990).

See also *Wooster Sauce*, the quarterly journal of the P. G. Wodehouse Society (UK), and *Plum Lines*, the quarterly journal of the Wodehouse Society (USA). Given that Wodehouse's works exist in numerous editions, unless otherwise stated, references to his texts are given by title and, where appropriate, chapter, rather than page number. A complete bibliography of Wodehouse's works can be found on the P. G. Wodehouse Society (UK) website http:// www.pgwodehousesociety.org.uk/.

Auden, W. H., *The Age of Anxiety* (1947), repr. in *Collected Poems*, ed.
Edward Mendelson (London: Faber, 2007).

Beevor, Anthony, and Artemis Cooper, *Paris after the Liberation 1944–1949*
(Harmondsworth: Penguin Books, 1995).

Crisswell, Colin, and Mike Watson, *The Royal Hong Kong Police Force*
(London: Macmillan, 1982).

Flannery, Harry, *Assignment to Berlin* (London: Michael Joseph, 1942).

Fury, David A., *Maureen O'Sullivan: No Average Jane* (Minneapolis:
The Artist's Press, 2006).

Jackson, Julian, *France: The Dark Years 1940–1944* (Oxford: OUP, 2001).

Jackson, Kate, *George Newnes and the New Journalism in Britain, 1880–1910*
(Aldershot: Ashgate, 2001).

Lean, E. T., *Voices in the Darkness: The Story of European Radio War*
(London: Secker & Warburg, 1943).

Leavis, Q. D., *Fiction and the Reading Public* (London: Chatto & Windus,
1932).

Lottman, Herbert R., *The People's Anger: Justice and Liberation in Post-War
France* (London: Hutchinson, 1986).

Moore, Lucy, *Anything Goes: A Biography of the Roaring Twenties*
(London: Atlantic, 2008).

Moorhouse, Roger, *Berlin at War: Life and Death in Hitler's Capital*
(London: Bodley Head, 2010).

Reynolds, Paul, *The Middle Man: The Adventures of a Literary Agent*
(William Morrow & Co. Inc.: New York, 1972).

Rushdie, Salman, *Imaginary Homelands* (London: Granta, 1991).

Taylor, D. J., *Bright Young People: The Rise and Fall of a Generation 1918–1940*
(London: Vintage, 2008).

Index